American Families

A Courses by Newspaper Reader

Edited by

Elizabeth Douvan
Helen Weingarten
Jane L. Scheiber

Courses by Newspaper is a project of
University Extension, University of California, San Diego

Funded by The National Endowment for the Humanities

KENDALL/HUNT PUBLISHING COMPANY
Dubuque, Iowa, USA • Toronto, Ontario, Canada

Courses by Newspaper
American Families in Transition

Academic Coordinator

Elizabeth Douvan
    Professor of Psychology and
    Director, Program on Family
    and Sex Roles
    Institute for Social Research
    University of Michigan

Editorial Director

Jane L. Scheiber
    University of California,
    San Diego

Research Associate

Helen Weingarten
    Faculty Member,
    School of Social Work,
    University of Michigan

Faculty Committee
University of California, San Diego

Paul D. Saltman, Chair
    Vice Chancellor,
    Academic Affairs
    Professor of Biology

Stanley A. Chodorow
    Professor of History

Doris A. Howell
    Professor of Community Medicine

Jacqueline P. Wiseman
    Professor of Sociology

Project Director

George A. Colburn
    University of California,
    San Diego

National Board

David P. Gardner, Chair
    President, University of Utah

Carl N. Degler
    Professor of History
    Stanford University

Robert C. Elliott
    Professor of Literature
    University of California,
    San Diego

Georgie Anne Geyer
    Columnist,
    Los Angeles Times Syndicate

Richard Leonard
    Editor, *Milwaukee Journal*

Thomas O'Connell
    President,
    Bellevue Community College

Paul D. Saltman
    University of California,
    San Diego

Gerald Warren
    Editor, *San Diego Union*

Cover Photo by Bob Coyle

Contents

iii

Preface

This is the thirteenth in a series of books developed for Courses by Newspaper (CbN). A national program, originated and administered by University Extension, University of California, San Diego, and funded primarily by the National Endowment for the Humanities, Courses by Newspaper develops materials for college-level courses that are presented to the general public through the nationwide cooperation of newspapers and participating colleges and universities.

The program offers three levels of participation: readers interested in self-learning can follow a series of weekly articles in one of the 450 participating newspapers; they can pursue the subjects further in this supplementary Reader and Study Guide; and they can enroll for credit at one of the more than 300 participating colleges or universities. In addition, many community organizations offer local forums and discussion groups based on the Courses by Newspaper series.

This volume supplements the fifteen newspaper articles written by noted experts from around the country especially for the thirteenth Course by Newspaper, "American Families in Transition." The weekly series was developed for newspapers throughout the nation, with a starting date of September 1980.

We would like to thank the hundreds of newspaper editors and publishers who have contributed valuable space to bring the newspaper series to their readers, and the faculties and administrations of the many colleges and universities participating in the program, who have cooperated to make credit available on a nationwide basis.

We would also like to acknowledge those who contributed to the development of this course. The authors of the newspaper articles—Jessie Bernard, Catherine Chilman, Milton Covensky, Nancy Datan, Natalie Davis, Kenneth Keniston, Barbara Laslett, Joseph Pleck, Lillian Rubin, Philip Slater, Catharine Stimpson, Marvin Sussman, Carol Tavris, and Robert Weiss—made valuable suggestions for this anthology and for the bibliographies which appear at the end of this volume. In addition, both the National Board and the CbN Faculty Committee made important contributions to the conception of the course.

Deserving special mention at the University of California, San Diego, is Paul D. Saltman, vice chancellor for academic affairs and professor of biology, who has chaired the Faculty Committee and guided the project since its inception, in addition to serving as the first academic coordinator in 1973. Special thanks also go to George Colburn, Project Director of Courses by

Newspaper, and the other members of the CbN staff—Yvonne Hancher, Stephanie Giel, Elliot Wager, Bethany Gardella, Beverly Barry, Sally Cirrito, and Donna Cheverton—who have played crucial roles in developing and administering the program.

Finally, we wish to express our gratitude to our funding agency, the National Endowment for the Humanities. The Endowment, a federal agency created in 1965 to support education, research, and public activities in the humanities, has generously supported this nationwide program since its inception.

Although Courses by Newspaper is a project of the University of California, San Diego, and is supported by the National Endowment for the Humanities, the views expressed in course materials are those of the authors only and do not necessarily reflect those of the funding agency or of the University of California.

Introduction

Interest in the family has surged during the last decade. Departments of sociology in major universities that had avoided course offerings in Marriage and the Family for twenty years (leaving them to schools of Home Economics or Social Work or Nursing) because they were not "theoretical" or "interesting" began to reintegrate them into the curriculum. Historians—who had never previously concerned themselves with the private affairs of ordinary people—began to see that family ties could affect the spread of Protestantism or patterns of migration or entry into the industrial labor force. Economists discovered the informal nonmarket exchanges that centered in family and neighborhood and represented value missed in their calculations of gross national product and other economic indicators. And the popular media—which had never found family life uninteresting or irrelevant—redoubled their coverage of family issues and assumed a more analytic approach to questions of family life and family stability.

Some of this renewed interest grew out of a sense of crisis: growing divorce rates seemed to say that the family was in trouble and in danger. And our society—certainly the media—is always interested in trouble and danger. They make lively, interesting copy.

Recent social and political movements also stimulated and focused interest in family questions. The counter-culture of the sixties challenged the model of the nuclear family and offered communal life as a preferable social arrangement. Conventional marriage was seen as an obstacle to love—an unnecessary legal invasion of the love life and sex life of individuals. The women's movement in its early stage cast the conjugal family, with its male "head of household" and sexual division of labor, in the role of enemy. If women were to realize their full potential, they would have to abandon or alter radically the structure of marriage and the family. Feminist historians, among others, sought and found evidence in the past that the conventional view of the family as a breadwinner husband, homemaker wife, and their dependent children had existed only in limited geographic areas for a short period in history, mainly since the late nineteenth century in England and the United States. In most eras in most cultures, both men and women were active in productive market work as well as the work of homemaking and child rearing.

The development of modern birth control—which brought reproduction firmly under individual control and offered such control for the first time in history both cheaply and safely—raised important moral questions about sex and reproduction. Spurred by the women's movement and reinforced by counter-thrusts from religious groups, issues of access to birth control, abortion, and women's right to self-determination in the reproductive realm became public political issues and the focus of political campaigns and demonstrations—another expression of public interest in the sphere of family life.

President Carter grounded his 1976 campaign on a strong family plank, promising to attend to the effects of government on family life and to work toward policies and programs that would support and strengthen American families. Early in his presidency, Mr. Carter assigned Vice President Mondale the task of overseeing family impact statements to accompany and balance legislative proposals. Carter further announced a White House Conference on Families to be held in 1980.

All of these factors, then, have played a part in the enlivened attention currently directed to family life. Interest and attention have led to a large and growing literature about family functioning, a literature that addresses itself to a wide array of questions and issues, including the following:

1. What is a family? What are its functions? In what ways are these the same in all cultures and in all historical periods? How do they vary?

2. Has the family lost some of its functions in contemporary America? Have family functions been absorbed by other institutions like schools, hospitals, nursing homes? Have other functions replaced those that have slipped from the family sphere?

3. What historical factors affected the form of the American family? How did our colonial past, the frontier, industrialization, and immigration shape the particular forms family life took in the United States? How did slavery, emancipation, and discrimination affect family life among black Americans?

4. How has the family been affected by developments and movements in the recent past—the massive increase in married women's participation in the labor force, the movement for population control and family planning, the "sexual revolution," the resurgence of feminism?

5. Is the American family in serious danger or decline? What do statistics about divorce, remarriage, childbirth, and illegitimacy really tell us? If families are experiencing strains, have facilities or services been developed to help families weather difficulties?

6. What do political and social leaders mean by "family policy"? Do government actions affect families and family stability? Should legislators be aware of these effects? Should government play an active role in developing programs to support families?

In the readings that make up this book, we have sampled from this burgeoning literature about the family. In cases in which a particular issue is still being debated—for example, the question of whether or not families have lost their functions—we have tried to represent both sides of the discussion.

The readings that follow are organized into four main parts. Part One includes an introduction, definitions, and a history of the family in America. Part Two is concerned with events and movements of the recent past that have affected family life—the development and spread of psychological knowledge and of expert advice about child raising, the human potential and human growth movements, the perfection of birth control and the movement for population control and family planning, challenges to traditional sexual morality and sex role definitions, the sexual revolution and the women's movement.

Part Three looks at the functioning of the family, the ways in which it intersects and interacts with other institutions in the larger society, changes in family functions through various life stages (from formation through child raising to the launching of children and the post-parenting couple), and the relationship of the child to the family during the socialization process. Finally we consider variations in family life in various ethnic, racial, and social class subgroups in American society.

The last major section of the book, Part Four, deals with signs of strain and efforts to meet family problems—either by suggesting new family forms or by providing new policies and services to help and support existing families. The last group of readings asks about prospects for the family in the future: Will the nuclear family survive in the years ahead and, if so, what changes is it likely to undergo?

No one can doubt that family life has been challenged in recent times. Signs of strain such as the increasing divorce rate and runaway wives and children are presented constantly in the media. "Alternate life styles"—communes, homosexual marriages, childless marriages, reconstituted and blended families, single-parent female-headed families—are discussed and even lobbied for by their proponents. Yet most people continue to live in families and to value family ties. In a recent national study of adults (Veroff, J., Douvan, E., and Kulka, R. *Culture and Conflict*, 1980), it was found that most people believe that they derive most meaning and satisfaction from family roles (spouse, parent), more so than from work or from leisure activities. The family may well be beleaguered, but it apparently continues to be the arena in which most of us find the satisfactions, the meaning, the self-affirmation that make life possible and significant.

Photograph by Crosby. Courtesy of Photophile.

Part One

DEFINITIONS AND HISTORICAL BACKGROUND

Introduction

The first part of this book serves to introduce our subject—the contemporary American family—and place it in historical context, tracing the roots from which it has come to its current condition. We have divided this first part into four chapters: (1) Introduction and Definitions; (2) The Family and Social Change; (3) The Meaning of Family in the Past; and (4) Postindustrial Society and the Family.

The opening article in Chapter One, "Saving the Family" from *Newsweek* magazine, describes current concerns about the family, which seems to be in a state of crisis. Subsequent articles set forth some definitions. What is a family? What functions define it? Psychologist Arlene Skolnick, in "The Intimate Environment," describes four different paradigms or models of families: nuclear, extended, communal, and cosmopolitan. The article by the distinguished anthropologist Clyde Kluckhohn also analyzes "Variations in the Human Family," but warns that we should not overlook the universal aspects of the family as an institution.

To make these definitions of the family more concrete and to enliven the sense of what this human arrangement is and what it does, we next present three vignettes of family life: "Life in Appalachia," by psychiatrist Robert Coles, and three sketches from "Family Types" by David Kantor and William Lehr of the Cambridge Family Institute.

Chapter Two, The Family and Social Change, addresses the question of how demographic and economic changes have affected the American family. How did industrialization—the removal of work from the home—influence relations among family members? How did our immigrant past—with its distinct ethnic patterns—and the change from a rural and small-town society to an urbanized society alter our family ties? Historian Tamara Hareven explores these questions in "Family Time and Historical Time," and points out that family life, in turn, has conditioned or altered the pace and particular forms of industrialization and urbanization.

The economic organization of society has profound implications for the way we live in families. In an agrarian society the family is the productive unit, and all members of the family, including very young children, contribute to production and share in what is produced. Many aspects of child rearing that we think of and worry about today did not have to be consciously considered under these circumstances. No one thought about baby sitters or day care centers for toddlers; parents raised toddlers in the fields or at home, where they worked side by side as soon as the children were able. Home and workplace were one. But when adults go away from home to an office or factory, the system of parent-child exchange is affected as their spheres are separated. Adults and children come to be thought of as very different kinds of beings. When economic conditions make it necessary—or attractive—for both parents to work outside the home, still further changes occur in the relationship among family members.

In "Stability of the Family in a Transient Society," psychologist Niles Newton considers the impact of demographic and economic changes on the family and on its capacity to meet human needs, suggesting some ways in which we can stabilize family ties in modern society. In the next article, "The Significance of Family Membership," sociologist Barbara Laslett focuses on changes in mortality, age of marriage, and fertility, arguing that these demographic factors have made the family more important to its members than in the past.

The Laslett article provides a transition to Chapter Three, which concentrates on the different ways in which family members relate to one another—the changes in the meaning of the family that have occurred in the wake of these demographic and economic changes in our society. Two letters from the Virginia Company in London, regarding the shipment of brides to the colony in the New World in 1621, provide a glimpse of seventeenth century attitudes toward marriage. The women were to be treated well, but clearly they were of financial value as well.

In "The American Family in Past Time," historian John Demos presents a broad picture of the meaning of family in our colonial past and of how that meaning has changed as we became an industrial, urban culture. He draws out common threads—ways in which even our current concepts of family relations are continuous with meanings developed by our colonial forebears—and shifts in the patterns that developed when we became an industrial "go-getter" nation of competitive entrepreneurs.

The next two selections give us sharply contrasting scenes of family life in the late nineteenth and early twentieth centuries. Cecyle Neidle, author of several books on immigrants, portrays the hard lives of Slavic wives and mothers in "America's Immigrant Women," while in "Genteel Backlash," sociologist Richard Sennett shows how the middle class reacted with fear to such "foreigners." This fear, according to Sennett, reflected insecurities and strains in family functioning that had in turn resulted partly from the schism between the public sphere of the business world and the private haven of the family.

Chapter Four presents various views of developments in our society in the twentieth century and the effect of contemporary, or postindustrial, society on family life. One feature of modern society is our extreme mobility, and sociologist Philip Slater discusses "Some Effects of Transience" on the family and on American culture. Such broad economic and social changes as mass education, mass production, mass consumption, and the development of technology, science, and the social sciences also had profound effects on the family. As a result of these developments, many of the functions that had previously resided in the family were given over to the state, specialized institutions, and experts: the education of children became the function of the schools, hospitals took over the function of caring for the sick, nursing homes developed to care for the old and infirm. In the process, argues historian Christopher Lasch in "The Family and Morality," families lost much of their authority as well as their functions, leaving the state in dangerous control of the individual.

Stripped of so many of its functions, the family appears to many observers to specialize only in providing social and emotional support to healthy members and in coordinating the services of other specialized institutions. Indeed, some critics have argued that the family is really no longer useful or necessary—that people can find their emotional satisfactions outside the family and that, in fact, the family is unnecessarily confining. In "The Family Out of Favor," Michael Novak, a philosopher, editor, and writer, addresses this attack directly and tells us what family life provides that no other sphere can supplant.

CHAPTER ONE

Introduction and Definitions

The root of the state is in the family.

Mencius, *Book IV* (372–289 BC)

Home is the place where, when you have to go there,
They have to take you in.

Robert Frost, "The Death of the
Hired Man"*

*From "The Death of the Hired Man" from *The Poetry of Robert Frost,* edited by Edward Connery Lathem. Copyright 1930, 1939, © 1969 by Holt, Rinehart and Winston. Copyright 1958 © by Robert Frost. Copyright © 1967 by Lesley Frost Ballantine. Reprinted by permission of Holt, Rinehart and Winston, Publishers.

KENNETH L. WOODWARD,
MARY LORD,
FRANK MAIER,
DONNA M. FOOTE, AND
PHYLLIS MALAMUD

Saving the Family

Our society has experienced both a crisis in family life and a crisis of conscience about the family. Late in the decade of the seventies many major journals issued special reports on the state of the family in America. The selection that follows is part of a special report in Newsweek *magazine summarizing the dimensions of the crisis in family life, trends in marriage, divorce, and childbirth, and some of the ways in which both families and experts were beginning to respond to the problems of family life.*

Only a decade ago, the beleaguered American family was being written off as obsolete. As society's basic institution, it was emotionally unstable, economically weak and not up to the task of raising children—or so the experts said. Lately, however, opinions have shifted: like Winston Churchill viewing democracy, the social critics are deciding that the family is the worst possible system, except for all the alternatives. "There is no better invention than the family, no super-substitute," says Rutgers University sociologist Sarane Boocock. The question now is not how to supplant the family, but how to support it.

That conclusion will hardly surprise most of the nation's 56.7 million families who have continued to raise their children, endure marital and economic stress and adapt with amazing grace to unprecedented social changes. "Sometimes it's really awful," says Rae Dufore, 45, a suburban Milwaukee mother of three daughters. "We discuss, we argue, we scream and holler. I understand why some people run away from home—both kids and adults. But almost anything of value demands effort. There's a richness to our lives that wouldn't have been if we'd decided not to have children."

Nevertheless, many parents feel increasingly harassed. Raising children has never been more costly—in time and money—and the interference from outside forces has never been more acute. Television, schools, the workplace, peer pressure and the family experts themselves have all invaded the family circle, robbing parents of much of their power without easing their responsibility. "Parents are not abdicating," says MIT psychologist Kenneth Keniston, "they are being dethroned by forces they cannot influence, much less control." The pressure is intense. "We're the ultimate nuclear family, and sometimes I feel as if someone is trying to split the atom," says Georgia Houser, 35, a Houston college administrator and mother of three. And on occasion, a parent's plight can be sadly ludicrous: a fortnight ago, a 24-year-old drifter in Colorado sued his parents for $350,000, charging that it was their failure that made him what he is.

Revolt in the Grass Roots

The family's plight is becoming [the new] cause. . . . The National Conference of Catholic Bishops designated 1980 "Family Year" and adopted plans for a decade-long program to support marriage and family life. . . . President Carter, who rode into office on a strong pro-family policy, . . . scheduled a . . . "White House Conference on Families" . . . and various experts are helping the government develop criteria for measuring the effect of current laws and programs on the family. "You need to look at very specific policies and trace them in terms of their specific impact on families," observes Marian Wright Edelman, head of the Children's Defense Fund. "We're trying to figure out how to stop the government from being harmful to families and children, and what are the ways government might do something to help them."

The U.S. is the only Western nation that does not have a formal family policy—the same thing, many say, as having an anti-family policy. But the impact of government and other outside agencies on the family is already so pervasive that it has provoked a grass-roots parents' revolt. The National Parents' Rights Coalition, formed [in 1977] in Chicago, promises that "anyone who has an impact on the family, from politicians and bureaucrats to educators and the media, will hear from us and face our power." In Washington, the Coalition of Family Organizations lobbies for tax breaks and other family support. Meanwhile, the American Family Society is promoting a slick new magazine, *Family Time,* devoted to self-help projects, and also puts out a checklist for locating possible sources of family instability.

Why is the family in trouble? One major reason is that traditions no longer dictate life patterns for most adult Americans. "Now people have more options—to get married or not, to have children or not, to stay married or not, to work or not," observes David A. Goslin, who directed a study of the family for the National Academy of Sciences. "These options are really at the heart of everybody's concern." A second reason is that the sheer cost of raising a child is enough to make any potential parent pause—and current parents shudder. At 1977 prices, a family of four, earning between $16,500 and $20,000 a year, can expect to spend $54,297 to support a child to the age of 18, excluding of expense of higher education.

Finally, parents feel increasingly powerless in the face of institutional interference. The growth of social services, health care and public education has robbed them of their traditional roles as job trainers, teachers, nurses and nurturers. And their control over their children's lives is threatened by the pervasive—and increasingly authoritative—influences of television, schools and peer groups. "Our oldest daughter is only 7, and already we can see the peer pressure at work," says Judy Syke, 31, a mother of two young children in exurban Galena, Ill. "She'll come home and tell us that so-and-so has this and why don't we? Tom and I know she needs social exposure, but at the same time we'd like to shelter her from other people's values—like television, easy money and the idea that you have to go here and go there to have fun."

In their confusion, parents have increasingly turned to experts for advice—and in the process ended up relinquishing more responsibility. "We can't feed our children, discipline them, select schools, books or games for them, even, it seems, have an ordinary conversation with them without consulting someone who claims to be in the know," observes Robert Coles. "This loss of self-respect and common sense is the principal reason why we turn to specialists, as if God had chosen to reveal Himself through them." In their preoccupation with disturbed and troubled families, some experts cannot even recognize a healthy family at work. A group of Dallas behavioral researchers have made a film of healthy and chaotic families interacting. When it is shown to mental health professionals around the country, "they nod and nudge each other when the chaotic family is shown—they recognize it," says psychiatrist John T. Gossett, who was involved in the project. "Their reaction to the healthy families is one of disbelief. They think we made it up."

"Various professional groups have been too eager to tell parents they weren't qualified to be parents," says Robert Mnookin, a law professor at

Berkeley. "Their message is that parents just aren't competent—and the sad thing is, parents bought it." Between their own expectations and the high standards set by the experts, many parents now feel they simply cannot measure up. "When parents believe that they should be the total providers of all that a child needs . . . any suggestion of unmet needs carries with it a sense of failure," says the Rev. Eileen W. Lindner, a staff associate for youth concerns at the National Council of Churches. "The myth of the self-sufficient, independent family is one of the most oppressive forces on the American family."

That myth of the self-contained, self-sufficient family has roots extending deep into Colonial America. From the outset, American families have been inspired by an ethos of autonomy—first through the Puritan image of the family as "a little commonwealth," and later by the Enlightenment ideals of individual rights as embodied in the U.S. Constitution.

Beginning in the nineteenth century, industrialization and urbanization gradually transformed the family. Women devoted themselves to nurturing children, and husbands regarded the family as private refuge from an increasingly impersonal and competitive world. Marriage became companionate—valued more for its emotional satisfactions than for its utility. For the first time in Western history, adolescence emerged as a distinct and prolonged period between childhood and adulthood, with parents assuming total responsibility for the socialization of youth at home.

This was the nuclear family model that European immigrants found when they arrrived in America, and—with one important embellishment—it was the model that most of them eventually adopted as their own. American scholars are only beginning to appreciate the importance of the extended family networks by which immigrant Irish, Jews, Slavs and other hyphenated Americans enriched the basic nuclear family. In the South, where industrialism proceeded more slowly, the plantation tradition provided many families with an almost mystical connection to the land and lineage of their fathers.

The Vanishing 'Ideal'

By the middle of the nineteenth century, however, Americans had already established the first and eventually the most powerful institutional counterpoise to the autonomous nuclear family: the compulsory, free public school. From that point on, schools were expected to do what educators assumed that families, especially those of immigrants, could not accomplish on their own—teach skills, develop work habits and instill approved social values. In the course of the following century, almost every other traditional function of the family passed out of the home and into the hands of institutions and professional providers, from care of the sick to support of the poor, from the preparation of food to instruction in leisure activities. "By convincing the housewife, and finally even her husband to rely on outside technology and the advice of outside experts, the apparatus of mass tuition—the successor to the church in our secularized society—has undermined the family's capacity to provide for itself," says University of Rochester historian Christopher Lasch.

The American family is clearly still in transition. Only about one family in four now conforms to the stereotypical image of breadwinning Dad, home-making Mom and dependent children. Now more than half of all married women with school-age children hold some kind of job. Couples with no children under 18 now make up 47 per cent of all families, which reflects both the longevity of American couples and the increasing number of those who are delaying or forgoing having children. At the same time, increases in divorce and illegitimacy have created millions of single-parent families while the rising rate of remarriage has produced the "blended" family. "All Americans must become aware that 'ideal' family barely exists and will never return as a significant force in American life," concludes a recent demographic profile of U.S. families by Zaida Giraldo and Jack Weatherford of the Center for the Study of the Family and the State at Duke University.

The Hidden Strengths

Nevertheless, there is an underlying stability to family life that often goes unnoticed. Statistics show that 98 per cent of all American children are raised in families and that, last year, 79 per cent of these were living with two parents. What's more, nearly two-thirds of all couples remain married until death, and of those who divorce, 75 per cent of the women and 83 per cent of the men remarry within three years.

The divorce rate—the highest in the world—may finally be leveling off. According to preliminary figures, the divorce rate increased only 2 per cent in 1976, compared with an annual average increase of 11.5 per cent over the past several years. And despite more relaxed attitudes toward "living in sin," only a fraction of 1 per cent of Americans admitted to cohabitation, according to a 1977 Census report—and most of them will eventually marry. "People are getting more various in their family behavior," says psychologist Arlene Skolnick of the University of California at Berkeley. "But more and more we are seeing a new commitment to child rearing and family control no matter what sort of family structure evolves."

From 'Deviant' to 'Variant'

Even so, many family structures are shaky. Thirty-eight per cent of all first marriages fail. As many as four children out of ten born in the 1970s will spend part of their childhood in a single-parent family, usually with the mother as head of the household; 17 per cent of all children under 18 are now living in single-parent families. Remarriage currently blends about 18 million step-children from the remnants of what used to be called "broken" families into new family units. "What was defined a decade ago as 'deviant,' " observes University of Massachusetts sociologist Alice S. Rossi, "is today labeled 'variant,' in order to suggest that there is a healthy, experimental quality to current social explorations 'beyond monogamy' or 'beyond the nuclear family.' "

Perhaps the most distressing development is the high tide of illegitimacy. Fifteen per cent of all births are illegitimate and more than half of all out-of-wedlock babies are born to teenagers. Illegitimacy is particulary high among blacks: of the 513,000 children who were born to black women in 1976, 50.3 per cent were illegitimate. And it is the illegitimate, both black and white, who are most likely to be impoverished, dependent on welfare, deprived of educational opportunities and destined to repeat the cycle with illegitimate children of their own. "In that sense, out-of-wedlock births really are a public problem," says Kristin Moore, a researcher at the Urban Institute in Washington, D.C.

How should government respond to such deep-seated problems? Over the past decade, the policy debate has tended to split along classic ideological lines, with liberal Democrats pushing activist intervention and Republican conservatives resisting. Thus in 1971, Richard Nixon vetoed a "comprehensive child-development program" on the argument that it would be "family weakening." On a similar ground, Gerald Ford in 1975 cut more than $1.6 billion from appropriations for food stamps, child health, Medicaid and social services. But positions have shifted in recent months, to the point where conservatives are now looking for ways to support family-oriented bills and liberals are abandoning such former goals as the setting up of a Federal family agency. "The last thing we need," Vice President Walter Mondale observed [in 1977], is for the Federal government to launch some ill-defined national crusade to 'save the family.' And I'm no more eager than any parent to be surveyed by some 'national bureau of family happiness' about how I'm getting along with my wife or how often I read to my children at bedtime."

Instead, the Carter Administration has pledged itself to a "strong, understandable, well-considered, deeply committed, pro-family policy." A definition of what that means has been deferred until the [1980] White House Conference on Families, but the trend now seems toward a pragmatic approach keyed not to any idealized vision but to the varying realities of U.S. life. . . .

A useful beginning might be to distinguish between problems affecting families in general, such as the trend to working mothers, and those that are primarily side effects of other problems, such as poverty and urban decay. As [former Secretary of Health, Education and Welfare] Califano himself told Carter in a campaign report in 1976, "The most severe threat to family life

FAMILIES IN PROFILE

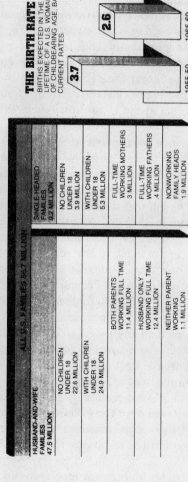

ALL U.S. FAMILIES 56.7 MILLION

HUSBAND-AND-WIFE FAMILIES 47.5 MILLION

- NO CHILDREN UNDER 18 — 22.6 MILLION
- WITH CHILDREN UNDER 18 — 24.9 MILLION
- BOTH PARENTS WORKING FULL TIME — 11.4 MILLION
- HUSBAND ONLY WORKING FULL TIME — 12.4 MILLION
- NEITHER PARENT WORKING — 1.1 MILLION

SINGLE-HEADED FAMILIES 9.2 MILLION

- NO CHILDREN UNDER 18 — 3.9 MILLION
- WITH CHILDREN UNDER 18 — 5.3 MILLION
- FULL-TIME WORKING MOTHERS — 3 MILLION
- FULL-TIME WORKING FATHERS — .4 MILLION
- NONWORKING FAMILY HEADS — 1.9 MILLION

THE BIRTH RATE

BIRTHS EXPECTED IN THE LIFETIME OF A U.S. WOMAN OF CHILDBEARING AGE, BASED ON CURRENT RATES.

- 1955-59 — 3.7
- 1965-69 — 2.6
- 1977 (EST.) — 1.8

WHAT CHILDREN COST

WHAT A FAMILY OF FOUR WOULD SPEND OVER EIGHTEEN YEARS TO RAISE A CHILD IN A NORTHEASTERN CITY. COSTS INCLUDE FOOD, CLOTHING, EDUCATION (EXCEPT COLLEGE) AND MEDICAL CARE AFTER BIRTH, AT 1977 PRICES.

- FAMILY INCOME UNDER $10,500 — TOTAL COST $24,727
- FAMILY INCOME $10,500-$13,500 — TOTAL COST $32,914
- FAMILY INCOME $16,500-$20,000 — TOTAL COST $54,207

THE MARRIAGE ODDS

OF ALL U.S. ADULTS

- 96% WILL MARRY
- 38% OF THOSE WILL DIVORCE
- 79% OF THOSE WILL REMARRY
- 44% OF THOSE WILL DIVORCE AGAIN

Newsweek, Inc., Bob Conrad.

stems from unemployment and lack of an adequate income." The consequences seem clear enough—in Flint, Mich., for example, alcoholism, drug abuse and child abuse all increased when the jobless rate hit 20 per cent—but it's not as clear that employment and income-supplement programs should be designed primarily as family measures.

Kenneth Keniston, author of the five-year Carnegie Council report, "All Our Children: The American Family Under Pressure," proposes putting more money directly into the hands of poor parents—through either tax-credits, child-care vouchers or a system of child-care allowances—and thus broadening parental options. But a recent experiment in Seattle and Denver, financed by the Department of Health, Education and Welfare, showed that income maintenance given to selected black and white mothers resulted in a sharp jump in family break-ups. Ironically, the most needy wives were also the most likely to leave their husbands when given a minimum-income guarantee.

A Bureaucratic Nightmare?

For most U.S. families, the problems are not that stark or the needs that clear. But every family is affected, to a greater or lesser degree, by the actions of government—a fact that has only recently been fully realized. Accordingly, many experts now favor a requirement for a family impact statement to assess the potential effects of all new legislation and government programs. Admittedly, that might turn into a bureaucratic nightmare, but it could at least provide a useful perspective. At George Washington University, a Family Impact Seminar has already identified 268 programs administered by seventeen Federal departments and agencies that have potential impact on families, plus another 63 that have explicit impact, such as direct aid.

One obvious area for family support would be help for working mothers who have not yet found a satisfactory way to combine their responsibilities to their children with the need for more income. Opinion is still divided as to how to do this. Even supporters of day-care programs cannot agree on whether they should be under school or community control. The government has allowed tax credits for day care by outsiders or by relatives who care for the child at home but who then cannot themselves be claimed as dependents.

Government and corporate officials are also studying the merits of "flextime" working hours and half-time jobs for both parents, which would allow at least one of them to be at home at all times without jeopardizing their careers. But there is a growing sentiment among some women—like child psychoanalyst Selma Fraiberg, author of *Every Child's Birthright: In Defense of Mothering*—that only a full-time mother figure can provide the nurture that children need. She proposes, for example, that welfare mothers should not be forced to work but be adequately subsidized so they can stay home with their young children.

On the whole, most advocates of family aid favor a delicate governmental hand, with incentives and discouragements rather than direct laws and regulations. But even that approach is still debated. Psychologist Nicholas Zill, of the Foundation for Child Development in New York City, says an answer to the illegitimacy problem might be to develop birth-control methods so that people would have to make a conscious decision to have children—and then to institute compulsory education on child-rearing and state-controlled birth licenses. Others argue that the family is a perfectly healthy institution that needs no help, and still others protest that families shouldn't be singled out for favorable treatment. Child advocates are so concerned that youngsters' rights will be overlooked that they have won a White House conference of their own.

In the long run, perhaps the wisest approach to the problem is to recognize that the family can best be served by nourishing those related institutions on which families have traditionally relied for primary support: neighborhoods, communities, churches and other such voluntary associations. Sociologist Peter L. Berger of Rutgers University sees these institutions as extensions of the family that serve as civilizing mediators between the private individual and the impersonal megastructures of big government, big business, big labor and big education. As a practical matter, Berger argues that parents should be empowered with vouchers to purchase local services—including religious education—for children and thus encourage the development of a vigorous and pluralistic community life.

"The most urgent thing facing us is the need to restore communities in this country," says anthropologist Margaret Mead, "—multi-generational, multi-ethnic and multi-occupational communities where you can take care of children, the old and the sick so that you don't have to segregate people by age and income into neighborhoods and institutions. The major function of a family is bringing up children to be full human beings, able to live in a world of two sexes, of different ages, of different personalities and temperaments."

Old Myths and Modern Drives

There are undoubtedly millions of families that serve this function in the U.S. today, but they escape the attention of social workers and mental-health officials, who typically see only troubled families. Over the past year, however, Robert Woodson, a resident fellow at the innovative American Enterprise Institute for Public Policy Research in Washington, D.C., has been observing what makes healthy families strong, with a view to having them teach "parent effectiveness" to less successful neighbors. As part of a long-term project organized by Cornell University psychologist Urie Bronfenbrenner, program director Frank Woolever is looking at ways in which black families in Syracuse, N.Y., can link together and rebuild decaying neighborhoods.

No organizer is likely to knock on the doors of middle-class families, much less ask how the well-to-do are getting along. Yet these families, especially, suffer from both the old myth of family self-sufficiency and the modern drive for individual fulfillment. "There's a real conflict between what's good for adults and for children, and possibly even between males and females," observes sociologist Boocock. "What nurtures the family unit is in conflict with what maximizes personal development. You just can't have it both ways."

Yet as any family member knows, such conflicts are the stuff of family life—the forge in which people learn how to live in the world. The family has survived thousands of years of that sort of internal strife, along with war, famine, pestilence and tyranny. Perhaps the most encouraging thought is that with that background, it can probably outlast its new friends and their remedies as well.

ARLENE SKOLNICK

The Intimate Environment

The nuclear family, consisting of a married couple and their dependent children, has been the dominant form of family in our society. But other family constructions are common in some cultures and in parts of our own society. Arlene Skolnick, a psychologist, defines four concepts of family or family types in this short selection from her widely used textbook The Intimate Environment.

Contrasting definitions of what the family *is* may . . . be said to be paradigms, or pictures of reality.

There seem to be at least four paradigms or programs or schemata for interpreting the experiences of family life in a society. They subdivide reality in different ways, define and group objects differently, and employ different concepts of space, time, and human nature. These paradigms include, first, the familiar nuclear or conjugal family model—what we mean in America by the term "my family." The second model of the family, based mainly on blood ties, is termed the consanguine family by anthropologists. It is also known as the extended family.

Some of Birdwhistell's (1966) Kentucky subjects, for example, who lived in interdependent or extended families, had very different conceptions and definitions of "family" from their friends, neighbors, and even spouses who had grown up in more nuclear or . . . segmented families. The interdependent family member seemed to define family in terms of blood kinship. He expected to continue all his life the intense involvement with kinfolk he had known as a child. He would not expect this involvement to be affected by reaching maturity, marrying, or work. In fact, the main purpose of Birdwhistell's research was to learn why some rural Kentuckians would migrate to other areas of the country and try to be "successful," while others who seemed much like them would remain behind in their hometowns. He believes he found the explanation in the different family patterns of the movers and nonmovers.

The family in the traditional extended-family model is a very different entity from the series of separate units in space and time that make up the nuclear-family model. The traditional family is continuous in space and time, unbounded by household walls, and immortal. Marriage, birth, maturity, even death do not reduce the central unit. The genetic family tree defines not only genetic connections, but ongoing obligations and involvements. Rather than the marriage of grown children leaving behind an empty nest, the in-law line may add additional family members:

> If the marriage is, in family terms, a good one, the affinal relatives/in-laws of the family member become one's own "almost like family." And as these affinal relatives meet at funeral, church, and family gatherings, they gain kinship status and are called by kinship terms. (Birdwhistell, 1966)

Furthermore, in the traditional-family system, the husband-wife pair is by no means the obvious core of the family. As a 39-year-old English mother of five put it:

> I couldn't get on without me mother. I could get on without me husband. I don't notice him.

Yet Birdwhistell's interviewees did not perceive the unique quality of their family life. When asked directly about their family relationships, the "interdependent" family people talked in the stereotyped terms and imagery of the nuclear-family model. It was as if the nuclear-family imagery had blotted out the experiences of those who had had a very different life style from the standard husband-wife, parent-child unit. And if there was any awareness of being different, it was stated with a sense of shame.

People who hold to one of the foregoing models may doubt that the other one is really a viable family. They are likely to see people in the other family model as not quite healthy or normal psychologically. For example, Birdwhistell notes that his nuclear-family subjects tended to define people with traditional-family ties as immature, dependent, and lacking in ambition. The traditional people, on the other hand, were likely to feel that people with the nuclear-family definitions were cold, selfish, and too driven by ambition. As for the family models we shall turn to next, the holders of both the traditional model and the nuclear model probably would think them mad and unworkable.

The first of these "deviant" family models is the communal one. The recent rebirth of the communal movement in the United States and other places has brought to many people an awareness that there are indeed alternatives to family life based either on blood kinship or the married couple and their children. This alternative is based on primary ties of mystic brotherhood or communion. The spread of the communal movement has also brought to light the fact that this form of family has a long and prolific history, reaching back to early Christian times at least. Within recent centuries the communal tradition has been associated in Europe with a number of Protestant sects as well as Utopian socialists and other idealists. The communes are often compared by both members and observers to the traditional extended family. Many contemporary communes consciously try to recreate the extended family on a nonkinship basis.

The fourth family paradigm is defined more by exclusion than by a focus on a particular family form. It makes no assumptions about a particular form of the family, or the family itself being necessary as the basic building block of society. The key difference between this paradigm and the others is that the individual is not defined by his place in a network of kin. He or she is not primarily a member of this clan or that tribe, as in the traditional family, nor primarily a son or father, mother or daughter, husband or wife, as in the second paradigm, nor a communal brother or sister. The family exists, of course, but it does not occupy all of the social space, nor is it the primary source of sociability. The two basic elements in this paradigm include the individual, considered apart from either blood or marriage ties, and an urban society, which supplies social density and a fairly high level of technology. Perhaps we should call it the "cosmopolitan model." Ralph Linton, the anthropologist, has written of how all kinds of family bonds are weakened in modern urban settings.

> Breakdowns of kin ties and of the close social integration of individuals and conjugal family groups are no new thing in history. They were an accompaniment of urbanization and suddenly increased spatial mobility in ancient as well as modern civilization. Nevertheless, there is another factor in the present situation which, if it is not altogether new, is at least of unprecedented importance. This is the progressive diminution of the economic dependence of spouses upon each other. . . .
>
> In the modern urban community the delicatessen, the steam laundry, ready-made clothes, and above all the opening to women of attractive and well-paid occupations have done more to undermine the sanctity of marriage than has any conceivable loss of faith in its religious sanctions. Under present conditions, adult men and women are at last in a position to satisfy their basic needs in the absence of any sort of familial association, either conjugal or consanguine. In the anonymity of city life and with the development of effective techniques for contraception even the sexual needs of both can be met without entering into permanent unions or entailing serious penalties. The revolutionary effect of these developments upon the family as an institution can scarcely be overrated.

Thus a person may be living in a torrent of social life, as in Aries' description of medieval life, or may combine public sociability with friend sociability, with family life and privacy. The common core underlying these models is the *individual* as the irreducible social atom, not the *family*. This model does not assume the close interdependence of family and society as in the other models. It does not assume a correspondence between kinship, living together, sexuality, and domestic functions such as child care, care of the sick, meal preparation. The emphasis on the individual implies that the family is *not* the building block of society.

Summary

The most familiar subjects are often the most difficult to study because we take them for granted. This is especially true of the family. In America the nuclear family—two parents and their minor children—in a home of their own is defined as *the family*. Variations from this pattern are seen as unfortunate and abnormal. It also has been widely believed that the nuclear family is universal.

When we look at family life in other societies, however, and our own historical past, we find that variations in family form and living arrangements are rather common. Nuclear-family members are often found living apart. The household may contain nonkin living together as a family. Households themselves may only be places where people sleep, while eating, child care, and other domestic functions occur elsewhere.

CLYDE KLUCKHOHN

Variations in the Human Family

The family varies widely in different human societies, yet underlying great variation are certain regular, universal themes: "The family was always and everywhere an agency for the protection and training of the child and for the care of the aged and the infirm . . . for the transmission of . . . culture." In this classic paper, a distinguished anthropologist considers variations in the form and functions of the family. The article, first published in 1949, still retains remarkable freshness and pertinence.

Variations in the human family are interesting and are important both from scientific and from practical standpoints. However, anthropology has tended to overemphasize the differences at the expense of the similarities. Fascinated with the exotic and obsessed with the new principle of cultural relativity, anthropologists have tried to show that the gamut of variability was limitless. Earlier systematic studies seemed to indicate that this was indeed the case. There was the discovery of the extended family system, of the fact that, even in Europe, ultimogeniture existed along with primogeniture; of "visit marriage" in which the man retains residence in his own group. There were those few societies in which two or more men might be married to one woman. But claims for a socially accepted complete promiscuity or for "group marriage" have not stood up under closer scrutiny. And matriarchy, in the strict sense of the term, has turned out to be a myth. What is true is that the formal and informal power of the mother—both within the family and in political and economic affairs affecting the group as a whole—is greater in some societies than in others. Similarly, the claim that there were groups in which the father had no social relationship to his children is now seen as an extravagant

From C. Kluckhohn, "Variations in the Human Family" in Community Service Society of New York, *The Family in a Democratic Society,* New York: Columbia University Press, 1949, by permission of the publisher.

overstatement of a considerable range of variation in the extent of that relationship.

The first generalization to be made, then, is that all variations in the form and functioning of the human family could, until recently, be seen as variations on a basic theme. No aspect of the universal culture pattern has been more clearly delimited than that of the family. The family was always and everywhere an agency for the protection and training of the child and for the care of the aged and the infirm. The manner and extent of this training and care varied considerably, but the basic function was constant. In every society the family was the fundamental institution for the transmission of those patterned ways of living which anthropologists call culture.

The past tense has been used advisedly in the preceding sentences; for the traditional philosophy of the family has been threatened in recent decades. Both in Europe and in the United States, the function of protection for the aged, the infirm, and the distressed is being taken over more and more by the state. Greatly increased geographical mobility, changed patterns in regard to employment of married women, and other economic developments make it impossible to regard this long-established functional continuity as still a constant. Under modern urban conditions, both men and women can enjoy opportunities (which previously were easily accessible only in family life) without surrendering their independence or assuming family responsibilities.

Every culture legalizes an enduring union between two or more persons of the two sexes explicitly for purposes of parenthood. This nuclear or biological family is never completely submerged in any extended family system. The social approval of sexual union does not in any society constitute in and of itself a marriage or a family. The legitimization of sexuality between husbands and wives, like that prohibition of sexual relations between all other members of the biological family which is an almost constant feature of the human family, is everywhere conceived, not as an end in itself, but as a means to [meet] the physical [needs] and cultural training of children.

There is nothing mysterious or supernatural about these pan-human regularities in cultural patterns for the family. They bear an understandable relationship to certain inescapable facts in the human situation. Children inevitably go through a period of helplessness. Sickness and old age render adults dependent again. These are biological "givens," which all cultures must face. In the same way, it is a biological fact that men are ordinarily stronger physically than women and that women are for longer or shorter periods incapacitated by events of their reproductive cycle. Sexual competition within the immediate family could hardly fail to lead to suffering and to disruption of the family. Hence, the restriction of sexuality to husbands and wives may be regarded as one of those aspects of the universal culture pattern that is based upon countless millennia of trial-and-error learning. Exceptions are limited to a few ruling groups and, possibly, to the society of old Iran.

With some qualifications, then, for the contemporary situation in Europe and America, it can be said that there are certain constants in the functions of the human family. There are also certain regularities in form. The ideal in all human groups has been long-term marriage—though not necessarily between only two partners. The elementary family has ever been conceived as based upon the primary relations of children and parents, with parents related to each other, in the last analysis, through their children. Finally, there are psychological universals. The Freudian description of the Oedipus situation and of sibling rivalry is basically right, even though there are formal variations of this psychological theme; that is, the older person of opposite sex to whom a male child is drawn may be the sister or an aunt, and the older person of the same sex toward whom there exist ambivalent feelings may be an uncle rather than the father. But psychoanalysis has correctly pointed to some inevitable features of the psychodynamics. These words from an Indonesian informant of Cora DuBois suggest one kind of basis for the universality:

> Wives are like our mothers. When we were small our mothers fed us. When we are grown, our wives cook for us. If there is something good, they keep it in the pot until we come home. When we were small, we slept with our mothers. When we are grown, we sleep with our wives. Sometimes when we are grown, we wake in the night and call our wives "mother."

It is no accident that in many cultures the term for "sweetheart" is identical with or similar to the word for "mother" or "sister."

Cross-Cultural Variations

Within this basic psychological-formal-functional pattern, variations are of three general types. The first may be termed cross-cultural and refers to those differences in blueprints for family living that are standardized as part of the historic tradition of a people. These cross-cultural variations relate in part to the form of the family, in part to its functions.

There are the well-known marriage forms of monogamy [marriage to one person at a time], polygyny [having more than one wife at a time], and polyandry [having more than one husband at a time]. These themselves have many variants. While every culture tends to define marriage as ideally permanent, there are many societies, such as our own, in which the behavioral pattern must be realistically described as "serial monogamy." Polygyny ranges from a standard of two or, at most, three wives to the Mohammedan limit of four or the hundreds held by certain African and Asiatic potentates. It is interesting, however, that in these cases only a few woman are ordinarily considered wives in the full sense. In some African tribes, for instance, there are only three legal wives— "the head," "the arm" and "the leg"—and the children of concubines are formally ascribed to one of these three. The plural marriage may be to sisters or to non-related women or to a woman and her daughter by a previous marriage. In polyandry, also, the marriage of the woman may be to brothers or to nonbrothers. Monogamy, on the whole, appears mainly in the simpler societies and in those where the normal sex ratio is not disturbed. [A study by] Hobhouse, Wheeler, and Ginsberg found monogamy in only 66 societies as against polygyny in 378 and polyandry in 31.

In addition to the marriage pattern, the form of the family is structured by the size of the group included in various social and economic arrangements. The biological family may customarily live alone with the occasional addition of a widowed grandmother or grandfather or collateral relative. Or, the family may be extended to include various relatives on the father's or mother's side of the family or both. Typically, a matrilineal extended family, is made up of a grandmother, her husband, her married daughters, their husbands, and their children. In many societes considered matrilineal, however, this typical picture is seldom actualized in all its details. One married daughter lives with her husband's people, or she and her husband and children live as an isolated family unit. One or more sons bring their wives and children to reside with the matrilineal group. In almost every case, membership in what W. Lloyd Warner has called the "family of orientation" continues to some extent when the adult joins in founding a new "family of procreation." Matrilineal, patrilineal, and bilateral families represent ideal types rather than clear-cut forms that apply without qualification to every family in a community.

The forms of family organization prescribed by cultural patterns have consequences that are in the strict sense social rather than cultural. A cultural pattern that provides for sisters and their husbands and children living together in one place determines the nature of interpersonal relations in ways other than dictating economic co-operation, stating that children of sisters shall call each other by sibling terms, behave toward each other as do biological brothers and sisters, etc. The sheer size of the face-to-face group of relatives makes for variation in family life. . . . Of course, this quantitative dimension is enormously complicated by the emotional quality of each given relationship.

It is convenient and in accord with usual practice to restrict the term "family" to that group of relatives who have habitual face-to-face dealings. Thus, only the biological families of orientation and procreation and the extended family are included, and such wider units as the clan . . . are excluded. But it should be noted that this conception is an artifact of the Western cultural tradition. The vocabularies of certain nonliterate languages do not include a term that corresponds to our biological family, and some fail even to distinguish the extended family from the whole group of individuals, whether personally known or not, whom one addresses by kinship terms. The distinction between actual mother and mother's sister or classificatory mother can always be and is expressed—when context makes it necessary—by such circumlocutions as "mother from whose body I came" and the like. Yet the concept of a particular group of individuals to whom one's actual biological relations are closest is often not explicit. The secondary parenthood and siblingship implied by a classificatory kinship terminology merges at every point with the relationships we call the "immediate family."

Two family systems can, of course, have approximately the same form but allot the functions within the family organization very differently. The families of the Navaho, Zuñi, and Hopi Indians are all extended, matrilineal, matrilocal. However, the cultural image of the ideal family is not identical in these three cases. The official head of the Navaho family is the father, though emotional and informal authority may actually rest largely with the mother. With the Hopi, authority is, in theory, divided between the mother and her brothers. In practice, the father has a good deal. The Zuñi system falls somewhere between the Navaho and the Hopi. In respects other than that of authority there is also a great and subtle range of variation, both formalized and unformalized. The obligations and expectations of each family member, the tolerated deviations, the stereotypes of ideal role fulfillment—all of these bear a relationship to the formal structure but cannot be predicted solely on the basis of knowledge of the forms.

Intracultural Variations

The second major type of variation may be called the intracultural. In spite of the existence of ideal patterns defining family life for a total society there tend to grow up behavioral patterns that differentiate local or regional groups, economic groups, religious groups, and class groups. In our own society, for example, the existence of a generalized pattern for family organization and behavior is attested to by uniformities in the picture portrayed in national advertisements, radio programs, and moving pictures. Yet the development of well-established, class-typed family patterns has been shown by Warner, John Dollard, Allison Davis, and others. Among the Navaho, polygyny is an accepted pattern of the aboriginal culture. But the actual incidence of polygyny varies widely as between regions where the primary economic base is agricultural, pastoral, or a mixture of these two.

Idiosyncratic Variations

The third principal type of variation may be called idiosyncratic. In no society, however homogeneous, nor in any given segment of that society, is any one family precisely identical with any other. No two individuals play the culturally defined role of mother in precisely the same way. In one family the mother happens, for reasons not culturally controlled, to be much older than the father. To another family the father brings the experience of a previous unhappy marriage. In societies where children are ordinarily born every two or three years, one parent is sterile for a period. Or, if some of the children in a sequence die at an early age, the constellation of that family is unmistakably altered. It is because of a combination of determinants of this order that no particular family ever passes on "*the* culture." Each family transmits its private variant of the culture. And herein lies a fertile source of culture change.

The cause of all these variations in human family life cannot be subsumed in any simple formula. There is some degree of correlation between economic patterns and family organization. Where population density is one to the square mile or less and where livelihood depends on intimate knowledge of the country, the normal form of the family is the simple patrilineal family, with families joined together in bands or hordes. But the correlation is by no means one to one. All kinds of cultural patterns have a way of persisting long after the institutions or circumstances which gave them adaptive value have disappeared. Family patterns may be radically altered as the consequence of widespread acceptance of a new religious cult. This acceptance, in turn, may be determined by a temporary set of economic conditions or other situational factors. Many cultural forms are the product of historical accidents. A variation in family life may, for instance, arise originally as an idiosyncratic variation. A father of a special constitutional type marries a woman who is psychopathic. They manage to work out a form of mutual adjustment for themselves and their children. Most often this particular form would disappear with the end of this particular biological family. But, if the father in question happens to succeed to the chieftainship through the accidental death of his older brother, or if a son of the family founds a new religion, an accidental variant might become the "sacred institution" of a whole people, to be blindly defended and carefully perpetuated.

The practical lessons to be drawn from the foregoing by the applied social scientist (the social worker, for example) would seem to be the following: First, the stuff of human nature is, after all, basically the same because of similarities in human biology and in the conditions of human life. The tailoring is different, and this is significant in making judgments as to how human needs can most effectively be satisfied, as to what incentives will work with one group and not another, as to the meaning of a specific human act. However, the applied social scientist must not be taken in by cultural stereotypes any more than by the simplest, commonsense view of human nature, which is ordinarily a projection of values and beliefs that are local in time and in space. There are patterned variations, whether regional or class or economic, within most cultures. Moreover, there are idiosyncratic variations that sometimes bear only the most general resemblance to the cultural blueprint. In other words, knowledge of a culture or of some segment of that culture can be very useful for general orientation, but one can never expect to drop a perpendicular from the abstracted culture patterns to the behavioral forms existing in a particular family. Finally, the applied social scientist will do well to remember the multifarious causes of variations in human family life. Knowing this, the social worker can steer a difficult but necessary middle course between proper respect for traditional ways of living, as related to the total life design of a group, and absolute acceptance of specific tailorings which usually turn out, after all, to be by-products of adventitious historical events.

ROBERT COLES

Life in Appalachia

In this description of a poor family in Appalachia, Robert Coles makes or implies important points about the family: that it lends meaning and organization to life even under extremely harsh circumstances; that a father can assert authority and receive respect even when he is severely restricted physically; that manners and civility are strong traditions which lend grace to lives under siege; that a sense of place and coherence in a social group contributes strength to individuals; that religion and ritual enrich and sustain group life and the individuals who participate in that life. Coles, a psychiatrist, demonstrates in this selection the sensitivity and respect for the integrity of lives which mark his award-winning series of books, Children of Crisis, *about Americans of different backgrounds.*

Hugh McCaslin is unforgettable. He has red hair and, at 43, freckles. He stands six feet four. As he talked to me about his work in the coal mines, I kept wondering what he did with his height down inside the earth.

Once he must have been an unusually powerful man; even today his arms and legs are solid muscle. The fat he has added in recent years has collected in only one place, his waist, both front and back.

"I need some padding around my back; it's hurt, and I don't think it'll ever get back right. I broke it bad working, and they told me at first they'd have it fixed in no time flat, but they were wrong. . . . I can't work, and even if I could, there's no work to do, not around here, no sir. They told me I'm 'totally incapacitated,' that's the words they used. They said my spine was hurt, and the nerves, and I can't walk and move about the way I should. As if I needed them to tell me!

"Then they . . . told me I was lucky, because even though I wasn't in shape to go in the mines, I could do anything else, anything that's not too heavy. Sometimes I wonder what goes on in the heads of those doctors. They look you right in the eye, and they're wearing a straight face on, and they tell you you're

Adapted from "Life in Appalachia—The Case of Hugh McCaslin," Part 8 of Chapter 6 of *Migrants, Sharecroppers, Mountaineers,* Volume II of CHILDREN OF CRISIS by Robert Coles (first appeared in *Transaction*). Copyright © 1967, 1968, 1969, 1971 by Robert Coles. By permission of Little, Brown and Company in association with the Atlantic Monthly Press.

sick, you've been hurt digging out coal, and you'll never be the same, but you're really not so bad off, because your back isn't so bad you can't be a judge, or a professor, or the president of the coal company or something like that, you know. . . .

"Then, you see, they closed down the mine itself. That shows you I wasn't very lucky. My friends kept telling me I was lucky to be alive, and lucky to be through with it, being a miner. . . . They'd come by here when I was sick, and they'd tell me I sure was a fortunate guy, and God was smiling that day, and now He'd be smiling forever on me, because I was spared a *real* disaster, and it was bound to come, one day or another. . . .

"After a while I thought maybe they did have something; and if I could just recover me a good pension from the company, and get my medical expenses all covered—well, then, I'd get better, as much as possible, and go fetch me a real honest-to-goodness job, where I could see the sun all day, and the sky outside, and breathe our air here, as much of it as I pleased, without a worry in the world.

"But that wasn't to be. I was dumb, real dumb, and hopeful. I saw them treating me in the hospital, and when they told me to go home I thought I was better, or soon would be. Instead, I had to get all kinds of treatments, and they said I'd have to pay for them, out of my savings or somewhere. And the pension I thought I was supposed to get, that was all in my mind, they said. They said the coal industry was going through a lot of changes, and you couldn't expect them to keep people going indefinitely, even if they weren't in the best of shape, even if it did happen down in the mines.

"Well, that's it, to make it short. I can't do hard work, and I have a lot of pain, every day of my life. I might be able to do light work, desk work, but hell, I'm not fit for anything like that; and even if I could, where's the work to be found? . . . We're doomed here, to sitting and growing the food we can and sharing our misery with one another.

"My brother, he helps; and my four sisters, they help; and my daddy, he's still alive and he can't help except to sympathize, and tell me it's a good thing I didn't get killed in that landslide and can see my boys grow up. He'll come over here and we start drinking. You bet, he's near 80, and we start drinking, and remembering. . . .

The McCaslins have five sons, all born within nine years. The oldest is in high school and dreams of the day he will join the army. He says he will be "taken" in, say, in Charleston or Beckley—in his mind, any "big city" will do . . . "anywhere that's good, and it'll be far away from here, I do believe that." Hugh McCaslin becomes enraged when he hears his son talk like that; with a few beers in him he becomes especially enraged:

"That's the way it is around here. That's what's happened to us. That's what they did to us. They made us lose any honor we had. They turned us idle. They turned us into a lot of grazing sheep, lucky to find a bit of pasture here and there. We don't *do* anything here anymore; and so my boys, they'll all want to leave, and they will. But they'll want to come back, too—because this land, it's in their bones going way back, and you don't shake off your ancestors that easy, no sir.

"My daddy, he was born right up the road in this here hollow, and his daddy, and back to a long time ago. There isn't anyone around here we're not kin to somehow, near or far. My daddy was the one supposed to leave for the mines. He figured he could make more money than he could dream about, and it wasn't too far to go. He went for a while, but some years later he quit. He couldn't take it. I grew up in a camp near the mine, and I'd still be there if it wasn't that I got hurt and moved back here to the hollow. . . .

"What choice did I have? I thought I might want to do some farming, like my grandfather, but there's no need for me, and my grandfather couldn't really keep more than himself going, I mean with some food and all. Then I thought it'd be nice to finish school, and maybe get a job someplace near, in a town not a big city. But everything was collapsing all over the country then, and you'd be crazy to think you were going to get anything by leaving here and going out there, with the lines standing for soup. . . .

"It could be worse, you say to yourself, and you resolve to follow your daddy and be a miner. That's what I did. He said we had a lousy day's work, but we got good pay, and we could buy things. My daddy had been the richest man in his family for a while. In fact, he was the only man in his family who had any money at all. . . . My daddy would hand out the dollar bills, one after the other. I can picture it right now. You feel rich, and you feel real kind."

Hugh McCaslin's life wouldn't be that much better even if he had not been seriously hurt in a mine accident. The miners who were his closest friends are now unemployed, almost every one of them. . . .

The McCaslins are early risers, but no one gets up earlier than the father. He suffers pain at night; his back and his legs hurt. He has been told that a new hard mattress would help, and hot baths, and aspirin. He spends a good part of the night awake— "thinking and dozing off and then coming to, real sudden-like, with a pain here or there." For a while he thought of sleeping on the floor, or trying to get another bed, but he could not bear the prospect of being alone:

"My wife, Margaret, has kept me alive. She has some of God's patience in her, that's the only way I figure she's been able to last it. She smiles when things are so dark you'd think the end has come. She soothes me, and tells me it'll get better, and even though I know it won't I believe her for a few minutes, and that helps."

So he tosses and turns in their bed, and his wife has learned to sleep soundly but to wake up promptly when her husband is in real pain. They have aspirin and treat it as something special—and expensive. I think Hugh McCaslin realizes that he suffers from many different kinds of pain; perhaps if he had more money he might have been addicted to all sorts of pain-killers long ago. . . . We will never know how Hugh McCaslin might have felt today if he had found suitable work after his accident, or had received further medical care. Work is something a patient needs as he starts getting better, as anyone who works in a "rehabilitation unit" of a hospital well knows. Hugh McCaslin lacked medical care when he needed it, lacks it today, and in his own words needs a "time-killer" as much as a pain-killer. . . .

He dwells on his children. There are five of them, and he wants all of them to leave West Virginia. Sometimes in the early morning, before his wife is up, he leaves bed to look at them sleeping:

"I need some hope, and they have it, in their young age and the future they have, if they only get the hell out of here before it's too late. Oh, I like it here, too. It's pretty, and all that. It's peaceful. I'm proud of us people. We've been here a long time, and we needed real guts to stay and last. And who wants to live in a big city? I've been in some of our cities, here in West Virginia, and they're no big value, from what I can see, not so far as bringing up a family. You have no land, no privacy, a lot of noise, and all that. But if it's between living and dying, I'll take living; and right here, right now, I think we're dying—dying away, slow but sure, every year more and more so."

He worries about his children in front of them. When they get up they see him sitting and drinking coffee in the kitchen. He is wide awake, and hungrier for company than he knows. He wants to learn what they'll be doing that day. He wants to talk about things, about the day's events and inevitably a longer span of time, the future: "Take each day like your life hangs on it. That's being young, when you can do that, when you're not trapped and have some choice on things." The children are drowsy, but respectful. They go about dressing and taking coffee and doughnuts with him. They are as solicitous as he is. Can they make more coffee? They ask if they can bring him anything—even though they know full well his answer: "No, just yourselves."

Mrs. McCaslin may run the house, but she makes a point of checking every decision with her husband. He "passes on" even small matters—something connected with one of the children's schoolwork, or a neighbor's coming visit, or a project for the church. She is not sly and devious; not clever at appearing weak but "manipulating" all the while. She genuinely defers to her husband, and his weakness, his illness, his inability to find work—and none of those new medical, social, or psychological "developments" have made her see fit to change her ways. . . .

Hugh McCaslin, as poor as one can be in America, not at all well-educated, jobless, an invalid, and a worried, troubled man, nevertheless exerts a strong and continuing influence upon everyone in his family. He is, again, *there*—not just at home, but very much involved in almost everything his wife and children do. . . .

"Let me tell you, if we had a chance, men like me, we'd vote for a different way of doing things. It just isn't right to use people like they're so much dirt, hire them and fire them and give them no respect and no real security. A few make fortunes and, the rest of us, we're lucky to have our meals from day to day. That's not right; it just isn't. . . .

They tell me sometimes I'm bitter, my brothers do, but they're just as bitter as I am—they don't talk as much, that's the only difference. Of course it got better here with unions and with some protection the workers got through the government. But you can't protect a man when the company decides to pull out; when it says it's got all it can get, so goodbye folks, and take care of yourselves, because we're moving on to some other place, and we just can't do much more than tell you it was great while it lasted, and you helped us out a lot, yes sir you did."

He does not always talk like that. He can be quiet for long stretches of time, obviously and moodily quiet. His wife finds his silences hard to bear. She doesn't know what they will "lead to." Every day she asks her husband whether there is anything "special" he wants to eat—even though they both know there isn't much they can afford but the daily mainstays. . . . Mrs. McCaslin defers to her husband, though; one way is to pay him the courtesy of asking him what he wants. I have often heard them go back and forth about food, and as if for all the world they were far better off, with more choices before them:

> "Anything special you want for supper?"
> "No. Anything suits me fine. I'm not too hungry."
> "Well, if that's it then I'd better make you hungry with something special."
> "What can do that?"
> "I thought I'd fry up the potatoes real good tonight and cut in some onions. It's better than boiling, and I've got some good pork to throw in. You wait and see."
> "I will. It sounds good."

He hurts and she aches for him. His back has its "bad spells," and she claims her own back can "feel the pain that goes through his." They don't touch each other very much in a stranger's presence, or even, I gather, before their children, but they give each other long looks of recognition, sympathy, affection, and sometimes anger or worse. They understand each other in that silent, real, lasting way that defies the gross labels that I and my kind call upon. It is hard to convey in words—theirs or mine—the subtle, delicate, largely unspoken, and continual *sense of each other* (that is the best that I can do) that they have. In a gesture, a glance, a frown, a smile they talk and agree and disagree:

> "I can tell what the day will be like for Hugh when he first gets up. It's all in how he gets out of bed, slow or with a jump to it. You might say we all have our good days and bad ones, but Hugh has a lot of time to give over to his moods, and around here I guess we're emotional, you might say. . . .
> "You know, when we were married he was the most cheerful man I'd ever met. I mean he smiled all the time, not just because someone said something funny. His daddy told me I was getting the happiest of his kids, and I told him I believed he was right, because I'd already seen it for myself. Today he's his old self sometimes, and I almost don't want to see it, because it makes me think back and remember the good times we had.
> "Oh, we have good times now, too; don't mistake me. They just come rare, compared to when times were good. And always it's his pain that hangs over us; we never know when he'll be feeling right, from day to day.

"But when he's got his strength and there's nothing ailing him, he's all set to work, and it gets bad trying to figure what he might do. We talk of moving, but we ask ourselves where we'd go to. We don't want to travel a thousand miles only to be lost in some big city and not have even what we've got. Here there's a neighbor, and our kin, always. We have the house, and we manage to scrape things together, and no one of my kids has ever starved to death. They don't get the food they should, sometimes, but they eat, and they like what I do with food. In fact they complain at church. They say others don't brown the potatoes enough, or the biscuits. And they like a good chocolate cake, and I have that as often as I can.

"When Hugh is low-down he doesn't want to get out of bed, but I make him. . . .

"When he feels good, though, he'll go do chores. He'll make sure we have plenty of water, and he'll cut away some wood and lay it up nearby. He'll walk up the road and see people. He has friends, you know, who aren't sick like him, but it doesn't do them much good around here to be healthy. They can't work any more than Hugh can. It's bad, all the time bad.

"We find our own work, though, and we get paid in the satisfaction you get. We try to keep the house in good shape, and we keep the road clear all year round. That can be a job come winter.

"A lot of the time Hugh says he wished he could read better. He'll get an old magazine—the *Reader's Digest,* or the paper from Charleston—and he'll stay with it for hours. I can see he's having a tough time, but it keeps him busy. He tells the kids to remember his mistakes and not to make them all over again. Then they want to know why he made them. And we're off again. He talks about the coal companies and how they bribed us out of our 'souls,' and how he was a fool, and how it's different now. When they ask what they'll be doing with their reading and writing, it's hard to give them an answer without telling them to move. You don't want to do that, but maybe you do, too. I don't know.

"Hugh fought the television. . . . The kids, they said everyone else didn't have the money, any more than we did, but somehow they got the sets, so why couldn't we? That started something, all right. . . . Well, then they mentioned it to their uncle—he works down there in the school, keeping it in order, and he's on a regular salary, you know, and lives as good as anyone around here, all things told, I'd say. So he came and told us he'd do it, get a set for us, because the kids really need them. They feel left out without TV.

"That got Hugh going real bad. He didn't see why the radio wasn't enough, and he wasn't going to take and take and take. He wanted help, but not for a TV set. . . . And he didn't want to go begging, even from kin. And we could just do without, so long as we eat and have a place to sleep and no one's at our door trying to drive us away or take us to jail.

"Finally I had to say something. I had to. It was one of the hardest things I've ever had to do. He was getting worse and worse, and the kids they began to think he was wrong in the head over a thing like TV, and they didn't know why; they couldn't figure it out. He said they wouldn't see anything but a lot of trash, and why should we let it all come in here like that? . . .

"Now, the kids could listen for so long, and they're respectful to him, to both of us, I think you'll agree. They'd try to answer him, real quiet, and say it wasn't so important, TV wasn't, it was just there to look at, and we would all do it and have a good time. . . .

"And finally, as I say, I joined in. I had to—and I sided with them. I said they weren't going to spend their lives looking at TV, no sir, but it would be O.K. with me if we had it in the house, that I could live with it, and I think we could all live with it. And Hugh, he just looked at me and didn't say another word, not that day or any other afterwards until much later on, when we had the set already, and he would look at the news and listen real careful to what they tell you might be happening. He told me one day, it was a foolish fight we all had, and television wasn't any better or worse than a lot of other things. . . .

On Sundays they go to church. Hugh says he doesn't much believe in "anything," but he goes; he stays home only when he doesn't feel good, not out of any objection to prayer. They all have their Sunday clothes, and they all enjoy getting into them. They become new and different people. They walk together down the hollow and along the road that takes them to a Baptist church. They worship vigorously and sincerely, and with a mixture of awe, bravado, passion, and restraint that leaves an outside observer feeling, well— skeptical, envious, surprised, mystified, admiring, and vaguely nostalgic. I think they emerge much stronger and more united for the experience, and with as much "perspective," I suppose, as others get from different forms of contemplation, submission, and joint participation. Hugh can be as stoical as anyone else, and in church his stoicism can simply pour out. . . .

After church there is "socializing." . . . I think there is a particular warmth and intensity to some of the meetings because, after all, people do not see much of one another during the week. Yet how many residents of our cities or our suburbs see one another as regularly as these "isolated" people do? Hugh McCaslin put it quite forcefully: "We may not see much of anyone for a few days, but Sunday will come and we see everyone we want to see, and by the time we go home we know everything there is to know." As some of us say, they "communicate efficiently."

There is, I think, a certain hunger for companionship that builds up. . . . Particularly at night one feels the woods and the hills close in on "the world." The McCaslins live high up in a hollow, but they don't have a "view." . . . When dusk comes there are no lights to be seen, only their lights to turn on. In winter they eat at about 5 and they are in bed about 7:30 or 8. The last hour before bed is an almost formal time. Every evening Mr. McCaslin smokes his pipe and either reads or carves wood. Mrs. McCaslin has finished putting things away after supper and sits sewing— "mending things and fixing things; there isn't a day goes by that something doesn't tear." The children watch television. They have done what homework they have (or are willing to do) before supper. I have never heard them reprimanded for failing to study. Their parents tell them to go to school; to stay in school; to do well in school—but they aren't exactly sure it makes much difference. They ask the young to study, but I believe it is against their "beliefs" to say one thing and mean another, to children or anyone else.

In a sense, then, they are blunt and truthful with each other. They say what they think, but worry about how to say what they think so that the listener remains a friend or—rather often—a friendly relative. Before going to bed they say good-night, and one can almost feel the reassurance that goes with the greeting. It is very silent "out there" or "outside."

"Yes, I think we have good manners," Hugh McCaslin once told me. "It's a tradition, I guess, and goes back to Scotland, or so my daddy told me. I tell the kids that they'll know a lot more than I do when they grow up, or I hope they will; but I don't believe they'll have more consideration for people—no sir. . . . I know it may not be necessary, but it's good for people living real close to be respectful of one another.

"Now there'll be fights. You've seen us take after one another. That's O.K. But we settle things on the same day, and we try not to carry grudges. How can you carry a grudge when you're just this one family here, and miles away from the next one? Oh, I know it's natural to be spiteful and carry a grudge. But you can only carry it so far, that's what I say. Carry it until the sun goes down, then wipe the slate clean and get ready for another day. I say that a lot to the kids."

Once I went with the McCaslins to a funeral. A great-uncle of Mrs. McCaslin's had died at 72. He happened to be a favorite of hers and of her mother. They lived much nearer to a town than the McCaslins do, and were rather well-to-do. . . . A real clan had gathered from all over, as well as friends. Of course it was a sad occasion, despite the man's advanced age; yet even so I was struck by the restraint of the people, their politeness to one another, no matter how close or "near kin" they were. . . . They were not exactly demonstrative or talkative, yet they were clearly interested in one another and had very definite and strong sentiments, feelings, emotions, whatever. . . .

A few days later Hugh McCaslin of Road's Bend Hollow talked about the funeral and life and death:

"I don't think much of death, even being sick as I am. It happens to you, and you know it, but that's O.K. When I was a boy I recall my people burying their old people, right near where we lived. We had a little graveyard, and we used to know all our dead people pretty well. You know, we'd play near their graves, and go ask our mother or daddy about who this one was and what he did, and like that. The other way was through the Bible: Everything was written down on pieces of paper inside the family Bible. There'd be births and marriages and deaths, going way back, I guess as far back as the beginning of the country. I'm not sure of the exact time, but a couple of hundred years, easy.

"We don't do that now—it's probably one of the biggest changes, maybe. I mean apart from television and things like that. We're still religious, but we don't keep the records, and we don't bury our dead nearby. It's just not that much of a *home* here, a place that you have and your kin always had and your children and theirs will have, until the end of time, when God calls us all to account. This here place—it's a good house, mind you—but it's just a place I got. . . . We worked hard and put a lot into it, and we treasure it, but it never was a *home,* not the kind I knew, and my wife did. We came back to the hollow, but it wasn't like it used to be when we were kids and you felt you were living in the same place all your ancestors did. We're *part* of this land, we were here to start and we'll probably see it die, me or my kids will, the way things are going. There will be no one left here and the stripminers will kill every good acre we have. I thought of that at the funeral. I thought maybe it's just as well to die now, if everything's headed in that direction. I guess that's what happens at a funeral. You get to thinking."

DAVID KANTOR AND
WILLIAM LEHR

Family Types

Short sketches of three nuclear families by David Kantor and William Lehr, who teach at the Cambridge Family Institute, demonstrate styles of family life. In the first family, life is highly organized and boundaries around the group are quite firm. The second family represents a looser form—in both its more fluid organization and more permeable boundaries. The third family lifestyle emphasizes the importance of individual members and is marked by spontaneity and a certain degree of chaos.

Closed Family: "They're back," calls out Maureen, the McKenzies' eleven-year-old daughter, from the window at which she has been watching for the family DeSoto. Immediately, the other children start gathering in the kitchen, breaking off their other activities. "Hey, how about some hands on these bags?" Father calls up the stairs. John, Stephen, and Kevin, the McKenzies' three oldest children at ages fourteen, thirteen, and twelve, hop down the stairs and accompany their father to the car where they pick up the family's grocery bags from out of the trunk. Each boy makes several trips with his bags up to the kitchen, where Maureen supervises their unpacking and Patty and Tina, the McKenzie "babies," help out by putting canned goods in pantries and cabinets, wherever they can reach. Bryan McKenzie, the ten-year-old, also helps with the unpacking until he notices a pack of Hershey bars in one of the bags. He tears off one bar, smacks his lips, and tosses the bar into the air. "Hey, you can't eat that now," Maureen shouts. "I know that," he replies. "I was just thinking how good it was gonna taste." He puts the bar back in the bag with the rest and resumes helping with the unpacking. When the last bag is picked up from the car, Mr. McKenzie locks up the trunk and says, "We'll be back in ten minutes." "Where are you and Ma going?" John asks. "That's none of your business," Father replies. "I bet it's a treat," Kevin says, "You'll all find out soon enough," Mother adds. By the time the parents

From David Kantor and William Lehr, *Inside the Family*. San Francisco: Jossey-Bass, 1975.

36

return with an angel food cake and some ice cream some ten minutes later, all the groceries are put away and the bags folded up neatly for subsequent use as waste basket liners. Mother slices the cake and Father scoops out the ice cream in quantities appropriate to the age of each of the children, who stand in line for the goodies. "You all did a very good job with the groceries," he says.

The senior McKenzies and their seven children live together in a six-room, four-bedroom apartment in a low-income housing project. The parents occupy the only bedroom with any architecturally built-in privacy, a privacy obtained solely by virtue of its being farthest from family gathering places and the flow of foot traffic. What privacy does exist is a credit to simply ingenuity, organization, and respect for boundaries. A second bedroom is occupied by the girls (Maureen, Patty, and Tina), a third by three boys (Stephen, Kevin, and Bryan) and the fourth by John, Jr., the eldest son. John's room doubles as storage space for large items such as bicycles (kept beneath his bed) and other objects displaced from more crowded rooms. Painstaking organization is the McKenzie's key to survival in inadequate physical surroundings, to reasonably peaceful coexistence as whites in a predominantly black housing project, and to successful access to the health, recreational, and educational resources of the community at large.

In every realm of life, the McKenzies work together like the parts of a simple and well-oiled machine. In addition to developing routines for physically maintaining the small apartment, the McKenzies manage to encourage athletic and academic achievements, which have resulted in some of the older children gaining recognition at school. In general, the family achieves maximal efficiency and productivity by ascertaining that each knows the parts he or she is to play, and can be depended upon to perform them accordingly. The entire McKenzie family believes firmly that the rights of individual members can be guaranteed only if the whole family's interests come first, if each individual is willing at all times to sacrifice personal interests for the collective balance.

John is the family's one source of imbalance, the only member who challenges the family's predilection for strict adherance to official policies. His interest in rock music and monster comic books is condemned by Mr. McKenzie, the member who is most rigidly observant of a system whose boundaries he helps to defend. John's deviations are viewed by his father as assaults on the carefully bounded family meaning sphere, especially since, in the family's traditional view of hierarchic authority, John has important example-setting responsibilities. As the eldest son, he also has certain rights and prerogatives, but these can only be exercised after he has satisfied the stronger claims of those above him in the authority structure, particularly the claims of his father. He fails to do so on occasion—actually, on rare occasion—but in the McKenzie household slight deviations may be subject to punishment.

John's younger brothers are more adept at deviating slightly and getting away with it. Stephen, a conformist to the family's established meanings, occasionally tests the family's time regulations with impunity because his outstanding academic achievements gain him an unofficial freedom from certain family restrictions. Kevin, an outstanding local basketball player, is also a good student. He is perhaps the most directly outspoken of the children, but seems to know better than John when and who to debate and challenge. . . .

Though discipline is often emphasized to the older children in particular, it is rigorously enforced throughout the family. The younger children, for instance, do not earn the right to a door key until they are judged responsible enough not to lose it. Failure to carry out responsibilities at any level can result in a loss of privileges. All of the children's comings and goings are closely screened and monitored. Children's friends, when they come to call, stop at the door, but do not enter. In general, the children tend to visit rather than be visited. The outsider feels the family's metaphoric system boundaries as walls of solid reality. . . .

The senior McKenzies are unquestionably the actual as well as the nominal heads of their household. They take unabashed pride in the fact that they run a tight ship, because its requisite discipline helps secure the family's island of safety in a sea of neighborhood violence and unrest. The parents also hope and believe that family discipline is a training ground for achievement at school and eventual financial betterment for their children. At the slightest provocation, or mere hint of interest, Mr. McKenzie will wax pontifical on these and other family matters. Mrs. McKenzie is more reserved, especially with strangers, but together they have built strong fortresses in defense of their physical and conceptual spaces. The children are better acquainted with their parents as a couple, or as spokesmen for the parental system, than with either one as an individual. What the parents usually share about their private lives is revealed not for the purpose of attaining stronger intimacy, but rather as a lesson in service of some family ideal or rule of order. In intelligence, aesthetic sensibilities, keenness of judgment, and social poise, Mrs. McKenzie would seem to be her husband's superior, but such is not what they choose to say to the world or to their children, and their differences are restricted to their private domain. The children seem to know when the fictional power features of their parental system are to be upheld and under what circumstances they can be ignored. . . .

Members' access to intimacy is regulated with the same discipline that is implemented in other spheres of their existence. Strong emotions are rarely expressed in public. Affection has a place in this family, but there is also an appropriate time for its expression. At the proper time and in the proper place, bids for affection are granted. Out-of-phase seeking of affection is at best discouraged, and, at worst, put down or punished. Overly invested demands for nurturance, closeness, or affection are strongly counteracted. The Mc-Kenzies' central message to members might be expressed as follows: "Process your most intense emotional needs indirectly, through faith in the family's meanings and goals. We do not have time for whiners or malcontents. Our efforts must be effectively distributed. So be strong and self-sufficient."

Open-Family: "What would you like for dinner?" Mrs. Cloud asks her nine-year-old daughter. "Steak or . . .?" "Cereal," replies Susanna who has recently decided to be a vegetarian. "Okay," replies Mrs. Cloud. "What about you, Pamela?" Mrs. Cloud asks Susanna's friend who is staying for supper. "Steak or something else?" "Steak," says Pamela. Susanna grimaces. "A little bit of steak and a big bowl of cereal," Pamela adds. Susanna smiles. During dinner, Mr. Cloud looks across the table and says, "Peter, I'm afraid I've got a bone to pick with you." "What's that?" "The mess from your mice is getting out of hand. I almost broke my neck in the hallway outside your room this afternoon. When we agreed to let you keep those mice it was on the condition that you clean their cages," "I do clean them," Peter counters, "once a week." "Well, it's not enough," Father says. "Their excrement's piling up on the floor." "That's because they're getting out of their cages," Peter replies. "Because you've got to many mice," says Father. "No, because you won't give me the money to buy new cages." "Wait a minute," interjects Mrs. Cloud. "Dad's right, Peter. Something's got to be done about the mess. But Peter's got a point too, Dad. Those cages are falling apart." "I'm glad somebody believes me," Peter remarks. "We can't afford new cages," says Father. "Well, what about the two of you getting together to repair the ones that are in there now? That might solve both your problems," says Mother. "On one condition," agrees Father. "You agree to clean them twice a week." "Agreed," says Peter.

The Clouds live on the first floor of a family-owned two-story frame house. Their flat, renovated by architect Oscar Cloud, consists of a large open public living room space (achieved by knocking down several walls), a large parents' bedroom, and two small children's bedrooms with a double bunk in each. The large, unobstructed public space of the flat is symbolic of the Clouds' family process. Friends and guests are frequently brought home by both parents and children. People may drop in or telephone at virtually any time of the day or evening without feeling uncomfortable. The parents' bedroom often becomes an extension of the family's public and semipublic space, partly because of its size and partly because members want to use it in that way. The television set is in there, as is Oscar's drafting table, so that the room draws in not only children and guests, but, on rarer occasions, business associates.

The Clouds, both individually and as a group, enjoy visiting with friends. At any point in the day, the four Clouds could be doing different things in different parts of town: Oscar meeting with a client, Muriel working on a terminal hospital ward, twelve-year-old Peter printing some photographs in a darkroom, and nine-year-old Susanna dressing up in costumes at a friend's. Partly as a strategy to bring themselves and their various jobs, hobbies, and activities together, the Clouds have purchased a farm jointly with another professional family, whose parents and children they consider part of their own "extended family." The idea is that the farm become something of a gathering place on weekends and holidays for both households.

Events frequently take place at the last minute, or close to it, in the Cloud household. Oscar's work pattern is one of taking it somewhat easy on a project and then launching a big, all-night push as his deadline nears. Muriel is also frequently behind schedule, whether she is cooking dinner, meeting her ride to work in the morning, or buying gifts for birthdays and Christmas. Yet somehow all these tasks are eventually done before it is too late. Muriel's tardiness is not due to laziness or lack of energy. Rather, it comes about because she has so much to do. There often don't seem to be enough hours in the day for her to satisfy all her duties as therapist, wife, friend, and mother. Yet, surprisingly, both Oscar and Muriel seem to invite interruption. They seem to experience little or no resistance to distraction from a task, even a task with an immediate deadline, and readily deviate from it in order to respond to the needs or enjoyment of another person.

Decisions, too, seem to be made at or near the last minute. They may be made earlier but go uneffected, so that the possibility of altering or reversing them is left open. On one occasion, for instance, whether Mr. Cloud is going to accompany the rest of the family on a holiday trip to see the grandparents is not firmly decided until an hour or two before the plane leaves. . . .

A corollary to this type of decision-making practice is that everyone is permitted to say what he or she thinks or feels about a particular subject. Such openness of discussion helps guarantee that too many promises don't go unkept. . . . Though the parents are the heads of the Cloud household, there is no permanent or static power hierarchy. Instead, each member has an egalitarian right to challenge and be heard within the family.

The Cloud apartment is filled with a number of plants and animals. A dog, two cats, a bowl of goldfish, several hamsters, some thirty mice, and a python snake are all part of the family scene. The plants belong to Muriel, who also finds herself feeding and taking care of many of the animals. There is thus a large variety of living things within the Cloud household, providing Muriel and Susanna at least with a strong sense of nurturing. Both respond affectionately to animals and feel it their mission to provide a home for them. Indeed, it is Susanna's love of animals that has prompted her to try out the life style of a vegetarian. Peter, who owns the mice and snake, deals with them in a more managerial fashion. He considers selling his surplus mice at a profit and trades one snake in for another more exotic one. With the exception of his favorites, Peter feeds the other mice to the python to keep him alive—one every other week. This feeding, as one might suspect, creates some tension in the household. Nevertheless, the family attempts to support and reward both children's ways of relating to animals, and each is permitted and encouraged to develop further his or her particular outlook.

The Clouds' approach to the target of identity is that any topic is suitable for discussion in the household, and family conversations range from a debate on men's and women's rights and obligations to a discussion of the Anglo-Saxon origins of curses and swear words. Everyone is encouraged to present his own point of view, though he must be willing to have that view subjected to criticism and at times ridicule, at least from Oscar. For the Clouds there is no such thing as an absolute answer to the problems of the day or of the family. There are, however, certain points of view that members generally hold to be true, one being that the happiness of family members is more important than their individual achievements.

Perhaps nowhere does the Cloud family system push its openness further than in its approach to the target of nurturance and intimacy. As a general rule, all requests for either joining or separating are viewed as legitimate. Peter, for instance, is free to determine when he will accompany the family to the farm and when he will stay in town with his friends. Such a procedure produces conflicts, but the Clouds are not afraid of conflict. The Cloud parents make very little attempt to prohibit their children from hearing them fight. The reason seems to be that they view their fighters as an important part of the decision-making process. Though feelings get hurt in such fights, the Clouds believe that negative feelings must be aired if more constructive arrangements are to result. In short, they contend that a family must be free to fight if it is also to be free to love.

Random-Family: "The bathroom door handle is off again," shouts Maria Canwin. "Teddy, will you fix it?" she calls to her nine-year-old son. "I'll do it," her husband Herbert volunteers. "That's what you said last week," retorts Mrs. Canwin. "I'm sorry, dear, I put it on the repair list, but I can't seem to find the list," he replies. Now Teddy, who, in spite of his young age, is more skillful than his father in most mechanical matters, starts looking at the door handle. Meanwhile, a huge toolbox stands as a monument of promise, blocking the doorway to Mr. Canwin's study. Melissa, recently turned thirteen, perches statuesquely on the toolbox. Dancing in gracefully slowed movements, she sings in falsetto to an unseen audience, laughing in uncensored self-admiration. Moments later, Maria Canwin answers the telephone. She lodges the receiver loosely between her ear and shoulder so she can continue stirring her dinner pots on the stove. Ringlets of smoke from the burning haddock in the oven play around her nose, but she fails to notice it. Waving a glass of wine in her free hand, she is deep in a fiery conversation, punctuated by raucous laughter. An old college chum, phoning on a layover from the airport, has just been stampeded into coming over. "We'll save dinner for you," Maria says, hanging up. "No you won't. You've burned the fish again," Herbert remarks, snorting under his breath. A shrieking Teddy, leaping from the stairs to a chair and onto his father's back in an impossible acrobatic sequence shouts, "I heard that, skunkhead." Enter Melissa, trying to peel her brother off her father's back. "Get off, jerk." She also tries simultaneously to pry her parents apart from a cluttered and obviously too energetic embrace. "Leave him alone, Mom. I want him now. You can have him later." Meanwhile Teddy shouts, "Put up your dukes, Herby!" "Stop it," roars Maria, suddenly overcome with the chaos. Sound and motion come to an instant stop. The three onlookers check in with each other: does she mean it? "One of you three children can set the table. We're having a guest."

Believing that they were entering a new phase of their life together, the Canwins decided to leave a fashionable neighborhood and buy an old house in a decidedly less affluent neighborhood. Over a period of months, the four Canwins met with an architect friend who was redesigning the house. Like many Canwin decisions, this one had both its beautiful and its stormy moments. Though the family supported each person's right to have his or her selfish needs represented in the architectural design, there were bitter disagreements over what would be sacrificed when the Canwin budget limited individual freedom. . . . The architectural result of these stormy deliberations is a house tailored to the predilections of a random collective. It is a house dominated by a completely open common living space with the view from the entrance covering four different levels. It is also a house accented with private spaces that have been designed to accommodate the interests of its occupants.

The Canwins' decision-making process reflects the family's belief in the viability of diverse meanings and images. Oftener than not in their deliberations, family-unit meanings give way or accommodate themselves to individual ones. Nevertheless, as their planning for a new house demonstrates, an amalgamation of meanings and images does take place.

The Canwin household is likely to be as cluttered with objects as it is with people. The hallway is typically strewn with clothes, yesterday's or last month's, forcing people to pick their way, as through a gentle minefield. Either the Canwins do not see the disarray or they are too preoccupied and cannot take the time to tidy up routinely. Mainly they do not seem to notice. . . ,

Life in the Canwin household is sparked by projects, planned and spontaneous, mostly spontaneous. In spite of their preference for spontaneity, the Canwins are ceremonially romantic about holidays and traditional events, which are rarely celebrated in the same way from one year to another. This past Halloween eve, for instance, the Canwins drove to their house in the country after the children finished trick-or-treating in the neighborhood. On the way, they stopped to visit a quiet graveyard along a dark country road where, with the aid of candles and flashlights, they inspected gravestones in search of one that touched some inward light. The family completed its game at the farm around a fire in a darkened room, where each person told a story whose central character was the person whose name appeared on a gravestone.

The individual Canwins frequently disperse to different private corners of the house, immersed in totally unshared activities which reflect four completely different tastes and styles. Although everyone endorses, at least in spirit, the idea of being together at table, it doesn't work out that way, even when all are in the household together.

The Canwins' mealtime dilemma is a prime example of the contradictions inherent in their random-type lifestyle. Herbert, Maria, Melissa, and Teddy all individually decry the fact that mealtimes do not provide a greater opportunity for emtional sharing and closeness. To set aside a specific time of day for their evening meal and to require each individual member to be present is not a strategy the Canwins care to impose, for it would imperil each person's right to be elsewhere, to be doing what he wants to do when he wants to do it. The upshot of this and other similar dilemmas is that the Canwins find themselves unable to formalize contexts in which emotional sharing and closeness will definitely take place. Closeness and intimacy do occur, but they occur spontaneously. . . .

The Canwin's handle property in much the same way they handled other power issues—erratically. The children meet and play with their friends in the parents' supposedly private bedroom. They also feel free to pick up and use any material item in the house. Yet Herbert's tools, wherever he can find them, are supposed to be private property. Moreover, no one is ever completely sure about which tools he will designate as "his" and which he will not. Melissa begins her day in her mother's closet, looking for something to wear to school. Maria Canwin doesn't object, for she has a dread of property and proprietorship. "Ownership of things is like imprisonment," she maintains. In addition, Melissa and Maria, who cannot keep a pair of socks together in their bureaus, wear those belonging to Herbert, who can. Such violations amuse Herbert, but appall his son, whose private room is off limits to everyone, including his parents. This appreciation of his own privacy doesn't deter Teddy from making enormous contraptions out of snowtires, encyclopedias, antique chairs, and pieces of junk gathered from the streets, and then placing them in positions where they dominate the basement and make it inaccessible to everyone else.

The ways in which the Canwin establishment regulates access to the power dimension are in some ways the least predictable of all their dimensional interactions. Herbert, and, to a lesser extent, Teddy at times make efforts to regulate access to power and wield control in a closed-style fashion. In fact, Mr. Canwin acknowledges a personal preference for a more traditional arrangement in which the parents exercise control, but usually accedes to the family's preference for a random-type regulation of the power dimensions, particularly in the interpersonal sphere. His occasional authoritarian harangues cause considerable confusion and uncertainty both to himself and to other family members.

The flow of energies in the Canwin home is dynamically erratic. Quiet times do, of course, occur, but silence is almost always breakable. Someone reading a book or thinking almost never objects to an escalation of noise and/or energy. During the family's high-energy periods, the Canwins appear to be, in the phrase of one of their friends, "connoisseurs of chaos." At such times too much seems to happen too fast, since no one member of the family has the surplus energy needed to counteract the momentum propelling them all forward into unknown events with increasing speed. At such times members either rein in their energies after some minor disaster or else slip into exhaustion after experiencing a creative high.

CHAPTER TWO

The Family and Social Change

Man may work from sun to sun
But woman's work is never done.

Old saying (anonymous)

Most of the Greeks I know in this family, and many outside it, came from
the tiny adjoining villages of Lia and Vavouria, in the northwestern
province of Epirus, near the Albanian border. Their collective story is at
once unique and universal. They came to Worcester for the same reasons
my own ancestors came from England in the seventeenth century and from
Ireland in the nineteenth; for the same reasons people now swarm in from
Haiti and Korea and Mexico. They came because things were tough at
home.

Jane Howard, *Families*

TAMARA K. HAREVEN

Family Time and Historical Time

We tend to think of developmental stages and decisions as individuals mat-
ters: a child reaches six and goes to school, at eighteen completes secondary
school, then leaves home to finish preparing for an occupation or to take a
job. Marriage follows and marks the individual's permanent separation from
the parents' home. The sequence and timing are orderly and individual except
in special circumstances. Historian Tamara Hareven points out in the fol-
lowing article that our assumptions about life stages are of relatively recent
origin. In earlier times decisions like marriage were much more embedded
in the life of the family group as a whole. A young person might not be able
to marry because she had aging parents to care for or because a widowed
mother needed help supporting and raising young children still at home.
Various ways in which individual time and family time intersected in the
past are described and contrasted with contemporary patterns.

Most activities in modern life are governed by specific and often rigidly enforced schedules, whether they result from personal relationships or other
kinds of social communication. Being early, late, or on time, juggling complicated schedules, and fulfilling a series of conflicting roles within time slots
have been essential characteristics of modern society, the product of urban,
industrial living. Timing has also become a central feature in the scheduling
of family events and the transitions of individuals into different family roles.
One of the most fascinating problems is that of the synchronizing of all the

different "time clocks" that govern both the movement of individuals and families through life and larger patterns of societal change. Historical time is generally defined as a linear chronological movement of changes in a society over decades or centuries, while individual lifetime is measured according to age. . . . How were typical lives "timed" in the past, and how did these life-course patterns fit into their economic, institutional, and demographic setting?

The understanding of "time" patterns along the life course provides an insight into one of the least understood aspects of family behavior—namely, the process of decision making within the family. Since we know that the structure of the family has persisted in its nuclear form over the past two centuries, examinations of how families time their behavior can reveal the important areas in which the major changes in family behavior have taken place.

The concept of "family time" designates the timing of events such as marriage, birth of a child, leaving home, and the transition of individuals into different roles as the family moves through its life course. Timing has often been a major source of conflict and pressure in the family, since "individual time" and "family time" are not always in harmony. For example, the decision to leave home, to marry, or to form one's own family could not in the past be timed strictly in accordance with individual preferences, depending instead on the decisions and needs of the family as a collective unit and on institutional supports. Research has only just begun to sketch some of the basic patterns of the timing of family transitions and to link them with "historical time"— that is, with changing social conditions.

The social values governing timing have also changed under different historical circumstances. For example, the age at which a young man is considered a "drop-out" or a woman an "old maid" varies in different societies and periods. . . .

Historical changes have impinged upon the timing of family events by providing the institutional or social conditions under which such transitions can be implemented or impeded. It would have been impossible, for instance, to enforce societal requirements for school attendance if public schools had not been readily available; similarly, it would have been difficult to impose compulsory retirement without institutionalized social security or old-age pensions. Institutions of social welfare and social control and public welfare programs have taken over many of the welfare functions previously performed by the family. Under historical conditions where most of the educational, economic, and welfare functions are concentrated in the family, the timing of transitions within the family was more significant than in modern society. . . . A variety of social and economic developments have also affected individual and family timetables. Wars and depressions have drastically altered patterns of family timing. Even on a smaller scale, . . . such events as migration or the shutdown of a factory . . . can have an important impact on timing for the families involved. . . .

[A] recurring theme in American history is that of the variation in norms by ethnic cultures. . . . These variations result from discrepancies and conflicts between the traditions and practices of different cultural groups and those of the dominant culture. Irish immigrants in late nineteenth-century Massachusetts, for example, married later than French Canadians or native Americans. Native Americans married earlier and commenced childbearing earlier than Irish immigrants, but they also stopped childbearing earlier, while Irish families had larger numbers of children spread over a longer time period.

. . . Family members converge or diverge at different stages of their individual development and such patterns relate to the collective experience of the family at different points of its development. Even the use of the word "children" within the family is ambiguous, because, in families with large numbers of children encompassing a broad age distribution, an older child will be in an entirely different position within the family vis-à-vis adults and siblings than either the younger ones or those in the middle. As the age configuration of children within the family changes, the status of each child in the family becomes different as well; for example, after the oldest child leaves home, the next child becomes the "oldest" and takes on a new status.

The distinctions are important because individuals fulfill [many] roles. They can simultaneously be members of their family of origin and their family of procreation. After forming his own family, an individual maintains some ties with his family of origin, but also forms a new allegiance with that of the spouse. The complexity of affiliations casts an individual into various overlapping and, at times, conflicting family roles, which continue to vary at different stations along the life course. . . . A son becomes a father; later, after his own children become independent and his parents have reached the age of needing assistance, he becomes a son again, sometimes even more intensively. . . .

As [sociologist] Talcott Parsons has pointed out, the kinship system of the United States is loosely structured so that most forms of assistance among kin are informal and voluntary. While the mutual obligations of husbands and wives or parents and children are clearly sanctioned and defined, relationships with extended kin are not. But under different historical and personal circumstances the interaction of individuals both with other members of the nuclear family and with extended kin can vary considerably, because the individual's position in his own family and his relationship to other family members and to more distant kin are entwined with the family's development as a collective unit.

Historical Differences in the Timing of Family Transitions

One widely held myth about the past is that the timing of family transitions was once more orderly and stable than it is today. . . . The historical record, however, frequently reveals precisely the opposite condition. Patterns of family timing in the past were often more complex, more diverse, and less orderly than they are today; voluntary and involuntary demographic changes that have come about since the late nineteenth century have in fact paradoxically resulted in greater uniformity in the timing of transitions. . . . The growing uniformity in timing has been accompanied by a shift from involuntary to voluntary factors affecting the timing of family events. The increase in life expectancy, the decline in fertility, and an earlier marriage age have, for example, greatly increased the chances for temporal overlap in the lives of family members. Families now go through a life course much less subject to sudden change than that experienced by the majority of the population in the nineteenth century.

The "typical" family cycle of modern American families includes early marriage and early commencement of childbearing, but a small number of children. Between 1810 and 1930 the birth rate declined from an average of 8 children per mother to slightly less than 3. Families following this type of family cycle experience a compact period of parenthood in the middle years of life, then an extended period, encompassing one-third of their adult life, without children; and finally often a period of solitary living following the death of a spouse, most frequently of the husband.

This type of cycle has important implications for the composition of the family and for relationships within it in current society: husbands and wives are spending a relatively longer lifetime together, they invest a shorter segment of their lives in child-rearing, and they more commonly survive to grandparenthood. This sequence has been uniform for the majority of the population since the beginning of the twentieth century. In contrast to past times, most families see their children through to adulthood with both parents still alive. . . . Prior to 1900, only about 40 per cent of the female population in the United States experienced this ideal family cycle. The remainder either never married, never reached marriageable age, died before childbirth, or were widowed while their offspring were still young children.

In the nineteenth century, the combination of a later age at marriage and higher fertility provided little opportunity for a family to experience an empty-nest stage. . . . Individuals became parents later, but carried child-rearing responsibilities almost until the end of their lives. The lives of parents overlapped with those of their children for shorter periods than they do in current society.

Under the demographic conditions of the nineteenth century, higher mortality and higher fertility, functions within the family were less specifically tied to age, and members of different age groups were consequently not so completely segregated by the tasks they were required to fulfill. The spread of children over a larger age spectrum within the family had important implications for family relationships as well as for their preparation for adult roles. Children were accustomed to growing up with larger numbers of siblings and were exposed to a greater variety of models from which to choose than they would have been in a small nuclear family. Older children often took charge of their younger siblings. . . . Youngest children were most likely to carry responsibilities for parental support, and to overlap in adulthood with a widowed mother. . . . One can better grasp the implications of these differences in age at marriage, number of children, assigned tasks, and generational overlap when one takes into consideration the uncertainties and the economic precariousness that characterized the period; these made the orderly sequence of progression along stages of the family cycle, which sociologists have observed in the contemporary American population, impossible for the nineteenth-century family.

Another comparison between what is considered the "normal" family cycle today and its many variants in the nineteenth century reverses one more stereotype about the past—namely that American society has been experiencing breakdown and diversification in family organization. In reality, the major transitions in family roles have been characterized by greater stability and conformity, because of the greater opportunity for generational continuities. The opportunity for a meaningful period of overlap in the lives of grandparents and grandchildren is a twentieth-century phenomenon, a surprising fact that runs counter to the popular myth of a family solidarity in the past that was based on three-generational ties.

The relative significance of transition into family roles also differed in the nineteenth century. In the nineteenth century, when conception was likely to take place very shortly after marriage, the major transition in a woman's life was represented by marriage itself. But, as the interval between marriage and first pregnancy has increased in modern society, the transition to parenthood has become more significant than the transition to marriage. Family limitation has also had an impact on the timing of marriage. Since marriage no longer inevitably leads to parenthood, postponing marriage is no longer needed to delay it. On the other end of the life course, transitions *out* of parental roles are much more critical today than they were in the past when parental or surrogate-parental roles encompassed practically the entire adult life span. Completion of parental roles today involves changes in residence, in work, and eventually, perhaps, removal into institutions or retirement communities.

Some familial transitions are also more easily reversible today than they were in the past. Marriages can now be ended by divorce, while, prior to the middle of the nineteenth century, they were more likely to be ended by the death of a spouse. . . .

Life-Course Transitions and Family Strategies

What factors guided these transitions and moves into different family roles, what constituted continuities and discontinuities in such transitions, and how did they affect family behavior? . . . Seemingly "disorderly" patterns in the timing of transitions in the nineteenth century were the result of the special role which the family fulfilled in the society and the prevailing view of its role and organization. The family was a corporate body operating as a collective unit, and the functions of the members within it were defined on that basis.

In modern society, we are accustomed to think of most family and work-career decisions as having been made by individuals. Even marriage is perceived as an individual decision, as an act resulting in independence from one's parents. But until recently these apparently individual transitions were treated as *family* moves and were, therefore, synchronized with other family needs and strategies. . . . The decision to marry, the choice of spouse, and the timing of the event all depended on calculations relating to the transmission of property, the finding of a job and housing, the support of aging parents, and to a wide variety of other family needs; it was not merely an impulse of romantic love. Collective family decisions took precedence over individual preferences. The careers of individuals were directed by the "familistic" ideology which remained powerful to the end of the nineteenth century, and which persisted in the lives of certain social groups into the twentieth century.

In Western society today, the major burdens of family relationships are emotional, while, in the nineteenth century, they were heavily weighted toward economic needs and tasks. . . .

Relationships between husbands and wives, parents and children, distant kin, and even family members and strangers were based on socially sanctioned mutual obligations that transcended personal affection and sentiment. Parents raised and supported their children with the dual expectations that the children would start to work as soon as they were able and that they would ultimately support the parents in old age. This "instrumental" view of family relationships has survived the industrial revolution, and it persists in the lives of working-class and rural families today. But in the absence of . . . public welfare, such instrumental exchanges between family members in the nineteenth century were essential for survival. They formed the backbone of familial relationships, providing continuity from one generation to the next.

Although the obligations that family members had for each other were not contractually defined, they rested on established social norms, and families had their own methods for enforcing them and for ensuring that the younger members in particular would not put their own interest before that of the family as a collective unit. In rural society, these sanctions were based on the inheritance of land, control of which offered aging parents the necessary leverage for securing old-age support from their sons. In industrial society, sanctions were less formal and were enforced mainly by the need for reciprocity dictated by the insecurities of urban life. . . .

One of the underlying goals of such reciprocal relationships was the maintenance of familial self-sufficiency. Families preferred to rely on each other for assistance rather than on strangers, even if the strangers were nearer. Individuals were expected to postpone or sacrifice their personal advancement if it jeopardized the family's autonomy as a unit, because the autonomy of the household was felt to be the foundation of family self-sufficiency. Regardless of class, occupation, or ethnic background, most American households in the nineteenth century were nuclear, as they are today, reflecting society's commitment to this autonomy. . . . If households became extended, it was usually only late in life. In most situations, even widows tried to maintain their own household by taking in strangers as tenants, rather than live in other people's houses. . . .

Mutual obligations and needs within the family imposed serious pressures on the timing of family transitions, and obviously caused trouble when individual preferences came into conflict with the family's collective timetable. Children had to leave school and start work early to support their younger siblings; sons and daughters often had to postpone marriage, or never marry, to support their aging parents. Individual wishes to leave home or to marry were frequently frustrated in the effort to sustain the family of origin. . . .

Historical Implications

What are the implications of these differences in the timing of individual transitions for the understanding of historical changes in the family generally? Slow and uneven transitions of individuals out of the family of origin and into independent adult roles were the result of a more continuous integration within the family of origin. This meant a greater continuity in the obligations of young people to their parents, which reached more deeply into their own adulthood and often overlapped with their own parental responsibilities. It also entailed a prolonged apprenticeship for future family roles which individuals carried out in their families of origin and, therefore, a less abrupt transition when they did marry and become parents. . . . Prior to the "affluent" society and the assumption of important familial functions by the welfare state, the family had mainly itself to rely on to meet its economic needs, to stave off dependency, and to cope with insecurities and disasters. Mutual help by family members was essential for survival. The modern notion of independent autonomous careers, linearly directed toward individual success and an almost exclusive investment in one's conjugal family, is dissonant with conceptions of family obligations in the past. Under earlier conditions when work careers were erratic and unpredictable, the insecurities of the market dictated a tight integration and an interchangeability of the tasks and functions of different family members. When occupational opportunities favored young women, a daughter was sent to work, and when they favored young men, a son was sent. When husbands and wives both found work outside the home, they shared household tasks as well; if only one could find work, the other carried the major burden of domestic responsibilities. This integration of individuals into the family's economic effort is characteristic primarily of rural society, but it also carried over into industrial society in the lives of the working class.

Individualistic patterns of family behavior first appeared in the nineteenth century among the urban middle class, and with them came patterns of segregation in family roles. Middle-class families were the first to follow a clear timing sequence for their children's entry into, and exit from, school, and to promulgate an orderly career pattern that led from choosing an occupation to leaving the parental household, marrying, and forming the new family. Orderly progression along the life course and structured transitions from one stage to the next were related to the "discovery" of childhood and, subsequently, adolescence as distinct stages of life. The segregation of age groups in accordance with their functions also occurred first among middle-class families. The emergence of the private, child-centered family consciously separating itself from the outside world brought about major redefinitions of traditional family roles and functions. This new family type placed emphasis on the family as a center for nurture and affection rather than as a corporate unit. Their wages no longer needed, women and children in the middle class were exempted from the labor force. Wives were expected instead to be the custodians of the family and to protect the home as a refuge from the world of work, and children, although expected to help with household tasks, were freed from serious work responsibilities until their late teens.

Members of middle-class, native-American families were the first to marry younger, to control fertility, and to space their children more closely. In their behavior, as well as in their mentality, they began to approximate the middle-class family type . . . so common in the twentieth century. Working-class and first-generation immigrant families, on the other hand, continued to hold on to traditional views of family roles, functions, and patterns of timing, at least in the first generation. The various ethnic groups and the working class thus lagged behind the middle class in adopting this new timing and in role segregation among ages. The influx of new groups from rural and small-town backgrounds continued to infuse pre-modern patterns of timing into an increasingly homogenizing society. As state institutions gradually took over the functions of welfare, education, and social control that had previously lodged in the family, there was greater conformity in timing. The gradual introduction of age-related requirements, such as compulsory school attendance, child-labor legislation, and mandatory retirement have all combined to impose more rigid patterns of timing in the larger society and, in the process, have also caused greater uniformity in the timing of family behavior.

NILES NEWTON

Stability of the Family in a Transient Society

The family has changed as the economic and social organization of our world has changed. Some of these changes are described and are placed in the context of human needs in the following articles. The author, a psychologist, suggests ways in which we can guard the life-sustaining qualities of the family.

Our traditional agricultural economy has gradually, in the past 200 years, been transformed into an industrial manufacturing economy, based on wages and salaries rather than home industry. Here is a list of changes within the family as our economic system has changed:

The role of men has changed markedly. Many worked at crafts and farming in or near the home. They were around and nearby to eat all meals with the family, to help in case of need, and they worked alongside their sons for a good part of the year, as soon as the boys could help in a simple way. The work load of men in traditional agricultural society was heavy, but it was shared. A whole group of people were working in unison to feed and clothe the family.

In contrast, the work tasks of the modern male are far away from the family in an office or factory, and what he earns there supports not only him but to a large extent the whole family. Most husbands and fathers get far less economic help from women and children and old folks in the home than they did two centuries ago. As a result, family members in the home, instead of being seen as economic help, may be seen as severe economic burdens that must be borne.

The role of women has changed possibly even more than that of men. My grandmother made soups and apple butter, bread and even soap. My great-great-grandmother still used a spinning wheel occasionally, and, awhile before that, housewifely arts included clothing manufacture and hand sewing of all clothes. Hard work, but requiring a very high level of skill, and challenge. This type of creative work is not demanded of women in homemaking today.

While the basic staples of the family, one by one, stopped being made at home, the birth rate dropped as well. American birth rates began dropping about 160 years ago. The changes have actually come gradually over many generations.

Most mothers would agree that the busiest time for mothers is the time when their children are under 5. There has been a tremendous drop of children in this age category since 1810, when U.S. Census reports indicated there were more than 1300 of such children to every 1000 white women aged 20–44.

Picking Cotton, Alabama, 1935. In agricultural societies, children tend to work along-side their parents. (From The Depression Years as Photographed by Arthur Rothstein. *Dover Publications.)*

By 1850, this amount dropped to about 900 children, and by 1900 there were fewer than 700 young children for every 1000 comparable childbearing women.

By 1940, after the very low birth rate of the depression years, the number of young children for comparable women was 419. Unfortunately, the U.S. Census Bureau does not appear to be issuing this statistic at the present time, but since our birth rate now has gone down even lower than the 1930 levels, the ratio of childbearing women to young children probably is even lower.

From 1300 to around 400 children under 5 is a major drop. Put in terms of men's activities, the impact would be similar to shortening their work hours from 45 to 15 hours per week.

The role of children has also changed radically. Instead of being baby-sitters, mother's and father's helpers, they now spend long hours, 5 days a week, many months of the year, away from their families, and when they are at home they are not often engaged in much family interaction, but have homework and television to keep them busy.

This contrasts with the fact that going to school was a minor activity of children even a hundred years ago. In 1870, only 57 percent of the children between 5 and 17 attended public schools, and then attended on the average of only 78 days per year. Instead of school, mothers and fathers worked together to train children in the skills of living.

Other public institutions were equally rudimentary and this, too, increased responsibilities on the family until fairly recently. The care of the vast majority of old and sick people was the cooperative effort of the whole, larger family group.

The family was a much larger family group in those days. In 1790, the time the first U.S. Census was taken, the median number of people living in one household group was about 5.7. In 1972, it had dropped to about 3.1 people, a decrease of nearly half. And now the most recent Census reports convey that the typical American household size is fewer than 3 persons per household—due in part to the increase in people living alone.

The larger households of yesteryear often included grandparents, in-laws, other relatives, hired hands on the farm, apprentices and lodgers and domestic servants. All of these non-nuclear family people have tended to disappear, especially domestic servants and dependent elders.

Basically, what this means is that homes used to have enough hands to help in times of crisis and to prevent young women from carrying the burden of baby and toddler alone day after day, as happens today.

With the lack of helping hands and increased industrialization have come radical changes in infant care, differing both from those of other mammals and from those used in traditional and preliterate societies.

Briefly, let me show you how our ideas have changed by sharing data gathered by Alice Judson Ryerson concerning medical advice on child rearing published between 1550 and 1900. Her sample was based on texts written in English or translated into English. No books by doctors about children for laymen originated in America until nearly 1800, and so Ryerson used only English sources published before that time. After 1800, she recorded only sources published in America, although these, too, sometimes were reprints of books by European authors.

With regard to the recommended age of weaning from the breast, all of three texts published between 1550 and 1650 recommended 2 years. Breast feeding until the age of 4 must have continued until 1725, because some books published that late mentioned it with disapproval. There was a marked drop in the recommended age in books of the mid-eighteenth century. . . .

Over these centuries there have been growing attempts to regulate the baby without regard for its own biologic rhythms. Schedules of feeding appear to have been invented in the early eighteenth century but did not really become popular until after 1825. With this there have come growing numbers of expressions of disapproval of masturbation and sex play. It may be noteworthy that expressed disapproval of masturbation and sex play came to the fore at a period when schedules were becoming popular and the weaning age was getting lower and lower.

Now let's look at the other end of life. The situation of the aged has changed radically within the family. In the years of large families, the so-called crises of middle and old age were muted.

Actually, a study done by Robert Wells of Quaker families in the eighteenth century, who appear to have been demographically similar to the rest of the American population, indicates that for them child rearing was a 40-year project, on the average. It took almost 40 years from the time of the marriage to the time the last child married and left home. Babies kept coming until mother reached her late thirties or forties. The median mother was 60 years of age when the last child left home.

In fact, when the wife or husband died, it was likely that there would be children in the home at the time of widowhood or widowerhood. The Quaker family statistics indicate that the median length of child rearing in the family was longer than the duration of 69 percent of the marriages, which in those days were almost always terminated by death. In fact, Quaker widows or widowers, if their experience held to the median, could expect to have children to care for 9 years after the death of the first spouse!

In the eighteenth century there was a different type of family instability. It was caused by the death not only of children but of spouses. This type of family instability has been conquered to a large extent by methods largely unknown and unforeseen in the eighteenth century—by the development of modern preventive medicine, and effective drugs.

This gives me hope that our family instability, which comes from such different causes, may also have solutions. The Industrial Revolution saved lives of babies, children, husbands and wives through the technology it developed, but at the same time the changes wrought in family living have accentuated a new kind of family instability.

Small and broken families, dependent on the industrial money economy, force some members to work away from the family for many hours a week and leave lonely and overstrained people at home.

Homo sapiens is not usually a solitary animal. We have evolved in groups and lived in groups as far back as recorded history. In fact, one of the worst punishments we can think of giving a person is to put him in solitary confinement, without human contact with others. We simply need other people to talk to, interact with and, above all, other people who really care about us and whom we care about.

The problem is that although most of the once normal communal economic activities of the family are gone, the psychologic need for family life still remains. Man is a social animal. What can be done now to encourage stronger human ties?

What can we do to stabilize family ties despite modern distractions?

Economic Issues

With the coming of the industrial economy, women and children have become increasing burdens. Insofar as money influences emotions, women and children may not be as beloved as formerly. What can we do about it without turning our backs to the Industrial Revolution?

1. Possibly we should consider elevating the status of part-time work. Currently, when women work outside the home part time, they often get lower pay per hour than if they were working at equally responsible jobs full time. Part-time workers often get no credit for vacations or retirement pay.

Much more of work currently done in the office could be done at home in a family context—typing, accounting, sales work by phone, anything you do alone without too much equipment. My daughter currently is writing her second novel with a friend. They get together three times a week in the afternoon while their four preschool children play together. The work schedule calls for the last chapter being finished the week before the next baby is due. Their arrangement illustrates that where there is concern about keeping mother and children together, a way often can be found to combine work and family care. . . .

My dream world is the world where the standard workweek for both men and women would be 25 hours. This amount of working time allows for free time for doing homemaking tasks and for plenty of interaction with the children. Those of us who enjoy work would take on two shifts of work, or 50 hours of working, during the years when home demands are low, if our energies are high. A man could retire to one unit of work from two in his sixties, when he wants to slow down, yet continue to contribute constructive energies to society. An energetic woman in her forties, whose children are gone and whose husband helps with the housework, might take on two units of work a week if she needs an extra challenge or wants money for her children's college or professional education.

Letting children work more might also be considered. Current minimum wage laws and the regulations that prohibit children under 16 working except with complicated permits overlook the fact that, *for children, work is a valuable education;* and part-time work, as long as it does not overfatigue, is highly desirable. It is far better to work as a stock boy or baby-sitter for 2 hours each afternoon than to sit passively in front of the TV for the same amount of time. It is better for self-esteem and self-support, helping the child both to contribute to the economy and to feel needed and wanted.

2. Another way to ease the economic burden brought on by the industrial money economy might be to pay very high child-care allowances to all women with children under 5, thus recognizing the social value of their work. They could, in turn, use the allowance to purchase day care privately, if they preferred not to look after their children themselves during portions of the day.

In our society we tend to distrust mothers. But I personally feel that mothers, as a group, should be less indifferent to the welfare of their children than would be unrelated and more superficially involved professionals. Mothers are in close, immediate contact with their children and see the effect of abuse or unhappy situations the very day they occur to their children at school or in day care.

3. As a third economic suggestion, we might consider income tax deductions for children that reflect realistically their actual cost to us.

I am aware that the last two points involve a great deal of tax money, but if families are strengthened, the cost of other social services is likely to go down as the families handle problems more directly and with fuller knowledge of the individuals involved and, most important, with fuller emotional commitment.

Since most of the other changes in family life appear to have occurred as a consequence of the economic revolution, it would be well to examine further the problem of children being economic punishment, which may have made them less beloved and secure in their parents' love.

Psychobiologic Issues

We often overlook the fact that the only way we human beings have of expressing love is through our bodies. We speak words of love through opening our mouths. We do acts of love by moving our bodies. Our bodies are fundamental to building a family life, and yet we often overlook ways in which bodies can be used to build strong families.

1. In the first place, good physical health leads to better mental attitudes and more energy to solve problems. It is possible to lead a happy family life if the members have too little sleep, have nutritional deficiencies of the type that influence behavior and are tense and tired from too little exercise, but this is very difficult and improbable. I would bet any time on the greater stability of a family that makes it a point to get enough sleep, enough exercise to minimize tension and a well-balanced diet.

2. Sexuality is another psychobiologic item that can be used to really strengthen family life, if it is enjoyed within the family. We hear a lot about open marriages nowadays, but the truth of the matter is that heavy love affairs and sexual friendships outside the home take time and energy away from spouse and children.

As a society, we readily accept the idea that love should lead to sex, but we overlook that the converse is equally true. Sex leads to love. The countries of the world that arrange marriages for their children count heavily on this inverse truth. The pleasure of sex leads to love and commitment. It is love and commitment outside the family rather than transient coitus that may be most disruptive to family life.

Sexuality is two-pronged, then, but a very potent factor. Good sex in a marriage can certainly greatly strengthen it. Good sex outside marriage tends to build auxiliary commitments that may interfere with family life in many instances.

Strangely, at the same time, we overlook an aspect of broader sexuality much enjoyed by our preindustrial ancestors, who experienced a lot more touching and body contact—the friendly, gentle type of love. In fact, they spent many hours each day touching each other in those big beds you see in museums. The big family bed with mother and father and young children used to be the pattern, the twin bed being a recent invention. Old child-care books warn that when the baby is weaned from the breast at 2 years and no longer sleeps with the parent, it is important to give the child a brother or sister or servant to sleep with so that he is not lonely.

Another aspect of touching is breast feeding. A number of studies suggest that mothers who nurse their babies completely may react differently toward their babies in other ways as well. Sleeping in bed with baby seems to go along with breast feeding. Dr. Caroline Rawlins and I found that 71 percent of mothers who breast feed their babies entirely reported sleeping in bed with their babies "sometimes" or "often." Only 26 percent of non-nursing mothers reported this. Another study found that rocking the baby "often" was reported by more than twice as many actively breast feeding mothers as mothers of same aged babies who were not nursing. . . .

One of the ironies of modern family life behavior is the strange reversal in areas of prudishness. Exotic sexual acts of all sorts now are acceptable, but simple family cuddling throughout the night has gone out of fashion. Even if double beds are used, few men now wear nightshirts, which make their bodies so much more accessible to contact, and even many women have now turned from nightgowns to pajamas, which limit easy skin contact.

Issues in Social Interaction

Before the Industrial Revolution, families used to work together. This still is a good way of building social interaction.

1. Working together can take many forms. A good place to start is family clean-up after supper. In our family, we have a firm rule—everybody but the person who did the cooking helps with the clean-up. It goes quickly and pleasantly that way. . . .

2. Communication is another very important aspect of family interaction. It may become necessary to set the time and place so that you get the most out of your communication time. Each family is different.

In our family, we have a social time in the early morning reading the papers, drinking tea and coffee and chatting on our big double bed. It's just a natural gathering time ever since the babies got their early morning nursing in bed. They have been coming back for pleasant visits at this time for the many years since then.

We also tend to visit when we come home at night, home after school, home after work. Any homecoming usually is a family visiting time, with even longer visits during the weekend at times that develop at odd moments. Shared breakfasts and dinners help our communication too. . . .

The art of communication does take time, a willingness to listen, a willingness to care and, above all, a willingness to inhibit destructive criticism. We all can learn from suggestions and reactions from other family members, but telling them that they are foolish or making derogatory remarks stops good communication for a long time.

3. Shared rituals and holidays do much to cement the family together. Special get-togethers for Christmas, trips to visit relatives or sightseeing are long remembered and give a feeling of solidarity.

Shared recreation is especially emphasized in our society and does have a place if the recreation involves interaction or group action. I am rather doubtful whether staring at TV together does much for family solidarity, when compared to recreation with more movement and interaction.

Issues Involving the Community

The community can help strengthen family life if it is used constructively. The points that come to mind are:

1. Make friends with other families on a family-to-family basis. Visit back and forth and really get to know one another well. The most solid

friendships are born when whole families know one another. Sharing and combining families may be particularly important when families are small, so that diversity of social contact can be fostered by the wider social group.

2. Join groups that are family oriented and give you a chance to be with others who are seeking strong family life. Some church and social action groups are like this. . . .

3. When seeking professional help, seek help that is family oriented. There are pediatricians who welcome fathers and like to discuss problems with the whole family. There are obstetricians who welcome fathers in their offices during pregnancy and in the delivery room, and there are psychologists and psychiatrists and social workers who like seeing the whole family together. They are showing you where their values lie.

4. Another point is to consider the source of the advice. Parents and professionals have a right to ask, "Is this person who is giving advice really experienced in the field?"

For instance, when you read a child-care book, ask yourself: "Has this person had any practical experience raising children? How much?" When you read a book on family relationships, ask yourself: "Does this person have a family life of the type I want?" Find out about his demonstrated capability in the field about which he is theorizing.

Finally, I would like to say that if families are to become strong in the United States again, it is not going to be done by professionals but by individuals within the context of their own families, each working to make his or her own family a better and more loving unit.

BARBARA LASLETT

The Significance of
Family Membership

Mortality, age at marriage, and fertility are three demographic factors that have affected the family. In this article, sociologist Barbara Laslett suggests that changes in these factors over the last century have made family relations more important in the lives of individuals.

Demography and Kinship

Three demographic factors are of particular importance in comparing the size and structure of the kinship group in past and present Western societies: mortality, age at marriage, and fertility. Although several types of kin will be considered, ascendant kin are most relevant for discussing the availability of persons likely to intentionally assume roles in the socialization process, particularly for children.

Mortality

In the past, people generally did not live long enough for there to be a sizable pool of older relatives with whom contact was possible. In 1900, the expectation of life at birth (for the white population) in the United States was 48.2 years for males and 51.1 years for females. In 1970, these figures had risen to 68.0 years for males and 75.6 years for females. Although some nineteenth-century American mortality data is available, questions have been raised about its adequacy; the decline in mortality in the twentieth century, however, when vital registration data have become increasingly available, is clearer.

Infant mortality made a major contribution to death rates in earlier times; nevertheless, higher mortality in the past affected adults as well as infants. At age 20, the life-expectancy of white males was 42.2 additional years in

Barbara Laslett, "The Significance of Family Membership" from *Changing Images of the Family,* edited by Virginia Tufte and Barbara Myerhoff. Yale University Press, 1979. Reprinted by permission.

1900 and 50.3 additional years in 1970; the comparable figures for white women were 43.8 and 57.8, respectively. One consequence of these changing mortality rates is that "the chances that today's typical bride and groom will both survive the next 50 years (to their golden wedding anniversary) are more than twice as great as were the chances of such survival for their counterparts in 1900–02."[1] Thus, fewer parents and grandparents were available in the past to participate in the socialization of their children and grandchildren.

Differential mortality by sex is also relevant to kin contacts. In twentieth-century America, there has been an increasing sex difference in life expectancy. While the length of life (at birth and older ages) of both sexes has increased between 1900 and 1970, the increase for women has been greater than the increase for men. Contemporary research shows the importance of parents for continued kin contact among their adult children, and the mother's survival may be particularly important in this respect since women are more active than men in maintaining family ties. Thus women's longevity may help to sustain contacts among related adults.

Age at Marriage

The median age at first marriage in the United States in 1890 was 26.1 years for men and 22.0 years for women; in 1950 it was 22.8 and 20.3 years; and in 1974 it was 23.1 and 21.1 years, respectively. The late nineteenth-century figures may well represent the high point of an upward trend, since available data indicate that people married at younger ages in the colonial period. In the twentieth century, however, compared to the late nineteenth, children are born (and are more likely to survive) earlier in their parents' life span. Under such circumstances, family members will be available both for more of the individual's life, because of increases in the life expectancy of the older generation, and for greater periods of the family life cycle, because new families begin at earlier ages.

Fertility

While the pool of potential kin may be affected by declining mortality and age at first marriage, changing fertility rates are also relevant for estimating the size and structure of the kinship group in the present compared to the past. Fertility in the United States has declined. The question, then, is whether lowered fertility offsets the effects of decreased mortality so that the number of living relatives per family in the present is no different than in the past.

Historical data that could illustrate this question directly are not available. However, Goodman, Keyfitz, and Pullum provide helpful material in their estimates of the number of living female relatives available to women of various ages. These researchers used the fertility and mortality data of the United States in 1967 and Madagascar in 1966, that is, a country with low

1. Metropolitan Life, *Statistical Bulletin 57* (Feb. 1976):4.

fertility and low mortality which illustrates the modern demographic profile was compared to a society with high fertility and high mortality, the preindustrial pattern. In general, the results show that in societies with low fertility and low mortality, older relatives are more available and younger relatives are less available. The advantage in terms of the size of the kinship pool does not appear to be marked for one type of society compared to another. Gray's application of the Goodman, Keyfitz, and Pullum model to 1920, 1930, and 1970 United States demographic rates shows, however, that to the extent that there is a difference more living kin are available to contemporary Americans than in earlier periods. Furthermore, it should be remembered that migration, a significant feature of American life throughout its history, is higher among younger than among older adults. Thus, although more young adults may have been alive in preindustrial times, they were less available to interact with other family members than their numbers alone would suggest.

The demographic factors reviewed here have implications for our understanding of patterns of family interaction and processes of socialization both within the household and within the extended kin group. [Paul] Glick says that "the larger the family the larger the proportion of time that children are likely to spend interacting with each other, whereas the smaller the family the greater the proportion of time the children are likely to spend interacting with their parents." Thus, changes in mortality, fertility, and age at marriage, as well as changes in household composition, are likely to affect the processes of role modeling and identification that occur within the contemporary family by increasing the impact of parents in the socialization process. Furthermore, demographic changes have also meant that more ascendant kin are available, particularly grandparents, uncles, and aunts, who may elaborate life-cycle models within the kinship group. Given the increased importance of family membership established in the early years of the socialization process, for both children and adults, and the improved means of contact and communication that technological advances have made available, kin contact may be more frequent than in earlier historical periods despite the lack of common residence.

Urbanization and Migration

Two factors relevant to the distribution of population that also affect the potential availability of kin with whom contact may occur are urbanization and migration. Rapid urbanization has been a feature in the American experience since the early nineteenth century, and the twentieth century has witnessed an increasing concentration of population into large metropolitan centers. Kin, therefore, may be concentrated in areas in which fairly frequent contact is possible, contact that is easier to make (and harder to avoid) because of the expansion of the highway system and the widespread availability of automobiles, air travel, and the telephone.

Migration, a characteristic of American life both past and present, has often been used to explain the absence of kin contact among mobile populations, because the act of migration (particularly overseas migration) reduces the pool of potential kin available both to the migrant and the non-migrant. Furthermore, the process of internal (versus overseas) migration can also thin the ranks of kin with whom contact is possible. Here again, literacy and the technology of communication are important, for once a relative leaves a community, contact between family members depends on what modes of communication are available. But the impact of migration may also vary according to whether it occurs earlier or later in the historical development of an area.

In earlier generations, migrating family members often established themselves in places that did not include members of their own kin group. First-generation migrants would be most severely restricted in terms of the availability of ascendant kin. The likelihood that kin would be found in the destinations of the next generation of migrants, however, was increased by the very fact that earlier migration of family members had occurred. It has been shown that nineteenth- as well as twentieth-century migrants chose their destinations in part because of the presence of kin group members in the new area. Thus, migration, particularly under modern technological conditions, does not necessarily reduce contact among kin to the degree suggested by earlier authors, although it does, perhaps, make it more voluntary.

To summarize, structural factors have created potential for family membership to become a more salient feature of personal identity in the contemporary period than in the Western, preindustrial past, through their effect on socialization within the household, on the increased number of ascendant kin, and on the spatial distribution of kin group members. In addition, developments in the technology of contact and communication, and increased literacy, make it easier for family members to be in touch with each other whether or not they live close together. In the earlier period, the co-resident domestic group was less often confined to primary kin group members alone, while in the present more households contain nuclear family members only. Thus, within the home, non-kin are not so likely to be available to diffuse identification with a particular family, and greater numbers of ascendant kin outside the home, with whom contact can easily take place, are available to amplify the identification developed within it.

The Ideology of Family Life

Beliefs about family life in contemporary American society tend to reflect and reinforce the intimacy and itensity that residential and demographic factors make possible. The early Puritan ideology in America emphasized the role of the family as guardian of the public as well as the private good. Not only did religion specify the approved type of relationships between family members, their duties and responsibilites to each other, but it also made it a sacred duty of members of the church to see that these edicts were carried out. It was not sufficient for people to be moral in public; they also had to be moral in private, and religion provided a legitimating ideology for minding other people's family affairs.

In contract to these beliefs, the idea of the private family and the home as a personal sanctuary grew throughout nineteenth-century America. Family life began to be characterized as an oasis, a retreat, a haven from the uncertainties, immoralities, and strains of life in a rapidly changing society. [Glen H.] Elder's suggestion that "the family as refuge" was one reaction of American families to the Depression of the 1930s indicates that this theme has continued into the twentieth century. Insecurities in public and occupational roles reinforced the belief that the family was the only place where meaningful relationships were possible.

The theme of the family as a retreat can also be found in recent discussions of contemporary nontraditional family forms such as communes and open marriages. These alternative family forms are thought to provide the opportunity for deep and meaningful personal relationships to a greater extent than other types of family living. Thus the family continues to be seen as a haven from the larger society. The ideology of family living, even in its most avant-garde forms, still views the family as a refuge from the larger society. The belief still prevails that it is only within the family that one can find intimate relationships and a sense of control over one's own life.

The relationship of the family to other social institutions reinforces this image of the family. One of the features that has been said to characterize modern industrial societies is an increase in the importance of achieved versus ascribed attributes. In the life of families in Andover, Massachusetts, in the seventeenth century, access to land was crucial to the adult life of sons, and the father's control over land affected many aspects of the son's adult behavior, including when he could marry. The growth of an occupational system that emphasizes an individual's educational achievements and the increasing availability of public education have loosened the constraints that these authority patterns and practices were likely to impose. Family contacts may therefore seem less crucial to achieving one's place in the modern occupational world. But the very fact that family contacts may no longer play such an important part in placing individuals in their public roles, thus reducing the instrumental usefulness of kin contacts, may increase their socio-emotional importance. In a society whose ideology values individual achievement and where favors won on grounds of kin ties are not generally considered legitimate, family membership may be prized simply because it does not have to be earned. The ascribed character of family membership may be experienced as a positive attribute for the very reason that it can be "taken for granted."

The socialization that occurs in today's American family is likely to contribute to the "taken for granted" character of family relationships. As social institutions have become more specialized, differences between the family and other institutions have sharpened. The fact that the contemporary family is private in character, providing a "backstage area" where persons can relax from performing their public roles, contributes to an ideology that defines the family primarily in socio-emotional terms. What is frequently forgotten in these formulations, however, is that performers not only relax backstage, but they also prepare for—and sometimes rehearse—their public roles. Potentially contradictory and confusing messages, a central focus of the recent developments in communication theory as it has been applied to the family, may create considerable discrepancy between the ideology and the actuality of contemporary family life.

Changes in economic organization within society in general may also have affected the emotional meaning of family relationships in other ways. In the past, when the family was the unit of production as well as the unit of consumption, work and family roles were intertwined. The systematic separation of home and work activities that began in nineteenth-century America, the decline in proprietorship in the contemporary period, and the increase in the salaried and bureaucratic sector of the economy meant that today fewer family members work together than before. In the past, relationships between employers and employees, between masters and servants or apprentices, and between parents and children had greater emotional similarity to each other than they do today. It is precisely the decline in the intertwining of what we now see as diverse social roles that permits the intensification of the emotional aspects of family relationships.

A similar argument can be made in relation to the family as educator. Before public schooling became widely available, much of a child's education took place in the home. When education was removed from the home, potential conflicts arising from the parents' responsibilities for both the intellectual development and the psychological well-being of the children were reduced. This is not meant to imply that parents are less concerned now than in the past about their children's educational achievement. Quite the opposite may in fact be the case. Alice Rossi has suggested that in the absence of clear-cut standards for parenting, mothers and fathers often look to children's report cards and pediatricians' reports as ways of judging their own performance as parents. The availability of institutions to foster children's attainment of cognitive skills outside the home permits and encourages greater concentration on the affective character of the parent-child relationship within it. Children's educational and occupational attainments are likely to take on a deeper psychological meaning for their parents, to become reflections or extensions of parental fantasies and ambitions for themselves. Thus the socio-emotional intensity of parent-child relations is even further reinforced.

Social contact outside the residential unit may help to confirm or diminish the importance of family membership for personal identity. Frequent interaction between extended family members provides a basis for the continuing reaffirmation of the sense of family membership generated within the residential group; many studies since World War II show the importance of contact between kin compared to non-kin in the United States. Thus, the importance of kinship is not only theoretical; it is also real, since kinship appears to provide the most significant basis for interaction when options are available.

Conclusion

The preceding analysis suggests the increasing importance of family membership in the United States. Changes in household composition and the demography of kinship, in the technology of communication and the spread of literacy, in the ideology of family life and the relationship of the family to other social institutions have affected the process of socialization in ways that have increased the salience of the family in the formation of personal identity. The fears of early writers that urbanization and industrialization would weaken "the bonds of kinship" have not materialized. On the contrary, the historical changes that have been described have resulted in an "intensified . . . weight of meaning [being] attached to the personal relations of the family."

How, then, are [current] family problems and strains . . . to be understood? Weigert and Hastings suggest that the contemporary family's "specialized function of affectivity and expressivity for the sustenance of emotionally charged personal identities" also makes it a particularly powerful source of pain and potential conflict. In addition the specialized and bureaucratic organization of modern life has made the family one of the few places where the expression of strong feeling is felt to be legitimate, and thus the likelihood that emotionally charged interactions, both positive and negative, will occur in the family is increased.

Perhaps, then, the most important question to ask about the modern family is not whether it is "here to stay" but whether it can sustain itself under the weight of the expectations placed upon it. The contradiction implied by characterizing the contemporary family as "here to stay, but not well" may reflect real contradictions that the family faces in modern American society. We must begin to ask if the family does, or can, have the means, both material and emotional, to satisfy the multitude of urgent demands confronting it today. An answer to this question may require a change in our understanding of the family—a change that focuses on the reality of the resources available rather than simply on the intensity of our desires.

CHAPTER THREE

The Meaning of Family in the Past

May the gods grant you all things which your heart desires, and may they give you a husband and a home and gracious concord, for there is nothing greater and better than this—when a husband and wife keep a household in oneness of mind, a great woe to their enemies and joy to their friends, and win high renown.

Homer, *The Odyssey*

To be honest, to be kind—to earn a little and spend a little less, to make upon the whole a family happier for his presence . . .—here is a task for all that a man has of fortitude and delicacy.

Robert Louis Stevenson,
A Christmas Sermon

Romantic love as it occurs in our civilization, inextricably bound up with ideas of monogamy, exclusiveness, jealousy, and undeviating fidelity, . . . is a compound, the final result of many converging lines of development in western culture, of the institution of monogamy, of the ideas of the age of Chivalry, of the ethics of Christianity.

Margaret Mead, *Male and Female*

The Purchase of Brides

The Puritans who settled New England in the seventeenth century came to the New World for a variety of religious and economic motives, but most of them came in family groups, for the family was central to their goal of establishing a commonwealth of God. Indeed, their strong sense of family was a major cause of the failure of the communistic society that the Pilgrims tried to establish at Plymouth. In contrast, the tobacco colonies in the South were initially regarded more as a commercial venture, and single men predominated. To ensure the permanence of the settlement, the Virginia Company in London sent shipments of brides, along with other provisions, to the colonists, as described in the following letters to the Governor and Council in Virginia.

Letter from the Virginia Company in London to the Governor and Council in Virginia, Aug. 12, 1621

We send you in this ship one widow and eleven maids for wives for the people in Virginia. There hath been especial care had in the choice of them; for there hath not any one of them been received but upon good commendations, as by a note herewith sent you may perceive. We pray you all therefore in general to take them into your care; and more especially we recommend them to you Master Pountis, that at their first landing they may be housed, lodged and provided for of diet till they be married, for such was the haste of sending them away, as that straitened with time we had no means to put provisions aboard, which defect shall be supplied by the magazine ship. And in case they cannot be presently married, we desire they may be put to several householders that have wives till they can be provided of husbands. There are near fifty more which are shortly to come, are sent by our most honorable

Virginia Company Records, III, 493–494, 505, 640.

Lord and Treasurer the Earl of Southampton and certain worthy gentlemen, who taking into their consideration that the Plantation can never flourish till families be planted and the respect of wives and children fix the people on the soil, therefore have given this fair beginning, for the reimbursing of whose charges it is ordered that every man that marries them give 120 lbs. weight of the best leaf tobacco for each of them, and in case any of them die, that proportion must be advanced to make it up upon those that survive. . . . And though we are desirous that marriage be free according to the law of nature, yet would we not have these maids deceived and married to servants, but only to freemen or tenants as have means to maintain them. We pray you therefore to be fathers to them in this business, not enforcing them to marry against their wills; neither send we them to be servants, save in case of extremity, for we would have their condition so much bettered as multitudes may be allured thereby to come unto you. And you may assure such men as marry those women that the first servants sent over by the Company shall be consigned to them, it being our intent to preserve families and to prefer married men before single persons. The tobacco that shall be due upon the marriage of these maids we desire Master Pountis to receive and to return by the first. . . . To conclude, the Company, for some weighty reasons too long to relate, have ordered that no man marrying these women expect the proportion of land usually allotted for every head, which to avoid clamor or trouble hereafter, you shall do well to give them notice of.

Letter from the Virginia Council in London to the Governor and Council in Virginia, Sept. 11, 1621

By this ship and pinnace called the *Tiger*, we also send as many maids and young women as will make up the number of fifty, with those twelve formerly sent in the *Marmaduke*, which we hope shall be received with the same Christian piety and charity as they are sent from hence. The providing for them at their first landing, and disposing of them in marriage (which is our chief intent) we leave to your care and wisdom to take that order as may most conduce to their good, and satisfaction of the Adventurers. . . .

"A Note of the Shipping, Men, and Provisions sent and Provided for Virginia . . . 1621"

[The voyage of the *Tiger* with its cargo of brides was anything but routine. Among the unusual occurrences of the year 1621 was noted:]

The admirable deliverance of divers ships, and namely of the *Tiger*, which being driven strangely near 200 leagues out of her course, fell into the Turks' hands and yet came safe to Virginia.

JOHN DEMOS

The American Family in Past Time

In his broad survey of the history of family life in America, historian John Demos describes a number of changes that have occurred since Colonial times: family life has become more isolated and disconnected from the life of the larger community, sex roles have become more sharply defined, childhood and adolescence have come to be recognized as distinctive life stages. He relates these changes to industrialization and to certain myths that developed about the nature of the social world. Demos argues that such changes led to an intensifying of family relationships and to certain problems we confront in contemporary family life.

The first Americans [held an] unquestioned assumption of a tight link between the family and the community at large. The individual household was the basic unit of everyday living, the irreducible cell from which all human society was fashioned. It formed, indeed, the model for every larger structure of authority; as one seventeenth-century author declared, "a family is a little church, and little commonwealth . . . a school, wherein the first principles and grounds of government and subjection are learned, whereby men are fitted to greater matters in church or commonwealth." Or—to reverse the metaphor—religious and political communities were only families writ large. The head of the family, normally the father, was also an agent of the state. . . .

But what did this mean in detail? It meant, first of all, that a man was not free to do entirely as he pleased within his own family. The larger community—the state—felt concerned in all his behavior toward his wife and children, and acted accordingly. Thus, for example, a disobedient child was not only punished with a thrashing at the hands of his father; he was also liable to action by the courts. Or—another example—colonial magistrates might remove a child from the care of "unseemly" parents and place it in some other family. Or, again, a local court could order the reunion of a husband and wife who had decided to live apart. . . . In general, individuals who lived by themselves were regarded as potential sources of disorder, and court records are full of directives to such people to find families in which to locate themselves. In all these ways the state might interfere in the sphere of family life. The word "interfere" expresses, of course, our own view of the matter, and the point is that people in the seventeenth century felt quite differently. They regarded such activity as a natural and vital prerogative of the state.

This pattern seemed appropriate because the premodern family performed a wide range of practical functions—both for its own members and for society at large. The household was, for example, the primary unit of economic production and exchange. The vast majority of the American colonists were farmers, and, as in most agricultural communities, there was ample work for everyone, right down to the very young. . . . The family was also the chief agency of education in colonial America. Schools were limited both in their number and in the character of their facilities, and colleges were for the wealthy few. It was, therefore, from parents that most children learned what they knew of the three Rs. And it was parents (or parental surrogates) who transmitted the vocational skills that would be essential to adult life, whether in farming or (less often) in some one of the skilled trades. In this connection the apprenticeship system precisely epitomized the larger significance of family life.

The family also provided a variety of social services that are now the prerogatives of other institutions. It was the usual place of recourse for sick persons and elderly. (Old people no longer able to care for themselves would sometimes move in with the family of a grown son, in exchange for a gift of money or land.) Orphans and the indigent were "placed," by local magistrates, in particular households. Even criminals were occasionally handled in this way—implying the effectiveness of the family both as an agency of restraint and as a setting for personal reform.

This range of activity and function, so different from that which obtains today, has encouraged the belief that the colonial family was different in its *composition* as well. Scholars have long thought that premodern society was organized into "extended households"—large kin-groups, including several conjugal pairs, and spanning three or four generations. A corollary assumption has connected our own "nuclear" pattern with the coming of the Industrial Revolution little more than a century ago. But recent demographic research has shown . . . that nuclear households have been the norm in America since the time of the first settlements, and in England for as far back as evidence survives. The fundamental unit, then as now, was husband, wife, and their natural children. Occasionally, to be sure, this group was modified through the temporary residence of an elderly grandparent . . . or of an apprentice, or of some charge on the community; but such arrangements were of limited impact overall. . . .

In a few cases, a *very* few, the local courts might sanction divorce. The acceptable grounds were limited to desertion (for a period of no less than seven years), adultery and impotence. (The third of these grounds reflects the important assumption that marriage should provide sexual companionship and yield children.) Incompatibility was recognized as a significant problem— an occasion sometimes for outside intervention, but not for divorce. Legal records reveal a variety of domestic troubles in frequently pungent detail: a man punished for "abusing his wife by kicking her off from a stool into the fire"; a woman charged with "beating and reviling her husband, and egging her children to help her, bidding them knock him in the head, and wishing his victuals might choke him"; a couple "severely reproved for their most ungodly living in contention with the other." In all such cases the courts stood ready to declare their interest—and to exert their authority.

. . . Family life was influenced by profound beliefs as to differences of age and gender. Concerning women, the thinking of this period was clear enough: in virtually every important respect theirs was the weaker, the inferior, sex. Their position in marriage was distinctly subordinate, their chief duty being obedience to their husbands. Their mental and moral capacities were rated well below those of men. . . . There is one other element in the colonial view of women that is hard to specify and even harder to analyze: an implicit, but unmistakable, undercurrent of suspicion and fear. . . . There was a sense that women were less than trustworthy. Thus one finds in legal and personal documents a comment like the following: "If you would believe a woman, believe me. . . ." Witchcraft was attributed far more often to women than to men. (There are cultures where the reverse is true.) Still, one must not overemphasize these alleged sex-differences. Colonial women were never truly set apart. Women's lives and characters overlapped with men's at many points; a whole world of thought and feeling and practical circumstance was effectively shared. Their experience from day to day was too similar, their partnership too profound, to support the more radical forms of sex typing that would develop in a later era.

And what of the young in colonial America? . . . A central theme . . .—especially, but not exclusively, in the writings of the Puritans—is the need to impose strict discipline on the child virtually from the beginning of life. . . . The child was regarded as coming into the world with an inherently corrupted and selfish nature, and this created *the* central problem for parents. Another urgent concern was the inculcation of religious principles—again, from an extremely early age. Cotton Mather's diary contains the following description of a conference with his four-year-old daughter.

I took my little daughter Katy into my study and then I told my child I am to die shortly and she must, when I am dead, remember everything I now said unto her. I set before her the sinful condition of her nature, and charged her to pray in secret places every day that God for the sake of Jesus Christ would give her a new heart. I gave her to understand that when I am taken from her she must look to meet with more humbling afflictions than she does now [that] she has a tender father to care for her.

. . . This passage startles us; the calculated appeal to fear affronts our sense of the needs and sensibilities of children. But there is a vital issue of context here. *Colonial society barely recognized childhood as we know and understand it today.* Consider, for example, the matter of dress: in virtually all seventeenth-century portraiture, children appear in the same sort of clothing that was normal for adults. In fact, this accords nicely with what we know of other aspects of the child's life. His work, much of his recreation, and his closest personal contacts were encompassed within the world of adults. From the age of six or seven he was set to a regular round of tasks about the house or farm (or, in the case of a craftsman's family, the shop or store). When the family went to church, or when they went visiting, he went along. In short, from his earliest years he was expected to be—or to try to be—a miniature adult.

. . . It is necessary . . . to consider more directly the ways in which their ideals and expectations were modified, and in some cases transformed, by various factors inherent in the American environment.

There was, first of all, the simple factor of space. Most of the colonists assumed that the proper way to live was in compact, little village-communities, such as their forebears in England had known for centuries. But in the New World, of course, the ecological context was wildly different. Out beyond the fringes of settlement there was land for the taking, seemingly limitless in extent and empty of "civilized" use or habitation. . . . For many people this presented an over-powering temptation—to move, and to live for and by oneself. Thus, by the early eighteenth century, the typical pattern of settlement was not a checkerboard of well-spaced villages, but rather a straggling, jumbled mosaic with houses strung out willy-nilly into the wilderness.

But the lure of empty land fragmented not only villages; families, too, were significantly affected. Movement away from the older centers of settlement was often accomplished in successive generations. Young people, as they approached adulthood, began to consider the possibilities of settling new land near the frontier. . . .

It was part of the New World experience that families should be continually divided, and that at least some elderly people should be left behind to fend for themselves after their children had moved on.

This altered balance between men and their environment would, in the long run, affect authority relations within the family. There are many scraps

Mobile Americans. Mobility has been one of the factors affecting families throughout American history. (Denver Public Library, Western History Department.)

of evidence to suggest that the position of the young was measurably strength-ened. If a child—an older child—felt unduly constrained by his family situ-ation, he could simply leave. Better still, he could use the threat of leaving as leverage in struggles or quarrels that might arise with his parents. There was also the fact that younger persons were often the most flexible and resourceful in meeting the challenges of the new land. Here, indeed, is the start of a central theme in the lives of immigrant families through the whole course of American history: parental authority is progressively undermined as the child discovers that he is more *effective* in the new setting than his foreign-born father and mother.

It also seems evident that the American environment worked to improve significantly the status of women. This process is most easily traced with respect to a woman's legal standing; her right to hold property, for instance, was extended well beyond the traditional limits of the Old World. Moreover, by the eighteenth century many women were active in business and profes-sional pursuits. They ran inns and taverns; they managed a wide variety of stores and shops; and, at least occasionally, they worked in careers like pub-lishing, journalism and medicine. More broadly, they seem to have interacted easily and informally with men, in all sorts of everyday encounters. There are, in the records of colonial America, no grounds for inferring a pervasive system of deference based on sex. . . .

One more topic, highly germane to family life, deserves special mention here—namely, the prevalent attitudes and behavior in regard to sexuality. . . . It is true . . . that the earliest settlers, especially in New England, maintained a firm moral code, which proscribed all sexual contacts outside of marriage. However, this code was directly violated by at least some individuals from the very start, and in the eighteenth century it was widely compromised. Gradually "fornication" ceased to be a crime that was taken into court; instead, legal dockets became filled with cases of "bastardy." In short, there was a growing tolerance for premarital sexual experience; the main problem was the disposition of those illegitimate children brought into the world as a result of this tolerance. There is other evidence bearing out the same trends. It is possible, for example, to obtain rates of bridal pregnancy by comparing the dates on which given couples were married with the dates of birth of their first children. (A "positive" case is recorded whenever the interval is eight months or less.) The results for colonial America are most interesting. Positive cases appear only rarely until the very end of the seventeenth century. In the early eighteenth century, however, the rate rises markedly. And by 1750 as many as one-third to one-half of the brides in some communities were going to the altar pregnant.

By the end of the eighteenth century it was clear that American family life had been considerably transformed. Some elements of the transformation have been sketched: . . . the break in the tight web of connections between the family and the larger community; the dispersion of the household group, with the young increasingly inclined to seek their fortune in a new setting; the improvement in the status of women; the erosion of parental authority; and a growing permissiveness in the area of sex. These changes were experienced by many people at the time as a kind of decline, and there is a nonpejorative sense, too, in which they represented a loosening of old commitments and standards. It is important to see the tendency whole, because the early nineteenth century marks a crucial transition point in the history of American family life—which, to some extent, entailed an effort to turn back the clock. . . . Broadly speaking, some of the trends discussed above were now reversed. Thus, for example, women's status began to decline again in certain respects; new attempts were made to subject children to stern discipline; and sexual mores swung back into a more restrictive mold. Above all, there developed a powerful movement to endow the family as *such* with new and deeper meaning.

The process was evident, first of all, in the growth after 1800 of a new literary genre, extolling the blessings of home and hearth in rapturous detail. Books of "domestic advice" fairly gushed from the presses, and their readership expanded dramatically. Trite and sentimental as they seem today, one can hardly doubt their salience for their own time. Their simple message, endlessly repeated, was the transcendent importance of family life as the fount of all the tender virtues in life. Love, kindliness, altruism, self-sacrifice, peace, harmony, good order: all reposed here behind the sacred portals of home. Here, and nowhere else—for it was widely agreed that the same virtues were severely threatened in the world at large. Indeed, if the home should give way, human life would be reduced to the level of the jungle. We should note well this assumed disjunction between home and the life of the individual family on the one hand, and the "outside world" on the other, for it was truly fundamental to many aspects of nineteenth-century culture. Hitherto perceived as complementary to one another, the two spheres were increasingly presented in the light of adversaries.

All this was related to a new, anxious and dichotomous view of the present quality and future prospects of American society. There was a mood of expansiveness abroad in the country, a sense of unlimited opportunities for individual enterprise, an impatience with institutions, a readiness to challenge all forms of traditional restraint. Americans of every sort believed that they were carrying out a uniquely wonderful experiment in human improvement, which would one day yield "perfectionist"—not to say, "millennial"—results. But there was also a darker side. Careful analysis of the popular culture of this period reveals deep undercurrents of fear, a sense that all meaningful bearings were slipping away.

Right here the family would play a pivotal role. The vision of worldly gain, the cultuvation of the "go-ahead" spirit (a favorite period phrase), was enormously invigorating, to be sure; but it also raised a specter of chaos, of individual men devouring each other in the struggle for success. Somewhere, the old values—especially the *social* values—had to be safely enshrined. One needed some traditional moorings, some emblem of softness and selflessness to counter the intense thrust of personal striving that characterized the age. There had to be a place to come in out of the storm occasionally, a place that assured both repose and renewal. That place, lavishly affirmed from all sides, was Home.

Rooted at the center of Home stood the highly sentimentalized figure of Woman. It was she who represented and maintained the tender virtues. Men, of course, had to be out in the world, getting their hands dirty in all sorts of ways; indeed, it was precisely because of this that their women must remain free of contamination. The literature of the time shows a consistent preoccupation with the career of the well-meaning but sorely pressed male, deeply involved in the work of the world, yet holding ever before his eyes the saintly image of the lady in his life. It was she—to quote from a popular sermon—"who, like a guardian angel, watches over his interests, warns him against dangers, comforts him under trial; and by her pious, assiduous, and attractive deportment, constantly endeavors to render him more virtuous, more useful, more honourable, and more happy." Such a creature was "a pearl beyond price," a fit centerpiece in what has been called "the cult of True Woman-hood."

. . . It would be quite erroneous to infer from such flattering rhetoric any genuine improvement in women's status. In fact, the nineteenth-century American woman, when compared to her grandmothers in colonial times, had given up a great deal. For example, women could no longer be permitted to work outside the home (except among the poorest classes where the issue was simple survival). Their position in life was defined in terms of a purity directly opposed to everything characteristic of the larger world. Thus the domestic hearth was both their altar, and, from another perspective, their prison. As one scholar has aptly written, nineteenth-century American woman was "a hostage to the old values held so dear and treated so lightly . . . the hostage in the home." And, like all hostages, she was not free to come and go as she pleased. . . .

The True Woman of the nineteenth century was only one-half of the most thoroughgoing system of sex-role differentiation ever seen in American history. It goes without saying that men, too, were typed to the point of caricature. As previously mentioned, they belonged preeminently to the world of affairs. And if this was their sphere, it called forth an appropriate character, which included strength, cunning, inventiveness, endurance—a whole range of traits henceforth defined as exclusively "masculine." The impact of these definitions on family life was truly profound. The man of the family now became the breadwinner in a special sense. Each day he went away to work; each night he returned. His place of work no longer bore any relation to his home envi-ronment. What he did at work was something of which other family members knew little or nothing. His position as husband and father was altered, if not compromised; he was now a more distant, less nurturant figure, but he had special authority, too, because he performed those mysterious activities that maintained the entire household.

Among their other attributes, American men of the nineteenth century were saddled with a heavy burden of libido. Sexual desire was regarded as an exclusively male, and mostly unfortunate, phenomenon. Women, in their pu-rity, were supposed to be passionless—not merely chaste, but literally devoid of sexual feelings. This complex of ideas was an invention of the age, with massive behavioral consequences. . . .

Given these conventions, it is hard to imagine that many married couples were gratified in their most intimate relations. But sex was merely an extreme case of a pattern that affected every sort of contact between men and women. When their appropriate spheres were so rigorously separated, when character itself appeared to be so gender-specific, what was the likelihood of meaningful communication? Gone was that sense of instinctive sharing, that implicit sexual symmetry, which had suffused the full range of experience in premodern society. Instead there was a new mode of partnership—formal, self-conscious, contrived. Men and women came together from opposite directions, as uncertain allies. Understandably, many of the alliances so formed did not survive. Divorce rates, which rose steadily after mid-century, barely hinted at the true dimensions of the problem. For every marriage that was ended in court, unrecorded others dissolved through tacit agreement between the parties themselves or through simple desertion of one by the other. . . .

Sex-role differentiation was paralleled by an increasing sensitivity to differences of age. And of all such differences those pertaining to childhood received the greatest attention. Now, for the first time in Western history, the child stood out as a creature inherently different from adults—someone with his own needs, talents and character. . . .

The most telling evidence of this trend was the astonishing growth, and distinctive content, of popular literature on child rearing. To be sure, there had always been some books of this type in circulation, but they were mostly imports from England or France, and were decidedly casual in tone. . . . The nineteenth-century literature, by contrast, dealt with the development of the child's character in a much deeper sense. Moreover, it was an exclusively native production; foreign models no longer seemed appropriate to the American scene. In part, this expressed a new spirit of truculent nationalism, but it was something else as well. For one feels in these works a note of extreme urgency—a reflection, presumably, of the fright and puzzlement of many parents faced with the task of raising children in the brave new world of nineteenth-century America.

What was it that gave to childhood both a more distinctive and a more worrisome aspect than for several generations before? There was, first of all, the factor of massive social and economic change. The nineteenth century spanned the transition from an agrarian, small-town social order to one that was characterized by large-scale industrialism and urbanization. But the view of the child that made him virtually a miniature adult was particularly appropriate—perhaps *only* appropriate—in an agrarian setting. On the farm he could, and did, take part in the work of the place from his earliest years; most likely, too, he would grow up to be a farmer himself. Thus it made sense to regard him as a scaled-down version of his father. Consider, by way of contrast, the position of a city-child in the mid-nineteenth century. His father works in an office or factory on the other side of town; the child himself knows hardly any of the details. He has no economic function in the household whatsoever. Moreover, his own future course—including his adult vocation—is shrouded in uncertainty. The diversified economy of the city opens up many possibilities, and there is no reason to assume that what he eventually does will bear any relation at all to what his father presently does. In short, circumstances seem to isolate the child in a profound way, and to create a gulf between the generations that had not been there before.

There were other reasons, too, for the heightened concern with child rearing. The weakening of traditional institutions appeared to leave the individual family very much on its own. If people failed in their duty as parents, there would be no one else to do the job for them. Everything depends on the child's home environment: this was the message of all the authorities on the subject. Yet on so much else these authorities spoke with a divided voice. What, for example, should be the long-range goals of child rearing? What type of character would a model home foster? Certainly there was much concern with the development of qualities like independence and resourcefulness—a readiness to assert one's own claims and interests. Because America had become an egalitarian society, open to talent, the child should be encouraged in a certain style of expressiveness, which would help him to realize his inner potentialities. It was this that led foreign visitors to regard nineteenth-century American families as unduly child-centered. There was, however, another side. The same writers on child rearing gave great emphasis to the values of order, discipline, control. Children must be hedged about with moral precept from an early age, and must learn implicit obedience to legitimate authority. . . . Only thus, would they develop the "sound conscience" and "steadfast principles" so necessary to ensure a straight course in the face of all the pitfalls they would encounter in later life. These two main criteria of development—expressiveness and control—were logically at odds with one another, and attempts to apply them simultaneously were bound to end in confusion. . . .

If there was one outcome toward which all of the above trends seemed to point, it was a deep intensification of the parent-child bond—or, to be more precise, of the mother-child bond. The careful rearing of children was . . . the most important activity of the True Woman. From virtuous homes came preachers, philanthropists, presidents ("All that I am I owe to my angel mother"—a favorite period cliché); from disorderly ones came thieves and drunkards. There was no doubting either the impressionable nature of the young or the decisive impact of the domestic environment. Yet if children were so deeply subject to the influence of their parents, there was also an opposite effect. A familiar character in novels from the period was the "errant" or "ungrateful" child. Although raised by solicitous parents in a morally scrupulous home, he yielded in later life to worldly temptation, and filled his days with crime and debauchery. When reports of his conduct filtered back, his parents were stricken with grief, and one (or both) took ill and died. This plot-line lays bare an innermost nerve of family life in nineteenth-century America. Father, mother and children were locked in a circle of mutual responsibility, and the stakes were literally life-and-death. . . .

When childhood and adulthood had been defined in such sharply different ways, it was harder to move from one to the other. Growth itself came to seem disjunctive and problematic—no longer a smooth ascent gradually accomplished, but a jolting succession of leaps and bumps. Adolescent behavior expressed the reluctance and doubt of young people about to undertake that last and longest leap of all, into adult life and responsibility. From a psychological standpoint, the critical issue was (and remains) "identity." Always, in premodern society, youth had received an adult identity in the natural course of things. The decisive change, in more recent times, has been the presence of so many alternatives—of career, of life-style, of moral and philosophical belief. In ever-growing numbers young people have faced demanding choices, which greatly complicate the preadult years. . . .

. . . There is no golden age of the family gleaming at us from far back in the historical past. And there is no good reason to construe recent trends in terms of decline and decay. To every point alleged as an adverse reflection on modern family life, one can offer a direct rejoinder. Consider, for example, the matter of divorce. We all know that the rate of legal divorce has been rising enormously in recent years. (In fact, the trend is more than one hundred years old.) But what does this tell us about marital failure? In earlier times countless marriages were ended by simple, and legally unrecognized, desertion. Hence the figures in question are partly an artifact of legal history—a more general access to the courts, and so forth. Even without this effect, troublesome problems of interpretation would remain. Perhaps we seek more from marriage than did our forebears—more intimacy, more openness, more deep-down emotional support.

But surely these comparative judgments, which purport to make one period better than another, are beside the point anyway. Far more important is the effort to understand how family life relates to larger historical processes. For the family continually interacts with other cultural institutions and, more especially, with the variable circumstances of its membership. There is a sense in which every historical era gets the family system it needs and deserves. Thus, in colonial America, the norm was a stable "peasant" household, gradually evolving toward looser internal forms to permit full exploitation of a novel environment. Thus, too, the nineteenth-century family experienced a wrenching transformation under the multiple impact of industrialization, urban growth, egalitarian ideology and demographic change. It is hard in fact, to avoid seeing the nineteenth century as a time of troubles—not to say tragedy—in the history of the family. Sex-role typing, the generation gap, a guilt-laden sense of domestic responsibility, tortured attitudes toward sexuality—the total situation was hardly a benevolent one. And yet we should remember that massive social change always exacts a high price in human suffering. The period from about 1820 to 1920 encompassed a veritable revolution in American life and culture, and the pressures on the family were necessarily extreme. Surely the vast majority of people who experienced all this found something immensely valuable in their domestic life. Perhaps, indeed, it was Home that kept the toll of misery from rising far higher. Who can say that any alternative pattern would have worked better?

CECYLE S. NEIDLE

America's Immigrant Women

The following descriptions of life of Croatian immigrant women by Cecyle Neidle, an expert on immigrants in America, remind us how different marriage and family roles were in our country in earlier times. The story of Manda Evanich also reminds us of the ingenuity and enterprise which characterized many immigrant women in their struggle with a new environment and an often harsh reality. While the cult of domesticity may have affected middle class native women, immigrant women managed their domestic affairs but also labored hard in the market to insure a living for their children.

Slavic girls were primarily "peasant girls." Poverty and meanness were their portion in America. "Work gives them no time to live," remarks Thomas Bell. Their homes were unpainted, ugly shanties made of scrap materials, and they considered themselves lucky to have a patch of ground on which to grow vegetables and to be able to keep a cow, a goat, and some chickens. Every room but the family room and kitchen was rented out to four or five bachelors who paid two to four dollars a month per room. This excluded the purchase of food, but included the cooking of it. Water had to be carried from a common fountain, and bread was baked at a communal bake oven.

Women served the males under their roofs like slaves. It was not unusual for husbands to beat their wives. On Saturday nights when men went to the tavern, "women waited in the passageways, shawled, quiet, patient, to take their husbands home."

Such was the even tenor of their days. When accidents came, it was with terrific suddenness. A siren or a bell announced an accident which brought all the women running. Thomas Bell tells of the death of a young miner, whose

The Immigrant Life. Conditions for immigrant women were usually harsh and dif-ficult. (United Press International Photo.)

wife, the mother of several young children, received compensation of $1,370, which was considered a large sum. In addition she was tubercular. Her duties bore down on her so heavily that in spite of the shock of her bereavement, the day after the funeral she had to do a large wash because it could not wait.

An even greater tragedy than the loss of a husband was the loss of a husband and son or sons in the same accident. One Croatian woman was said to have lost three or four sons in the same mine disaster. The Croatian artist,

Maxo Vanka, who had been professor of painting at the Zagreb Academy of Art and a pupil of Ivan Mestrovic, was so affected by the misfortunes of Croatian mothers in America that he devoted one of his murals on the walls of the Saint Nicholas Croatian Church at Millvale, Pennsylvania, to the picture of a mother weeping over the body of a son killed in a mine accident.

No discussion about Slavic wives and mothers can ignore their behavior during the fierce strike of the late nineteenth and early twentieth centuries. Contrary to allegations that the Slavs did not support their strikes, recent historiography maintains that rather than being strikebreakers, they made heroic sacrifices in support of their unions.

Women played an extraordinary role in the "Long Strike" of 1875 and the "Latimer Massacre" of 1897, when strikers were fired upon and brutally manhandled. To ascertain whether their husbands and sons were among the dead or the injured

> Frantic, kerchiefed women, trailing bewildered children behind, searched among the blood-spattered beds for their husbands and sons. When they found the ones they sought a pitiable wailing arose.

A woman of heroic stature was "Big Mary" Septek. Employing the tactics of Mother Jones, who was a well known strike leader among miners, "Big Mary" placed herself at the head of a caravan of women supplied with rolling pins and pokers, some carrying their infants, and prevented strikebreakers from entering the mines. According to Professor Greene:

> At five separate points . . . a score of women armed with clubs, rolling pins and pokers led over a hundred men and boys in chasing immigrant workers on the South Side.

Louis Adamic tells a more optimistic story about a Croatian woman whom he calls Manda Evanich. Manda worked just as hard as any woman among the Slavs, but she succeeded in bringing her husband and sons to a peak of responsibility and affluence.

Manda was, like so many of her countrywomen, unusually strong; she could haul, lug and lift as well as any man. She could also read and write, which many Slavs, men and women, could not, and she was adept at healing, at setting bones and taking care of injuries. This was greatly valued in any immigrant colony.

Her marriage to Mike Evans at nineteen was her second marriage, and she had a child from a previous marriage. Mike Evans preceded her to Michigan by two years. The first Croatian in Michigan, he worked in the copper mines. His intention was to return to his homeland. But when he contracted an eye disease no doctor seemed able to diagnose, he wrote to his wife to come posthaste with her herbs so that he might be cured.

Upon her arrival she found an abandoned log cabin waiting, which her husband and a dozen prospective boarders had made ready for her. In two weeks her husband's eye infection was cured.

His daily wage was a dollar and twenty-five cents, but with the income from the boarders they were able to save six hundred dollars. For three dollars a month she cooked, baked, cleaned, washed and ironed for them, working sixteen to eighteen hours a day. In addition she nursed their colds, stomach-aches and injuries such as broken arms and open wounds. She offered an additional service to her boarders, washing their feet once a week.

She was alert to every opportunity to improve their situation. When she heard that other mines paid better, she prevailed upon her husband to change his place of work. Then she found another home, her boarders faithfully following her. Later she bought a large house in Calumet. By then she had saved twenty-five hundred dollars, with which they decided to open a saloon, a business much favored by Slavs. She was then in her early thirties and had spent eight years in America.

In the meantime several American-born children—all sons—had made their appearance. Twelve of them grew to manhood. When the last, a pair of twins, were born, President Theodore Roosevelt wrote her a letter of congratulations.

A saloon keeper was expected to act as an intermediary for his country-men. He sold not only beer and wine, but provided a social center where meetings and weddings took place. The saloon keeper cashed paychecks, often collected union dues, sold steamship tickets and money orders, wrote letters, acted as banker, prepared people for naturalization, and accompanied would-be citizens to the place of examination. Gambling was not allowed at the Evans saloon, and Mrs. Evans herself was capable of disposing of drunks.

As the saloon became a thriving establishment, Manda was busier than ever, attending to a variety of duties with the help of girls she kept bringing over from Croatia. They stayed with her until they were married. She promoted the building of a Roman Catholic Croatian church, organized a Croatian Women's Club, and at the same time kept an eye on her twelve sons.

One of her jobs was to go to Chicago twice a year to purchase at wholesale the wearing apparel twelve growing sons required. Guided by her good sense she cautiously bought copper stocks which eventually added considerably to the family wealth.

After twenty years she began to think of giving up the saloon and returning to farming. The Canadian government was offering one hundred and sixty acres in Saskatchewan to every adult male who would settle on the land and improve it. With twelve sons she visualized a princely estate of several thousand acres. Her husband and several sons had already begun the building of a home when Mike took ill and died. The undertaking was dropped. It was the only plan she had ever abandoned.

Mrs. Evans's greatest achievement was that all her sons became successful and respected men. Several were sent to college and law school. Three became lawyers, one ending up as a well-thought-of member of the Chicago Bar. One served in the legislature of Wisconsin, another in the state government of Michigan. However, none became a priest, though three were sent to the seminary. One struck oil in Texas. At eighty-one Mrs. Evans was still alive, a financially independent woman who was still practicing her healing art.

RICHARD SENNETT

Genteel Backlash

A violent incident in Chicago in 1886 is investigated by sociologist Richard Sennett in the article below for the sources of fear—and particularly fear of "foreigners"—which marked the reaction to it. Sennett looks at the nature of middle class family life—its conflicting desires to succeed in, and to escape from, the city—and describes how it led to insecurity and fear in its members, which in turn led to suspicion of all who differed from one's self and one's family. Herein, Sennett argues, lay the dread of foreign elements that led to the peculiar response of the Union Park neighborhood to an outbreak of crime.

Crime in the Streets

On Thursday, February 9, 1888, the *Chicago Tribune* gave its lead space to the following story:

> Amos J. Snell, a millionaire who lived at the corner of Washington Boulevard and Ada Street, was shot to death by two burglars who entered his house and made off with $1,600 worth of county warrants and $5,000 in checks. The murder was committed at about 2 A.M. and discovered by a servant at about 6:30 A.M.

Snell had been a resident of the area since 1867, when he built a home in Union Park and bought up many blocks of desirable real estate around it.

The murder of Snell climaxed a tense situation in Union Park that had existed since the beginning of the year 1888. Since New Year's Day, "between forty and fifty burglaries have been committed within a radius of half a mile from the intersection of Adams and Ashland Avenues," the editor of the *Tribune* wrote the day after Snell's death. . . .

The Snell murder brought public discussion of the robberies, and how to stop them, to a high pitch. Especially in Union Park, the vicinity of Snell's residence, the community was "so aroused that the people talked of little else than vigilance committees and frequent holdings of court . . . as a panacea for the lawless era that had come upon them." Gradually, the small-town

Richard Sennett, "Genteel Backlash: Chicago 1886," from *Nineteenth Century Cities*, edited by Stephen Thernstorm and Richard Sennett. Yale University Press, 1969. Reprinted by permission.

vigilante idea gave way to a new attitude toward the police, and how the police should operate in a large city. "It is no use," said one member of the Grant Club, the West Side club to which Snell himself had belonged, "to attempt to run a cosmopolitan city as you would run a New England village." He meant that the police had up to that time concentrated on closing down gambling houses and beer parlors as a major part of their effort to keep the town "respectable" and "proper." Thus they didn't deal effectively with serious crimes like robbery and murder because they spent too much time trying to clean up petty offenses; the main thing was to keep the criminal elements confined to their own quarters in the city. In all these discussions, the fact of being burglarized had been forgotten. The search turned to a means of separatism, of protection against the threatening "otherness" of the populace outside the community. . . .

What Union Park wanted, and what it got, was a garrison of police to make the community riotproof and crimeproof. For the police did indeed abandon the search for the killers, and concentrated on holding the security

19th Century Family Portrait. Printed from a cracked glass negative, this photograph shows a midwestern family in the 1890s. (United Press International Photo.)

of Union Park, like an area under siege. In this way, the original totally suburban tone of the parks and mansions was transformed; this respectable neighborhood felt its own existence to be so threatened that only rigid barriers, enforced by a semimilitary state of curfew and surveillance, would permit it to continue functioning.

The characteristics of their reaction to violence could only lead to such a voluntary isolation: everyone "knew" immediately what was wrong; and what was wrong was overwhelming: it was nothing less than the power of the "foreigner," the outsider who had suddenly become dominant in the city. Isolation, through garrisons and police patrols, was the only solution. . . .

The facts of the rationality of the enemy and his limited purpose, although acknowledged, were not absorbed; he was felt to be something else—a nameless, elusive terror, all-threatening—and the people reacted with a passion equal to his. . . .

What I would like to explore—and I certainly do not pretend to prove it—is how, in an early industrial city, the fears of the foreign masses held by a middle-class group may have reflected something other than the actual state of interaction between bourgeoisie and proletariat. These fears may have reflected instead the impact of family life on the way the people like those in Union Park understood their places in the city society.

If it is true that in the character one ascribes to one's enemy lies a description of something in one's own experience, the nature of the fear of lower-class foreigners among Union Park families might tell something about the Union Park community itself. The Union Park men, during the time of the riot and robberies, accused their chosen enemies of being lawless anarchists whose base passions pushed them outside the bounds of acceptable behavior, which finally sent them emotionally out of control. If the poor were reasonable, if they were temperate, ran the argument, these violent things would not have come to pass.

What about the Union Park people themselves, then? Were they masters of themselves? . . . It is the dimension of stability in these family patterns, I believe, that shaped their reaction to violence in their city.

A Close and Happy Home?

In 1880, on a 40-square-block territory of Union Park, there lived 12,000 individuals in approximately 3,000 family units. The latter were of three kinship types: single-member families, where one person lived alone without any other kin; nuclear families, consisting of a husband and wife and their unmarried children; and extended families, where to the nuclear unit was added some other relative—a brother or sister of the parents, a member of a third generation, or a son or daughter who was married and lived with his spouse in the parental home. The most common form of the extended family in Union Park was that containing "collateral kin," that is, unmarried relatives of the same generation as the husband or wife.

The dominant form of family life in Union Park was nuclear, for 80 percent of the population lived in such homes, with 10 percent of the population living alone in single-member families, and the remaining 10 percent living in extended family situations. A father and mother living alone with their growing children in an apartment or house was the pervasive household condition. There were few widowed parents living with their children in either nuclear or extended homes, and though the census manuscripts on which my study of the year 1880 is based were inexact at this point, there appeared to be few groups of related families living in the same neighborhood but in separate dwellings.

Family Sizes

The size of the Union Park family was small. Most families had one or two children; it was rare for a family to have more. And, the size of poorer families was in its contours similar to the size of the wealthier ones: few families were larger than six members. . . .

The nuclear, small-size families during the year 1880 were very cohesive in relations between husbands and wives, parents and children. Whether rich or poor—and about 25 percent of the community fell into a working class category—the young men and women from such homes rarely broke away to live on their own until they themselves were ready to marry and found families, usually when the man was in his early thirties. The families of Union Park, observers of the time noted, were extremely self-contained, did little entertaining, and rarely left the home even to enjoy such modest pleasures as a church social or, for the men, a beer at the local tavern. The small family, containing only parents and their immediate children, resisted the diverse influences either of other relatives or extensive community contacts. These intensive families would seem to epitomize stability among the people of Union Park.

Mobility and Family Stability

Nevertheless, my study of intergenerational mobility in work and residence from 1872 to 1890 did reveal a complicated, but highly significant pattern of insecurity in the dominant intensive families as compared to the smaller group of less intensive families.

The first insecurity of these families was in the rate of desertion. While divorce was rare—it was an act carrying a terrible stigma a hundred years ago—practical divorce in the form of desertion did occur. In Union Park, the rate of desertion was twice as high as that of *poorer* communities—in nearly one out of ten families husband or wife had deserted. A more subtle pattern of insecurity was at work as well.

In the nuclear-family homes and in the smaller families the fathers were stable job holders, as a group, over the course of the 18 years studied; roughly the same proportions of unskilled, skilled and white-collar workers of various kinds composed the labor force of these nuclear fathers in 1890 as in 1872. Given the enormous growth of Chicago's industrial production, its banking and financial capital, retail trade volume, as well as the increase of the population (100 percent increase each ten years) and the greatly increasing proportion of white-collar pursuits during this time, such stability in job distribution is truly puzzling.

But equally puzzling is the fact that this pattern of job holding among the fathers of intensive families was not shared by the fathers in extended families or fathers of larger families living in Union Park. For, unlike their neighbors, fathers of these more complex and extensive families were mobile up into exclusively bureaucratic, white-collar pursuits—so much so that by 1890 virtually none of these fathers worked with their hands. They gradually concentrated in executive and other lesser managerial pursuits and decreased their numbers in shopkeeping, toward which, stereotypically, they are supposed to gravitate.

Even more striking were the differences between fathers and sons in each of these family groups. The sons in the dominant family homes were, unlike their fathers, very unstable in their patterns of job holding. As many moved down into manual pursuits over the course of the 18 years as moved up into the white-collar occupations. One is tempted to explain this simply as a regression toward the mean of higher status groups in time. But the sons of extended and large families did not move in this mixed direction. Rather, they followed the footsteps of their fathers into good white-collar positions, with almost total elimination of manual labor in their ranks as well. This pattern occurred in small-family sons versus large-family sons and in nuclear-family sons versus extended-family sons. The difference in the groups of sons was especially striking in that the starting points of the sons in the occupational work force had virtually the *same* distribution in all types of families. Stephan Thernstrom has pointed out that economic aid between generations of workers is more likely to manifest itself at the outset of a young person's career than when the older generation has retired and the young have become the principal breadwinners. But the fact is that in Union Park, both extended-family and nuclear-family sons, both large- and small-family sons, began to work in virtually the same pursuits as their fathers, then became distinctively different in their patterns of achievement. This strongly suggests that something *beyond* monetary help was at work in these families to produce divergences in the work experiences of the different groups of sons.

The residence patterns of the generations of the intensive and less intensive families also bears on the issues of stability and instability in the lives of the people of Union Park. Up to the time of violence in the Union Park area, the residence patterns of the two kinds of families, in both the parents' and the sons' generations, were rather similar. In the wake of the violence, however, it appears that within the parents' generation there was significant movement back into the Union Park area, whereas for the half decade preceding the disturbances there was a general movement out to other parts of Chicago. It is in the generation of the sons that differences between the two family groups appeared. In the wake of the violence, the sons of large families and of extended families continued the exodus from Union Park that began in the early 1880s. The sons from intensive families did not; in the years following the violence they stopped migrating beyond the boundaries of the community they had known as children, and instead kept closer to their first homes.

Family Background and Making It

These observations have an obvious bearing on an important debate over what form of family life best nurtures the kind of children who can cope with the immensely dynamic and risky world of the industrial city. [Sociologist] Talcott Parsons has argued that the small nuclear family is a kinship form well adapted to the industrial order; the lack of extensive kin obligations and a wide kin circle in this family type means, Parsons has contended, that the kinship unit does not serve as a binding private world of its own, but rather frees the individual to participate in "universalized" bureaucratic structures that are urban-wide and dynamic.

The cultural historian Philippe Ariès, in *Centuries of Childhood,* has challenged this theory by amassing a body of historical evidence to show that the extended kinship relationships in large families, at least during an earlier era, were actually less sheltering, more likely to push the individual out into the world where he woud have to act like a full man on his own at an early age, than the intense, intimate conditions of the nineteenth-century home. In intensive homes, the young person spent a long time in a state of dependence under the protection and guidance of his elders. Consequently, argues Ariès, the capacity of the young adult from small nuclear homes to deal with the world about him was blunted, for he passed from a period of total shelter to a state in which he was expected to be entirely competent on his own.

The data I collected on Union Park clearly are in line with the argument made by Ariès. The young from homes of small scale or from homes where the structure of the family was nuclear and "privatistic," in Ariès' phrase, had an ineptness in the work world, and a rootedness to the place of their childhood not found to the same degree among the more complex, or larger-family situations. . . . But the conditions that faced Union Park families in a new kind of city, a city at once disorganized and anarchic, set the stability of the family against adaptation to city life. For it is clear that the nineteenth-century, privatistic, sheltering homes Ariès depicts, . . . homes that observers of the time pointed to as a basic element in the composition of the "dull respectability" of Union Park, could themselves have easily served as a refuge from the confusing, dynamic city that was taking shape all around the confines of Union Park.

And what is more natural than that middle-class people should try to hold onto the status position they had in such a disrupting, growing milieu, make few entrepreneurial ventures outside their established jobs, and withdraw into the comfort and intimacy of their families. Here is the source of that job "freeze" to be seen in the mobility patterns of fathers in intense-family situations; the bourgeois intensive family in this way became a shelter from the work pressures of the industrial city, a place where men tried to institute some control and establish some comforting intimacies in the shape of their lives, while withdrawing to the sidelines as the new opportunities of the city industries opened up. Such an interpretation of these middle-class families complements Richard Hofstadter's interpretation of middle-class political attitudes in the latter part of the nineteenth century. He characterizes the middle-class as feeling that the new industrial order had passed them by and left them powerless. It is this peculiar feeling of social helplessness on the part of the fathers that explains what use they made of their family lives.

But the late nineteenth century was also the world of Horatio Alger, of "luck and pluck"; it was no time for withdrawal. The idea of seizing opportunities, the idea of instability of job tenure for the sake of rising higher and higher, constituted . . . the commonly agreed-upon notion among respectable people of the road to success. One should be mobile in work, then, for this was the meaning of "opportunity" and "free enterprise," but in fact the overwhelming dislocations of the giant cities seem to have urged many men to retreat into the circle of their own families, to try simply to hold onto jobs they knew they could perform.

Conditions of privacy and comfort in the home weakened the desire to get ahead in the world, to conquer it; since the fathers of the intensive families were retreating from the confusions of city life, their preparation of their sons for work in Chicago became ambiguous, in that they wanted, surely, success for their sons, yet shielded the young, and did not themselves serve as models of successful adaptation. The result of these ambiguities can be seen directly in the work experience of the sons, when contrasted to the group of sons from families which, by virtue either of family form or size, were more complex or less intense. Overlaid on these family patterns was a relatively high rate of hidden marital breakdown in Union Park—one in every ten homes—while the expectation was, again, that such breakdowns must not occur, that they were a disgrace.

Because the goals of these middle-class people were bred of contradictory desires to escape from and succeed in the city, the possibility of a wholly satisfying pattern of achievement for them was denied. The family purposes were innately contradictory. A family impulse in one direction inevitably defeated another image of what was wanted. This meant that the sources of defeat were nameless for the families involved; surely these families were not aware of the web of self-contradictions in which in retrospect they seem to have been enmeshed; they knew only that things never seemed to work out to the end planned, that they suffered defeats in a systematic way. It is this specific kind of frustration that would lead to a sense of being overwhelmed, which, in this community's family system, led easily to a hysterical belief in hidden, unknown threats ready to strike at a man at almost any time.

What I would like to suggest is that this complex pattern of self-defeat explains the character of the Union Park reaction to violence. For the dread of the unknown that the middle classes projected onto their supposed enemies among the poor expressed exactly the condition of self-instituted defeat that was the central feature of the family system in Union Park. And this dread was overwhelming precisely because men's own contradictory responses to living in such a city were overwhelming. They had defined a set of conditions for their lives that inevitably left them out of control. The fact that in Union Park there was a desire to destroy the "immigrant anarchists" or to garrison the neighborhood against them, as a result of the incidents of violence, was important in that it offered an outlet for personal defeats, not just for anger against lawbreakers. This response to violence refused to center on particular people, but rather followed the "path of hysterical reaction," in Freud's phrase, and centered on an abstract class of evildoers. The fear of being suddenly overwhelmed from the outside was really a sign that one was in fact in one's own life being continually overwhelmed by the unintended consequences of what one did.

The terrible fear of attack from the unbridled masses was also related to the fear of falling into deep poverty that grew up in urban middle-class families of this time. To judge from a wide range of novels in the latter half of the nineteenth century there was a dread among respectable people of suddenly and uncontrollably falling into abject poverty; the Sidwells in Thackeray's *Vanity Fair* plummet from wealth to disorganized penury in a short space of time; In Edith Wharton's *Age of Innocence,* Lily Bart's father is similarly struck down by the symbol of entrepreneurial chance in the industrial city, the stock market. This feeling of threat from the impersonal, unpredictable workings of the city economy was much like the sense of threat that existed in the Union Park families, because the dangers encountered in both cases were not a person or persons one could grapple with, but an abstract condition, poverty, or family disorder that was unintended, impersonal and swift to come if the family should once falter. Yet what one *should* do was framed in such a self-contradictory way that it seemed that oneself and one's family were always on the edge of survival. The growth of the new industrial city, with its uncertainties and immense wastes in human poverty, not all victims of which were easily dismissed as personal failures, could surely produce in the minds of middle-class citizens who were uneasy about their own class position and lived out from the center of town, the feeling that some terrible force from below symbolized by the poor, the foreigner, was about to strike out and destroy them unless they did something drastic.

The reaction among most of the families to the eruption of violence bears out this interpretation of events. With the exception of the upwardly mobile, extended-family sons, most family members did not try to flee the community as a response to the threats of riot and the organized wave of crime. There was a renewed feeling of community solidarity in the face of violence, a solidarity created by fear and a common dread of those below.

The relations between family life and the perception of violence in this Chicago community could be formed into the following general propositions. These were middle-class families enormously confused in what they wanted for themselves in the city, both in terms of their achievements in the society at large and in terms of their emotional needs for shelter and intimacy. Their schema of values and life goals was in fact formed around the issues of stability and instability as goals in a self-contradictory way. The result of this inner contradiction was a feeling of frustration, of not really being satisfied, in the activities of family members to achieve *either* patterns of stability or mobility for themselves. The self-defeat involved in this process led these families to feel themselves threatened by overwhelming, nameless forces they could not control, regardless of what they did. The outbreak of violence was a catalyst for them, giving them in the figure of the "other," the stranger, the foreigner, a generalized agent of disorder and disruption.

It is this process that explains logically why the people of Union Park so quickly found a communally acceptable villain responsible for violence, despite all the ambiguities perceived in the actual outbreaks of the disorders themselves. This is why the villain so quickly identified, was a generalized, non-specific human force, the embodiment of the unknown, the outside, the foreign. This is why the people of Union Park clung so tenaciously to their interpretation, seemed so willing to be terrorized and distraught. . . .

CHAPTER FOUR

Post-Industrial Society and the Family

Despots have ever found families a vexation, if not an outright threat. The
states of the world, after all, attempt or pretend to be "rational," which
families by their very nature can never be. The more "rational" and
bureaucratic the world becomes, in fact, the more families matter, the
greater the need for the passionate and irrational connections which
families exist to supply.

                                                    Jane Howard, *Families*

Under the strains of modern living the
American family has been showing signs
of coming apart.

                              George W. Pierson, "A Restless Temper"

PHILIP SLATER

Some Effects
of Transience

Mobility has long characterized American society. The earliest colonists had moved from their ancestral lands, and successive generations of Americans moved westward in search of new opportunities, settling a continent in the process. As early as 1831, the French observer Alexis de Tocqueville commented on "the restless temper" of the American people. But more than ever before, ours now is a mobile society. Young families move for opportunities in work. The success ethic requires personnel to move when their company transfers them or promotes them to higher positions in distant branches. And the family must be ready to pull up roots to follow success. Older couples move to find a place in the sun when they retire, leaving children, grandchildren, and friends behind. Sociologist Philip Slater analyzes the effects of constant movement—and expectation of frequent moves—on American character and society.

We live in the most mobile society that has ever existed. It is true that there have been many societies that continually moved from place to place. But these nomadic tribes moved as a group and usually over a fixed route. They carried their possessions, their relationships, their entire way of life along with them, unchanged. In most cases, even the land did not really change since every part of the route was re-encountered at predictable intervals. Nomadic tribes are just as rooted to the land as a peasant farmer, but to a corridor instead of a site.

Mobility in modern society is quite another matter. Here individuals or family units are plucked out of their social context and transplanted. They may never live in the same place twice. While they may stay within the same society (and even these boundaries may weaken in the future), they must form new relationships, adapt to a new physical environment, new norms, and so on. Those who remain behind must repair the social fissure that the transients have created.

The effects of mobility on our culture have been profound. George Pierson has argued with great force that most of what is distinctively American can be traced to it. Optimism, conservatism, other-directedness, individualism egalitarianism, superficiality, identity diffusion, gregariousness, alienation, homogeneity, money-mindedness, loneliness, nostalgia, anxiety, conformity, activity, achievement orientation, pragmatism, love of novelty, materialism, youth worship—all these real or imagined qualities bear some relationship to the tendency of modern Americans to uproot themselves frequently. Constant moving about tends to detach the individual from enduring and significant relationships. But the difficulty of continually forming new bonds and breaking old ones can be eased by learning to speed up the process of making friends— developing an informality, an easy friendliness, a capacity for ready, if superficial, ties.

Human beings are all equipped with the same emotional repertoire, the same basic needs, the same basic defenses. Out of these evolve more idiosyncratic patterns that we call personality or shared patterns we call culture. These differences help maintain boundaries between individuals and between groups, but at the cost of some violence to the emotional life of the individual. My body may tell me, as a human being, to respond in a given way to a punch in the nose, a sexual stimulus, a loss, or a rejection, but I may have learned, as a member of a specific culture or as one playing a special role within that culture, not to react in this human way but in some way that defines me "uniquely."

To be more individual, in other words, is to be less human, more of a social artifact. One person learns to lose the capacity to respond with love, another person with anger, another with jealousy, another with tears, and so on. This process of emotional crippling we call personality development. Its effect is to create a kind of emotional specialization between people. In a permanent group the alienation that comes from a man's specialized response system is eased by his contact with other specialists, who express his needs and feelings for him as he does for them. In a culture in which a man cannot weep, his women may weep for him. If he is a group jester, there will be some dour compatriot to feel gloomy for him, and so on. And where the group as a whole warps human feeling in a given direction, defining its differentness from other groups, his similarity with those around him relieves his sense of alienation from his feelings.

When a man loses a permanent role in a permanent group, his specialization becomes pointless and somewhat burdensome. He becomes a part in search of a whole, feeling unlike others and therefore alone and lost but having no sense of himself as a separate entity firmly fixed in a pattern of other such entities. In a society that places a value on individualism, this inability to experience oneself leads paradoxically to a cry for *more* uniqueness, more eccentricity, more individuation, thus increasing the symptoms.

The solution to this problem, to put it bluntly, is the obliteration of differences by increasing uniformity and sameness among people. But uniformity could only be tolerated if people were all transformed into full human beings rather than remaining specialized semipersons as we are now. Fantasies of uniformity have always assumed that all humans would affect some specialized posture: the gregarious suburbanite, the submissive peasant, the Prussian officer. We imagine with horror everyone being forced to assume some narrow role now played by only a few. But such a uniformity would not work since (1) it would retain the same constraints under which we now suffer without providing the assurance that others will express the stunted sides of ourselves; and (2) the advantages of a social division of labor would be lost, and the society as a whole would suffer from the loss of variety, the lack of human resources. Attempts to evolve this kind of uniformity may be (and are being) made, but a society so structured will fail. A viable society needs a great variety of contradictory human responses. If members of that society are to be limited in the ways they can respond, then each must be limited in different ways; otherwise generalized shortages will (and do) arise. On the other hand, if a society is to function with uniform participants, each one must be individually complex and comprehensive in his or her available responses. Each must have the capacity to be introverted *and* extroverted, controlled *and* spontaneous, independent *and* dependent, gregarious *and* seclusive, loving *and* hostile, strong *and* weak, and so on.

This is, of course, utopian. Human beings will never attain this degree of humanness; nor, happily, will complete uniformity ever be achieved. I am merely saying that if uniformity is the goal, specialization and incompleteness must be avoided. Less variety from person to person requires more variety within each person. The individual will be more changeable, less predictable from moment to moment and from situation to situation, less able to play the same tune all his or her life long.

Now if one must make and break relationships rapidly, then it becomes increasingly important that people be as interchangeable as possible, like the motel. An American today can travel almost anywhere in the country, stop at a motel, and find himself in an entirely familiar environment. He would, indeed, be hard put to distinguish one from another. As relationships become increasingly temporary, the need to establish such instant familiarity will correspondingly increase.

But people are not motels. We have already pointed out the necessity for an enrichment of the individual before interchangeability can exist. Transience also makes it more necessary to take people as we find them—to relate immediately, intensely, and without traditional social props, rituals, and distancing mechanisms. Distance is provided by transience itself, and the old patterns of gamesmanship, of extended, gradual, and incomplete unmasking, become inappropriate. By the time the individual reaches his "here is the real me" flourish, he finds himself alone again. It has often been observed that encounter groups are adapted to a transient world since they emphasize openness, feedback, immediacy, communication at a feeling level, the here and now, more awareness of and ability to express deeper feelings, and so on. Members of such groups often express surprise and chagrin at their capacity to respond warmly to people they would in other situations have regarded with indifference, fear, or contempt. After the initial shock has worn off, the old preferences are rediscovered, but there remains a sense of how often opportunities for significant relationships are wasted by casual stereotyping.

Another effect of transience is the development of more flexible moral patterns. Mobility and change rule out the effectiveness of any permanent system of social control. *External* controls depend on the permanent presence of the individual in the same social unit, a condition that has largely vanished from the civilized world. Even *internalized controls of a fixed kind* rapidly become irrelevant to a changing social environment. Our society has long required, and obtained, a system of internalized controls that incorporates moral relativism—what David Riesman has called "other-direction." The individual must both be capable of self-restraint and, at the same time, recognize that groups vary in what they consider desirable and undesirable social behavior. He or she must be acutely sensitive and responsive to group norms, while recognizing the arbitrariness, particularity, and limited relevance of all moral rules.

This idea is offensive to many and generated a whole tradition of angry nostalgia among postwar critics of American society. But the "inner-directed" individual is like a wind-up toy, programmed at birth to display a limited range of responses in all situations regardless of environmental variation, and while this may well be considered heroic, it is, like all heroic traits, excessively simple-minded.

Greater complexity is also required at the marital level. Two married persons in a stable and permanent social context need seek little from each other. Pyschological and interpersonal needs can be satisfied in a variety of other relationships—kin, neighborhood, friendship. In many societies and subcultures, deeply entrenched patterns of sex segregation make intimate communication between the sexes difficult or impossible; men and women literally live in different worlds. Wherever this stability begins to break down, husband and wife tend to increase their emotional demands on each other. The transition from working-class to middle-class status and from "urban village" to suburban environments often brings about a loosening of social relationships and is therefore usually associated, as we have seen, with an increase in the intensity and intimacy of the marriage and a decrease in role specialization.

Sociologists have generally argued, with good reason, that higher income, education, and other attributes of middle-class standing are stabilizing forces for marriage. But we could also anticipate that the greater burden placed on the marriage by the reduction of other intimate and lasting relationships would increase marital discord. In a nonmobile society, one expects of marriage only a degree of compatibility. Spouses are not asked to be lovers, friends, and mutual therapists. But it is increasingly true of our own society that the marital bond is the closest, deepest, most important, and supposedly the most enduring relationship of one's life. Therefore, it is increasingly likely to fall short of the demands placed upon it and to be dissolved. As emotional alternatives are removed, the limitations of a marriage become less and less tolerable. The social ties of modern Americans are becoming so transitory that a permanent point of reference seems essential, and this perhaps accounts for the heroic effort made in our society—through marriage manuals, counselors, psychotherapists, magazine articles, and so on—to find ways of enabling the marriage relationship to bear the enormous emotional burdens placed upon it.

The most obvious strain in a transient society is produced by each partner having a career. This means that at any moment competing job requirements or opportunities threaten to separate the couple geographically. This is an increasing problem in a world in which more and more professional couples are appearing. Unless one or the other is willing to assume subordinate status, it is often difficult for the couple both to find desirable positions in the same community.

Yet the decline in the specialization of marital roles constitutes a powerful force for feminine equality, and a mobile society must either tolerate the pull of competing careers or the push of feminine discontent. For decades our society chose the latter, and one result has been an exaggerated investment of feminine energy and ambition into the child-rearing process. While the social costs of either solution are high, it is difficult to envision a more serious social risk than that which results from children having to validate their mothers' competence through their own successes, creativity, and mental health.

The "problem" of the working mother is often discussed as if the mother's presence in the home were an unqualified blessing. Child rearing, however, has never been, throughout history, either a full-time or a one-person task, but rather the adjunct of an otherwise full life. The children, meanwhile, have been their own heroes, not merely the central character in their mother's drama. No one ever asks the victims of our American pattern whether they might not have preferred to see a little less of their mothers and let both mother and child win their own rewards.

CHRISTOPHER LASCH

The Family
and Morality

Historian Christopher Lasch sees industrial development and the technology
of advertising, mass education, and the rise of the experts in education and
child development as forces that have undercut family authority and indi-
vidual conscience. He argues that mass socialization leaves the individual
unguarded against authoritarian control by the state. His is a controversial
and extreme view, but it has been widely publicized and influential. Other
observers do not accept his view that family authority has been destroyed or
that permissive child rearing has produced a generation of dependent young
people without consciences. John Demos and Philip Slater also question
Lasch's belief that permissiveness in child rearing is new.

The survival of any form of human society depends on two things, the production of the necessities of life and the reproduction of the labor force itself.

Reproduction includes not merely the propagation of the species, but the
care and nurture of the young—education, training, discipline, and cultural
transmission.

In the early days of capitalism, the work of socialization took place largely
in the family. The patriarchal family, in which the father's authority was
unquestioned, was responsible not only for imparting ethical norms—standards of right and wrong—but also for instructing the child in the prevailing
social rules. It thus served as the primary agency for shaping the child's
character.

The capitalist made little effort to interfere with this central position of
the family. He attempted to supervise his workers' lives on the job, but his
control ended when the workers left the factory at closing time. Only a handful
of employers in the early twentieth century understood that the success of the

From *Moral Choices in Contemporary Society: Articles for the Sixth Course by Newspaper.*
Copyright © 1976, 1977 by the Regents of the University of California.

"IT'S VERY NICE, DEAR, but DON'T YOU THINK YOU SHOULD HAVE ASKED DADDY SINCE IT'S HIS CAR?"

mass production economy now required not only the capitalistic organization of production but the organization of consumption and leisure as well.

One of the first business leaders to recognize the need for a new kind of social education for the young was Edward A. Filene, the Boston department store magnate. "Mass production," he said in 1919, "demands the education of the masses; the masses must learn to behave like human beings in a mass production world." In other words, the mass production of commodities in ever-increasing abundance demands a mass market to absorb them.

Transformation of the Family

Today, the "education" of masses of people has proved to be one of the most important elements not only in the emergence of an economy based on mass consumption, but in the transformation of the family. In the course of bringing Filene's bargain-basement "culture" to the consumers of it, the advertising industry, the school, and the mental health and welfare services have taken over many of the socializing functions of the home. The ones that remain have been placed under the direction of modern science and technology.

While glorifying domestic life as the last haven of intimacy, these agencies of mass tuition have propagated the view that the family cannot provide for its own needs without outside assistance.

The advertising industry insists that the health and safety of the young, the satisfaction of their daily nutritional requirements, their emotional and intellectual development, and their ability to compete with their peers for popularity and success all depend on consumption of vitamins, Band-Aids, cavity-preventing toothpaste, cereals, mouthwashes, and laxatives.

"Domestic science" urges the housewife and mother to systematize housekeeping and to give up the rule-of-thumb procedures of earlier generations. Modern medicine orders the abandonment of home remedies. The mental health movement teaches that maternal "instinct" is not to be trusted in childrearing.

Even the sex instinct has come to be surrounded by a growing body of scientific analysis and commentary, according to which sexual "fulfillment" depends on study, technique, discipline, control.

The New Social Welfare

The diffusion of the new ideology of social welfare and "civilized" consumption has had the effect of a self-fulfilling prophecy.

By convincing the housewife, and finally even her husband as well, to rely on outside technology and the advice of outside experts, the apparatus of mass tuition—the successor to the church in our secularized society—has undermined the family's capacity to provide for itself. The agencies of mass socialization have thereby justified the continuing expansion of health, education, and welfare services.

Yet rising rates of crime, juvenile delinquency, suicide, and mental breakdown belatedly suggest to many experts, even to many welfare workers, that welfare agencies furnish a poor subsitute for the family. Dissatisfaction with the results of socialized welfare and the growing expense of maintaining it now prompt efforts to shift health and welfare functions back to the home.

The Demise of Family Authority

It is too late, however, to call for a revival of the patriarchal family or even of the less authoritarian family that replaced it. The socialization of reproduction has fatally weakened not only the father's authority but that of the mother as well.

Instead of imposing their own standards of right and wrong, now thoroughly confused, parents influenced by psychiatry and the doctrines of progressive education seek to understand the "needs" of the young and to avoid painful confrontations. Instead of guiding the child, the older generation struggles to "keep up with the kids," to master their incomprehensible jargon, and even to imitate their dress and manners in the hope of preserving a youthful appearance and outlook.

Under these conditions, children often grow up without forming strong identifications with their parents. Yet it was precisely these identifications that formerly provided the psychological basis of conscience or superego— that element of the psyche which internalizes social prohibitions and makes submission to them a moral duty. Lacking an internalized sense of duty, children become "other-directed" adults, more concerned with their own pleasure and the approval of others than with leaving their mark on the world.

The ease with which children escape emotional entanglements with the older generation leaves them with a feeling not of liberation but of inner emptiness. Young people today often reproach their parents with indifference or neglect, and many of them seek warmth and security in submission to spiritual healers, gurus, and prophets of political or psychic transformation.

Permissive styles of childrearing, instead of encouraging self-reliance and autonomy, as might have been expected, appear instead to intensify the appetite for dependence.

Superstate

The only alternative to the superego, it has been said, is the superstate. Formerly, the absorption of parental values enabled the young to overcome childhood dependency and to become morally autonomous.

Today, the wish for dependence persists into later life, laying the psychological foundations of new forms of authoritarianism.

At first glance, the decline of conscience might appear to make it more difficult for the authorities to impose themselves on the rest of the population. Not only parents, but all those who wield established authority—teachers, magistrates, priests—have suffered a loss of "credibility."

Unable to inspire loyalty or even to command obedience, they therefore attempt to impose their will through psychological manipulation. Government becomes the art of personnel management, which treats social unrest as a kind of sickness, curable by means of therapeutic intervention.

Yet, in many ways the new forms of authoritarianism and social control work more effectively than the old ones. As religion gives way to the new antireligion of mental health, authority identifies itself not with what ought to be but with what actually is, not with principles but with reality. The individual's conduct is governed less by his superego than by his conception of reality; resistance to the status quo becomes not "unprincipled," but "unrealistic."

Political authority no longer rests on the family, which formerly mediated between the state and the individual. Indeed, the state has accommodated itself so well to the weakening of parental authority that efforts to strengthen the family are likely to be perceived as threats to political stability.

Through the proliferating apparatus of mass socialization, the state now controls the individual more effectively than it controlled him through appeals to his conscience. Even though the new methods of social control might exact a mounting economic, social, and psychological price, those methods will be discarded only when the price threatens to become altogether unbearable.

MICHAEL NOVAK

The Family Out of Favor

The myths of individual autonomy and individual fulfillment are leading us astray, says Michael Novak, author and former editor of Christian Century. *It is our attachments to others and the concrete experiences of daily life in our families that make us whole and fully human. It is in this homely reality that we find meaning and joy; it is in the family that we find our institutional strength.*

Theories of liberation deserve to be studied in the light of flesh, absurdity, and tragedy. There is a pervasive tendency in Western thought, possibly the most profound cultural undercurrent in 3,000 years (compared to it, C.S. Lewis said, the Reformation was a ripple on the ocean), in which liberation is imagined as a breaking of the bonds of finiteness. Salvation comes as liberty of spirit. "Don't fence me in!" The Fall results from commitments that "tie one down," that are not subject to one's own controlling will. One tries to live as angels once were believed to live—soaring, free, unencumbered.

The jading of everyday, the routines of weekdays and weekends, the endless round of humble constraints, are, in this view, the enemies of human liberty.

In democratic and pragmatic societies, the dream of the solitary spirit often transfers itself into a moral assault upon institutions, traditions, loyalties, conventions. The truly moral person is a "free thinker" who treats every stage of life as a cocoon from which a lovely moth struggles to escape the habits of a caterpillar. This fuzzy sentiment names each successive breakaway "growth" and "development." It describes the cumulative process as "liberation."

There is, of course, a rival moral tradition. I do not mean the conventional variant, which holds that fidelity to institutions, laws, conventions, and loyalties is sufficient. The more compelling alternative—call it "realist"—differs from the romantic undercurrent by associating liberation with the concrete toils of involvement with family and/or familial communities. The romantic undercurrent takes as the unit of analysis the atomic individual. The realist alternative takes as the unit of analysis the family. To put it mythologically, "individual people" seek happiness through concentration upon themselves, although perhaps for the sake of service to others. Most television cops, detectives, cowboys, and doctors are of this tribe. The "family people" define themselves through belonging to others: spouse, children, parents, siblings, nieces, cousins, and the rest. For the family people, to be human is to be, so to speak, molecular. I am not solely I. I am husband, father, son, brother, uncle, cousin; I am a family network. Not solitary. On television both *All in the Family* and *Good Times* have as a premise the molecular identity of each character. The dramatic unit is the family.

There is, beyond the simplicities of half-hour television, a gritty realism in family life. Outside the family, we choose our own friends, like-minded folk whose intellectual and cultural passions resemble ours. Inside the family however, divergent passions, intellections, and frustrations slam and batter us. Families today bring together professions, occupations, social classes, and sometimes regional, ethnic, or religious differences. Family life may remain in the United States the last stronghold of genuine cosmopolitanism and harsh, truthful differences.

So much of modern life may be conceived as an effort to make ourselves pure spirits. Our meals are as rationalized and unsensual as mind can make them. We write and speak about sexual activity as though its most crucial element were fantasy. We describe sex as though it were a stage performance, in which the rest of life is as little as possible involved. In the modern era, the abstract has grown in power. Flesh, humble and humbling, has come to be despised.

So it is no surprise that in our age many resistant sentiments should war against marriage and family. Marriage and family are tribute paid to earth, to the tides, cycles, and needs of the body and of bodily persons; to the angularity and difficulties of the individual psyche; to the dirty diapers, dirty dishes, and endless noise and confusion of the household. It is the entire symbolic function of marriage and family to remind us that we come from dust and will return to dust, that we are part of the net of earth and sky, inspirited animals at play for our brief moment on this planet, keeping alive our race. The point of marriage and family is to make us realistic. For it is one of the secrets of the human spirit that we long *not* to be of earth, not to be bound by death, routine, and the drag of our bodies. We long to be other than we are.

A generation ago, the "escape from freedom" was described in terms almost the reverse of those required today. In those days, as writers like Erich Fromm rightly worried, many persons were afraid of risks and responsibilities; many sought shelter in various fixed arrangements: in collectivism, in religion, in family. But dangers to freedom change with the generations. In our own time, the flight most loved is flight from flesh. The restraints Fromm worried about have proven, under the pressures of suburbs, automobiles, jet planes, television, and corporate mobility, all too fragile. Today the atomic individual is as free as a bird. The threat to human liberation today is that the flesh, the embodied psyche, earthy roots, bodily loyalties, will be dismissed with contempt.

The consequence of this freedom is likely to be self-destruction. Whoever nourishes spirit alone must end by the ultimate denial of the flesh. A flaming burst of destruction and death is the image that fascinates us (as in *The Towering Inferno*), that most expresses our drift of soul. For fear of the flesh is fear of death. A love for the concrete and humble gestures of the flesh meant, even in the concentration camps, spiritual survival.

A return to the true conditions of our own humanity will entail a return, on the part at least of a dedicated few, to the disciplines and terrors of marriage and family. Many will resist these disciplines mightily. (Not all, of course, are called to marriage. The single life can have its own disciplines, and celibacy its own terrors. What counts is the governing cultural model. The commitment of "the family people" to the demands of our humanity provide a context within which singleness and even celibacy have a stabilizing strength; and the freedom and dedication of the single, in turn, nourish the family.)

People say of marriage that it is boring, when what they mean is that it terrifies them: too many and too deep are its searing revelations, its angers, its rages, its hates, and its loves. They say of marriage that it is deadening, when what they mean is that it drives us beyond adolescent fantasies and romantic dreams. They say of children that they are piranhas, eels, brats, snots, when what they mean is that the importance of parents with respect to the future of their children is now known with greater clarity and exactitude than ever before.

Marriage, like every other serious use of one's freedom, is an enormous risk, and one's likelihood of failure, is rather high. No tame project, marriage. The raising of children, now that so few die in childbirth or infancy, and now that fate takes so little responsibility out of the hands of affluent and well-educated parents, brings each of us breathtaking vistas of our inadequacy. Fear of freedom—more exactly, fear of taking the consequences—adds enormously to the tide of evasion. The armies of the night find eager recruits.

It is almost impossible to write honestly of marriage and family. Who would like the whole world to know the secret failures known to one's spouse and one's children? We already hate ourselves too much. Given our affluence and our education, we are without excuses. We are obliged by our own vague sentiments of progress and enlightenment to be better spouses, better parents, than our ancestors—than our own parents, or theirs. Suppose we are not? We know we are not. Having contempt for ourselves, we want desperately to blame the institution which places our inadequacy in the brilliant glare of interrogation.

Still, just as marrying and having children have today the force of public political and moral statements, it is necessary to take one's private stand. Being married and having children has impressed on my mind certain lessons, for whose learning I cannot help being grateful. Most are lessons of difficulty and duress. Most of what I am forced to learn about myself is not pleasant.

The quantity of sheer impenetrable selfishness in the human breast (in *my* breast) is a never-failing source of wonderment. I do not want to be disturbed, challenged, troubled. Huge regions of myself belong only to me. Getting used to thinking of life as bicentered, even multicentered, is a struggle of which I had no suspicion when I lived alone. Seeing myself through the unblinking eyes of an intimate, intelligent other, an honest spouse, is humiliating beyond anticipation. Maintaining a familial steadiness whatever the state of my own emotions is a standard by which I stand daily condemned. A rational man, acting as I act? Trying to act fairly to children, each of whom is temperamentally different from myelf and from each other, each of whom is at a different stage of perception and aspiration, is far more baffling than anything Harvard prepared me for. (Oh, for the unselfconscious box on the ears used so freely by my ancestors!)

My dignity as a human being depends perhaps more on what sort of husband and parent I am, than on any professional work I am called upon to do. My bonds to them hold me back (and my wife even more) from many sorts of opportunities. And yet these do not feel like bonds. They are, I know, my liberation. They force me to be a different sort of human being, in a way in which I want and need to be forced.

Nothing, in any case, is more poignant and private than one's sense of failing as a father. When my own sense of identity was that of a son, I expected great perfection from my father. Now that I am a father, I have undergone a psychic shift. Blame upon institutions, upon authorities, upon those who carry responsibilities, now seems to me so cheap. Those who fail in their responsibilities have a new claim upon my sympathies. I know the taste of uncertainty. To be a father rather than a son is to learn the inevitability of failure.

Family Politics

It would be a lie, however, to write only of the difficulties of marriage and family, and not of the beauty. The joys are known. The more a man and a woman are in love, the more they imitate the life of husband and wife; long, sweet affairs are the tribute romances pay to matrimony. Quiet pleasures and perceptions flow: the movement of new life within a woman's belly; the total dependence of life upon the generosity and wisdom of its parents; the sense that these poor muscles, nerves, and cells of one's own flesh have recreated a message to the future, carried in relays generation after generation, carried since the dim beginnings. There may not be a "great chain of being." But parents do forge a link in the humble chain of human beings, encircling heirs to ancestors. To hold a new child in one's hands, only ounces heavy, and to feel its helplessness, is to know responsibilities sweet and awesome, to walk within a circle of magic as primitive as humans knew in caves.

But it is not the private pleasures of family life that most need emphasis today. Those who love family life do not begrudge the price paid for their adulthood. What needs elucidation is the political significance of the family. A people whose marriages and families are weak can have no solid institutions.

In intellecutal terms, no theme is so neglected in American life and thought. The definition of issues given both by our conservatives and by our liberals is magnetized by two poles only: "the state" and "the individual." Both leave the family out. Emphasis on the family appears to conservatives a constraint upon the state, and to liberals a constraint upon the individual. Our remarkable humanitarianism holds that attention to family weaknesses will stigmatize those who suffer. No concept in the heavens of theory is as ill-starred. Turning toward the family, our minds freeze in their turning.

The time to break taboos in our minds must surely come. Every avenue of research today leads to the family. Do we study educational achievement? nutrition? the development of stable and creative personalities? resistance to delinquency and violence? favorable economic attitudes and skills? unemployment? sex-role identification? political affiliation? intellectual and artistic aspiration? religious seriousness? relations to authority and to dissent? In all these instances, family life is fundamental. A nation's social policies, taken as a whole, are most accurately and profoundly to be engaged by their impact upon the families that make up that nation.

There are three critical points in American political life today at which a more profound consideration of the politics of the family is closer to the essence than in any previous era: among white ethnics (some 70 million); among blacks (some 22 million); and among upper-class "opinion leaders" of all races (perhaps 10 million).

The meaning of Left and Right has, in recent years, come to be defined according to the tastes, interests, and prejudices of the upper 10 percent of the American population, that (roughly) 10 percent that has a four-year college education, an annual income over $20,000; and professional standing, so as to be paid monthly (not weekly), to possess travel privileges and expense accounts, and a considerable degree of control over the conditions of their work. Thus, Left and Right are now defined by culture rather than by economics, by attitudinal issues salient to those whose economic needs are well beyond the level of survival. The governing language of upper-class attitudes, therefore, distorts the true political struggle. The competition between the left and right wings of the upper 10 percent is interesting and important. It hardly begins to touch the restlessness of the bottom 90 percent.

In this context, the true political leanings and energies "of the white ethnics" are consistently misperceived. Richard Hamilton, in *Restraining Myths,* for instance, describes related gross distortions in the conventional wisdom. Suffice it to say that white ethnic voters, traditionally more Democratic than the national average and now more independent, are economic progressives. But in matters touching the family, they are fiercely traditional. The bulwark of conservatism in America is the white Anglo-Saxon Protestant—68 percent for Nixon in 1972; 16 percent for Wallace in 1968 (compared to 7.7 percent of the Catholic vote). Slavic-Americans gave George McGovern 53 percent of their vote in 1972 (down from 80 percent for Lyndon Johnson, and 65 percent for Hubert Humphrey). The white ethnics are becoming increasingly impatient with both Republicans (their traditional opponents) and Democrats (their former allies). Neglect of the politics of the family is the central issue. It is on this issue that "a new majority" will—or will not—be built.

For a thousand years, the family was the one institution the peoples of Eastern and Southern Europe, the Irish, and others could trust. The family constitutes their political, economic, and educational strength. The public schools of the United States failing them, they reached into their families and created an astonishingly successful system of parochial schools. Hardly literate, poor, and diffident peoples, they achieved something of an educational miracle. Economically, the Jews, the Greeks, the Lebanese established one another in as many small businesses as they could open. The Italians, the Poles, the Slovaks, the Croatians gave each other economic help amounting to two or three thousands of dollars a year per family. Cousin Joe did the electrical work; Pete fixed cars; Emil helped paint the house; aunts and uncles and grandparents canned foods, minded the children; fathers in their spare time built playrooms, boats, and other luxuries in the basements of row houses.

The family network was also a political force in precinct, ward, or district. People of the upper classes could pass on to their children advantages of inheritance, admission to exclusive schools, and high-level contacts. Children of the immigrants also made their families the primary networks of economic and political strength. Kinship is a primary reality in many unions and in all urban political "machines." Mothers and fathers instructed their children simultaneously, "Don't trust anybody," and "The family will never let you down."

In contemporary conditions, of course, these old family methods and styles have atrophied. There is no way of going back to the past. (Not everything about the past, in any case, was attractive.) Education media help children to become sophisticated about everything but the essentials: love, fidelity, childrearing, mutual help, care for parents and the elderly. Almost everything about mobile, impersonal, distancing life in the United States—tax policies, real-estate policies, the demands of the corporations, and even the demands of modern political forms—makes it difficult for families that feel ancient moral obligations to care for their aged, their mentally disturbed, their retarded, their needy.

It is difficult to believe that the state is a better instrument for satisfying such human needs than the family. If parents do not keep after the children to do their schoolwork, can the large, consolidated school educate? Some have great faith in state services: in orphanages, child-care centers, schools, job-training programs, and nursing homes. Some want the state to become one large centralized family. Such faith taxes credulity. Many of the popular resistance to federal child care arises from distrust of social workers and childhood engineers who would be agents of state power. Families need help in child care, but many distrust the state and the social-work establishment.

Almost everything about both "liberal" and "conservative" economic thought neglects, ignores, or injuries family networks. It is not benign neglect. Millions of dollars are spent on the creation of a larger and larger state apparatus. Resources are systematically taken from the family. Is this an accident? One by one, all centers of resistance to the state are being crushed, including the strongest family. The trend does not augur well for our liberties.

An economic order that would make the family the basic unit of social policy would touch every citizen at the nerve center of daily life. No known form of social organization weds affect to efficiency in so powerful a way. The family is the primary teacher of moral development. In the struggles and conflicts of marital life, husbands and wives learn the realism and adult practicalities of love. Through the love, stability, discipline, and laughter of parents and siblings, children learn that reality accepts them, welcomes them, invites their willingness to take risks. The family nourishes "basic trust." From this spring creativity, psychic energy, social dynamism. If infants are injured here, not all the institutions of society can put them back together. Familial arts that took generations to acquire can be lost in a single generation, can disappear for centuries. If the quality of family life deteriorates, there is no "quality of life." Again, emphasis on family life is politically important because it can unite people of diverse religious, ethnic, regional, and racial traditions. Families differ in their structures, needs, and traditional inclinations; but they share many basic economic and political necessities.

A politics based on the social unit of the family would have a revolutionary impact on the sterile debate between Democrats and Republicans, and between libertarians and socialists. To strengthen the family through legislative reform is, indeed, a social intervention, but one which creates a counterpoise to the state. It is the forgotten lever of social change.

In particular, a fresh approach here promises unparalleled gains for blacks. "The repair of the black condition in America disproportionately depends upon the succor of strong families," Eleanor Holmes Norton told the Urban League in Atlanta [in 1975]. "We must make marriage and family life unabashedly a tool for improving all our lives." The stunting of black progress in America, she held, was done most effectively through tearing asunder the black family both in slavery and by discrimination. No institution, she observed, had so nourished blacks in the darkness of slavery; none had helped them to joy, laughter, and affirmation through the bitter days, as had the family. No institution is so beloved in black consciousness. None is more at the heart of social hope. "Were it not for law-enforced slavery and discrimination," she said, "our families would have thrived like most others and our time in America would have waxed into prosperity as for all other immigrant groups." She told the assembly, in sorrow, that the percentage of black households headed by women increased to 35 percent in 1975. (By the age of sixteen, two-thirds of all black children have spent some years without a father. In 1973 46 percent of all black children were born outside of wedlock.) The psychological and economic penalties, she argued, are immense. She called for a resurgence of the love and loyalty that had carried blacks in America through the centuries.

Such a call instantly makes possible alliance between the white and black working class. The families of both are in trouble; the difference in degree does not remove the similarity in root and remedy. Our media exalt the flashy, the hedonistic, the individualistic; they dwell upon the destructive orbits of the doomed: James Bond and Patty Hearst. Destruction, hustling, and defiance—one side of the Black Panthers—is picked up; the feeding of children and the nourishing of families receives no public praise. Love between a husband and wife, discipline in children, virtues of work, effort, risk, and application—these now visibly embarrass, as pornography once did. Yet these are the substance of working-class morality. They are the base of all advantage.

A Choice for Survival

Why does the preferred liberal solution for the sufferings of blacks look to every avenue of approach—school buses, affirmative action, welfare—except the family? Could it be that the family is too truly at the center, and is the one thing that liberals themselves cannot supply? That the family is the one social standing place for independence?

Economic and educational disciplines are learned only in the home and, if not there, hardly at all. Discipline in black families has been traditionally severe, very like that in white working-class families. Survival has depended on family discipline. Working-class people, white and black, cannot count on having their way; most of the time they have to be docile, agreeable, and efficient. Otherwise, they are fired. They cannot quit their jobs too often; otherwise their employment record shows instability. Blacks as well as whites survive by such rules, as long as authority in the home is strong. From here, some find the base for their mobility, up and out. Without a guiding hand, however, the temptations to work a little, quit, enjoy oneself, then work a little, are too much encouraged by one's peers on the street. *Either* the home *or* the street: This is the moral choice. Liberals too seldom think about the economic values of strong family life; they neglect their own source of strength, and legislate for others what would never have worked for themselves.

Consider the figures for unemployment for teenagers. The figure frequently given for blacks in New York is 40 percent. The huge number of female-run households among blacks correlates with the unemployment rates. The rough discipline of Slavic, Italian, and Irish fathers regarding the employment of their sons is an economic advantage. One of the requirements for obtaining and holding a job, especially at the unskilled level, where jobs abound, is a willingness to accept patriarchal discipline. Many young black males find such disciplines both unfamiliar and intolerable. Many will not take available jobs; many others quit.

Consider, as well, the educational preparation of black children as they leave their homes, before they enter school. Among successful blacks, patterns are like those among whites. Parents watch over their children. Books and papers are available in the home. Where the parents take education seriously, there is high probability that children will. Where the parents do not, schools cannot reasonably be expected to reach the psyches of the young. Why, then, do we habitually try to help schools, but not families? For both blacks and whites of the working class and all the more for the still more needy "underclass," the provision of books and newspapers to the home, and sessions to assist parents in teaching their children, might be more profitable than efforts in the school.

In a word, a politics aimed at strengthening families, white and black, would be a politics of unity rather than of division. It would also have higher prospect of success. The chief obstacle in its execution is the mysterious contempt liberals unthinkingly manifest toward their own greatest source of advantage.

As Jean-Paul Sartre has taught us, it is bad faith to plead "to each his own," to permit intellectual laissez-faire. Actions speak louder than shrugs of the shoulder. To marry, to have children, is to make a political statement hostile to what passes as "liberation" today. It is a statement of flesh, intelligence, and courage. It draws its strength from nature, from tradition, and from the future. Apart from millions of decisions by couples of realistic love, to bring forth children they will nourish, teach, and launch against the void, the human race has no future—no wisdom, no advance, no community, no grace. Only the emptiness of solitary space, the dance of death.

It is the destiny of flesh and blood to be familial.

United Press International, Inc.

Part Two

FORCES
FOR
CHANGE

Introduction

Part Two of this book considers three important movements that have occurred in our society over the last thirty years and that have been forces for change in the way we think about, and play our roles in, marriage and the family. They are (1) the psychological revolution, or individualism and the "personal growth movement"; (2) the sexual revolution; and (3) the feminist revolution. They have been interlocking developments, each influencing the others and all carrying profound implications for family life. How can we characterize and understand them?

The psychological revolution, addressed in Chapter Five, was both a cause and a result of an overall change from a merger of the family and society, in both interests and functions, to a separation of the two and a growing emphasis on personal happiness as the goal of family life. Central to this change was a belief in individualism and in the notion that the family, rather than society, was the best vehicle for achieving individual happiness.

The individual orientation of our culture has reached new heights in recent years with the "personal growth movement" and the narcissism, or concern with one's self, of the "me" generation. But the roots of this individualism go back to the nineteenth century and to such factors as urbanization and industrialization. Before discussing the readings for this chapter, it may be useful to examine some of these roots.

Urbanization and geographic mobility are certainly among the most important roots of individualism. When people lived mainly in small towns or rural areas and spent their lives—like the McCaslins described in Robert Coles' article in Chapter One—more or less continuously in touch with the same community of neighbors, friends, and kin from childhood through adulthood and old age, they had a strong sense of place and continuity. They also had a strong sense of self based on family and on individual characteristics expressed in a range of activities and social exchanges that remained stable over time. Change occurred because one grew up and took on new roles (wife, mother, grandmother), but there was extraordinary stability in the social setting within which one acted. Mrs. McCaslin, for example, knows that Hugh is a cheerful, good-natured man—everyone knows it—because over the years she and others have seen him behaving in ways that bespeak a cheerful and jolly disposition. A young person in the hollow who behaves with characteristic good cheer gets responses from his small but stable audience that affirm he is good natured. He feels comfortable and rewarded in his cheerfulness and develops a strong sense of what he is.

When Hugh is out of sorts or angry, people who know him are likely to interpret this unusual behavior as somehow less real than his cheerfulness. They think that "Hugh is not himself today," or they may discount the unusual mood entirely and not even note it. They—and Hugh—have a strong sense of what he really is.

The point is, in a stable community people can be what they are. A stable community is very much like a family in this respect. Since both you and everyone else knows you and knows what you are, there is a seamless quality to your identity.

When, on the other hand, you move into a world of strangers, there are both more opportunities to change, to try different ways of being and behaving, and more incentives to "present" oneself, to act in ways that are likely to bring quick approval and acceptance. There may, then, develop a gap between what you are and what you appear to be. As Philip Slater pointed out in Chapter Four, constant moving imposes on people the special requirement to develop those skills which will allow them to form new friendships easily. But these skills—charm, cheerfulness, affability, agreeableness, optimism—will not always coincide with what they believe to be their true innermost selves. And this opens the possibility of alienation from the self, the sense of the self as an object that can be changed, improved, hidden, enlarged, and loved or despised. The self is no longer taken for granted. It becomes regnant in consciousness. People become self conscious.

Industrialization and the division of labor underscore self consciousness. When one both worked and lived in the company of the same group of kin and neighbors, there was no compelling reason to alter one's behavior or self at work. When the two spheres are separated, there is more possibility of systematic differences developing between the "self-at-work" and the "self-at-home." Many parents have discovered this differentiation in a child's self when they have a first conference with a teacher and discover that the child they have known at home as the most difficult and obstreperous of their children is known at school as the most polite and accommodating child in the class.

Division of labor is even more imposing because certain work roles demand only one kind of behavior and attitude. A "straw boss" must be tough and unfeeling in his interaction with the workers he supervises. A saleswoman is supposed to say that the hat looks lovely on the customer irrespective of what she privately thinks. A surgeon must not cry or faint when he sees people in pain. All such role requirements heighten the distinction between "what I say and do" and "what I really am."

The competitive ethic of nineteenth century business, supported by the myth of social Darwinism—that those who "beat out" competitors, regardless of methods, were naturally the "fittest"—contributed to and heightened individualism. The churches and social critics worried that this rampant individualism might lead to social chaos; and, as John Demos' article in Chapter Three pointed out, it was in response to such fears that the home—along with the church—was assigned the role of tempering the selfish ethic of the world and preserving the traditional, gentler, more social and altruistic values.

In our own era, the role of the churches has declined and the effective force of religion in people's daily lives has diminished. Certainly, compared to our Puritan forbears, modern man is not constrained by fear of damnation if he believes or acts in morally or ethically questionable ways. The growth of knowledge and the ascendance of science as the measure of truth and reality have undercut traditional religion as a check on individualism and as a source of meaning.

The family has remained as the one institution that could provide this sense of meaning. In the readings that follow, sociologist Richard Sennett, in "The Brutality of Modern Families," describes how the separation of home and work spheres that accompanied urban industrialization—and increased with "suburbanization"—led to the "intensive" family, isolated from the larger community and conceiving itself as a microcosm of all that was meaningful in life. The intensity of emotional investment and the isolation of the family, however, required the suppression of conflict within the family. If all meaning hinged on the family, conflict became too dangerous, since it might destroy this last vessel of significance.

Philip Slater, in "The Pursuit of Loneliness," is concerned with the ways in which the intensive family socialized its children. The goals of child raising, he asserts, have changed from compliance to the creation of proper attitudes and motivation. Less emphasis is placed on behavior and more on the individual psyche.

Kenneth Keniston, in "The Weakened Executive," looks at somewhat different consequences of the separation of family and society. Not only was the family increasingly isolated from society, it also lost many of its former functions, such as education and the care of the sick and aged, to social institutions. Since the family nevertheless retains the critical responsibility for its members' growth and welfare, it faces the problems of coordinating the services of other institutions over which it has no final authority.

If the family lost its role as a work unit and is no longer necessary for physical survival, its primary role has become that of meeting the emotional needs of its individual members. In "Mirages of Marriage," William Lederer, a journalist, and Don Jackson, a mental health expert, examine the reasons for marriage, and find "being in love" to be the main one. According to the authors, however, this is one of many myths that have affected our beliefs about marriage.

The family has, of course, traditionally provided for the legitimate expression of sexual desire. But this, too, is changing. Chapter Six deals with the sexual revolution, the changes developing in people's sexual behavior, and controls on sexuality over the last thirty years. Again the change is one from control by fear (fear of pregnancy and fear of social stigma or of consequences to one's soul in a religious context) to control based on some individually developed standards and values. The introduction of safe, inexpensive, and effective birth control must be seen as the material condition for such change. Oral contraceptives created the possibility of absolute separation of sex and pregnancy and thus removed one of the consequences which might inhibit sexual expression. The ascendance of science and knowledge augmented the change: the Kinsey studies, widely distributed and publicized in the media, revealed a picture of the sex lives of American adults which dispelled ignorance and revealed much more active and varied sex lives than had previously been imagined as the norm. The report and increasing dispersion of information about the intricacies of sexual "performance" and practice in America undermined social norms that had opposed sexual expression outside of marriage. The stage was set for radical changes in sexual behavior and attitudes, and experts agree that at least among younger members of our society, changes did indeed occur.

One change that resulted from the ability to separate sex and reproduction was the explosion of what journalist Betty Rollin, in "Motherhood: Who Needs It?" refers to as the Motherhood Myth—the idea that all women instinctively want and need children.

Another consequence is traced by psychologist Bruno Bettelheim, who argues that women's new control over their reproductive lives made them more independent of their husbands, loosening bonds and "Untying the Family."

Experimentalism in sex, as in many areas of life in the 1960s and 1970s, attracted its adherents, who created a new literature of "sexual growth"— urging such innovations as open marriage, group marriage, swinging, and "recreational" sex. Sex become another arena for expressing one's self, and we were urged to "do our own thing," "do it if it feels good," and "do it in the street." Relatively little attention was paid in this literature to the meaning of sex within the context of love, its effect on others, and its ability to bind people to each other. In "Sex Outside Marriage," social psychologist Carol Tavris compares old attitudes and practices regarding premarital and extramarital sex with those of the mid-1970s, while marriage expert Morton Hunt analyzes attitudes toward "The Affair." Jean Lipman Blumen, in "The Dilemmas of Sex," considers the relationship among sex, intimacy, and responsibility.

The availability of reliable birth control affected not only sexual behavior, but sex roles and norms governing them, as well. Women no longer had to spend most of their lives caring for children. Education had prepared women for activities and work roles which they were proscribed from realizing because of traditional attitudes toward the "woman's role."

It was only a matter of time before the discrepancy between women's training and the roles to which they were assigned and largely restricted would give rise to resurgent feminism. Betty Friedan struck a responsive chord in 1963 when she attacked "the feminine mystique"—the notion that women could find fulfillment in—and only in—the role of wife and mother. The growth of the new feminism thus led not only to the development of a major movement for women's rights, but also to an open challenge to established sex role arrangements and patriarchal family structure. Married women entered the labor force in massive numbers. Women—along with minorities and gay people—challenged discriminatory practices and brought suits to press their claims for equal treatment. These developments brought pressure on families to accommodate to the new aspirations of their wives and mothers, to recognize them as individuals. These pressures are discussed in Chapter Seven, The Feminist Revolution.

In "Changing Family Life Styles: One Role, Two Roles, Shared Roles," sociologist Jessie Bernard discusses changing attitudes towards women's participation in the work force and urges the adoption of policies that would enable men and women to share both the traditionally male market role and the traditionally female family role.

In "Feminists Against the Family," political scientist Jean Bethke Elshtain argues that feminism has turned the family into a political issue and, in the process, has undercut its strengths. Columnist Ellen Goodman discusses the different impact that feminism has had on men and women, as well as how feminist attitudes toward the family have changed in recent years. And finally, critic Carolyn Heilbrun, in "On Reinventing Womanhood," urges that women combine their femaleness with their drives for equality in the workplace, not sacrificing one to the other.

The drive for sexual equality (as for equal treatment for minorities) has thus reinforced our self-orientation and individualism. Women are no longer willing to take themselves and their "place" for granted, but neither are they necessarily willing to deny their role as women, as wives and mothers.

CHAPTER FIVE

The Psychological Revolution

God setteth the solitary in families.

Psalms 68:6

A child may have too much of his mother's blessings.

English proverb

Home life as we understand it is no more natural to us than a cage is to a cockatoo.

George Bernard Shaw, *Getting Married*

RICHARD SENNETT

The Brutality of
Modern Families

The shift from city life to suburbs that occurred after the Second World War
changed the setting of the family from the diversity of the city, in which
there were daily contacts with people of widely different economic and cul-
tural backgrounds, to the uniformity of middle class suburbs, where it was
possible to live in contact only with others very similar to oneself in age,
social class and cultural perspective. At the same time, and in consequence
of this shift, family life has become intensive—that is, the family comes to
be seen as a microcosm of society and the setting for all activities that have
meaning and value. With family members investing so much time and emo-
tion in each other, normal conflict and hostility within the family become
feared as indications of pathology. The fear of conflict converts ordinary
problems into exaggerated and real problems. These developments are the
subject of the following selection by the historical sociologist Richard
Sennett.

The life of a child on Halstead Street [in Chicago's immigrant ghetto] in
1900 would seem odd to us, not to say frightening. The child of ten or eleven
would be wakened early in the morning, scrubbed and sent off to school. Until
three in the afternoon he would sit at a high desk reciting and memorizing.
This experience is not strange to us, but again, his life after school would be.
For if he did not come home to work, and many did not, he would be out on
Halstead Street selling or hawking in the stall of someone much older, who
sold and cajoled the passing traffic just as he did. . . . Many youths would,
with the tacit consent of their parents, enter into the more profitable after-
school activity of stealing—we read, for instance, in the letters of one Polish

family of great religious piety, of the honor accorded to a little son who had stolen a large slab of beef from a butcher on the corner. Life was very hard, and everyone had to fight for his needs with whatever weapons were at hand.

This life on Halstead Street required an urbanity of outlook, and multiple, often conflicting points of social contact, for these desperately poor people to survive. They *had* to make this diversity in their lives, for no one or two or three institutions in which they lived could provide all their needs. The family depended on political favors, the escape valve of the coffee shops and bars, the inculcation of discipline of the *shuls* and churches and so forth. The political machines tended in turn to grow along personal lines, to interact with the shifting politics of church and synagogue. This necessary anarchy took the individuals of the city outside the ethnic "subcultures" that supposedly were snugly encasing them. Polish people who belonged to steel unions often came into conflict with Polish people who had joined the police. It is the mark of a sophisticated life style that loyalties become crossed in conflicting forms, and this sophistication was the essence of these poor people's lives. . . .

The city of necessity broke apart the self-contained qualities of the various ethnic groups. The groups were not like little villages massed together in one spot on the map; rather they penetrated into each other, so that the daily life of an individual was a journey through various kinds of group life, each one different in its function and character from the others. . . .

In the last half-century, a majority of the ethnic groups in the city have achieved a state of prosperity for themselves far beyond what the first immigrants ever dreamed of. In the process, this necessary anarchy, this necessary sophistication, has died out; in its stead, social activities have become more coherent, more simple, and the social bond itself has become less compelling. The reason for this change is to be uncovered, I believe, in the transformation that family life has undergone as a majority of white urban Americans have achieved relative affluence. It is in the family lives of urban men today that one finds the expression of those forces that eroded the urbanity of city life in the past, eroded the necessary anarchy of the city and the complexities of feeling it exacted in ordinary experience.

When I first began to do research on the structure of city family life, I encountered over and over a popular stereotype: the idea that city conditions somehow contribute to the instability of the home. Evidently, the assumption is that the diversity of the city threatens the security and attachment family members feel for each other. Especially as suburban community life has come to dominate cities, there has grown up a mythological family image of affluent homes where Dad drinks too much, the kids are unloved and turn to drugs, divorce is rampant and breakdowns are routine. The good old rural families, by contrast, were supposedly loving and secure.

The trouble with this popular image is that it simply isn't true. Talcott Parsons has amassed evidence to show that the rate of divorce and desertion was much higher "in the good old days" at the turn of the century than it is now. William Goode has taken the idea a step further by showing how divorce is *less* frequent in affluent homes than in working-class homes. There may still be a great deal of unrest and tension in these suburban families, but it cannot be allied to their structural instability. In fact, we shall see, it is the juncture of great formal stability with deep and unresolved tension that now marks these families. . . .

There is an important history to this stereotype of the city's threat to the home. At the turn of the century, the bulk of the population of American cities was working-class, people whose origins and urban experience was of a piece with the residents of Halstead Street. But there was a numerically smaller group of middle-class families in cities like Chicago whose family patterns were very different, much closer to the narrowness of the life of the affluent middle class in today's metropolitan areas. In *Families Against the City* I explored the lives of one such middle-class community and what the history of these people revealed was that the common stereotype of the city's impact on the family has to be reversed for middle-class homes. For the disorder and vigor of city life in the first decade of this century frightened middle-class families, but, unlike working-class people, they had the means to do something about their fears. They drew in upon themselves: there was little visiting outside the confines of home; voluntary groups like churches and political clubs claimed few bourgeois participants; in America, unlike France or Germany, the urban middle class shunned public forms of social life like cafés and banquet halls. The home became for these early middle-class city dwellers a sanctuary against the confusions of the outside world.

Family Intensity

That kind of family isolation has abated in modern times, particularly when a family is in crisis. But there was something about such urban middle-class families at the opening of the twentieth century that has survived over time. These families possessed a character that now typifies families in middle-class suburbs as well as the middle-class islands within the central city; it is a quality of living that unites newly middle-class families whose parents were immigrants with the native-born urban middle-class families that have always lived in large cities. This characteristic of family life is the intensity of family relations. It links the variety of groups and backgrounds of people lumped together as middle-class, and the reach of this phenomenon extends beyond the city proper into the suburb and the town.

What is meant by an "intense" family life? There are, I think, a state of mind and a style of living that define the family intensity now found in many if not most segments of the urban population. The state of mind is that family members believe the actions and feelings that transpire in the family are in fact a microcosm of the whole range of "meaningful" actions and feelings in the world at large. The belief is, as one middle-class mother in Queens explained to an interviewer recently, that nothing "really important" in human relationships occurs that cannot be experienced within the boundaries of the home. People who think in this way can therefore conceive of no reason for making social forays or social contacts that cannot be ultimately reconciled or absorbed in family life.

The style of living that makes for an intense family life is the reduction of family members to levels of equality. This characteristic is much more pronounced in American urban families than in European ones. The feeling consists, most vulgarly, in fathers wanting to be "pals" to their sons and mothers wanting to be sisters to their daughters; there is a feeling of failure and dishonor if the parents are excluded from the circle of youth, as though they were tarnished by being adult. A good family of this sort is a family whose members talk to each other as equals, where the children presume to the lessons of experience and the parents try to forget them. That the dignity of all the family members might lie exactly in mutual respect for separateness and uniqueness is not conceived; dignity is conceived to lie in treating everyone equally. This brings the family members into a closer relation to each other— for there are taken to be, ideally, no unbridgeable gaps.

Both the state of mind and the life style have become in fact structures for limiting the sophistication and tolerance of the people who live in such homes.

The conviction that a family is the whole social arena in microcosm stifles parents and children both in an obvious and in a subtle way. Clearly, no band of four or five people represents the full spectrum of attitudes and human traits to be found in the wider society. The family as a world of its own can therefore become highly exclusive. Studies of intense family attitudes toward strangers reveal that the outsiders are judged to be "real," to be important and dealt with, only to the extent to which they reflect the particular attitudes and personalities found within a family circle. . . .

Conflict Is a "No-No"

The subtle way in which families, feeling themselves a microcosm of the society, become self-limiting has to do with the base of stability on which such families rest. This base is the existence, or the belief in the existence, of long-term trust. For families to believe they are all-important there has to be the conviction that no betrayal and breakup will occur. People do not concentrate all their energies in one place and simultaneously believe it may one day shatter or betray them. . . . An intense family life must refuse to grant worth to that which is shifting, insecure or treacherous, and yet this is exactly what the diversity in society is built of.

When people in a family believe they must treat each other as equal in condition, the same self-blinding, the same limitation, occurs. A recent project made psychiatric interviews in homes of "normal," "just average" families in a modest suburb outside a large city. Over and over again in these interviews adults expressed a sense of loss, sometimes amounting to feelings of annihilation, in the things in their lives they had wanted to do and could afford to do but refrained from doing for fear of leaving out the children. These sacrifices were not dictated by money; they were much more intimate, small-scale, yet important things: establishing a quiet spot in the day after work when a man and his wife were alone together, taking trips or vacations alone, eating dinner after the children were put to bed. . . . Such burdens are acquired, so many daily chances for diversity and change of routine are denied, out of the belief in the rightness of treating children as much as equals as possible, especially in early and middle adolescence. . . .

A few students of the family have recently been at pains to unravel what is awkwardly called "the guilt-over-conflict syndrome." This syndrome appears in the attitudes of many intense family members toward their families. The syndrome is simple to state, but not simple to overcome by people painfully caught up in it: to most people it appears that good families, upright families, ought to be happy, and it also appears that happy families ought to be tranquil, internally in harmony. What happens then when conflict or serious fights erupt? For many people, the emergence of conflict in their family lives seems to indicate some kind of moral failure; the family, and by reflection the individual, must be tarnished and no good. . . . But a body of evidence about conflict and mental illness in families has accumulated sufficiently to make this middle-class notion untenable; the facts indicate that families in which abrasive conflicts are held down turn out to have much higher rates of deep emotional disorders than families in which hostilities are openly expressed, even though unresolved.

But the guilt-over-conflict syndrome is significant because it is so deeply held a presupposition about family life: people look, for example, at conflicts between generations as an evil, revealing some sort of rottenness in the familial social fabric, rather than as an inevitable and natural process of historical change. . . . Put another way, anxiety and guilt over family conflict really express the wish that for the sake of social order, diversity and ineradicable differences should not exist in the home.

Islands in Metropolis

But this guilt about conflict, produced by the desire for intense family relations, helps explain a much broader social phenomenon: the ways in which the family group brutalizes its members, both young and old, in their dealings with the larger society. The link between family life of this kind and the society beyond it can be understood by posing this question: is there any reason to call an intense family life, fearful of conflict, an "urban" condition? Could it not simply be the way in which families live today in America, and since most families live in urban areas, be an "urban" family trait by location only?

There is an intimate relation between the desire for family intensity, the guilt it produces over conflict or disorder in intimate affairs and the social structure of a city. For, as the intensity of family relations grows, freshening of one's perceptions through diverse experience in the outside world diminishes. Intense families wall in the consciousness men have of "significant" or "important" experiences in their lives. One special social institution—the family group—becomes the arena of what is real. Indeed, the guilt that family intensity produces about experiences of disorder or conflict makes this absorption into the home appear as a moral or healthy act. The diversity of the city world beyond, as an older generation of immigrants or blacks knew it, never fit together in an orderly way; men were continually becoming involved in messy situations or having to change the face they presented to the world. In the new order of affluence, significant social life can be more proper, more dignified, by virtue of a more narrow order. One affluent working-class father told me recently, "When I was a kid, I had to be on my toes all the time, see, because in the slums of Boston you couldn't take anything for granted if you wanted to survive. Now that I've got some money, I can live respectably, you know, take care of the house and kids and not worry about what's happening outside. Maybe I'm not as sharp, but I've got more respect."

The essence of intense family life is this absorptive capacity, a power to collect the interests and attention of the individual in the tight-knit band of kin. Historically, the last half-century of city life has been marked exactly by such intimacy-making. This spells a decline in the sophisticated anarchy of association for most city men and the rise of an urban isolationism for the masses—an isolationism once encircling only the small, native-born, middle class.

Suburban Closeness

The vehicle for replacing the sophistication of an older urban life by the suffocation in the family today is the growth of middle-class suburbs in this country. The shrinking of diverse community life into the family is the hidden history of suburban places—which seem so empty of secrets; this history makes sense of their simplicity and their great appeal to Americans.

The classic pattern of industrial city-suburb arrangements up to the Second World War was the pattern still extant in Turin or Paris. Cities were arranged in rings of socioeconomic wealth, with the factories at the outskirts of town, workers' suburbs or quarters next to them and then increasingly more affluent belts of housing as one moved closer to the center of the city. . . .

Fights are bad?

Published by permission of Transaction, Inc. from *Society,* Vol. 7, No. 11, 1970. Copyright © 1970 by Transaction, Inc.

When the flight to the suburbs first began in massive numbers after the Second World War, it was commonly thought that its causes were related to the depression and to the population dislocation of the war. But this explanation is simply inadequate to explain the persistence of the event over the course of time. . . .

The historical circumstances of depression, war, land value and racial fear all have played a role, but they are offshoots of a more central change in the last decades that has led to the strength of suburban life. This deeper, more hidden element is a new attitude about the conduct of family life within and without the city.

A variety of recent books on suburbs, like Herbert Gans' *The Levittowners* or John Seeley's *Crestwood Heights,* reveal that people who now live in suburbs value their home settings because they feel that closer family ties are more possible there than in the city center. The closeness is not so much a material one—after all, families in city apartments are extremely close physically. Rather, as is now being learned, it is the simplification of the social

environment in the suburbs that accounts for the belief that close family life
will be more possible there than in the confusion of the city.

In most American suburbs, physical space has been rigidly divided into
homogeneous areas: there are wide swatches of housing separated from
swatches of commercial development concentrated in that unique institution,
the shopping center; schools are similarly isolated, usually in a parklike setting.
Within the housing sectors themselves, homes have been built at homogeneous
socioeconomic levels. When critics of planning reproach developers for con-
structing the environment in this way, the developers reply truthfully that
people want to live with people just like themselves; people think diversity in
housing will be bad for social as well as economic reasons. In the new communal order made possible by affluence, the desire of people is for a func-
tionally separated, internally homogeneous environment.

Homogeneous Zones

I believe this homogeneous zones idea in suburbs is a brutalizing community
process, in contrast to the urban situation that preceded it in time. For the
homogeneous zones of function in a suburb prohibit an overlay of different
activities in the same place; each place has its own pre-defined function. What
therefore results is a limitation on the chance combination of new situations,
of unexpected events, of unlikely meetings between people that create diversity
and a sense of complexity in individual lives. People have a vision of human
variety and of the possibility of living in a different and better way only when
they are challenged by situations they have not encountered before, when they
step beyond being actors in a preordained, unchanging routine. This element
of surprise is how human growth is different from the simple passage of time
in a life; but the suburb is a settlement fitted only to muffle the unknown, by
separating the zones of human activity into neat compartments.

This prohibition of diversity in the arrangement of suburban areas permits, instead, the intensity of family relations to gather full force. It is a
means for creating that sense of long-term order and continuity on which
family intensity must be based. In a stable family, where longe-term trust
between pretend-equals exists, the "intrusions" of the outside must be diminished, and such is the genius of the suburban mode. The hidden fear behind
this family life in the suburbs is that the strength of the family bond might
be weakened if the individual family members were exposed to a richer social
condition, readily accessible outside the house.

When the suburbs began to grow rapidly after the Second World War,
some observers, such as David Riesman, were moved to criticize them for an
aimlessness and emptiness in communal relations. But there was and is a
peculiar kind of social bond made possible by this very emptiness, this lack

of confusion. The bond is a common determination to remain inviolate, to ensure the family's security and sanctity through exclusionary measures of race, religion, class. . . .

This kind of family living in the suburbs surely is a little strange. Isn't the preference for suburbia as a setting for family life in reality an admission, tacit and unspoken to be sure, that the parents do not feel confident of their own human strengths to guide the child in the midst of an environment richer and more difficult than that of the neat lawns and tidy supermarkets of the suburbs? If a close, tight-knit family emerges because the other elements of the adult and child world are made purposely weak, if parents assume their children will be better human beings for being shielded or deprived of society outside the home and homelike schools, surely the family life that results is a forced and unnatural intimacy. . . .

This society of fear, this society willing to be dull and sterile in order that it not be confused or overwhelmed, has become as well a model for the rebuilding of inner-city spaces. . . .

In the name of establishing the "decencies" of life as regnant, the scope of human variety and freedom of expression is drastically reduced. The emotions shaping the rebuilding of inner-city living-places run much deeper than protection from the blacks or from crime; the blacks and the criminals are a symbolic cover under which the family can turn inward, and the family members withdraw from dealing with the complexities of people unlike themselves.

The Morality of Being Passive

This urban transformation has now a frightening impact on the social and political life of adult city men as citizens. In the collapsing of multiple, interwoven points of social contact as the majority of city families have come to live in intense situations, lies an urban crisis as important as the crises of life faced by city people who are still oppressed and without economic power. . . .

This new configuration of polarized intimacy in the city provides the individual with a powerful moral tool in shutting out new or unknown social relations for himself. For if the suburbanized family is a little world of its own, and if the dignity of that family consists in creating bases of long-term stability and concord, then potentially diversifying experiences can be shut out with the feeling of performing a moral act. For the sake of "protecting the home" a man refuses to wander or to explore: this is the meaning of that curious self-satisfaction men derive in explaining what they gave up "for the sake of the children." It is to make impotence a virtue.

The glorification of passivity makes clearer the willful indifference or the hostility that most middle-class urbanites show toward programs aimed at eradicating conditions of poverty in the city. . . . It isn't that the poor are black that rankles so much, it isn't even that they are poor; what hurts is that middle-class people are asked by programs such as school bussing to be more than passive onlookers in the social process, they are asked to interact with people who are different, and that kind of interaction they find too painful. It is this same inner-turning little world of family affairs, unused to the daily shocks of confrontation and the expression of ineradicable differences, that reacts with such volatility when oppressed groups in the city become disorderly. It is a short step from concentrating on one's own home affairs to sanctioning terrible repression of disturbances from below: if the poor are silenced, then there need be no intrusions on the "meaningful" circle of one's own life, the intimate relationships between Pop, Mom and the kids.

In these ways, affluent city life has created a morality of isolationism. The new virtue, like the religious puritanism of old, is a ritual of purifying the self of diverse and conflicting avenues of experience. But where the first puritans engaged in this self-repression for the greater glory of God, the puritans of today repress themselves out of fear—fear of the unknown, the uncontrollable. The intense family is the *via regia* by which this fear operates: such a family creates in men's intimate lives the necessity for known functions and well-worn routines. It is this kind of family life that explains, I believe, why so many white Americans can accept with equanimity the remaining injustices and oppressive poverty faced by blacks and Puerto Ricans in our cities.

KENNETH KENISTON AND
THE CARNEGIE COUNCIL ON CHILDREN

The Weakened Executive

While some family functions have been absorbed by other institutions and agencies, the family remains the "executive" agency, in charge of insuring, coordinating, and conditioning the services and influences of other institutions on its members, particularly on its children. While parents, thus, have enormous responsibility for the welfare of the child, they do not always have the power they need to discharge their responsibility. This imbalance must, according to psychologist Kenneth Keniston, be redressed by supporting and strengthening parents. The following selection is excerpted from All Our Children, *a study undertaken by Keniston and the Carnegie Council on Children, which was created in 1972 to examine the way children grow up in America.*

At the same time that families have been shorn of many traditional roles with children, new expectations about children's needs have arisen and, along with them, new specialists and institutions to meet the expectations. Part of the change of family functions, which carries with it a new dependence on people and institutions outside the family, rests on the family's needs for forms of help and expert assistance that are the creations of the last century.

Not all the family functions that seem to have been transferred outside the family—or that romantics sometimes yearn to bring back—were there in the first place. It is often claimed that "extended families" (with three generations at home, aunts and uncles included) were the rule, and that they have now been replaced by "nuclear" families. But actually most Americans have always lived in families consisting only of parents and children, and in colonial days, just as today, most children moved away from their parents' homes to set up households of their own. Nor is the mobility that scatters kinfolk to widely separated regions a new thing; historical studies indicate that frequent moves to new places have always been the rule in American life.

The genuine shifts in traditional family functions do not leave families with nothing to do. On the contrary, some needs and tasks appear even more concentrated in families than in the past. Among these is fulfilling the emotional needs of parents and children. With work life highly impersonal, ties with neighbors tenuous, and truly intimate out-of-family friendships rare, husbands and wives tend to put all their emotional hopes for fulfillment into their family life. Expectations of sharing, sexual compatibility, and temperamental harmony in marriage have risen as other family functions have diminished.

Most important, parents today have a demanding new role choosing, meeting, talking with, and coordinating the experts, the technology, and the institutions that help bring up their children. The specific work involved is familiar to any parent: consultations with teachers, finding good health care, trying to monitor television watching, and so on. No longer able to do it all themselves, parents today are in some ways like the executives in a large firm—responsible for the smooth coordination of the many people and processes that must work together to produce the final product.

This job is crucial for parents because they are usually the world's outstanding experts on the needs and reactions of their own particular children. Teachers, doctors, TV producers, all deal with a piece of the child, and are often more beholden to the interests of educational bureaucracies, medical societies, and the needs of advertisers and networks than to the child as a particular person with unique needs. Only parents are in a position to consider each influence in terms of a particular child and to judge how these outside influences should interact.

But, as an executive, the parent labors under enormous restrictions. Ideally, an executive has firm authority and power to influence or determine the decisions of those whose work needs coordination. Today's parents have little authority over those others with whom they share the task of raising their children. On the contrary, most parents deal with those others from a position of inferiority or helplessness. Teachers, doctors, social workers, or television producers possess more status than most parents. Armed with special credentials and a jargon most parents cannot understand, the experts are usually entrenched in their professions and have far more power in their institutions than do the parents who are their clients. To be sure, professionals would often *like* to treat each child in accordance with his or her unique needs, and professional codes of conduct urge that they do so, but professionals who really listen to parents or who are really able to model their behavior in response to what parents tell them are still few and far between.

As a result, the parent today is usually a coordinator without voice or authority, a maestro trying to conduct an orchestra of players who have never met and who play from a multitude of different scores, each in a notation the conductor cannot read. If parents are frustrated, it is no wonder: for although they have the responsibility for their children's lives, they hardly ever have the voice, the authority, or the power to make others listen to them.

What light does this analysis of changing families shed on parental worries? . . . Recall the "problem" of working mothers. Their entry into the labor force is not a product of selfish eagerness to earn pin money but is related to the disappearance of the family as an economically productive unit. Mothers on traditional farms played too vital a role in keeping the farm afloat to work for wages anywhere else. Stay-at-home mothers with wage-earning husbands, in contrast, are important to their families and indeed work hard at housekeeping and child rearing, but many find it hard to maintain the sense of self-worth that can come from doing work society values and pays for, and they do not contribute directly to the family cash flow.

The economic drain children now represent adds to the new economic pressures on families. Since most children now use family income for seventeen to twenty-five years and few yield significant income in return, the years of child rearing are the years of greatest financial stress on families; that stress helps push women out into paid jobs to maintain the family standard of living. This is particularly true of single-parent families headed by a woman; her work is a necessity if the family is to avoid welfare and the stigmas that accompany it. In 1974, the median family income was $16,928 if the wife also worked, $12,028 when she did not. Many families are above the poverty line not because wages have kept abreast of needs and inflation, but because wives have gone to work to make up the difference. Mothers work outside the home for many reasons, but one of them is almost always because their families need their income to live up to their standards for their children.

At the same time, rising expectations have inflated most Americans' definition of a reasonable standard of living. A private home, labor-saving appliances, time and money for entertainment and vacations have all become part of normal expectations. Some of these components of a good life in turn make work outside the home more possible for those who can afford them: freezers can reduce shopping to once a week; automatic washers and dryers have eliminated long, hard hours at the washboard and clothesline, store-bought bread eliminates the need to bake. All of these add up to a greater opportunity to work yet in a circular fashion make the income from work more necessary.

We see the same circle connecting mothers' employment to schools. If a mother must work, having children in school for 200 days a year leaves her many childless hours during which she can work without neglecting them. School thus permits mothers to enter the paid labor force by indirectly providing the equivalent of "free" baby-sitting, making working possible without expensive child-care arrangements.

Finally, the changing nature of the job market has opened up millions of jobs to women. What sociologists call the "service sector"—jobs that consist primarily in providing personal services, help, and assistance such as nursing, social work, waiting on tables in restaurants, teaching, and secretarial work— is growing more rapidly than any other sector of the American economy. Many jobs in this sector have traditionally been held by women. In a number of service jobs, qualities such as physical strength that favor men are irrelevant, and stereotypically "female" qualities such as helpfulness, nurturance, or interpersonal sensitivity are thought necessary and therefore employable. These jobs pay less than those usually taken by men—one reason for the poverty of female-headed households—but they are all that is available to most women, who have taken them for lack of anything else.

Most mothers work because they need the money. To be sure, other factors are important as well: for example, greater cultural acceptance of women being gainfully employed, and the new insistence on women's right to independence, security, and fulfillment in work. Birth control and increased longevity also play a role that is often overlooked. Whereas formerly many women kept on having children as long as they were fertile, women now have fewer children and space them closer together, so that on the average their last child is in school by the time they are in their late twenties or early thirties. Faced with the prospect of living to seventy-five instead of, say sixty-five, a woman in her twenties today knows that the days are gone when her role as mother would occupy most of her adult years. A job, even when children are at home, is, among other things, a way of preparing for the decades when the nest is empty.

Over time, however, economic pressures and the way we define economic well-being have had the most pervasive—and most often ignored—influence on mothers working for wages. It follows that it is addressing the wrong issue to point to ignorance, selfishness, or immorality in explaining it.

Or consider the "problem" of the rising divorce rate against the backdrop of the changes in the family. The one crucial factor behind the increase in divorce rates is the reduction in the number of bonds that tie husband, wife, and children together. When family members had more tasks to perform together—and especially when they were united around work as a family— lack of emotional satisfaction with the marriage partner still left family members with much to do in common. Furthermore, parents by and large had less elevated expectations about finding complete emotional, sexual, and interpersonal fulfillment in marriage. Men and women alike were more willing to accept sexual dissatisfactions or frustrations in marriage; temperamental incompatibilities may have caused equal misery but less often led to divorce. A happy, long marriage was, then as now, a blessing and a joy; but an unhappy marriage was more likely to be accepted as simply a part of life.

Finally, in earlier times, the collapse of a marriage was far more likely to deprive both spouses of a great deal more than the pleasure of each other's company. Since family members performed so many functions for one another, divorce in the past meant a farmer without a wife to churn the cream into butter or care for him when he was sick, and a mother without a husband to plow the fields and bring her the food to feed their children. Today, when emotional satisfaction is the main bond that holds marriages together, the waning of love or the emergence of real incompatibilities and conflicts between husband and wife leave fewer reasons for a marriage to continue. Schools and doctors and counselors and social workers provide their supports whether the family is intact or not. One loses less by divorce today than in earlier times, because marriage provides fewer kinds of sustenance and satisfaction.

Even the presence of children in a family is less of a deterrent to divorce than in the past. One reason, as we have said, is that other people and institutions provide more continuity in children's lives when a marriage breaks up. Furthermore, many parents today believe what research usually confirms, namely that preserving an unhappy marriage "for the sake of the children" may be doing the children more harm than good. And finally, the financial effects of divorce on children, though still very bad, are by no means as disastrous as they once were. The greater availability of jobs for women means that more middle-class children today survive their parents' divorce without a catastrophic plunge into poverty.

The entry of women into the paid work force, moreover, has its own effects on divorce rates. A positive by-product of women's economic independence is that a woman who can earn a decent living herself does not have to remain trapped in an impossible marriage because of money alone. And a husband who knows that his wife can earn a good salary is less likely to be deterred from divorce by the fear that he will have to support his ex-wife financially for the rest of her life. Moreover, wives' employment subtly alters relationships of power and submission within marriage. A wife's new independence can strengthen the husband-wife relationship, but increased equality also can produce new stresses or cause old stresses and resentments to surface. Women who are less submissive by and large will put up with less and expect more. One consequence may be the realization that a marriage has not lived up to the high hopes of husband or wife and a decision to end it, particularly when cultural attitudes toward divorce make it far less socially shameful than it once was.

As we have said, none of these changes is the result of an increase in selfishness, ignorance, or weakness in parents. This is not to say that parents are perfect. But few of these changes are within the power of individual parents to influence. Nor do these changes equal the "breakdown" or the "death" of families, as some claim. Most Americans marry and most marriages produce children. Most divorced people remarry in time, as if to demonstrate that their discontent was with their former partner and not with marriage itself.

What has changed is the content and nature of family life. Families were never as self-sufficient or as self-contained as the myth made them out to be, but today they are even less so than they used to be. They are extraordinarily *dependent* on "outside" forces and influences, ranging from the nature of the parents' work to the content of television programming, from the structure of local schools to the organization of health care. All families today need and use support in raising children; to define the "needy" family as the exception is to deny the simplest facts of contemporary family life.

There is nothing to be gained by blaming ourselves and other individuals for family changes. We need to look instead to the broader economic and social forces that shape the experience of children and parents. Parents are not abdicating—they are being dethroned, by forces they cannot influence, much less control. Behind today's uncertainty among parents lies a trend of several centuries toward the transformation and redefinition of family life. We see no possibility—or desirability—of reversing this trend and turning the clock back to the "good old days," for the price then was high in terms of poverty and drudgery, of no education in today's sense at all, and of community interference in what we today consider private life.

At the same time, however, most American parents are competing on unequal terms with institutions on which they must depend or which have taken over their traditional functions. To be effective coordinators of the people and forces that are shaping their children, parents must have a voice in how they proceed, and a wide choice so they do not have to rely on people or programs they do not respect. Parents who are secure, supported, valued, and in control of their lives are more effective parents than those who feel unsure and who are not in control. Parents still have primary responsibility for raising children, but they must have the power to do so in ways consistent with their children's needs and their own values.

If parents are to function in this role with confidence, we must address ourselves less to the criticism and reform of parents themselves than to the criticism and reform of the institutions that sap their self-esteem and power. Recognizing that family self-sufficiency is a false myth, we also need to acknowledge that all today's families need help in raising children. The problem is not so much to reeducate parents but to make available the help they need and to give them enough power so that they can be effective advocates with and coordinators of the other forces that are bringing up their children.

PHILIP SLATER

Women and
Children First

*In traditional societies women raise children while they work. In our society
after the Second World War, women were urged to leave the labor force and
devote themselves wholly to the tasks of homemaking and childrearing. This
was done, in part, by changing the nature of childrearing—from a system
designed to obtain obedience and conformity in* behavior *to one that set out
to mold the* psyche, *to mold the child's motivation and attitudes. Philip
Slater describes these changes and some of their effects in this next selection,
excerpted from his bestseller* Pursuit of Loneliness.

For any generation born before World War II, rituals, ceremonies, and social
institutions have an inherent validity that makes them intimidating—a validity that has priority over human feelings. One would hesitate to disrupt a
serious social occasion for even the most acute and fateful need, unless it could
be justified in social rather than personal terms. Doris Lessing and Shelley
Berman have both observed (in the case of people confronted with aircraft
whose integrity has been cast in doubt) that most people would die quietly
rather than make a scene.

Many younger people no longer share this allegiance. They don't see
social occasions as having automatic validity—social formality is deferred to
only when human concerns aren't pressing. Stoicism is not valued. . . .

This change was responsible both for the character of radical protest in
the sixties and for the angry responses of older people to it. Sitting-in at a
segregated restaurant, occupying a campus building, lying down in front of
vehicles, pouring blood in office files—all depended heavily on a willingness
to make a scene and not be intimidated by a social milieu. And this was

precisely what so enraged older people. They were shocked not so much by the radicalism of young people as by their bad form. That students could be rude to a public figure was more shocking to parents than that the public figure was sending their children to their deaths in an evil cause.

Yet the change was one that the parents themselves had created, for it was based on child-centered family patterns. While Europeans have always felt that American parents gave far too much weight to their children's needs and far too little to the demands of adult social occasions, Dr. Spock's emphasis on allowing the child to develop according to her own potential carried the trend even further. It focused the parents' attention on the child as a future adult, who could be more or less intelligent, creative, and healthy according to how the parents behaved toward her. This was unlike the older view that the child had a fixed personality to which the parents tried to give a socially acceptable wrapping. The old method was based on the military model: you take people who are all different and get them to behave outwardly in a uniform manner, whether they're inwardly committed to this behavior or not. Thus there was a sharp distinction between one's outer and inner worlds. The child or recruit was *expected* to harbor inner feelings of rebellion or contempt, so long as these were not expressed outwardly.

The new method gives much more responsibility to the parents, who must now concern themselves with the child's inner state. They are no longer trying merely to make the child well-behaved—for them personality is not a given, but something they can mold. The parents under the old method felt they had

"Do you want to talk about it?"

Drawing by Koren; © 1974 The New Yorker Magazine, Inc.

done their job well if the child was obedient, even if he turned out dull, unimaginative, surly, sadistic, and sexually incapacitated. Spockian parents feel it's their responsibility to make their child into the most all-around perfect adult possible, and although what this leads to may look like "permissiveness," it's actually more totalitarian, for the child no longer has a private sphere. His entire being has been taken over by parental aspirations: what he is *not* permitted to do is take his own personality for granted.

Under the old system, for example, the parents would feel called upon to chastise a child defined as bright but lazy, and if they forced him to spend a fixed amount of time staring at a book—whether he learned anything or lost all interest in learning—they would feel justified and relieved of all moral responsibility for him. ("I don't know why he's so bad, I beat him every day.") Today parents feel required not just to make him put in time but to "motivate" him to learn.

The tradeoff for having her whole personality up for grabs is that the child's needs are paid much more attention. The old method demanded that these needs be subordinated to social reality: in the most casual social encounter the parents would be willing to sacrifice the child's sense of truth and fair play ("kiss the nice lady"), her bodily needs ("you'll just have to wait"), and even parental loyalty ("she's always stupid and shy with strangers"). For the parent who loves her, to throw her to the dogs for something so trivial as etiquette makes a deep impression on the child. She sees the parent nurturant and protective in situations that seem much more important and dangerous, so why not here? Since she can't *see* anything important enough to justify this betrayal, all social situations tend to acquire a sacred, intimidating air. When the parents put this mysterious situation above all else, it acquires the same importance for the child.

But Spock-taught parents, fired with the goal of molding the child's total character, were much less inclined to sacrifice her to the etiquette concerns of strangers—the artist working on a masterpiece doesn't let guests use it to wipe their feet on. As a result, their children have grown up feeling that human needs have validity of their own. Social occasions are less sacred to them than they were to earlier generations. . . .

Spock's Impact

It would be unfair either to credit or to blame Dr. Spock for changes in the American character. His books on child-rearing would not have been so popular and influential had they not been firmly rooted in existing American values and attitudes. At the same time, however, they strengthened and nourished those attitudes. In particular, they reinforced three trends in American family and child-rearing patterns: permissiveness, individualism, and feminine domesticity. The first two have been with us for at least two centuries, but the last was a post-World War II phenomenon—a twenty-year interruption of an older trend in the opposite direction.

Often it's assumed that permissiveness in child-rearing is a recent American development, but this is clearly not the case. While every generation of Americans since the first landing has imagined itself to be more permissive than the previous one, foreign visitors have refused to notice any ups or downs in the unremitting stream of American laxity: They have stoutly and consistently maintained since the seventeenth century that American children were monstrously undisciplined. Spock, in any case, has always emphasized the child's need for parental control and the importance of not letting him become a tyrant in the home. The areas in which he reinforced "permissiveness" had to do not with social behavior but with such matters as feeding schedules and toilet training, and even here he merely revived practices current in America and England prior to the middle of the eighteenth century. While Spock has become a *symbol* of permissiveness in child-rearing, I think we'll learn more about his impact by looking at the other two patterns: individualism and feminine domesticity.

Spock's work is in the old American tradition that every individual is unique and has a "potential." This potential is viewed as innate, partially hidden, gradually unfolding, and malleable. The parent cannot simply coerce the child into a set pattern of behavior because it's important to our achievement ethic that a child realize her maximum potential, and that means taking into account real or imagined characteristics of her own. The parent is given not clay but some more differentiated substance with which to mold an adult.

Spock is concerned about what he feels to be our excessive child-centeredness, but he sees no escape from it: "I doubt that Americans will ever want their children's ambitions to be subordinated to the wishes of the family or the needs of our country." He suggests that children would be happier if parents would stick to whatever principled guns they have, but this hardly balances the general thrust of his work. From the very beginning Spock's books have encouraged Pygmalionesque fantasies in mothers—stressing the complexity and importance of the task of creating a person out of an infant. His good sense, tolerance, humanity, and uncanny ability to anticipate the anxieties that everyday child-rearing experiences arouse in young mothers seduce them into accepting the challenge. Deep in their hearts most middle-class, Spock-taught mothers believe that if they did their job well enough, all their children would be creative, intelligent, kind, generous, happy, brave, spontaneous, and good—each, of course, in his or her own special way.

It was this challenge and this responsibility that led mothers to accept the third pattern that Spock reinforced—feminine domesticity. For until quite recently, when he finally bowed to the demands of feminists and acknowledged the legitimacy of their resentments, he has always maintained that a woman's place is in the home. He emphasized the importance and the difficulty of the task of child-rearing and gave it priority over all other possible activities. He suggested government allowances for mothers compelled to work on the grounds that it "would save money in the end"—implying that only a full-time mother could avoid bringing up a child who was a social problem. . . . Otherwise Spock tried to induce guilt: "If a mother realizes clearly how vital this kind of care is to a small child, it may make it easier for her to decide that the extra money she might earn, or the satisfaction she might receive from an outside job, is not so important after all."

American women have always had a reputation for independence—Tocqueville commented upon it in 1830. Our culture as a whole tends to exert a certain pressure for sexual equality, and American women in the nineteenth century were not as protected as women in Europe. In frontier settings they were too important to yield much power or pay much deference to husbands, and among immigrant groups they were often more employable than their husbands. . . .

After World War II, however, a strange thing happened. Although more women were working than ever before, this was not true in the professions. Despite more women going to college, a smaller percentage were using this education in any way. In short, while single middle-class women were becoming more and more liberated, married middle-class women were embracing a more totally domestic existence than ever before. But how was this achieved? How could educated women devote their entire lives to a task so shrunken? How could they make it fill the day, let alone fill their minds? . . .

The main factor in the domestication of the middle-class American woman was the magnification of the child-rearing role. Child-rearing is not a full-time job at any age in and of itself. In every other society throughout history women have been busy with other tasks, and reared their children as a kind of parallel activity. The idea of devoting the better part of one's day to child care seldom occurred to anyone because few women ever had time for it before, and when they did, they usually turned the job over to a servant. . . .

This is not to say that child care *cannot* fill a day. The modern suburban home is neither built nor equipped in a way that allows for the comfortable or healthy management of an eighteen-month-old child. Living in the suburbs also forces the mother to be constantly driving her children about from one activity to another. Anyone could add to the list of anomalies created by our being a child-oriented society in the face of a technological environment that is antagonistic to children. One has only to see a village community in which women work and socialize in groups with children playing nearby, also in groups—the older children supervising the younger ones—to realize what's awkward about the domestic role in America. Because the American mother is isolated, she can engage in only one of these three activities (work, social-izing, child-rearing) at a time, with effort, two—hardly a satisfying occupation for a civilized woman.

But most important, the American mother has been told: "You have the capacity to rear a genius, a masterpiece. This is the most important thing you can do, and it should rightfully absorb all of your time and energy." With such an attitude it's easy to expand child-rearing into a full-time job. For although Spock has many sensible passages about not martyring oneself to one's children ("needless self-sacrifice sours everybody"), the temptation to do so is enormous when there's so little else. In the tedium of domestic chores, this is the only thing important enough to be worthy of attention. We are a product-oriented society, and the American mother has been given the op-portunity to turn out a really outstanding product.

Unfortunately, however, there really isn't much she can do to bring this about. At first the child sleeps most of the time, and later spends more and more time playing with other children. . . . Since she really doesn't know how to create an outstanding adult, and perhaps recognizes, deep in some uncorrupted sanctuary of good sense, that the more actively she seeks it the less likely she is to attain it, the only time she'll feel she's doing her job is when she's meeting minor crises. Naturally this creates a great temptation to induce such crises, indirectly and, of course, without conscious intent.

I once suggested that jovial references to the many roles played by house-wives in our society are a way of masking the fact that the housewife is a nobody. A similar effect is achieved by the Story of the Chaotic Day, in which one minor disaster follows hard upon another, or several occur simultaneously (". . . and there I was, the baby in one hand, the phone and doorbell both ringing . . ."). These sagas are enjoyed because they conceal the fundamental vacuity of the housewife's existence. . . .

The emotional and intellectual poverty of the housewife's role is nicely expressed in the universal complaint: "I get to talking baby talk with no one around all day but the children." There are societies in which the domestic role works, but in those societies the housewife is not isolated. She is either part of a large extended family household in which domestic activities are a communal effort, or participates in a tightly knit village community, or both. The idea of imprisoning each woman alone in a small, separate, and self-contained dwelling is a modern invention, dependent on an advanced tech-nology. . . .

For a middle-class woman this is in striking contrast to her premarital life. In school she's embedded in an active group life with constant emotional and intellectual stimulation. Marriage typically eliminates this way of life for her, and children deliver the *coup de grâce*. Her only significant relationship tends to be with her husband, who is absent most of the day. Most of her social and emotional needs must be satisfied by her children, who are hardly equal to the task. Furthermore, since she's supposed to be molding them into superior beings, she can't lean too heavily on them for her own needs, although she's sorely tempted to do so.

This is the most vulnerable point in the whole system. Even if the American housewife were not a rather deprived person, it would be the height of vanity for anyone to assume that an unformed child could tolerate such massive inputs of one person's personality. In most societies the impact of the mother's character defects is diluted by the presence of many other nurturing agents. In middle-class America the mother not ony tends to be the exclusive daytime adult contact of the child, but also has a mission to create a near-perfect being. This means that every maternal quirk, every maternal hangup, and every maternal deprivation is experienced by the child as heavily amplified noise from which there is no escape.

WILLIAM J. LEDERER
AND DON D. JACKSON

The Mirages
of Marriage

Throughout much of history, and in many parts of the world, young cou-
ples—or even children—married primarily for economic or social reasons.
Parents frequently arranged marriages, often for a price and often without
even consulting the couple involved. Arranged marriages are still customary
in many societies, particularly in India and the Far East. But in contemporary
Western society, most young people choose their own marriage partners, and
love is regarded as the major reason for marriage. In this article, a journalist
and a family therapist look at concepts of love and ask whether love is,
indeed, usually present in marriages today, whether people marry for love,
and whether love is even necessary for a satisfying marriage.

Marriage used to be an institution for the *physical* survival and well-being of
two people and their offspring. This function gave rise to a particular rule-
governed structure suitable to the situation. Today, except in time of war or
accident, the struggle for survival in industrialized societies does not require
purely physical strength. Instead, we have primarily the struggle for *psycho-*
logical and *emotional* survival. The family unit is the natural unit for human
survival regardless of what the hazard is. But so far, the changes in the
structure, form, and processes of marriage have been too few and too unsys-
tematic to cope with the new psychological and emotional problems. Marriage
still is an anachronism from the days of the jungle, or at least from the days
of small farms and home industries.

WIZARD OF ID by permission of Johnny
Hart and Field Enterprises, Inc.

Divorce, marital strife, desertion, and emotional and physical illness are
a few symptoms of this cultural lag in the institution of marriage, and they
seem to be on the increase. We cannot return to the "simple" life of an
agricultural or primitive community in this industrial age; we must modify
our outmoded attitudes, beliefs, and institutions to accommodate current social realities.

Marriage is still a necessary institution. But it must be adjusted to new
social and economic conditions. Above all, the new roles and relationships of
men and women must be recognized. It is not surprising that an anachronistic
social institution cannot function; nevertheless, it is tragic that so many marriages fail and so little is being done about it.

One young woman said, "Marriage is not what I had assumed it would
be. One premarital assumption after another has crashed down on my head.
I am going to make my marriage work, but it's going to take a lot of hard
work and readjusting. Marriage is like taking an airplane to Florida for a
relaxing vacation in January, and when you get off the plane you find you're
in the Swiss Alps. There is cold and snow instead of swimming and sunshine.
Well, after you buy winter clothes and learn how to ski and learn how to talk
a new foreign language, I guess you can have just as good a vacation in the
Swiss Alps as you can in Florida. But I can tell you, doctor, it's one hell of
a surprise when you get off that marital airplane and find that everything is
far different from what one had assumed."

This realistic and candid young woman is now happy in her marriage.
But for her to reach this point required two years of patient working and
changing, and of expensive visits by herself and her husband to a competent
marriage counselor for a once-a-month "checkup." She learned that the institution of modern marriage is based on many false assumptions and untrue
beliefs. . . . We believe that if men and women were acquainted with the
realities of marriage before they entered it, and if they accepted these realities,
the divorce rate in the United States would diminish markedly.

To understand the realities of the marital relationship it is essential first to recognize the unrealities. What follows is a discussion of [some] of the major myths of marriage.

The first myth is the belief that people get married because they are "in love." It is extremely difficult to define love satisfactorily. Dictionaries disagree. . . .

The definition . . . most cherished in the Western world is the one given by St. Paul in the thirteenth chapter of First Corinthians. True, it is a Christian definition; but it is so universal that its almost exact equivalent is used by Muslims, Hindus, Buddhists, and Jews.

> Love* suffereth long, *and* is kind; love envieth not; love vaunteth not itself, is not puffed up,
> Doth not behave itself unseemly, seeketh not her own, is not easily provoked, thinketh no evil;
> Rejoiceth not in iniquity, but rejoiceth in the truth;
> Beareth all things, believeth all things, hopeth all things, endureth all things.
> Love never faileth.

The authors have never met a person who is consistently loving according to St. Paul's definition. We have known many decent people, people who have integrity and who are kind most of the time; but they are not consistently loving in this biblical sense. It is our opinion that it would be too difficult for spouses to practice this kind of relationship described by St. Paul—unless both were saints.

A more practical definition of love has been given by the great American psychiatrist Harry Stack Sullivan: *"When the satisfaction or the security of another person becomes as significant to one as is one's own satisfaction or security, then the state of love exists."*

The state of love described by Sullivan is possible in marriage—but few spouses are prepared for it, or capable of experiencing it, right after the wedding. Its coming, if it comes at all, is the result of luck or of years of hard work and patience. . . .

It is a false assumption that people marry for love. *They like to think of themselves as being in love;* but by and large the emotion they interpret as love is in reality some other emotion—often a strong sex drive, fear, or a hunger for approval.

If they are not in love, then why are they impelled to marry?

There are several reasons.

During courtship, individuals lose most of their judgment. People who believe themselves to be in love describe their emotion as ecstasy. "Ecstasy"— from the Greek *ekstasis,* which means "derange"—is defined as the "state of

---

*Some versions use the word "charity" instead of "love." But they mean the same thing. Both refer to the act of cherishing dearly and giving unstintingly without wishing anything in return.

being beside oneself; beyond all reason and self-control." When an emotional courtship starts, the man and woman appear to relinquish whatever sense of balance and reality they ordinarily possess.

Courtship—the time of ecstatic paralysis—has been cleverly designed by Nature to lure members of the species into reproducing themselves. Courtship is a powerful manifestation of sexual excitement. In Western culture, it has well-defined rituals; these are simple steps leading up to the ultimate goal— legal breeding. The man and the woman are in a trance. By the magic of Nature, they have become wonderfully attractive to each other.

It is marvelous to observe how ruthless and cunning Nature is in her effort to perpetuate the species. Individuals are in such a dizzy state they they become reckless. The problems of marriage are not noticed or considered. The frightful divorce statistics mean nothing; it seems obvious that bad marriages, like death, are for others only. Frequently, the partners-to-be know that they are marrying the wrong persons, but they are in such a passion (some call it romance), and are being driven so hard by the applause of society, that they cannot help themselves. For example, they may realize that the man is unable, as yet, to earn a living; or that the woman is incompetent to manage a home; or that each has radically different tastes and values from the other. These and many other obstacles to a workable marriage usually have no significance to a couple in the courtship stage. The courting individuals are obsessed by one desire only—to mate. And society ordains that a ceremony must sanctify the mating. Although in a majority of marriages the magic and marvelous attractiveness of courtship diminishes (and often vanishes entirely) within a brief time after the honeymoon, it is obvious that the instinct to reproduce— the sex drive (which mistakenly is called love)—lures a great many individuals into marriage.

People often marry because society expects it of them. In our society a spinster is frequently regarded as an unattractive failure; and a middle-aged bachelor is suspected of being a homosexual, or of having a mother complex. Society encourages marriage in many ways and for many reasons. . . .

For the clergy and for officials, marriage is a source of power and control, a means of perpetuating loyalty to the Church through the children. Certain historical necessities—which in point of fact may no longer exist—are also reflected in the attitudes of society. For example, in earlier days, when mortality rates were high, a "big family" meant more people in the community and thus a greater chance for survival; and marriage was prerequisite for the existence of the big family. Though circumstances have changed now, the approbation of marriage has not. In short, almost all segments of society disapprove of the single state but approve of marriage. This universal attitude tends to cause people who think they are in love to be impetuous, hurried, and careless in getting married. Marriage, they have been taught, is a "good thing."

The pressures and the maneuverings of parents often push their children into premature and careless marriages. Parents maneuver, manipulate, and meddle. Fathers and mothers claim that they meddle for their children's benefit. The truth is that parents often feel failure or disgrace if their children aren't married at the conventional age. . . .

Romantic literature, tradition, and social hysteria have given marriage false values which the excited male and female often accept as true. They enter wedlock expecting a high level of constant joy from that moment on. Although they take an oath to love and cherish each other throughout all adversity, in fact they do not expect any serious adversity. They have been persuaded that love (which they cannot even define) automatically will make it possible to solve all problems.

Loneliness often drives people into marriage. Many individuals simply cannot bear to be alone. They get bored and restless, and they think that having somebody of the opposite sex in the house will stop them from being miserable. Thus they marry because of desperation, not love.

Many people are fearful concerning their economic future. Men may believe that the responsibility involved in supporting a wife and children will automatically motivate them to produce more than they would if they remained single. Women often feel they will find financial security through marriage, regardless of the current ability of their fiancés to provide for their needs.

Some individuals marry because of an unconscious desire to improve themselves. Almost all human beings have a mental image—called the ego ideal—of what they would like to be. In reality an individual seldom develops into this ideal person. But when he meets someone of the opposite sex who has the qualities which he desires, then up pops another false assumption. The individual unconsciously concludes that if he marries, he will, without effort, acquire the missing desirable characteristics or talents. . . .

Many marriages are motivated by neuroses. Certain individuals pick as mates those who make it possible for them to exercise their neuroses. These people do not wish to be happy in the normal sense. If they enjoy suffering, they unconsciously choose partners with whom they can fight, or who will abuse or degrade them. . . .

Some people miss their father or mother and cannot live without a parental symbol. Therefore they find—and marry—a person of the opposite sex who will play the parental role.

In summary, then, it may be said that people generally enter matrimony thinking they are in love and believing that marriage will bring them "instant happiness," which will solve all problems. Actually, in most instances they are swept into marriage on a tidal wave of romance, not love. Romance is usually ephemeral; it is selfish. Romantic "lovers" are distraught and miserable when separated, and this misery is caused by selfishness of the most egocentric type. The "lover" is sorry for himself and is grieving over his loss of pleasure and intimacy. This state of mind is closely related to another selfish emotion—jealousy. Romance is exciting—but it is no relation to love, no kin to that generous concern for someone else which Harry Stack Sullivan defines as love. . . .

One reason for marital disenchantment is the prevalence of the mistaken belief that "love" is necessary for a satisfying and workable marriage. Usually when the word "love" is used, reference is actually being made to romance— that hypnotic, ecstatic condition enjoyed during courtship. Romance and love are different. Romance is based usually on minimum knowledge of the other person (restricted frequently to the fact that being around him is a wonderful, beatific, stimulating experience). Romance is built on a foundation of quick- silver nonlogic. It consists of attributing to the other person—blindly, hope- fully, but without much basis in fact—the qualities one *wishes* him to have, though they may not even be desirable, in actuality. Most people who select mates on the basis of imputed qualities later find themselves disappointed, if the qualities are not present in fact, or discover that they are unable to tolerate the implication of the longed-for qualities in actual life. For example, the man who is attracted by his fiancée's cuteness and sexiness may spend tormented hours after they are married worrying about the effect of these very charac- teristics on other men. It is a dream relationship, an unrealistic relationship with a dream person imagined in terms of one's own needs. . . .

To live with another person in a state of love (as defined by Sullivan) is a different experience from whirling around in a tornado of romance. A loving union is perhaps best seen in elderly couples who have been married for a long time. Their children have grown, the pressure of business has been relieved, and the specter of death is not far away. By now, they have achieved a set of realistic values. These elderly spouses respect each other's idiosyncracies. They need and treasure companionship. Differences between them have been either accepted or worked out; they are no longer destructive elements. In such instances each has as much interest in the well-being and security of the other as he has in himself. Here is true symbiosis: a union where each admittedly feeds off the other. Those who give together really live together!

But it is possible to have a productive and workable marriage without love (although love is desirable) as well as without romance. One can have a functioning marriage which includes doubts and criticisms of the spouse and occasional inclinations toward divorce. The husband or wife may even think about how much fun it might be to flirt with an attractive neighbor. Such thoughts can occur without being disastrous to the marriage. *In many work- able marriages both spouses get a good deal of mileage out of fantasy.*

How, then, can we describe this functional union which can bring reasonable satisfaction and well-being to both partners? It has four major elements: tolerance, respect, honesty, and the desire to stay together for mutual advantage. One can prefer the spouse's company to all others', and even be lonely in his absence, without experiencing either the wild passion inherent in romance, or the totally unselfish, unswerving devotion that is basic in true love.

In a workable marriage both parties may be better off together than they would have been on their own. They may not be ecstatically happy because of their union, and they may not be "in love," but they are not lonely and they have areas of shared contentment. They feel reasonably satisfied with their levels of personal and interpersonal functioning. They can count their blessings and, like a sage, philosophically realize that nothing is perfect. . . . .

CHAPTER SIX

The Sexual Revolution

In the culture in which we live it is the custom to be least informed upon that subject concerning which every individual should know most, namely the structure and functions of his own body.

Ashley Montague, *Anthropology and Human Nature*

The great question . . . which I have not been able to answer, despite my thirty years of research into the feminine soul, is, "What does a woman want?"

Sigmund Freud, quoted in Charles Rolo, *Psychiatry in American Life*

The psychology of adultery has been falsified by conventional morals, which assume, in monogamous countries, that attraction to one person cannot coexist with a serious affection for another. Everybody knows that this is untrue.

Bertrand Russell, *Marriage and Morals*

BETTY ROLLIN

Motherhood: Who Needs It?

In this article a journalist looks at the evidence for and against a "maternal instinct" and concludes that the "need" to have children is the result of the way we socialize little girls and young women. Written in 1971, this article was one of the first and clearest critiques of pro-natal norms (that is, the idea that all women should have children), sharply calling into question the value of children in the lives of women.

Motherhood is in trouble, and it ought to be. A rude question is long overdue: Who needs it? The answer used to be (1) society and (2) women. But now, with the impending horrors of overpopulation, society desperately doesn't need it. And women don't need it, either. Thanks to the Motherhood Myth—the idea that having babies is something that all normal women instinctively want and need and will enjoy doing—they just *think* they do.

The notion that the maternal wish and the activity of mothering are instinctive or biologically predestined is baloney. Try asking most sociologists, psychologists, psychoanalysts, biologists—many of whom are mothers—about motherhood being instinctive; it's like asking department-store presidents if their Santa Clauses are real. "Motherhood—instinctive?" shouts distinguished sociologist-author Dr. Jessie Bernard. "Biological destiny? Forget biology! If it were biology, people would die from not doing it."

"Women don't need to be mothers any more than they need spaghetti," says Dr. Richard Rabkin, a New York psychiatrist. "But if you're in a world where everyone is eating spaghetti, thinking they need it and want it, you will think so, too.". . .

There is, surely, a wish to pass on love if one has received it, but to insist women must pass it on in the same way is like insisting that every man whose

"Do you know of any reason why she might have run off?"

father is a gardener has to be a gardener. One dissenting psychoanalyst says
simply, "There is a wish to comply with one's biology, yes, but we needn't
and sometimes we shouldn't." . . .

Anyway, what an expert cast of hundreds is telling us is, simply, that
biological *possibility* and desire are not the same as biological *need*. Women
have childbearing equipment. For them to choose not to use the equipment
is no more blocking what is instinctive than it is for a man who, muscles or
no, chooses not to be a weightlifter.

So much for the wish. What about the "instinctive" *activity* of mothering?
One animal study shows that when a young member of a species is put in a
cage, say, with an older member of the same species, the latter will act in a
protective, "maternal" way. But that goes for both males and females who
have been "mothered" themselves. And studies indicate that a human baby
will also respond to whoever is around playing mother—even if it's
father. . . . And, to turn the cart (or the baby carriage) around, baby ducks
who lovingly followed their mothers seemed, in the mother's absence, to just
as lovingly follow wooden ducks or even vacuum cleaners.

If motherhood isn't instinctive, when and why, then, was the Motherhood Myth born? Until recently, the entire question of maternal motivation was academic. Sex, like it or not, meant babies. Not that there haven't always been a lot of interesting contraceptive tries. But until the creation of the diaphragm in the 1880s, the birth of babies was largely unavoidable. And, generally speaking, nobody really seemed to mind. For one thing, people tend to be sort of good sports about what seems to be inevitable. For another, in the past, the population needed beefing up. Mortality rates were high, and agricultural cultures, particularly, have always needed children to help out. So because it "just happened" and because it was needed, motherhood was assumed to be innate.

Originally, it was the word of God that got the ball rolling with "Be fruitful and multiply," a practical suggestion, since the only people around then were Adam and Eve. But in no time, supermoralists like St. Augustine changed the tone of the message: "Intercourse, even with one's legitimate wife, is unlawful and wicked where the conception of the offspring is prevented," he, we assume, thundered. And the Roman Catholic position was thus cemented. So then and now procreation took on a curious value among people who viewed (and view) the pleasures of sex as sinful. One could partake in the sinful pleasure but feel vindicated by the ensuing birth. Motherhood cleaned up sex. Also, it cleaned up women, who have always been considered somewhat evil, because of Eve's transgression (". . . but the woman was deceived and became a transgressor. Yet woman will be saved through bearing children . . . ," I Timothy 2:14–15), and somewhat dirty because of menstruation.

And so, based on need, inevitability and pragmatic fantasy—the Myth worked, from society's point of view—the Myth grew like corn in Kansas. And society reinforced it with both laws and propaganda—laws that made woman a chattel, denied her education and personal mobility, and madonna propaganda that said she was beautiful and wonderful doing it and it was all beautiful and wonderful to do. (One rarely sees a madonna washing dishes.)

In fact, the Myth persisted—breaking some kind of record for long-lasting fallacies—until something like yesterday. For as the truth about the Myth trickled in—as women's rights increased, as women gradually got the message that it was certainly possible for them to do most things that men did, that they live longer, that their brains were not tinier—then, finally when the really big news rolled in, that they could choose whether or not to be mothers, what happened? The Motherhood Myth soared higher than ever. As Betty Friedan made oh-so-clear in *The Feminine Mystique,* the 1940s and '50s produced a group of ladies who not only had babies as if they were going out of style (maybe they were) but, as never before, turned motherhood into a cult. First, they wallowed in the aesthetics of it all—natural childbirth and nursing became maternal musts. Like heavy-bellied ostriches, they grounded their heads in the sands of motherhood, coming up for air only to say how utterly happy and fulfilled they were. But, as Mrs. Friedan says only too plainly, they weren't. The Myth galloped on, moreover, long after making babies had turned from practical asset to liability for both individual parents and society. With the average cost of a middle-class child figured conservatively at thirty thousand dollars (not including college), any parent knows that the only people who benefit economically from children are manufacturers of consumer goods. Hence all those gooey motherhood commercials. And the Myth gathered momentum long after sheer numbers, while not yet extinguishing us, made us intensely uncomfortable. Almost all of our societal problems, from minor discomforts like traffic to major ones like hunger, the population people keep reminding us, have to do with there being too many people. And who suffers most? The kids who have been so mindlessly brought into the world, that's who. They are the ones who have to cope with all of the difficult and dehumanizing conditions brought on by overpopulation. They are the ones who have to cope with the psychological nausea of feeling unneeded by society. That's not the only reason for drugs, but, surely, it's a leading contender. . . .

If reproduction were merely superfluous and expensive, if the experience were as rich and rewarding as the cliché would have us believe, if it were a predominantly joyous trip for everyone riding—mother, father, child—then the going everybody-should-have-two-children plan would suffice. Certainly there are a lot of joyous mothers, and their children and (sometimes, not necessarily) their husbands reflect their joy. But a lot of evidence suggests that for more women than anyone wants to admit motherhood can be miserable. ("If it weren't," says one psychiatrist wryly, "the world wouldn't be in the mess it's in.")

There is a remarkable statistical finding from a recent study of Dr. Bernard's, comparing the mental illness and unhappiness of married mothers and single women. The latter group, it turned out, was both markedly less sick and overtly more happy. . . . "Many women have achieved a kind of reconciliation—a conformity," says Dr. Bernard, "that they interpret as happiness. Since feminine happiness is supposed to lie in devoting one's life to one's husband and children, they do that; so *ipso facto,* they assume they are happy. And for many women, untrained for independence and 'processed' for motherhood, they find their state far preferable to the alternatives, which don't really exist." Also, unhappy mothers are often loath to admit it. For one thing, if in society's view not to be a mother is to be a freak, not to be a *blissful* mother is to be a witch. Besides, unlike a disappointing marriage, disappointing motherhood cannot be terminated by divorce. . . . The realities of motherhood can turn women into terrible people. And, judging from the fifty thousand cases of child abuse in the United States each year, some are worse than terrible.

In some cases, the unpleasing realities of motherhood begin even before the beginning. In *Her Infinite Variety,* Morton Hunt describes young married women pregnant for the first time as "very likely to be frightened and depressed, masking these feelings in order not to be considered contemptible. The arrival of pregnancy interrupts a pleasant dream of motherhood and awakens them to the realization that they have too little money, or not enough space, or unresolved marital problems. . . ."

Every grown-up person expects to pay a price for his pleasures, but seldom is the price as vast as the one endured "however happily" by most mothers. We have mentioned the literal cost factor. But what does that mean? For middle-class American women, it means a life style with severe and usually unimagined limitations; i.e., life in the suburbs, because who can afford three bedrooms in the city? And what do suburbs mean? For women, suburbs mean other women and children and leftover peanut-butter sandwiches and car pools and seldom-seen husbands. . . . But it is simply a fact that a childless married woman has no child-work and little housework. She can live in a city, or, if she still chooses the suburbs or the country, she can leave on the commuter train with her husband if she wants to. Even the most ardent job-seeking mother will find little in the way of great opportunities in Scarsdale. Besides, by the time she wakes up, she usually lacks both the preparation for the outside world and the self-confidence to get it. You will say there are plenty of city-dwelling working mothers. But most of those women do additional-funds-for-the-family kind of work, not the interesting career kind that takes plugging during "childbearing years."

Nor is it a bed of petunias for the mother who does make it professionally. Says writer-critic Marya Mannes:

> If the creative woman has children, she must pay for this indulgence with a long burden of guilt, for her life will be split three ways between them and her husband and her work. . . . No woman with any heart can compose a paragraph when her child is in trouble. . . . The creative woman has no wife to protect her from intrusion. A man at his desk in a room with closed door is a man at work. A woman at a desk in any room is available.

. . . One of the more absurd aspects of the Myth is the underlying assumption that since most women are biologically equipped to bear children, they are psychologically, mentally, emotionally and technically equipped (or interested) to rear them. . . . To assume that such an exacting, consuming and important task is something almost all women are equipped to do is far more dangerous and ridiculous than assuming that everyone with vocal cords should seek a career in the opera.

A major expectation of the Myth is that children make a not-so-hot marriage hotter, and a hot marriage hotter still. Yet almost every available study indicates that childless marriages are far happier. One of the biggest, of 850 couples, was conducted by Dr. Harold Feldman of Cornell University, who states his finding in no uncertain terms: "Those couples with children had a significantly lower level of marital satisfaction than did those without children." Some of the reasons are obvious. Even the most adorable children make for additional demands, complications and hardships in the lives of even the most loving parents. If a woman feels disappointed and trapped in her mother role, it is bound to affect her marriage in any number of ways: she may take out her frustrations directly on her husband, or she may count on him too heavily for what she feels she is missing in her daily life.

". . . You begin to grow away from your husband," says one of the ladies. "He's working on his career and you're working on your family. But you both must gear your lives to the children. You do things the children enjoy, more than things you might enjoy." More subtle and possibly more serious is what motherhood may do to a woman's sexuality. Even when the stork flies in, sexuality flies out. Both in the emotional minds of some women *and* in the minds of their husbands, when a woman becomes a mother she stops being a woman. It's not only that motherhood may destroy her physical attractiveness, but its madonna concept may destroy her feelings of sexuality.

And what of the payoff? Usually, even the most self-sacrificing maternal self-sacrificers expect a little something back. Gratified parents are not unknown to the Western world, but there are probably at least just as many who feel, to put it crudely, short-changed. The experiment mentioned earlier where the baby ducks followed vacumm cleaners instead of their mothers indicates that what passes for love from baby to mother is merely a rudimentary kind of object attachment. Without necessarily feeling like a Hoover, a lot of women become disheartened because babies and children not only are not interesting to talk to (not everyone thrills at the wonders of da-da-ma-ma talk) but are generally not emphathetic, considerate people. Even the nicest children are not capable of empathy, surely a major ingredient of love, until they are much older. . . . When the "returns" are in, the "good mother" suffers most of all. It is then she must face a reality: the child, the appendage with her genes, is not an appendage but a separate person. What's more, he or she may be a separate person who doesn't even like her—or whom she doesn't really like.

So if the music is lousy, how come everyone's dancing? Because the motherhood minuet is taught free from birth, and whether or not she has rhythm or likes the music every woman is expected to do it. Indeed, she wants to do it. Little girls start learning what to want—and what to be—when they are still in their cribs. . . .

By the time they reach adolescence, most girls, unconsciously or not, have learned enough about role definition to qualify for a master's degree. In general, the lesson has been that no matter what kind of career thoughts one may entertain, one must, first and foremost, be a wife and mother. A girl's mother is usually her first teacher. As Dr. Goode says, "A woman is not only taught by society to have a child; she is taught to have a child who will have a child." A woman who has hung her life on the Motherhood Myth will almost always reinforce her young married daughter's early training by pushing for grandchildren. Prospective grandmothers are not the only ones. Husbands too can be effective sellers. After all, they have the Fatherhood Myth to cope with. A married man is supposed to have children. . . . Children are a sign of potency. They help him assure the world—and himself—that he is the big man he is supposed to be. Plus, children give him both immortality (whatever that means) and possibly the chance to become "more" in his lifetime through the accomplishments of his children, particularly his son. . . .

Friends too can be counted on as myth-pushers. Naturally one wants to do what one's friends do. One study, by the way, found an absolute correlation between a woman's fertility and that of her three closest friends. . . .

In case she has escaped all of those pressures (that is, if she was brought up in a cave), a young married woman often wants a baby just so that she'll (1) have something to do (motherhood is better than clerk-typist, which is often the only kind of job she can get, since little more has been expected of her and, besides, her boss also expects her to leave and be a mother), (2) have something to hug and possess, to be needed by and have power over, and (3) have something to be—e.g., a baby's mother. Motherhood affords an instant identity. . . .

What's the point? A world without children? Of course not. Nothing could be worse or more unlikely. No matter what anyone says, motherhood isn't about to go out like a blown bulb, and who says it should? Only the Myth must go out, and now it seems to be dimming.

The younger-generation females who have been reared on the Myth have not rejected it totally, but at least they recognize that it can be more loving to children not to have them. And at least they speak of adopting children instead of bearing them. Moreover, since the new nonbreeders are "less hung up" on ownership, they seem to recognize that if you dig loving children, you don't necessarily have to own one. The end of the Motherhood Myth might make available more loving women (and men!) for those children who already exist.

BRUNO BETTELHEIM

Untying the Family

Many forces in modern life have affected the organization and resilience of the family. Most of these, psychologist Bruno Bettelheim speculates, can be traced to two underlying changes: affluence and modern birth control. Conception and pregnancy, now in the control of the individual woman, no longer stand as inhibiting consequences of sexual intercourse. The separation of sex and conception has led not only to changes in sexual morality and behavior, but also to greater freedom for the woman to control her own life and to spend more of that life in the labor force. This, in turn, has meant a weakening in the dependence and interdependence of family members for survival, and consequent strains on the family as a unit.

In the past, survival of the species and protection of the parents in sickness and old age depended on women having many pregnancies. On the average, at least six were needed, not just to maintain the population but to raise one son who reached maturity and hence could take care of the parents. Since children were breast-fed, and the ability to procreate began roughly at age eighteen, and allowing about two or three years for each pregnancy and nursing period, some twelve to eighteen years of a woman's life were fully taken up with the exhausting task of bearing children. When this period in her life ended—somewhere between the ages of thirty-five and forty-five—she was spent, and for most women life had ended. Her husband, too, was exhausted by the hard labor required of him when man's physical strength alone powered the economic process. He had to work hard for some ten to twelve hours a working day, as had she, to provide the necessities which permitted survival. Psychological difficulties existed then as now, but they did not loom so large when at the day's end one was so tired that all one craved was rest.

Today, when most children are bottle-fed, when a family has, on the average, two children, when a woman's life expectancy is not thirty but at

Bruno Bettelheim, "Untying the Family." *The Center Magazine,* September–October 1976. Reprinted by permission.

"WAS SHE ON FERTILITY DRUGS?"

By permission of V. Gene Myers and *Good Housekeeping.* © 1979.

least sixty years, and when the childbearing age begins not at eighteen but at sixteen, or sooner, only a small segment of woman's mature life is taken up with procreation: barely some six out of more than forty years. During the other long years there is no compelling reason why there should be any economic, social, and, in most respects, any psychological separation between the functions of males and females in family and society. Even what used to be considered men's work no longer requires much greater muscular strength than most women also possess. Cooperation based on division of labor has become largely replaced by its absence, often by competition. Still, the expectation is that husband and wife should live as smoothly together as they did when each had his and her very special and very own sphere of functions.

Children are expected to fit themselves as easily into family life as they did when most of their life was spent within the family circle. But today, from an early age most children's lives proceed outside of the family.

While many and far-reaching changes have occurred in the social, economic, and psychological bases of the family—only some of which I have mentioned—in the last analysis these can be traced back to two relatively independent, although related, developments, both quite recent and most marked in the Western middle classes. The first of these is affluence, which is no longer restricted to the extremely small minority that formed the upper class, but now, for the first time in history, is true of the majority. This affluence enables each family member to survive independently from a support system consisting of other family members. The second is birth control. Whether or not to have children and, if so, how many, and how spaced, has become a matter of relatively easy choice, since it no longer requires such hardships as abstinence or coitus interruptus. Affluence and control over the number of children are, of course, closely connected; the small size of a family is a major ingredient of its affluence. This, incidentally, is another of the recent reversals to which we have not yet made the requisite emotional adjustment. Throughout most of history, having many children more often than not spelled both psychological and economic security, as I have said. It required at least six childbirths to raise one son into adulthood so that he could provide for his parents in old age, which began around the age of forty-five. Now, having many children produces economic insecurity although it still provides psychological security for the family. Hence there is now a contradiction between the two, where before there was congruence.

I shall avoid a discussion of the changes in the family brought about by the changed role of women in society, short of mentioning that change would not have been possible if easy contraception and abortion had not become available, and if the progress of medical science, hygiene, nutrition, housing, etc., (made possible by affluence) had not done away with the need for many childbirths to have at least a few children survive into adulthood. The reason I feel no need to elaborate on the consequences of the women's-rights movement for the family is that these are widely discussed and so new that we do not know in which direction these will take women and families.

Suffice it to say that in the Israeli Kibbutzim, in which childrearing is not a family but a communal obligation and where women have been fully liberated for some three generations, they tend to choose to work in what have been traditionally viewed as female occupations. They do so mainly because they prefer it, and partly because it does not bring with it any economic, social, or psychological disabilities. If these disabilities are removed from traditional women's occupations, the same phenomenon may occur here.

I might also mention that at first the institution of marriage was looked at critically in the Kibbutz because, as the family was generally organized, marriage implied discrimination against women and undue and arbitrary domination of the children. Now, two or three generations later, marriages in the Kibbutz are the rule and, by comparison to the Western world, very stable. This suggests that once a new and different *modus vivendi* between husband

and wife and a different method of childrearing have become established, based on the modern conditions of what now can be the foundation of family living, and when age-old expectations no longer interfere with modern adjustments, then a new form of family living may appear which will be as viable as the ancient one. However, as with all forms of family living, the new form will not be without its probems. The Kibbutz example suggests that when antiquated notions about the family stop making people dissatisfied with its present reality, then companionship and intimacy may be accepted as satisfactory justification for the modern family; it will be viewed—as it is in the Kibbutz—as meeting its purposes, and this view in turn will cement it.

Among other changes that have occurred in the last century or two, it might be worth mentioning that the freedom to choose one's occupation at will is nearly as new for males as it is for females. Only a few generations separate the two sexes in this respect in the Western world, and it is still not possible in most parts of the rest of the globe. Choice became available only when affluence no longer required the coordinated labor of all family members to guarantee their survival. This is something quite new for the majority of people. Even more recent is that the labor of one parent is now sufficient to provide for his and his children's livelihood. Only in the last decades has our social security system made us independent in our old age of the need of support by our marital partner or our children. With so many reasons for its existence removed, marriage necessarily becomes more problematic.

All this is well known. What are not so well known are changes which have occurred during the last few generations due to advances in medical sciences and alterations in the life cycle of the individual.

Much has been written about the new sexual morality, or freedom, which no longer requires dependence on one marital partner for sexual satisfaction. But it was not a morality of sexual freedom which brought about the significant changes in our views of marriage and family relations. Rather, it was progress in the medical sciences: ease of contraception and control of venereal disease. Monogamy was most powerfully buttressed by the fear that satisfying—that is, completed—intercourse was likely to lead to pregnancy, and by anxiety about who would take care of the mother during and after pregnancy, and of the child after his birth, if marriage did not tie a male to his family.

In promiscuous relations there was the great danger of contracting venereal disease, a horrible and often lethal sickness. Only in sexual relations with one's marital partner could one feel reasonably protected against this danger.

Before the appearance of the pill and similar contraceptive devices and the ready availability of abortion, it was essentially up to the male to see to it that sexual relations did not result in pregnancy. The female's ability to protect herself against this danger was much more limited. If the male was the one who alone could protect the female against such danger—short of her giving up a normal sexual life—how understandable that such a socially and psychologically protective role often became tantamount to a dominating role. Often the survival of mother and child depended on the husband-father providing much of the livelihood, especially during the last stages of pregnancy and during the nursing period. This dependency was another reason for the male to assume and the female to accept his protective role, which again easily became one of dominance in important respects. Marital relations were built on this role of the male and on the female's catering to it through accepted or assumed submission.

Modern contraceptive devices have put the woman in control over her pregnancies. No longer does she have to rely either on foregoing normal and complete sex experiences or on the man acting with responsibility. It is she who now has full control over and responsibility for childbirth. This is a reversal of roles which necessarily must lead to far-reaching changes in marital relations. Changes are already taking place, since the person who carries major responsibility naturally becomes the more dominant in a relationship. If children make for the family, the person who decides whether, how many, and when children will be born has the final say in regard to family matters. This is today's reality. But, again, the expectations of both males and females are in many cases still the old ones: that the male should be the protector and the person who decides; that the female should be the one who is part of the decisions but should not make them on her own. These expectations fly in the face of what has become their basis for sexual reality.

With venereal disease readily curable, a much greater barrier against promiscuous relations has been removed than we are ready to realize. Our self-love and high opinion of ourselves suggest to us that modern sexual freedom is due to our greater enlightenment. Actually, it is largely due to the removal of fear of the consequences of promiscuity. Still, the fact remains that that fear was a powerful reinforcer of the marriage bond and that it helped strengthen the family. Now, the family will have to survive without being buttressed by fears often camouflaged as higher morality.

A consequence of effective contraception and ease of abortion is that having a child is truly the parents' free decision, most of all the mother's. It is a decision which is all the more difficult to make since foregoing having children no longer interferes with sexual pleasure. To become pregnant was viewed as an act of God. It is much easier to accept God's will than to have to live with the consequences of one's free decisions. The question, did I really want to have this child, when seriously raised, often becomes difficult to answer with certainty. The same goes for the spacing of children, which today is a difficult and often bothersome problem, whereas before it was due to the exigencies of nature.

Children, too, at a relatively early age, know that their parents had a choice in the matter of their being born. Today they can rightly throw into a parent's face the fact that they had not asked to see the light of day. At a time when having children was much less of a choice, the child accepted implicitly that he could not expect his parents to forego sex so that he would not be born. Now the responsibility of having children weighs so much more heavily, since not having them no longer requires abstinence. It is a new and difficult responsibility being added to the burdens of marriage, and this at a time when there is much less compelling reason to engage in marriage.

There are other changes due to our living longer. For example, less than two hundred years ago, the average length a couple remained living together was seventeen years, largely because so many women died as a consequence of pregnancies and because men on the average died much earlier than now. Despite the frequency of divorces, in 1960 the average duration of a middle-class marriage in the Western world was thirty-nine years. Obviously it is much more demanding of two persons to live together in a marriage for thirty-nine years than for less than half of that time. Thus, even in a good marriage the strains are much greater than ever before. Nevertheless, the current expectation is that a marriage lasting more than twice as long should be as smooth as was one of much shorter duration.

A consequence of longevity is that we live much longer not only with each other, but also with our children. Two hundred years ago, the average age of a child on losing one parent through death was fourteen; in 1960 it was forty. Even today, very few parents run into serious troubles with their children before the age of fourteen. If only one parent remains alive, this poses hardship also for the child; but at least he cannot play one parent against the other, a frequent source of family difficulties. And difficulties in growing up and seeking independence could not arise between both of the parents and their child when one of the parents was no longer living.

Only a few generations ago, most children left their homes at the beginning of puberty. Again, few serious conflicts occur between children and their parents before that time. When they were twelve years old, or a bit older, children were apprenticed out or they joined the labor force in some other form. They were no longer treated as children, although not yet necessarily viewed as fully grown up. It is something entirely new that most children are kept economically—hence also socially—dependent on their parents until they are twenty or older. Yet, again, the tacit expectation is that things should proceed as smoothly in today's family when children remain dependent up to the age of eighteen and beyond, as they did when the child remained part of the family only up to about the age of thirteen.

As if all this would not be sufficient to explain the tremendously greater social and psychological strains from which the family suffers because so much more is expected of it—and this when it fulfills fewer necessary functions—children also mature much sooner than ever before and, at the same time, they are kept dependent so much longer. At the end of the eighteenth century the average age of the girl at the onset of menarche was over seventeen. At the beginning of this century in the United States, it was over fourteen. Today it is just over twelve. Thus, children become physiologically and sexually mature five years earlier than some 150 years ago. At the same time they are kept dependent for at least five years longer.

CAROL TAVRIS

Sex Outside Marriage

In two short lists from The Redbook Report on Female Sexuality, *Carol Tavris, a social psychologist, summarizes changes and stabilities in premarital and extramarital sexual practices.*

The Premarital Scene: Old News and New News

Old News	*New News*
1. Most women still have premarital sex only with their fiancés . . .	1. . . . but more and more women are having premarital sex, which is expected soon to be a virtually universal experience.
2. Most teenage girls do not have sex on a casual or promiscuous basis . . .	2. . . . but teenage girls are having their first sexual intercourse at younger ages.
3. Most girls still need time, love, and learning before they become regularly orgasmic . . .	3. . . . but fewer girls are nonorgasmic in their premarital sex experiences than women were in previous generations.
4. Many women still cling to the double standard for their children . . .	4. . . . but premarital sex with love has become the accepted behavior for both sexes.
5. Girls who begin intercourse at fifteen or younger are more likely to have numerous lovers (before and after marriage), to be sexually adventuresome, and be less happy with their marriages and sex lives . . .	5. . . . but this has always been true of girls who have an early sexual initiation; it is not necessarily the wave of the future.
6. Premarital sex does not affect a woman's satisfaction with her marriage or her married sex life.	6. Premarital sex does not affect a woman's satisfaction with her marriage or her married sex life.

Berry's World

"Let's play housemates. You be Lee Marvin and I'll be Michelle Marvin."

Reprinted by permission. © 1979 NEA, Inc.

The Extramarital Scene: Old News and New News

Old News	*New News*
1. About the same number of wives are having extramarital sex now as in Kinsey's era . . .	1. . . . but they are starting earlier in their marriages.
2. Most wives who have extramarital sex are dissatisfied or bored with their marriages . . .	2. . . . but a substantial minority happily enjoy their husbands *and* their lovers.
3. Women who have extramarital sex are not having more partners than they ever did (still very few) . . .	3. . . . but they tend to have a casual dalliance rather than a long-lasting love affair.
4. Women anticipate more guilt . . .	4. . . . than they usually feel.
5. Religious devoutness still acts to inhibit extramarital sex . . .	5. . . . but religious devoutness tends to decline with age, length of marriage, and the opportunity for an affair.
6. The double standard still lives in people's attitudes . . .	6. . . . but men and women are behaving in more similar ways.
7. The great majority of American wives are monogamous and would like to stay that way.	7. The great majority of American wives are monogamous and would like to stay that way.

MORTON HUNT

The Affair

The Kinsey reports of 1948 and 1953 publicized the commonness of extra-marital sexual relationships. In the following excerpt from his book The Affair *(1969), Morton Hunt, who has written extensively on marriage, considers the ambivalence and conflicting attitudes of Americans about the idea of sex outside of marriage. He concludes that there exists a schism between code and reality which may diminish over the next several generations.*

To date there is still only one major source of sound statistical information on extramarital sexual activity in the United States—the first and second volumes written by Alfred Kinsey and his associates, of the Institute for Sex Research at Indiana University. Despite the limitations of Kinsey's methodology and sampling procedures—his sample, critics have said, is overweighted with the too-willing; it is more a group of the self-selected than the randomly selected—these reports do say how many men and women in a very large, more-or-less national, sample have ever experienced sexual relations outside their marriage. In brief the findings are these: In each five-year age group of married men, somewhere around a third (27 percent to 37 percent) had at least some—that is, at least one—extramarital experience, while the cumulative figure—the total percentage of men who had extramarital experience at any time during their married lives—was a good deal larger. As the authors wrote, in their celebrated estimate, "On the basis of these active data, and allowing for the cover-up that has been involved, it is probably safe to suggest that about half of all the married males have intercourse with women other than their wives, at some time while they are married." For women, in each five-year age group between the ages of 26 and 50, somewhere between one in six and one in ten had at least some extramarital experience; the cumulative incidence was calculated at about one in four, although it is possible, according to the authors, that the true figures might be still higher due to cover-up.

These are the best, and almost the only credible, figures available. But since *Sexual Behavior in the Human Male* was published in 1948 and *Sexual Behavior in the Human Female* in 1953, I returned to the same source to ask what the figures might be today. Dr. Paul Gebhard, successor to Kinsey and present director of the Institute, said that he and his staff, on the basis of their recent work and their general impressions, feel there has been a continuation of previous trends. To quote Dr. Gebhard:

> If I were to make an educated guess as to the cumulative incidence figures for 1968, they'd be about 60 percent for males and 35 to 40 percent for females. This is change, but not revolution. The idea that there has been a sexual revolution in the past decade or two comes from the fact that we have so rapidly become permissive about what you can say and print. That isn't the same as actual change in behavior; still, all this talk *is* going to change the overt behavior of the next generation.

But how much it will do so, and whether men, women, and marriage will prosper or suffer from the changes, is not scientifically predictable; perhaps, though, we will feel entitled to make some reasonable guesses about the future after we have looked at the present more closely.

The ambiguity of the term "extramarital affair" is part of the general American ambivalence toward such relationships. Despite the immense change in what it is permissible to say and to print, the United States still has a dominant sexual code which disapproves of premarital sex and condemns common-law marriage, illegitimacy, abortion, sexual variations and deviations of most sorts, and, of course, adultery. We hear a great deal today about those growing minorities that openly flaunt the code—the undergraduates who openly sleep together and even room together, the show-business celebrities who freely speak of their love affairs, the homosexuals who publicly indicate their bent through clothing, speech, and the companions they are seen with. What is much more significant, there continues to exist a vast underground of good middle-class citizens who overtly accept the code but in fact secretly disagree with, and violate, one or more parts of it.

In *The Significant Americans,* a study of the sexual mores of upper-middle-class people, sociologist John F. Cuber and his co-author, Peggy B. Harroff, term the traditional code a "colossal unreality" based on "collective pretense" and on the systematic misrepresentation, by most people, of what they think and do sexually. They are not alone in this finding: Virginia Satir, a leading family therapist and co-founder of the Esalen Institute at Big Sur, told the 1967 convention of the American Psychological Association that "almost any study of sexual practices of married people done today reports that many marital partners do not live completely monogamously. . . . The myth is monogamy. The fact is frequently polygamy."

There are widespread indications of this schism between code and reality. Christian and particularly Calvinist tradition continues to make adultery a punishable offense in the criminal codes of 45 of the 50 states; maximum penalties range from a $10 fine in Maryland to a five-year jail term, plus substantial fines, in Maine, Vermont, South Dakota, and Oklahoma—yet these laws are almost never enforced except when, as very rarely happens, some aggrieved third party introduces a complaint on which the state must act. Prior to 1967 the only ground for divorce in New York was adultery, and accordingly the State granted some 7,000 to 8,000 divorces annually on this ground (the law has since been liberalized), but even though all the defendants were shown in divorce court to have done something that constituted a criminal act, the county district attorneys prosecuted none of them. Legislators, however, continue to reflect the hypocrisy of their constituents: During New York's penal code revision of 1965, it was proposed that the unenforced and outmoded criminal statute against adultery be removed, but the legislators rejected the suggestion by a three-to-one vote. Even in Illinois, a state which has modernized some of its sex statutes, adultery continues to be a crime if "open and notorious"; in other words, it is criminal if made public knowledge, but noncriminal if kept quiet.

Whatever disapproval most Americans exhibit toward infidelity, their fascination with it is evidenced by the ubiquitousness of the subject in movies, television, novels, and drama; significantly, in these media it is often presented as an exciting and beautiful experience, and even in the movies is no longer required invariably to end in disaster. A story like Elia Kazan's *The Arrangement,* in which adulterous lovers eventually find happiness together in marriage, might have pleased the bohemians and radicals of thirty or forty years ago, but could hardly have been a national bestseller. Yet when the kind of people who read and enjoy this novel today are asked to state how they feel about adultery—even by professional pollsters guaranteeing them anonymity—they tend to give lip service to the traditional code. Are they deliberately lying? Probably not; more likely, they are of two minds about it all, and can find justifications or excuses for it in some cases (including their own, if they have been unfaithful), while condemning it on principle.

A large majority of the respondents to my own questionnaire said they always or usually disapprove of adultery; those who had had affairs themselves were somewhat more tolerant, although even in this group over half were generally disapproving. Other and larger attitude surveys have shown the same thing. As recently as 1958, sociologist Harold Christensen reported that only 6 to 12 percent of a sample of midwestern college students thought adultery ever justifiable for men; the figures may have grown in the past eleven years, but not much, if we may judge by other sex-attitude surveys. A national poll conducted for *McCall's* magazine in 1966 showed somewhat larger percentages tolerant of adultery where home life was miserable, the marriage sexless, and the like, but a large majority still condemned it under almost all circumstances. Half of all the *McCall's* respondents, in fact, said they had *never* felt any sympathy with, or tendency to condone, the extramarital affairs even of friends or acquaintances. Where then, we must ask ourselves, do all those avid movie-goers and TV-watchers, never tired of infidelity as a theme, come from? One can only suppose that what people say they feel about the matter, or even what they think they feel, is only part of what they actually feel.

The most common American attitude toward extramarital affairs is somewhat like the American attitude toward paying one's income tax: Many people cheat—some a little, some a lot; most who don't would like to, but are afraid; neither the actual nor the would-be cheaters admit the truth or defend their views except to a few confidants; and practically all of them teach their children the accepted traditional code though they neither believe in it themselves nor expect that their children will do so when they have grown up.

This is what the disjunction between code and reality looks like, when one penetrates the facade:

—On a Saturday night, in a meagerly furnished apartment in a large Southern city, a young man and woman sit in stony silence watching television. They had been separated and now are attempting a reconciliation, largely because they have a one-year-old son; it is not going well, however, and despite the effort to live with him again, she is still secretly seeing a man she had had a relationship with during the separation and avoiding her husband's sexual advances whenever possible. Toward midnight they go to bed; he makes a feeble try, she pleads weariness, and he turns his back on her in anger and eventually falls asleep without another word. She lies awake, watching the hands of the luminous clock on the night table. At about 1:30 A.M. a car drives up and stops almost under their window; she recognizes the sound, and swiftly slips out of bed, throws on a coat, and hurries downstairs. The man at the wheel drives off to Lovers' Lane, where the two of them feverishly make love in the cramped back seat. At 4 A.M. she slides herself back between the sheets of the bed, sleeps until the clock goes off at 7:30, and then rises, dresses, and makes breakfast. At 9:30 A.M. she is sitting in front of a classroom full of eight-year-old children at the Methodist church, and beginning the lesson on the meaning of communion.

—In a well-to-do suburb of Philadelphia, a slender, somewhat overdressed and over-coiffed woman of thirty-eight speaks of some new facts she has learned about life since her separation from her husband:

> You could ask all these married couples around here and they'd lie in their teeth denying that anything happens except for a little fooling around at parties. But I learned the truth when my husband and I broke up. The first couple of months, about ten of my friends' husbands called me with one excuse or another—some didn't even bother with an excuse—and wanted to take me to dinner, or openly told me what they were after. It shook me up—I didn't know what to believe in any more. Since then, I've noticed things I never used to notice—I've seen Frank's

car parked at the Marriott Motel in the afternoon, and Joe Goodbody's car a half block from Lynn's house one night when Lynn's husband was on an out-of-town trip. God! Sometimes I feel so bitter and cynical. I lived in the middle of this for years and never knew what was going on; it was all a lie around me.

—A salesman who represents several small manufacturers tells how he began his infidelities at thirty, after nine years of happy marriage:

It never occurred to me to fool around; I didn't know any different, and none of my friends in our town were doing anything, as far as I knew. Then I started in for myself as a freelance sales representative in New York, and I saw for the first time how things really were. Everybody was screwing anything they could, whenever they had the chance. People I was doing business with would come to town and expect me to fix them up, or they'd want me to go cruising the bars with them and help them find something. I learned about human nature; I saw it the way you don't see it until you're behind the scenes. And it seemed like everybody was having fun and not getting hurt. So I was *ready*. One night I was having a drink with one of the out-of-town manufacturers I represented, and he sent a note over to two girls in the far corner, and first thing you know we were with them, and it was great fun. Later, I took mine home in a cab and put an arm around her, and the next thing I knew I was making it with her three or four times a week, and really living it up. It was tremendous. I never wanted any of that originally—all I wanted was to be a smalltown boy and love my wife.

—In Washington, D.C., a forty-four-year-old woman sums up the effects of the dozen affairs she has had during her very happy marriage to a man she has never thought of leaving, and who is unaware of her way of life:

When I compare my life to the lives of women I know who haven't had affairs, I feel I'm happier than most of them and my marriage is better than most of theirs. Not that I would ever dare admit it, or urge anyone else to do the same thing. Besides, to tell you the truth, I don't even approve of affairs, on the whole. I feel that most people can't handle them and still have a good solid marriage. But I can, and I don't regret a single one.

—A late-night disc jockey on a southwestern radio station, plump, boyish, and thirty-seven:

One day my wife told me she was going to have dinner and spend the night with some friends who live forty miles away; the maid would sleep in and take care of the kids. So I went to see this girl I was making it with, and because my wife wasn't home and I didn't have to get back any special time that night, I forgot to wake up until early the next morning. When I did, I thought, "Oh God, if Deirdre gets home first, she'll see that I haven't been there and the fat will be in the fire." So even though this eager girl is lying next to me naked and waiting, I'm dialing the phone, sweating and trembling and praying I reach Deirdre at her friends' house before she starts home. But when I get the number at last, her friends sound puzzled and say she isn't there and hasn't been, and they hadn't been expecting her.

So then I knew. I'd wondered for weeks whether she might not be having an affair with my best friend, and now I knew. I left that naked girl right where she was, and threw on my clothes and rushed out to beat Deirdre home and establish my own innocence while confronting her with her lies and her cheating. I was boiling with rage. I drove home like a maniac and she wasn't there, so I mussed up the bed, talked to the maid and the kids for a minute, and then cleared out. In the afternoon she called me at the studio and I told her not to tell me any lies because I knew she hadn't been where she was supposed to have been; I sounded like a hellfire-and-brimstone preacher when I said it. She was quiet for a while and then just said, "I guess there's nothing to say," and hung up. Before dark, she and the kids had moved to her parents' house; I came home to an empty house that night and walked around looking at everything and seeing my whole life in ruins. She had been cheating on me with one of my closest friends and didn't even want to be forgiven! That night I woke up with what felt like an immense stone crushing my chest and I grabbed the phone; half an hour later I was in the hospital under an oxygen tent. The attack kept me flat on my back for three weeks. By the time I got out, she had seen a divorce lawyer—she didn't want to come back and didn't give a damn what I thought or felt about it. She actually married that bastard after a while.

It may well be that within a generation or so, the schism between code and reality will greatly narrow and the ambivalence felt by so many Americans about the matter will diminish. The theoretical liberalism of one generation is often absorbed into the feelings of the next one, and what had been permissible only in thought becomes so in action. Yet revolutions, sexual as well as political, change the outward appearance and structure of things more quickly than they do the deeply internalized emotions and habits that constitute much of the stuff of each culture. Fifty years of socialism in Russia have transformed the economy and the power structure of that nation, but most Western observers find the Russians still rather puritanical, submissive, dogged, and given to alternating between moodiness and gaiety. Similarly, the so-called sexual revolution in America will produce certain outward changes—particularly in the direction of greater tolerance of whatever other people do—but much smaller changes in how most people feel about their own behavior; the ambivalence is deep-seated in our character. Significantly, the considerable increase in premarital sexual freedom has not radically altered the basically monogamous nature of the male-female relationship: Young men and women today expect and require fidelity of each other in their premarital love affairs, and infidelity among them remains, by and large, concealed and guilt-producing. Although it does seem likely that there will be some increase in the incidence and openness of extramarital activity in the next few decades, most Americans will probably continue to keep their unfaithful longings and acts secret, and to profess personal allegiance to the ideal of fidelity.

JEAN LIPMAN-BLUMEN

Dilemmas of Sex

Sexual intercourse is "the physical epitome of intimacy," a relationship that exposes the deepest vulnerabilities of partners. It inevitably raises the complex interaction of intimacy and responsibility. In the article that follows, Jean Lipman-Blumen, an expert on the role of women in society, considers the tension between these elements and the effects of technological changes on the development of intimacy.

Most twentieth-century analysts forget they are not the inventors of the moral dilemmas surrounding sexuality. The issues of morality that infuse sexual behavior have always been with us. Technology and changing values merely create the illusion that the current crop of problems are new and different.

Mass media's obsession with details of pre-, post-, extra-, intra-, and inter-marital sex, in pairs, trios, small groups, or large crowds, falsely emphasizes their diversity and obscures their commonality. We lose sight of the important understanding that all forms of sexual behavior are linked by the same underlying moral issue: the relationship between intimacy and responsibility.

When procreation was seen as the essential rationale for sexual relationships, the responsibility bred by intimacy was apparent. With advanced medical technology and forms of birth control, the nonprocreative aspects of sex have become the major and often disproportionate focus of concern. Our interest is more readily titillated by details of the latest fads in sexual behavior than by the "heavy" subject of responsibility. But the question of responsibility and intimacy barks at our heels.

While technological change has reduced some previous difficulties involved in human relationships, it has substituted others. The telephone, the automobile, the plane, and improved contraception create the possibility to meet, communicate, and develop seemingly intimate relationships with a speed and frequency previously impossible.

*"I love the fact that you actually went through with
this, Phil. I mean, it's such a romantic gesture."*

Drawing by W. Miller; © 1977 The New
Yorker Magazine, Inc.

Mass media, another outgrowth of technology, provide the knowledge, examples, and value context within which relationships grow. The incubation period for intimacy thus has decreased drastically, and often we find ourselves catapulted into seemingly intimate relationships before we are "ready."

Separateness and Union

In one sense, we are never quite "ready" for intimacy. The human condition is one of polarity between essential separateness or uniqueness and union or communion with others. Because we are never totally "ready" for intimacy—never totally prepared to relinquish our separateness—the question of responsibility looms large.

Sexual union expresses the duality of human separateness and connectedness. It represents striving after confirmation of our uniqueness as an individual, at the same time that it reaffirms our loss of self in a larger cosmic process. This is true with regard both to the immediate sexual act with our partners and to the new life that may result from such a union.

Sexual relationships, the physical epitome of intimacy, inevitably breed responsibility, whether or not we choose to recognize it. Sexuality creates responsibility because our sense of ourselves as sexual beings—particularly sexually acceptable, attractive, and adequate beings—is central to our human identity. And it is the exposure of our essential being, our core meaning, that creates responsibility in ourselves and in the individuals who would accept our offer of intimacy.

Sexual relationships involve exposing our most vulnerable selves to one another. Protecting the other person's vulnerable self from harm, humiliation, rejection, and embarrassment is a serious responsibility. The degree to which we do this is one measure of our own humanity.

While we may be mature in years, sexual maturity is a long, complicated process not systematically linked to physiological and chronological development. In fact, in modern societies, the individual's sexual self is the *least* and *last* explicitly developed dimension of self.

Unlike the social and intellectual dimensions of the self, which are involved in human interaction and growth from the day of birth, the sexual self in modern society usually is protected from deliberate and conscious development and experience at least until adolescence. Perhaps our awareness of the disparity between the childlike state of our sexual being and experience and the sophistication of our intellectual, social, even political selves complicates the problem.

Vulnerability

Novelists from F. Scott Fitzgerald to J.D. Salinger have portrayed the anxiety of the young man's first sexual encounter. It is a picture that arouses sympathy, horror, and humor because we recognize his "brand newness," his raw vulnerability. It is this very vulnerability—both in women and men—that creates responsibility.

Often, we are so concerned with self-protection that we fail to recognize the other person's equally great need. Opening oneself to another person, revealing an aspect of oneself that is at the center of one's identity, is an act fraught with both danger and great potential. There is the danger of being diminished by rejection, the potential of being enhanced by confirmation and union. The possibility of self-reduction by treating others without responsibility adds still another level of intricacy to sexual relationships.

The responsibility we assume for both the other person and ourselves can act as a heavy burden or as a source of great joy, growth, and awareness, depending in part on the motivation behind sexual relationships. The feminists have been quick to see that the moral issue at the heart of sexual intimacy is not *if* but *why* we establish sexual relationships.

Motives for Sexual Relationships

Do we seek sexual relationships simply because we perceive the person as a "sex object," someone who "turns us on"? Does the relationship mean the creation of "convenience sex," not unrelated to "convenience foods" in an increasingly plastic society? Does the relationship signify a conquest, a power or ego "trip"?

Do we enter sexual relationships because refusing may label us as unsophisticated, unliberated, repressed, unmanly, unwomanly? Or do we engage in sexual relationships because we fear refusal will jeopardize other valued aspects of the relationship? Do we do so because we sense that denial will damage the other person's sense of self?

Do we enter such relationships to transform ourselves and others? Do we seek sexual union to create new life or instill vitality in old lives? Do we enter sexual relationships in order to give or to take or to establish a balance between the two?

Very often the emotional and intellectual intimacy that we seek with another person is absent, and we attempt to create it artificially through sexual intimacy. But when sexual intimacy stands alone, unintegrated with the development of knowing, caring, and feeling, we face the "depersonalization," the anonymity of sex.

Sex Object

The new "buzzwords"—"depersonalization" and "sex object"—bespeak our concern with protecting our sense of self. When our sexual identity is reduced to sexual functioning, replaceable bodily parts, we experience the anomie, the existential isolation that transforms sexual relationships into a parody of human existence.

Only the responsibility that we take for protecting one another's unique individuality and self in sexual relationships insures us against the tragic realization that our most central self is simply "another body," not a special unique being to another person.

Trust is an important component of responsibility. When we enter sexual relationships before we have exposed the nonsexual aspects of ourselves, it is impossible to guarantee responsibility for protecting this unknown, unique individuality of another person. And when one individual cannot hold out the promise of responsibility, the other individual cannot hold out the expectation of trust.

Yet, getting to know another person takes time. Marathon self-revelation is no substitute for seeing an individual's personality reveal itself under different circumstances over time. When we telescope the interpersonal aspect of knowing another person and enter a sexual relationship on the basis of "instant understanding," we cannot guarantee that we will truly like, respect, and be responsible for this individual whom we shall know differently as time passes. The disjuncture between the physical intimacy and the interpersonal anonymity takes its toll in loneliness and despair.

The relationship between responsibility and intimacy is obviously very complex. The complexity arises from the interweaving of responsibility, trust, and intimacy, uniqueness and commonality, isolation and communion, self and other. The moral dilemmas posed by this relationship cannot be reduced or understood by separating the inseparable parts.

CHAPTER SEVEN

The Feminist Revolution

When I was single I wore a plaid shawl
Now that I'm married, I'm nothing at all.

Old folk song

The domestic career is no more natural to most women than the military career is natural to all men; although it may be necessary that every able-bodied woman should be called upon to risk her life in child-bed just as it may be necessary that every man should be called upon to risk his life in the battlefield. . . . If we have come to think that the nursery and the kitchen are the natural sphere of a woman, we have done so exactly as English children come to think that a cage is the natural sphere of a parrot—because they have never seen one anywhere else.

George Bernard Shaw, *The Womanly Woman*

We can no longer ignore that voice within women that says: "I want something more than my husband and my children and my home."

Betty Friedan, *The Feminine Mystique*

JESSIE BERNARD

Changing Family Life Styles: One Role, Two Roles, Shared Roles

Jessie Bernard, America's premiere analyst of family life, looks at the roles that dominate women's lives and the ways in which they have been organized. She sees the emergence of the sharing of family roles (homemaking and child-rearing) by husband and wife and adaptation of work arrangements allowing both males and females to carry two roles—a market role and family role—simultaneously. Policy proposals are offered to make the two-role option more available and manageable.

In 1957 the National Manpower Council concluded a survey of the employment status of women by noting that the major concerns of those seeking to advance the interests of women at that time had to do with equal-pay legislation and an equal-rights amendment. The authors commented on the absence of interest in both maternity leave and the expansion of child-care facilities to make employment easier for women. They took it for granted that recent changes would influence future public-policy issues, but as of that moment "the form these future developments may take . . . [was] still obscure." Fifteen years later, the issue of the equal-rights amendment is still hot. And interest in the expansion of child-care facilities has become salient.

Reprinted with permission of the New York State School of Industrial and Labor Relations, Cornell University. Copyright © 1970, Cornell University.

I venture here to suggest that future public-policy developments must deal with hours. Not hours in the traditional form of rescinding special protective legislation which can be used as a means of evading antidiscrimination legislation—currently an active issue—but rather concern with implications and ramifications of hours that are far more revolutionary: a concern not so much with the impact of hours of work on productivity or on the economy as with their impact on the relations between the sexes in the family, vis-à-vis one another, vis-à-vis children. Our new concern will ask industry to accommodate to the family rather than requiring the family to accommodate to industry. It calls for extensive increase in the availability of part-time work for both men and women so that fathers and mothers can share roles providing income, child rearing and socialization. It challenges as dysfunctional for men, for women, for children and for marriage itself the exclusive assignments of the child-rearing function to women and the provider role to men, on which all public policy with respect to employment rests.

The One-Role Ideology

Until not too long ago no woman was supposed to work outside the home unless she had absolutely no other source of support. Only one role was appropriate for any woman, a domestic one which encompassed a variety of related functions, especially childbearing, child rearing and housekeeping, along with productive activities. Economic necessity was the only acceptable reason for assuming the provider role which belonged to men. Later on it became acceptable for women to hold jobs before they were married but not after, unless, again, they had absolutely no other source of support; married women still had only one proper role.

As recently as 1969, one respondent in a Gallup poll was still expressing the one-role ideology: "Women should stay home and take care of their families. Even if the kids are in school, a woman's obligation is still to make a home for her husband." The one-role ideology could prevail so long as all the functional assignments of women—childbearing, child rearing, and industrial production—could be combined in one role. When they no longer could—as more and more of the industrial production of the economy was removed from the home—a two-role ideology gained recognition. The function of industrial production—though not of housekeeping services—was split off from the domestic role and a separate worker role for women developed.

When more than half of all the women in the labor force were married, husband present, and when about half of mothers with school-age children were in the labor force, the opinion of the Gallup poll respondent sounded quaint. It has taken some people quite a while to catch up with the twentieth century. Quaint as they may seem, such attitudes cannot be ignored, for all analyses of labor-force participation by women pay their respects to "social values and attitudes" which "exert a pervasive influence upon women's employment." These attitudes "are deeply rooted and resist change, but they are far from immutable."

The Two-Role Ideology

The twentieth century was almost half over when the fallacy of the one-role ideology in this day and age was officially recognized. By that time it was becoming obvious that a modern industrialized society had no choice in the matter; it could not operate without the contribution of women. Thus, in 1949 a Royal Commission on Population in Great Britain reported that it would be harmful to restrict the contribution that women could make to the cultural and economic life of the nation and therefore "a deliberate effort should be made to devise adjustments that would render it easier for women to combine motherhood and the care of a home with outside activities." This was not the reason likely to be given by women themselves if asked, but certainly it was

"I've been a housewife for twenty-five years now, and I've decided to retire next month."

Courtesy, *Good Housekeeping* Magazine, © 1979.

a legitimate rationale for policy. At any rate, the Commission's report marked the recognition of the two-role, or double-track, ideology. Now, in addition to self-support, the contribution which women made to the economy was a legitimizing sanction for labor-force participation even by married women.

President John F. Kennedy went along with this ideology. In establishing his own Commission on the Status of Women in 1961, he prefaced his order with a statement including the necessity of making the most efficient and effective use of the skills of all persons to promote the economy, security, and national defense. President Lyndon B. Johnson also played up the we-need-their-services justification for the two-role ideology, pointing out how badly off we would be if women were not encouraged to enter the labor force.

Not until the second half of the century did a third reason for labor-force participation by women, including married women, enter the accepted repertoire of arguments. It was presented in 1956 by Alva Myrdal and Viola Klein in their book *Women's Two Roles*. This book supplied the sober social-science underpinnings for the we-need-them aspect of the two-role policy. It added also that it would be unrealistic to suppose that all the postmaternal years of a woman's life could be left vacant, unfilled. But this book was important because it also added another support for the two-role ideology. Women, no less than men, needed not only "emotional fulfillment in their personal relations" but also "a sense of social purpose." And President Kennedy included self-fulfillment as an acceptable reason for employment also; women "should be assured the opportunity to develop their capacities and fulfill their aspirations." Agreeing with the Royal Commission on Population, he thought women should be helped by provision of services "to enable women to continue their role as wives and mothers" while at the same time "making a maximum contribution to the world around them."

The self-fulfillment basis for the two-role ideology had good research support. There was convincing evidence that if wives wanted to work and did, their marriages were better; in some cases having a job made motherhood itself more satisfying. Many women who gave economic reasons for working said they would want to work even if they did not have to. And in a study of mothers receiving Aid to Families with Dependent Children, four-fifths said they would prefer to work even if they had incomes of their own. Some form of the two-role pattern was the preferred one by both young men and women among both black and white students.

Especially persuasive research support for the two-role ideology came from a classic study of marriage inaugurated a generation ago. E.W. Burgess and Paul Wallin had interviewed a thousand couples in the late 1930s and early 1940s; in the late 1950s, four hundred were reinterviewed. Among the most important findings of this unique and unparalleled study was one to the effect that marriages with the greatest role *differentiation between spouses were the least satisfactory,* most likely to have deteriorated into "empty shells."

Actually, the self-actualization or self-fulfillment argument in favor of the two-role ideology has never been taken seriously by legislators. The nearest recognition of its validity has been the antidiscrimination legislation, and that came almost accidentally; administration has been far from crusading in nature. Self-support, especially in the case of women on assistance rolls, has been aggressively implemented by insistence that women work if at all possible—a policy mean-spirited, almost punitive. The contribution of women to the economy as a basis for the two-role ideology has been given lip service, but, despite the persistent and continuing efforts of women, the facilities in the form of child-care services that would make it feasible have been niggardly. In the case of women pejoratively labeled "career" women, policy has been resistant; one might even say sullen and resentful.

This, in general, was where our thinking stood in the 1960s. A kind of unwilling acceptance by policy-makers of the basic fact of twentieth-century life: that women's place was not exclusively in the home, that families did not have exclusive claim to the entire lives of women, that, like it or not, labor-force participation was going to play an increasing part in the lives of more and more women.

In the late 1960s and early 1970s a new angle began to appear in the discussions of the employment of women. A new rationale was emerging to add to those which legitimize the employment of women, this time an antinatalist argument.

Two-Role Ideology Becomes Antinatalist Ideology

It had long been known . . . that marriage and children were the major determinants of labor-force participation by women, the second more than the first. Arguments against the employment of women had been based on its deleterious effect on the birth rate, the assumption being that labor-force participation was the independent variable. Others saw the decline in the birth rate as the independent variable and labor-force participation as the dependent variable.

For policy purposes, labor-force participation was viewed as the independent variable. Studies of developing countries around the world showed that participation in the labor force by women was related to fertility; thus it came to be argued that women should be encouraged to get jobs as, in effect, a form of birth control. This view not only would discourage anything that interfered with the participation of women in the labor force, but also would positively encourage anything that facilitated it. "As white-collar employment is strongly related to a later age at marriage as well as lower fertility, normative barriers against the employment of women in professional and other white-collar employment should be undermined by government policy whenever possible. Although the employment of women outside the home as well as that of married women should be encouraged, the provision of employment for young unmarried females upon graduation may lead to an increase in the age at marriage." Employment, in brief, was to be made an attractive alternative to motherhood as a life career for women. Fewer rather than more children was the goal to strive for. Women were, in effect, to be bribed by attractive jobs to enter and remain in the labor force quite aside from their possible contribution to the gross national product—even, in the case of women who wanted children, quite aside from self-fulfillment by way of motherhood. . . .

Strange as it may seem, however, despite the logic of the antinatalist argument for the two-role ideology, it did not seem to work out. For women in the 1960s were learning how to cope with both babies and jobs. Mothers of preschool children were increasingly participating in the labor force, almost a third being in the labor force in the late 1960s. Either jobs were not interfering with having babies or having babies was less and less interfering with labor-force participation. . . .

Just as, on whatever grounds, the two-role ideology was becoming accepted and even positively advocated by antinatalists, it was coming under attack by avant-garde women.

One of the most salient issues in the near-future of industrial societies is being gradually formulated not by government, labor or academic economists, but by young radicals, especially avant-garde women, and family sociologists. It is being thought through not in terms of the economy but in terms of the sexual specialization of functions and the roles which implement it. . . . Implementation will be worked out in terms of hours of work or part-time work; sooner or later the economists will turn the engines of their analyses to show how the goals set up by the critics can be met. For labor-force definition and analysis have always been determined by the needs of social policy. The needs, in this instance, of updating the sexual specialization of functions and the consequent sharing of roles. . . .

As long as the two-role ideology prevailed, women could not really expect equality; discrimination against them was inevitable. There were two fronts in this battle, one in the labor force and the other in the home. No one-front attack could win; both had to be won. In the labor force it involved a more flexible policy, including part-time work; and in the home, a reassignment of functions: not an exchange of functions, . . . but a sharing of them; not a mere tinkering but a radical restructuring of both labor force and family.

Mothers were to be released from exclusive responsibility for child care, and fathers to be given the opportunity to share in child rearing. Everyone, fathers as well as mothers, should share the functions now encompassed in the domestic role.

The net effect of this new look at family and work roles of both men and women has been the emergence of a shared-role ideology to be implemented by some form of part-time work for both men and women. . . .

Part time [work] in the new context of shared role for both men and women was quite a different matter from part time for women only as a way to make possible the performance of all their functions. The argument now was that child rearing and socialization were far too important to entrust to one sex alone; both parents should participate. If men were to share this function, then they would have to be relieved of part of the responsibility of support. Thus both should have the option of part-time participation in the labor force.

The details for implementing the shared-role ideology have by no means been worked out. Some argue for part time on a daily basis, each working half a day; others argue for an annual basis, each alternating every, let us say, six months. . . . Economists have been examining hours of work for many years and have accumulated considerable knowledge on the subject under current conditions. A survey of economies around the world leads to the "connection . . . between shorter hours and higher participation rates. Shorter hours—including more part-time jobs—make it easier for more members of a household to take jobs; and reciprocally, a given standard of living can be maintained with shorter hours per worker when the participation rate is higher." A tenth of the labor force in the country today works on a part-time basis.

Official policy of necessity lags behind avant-garde thinking. But in this case, not very far behind. By 1968 the shared-role point of view had become official policy in Sweden. In a report to the United Nations in that year, the Swedish government stated that it was

> necessary to abolish the conditions which tend to assign certain privileges, obligations or rights to men. No decisive change in the distribution of functions and status as between the sexes can be achieved if the duties of the male in society are assumed *a priori* to be unaltered. The aim of reform work in this area must be to change the traditional division of labour which tends to deprive women of the possibility of exercising their legal rights on equal terms. The division of functions as between the sexes must be changed in such a way that both the man and the woman in a family are afforded the same practical opportunities of participating in both active parenthood and gainful employment.

Hours of work tend to become so highly institutionalized, so much a part of the social structure, so determinative of other aspects of life, so widely ramifying, that change tends to come slowly. And then, say Brown and

Browne, only when "workers' preferences for them have had some time to build up and the scope for them has become fairly wide." Avant-garde women, young radicals and academic critics are now, I believe, beginning the buildup of attitudes favorable to the shared-role ideology which in the not too distant future will affect the workers' preferences.

It is, in fact, hard to remain avant-garde very long in a fast-paced society like ours. In June 1970 a television program, *The Advocates,* was already debating "women's liberation" in the form of this question: "So that women may work and men share the family tasks, should unions demand that everyone be given the option to work full or half time?" A surprising 46 percent of the studio audience and a whopping 75.4 percent of the national television audience favored the affirmative. Esther Peterson, the judge in this debate, pointed out the complexity of the problem and the inadequacy of the way the question was formulated. Then came her conclusion:

> My vote goes to those who are working for a society where no one is forced into a predetermined role on account of sex; a society where men and women have the option to plan and pattern their lives as they themselves choose. This society will require many things: a new climate of opinion which accepts equality of the sexes while still recognizing human and biological differences; a society which provides day care and supplementary home services which make choice possible; a society where non-merit factors in employment such as sex do not count; a society which provides a new concept of training for both young men and women with an eye to employment and social usefulness along with active parenthood. And most important, a society that provides a shortened work day and work week with adequate pay for all workers—thus permitting time for families to be together, for fathers to participate in family activities (including the care and raising of children) where both parents can develop to their fullest as human beings. It's a long way down the road, but it's coming.

Not necessarily such a long way down the road, for, labor economists tell us, once a momentum has been achieved, hours have "been reduced substantially in a movement that runs through many industries in the course of only a few years."

Although the criticisms made by avant-garde women and their demands that men share in the child-rearing function may sound shrill to some, still even sober economists agree that the shared-roles ideology implemented by way of part-time work could have imponderable benefits for our society. Their studies give them "reason to believe that as time goes on, a labor force that works shorter hours will develop its capabilities as it broadens its interests and education. . . . The hours set free, moreover, although they do not add to the measured national product, are used in practice to add something to the unmeasured amenities of households and to the goodness of life." And, may we add, to the welfare of children?

JEAN BETHKE ELSHTAIN

Feminists Against the Family

The feminist movement has defined the family as a system of power relations in which women are the losers. By converting the family into a political arena, the movement has undercut the strength of family relationships without offering meaningful alternatives, says Jean Bethke Elshtain, a political scientist, in this next article.

Whatever its sins against generations of mothers and daughters, the family has served the women's movement well: located by feminists as the key to female oppression, it has been offered up as *the* institution to reform, revolutionize or destroy if feminist aims are to be realized. As a catalyst for rethinking the terms of public and private reality, the family has also provided feminist thinkers with inexhaustible material for dissecting the human condition from the vantage point of this, its central bête noire.

Much that is exciting and fruitful emerged from this ferment. Connections between sexuality, authority and power were opened up for debate in a provocative way. Women were encouraged to create conceptual and linguistic tools to help them pierce the patterns of social reality. Through consciousness-raising, hundreds of women began to view themselves less as passive recipients of revocable privileges and more as active, responsible human beings. But from the start something was terribly wrong with much of the feminist treatment of the family. By "wrong" I don't mean so much careless or unscholarly by traditional canons of historic and social science methodology, though one saw evidence of both. I refer instead to an imperative more deeply rooted and bitter, which erupted from time to time in mean-spirited denunciations of all relations between men and women and in expressions of contempt for the female body, for pregnancy, childbirth and child-rearing.

195

In my view, the feminist movement has contributed to the discrediting of what Dorothy Dinnerstein, a psychoanalytic feminist thinker, calls the "essential humanizing functions of stable, longstanding, generation-spanning primary groups" and the "virulent, reckless, reactive quality of much feminist rhetoric against the biological family, against permanent personal commitments of adults to childhood . . . against childbearing itself [has occurred] ironically, when women and men have been in the best position to minimize the oppressive features of human biology." The result has been the creation of what I shall call a *politics of displacement,* which erodes personal life even as it vitiates the emergence of a genuine public life. This feminist politics of displacement, in turn, helps to provoke a troubling mirror-image. How has this come about?

The key to feminist politics lies in a phrase that has served simultaneously as an explanatory principle, a motto and an article of faith: "The Personal Is Political." Note that the claim is not that the personal and the political are interrelated in important and fascinating ways not yet fully explored and previously hidden to us by patriarchal ideology and practice; nor that the personal and the political may be fruitfully examined as analogous to one another along certain touchstones of power and privilege, but that the personal *is* political. What is asserted is an identity: a collapse of the one into the other. Nothing "personal" is exempt, then, from political definition, direction and manipulation—neither sexual intimacy, love, nor parenting.

By reducing politics to what are seen as "power relations," important thinkers in all wings of the women's movement, but centered in the radical feminist perspective, have proferred as an alternative to the malaise of the present a rather bleak Hobbesianism rejuvenated in feminist guise. For if politics is power and power is everywhere, politics is in fact nowhere and a vision of public life as the touchstone of a revitalized ideal of citizenship is lost. These are serious charges and I shall document them by turning to the manner in which radical feminist images of the "sex war," centered in the family, are served up as a substitute for social and political struggle.

To have a war one needs enemies, and radical feminism (as distinguished from liberal, Marxist or socialist, and psychoanalytic feminism) has no difficulty finding him. The portrait of man which emerges from radical feminist texts is that of an implacable enemy, an incorrigible and dangerous beast who has as his chief aim in life the oppression and domination of women. Ti-Grace Atkinson attributes this male compulsion to man's a priori need to oppress others, an imperative termed "metaphysical cannibalism" from which women are exempt. Susan Brownmiller's male is tainted with an *animus dominandi* which makes him a "natural predator." Mary Daly's male is less bestial, more ghoulish, a vampire who feeds "on the bodies and minds of women. . . . Like Dracula, the he-male has lived on women's blood." Women, however, escape the curse of original sin, being accorded a separate and divergent ontological status. In their views on male and female nature, radical feminists sadly confuse "natural" and "social" categories (as they accuse apologists for patriarchal privilege of doing by manipulating the terms "nature" and "culture" for their own ideological ends). For if male and female roles in society flow directly from some biological given, there is little or nothing politics can do to alter the situation.

Although women escape the curse of an unblessed birth, they are treated to considerable scorn by radical feminists under the guise of "demystifying" their "biological functions." Pregnancy is characterized as "the temporary deformation of the body for the sake of the species." Shulamith Firestone rubs salt into the wound by relating a story of a group of malicious children who point their fingers at a pregnant woman and taunt mercilessly, "Who's the fat lady?" The fetus is labeled variously a "tenant," a "parasite" and an "uninvited guest." Heterosexual sex is reduced to "using people, conning people, messing over people, conquering people, exploiting people." And love? A "pathological condition," a "mass neurosis" which must be destroyed. Childbirth is painful and hideous. Motherhood is portrayed as a condition of terminal psychological and social decay, total self-abnegation and physical deterioration. The new mother is "barely coherent . . . stutters . . . bumps into stationary objects." What has all this to do with politics? The answer, for radical feminists, is everything, given that the "personal is political."

United Press International, Inc.

The only way to stop all this, they go on, is to eliminate the patriarchal nuclear family. The argument runs something like this: because "tyranny" begins in biology or nature, nature itself must be changed. *All else* will follow, for it is biological "tyranny," the sex distinction itself, that oppresses women. Having accepted as a necessary and sufficient condition for social change the total "restructuring" of relations between the sexes, Firestone, for example, fizzles into a combination of trivial self-help ("a revolutionary in every bedroom") and a barbaric cybernetic utopia within which every aspect of life rests in the beneficient hands of a new elite of engineers, cyberneticians animated by the victorious Female Principle. Brownmiller's solution to the sex war lodged in male biology and the "rape culture" that is an automatic outgrowth of man's unfortunate anatomy is a loveless Sparta, a "stalemate" in the sex war in which women have been "fully integrated into the extant power structure—police, national guards, state troopers, local sheriffs' offices, state prosecuting attorneys' offices, armed forces"—in other words, just about any male activity that involves a uniform, a badge, a gun or a law degree.

These suggested solutions to masculine perfidy and biological "tyranny" exemplify a politics of displacement for they cannot be specified with any concreteness nor acted upon, remaining utopian and abstract; at other times they envisage a female takeover of the extant "power structure," thus vitiating consideration of the structural dimensions of our current crisis, which lie in the specific practices of production, the nature of life work, the problems of political accountability and of social stratification along lines of ethnicity, class and race as well as sex.

Except for its ludicrous caricature of the married person as a family fanatic busily engaged in putting single people down, a more recent and sophisticated treatment of radical feminist themes, Ellen Willis's *Village Voice* article, "The Family: Love It or Leave It," avoids many of the crude oversimplifications I have cited. Willis expresses much of the richness and ambivalence internal to family life and to an honest contemplation of that life. Finally, however, her essay collapses under the weight of several contradictions. She insists, for example, that familial matters include public issues that should be the grounds for political decision making. Yet she provides no basis for genuine political action because her strategy remains steadfastly individualistic. ("If people stopped. . . . If enough parents. . . . If enough women. . . .")

Indeed, it is difficult to determine how and why "people, enough parents, women" could mount an effective assault on the public issues Willis finds embedded in our private lives if one of her other claims, that capitalists "have an obvious stake in encouraging dependence on the family," is as overriding as she says it is. She fails to realize that one could make precisely the opposite case—with strong support from historic case studies, something Willis never sees fit to provide—that capitalists have historically had an interest in breaking up family units and eroding family ties. The capitalist ideal is a society of social atoms, beings not essentially connected to one another, to a time, or to a place, who could be shunted about according to market imperatives alone.

Liberal feminism's indictments of family life and men are less blood-curdling, although Betty Friedan couldn't resist the alliterative "comfortable concentration camp" as a description of suburban housewifery. Friedan's women vegetated as menfolk went off to the city and "kept on growing." Friedan's presumption that the world of work within capitalist society is infinitely preferable to the world of the home is a linchpin of liberal feminism and serves to highlight the class-bound nature of their reflections. Friedan certainly didn't have eight hours a day on an assembly line in mind when she denigrated familial life and celebrated work life. Elizabeth Janeway, another liberal thinker, insists that a man has it over a woman in contemporary society because he knows where he stands; he receives rewards according to pre-existing standards of judgment in the marketplace. Women, however, out of the running for the prizes, are confused as to their "true value" (i.e., market worth). Women can take care of this unfortunate state of affairs as individuals, acting alone and being political simply by being "role breakers," a move that simultaneously puts them into the market arena and "threaten[s] the order of the universe."

Marxist feminists put forth conflicting views of family life, but those operating within an orthodox Marxist-Leninist framework are locked into a narrow econometric model that sees both the family and politics as epiphen-omenal, having no autonomous nor semiautonomous existence of their own. Within this perspective, politics is displaced onto economic concerns exclu-sively and, paradoxically, depoliticized as a result. Mothering becomes "the reproduction of the labor force" or "the future commodity labor power." Should a mother take umbrage at this characterization of her alternately joyous and vexing activity, it is taken as evidence of her "false consciousness." (There are, however, feminists working within the Marxist tradition who have a more complex image of familial life, and I discuss their views briefly below.)

Taken all in all, the image that emerges from contemporary feminism's treatment of the family is that of a distortion so systematic that it has become another symptom of the disease it seeks to diagnose. One of the key symptoms of this disease—this "legitimation crisis"—is a widespread draining of soci-ety's social institutions, public and private, of their value and significance. In stripping away the old ideological guises that celebrated motherhood and denigrated women, extolled the dignity of private life yet disallowed parents the means with which to live in decency and with dignity, feminists performed a necessary and important service. But unmasking an ideology and construct-ing a sound theory are not the same activity. Ironically, a new feminist ideology has emerged to replace the old patriarchal one. It, like the old, exerts a silencing effect over free and open debate on a whole range of issues having to do with female sexuality, the conflicting demands of contemporary hetero-sexuality, pregnancy, childbirth and child-rearing, and family life, even as it provides no alternative vision of a revitalized concept of "citizenship."

My concern is with that anti-familial feminist ideology that has become linked in the popular mind with efforts to erode or destroy the meaning and relations of family life *in the absence of any workable alternative*. I have described the complex process at work as a politics of displacement, a form of pseudopolitics in which the symptoms of social breakdown are construed as the disease itself, allowing the deeper dimensions of the crisis to go un-challenged.

Feminist thinkers, in their quest to identify the breeding ground of pa-triarchal privilege, found a sitting duck in the family. But this is as much attributable to our confusion and malaise over the family's proper social role as it is to feminist prescience. Since the advent of the Industrial Revolution, Western society has faced a "crisis in the family" with each successive gen-eration. The chain of events set in motion by industrialism eventually stripped the family of most of its previous functions as a productive, vocational, reli-gious, educative and welfare unit. As these functions were absorbed by other social institutions and practices, the family remained the locus of intimate, long-term reproductive relations and child-rearing activities. The strains of these shifts are reflected historically in the works of great novelists, political and social theorists and the theory and practice of psychoanalysis.

The feminist movement is, then—at least in part—a direct outgrowth of the intensification of contradictory burdens and demands on family members. The family is a product of uneven development, existing as a purposeful and vital unit within *every* extant society, yet resisting, within capitalist society, total domination by relations of exchange and the values of the marketplace. Diverse aspects of social practices collide within the family: little girls, for example, may be inculcated with the American ideology of equality of op-portunity, receive an education identical to that of their brothers yet, simul-taneously, learn an ideology of womanhood and domesticity incompatible with the other ideological imperatives they also hold. Nevertheless, the family, however shakily and imperfectly, helps to keep alive an alternative to the values which dominate in the marketplace. It serves, in the words of Eli Zaretsky, as a reminder of the hope that "human beings can pass beyond a life dominated by relations of production." This vital role played by the family in modern life is recognized by a minority of feminist thinkers who hold the socialist and psychoanalytic perspectives. Indeed, one of the most lyrical evoc-ations of the importance of holding on to that which is valuable in family life, if social relations are not to become thoroughly brutal, may be found in the words of Sheila Rowbotham, a British Marxist feminist, who writes of the family as a "place of sanctuary for all the haunted, jaded, exhausted sentiments out of place in commodity production. . . . The family is thus in one sense the dummy ideal, the repository of ghostly substitutes, emotional fictions. . . . But this distortion of human relations is the only place where human beings find whatever continuing love, security, and comfort they know."

Each child taught to see himself or herself as unique and unconditionally loved, a being (to draw upon Kant) having "dignity," not merely a "price," represents a challenge to the terms of the market system, just as noninstrumental human intimacy is a similar affront to increasingly sophisticated attempts to merchandise every area of human sexual life. Yet these family ties and relations are fragile, subject to strains and breakdowns and to a coarsening that reflects in miniature the abuses of the world outside. Reported incidents of child abuse, for example, rise dramatically during periods of widespread unemployment and economic despair as outward frustrations, in another variant on the politics of displacement, are displaced privately onto the family's most vulnerable members.

The politics of displacement is nothing new under the political sun. Past examples that spring to mind include the policies of the Romanov czars who, over the years, implicated Russia in some external imbroglio whenever they wished to shift public attention away from their domestic politics. A more sinister instance is the use of German Jews as scapegoats for the widespread social dislocation and hardship that followed the end of World War I, a politics of displacement perfected by fascism. In the history of American capitalist expansion and labor strife, one finds the frequent pitting of poor white and black unemployed against each other in such a way that each group saw the other as the source of its misery and corporate oligarchs escaped serious political challenge. Feminism's politics of displacement reveals its true colors when a feminist thinker assaults a social unit, already vulnerable and weakened by external and internal strains, as both *cause* and *symptom* of female subordination. In so doing, those feminists direct attention away from structural imperatives and constraints and promote a highly personalized sexual politics that is simultaneously depoliticizing, individualistic and potentially pernicious in its implications.

The implication of a feminist politics of displacement for politics itself is simply this: a displaced pseudopolitics vitiates attempts to articulate an ideal of public life as the deliberate efforts by citizens to "order, direct, and control their collective affairs and activities, to establish ends for their society, and to implement and evaluate these ends." Feminism's politics of displacement renders politics hollow, first, by finding politics everywhere; second, by reducing politics to crude relations of force or domination, and third, by stripping politics of its centrality to a shared social identity. It erodes private life by construing it as a power-riddled battleground, thus encouraging a crudely politicized approach toward coitus, marriage, child-rearing, even one's relationship to one's own body. It shares with all spinoffs of classical liberalism the failure to develop a vision of a political community and of citizenship that might serve as the touchstone of a collective identity for males and females alike. As Michael Walzer put it recently: "What made liberalism endurable for all these years was the fact that the individualism it generated was imperfect, tempered by older restraints and loyalties, by stable patterns of local, ethnic, religious or class relationships. An untempered liberalism would be unendurable." Feminist thinkers have yet to confront this sobering realization.

ELLEN GOODMAN

Feminism and the Family

*Author and columnist Ellen Goodman has fresh things to say about family
life and feminism. In the two columns reprinted here, she talks about the
different ways men and women are taught to think about their lives and
accomplishments and about the changing attitudes of the women's movement
toward families.*

Why Men Feel Like Failures and Women Don't

I had just finished another one of those articles about the '70s that made me
feel guilty for not being depressed.

It said that depression has been to the '70s what anxiety was to the '60s
and passivity was to the '50s—the Mood of Our Time. It even quietly suggested that anyone who wasn't depressed was probably shallow, insensitive
and maybe even a touch stupid.

With that thought in mind, I called up my friendly neighborhood touchstone on these matters and asked her if she thought that everyone was really
all that depressed.

"Not everyone," she yelled in her abrupt fashion into one of those horrible
little telephone boxes on her desk. "Just the men."

Well, I started ambling down the list of people I know—this was not a
scientific poll, you understand—and it seemed to me that she was more or
less right. While the women I know seem energized and even a touch manic,
depression is running through the male half of the species like an Andromeda
strain.

An outrageous number of men, especially in the over-35 age group, seem
to live with a sense that somehow they haven't measured up. It doesn't actually

matter what they are doing. The sense of a failed being comes from their internal measuring rod. It has more to do with expectations than achievement.

"All the men I know were raised to be President of the United States, while all the women I know were raised to be their mothers," bellowed my friend into her machine. "If you're a woman doing more than your mother did, you feel successful. If you're a man and you're not President, you feel like a failure."

While that is a bit simplistic, it does seem that a vast number of men were raised by books with nagging titles like *Why Not the Best?* They often spend their adult lives convinced that they are second-best. Women, on the other hand, often have such low ceilings on their hopes that they feel enormously proud if they get out of the basement. It's all, as they say, a matter of relativity.

I have two friends in their late 30s, for example, who are both writers. They have the same number of book titles, the same degree of fame, the same incomes. She thinks that what she has accomplished is terrific. He thinks that what he has done is barely sufficient.

"He compares himself to someone who wins the Pulitzer Prize," she explains. "I always thought that if I could be married, have two children and just have a job, any job—writing obituaries for a small-town weekly—it would be a big thing."

The truth is that she considers herself an overachiever and is, at times, excited about it. He considers himself an underachiever and is, at times, depressed about it.

A teaching couple I know suffer the same syndrome. She is tickled to have tenure, while he flagellates himself regularly for not having written the Definitive Work.

I have the sense that a lot of men were set up for disappointment. So few could "measure up," so many were given the chance to "fall short." It reminds me of a bumper sticker I once saw: Life Is a Failure Opportunity.

I don't think this mass case of depression is part of a sexual seesaw—as women move up in the world, men feel relatively lower—although there may be some of that. Men are still suffering from expectations that were not only too high but too narrow. On the other hand, women at this moment in history have suddenly outreached their childhoods. But they have widened their definition of success, rather than transferring it. To the women in this transitional time, success is graded on a point system that counts personal as well as professional values.

Of course, it is possible that women are just a generation or two behind men. It is possible that as girls are raised to go for the top, a few will reach the Senate Chamber and the rest will reach a mid-life downer.

But it would be nice, if, for once, today's women were the role models for the future. The alternative is, after all, rather depressing.

B.C.  by johnny hart

B.C. by permission of Johnny Hart and Field
Enterprises, Inc.

Concept of Family Changes; So Does Women's Movement

Ten years ago it would have sounded like the title of a farce or fantasy. A feminist conference on the future of the family? In 1970, women liberationists would have produced a wake instead of a day of seminars.

But [as the decade closed], Betty Friedan told those assembled at the NOW Legal Defense and Education Fund event that, "Today we turn the page to a new future." She officially staked out the family as feminist turf.

There has been a sea change in the women's movement.

At the first crest, many women saw the family they grew up in or lived in as an indoctrination center or prison of the female spirit. Younger and radical women, in particular, talked as if the future of the family belonged to the archaeologists.

The feminine mystique had told women only to view themselves in the context of their families. Feminism told women to view their "selves" totally outside of that context. The feminine mystique taught women to ask: "What do others want?" Feminism taught women to ask: "What do I want?"

But, over time, the women who asked themselves what they wanted added something to the list: a rich family life. Over time, women who explored their selves found that they wanted others. Many who grew confident and independent could risk and embrace mutual dependency; others acknowledged or rediscovered the pleasures of nurturing along with achieving.

Moderate feminists like Friedan had long warned against exchanging the feminine mystique with a feminist mystique, but other women simply changed. Now, when you look around at the old radicals, you see more mothers.

Phyllis Chesler, the author of *Women and Madness,* has published a rich, honest diary of the explosive mix of feelings about child-bearing, *With Child.*

Jan Peterson, a member of the first radical consciousness-raising group, attended this seminar with her baby, talking about homemaking. Still others have reconnected with their families, reconfirming the organic parts of their own identities.

This has happened naturally. There is a rhythm to most ideologies that move from 12-point programs to complexity, from intellectual purity to humanity.

But feminism has evolved against a backdrop of political change. While feminists were preparing for this sea change, the conservative, anti-feminist movement had grabbed the family as their issue. "The Family," as they portray it, is one with a father-breadwinner, mother-homemaker and children. It is a traditional vision rooted in nostalgia more than reality. But it is the ideal they defend.

Sooner or later, feminists with their renewed sense of family as a priority—but a very different definition of family—would engage in a debate. Today, curiously, feminist and anti-feminist are each out "pro-familying" the other.

There is, in short, a basic argument going on about who is For What Family. At the NOW conference, virtually every speaker noted that only seven percent of the families in the country are what traditionalists persist in thinking of as The Family. They noted that by 1990, according to the Urban Institute, one-half of all the mothers of preschool children would be working. They noted the statistics on single parent families.

The anti-change people look at these statistics and see the family as an endangered species that can only be protected by making alternatives difficult and painful, by marketing guilt against employed mothers, and by lobbying against day care for the children of working parents.

The women's movement, on the other hand, sees in these new realities the family surviving in a range of new forms. In the seminars, they explored ways to bring emotional or corporate or public support to alleviate stress: From extending flextime at work, to improving the status of homemakers, to creating new housing environments, to balancing the demands of work and home.

So, while one group rages against the change in the game of the family, another carries into this future a new sense of the importance of this belonging.

As Friedan said, "There was hypocrisy about the family, a denial of personal truths from extremists of our own movement. We must ground ourselves again in our personal lives. We have the need to love and be loved. To nurture and be nurtured. We are not turning our backs on the future of the family.

They have, in fact, formally and publicly laid claim to the leadership of the "pro-family" movement.

CAROLYN G. HEILBRUN

On Reinventing Womanhood

Carolyn Heilbrun, a distinguished critic and professor of literature, thinks that women in the past have been unable to achieve the goals of feminism because successful women have not bonded with other women or encouraged younger women. Rather, in their search for achievement, they have become "honorary men." She urges a new, full ideal of womanhood to help women realize true equality.

I was in my fiftieth year when I began *Reinventing Womanhood* (W.W. Norton & Co., Inc., 1979)—a time of flowering. A friend wrote to me at Cambridge, after we had dined in New York: "You are in your prime." Women seldom think of themselves as in their prime at fifty, but I think it is often so. (Charlotte Perkins Gilman wrote: "One day the girls were discussing what age they would rather be, for life. Most of them agreed on eighteen, which many of them were at that time. When they asked me I said fifty. They didn't believe it. Why? they demanded. 'Because,' I explained, 'when I'm fifty, people will respect my opinions if they are ever going to, and I shall not be too old to work.' " She remembered this when starting the *Forerunner* at fifty.)

I was devoting myself to a task for which my life had prepared me (but this is no doubt always true of welcome tasks). I wished to name, if I could, those strictures not wholly societal or cultural that inhibit women from the full formation of a self. Obviously, there were many ways in which I was not professionally qualified for this task, but I had come to recognize a unique qualification. I felt that, unlike so many of the women I had read of and known personally, I had been born a feminist and never wavered from that position. I do not mean, of course, that I expressed feminist views in the dreary masculinist years after World War II. But I never denied the pain to myself, or lied about my anger.

We are, for example, only now beginning to understand that the sanctification of motherhood, which prevented mothers from ever admitting to feelings of ambivalence toward their children, is not necessarily good for the child but may induce profound anxiety. Thus I can only now recognize how clear had been my mother's message about the importance of autonomy for women, clear and free of the ambiguity of most such messages from mothers to daughters. She seems to me, in retrospect, almost unique in her honesty, her ability to describe her pain, her subtle refusal to induce me to share it. She spoke to me of what she knew, of what, through great suffering, she had concluded. But she was never free to act on her own knowledge.

I believe that had there been some form of group support from women, she might have found the impulse to action. None such existed. In the thirties came the depression, in the forties war, and after the war, the return to the feminine mystique. Her childhood, poor but with that "upward" aspiration to a "higher" class, is almost a model of how convention imprisons women. She achieved the status she sought, but never denied the burden of futility she carried with her until her death. Her lasting gift to me was a message remarkably clear, uncontradictory: Be independent, make your own way, do not pay with your selfhood for male admiration and approval; the price is too high. Most mothers give a double message: Succeed, but not at the price of imperiling your "feminine allure." Mine did not.

I was, moreover, now, at fifty, provided with the ideal conditions for the work I had undertaken. Our children were in college; I had in some measure resigned responsibility for their destinies, not, of course, as far as money or affection or readiness for consultation were concerned, but my husband and I had quite consciously, when the youngest reached college age, abdicated any further day-to-day responsibility for them. My marriage, probably the single most fortunate factor in my life, allowed itself to develop into new forms and patterns, both of us discovering new individuality and intimacy. In having been made a Fellow of the Radcliffe Institute for Independent Study in 1976–77, I found myself simultaneously endowed with three rare blessings: I was placed in ideal working conditions; I was, for the first time in my life, part of a community of professional women; and I had the opportunity to learn from highly competent and informed people in all disciplines the fruits of their studies of women.

I decided in outlining *Reinventing Womanhood* that I could not speak of the problems of women today without speaking of my own life. Through most of my career as a professor of English literature, the prevailing literary cult has dictated that the personal be subdued. I have been a most eager and persistent follower of this ideal. Professionally trained in the so-called New Criticism, that close attention to the text that denies the relevance of any factors outside it, I found that this criticism nicely reinforced my need for impersonality.

That I managed to keep my personal and professional lives so separated permitted me to survive. My job, as I saw it, was to struggle through to the greatest accomplishment of which I was capable, ignoring, as far as possible, both my Jewishness and my femaleness. Which is not to say that I denied either. What I denied was the power they had to limit *self*-development, to force me humbly, rather than arrogantly, to suffer.

Being a woman and a Jew were in no way of comparable importance in my life. The first was infinitely more pervasive; not only because it was impossible to deny or change, but also because I recognized the condition of femaleness to be for me that which Yeats described as the greatest obstacle to achievement one might confront without despair.

Contemplating this in my fiftieth year, I recognized for the first time the degree to which women have been outsiders in ways unique to them. Had I been an outsider? I began to understand that having been a Jew, however unobserved that identification was, however fiercely I had denied the adamant anti-Semitism all around me as I grew up—still, having been a Jew had made me an outsider. It had permitted me to be a feminist.

It seemed to me, furthermore, essential to discover, if I could, why the woman's movement had been ready to defeat itself after each flowering with so little help from the opposition. Each cycle of progress for women seems to end after a decade or two with precious little real advance toward equality. The complacency in women that a few steps forward induces drains the movement of its energy. Progress halts, or is even reversed.

Why does this inevitably happen? Why is every gain women make followed by a fearful step backward into the shadow of male protection? Women have conspired in the (perhaps unconscious) policy of the male establishment to let a few women in—more, perhaps, in times of feminist pressure—but few enough so that when the inevitable female retreat occurs, the male establishment will be left essentially unchanged in its evident maleness.

Support systems, or networks of women, have for the most part operated in the crises of the conventional womanly life, birth, death, imposed loneliness, but they have rarely encouraged greater female autonomy. The failure of woman's movements, past and present, to retain the momentum of the years of highest accomplishment can be attributed to three causes: the failure of women to bond; the failure of women to imagine women as autonomous; and the failure of even achieving women to resist, sooner or later, the protection to be obtained by entering the male mainstream. Among these causes, the failure of women to find "support systems" among themselves is certainly close to the heart of the problem.

Womanhood must be reinvented. Woman has too long been content to accept as fundamental the dependent condition of her sex. We avoid aggressive behavior, fear autonomy, feel incomplete without the social status only a man can bestow. In the past those women who have made their way successfully into the male-dominated worlds of business, the arts, or the professions have done so as honorary men, neither admiring nor bonding with other women, offering no encouragement to those who might come after them, preserving the socially required "femininity," but sacrificing their womanhood.

What I suggest is that women, while not denying to themselves the male lessons of achievement that almost all our literature and history can afford, recognize the importance of taking these examples to themselves *as women,* supporting other women, identifying with them, and imagining the achievement of women generally. I wanted, therefore, to examine not only how, outside of the brief periods of high feminism, women have achieved positions in male-dominated worlds against great odds, but also how, in the future, they might in larger numbers repeat these accomplishments without being co-opted as honorary members of a male club.

Central to this whole question is the family; its condition, its survival, its essential nature. At the heart of women's problems (to say nothing of men's) is the nuclear family, where the nurturing is done almost entirely by the mother, while the representative of the outer world, the only alternative to the nurturing female, is inevitably male. As Nancy Chodorow concisely puts it, Freud and his followers demonstrated how this family works "with boys appropriating their masculine prerogatives and girls acquiescing in their feminine subordination and passivity." This family structure no longer successfully operates even for the fulfillment of its own aims. I believe that parenting must become the work of both sexes, and of more than a single individual, but I do not believe that Freud's essential insights about the development of the individual need therefore be sacrificed or abandoned.

Certainly conservatives voice a profound fear of the dissolution of the "family" and the loss of what they call traditional "moral values." At a deeper level, what they in fact fear, I think, is the necessity of living with change, with the risks and terrors and pain and reinvention. They have, of course, always retained an exceptional capacity for tolerating the pain of others. I mention conservatives because it is they who most often, and with most publicity, speak as though the nuclear family that we all grew up in were the indispensable pillar of Western civilization, and women, in their passivity and submission, the irreplaceable foundation of the nuclear family. I do not believe this to be true.

The major danger lies in women's fear: the fear of being called inhuman. In the past, womanhood has served importantly to define manhood: boys and men defined themselves, from their first separation from the mother, as *not* feminine, *not* womanly. Men fear, perhaps, having nothing to define themselves against. Yet the rewards for them could be very great. Because of man's relation to his mother in the present family structure, men come to women looking for "narcissistic, phallic reassurance," not for intimacy, or companionship, or love. Both sexes, I believe, will gain enormously by ceasing to define themselves negatively against the other.

Today, as in the wake of all periods of high feminism, women are tempted to forsake the imagination of wholeness, almost before they have begun to embrace it. Woman is again reminding herself of what she has been told through the ages, at least through all recorded history: Keep ambition and womanhood separate, do not let them near one another. (Some women are saying: Combine your ambition and womanhood, but separate yourself from men.)

Men have monopolized human experience, leaving women unable to imagine themselves as both ambitious and female. If I imagine myself (woman has always asked) whole, active, a self, will I not cease, in some profound way, to be a woman? The answer must be: *Imagine,* and the old idea of womanhood be damned. Womanhood can be what we say it is, not what they have always said it was.

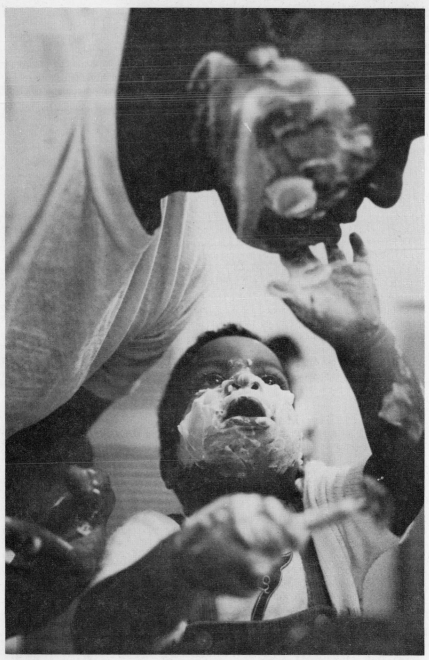

Photograph by Burk Uzzle. © Magnum Photos,
Inc.

Part Three

FUNCTIONS AND
FORMS OF
FAMILY LIFE

Introduction

Part III looks at how the family functions as an institution in society as well as internally, considering various family stages and the special role of the child. It also discusses variations in family patterns among various subgroups in our pluralistic society.

In Chapter Eight, the family is considered in relation to other institutions and the larger society. Families exist in, and are influenced by, the larger social context. We have seen in earlier chapters of this book how our history and economic organization in various periods affected particular forms of American family life, and how recent changes in values and mores have brought new pressures on families. Now we will take a closer look at contemporary social structure and the way in which certain aspects of that structure influence (or may in the future influence) our family forms.

In earlier times, there was less of a division between the public life of the society and the private life of the family than there is today. As the article by John Demos in Chapter Three pointed out, the community did not hesitate to intervene in the life of the family. One consequence of modern family privacy is that much of our knowledge about what other families are doing is indirect—it is based on media images of the family. In an era when television has become so pervasive that it has been referred to as "the flickering blue parent," these images can have tremendous impact on what are perceived to be family norms and, consequently, on family behavior. These themes are explored by psychologist Arlene Skolnick in "Public Images, Private Realities: The American Family in Popular Culture."

While the family may well have been left to function in private in recent years, it is also true that fewer and fewer functions have been left to the family. The family is, in Kenneth Keniston's phrase, an "executive" trying to coordinate and control the interactions between itself and other institutions and the effects of these institutions on its individual members. This trend toward institutionalization of family functions has already been noted in earlier articles in this book, particularly those by Demos and Lasch as well as Keniston. Corporations, schools, government organizations, the courts, and hospitals are among the bureaucratic institutions that are taking over tasks formerly belonging to the family. In "The Institutionalized Family," Amitai Etzioni, a sociologist, discusses the impact of these trends, which he sees as leading to less humane care of family members and a weakening of the family itself.

However, it should be noted that the family is still responsible for overseeing the quality of services provided by other social agencies and integrating their effects on family members. If the school provides skill training but not the religious and moral education that parents want their children to have, the family must arrange for membership in a religious organization or supplement the child's education at home. If an elderly parent in a nursing home has no access to needed physical therapy, the family must make arrangements for this additional treatment. The family is still the first line of defense in times of trouble and intervenes for family members in encounters with other institutions.

In some cases, the family functions to absorb and deflect pressure from other institutions. For example, when the work life of one family member (often the husband-father) interferes with his time to meet family obligations, other family members (often wife-mother) step in and absorb these functions temporarily. When work creates tension and anxiety, the family often provides solace or at least relief and relaxing distraction. As we will see in the article by Kathy Weingarten in Chapter Thirteen, when both husband and wife are working, it is sometimes a delicate task to balance the needs of family members. Sometimes work pressure exerts unrelenting and hazardous pressure on family life. The relationship between work and the family is explored in the next two articles in this chapter. In "Work and Family in the United States," sociologist Rosabeth Moss Kanter describes the various ways in which our work lives and family lives have intersected as we have changed from an agricultural to an industrial to a postindustrial society. One particular kind of work, that of the business executive, is the focus of E. Jerry Walker's article, " 'Til Business Do Us Part?" In the post-World War II period, the "corporation wife" has become as much of a stereotype as "the man in the grey flannel suit." Walker, a minister and family counselor, emphasizes the need for both large corporations and family members to work together to ease the stresses placed on family relationships.

Finally, it should be mentioned that the family also interacts with political institutions in various ways. Certain policies of government (for example, tax and welfare legislation) affect families directly and forcefully, and family issues are often converted into political issues (as, for example, abortion, day care, and the Equal Rights Amendment). Some of these have already been discussed; others will be discussed in Chapter Fourteen. In these and other ways, the family makes contact with, and exists in the context of, other institutions.

Families change in response to external forces, but they also change because of developmental processes occurring within the family itself and in its members. Families, in other words, undergo changes in form and function as their membership changes and develops. These changes, the "family life stages," are the focus of Chapter Nine. A couple marry and form a family, they have children and the family enlarges its functions as well as its size, children grow through various developmental stages with needs which the family adds to its repertoire of functions, children achieve independence and leave home and the family shrinks again to the marriage partners, the post-parental couple. In old age one or both of the original couple may be absorbed into the family of one of their children. The readings in this chapter look at decisions and challenges presented at different stages in the life course of the family.

Claudia Dreifus, a writer, explores the dilemma faced by many young women today after the birth of a child in "Shall I Go Back to Work?" With the widespread use of birth control in our society, many young couples postpone having children until they have worked for several years and are well established. Many women who do not have to return to their jobs after childbirth for financial reasons may nevertheless have planned to be working mothers, but the decision can be a difficult one to make after the baby arrives.

The "generation gap," the conflict between young people and their parents, is an old problem, although it may be newly publicized and have assumed new dimensions. This is the focus of Elizabeth Douvan's article, "What Happens to Parents?"

But children do grow up, and with fewer children born to each family and greater longevity for adults, middle-aged couples are likely to face the "empty nest" syndrome. The problem can be particularly acute for women whose major function has been that of raising children. Sociologist Lillian Rubin gives a moving account of her struggle to deal with this situation in "Women of a Certain Age."

Men, too, frequently face problems in middle age, and, in Suggestions for Further Reading, we have included two books—Levinson and Sheehy—concerned primarily with the male crises of adulthood. (See page 473.)

"Families in Later Life" are discussed by a group of researchers in the field, Lillian Troll, Sheila J. Miller, and Robert C. Atchley. The aged are becoming an ever-increasing portion of our population, and their relationships with their grown children and their problems as they face widowhood are the focus of this article. The relationship of older people to their grandchildren is discussed by Bernice Neugarten and Karol Weinstein, who point out that grandparents today are often not old at all, and we can perhaps better understand certain attitudes and behaviors if we view grandparenthood as a "middle-age" stage.

Chapter Ten concentrates on one of the two traditional functions of the family—socializing children—and asks a number of questions about that performance. What is the process like? What powers and resources does the family bring to the socialization task? How does the child experience the family?

The first readings in this chapter, colonial statutes relating to children, make it clear that obedience was expected of children and would be enforced by law, a sharp contrast to today's increasing emphasis on children's rights. Given this attitude, it is doubtful whether anyone in colonial society would even think to ask children what they thought of the family. However, children's views of the family today are the focus of a recent study conducted by Nicholas Zill. As reported in *Science News* and reprinted here, this research concludes that "U.S. Children Give Families High Marks."

The problems of "Raising Black Children" in a white society are reported by Andrew Billingsley, a sociologist. To some extent, all ethnic groups in America have faced the problems of socializing their children to a culture that was different from their own; in many cases, the schools were the primary socializing agencies and the children, having learned American ways, actually ended up by socializing their immigrant parents. Often the parents were torn between wanting to keep their own culture and adopting a new one. The problems for black families, however, have been unique, as their children have faced racial as well as cultural discrimination, which was long supported by the legal structure of society.

One of the most crucial problems in raising children today is the provision of child care. What are the options for working mothers, who now constitute a majority of all mothers? On what basis should they make their choices among those options? These questions are answered by Mary Rowe, an expert in problems of women and work, in "Choosing Child Care: Many Options."

One form of child care—one that is strikingly different from American methods—is examined by psychiatrist Bruno Bettelheim in "Communal Education: The Case of the Kibbutz." Bettelheim contrasts the methods and results of this Israeli style of child raising with those prevailing in nuclear families in the United States.

Of course, not all nuclear families in the United States are the same. While all families share certain characteristics and functions, there is, as we have seen in Part One, a great deal of variation among families. We can legitimately speak of a mainstream family, but America is a pluralistic society with several more or less distinct traditions and forms that have developed from the histories of different groups. These subcultural variations are considered in Chapter Eleven, Varieties of Family Patterns.

Andrew Billingsley is concerned with both middle-class and poor black families. He emphasizes that the great majority of blacks are working, not on welfare, and analyzes different patterns of family life among the various socioeconomic levels. The problems facing black families at the beginning of the

1980s are further described in an exchange of views between sociologist Nathan Glazer and historian Herbert Gutman. Another distinct ethnic group, Italian-Americans, are the focus of sociologist Herbert Gans' article, "The Urban Villagers," while Lillian Rubin in "Worlds of Pain" contrasts differences in family patterns between lower-class and middle-class families. These selections make it clear that the degree to which the nuclear family relates to a larger, extended family or kin group varies widely among different cultures.

CHAPTER EIGHT

The Family in Society

My soul knows that I am part of the human race, my soul is an organic part of the great human race, as my spirit is part of my nation. In my own very self, I am part of my family.

David H. Lawrence, *Apocalypse*

The family only represents one aspect, however important an aspect, of a human being's functions and activities. . . . A life is beautiful and ideal, or the reverse, only when we have taken into our consideration the social as well as the family relationship.

Havelock Ellis, *Little Essays of Love and Virtue*

ARLENE SKOLNICK

Public Images, Private Realities: The American Family in Popular Culture

Family life is influenced by images, fantasies, and expectations people have of what a family should be. These images are presented to us in the media and in the writings of "experts," particularly when these are given wide currency in the media. Arlene Skolnick, a psychologist, looks at popular images of the American family in the past and in our own time and describes the effects these images may have had on families and the experience of the family.

Within the past hundred years, our lives have become immersed in images and messages. The technology of modern communications has created an "information-rich" society in which most of what people know is learned vicariously, rather than through direct experience. Much of this vast flood of imagery deals with family life and is aimed at families. The mass media entertain us with endless dramatizations of family normality and deviance.

Arlene Skolnick, "Public Images, Privates Realities: The American Family in Popular Culture and Social Science," from *Changing Images of the Family* edited by Virginia Tufte and Barbara Myerhoff. Yale University Press, 1979.

Advertising exhorts us with glamorous visions of the good family life. A variety of advice-givers—in television, in print, and in person—offer prescriptions for home management and family living. And, at the furthest end of the spectrum from commercial mass culture, social scientists and other scholars develop theories of family life that eventually find their way into the mainstream of the popular culture. . . .

The tendency to treat the family as an abstract essence has been exacerbated by the norm of family privacy. In contemporary Western society, the family is a "backstage" area, to use Goffman's term, where people are free to act in ways they would not in public. Family privacy has strong effects on family life and individual family members—and it makes research difficult. Privacy results in pluralistic ignorance—we have a backstage view of our own families, but can judge others only in terms of their public presentations. The gap between public norms and private behavior can be wide; marital relationships tend to be even more private and "invisible" than those between parents and children. Waller observes that the true nature of a couple's interaction is hidden from even close friends. More recently, Berardo notes that "the impulse to maintain a public facade of solidarity persists even in those marriages which are deteriorating . . . once the marital difficulty is made public, the processes of deteriorating may be accelerated."

The strong moral and legal norms surrounding family life have also blurred the distinction between image and reality. Judges and clinicians are likely to evaluate the families that come before them in terms of an ideal standard; ethnographers have often written descriptions of family life in terms of the rules for family behavior, a tendency which idealizes and camouflages family processes.

. . . People themselves may not be accurate informants about their own families. Anthropologists often find discrepancies between observable behavior and the accounts people give of their family lives. Marvin Harris, for example, observes that there is "a vast literature in anthropology and related disciplines which indicates that norms and events never quite match and that, not infrequently, the main function of the norms is to obscure the reality.". . .

The fact that images are incongruent with behavior does not mean that they are unimportant. . . . Images may not correctly represent the social order, but they influence what people do, what they think they are doing, and what they say they are doing.

While gaps between norms and behavior may be the rule rather than the exception in the world's cultures, such discrepancies seem to be particularly disturbing to contemporary Americans. In traditional societies, there exists what Keniston has called the "institutionalization of hypocrisy"; customary violations of cultural rules are justified by a set of customary rationalizations or denials that violations are in fact taking place. In a rapidly changing modern

Leonard McCombe, *Life* Magazine, © 1948,
Time Inc.

society such as ours, new cultural norms emerge without an accompanying
set of rules to justify deviations. Modern parents trying to follow the latest
expert advice on child-rearing have no new rationalizations to sustain them
when they fail to live up to the new principles.

The privacy of modern family life distinguishes it in another even more
crucial way from family life in the past. In traditional cultures and our own
past, much of daily life within the family was visible to outsiders. Besides
regulating family life through observation and the threat of gossip, the premodern community could often intervene directly. Perhaps the most dramatic
example of community intrusion into family life was the practice called the
"charivari" or several other names, prevalent in Western Europe and America
until the nineteenth century. Charivari were noisy public demonstrations used
to discipline wayward family members by humiliating them: "Sometimes the
demonstration would consist of masked individuals circling somebody's house
at night, screaming, beating on pans, and blowing cow horns. . . . On other
occasions, the offender would be seized and marched through the streets,
seated perhaps backwards on a donkey or forced to wear a placard describing

his sins." The sins that attracted such punishment were unusual sexual behavior, marriages between people of grossly discrepant ages, deviations from
proper sex roles, or simply "household disorder." Although this extreme form
of community regulation did not persist far into the nineteenth century, the
degree of family privacy we know today is relatively recent. . . .

Ironically, the external influences on family life did not disappear with
the emergence of the private family; they merely became more shadowy.
Instead of regulation by gossip and the direct intrusion of neighbors, family
life came under the guidance of images and prescriptions derived from the
mass media, and from a vast literature of books, magazines, pamphlets, as
well as from doctors, educators, and other professional "experts" and social
reformers.

The removal of family life from public scrutiny seems to have pushed
family ideals and realities in opposite directions. . . . The more behavior is
immune from observability, the more deviation from the norms is likely to
occur. Laslett observes that the private family lacks both social control and
social support, except in the unusual situation where family behavior comes
to the attention of the community—people are no longer censured for departing from the norms, nor are they supported by the community for fulfilling
them.

While family *behavior* has acquired the potential for greater deviance,
family *norms* have become more demanding. One reason, as noted earlier, is
that privacy allows families to overestimate how much other families conform
to ideal norms, since we have access only to other families' public performances. Moreover, the images and prescriptions for family life that began to
be promoted by the new mass media of the nineteenth century were both
vague and perfectionistic. Instead of avoiding violations of family decorum,
the modern family came under pressure to live up to elusive and abstract
standards. Having internalized such standards, the modern middle-class
spouse or parent was confronted with a superego far more severe and scruti-
nizing than the traditional community had been. As one father put it, "Every
time I yell at my kids, I have the feeling I'm being reported to some secret
psychiatric police force."

Traditional and Modern Images of Family Life

The family has always been a pervasive theme in Western literature, but
before the nineteenth century many of the most vivid portrayals of family life
had been negative or at least ambivalent. In what could be called the "high
tragic tradition"—including not only the dramas of the Greeks and Shake-
speare, but the Bible, fairy tale literature, and the novel—the family is portrayed as a high-voltage emotional setting, laden with dark Freudian passions

of love and hatred. Freud himself was fond of stating that the essential themes of his theories could be found in the works of poets, novelists, and playwrights. While to the psychoanalyst such figures as Cain and Abel, Oedipus and Medea, Hamlet and Lear, and the witches and ogres of fairy tales present disguised versions of the emotions of ordinary family life, to the audiences such figures serve . . . as horrible examples, deviants whose actions go beyond the boundaries of permitted behavior.

Another tradition is that of low comedy—the world of henpecked husbands and tyrannical mothers-in-law. George Orwell once pointed out that this kind of humor is as traditional a part of Western European consciousness as Greek tragedy. Among the conventions he finds in this brand of humor are the following: (1) Marriage benefits women only; every woman is plotting marriage, and every man, seduction; (2) there is no such thing as a happy marriage; and (3) no man ever gets the better of a woman in an argument. This imagery, like that in the tragic tradition, presents negative examples of family behavior. The stock figures of low comedy were, in fact, once used (as in the charivari) to humiliate publicly those who had violated community norms. For many in the audience, such negative imagery of family life probably served a cathartic function, draining away some of the tensions that could not be expressed in daily life. For others, buried passions might be stirred to awareness. Yet no one watching either tragedy or comedy would experience an idyllic image of family perfection that would make their own family life seem flawed by contrast.

But the new "sentimental model" of the family, which arose in response to massive social changes, introduced impossible ideals that did indeed make normal family life seem flawed. . . . When production moved from home to factory, the family was no longer a group of interdependent workers. Men went out into the world and became "breadwinners"; wives and children became dependents. The home was placed in an ambiguous position outside the realm of economic necessity. The new ideology of the family filled the void by idealizing the home and the woman's role in it. Many of our traditional notions about femininity and family life were emphasized by industrialization: the idea that woman's place is in the home; the idea that the essence of femininity lies in ministering to the personal and psychological needs of husbands and children; the idea that mothers have a Pygmalion-like influence on their children.

The Sentimental Model and Its Variations

Over the course of a century and a half, the new ideology of the family took several forms. The earliest and most saccharine form appeared in the new mass media that proliferated during the second quarter of the nineteenth century—the novels, tracts, newspaper articles, and ladies' magazines that represented the beginnings of modern mass culture. Middle-class women and liberal Protestant clergymen, both newly disenfranchised by the development of an aggressively materialistic society, became the custodians of femininity and domesticity. They elaborated a "cult of true womanhood" with religious piety, submissiveness, and domesticity as the core of virtuous femininity. Women were placed on a pedestal and made into objects of almost religious worship. . . .

Later in the century, science replaced religion as the justification for domesticity. Child care and housework were seen not as woman's "special mission" or "beautiful errand," but as a full-time career. The professionalization of the housewife took two different forms. One was concerned with motherhood and the socialization of children according to the scientific understanding of their physical and emotional needs. The other was the domestic science movement, which focused on the woman as full-time homemaker, applying "scientific" and "industrial" rationality to housework. The new ideology brought about a series of cultural splits that have remained ever since. The world was divided into man's sphere and woman's sphere. Toughness, competition, and economic expansion were the masculine values that ruled the world outside the home. But the softer values banished from the larger society were worshiped in the home and the church. The clergymen and middle-class women who promoted the cult of true womanhood disdained the materialistic, competitive forces in the larger world from which both were excluded. As Ann Douglas observes, sentimentality "asserts that the values a society's activity denies are precisely the ones it cherishes . . . [it] provides a way to protest a power to which one has already capitulated." Despite this "capitulation," the sentimental model of the family contained a profound critique of the social and economic order that had spawned it. . . .

By separating work and family, industrial capitalism both undermined the home and at the same time increased its attractions as the only place where security and emotional release could be found. The home came to be seen as both the mainstay of the social order and, at the same time, a precarious enterprise in need of constant shoring up. Any challenge to the prevailing ideology provoked an angry response. The woman was held in the home as hostage to the values that men both cherished and violated in their daily lives. . . .

What is striking as one looks at the writings of popular moralists and advisers of the nineteenth century—the physicians, clergymen, phrenologists, and "scribbling ladies"—is how little their essential message differs from that of the sociologists, psychiatrists, pediatricians, and ladies' magazine writers of the twentieth century. The language has become less flowery, and the whole framework of analysis and justification has become scientific, rather than religious or moral, but the ideas remain the same. The idealized family of the nineteenth century has become the "normal" family of the twentieth century. Until recently, most family studies accepted the sentimental family as reality. . . . Instead of men's and women's spheres, soiologists speak of "instrumental" and "expressive" functions and roles. The idea of the family as retreat from and regenerator of the outside social order reappears in the form of the sociological concept of "functional differentiation"—the family has become a specialized agency ministering to the psychological needs of its members: preparing adjusted, well-socialized children to take their places in the social order, and soothing the tensions acquired in the competition of the office or factory.

Even studies of presumably pathological families have reinforced rather than challenged the sentimental model. As Ruesch and Bateson point out, clinicians tend to construct norms by assuming the general population is marked by the exact opposite of the features they find in their patients. The result of this kind of thinking is the assumption that there are two distinct types of families—the normal and the deviant—with little in common, and that the deviant type is responsible for all our ills. . . .

The sentimental ideology of the family in all its forms assumed the family must compensate for the harsh realities of life outside the home.

Paradoxes of Perfectionism

None of those who formulated the modern ideology of the family considered the ironic possibility that the idealized images of family life they presented could introduce new tensions into the home. By either denying that daily family life is inevitably punctuated by tension and ambivalence or suggesting that all problems are easily solved if the proper methods are followed, the sentimental image of the perfect, happy family makes failure inevitable. The molehills of ordinary troubles become magnified into mountains of pathology. As family therapist John Weakland observes:

> There are countless difficulties which are part and parcel of the everyday business of living for which no known ideal or ultimate solutions exist. Even when relatively severe, these are manageable in themselves but readily become "Problems" as a result of the belief that there should, or must, be an ideal solution for them.

If we choose to avoid the pain and stigma of failure to live up to the ideal image by sweeping problems under the rug, we open ourselves to a deeper kind of trouble: " . . . the husband and wife who insist their marriage was made in heaven, or the parents who deny the existence of any conflicts in their children . . . are likely to be laying the groundwork for some outbreak of symptomatic behavior."

An example of the kind of everyday difficulty that can be made into a problem through exaggeration or denial is provided by marriage counselor

David Mace. He reports that the single biggest cause of the marital troubles he has witnessed is the spouses' failure to deal with anger. Although anger is an inevitable component of intimate relations, most people think that something is wrong with their spouse or their marriage if angry conflict occurs. Eventually, the angry feelings in both parties may crowd out the positive ones, and the result is a corroded relationship full of bitterness.

. . . In the past, a parent could spank a child for misbehavior and, because it was socially approved, could do it in a controlled manner. Now, parents try not to spank their kids, but when they almost inevitably do, it is outside any context of approved parental behavior. The parent's guilt is likely to increase his or her outrage, and may result in an out-of-control attack.

By prescribing inner states rather than behavior, modern standards of family perfection make success almost impossible to achieve. They are like religions of faith, rather than religions of deeds. Family members, if their family is to be regarded as normal, healthy, adjusted, and so forth, are supposed to experience emotional states such as love, happiness, joy, fun, and good orgasms. . . . In former days, the proper performance of family roles was a matter of duty—carrying out tasks properly. If your child was clean and reasonably obedient, you had no cause to look further into his or her psyche. By contrast, the modern mother's self-evaluation can no longer be based on whether she is doing the right and necessary things, but involves nuances of feeling that cannot be controlled voluntarily. It is little wonder that surveys of middle-class mothers (such as that conducted by Sears *et al.*) reveal widespread guilt and anxiety over child-rearing. . . .

The goals of parenthood have become elusive and psychological. Around the turn of the century, a mother's concerns about feeding her child were physical ones—was the food clean and nourishing? Was the child chewing it properly? By the time of Dr. Spock, feeding a child became embroiled in issues of personality development. As historian Nancy Weiss observes: "Checking the bread and milk a child eats and seeing that he or she chews it well are concrete labors mothers can complete. The permissive tasks of enjoying a child at the table, and considering the learning element in feeding, are by their nature less susceptible to being finished. These are tasks that linger, and ones of Sisyphean proportions."

The task of twentieth-century parents has been further complicated by contradictions in the advice offered them. The experts disagree with each other, and they often contradict themselves. . . . However contradictory the advice offered them, parents seem to have acted upon it. A review of child-rearing research by Bronfenbrenner revealed that middle-class parents reflected in their actual child-rearing practices the swings in expert opinion. During the first half of the twentieth century, middle-class parents tended to be more strict with their children than working- and lower-class parents, but by the fifties they had crossed over and become more permissive. Attributing these changes to the great sensitivity of middle-class parents to expert opinion, Bronfenbrenner observes that child-rearing practices are likely to change most quickly among those who have closest access to the agencies or agents of change such as public media, clinics, physicians, and counselors.

After a century and a half, the web of beliefs and attitudes that made up the sentimental model of the family appears to be unraveling. The postwar era of togetherness and the feminine mystique, of the baby boom and the rise of suburbia, seemed to represent its fullest realization. Yet both the prosperity and the social tranquillity of the period turned out to be fragile and illusory. The tensions simmering just below the calm surface of the fifties were later to erupt in the youth revolts of the sixties and the rebirth of feminism.

The sense of malaise about the family today, the widespread feeling that it is falling apart, may be seen as a response not only to rapid and profound social change, such as the steep rise in the divorce rate and the increase in women working, but also to the weakening of the sentimental model. Many people, faced with the obvious discrepancy between the realities of today's family life and the model, refuse to give up the dream of domestic perfection, and project it back into the past. A fierce nostalgia for some lost golden age of the family afflicts a large segment of the public and a few family scholars as well. For most contemporary students of the family, however, there is a growing awareness that the image of the stable, harmonious family is a myth or, at best, a half-truth. Within the social sciences there has been a rebirth of theories that see conflict and change as inherent aspects of social life, not perturbations arising from outside the system. Also emerging from a number of fields is the view that family problems arise out of the processes of family life itself—not necessarily from quirks of the individual psyche. In many ways, we are witnessing a resurrection of the tragic view of the family, a return to the kind of models of family life suggested by Freud and Simmel around the turn of the century. Rather than viewing the family as a haven of perfect peace and tranquillity, we have begun to realize that intimate relations inevitably involve antagonism and hostility as well as love. Indeed, the two aspects are inseparable—intimate relations provide more occasions for conflict than less close relationships, and conflicts between intimates are usually more intense than those between nonintimates. . . .

Although researchers in a variety of areas of family study are dismantling the old sentimental model of family, new ones are appearing to take its place. Thus, in recent years we have seen communes and open marriages presented as routes to individual salvation, social regeneration, or both. Recent works on sex have opened up whole new areas in perfectionist standards. At the same time, many people still hold to the traditional notions about family.

Given the uncertainty of family norms and family life, plus their private character, illusions can flourish and be sustained here more readily than in other areas. . . .

The sentimental model has encouraged the American frontier tendency to deal with social problems by running away from them. As Jeffrey observes, "When middle-class Americans increasingly opted for retreat rather than active engagement in the life of their society, they thereby ensured that the abuses they perceived would be perpetuated and that their reasons for despairing about their society would grow ever stronger."

Thus, I see in the current disillusion with family life some hope for the future. Lowered expectations of family life may increase our ability to cope with the strains and irritations of marriage and child-rearing. Further, once we are no longer convinced that we may find heaven by withdrawing from the world, we may try harder to change it.

AMITAI ETZIONI

The Institutionalized Family

Most observers agree that functions at one time performed by the family have been taken over by specialized institutions outside the family; they are not, however, in complete agreement about the extent to which this process has occurred nor about the overall effect it has had. In the following article, Amitai Etzioni, a sociologist, takes the position that institutionalization has gone too far and that we must think of ways to help the family perform its functions rather than let those functions drift to outside agencies.

In those glowing notes reserved only for blessed news, a news station recently reported that New Haven [was to] have a new hospital for dying cancer patients by March of 1979. This, unlike existing hospitals, [would] have plenty of room for families of dying patients to spend the last days with their loved ones, all gathered together in this reconstituted, "opened up," informalized hospital.

There is room here for a few encouraging notes. To wit, dying cancer patients will presumably not be shunted and isolated nor their families restricted to visiting hours. Relatives, instead, will be made to feel as if they belong to the scene rather than being treated as troublesome intruders underfoot.

Unfortunately, this "blessed news" also indicates a tendency to expand the trend to institutionalize the parts of America not yet relegated to institutions. Ever more social responsibilities are being transferred from home and family to corporations, organizations, bureaucracies—in short, to institutions. Fast-food chains replace family meals at home; child-care centers instead of

Amitai Etzioni, "The Institutionalized Family." *Human Behavior,* May 1978. Reprinted by permission of the author.

babysitting by the extended family; nursing homes instead of family care for the elderly; and, now, hospitals bring the family to live in instead of allowing death to occur at home.

Each of these developments is perceived, quite correctly, as having liberating effects. Fast-food chains, and slow ones, make home cooking an option rather than a requirement. Child-care centers make it easier for both parents to work full-time. Putting elderly persons into nursing homes allows their kin greater freedom. And hospitals for dying patients *and* their relatives make it easier to cope with tragedy.

It is less evident whether or not this trend of expanding institutionalization is wise in the longer run and its accumulative effects. While the merits—which *are* there—have often been touted, some major societal consequences have less often been considered. These are best seen in historical perspective.

Without attempting a full account here, it should be noted that the trend of modern society has basically been to take ever more functions out of the home and invest them in specialized, bureaucratized, professionalized institutions. In preliterate and even traditional societies, production was carried out largely by the family, in the home, on the farm; now it is done mostly in factories and offices. Education, once mainly integrated into parental roles, is—in modern society—a job for schools. Welfare and charity, once taken care of by the extended family or religious or voluntary associations, is more and more a matter for HEW, state and city administrations and private foundations. This transition resulted in ever greater reliance on bureaucratized, often inefficient, institutions delivering poor service to the needy but large amounts of public funds to those who prey on the poor, from nursing-home owners to "medical mills" physicians. The multi-billion-dollar public costs involved have risen to the point that additional tax increases, needed to finance new or expanded institutions, are harder and harder to come by. Tax cuts and institutional *cuts,* or "deinstitutionalization," are what most people seek, from Willowbrook to mental institutions to prisons. Another outcome is that the nuclear family, the extended family, neighborhoods and communities are being rendered more fragile, left with fewer responsibilities.

The most recent expansion of institutionalization is characterized by (1) institutions taking over, not work or education, but the family's caring responsibilities; and (2) cutting into what in most, if not all, societies is the foundation of the nuclear family (the care of young children) and of the extended family (the care of the old and disabled).

To examine where continued institutionalization of the family's responsibilities is leading us is not to ignore the reasons that propel the movement or its liberating merits cited earlier; it is to ask if the same progress cannot be achieved by other means. Thus, one can favor securing the right of women to work outside the home, and equal division of labor between husband and wife within the home, but still advocate child care by the parent (not just by the mother) rather than by child-care centers. Flexitime and half-time jobs without career penalties (such as slow promotion, no tenure, fewer fringe benefits) are steps in this direction. Home-health services (which provide older and disabled persons with nursing care, meals, shopping and other needs in their own homes) are more compatible with old people's preferences than nursing homes, help maintain the family and curb public expenditures. Food delivery to homes is preferable to going out to restaurants, and a professional who would make house calls to the family of a person dying at home may both help the family cope and not require institutionalization.

In short, more effort has to go into finding ways to respond to the legitimate needs of working parents, children, the elderly and the dying, without further increases in the reliance on institutions. Institutions are less humane and more costly than most families, and their continued expansion will leave the family without a significant social role. This, in turn, may well lead not to a utopia but to the ultimate bureaucratization of society.

ROSABETH MOSS KANTER

Work and Family in the United States

Work and family can be separated or connected in various ways. Sociologist Rosabeth Moss Kanter, in the following article, describes the increased separation of work from family that developed in our society over the last century. She also suggests research that should be undertaken to determine the effects of integration and separation of the spheres of work and family and to serve as a base for policy.

For the white-collar classes, the growth pattern of cities helped separate the family. Because industrialization was not a pleasant process, an ideology of home and hearth as the preserve of tradition and humanity grew through the nineteenth century—what has [been] called the "home as utopian retreat from the city." Those who could afford to remove their residences to "pastoral" surroundings far from places of employment often did so, also removing, in the process, points of contact between the rest of the family and the organization. (If the family realm represented a retreat from the urban-industrial jungle, however, the separate workplace also represented for men a possible retreat from intimacy, as it may continue to do today for some people.) It was the well-paid people—the least replaceable, with the most control over the organization's resources—whose loyalty, and hence freedom from particularistic ties, organizations needed most. And it was these same workers who perhaps tended to have the strongest degree of work-family territorial separation.

Territorial separation between residential and commercial/industrial districts, reinforced in the twentieth century by the advent of zoning, . . . confirmed the tendency to see work and family as entirely separate. It is the middle-class family, after all, upon which many society-wide images of America are based, and suburbia has in many ways become the American version of "traditional society." It is hardly surprising to notice, . . . that for much of the time suburbia is populated only by women and children, the people who transform an individual worker into a "family" with "family life," and the man is plugged in when he appears, but *not* seen as carrying with him family membership when he goes off to work. (Working women *are* seen as always carrying a family, however.) That the activities and attitudes of only women could be studied as constituting family life reinforced the myth of separate worlds and led some critics to conclude that we had "his" and "hers" marriages or a "wives' family sociology" rather than a "family sociology."

Separation of the occupational and family sectors of society came to be considered, by modern theory as well as conventional wisdom of the post-World War II period, essential to the smooth functioning of each institution and thus to the integration of society as a whole. This view rested, first, on a definition of the norms of each sector as "incompatible." Occupational life in this perspective is organized around impersonal and objective standards of competence linked to the technical content of a function. These norms are directly opposed . . . to those of the family, which instead rest on custom and particularistic and emotional standards and define roles by age and sex categories rather than "objective" performance criteria. . . . A strong separation of the two institutions permitted each to function with minimum interference from the conflicting standards of the other. The work world's interests were served in theory by making sure that only *one* member of a conjugal family unit played a "fully competitive" role in the occupational system and that workplaces were clearly distinct from residences. The family's interests were also served by this separation (and exclusion of married women from careers), for intimacy and solidarity can be retained, the theory held, only if husband, wife, and children do not engage in direct competition for prestige or rate performance by impersonal standards.

If other institutions, ideologies, and patterns facilitated the isolation of family ties from the world of organizations, it was still the organizations themselves that had the major stake in creating and preserving it. Capitalism and the growth of large work organizations only made "necessary" for more people a process of control of the family that other large loyalty-exacting organizations (such as the military and the Roman Catholic church) had also found supportive of an organization's power. But the vast majority of modern organizations are not total institutions, such as the priesthood or a monastery or a military base. They can do no more than push the family aside and exclude it from "business"; they cannot eliminate it completely. (Indeed, corporations at least began to put a premium on married men in management; presumably their "family responsibilities" made them less likely to behave uncooperatively or unpredictably and risk loss of promotion.) The compromise put into effect by the modern organization could be phrased as a dictate to members: "While you are here, you will *act as though* you have no other loyalties, no other life." (The demands made on key members, of course, reflect the consequences of this dictate.)

The "act as though" principle was reinforced by the myth of individual achievement: that people in American society rise or fall on their own. Thus the family as helper (a subject I will return to) could no more be taken into account than the family as a competing loyalty. Nor could the person-on-the-rise implicate his or her family (usually "his" because this is more allowable for women) without looking like something less honorific than the independent achiever.

If the territories of the organization and the family remain separate (as they do for large employers but *not* for many small businesses and family proprietorships), and if the only people to move physically between the two are directed to "act as though . . . ," then it is not surprising that attempts by researchers to discover connections between work and family by asking people about them directly might result in denials and refusals.

Research Priorities

Five areas stand out as priorities for research and theory.

1. Patterns of work-family connection and the characteristic benefits, costs, and dilemmas associated with each.

Work and family are separated or connected in many different ways for people in this society, but the consequences of each pattern are not well-known. Social critics of the past decade often pointed out the negative effects (especially on housewives and children) of the extreme separation of work and family in some occupations. But there may be advantages as well as costs, for some people, under some conditions, to a degree of separation of home life and work life. At the same time, highly integrated conditions (such as small family businesses) may bear their own particular possibilities for stress as well as benefits to the family. Models need to be developed, and they need to be proposed in terms of *dilemmas*—the kinds of situations that must be managed within each pattern. Social organization does not automatically determine human responses, but it does set limiting conditions and confront people in various locations with characteristic sets of problems and choices. . . .

2. Nepotism and anti-nepotism.

The history and effects of anti-nepotism rules as well as the issues that arise when family members are employed in the same organization or work group would be a valuable research topic. Such questions arise particularly as the number of married women in the labor force continues to grow and as organizations experiment with new work patterns, such as "shared jobs."

3. Occupational situations and organizational arrangements as structural constraints on personal and family development.

. . . Of particular importance as structural constraints are time and timing. Since time is a scarce resource, and families or personal priorities too often get what is "left over" after work, quantity of time and its scheduling can have a major impact on family life and private relationships. Research on this topic could also be integrated with new psychobiological and sociobiological investigation of temporal rhythms and other time effects.

A second critical area is the nature of occupational demands as constraints on personal life. More research on absorptive occupations is warranted. Threads from the important labor-leisure investigations of the 1950s and early 1960s should be picked up, with examination of a range of occupations and associated conditions within the family or personal life-styles. Those occupations that absorb people "negatively"—that is, "burn them out" and leave them with little energy for personal life—should also be examined.

4. The effects of adult career development or work progression on personal and familial relations.

How do people change in the course of their work experiences, and how do these changes facilitate or disrupt personal relations or constitute dilemmas that require resolution? The current wave of research on adult development should be encouraged to continue but with a special focus on work experiences and the attainment of new positions at work as "socializers" which may affect the ways people view and handle their marital, parental, or community roles. The effects of congruent or incongruent experiences among family members should also be investigated.

5. Joint effects of work and family on disruptions of personal well-being.

Wherever health or illness is considered in social context, it would be important to consider it as a joint outcome of participation in at least two systems: a system of family relations and a work system (in which some but not all family members, including the individual in question, participate). For example, as family psychotherapy continues to grow and family medicine gains prominence as a field, practitioners as well as researchers should also view the family (or the intimate system) in the context of its work location, organizational situation, and employment conditions. Practitioner training should include understanding of economic, organizational, and occupational stresses on individuals and families.

Social Policy Innovations and Experiments

There is also a need for policy experiments and research into their effects. A number of such innovations and interventions can be identified.

1. Flexible (flexible working hours).

. . . Flextime plans are growing in the United States (they are much more common in Europe), but they need further encouragement. In particular, the effects of increased temporal flexibility on personal life need to be researched, and if (as preliminary evidence suggests) the benefits to families, community and political participation, and the personal health and growth of individuals can be demonstrated, such benefits should be widely publicized in order to encourage further implementation of flexible time policies. Flextime would seem especially critical for married women with family responsibilities and for single parents. It might also help those who would like to care for the sick or the elderly within the family rather than in outside institutions.

2. Organizational change and job redesign.

If certain absorptive occupations unduly constrain personal and family life, and if certain low opportunity, low autonomy, and low skill occupations have negative effects on mental health and create a source of tension that may manifest itself in hostility within the family, then jobs need to be redesigned. For those in low opportunity, low autonomy situations, worker participation, job enrichment, and increased opportunities for job control and growth may be necessary not only to ensure equity in the workplace but also to generate greater satisfaction for the worker in the family context. Similarly, redefining "success" for those at the top and redesigning reward structures so as to discourage rather than to encourage "work-aholics" may be equally necessary for other families to prosper. In this connection, the effects of experimental kinds of organizations (such as work cooperatives, worker-controlled and managed firms, or nonhierarchical and decentralized firms) on personal and family relations should be investigated. The possibilities for change in the organization of work life in order to improve the quality of *all* life is an extremely high priority.

3. Joint family and work-group meetings and workshops.

In keeping with my assumption that policy should help people build their own strengths, another step would be to encourage the families of people in ongoing work units to meet together to define their own issues and develop their own solutions. At the very least, such occasional or routine meetings would help other family members feel included in and more knowledgeable about what the worker does at work, and it would help them build connections with others in a similar situation. At most, such meetings might result in policy suggestions to employers or a greater voice for workers and their families in organizational policies. Where these kinds of workshops have been conducted, they have tended to be extremely well received by workers and families, although many organizations are reluctant to sanction or support them. (One program with which I was associated brought together men in a high demand work unit who complained of tensions at home and their wives who increasingly felt excluded and distanced from their husbands. Though not all problems were solved, effective support systems were built for both parties.)

4. Bringing children (and spouses) to work.

On-work-site day care is a policy issue that others have dealt with at great length. Here it may be suggested only that the opportunity for children (and even excluded spouses) to share some time at workplaces with workers has potential value that should be investigated. Single parents, especially, might appreciate the opportunity to bring their children to work for part of the day.

5. On-work-site counseling.

More and more employing organizations are making some psychological as well as medical counseling available to people on the work site. How this opportunity affects personal out-of-work relations is still a question. Perhaps the value of this may lie in the recognition that personal crises can affect work life and need to be acknowledged, with supportive help provided. But the "paternalism" inherent in such a policy, issues of confidentiality and effects on careers, all raise uneasy questions that must be answered. And, if some stresses arise from the nature of jobs, it is important to ask whether the Band-Aid solution of counseling is really an adequate substitute for organizational reform or job redesign.

6. Community supports for employed women.

If one major issue for married employed women with children is managing their multiple involvements, attention needs to be given to community services that will provide aid and support, especially for single parents without familial supports and for working women whose husbands fail to give it to them.

7. Leaves and sabbaticals.

A wide variety of personal leaves and sabbaticals can be considered. Maternity and paternity leave are the most obvious, but beyond these, there are a number of situations in which career flexibility and the possibility for brief "interruptions" could aid personal and family life.

8. Workman's compensation for families of work "victims."

Recent court decisions have extended workman's compensation to exec-utives, managers, and other white-collar workers, as well as to widows whose husbands had fatal heart attacks in the course of executive pressures (Stessin, 1976). There are large implications here. The legal issues and financial costs of such extensions need to be investigated. The feasibility of allowing families in general to claim compensation (such as for the costs of psychotherapy to handle stresses introduced by work situations) should be examined. Such policies might also serve as a deterrent, forcing employers to make changes in family-stress-producing situations.

9.   *"Family responsibility statements" by organizations.*

The suggestion of a "family impact statement" attached to governmental legislation, which Vice President Mondale made while serving as a Senator, is still under review. However, as Gerzon (1973) pointed out, government programs, such as the Social Security Administration, have played a major role in shaping the environment for families and children. But perhaps another arena may be proposed: "family responsibility statements" filed by employing organizations. If, as I suspect, the nature of the work world plays a dominant role in the possibilities for families and for personal satisfaction in out-of-work life, then the organizations in which most Americans work might begin to take some responsibility for their effects on families and personal relations. Organizations could file a "family responsibility" document in the same way as an affirmative action plan, although without much of the statistic-gathering and paper work that the latter entails. The statement could include a summary of major organizational policies (such as the timing of work, promotion practices, job control, and executive transfers) along with consideration of how they might affect families and how the organization intends to alleviate major stresses.

The human impact of work organizations—on the workers and on those related people linked to the organization through them—needs the full attention of policy makers.

E. JERRY WALKER

'Til Business Do Us Part?

A minister and family counselor discusses the demands that ambition and career goals of young executives—combined with certain policies and practices in business—place on family relationships. Businesses, he says, are beginning to admit the needs of the executive's family, and families themselves are becoming less willing to be ignored or treated as appendages. Open communication, Walker argues, can help executive couples to face and solve some of their problems.

Midway through a week-long seminar for executive couples one wife said to a woman's group, "I came here saying I am *not* a corporation wife. Now I've been here two days and I find I *am* one—with all the good and the bad that seems to imply. I accommodate the children and myself to his job. I'm gracious to his friends. I'm so cooperative that I've even picked up on a week's notice and prepared to move halfway across the country to some town where I knew nobody. And," her voice was steady, carefully controlled, "I guess sometimes I cry a lot."

A young, attractive women, whose husband was obviously on a "fast track" in a major international corporation, blurted, "I know what you mean. The damned corporation always comes first!" Then tears welled in her eyes as she realized the dissatisfaction that she had expressed for perhaps the first time in her married life.

These women, like other wives of promising young executives, are no longer willing to be third-party bystanders witnessing their husbands' seduction by corporate mistresses up increasingly lonely career paths. They want

240

to share more of their husbands' lives. But, according to Fernando Bartolomé, high-achieving executives as a rule are caught in a stereotype of being "super-masculine, super-tough, super-self-sufficient, and super-strong" on the job. And at home these executives avoid expressing their needs, dependencies, and tender feelings for fear that their wives will think them weak and, consequently, that their wives will be "turned off" by them.

Is the apparent conflict between corporate success and happiness at home unresolvable?

I do not think so. For a number of years I have been studying the marriage/career relationships of business executives and their wives and have found that conflict often rests on two misperceptions: one, the wife's view of her husband's career, and two, the husband's view of himself. In presenting my observations of some of the dynamics between business executives and their wives that contribute to the conflict, I also draw some implications for the corporation. For if issues of great importance affect an individual's personal life, there is no doubt that his work will be affected as well.

Wife vs. the Company

The clinical evidence I have been gathering over the years not only supports the suggestion of a management stereotype but also indicates that there is a pattern among executive wives. For one thing, groups with whom I have been associated are not laced with activists from women's lib, although today the wives are expressing a desire for more consideration in company decisions affecting them and their families. Despite occasional outbursts of resentment and frustration, and revelations of loneliness, most executive wives seem acutely aware of the bargain they made in marrying a high achiever; they may not totally like it and they may hope to modify it, but they understand the pattern described by William Lederer and Don Jackson:

> "The person who is looking for a helpmate in his quest for success is not giving love, but is expecting his spouse to accept status and achievement as reward enough for her efforts."

Dr. Robert Seidenberg, psychiatrist and author on marriage/career relationships, notes that "until the last few years, business literature always emphasized how [the executive wife] could be of help to the company and assumed that all her needs could be met through her husband."

Also, the corporate wives I have talked with do not for the most part want to trade off even minimal marital satisfactions for more freedom to find other satisfactions elsewhere. What I am hearing is the opposite. Many want just one thing: a deeper, more complete companionship with their husbands. Recognizing the limited time they have together, the wives are anxious to maximize it and make it more meaningful. It is at the point where career demands are destructive to any semblance of companionship that there appears to an emerging revolt by some, especially younger, corporate wives. However, I believe this revolt is frequently misunderstood, especially by the wife herself.

In an effort to deepen her relationship with her husband a wife may strike out at the company. A typical example is the woman whose husband recently was offered an advance from assistant store manager to store manager—an advance that would also mean relocating. His wife's response was "We've only been here less than a year and I'm not about to let that company do this to you and your family again. Furthermore, I will not move to that stinking city." What she thought she was fighting was the unreasonable demand of her husband's company. What she was actually attacking was her husband's commitment to his own career.

The Career Comes First

In groups of all-male managers, the deep, essential meaning of career success becomes evident. To a high achiever career success is an entity in itself, it becomes the essence of his self-image. While many executives pay lip service to being a good provider, good husband, and good father, these are not the driving motivations behind their efforts. For most executives career success appears as a goal in and of itself.

"When we married," said one dynamic, self-assured young man in his late thirties, "I was frank with Linda. I told her I planned to get to the top and that I'd selected one of the largest, toughest, corporations in the world in which to do it. I simply told her that I was going to be on a fast track and if she wanted to take the ride with me, I'd love to have her. But if ever the pace became too much and she wanted off, well—I'd understand."

After four significant relocations, which have brought him in his calculations to within three moves of the home office, he is well on his way. His marriage? He guesses that it is okay, although he sees his two young sons only on weekends, because they are always in bed by the time he makes it home on weekdays for an eight o'clock supper. "Suppose," I asked, "that ten years from now when you are at the home office and settled into the key management group, she has decided somewhere along the way to get off the track, and she and the kids aren't with you?"

He thought about that before responding. I sensed his struggle and watched his face. At first he frowned, but shortly his expression cleared to its usual pleasant, unruffled one, and he said with a smile, "Well, I just don't think that would happen."

Nor, in his case, do I. He and his wife may have a marriage with minimal personal satisfactions beyond the material benefits of career success, but they have come to terms with it. And they have taken the very large risk of beginning to be honest about it. The stongest prognosis for their staying together is Linda's recognition that it is not the demands of the company that cause her frustrations but her husband's commitment to achieving a significant career in top-level management.

This is quite a different matter from the wife who blames the company for demanding that she and her family relocate again within a year of their most recent move. She does not recognize that this is her husband's personal career decision and not, as she sees it, a corporate insensitivity. It is not the company's demands on her husband but his demands on himself that she is fighting.

But how would her recognition that what comes between them is not the company but her husband's need for success help the executive to resolve the home/career conflict? It would not help unless he recognizes his own misperceptions.

The Executive vs. Himself

If male executives, particularly, could overcome their fear of revealing their feelings to their wives, they could avoid many unhappy situations and open up a whole new dimension in their marriages. In the counseling professions it is axiomatic that persons only reach maturity through an acceptance of dependence as well as through the achievement of self-sufficiency; yet Western culture trains men to hide their dependencies, to be doers, and to succeed in a world of action while denying the world of emotions. As one businessman put it quite plainly, "Feelings of dependence are identified with weakness or 'untoughness' and our culture doesn't accept these things in men."

Three months after our final meeting together, one wife wrote me, "I can say I'm happier and Harry shows me he is. Best of all, we realize we have a good marriage and we're improving it. Wasn't it funny, though, how all the men at that meeting disagreed that there even is an executive stereotype? Harry will never admit that he has any of the tough and unfeeling traits of the 'typical' executive. He may be an executive at work, but he's convinced he's a loving husband and father at home!"

At the time when I met Harry and his wife, Harry related the following incident with a good deal of humor, showing what used to happen.

One day, Harry came home from work tired, his mind filled with unfinished business at the office. He found his wife, Peg, upset and ready to blow up because of her day's frustrations.

"So what's with you?" he demanded.

"It's this dress," she said, holding up a full-length formal skirt she was making for the symphony ball that weekend. "I just can't get this zipper to go in," and she flung it down on the table, her chin quivering.

"Good Lord!" he said, with obvious feeling. "All that fuss for a lousy little zipper! You should have *my* problems. Look, it's not worth it. Forget it! I'll buy you a dress."

Harry had dealt with what had triggered Peg's feelings but not with her feelings themselves, and he had assumed that they were not as important as his own. He was still the obtuse, arrogant, problem-solving expert, and in using his executive talents on her he had only hurt and angered her further— and, worst of all, diminished her self-esteem. Her feelings, not their cause, were crying for his concern.

Now, according to Peg's letter, Harry was experimenting with his and Peg's feelings in at least a small way, and he was realizing that this new concern did not diminish his ability to be a hard-driving executive.

The ironic fact is that Harry never saw himself as strong, tough, and self-sufficient. Nor did the other men in his group; they all felt vulnerable and exposed, and used the male stereotype as a defense against those feelings. Perhaps it is too great a risk for them to express inner feelings, lest their emotions get out of hand, they appear weak, and therefore they be rejected.

In one group, someone commented to a particularly personable but hard-driving corporation vice president, "You know, Bob, I've been with you for three days now. And I find you a sensitive, tender person—secretly." For high-achieving male executives, it is the process of extending those feelings that becomes scary. Somehow, they fear that their feelings may be destructive to their career.

Because the office is so representative of male competition, which to most men implies toughness, it seems to be difficult for people to explore their feelings there. So the home would seem to be the best place to experiment with feelings, as the climate there tends to be more open.

But the man who is practiced in hiding his feelings and who virtually never talks about them will find experimenting at home a high-risk change. Even in our egalitarian age men may not be ready yet for equality. While many women are speaking out for equality of the sexes, especially in what used to be called a man's world, men may be a long way from being ready for it in the world of emotions, which has customarily been identified with women. It is just a conjecture, but women may be able to move into a world of harsh competitiveness with more ease than men can learn to express emotion. In the interchange, as he sees it, she gains and he loses.

There is a realistic quality about the marital predicament of Robert Slocum, business-executive hero of Joseph Heller's novel *Something Happened*. He says about his wife, "She's really a better and stronger person than I am, but I must never let her find out." The author amplifies, "What I'm saying about Slocum is in the character of almost every man I know." . . .

Perhaps, as psychiatrist Robert Coles writes, "there should be a little more blurring of the roles" between husband and wife, especially the roles of father and mother. Unfortunately, many men would be uncomfortable with this, having been brought up to believe that warmth and affection compromise their masculine dominance. So the stereotype—really, the double stereotype—is perpetuated.

One couple, each having sublimated, strong, individual desires, reported later how they came to grips with this. "We have just begun to understand what marriage means to us," the wife wrote. "We had forgotten who we were as individuals, and now we have become more aware of each other and our feelings as Joanne and Gene, not as Mother and Father, or wife and husband."

Significantly, she noted that this was just the beginning of their new relationship. She went on to say, "In learning to talk about our feelings we have opened up a communication process that has enhanced our marriage so greatly that we are amazed it took us so long to find out what we had been missing."

Working Together

The one thing that invariably comes through on follow-up correspondence with executive couples is this discovery: "We are learning to communicate." Trite as this may sound, marriage literature and research place noncommunication at the top of the pile of marriage busters. In a recent study conducted by the Family Service Association of America, 87 percent of the married couples interviewed said that communication was a major area of conflict in their marriage. Sex at 44 percent and money at 37 percent trailed far behind.

When lack of communication builds up over the years, a husband and wife are likely to experience a heartbreaking trauma in later life. I sat recently with a senior vice president of a major component of the Bell System. "I've been 40 years with my company," he told me. "And in my rise through the ranks we moved 26 times. Whenever I was offered a relocation, I went home and talked it over with my wife, and she said, 'We're in this together, Ralph. If it's good for you, it's good for me'. So I made decisions, all 26 of them, thinking she was right there with me. Now I'm facing retirement. We are going to be living together a lot more hours of every day. And suddenly I discover she's carrying a big bundle of resentment and hostility that has been building up over all these years."

"What do you figure went wrong?" I asked.

"Simple," he said. "Every time we moved, I moved up. Better salary, more status, increased attention from the corporation. But every time we moved, she had to go back down and start all over again in a new community. And I never realized it because we never talked about it."

He snubbed out the cigarette that was burning his fingers. "I guess it's too late to do anything about us," he said. "But I'd like to see something done to make it better for our younger managers. And you know, to be honest, I don't know what or how. In this company moving up means moving around. If a man doesn't relocate, he stagnates. It's a part of the game."

As I listened to this older man, I thought of an evaluation from a brilliant young manager who is on the move in another large corporation, Atlantic Richfield. Recently, he relocated from Dallas to Los Angeles. He spoke of the new insights that a vital, real communication process would bring to his marriage on his *next* relocation.

"Here's the difference," he said. "Before we moved to Los Angeles, Martha and I went there at company expense. They took us to the executive vice president's office—where I was going to have maybe a cubicle. They took us for lunch at the country club—which would be off limits for my noon hours. So, on an interview, she never really saw what my real job would be like. In effect, I made the decisions for both of us after she gave a perfunctory, 'I'll go along with whatever you think is right for us, Mike'. And," he added, "this put me in a terrific bind. Suppose I failed? Then I not only have responsibility for failing the trust the company put in me; I also fail my wife and my family and myself. That's a heavy bundle to carry!"

How would an open system of intramarital communication change this? Mike expressed it this way: "Because of women's increasing awareness and concern about their role in life, companies can no longer assume that a male employee should 'manage' his family affairs so that his wife and family will 'adjust to' his career commitments. To an increasing extent wives are becoming more vocal about and influential in the career decisions of their husbands. If one buys this concept, then it is important to have the wife know as much as possible about her husband's career, to give her an opportunity to 'buy in' on his career commitment. I can think of no way for a wife to become familiar, at a feeling level, with what career decisions mean to her husband unless the couple has a real ability to communicate. For most people, Martha and me included, such communication doesn't just happen. It has to be learned and worked at."

According to marriage counselors Rover Lee and Marjorie Casebier, marriage is like space travel:

"Space scientists point out that a slight midcourse correction is essential for a successful flight, and that a little change in midcourse has vast consequences later on. Similarly, a midcourse correction involving mutual change for middlescent marriages will bear significant fruits later on. . . . Perhaps nothing 'new' can be introduced into a marriage at middle age, but there can be a rearrangement of what there is . . . around which the marital relationship is renewed and rebuilt."

On this premise there is still hope for the about-to-retire senior vice president referred to earlier. But how much more exciting are the new horizons that open to the younger, high-potential couples when the wife finds a way, as Mike indicated, to "buy in," on terms she helps set, to her husband's career.

Benefits to the Career

What Mike was saying ties together the critical issues I have been discussing. In the future, for a man to succeed in business as well as in his marriage, it is going to be more and more necessary that his wife really understand and accept his deep commitment to his career. This understanding cannot occur unless husbands and wives learn to talk to each other on a more basic level than my experience shows that they do now. Through this communication husbands may find that sharing their feelings with their wives can be strengthening rather than weakening, supporting rather than debilitating; and both career and home life may be enhanced. But is this true?

While it is fairly easy to identify how better communication would benefit a marriage, it is somewhat more difficult to see how it would improve a person's growth in the job. Personal growth is not so easily measured as management skills. It is easier to focus attention on tasks and behavioral demands on the job than it is to improve an executive's performance in his personal manner of relating to others. Because the former can be measured while the latter cannot, most training, development, and evaluation tend to be task-oriented.

One division vice president was disappointed that a participant from his company had not returned from a growth seminar with a notebook full of new ideas that could be shared in a staff meeting. However, on the positive side, many participants have repeated one husband's pleasure over the "good feeling toward the company on the part of my wife" that the experience engendered. Another put it even more bluntly in his report to his superiors, saying "My wife says it's the first time in 15 years the company ever did anything for *her*."

But this still does not get at the question of the seminar's effect on job performance and the company's perception of the role marriage can play in an employee's life. Nor do I have any way of measuring this. However, I have seen some encouraging signs. A company president later confessed that he sent a top salesman and his wife to the program because he thought marital tension was draining his man's energies away from his work. Meanwhile, a vice president for personnel plans at IBM asserts, "Our people who have attended feel it is a very worthwhile experience, and the new ideas are certainly of interest." And the management development team at Northwestern Bell has made the effects of frequent relocation on the family a vital part of its research and training program.

A division vice president of the Dayton Hudson Company decided that if learning to listen could be so helpful to his marriage, it might do the same in his office. Now, once a month, he holds a coffee hour with his entire staff, secretaries included; there they "let it all hang out," and there are no reprisals. "It's meant a lot to the morale of my department," he writes. And a manager from the Peavey Company notes, "There is a fine line between good and great managers and between good and great companies. This line is attitude. A good manager with a positive attitude and secure home life becomes a great manager, and the company profits. That's what needs building—positive attitudes and honest people; I mean people who are honest with themselves. Once a person has this, he is free to make decisions." . . .

The climate of the times seems to presage a change in those corporate policies that tacitly deny the existence of an executive's family, literally treating the male executive as though he were a bachelor with little more than suitcases to pack in response to the call to higher achievements. Men do want to achieve. Their career is an entity in and of itself. But for the family man, there are dual priorties, and the corporation can no longer treat his wife and family as just an adjunct to his life. If corporations want to get the best out of one partner in a marriage, they would do well to ensure that the other partner is getting something out of that relationship as well.

CHAPTER NINE

From Infancy to Old Age: Family Stages

Train up a child in the way he should go: and when he is old, he will not depart from it.

Proverbs 22:6

Little by little the child in her dies.
You say, "I have lost a child, but gained a friend."
You feel yourself gradually discarded.

Randall Jarrell, "The Lost Children"

Grow old along with me!
The best is yet to be,
The last of life, for which
The first was made.

Robert Browning, "Rabbi Ben Ezra"

CLAUDIA DREIFUS

Shall I Go Back to Work?

Several young, highly educated women talk to writer Claudia Dreifus about their concerns and efforts in the difficult task of harmonizing their mother-hood with already-established careers. These are all women who have some choice about working and are committed to their jobs. Yet they face problems and conflicts. One of the most engaging things that emerges in the discussion is the extent to which these highly developed women found motherhood compelling and captivating. To some, this came as an unanticipated claim on their emotions and plans.

Note: More and more young women today are choosing to establish themselves in a job or career before starting a family. Their idea is to wait to have a child until they're in their 30s and then, after a few months or a year, return to work. But though this plan may sound fine in theory, in practice it can present unexpected conflicts. To find out how some of these new mothers are faring, *McCall's* invited a group of them to share their experiences with writer Claudia Dreifus. Participating in the discussion were: ISABEL, 36, the director of an anti-poverty organization and mother of Miriam, six months old; MARGARET, 31, a second-year psychiatry resident, mother of two-month-old Justin; ELIZABETH, 39, an executive secretary, mother of Peter, 20 months; ALICE, 34, a teacher, mother of Eleanor, six months old; and JOANNA, 33, an art historian, mother of six-month-old Steven.

JOANNA: I'm going through a crisis . . . and it's a bad one, and it hurts. Six months ago, when my son Steven was born, I took a leave of absence from my job. I'm supposed to go back part time on Monday, and now the

Reprinted by permission of the McCall Publishing Company from the October 1979 issue of *McCall's*.

thought of being away from Steven is turning me into an absolute wreck. For much of the day I've been debating calling my boss and telling him, "Forget it. There's no way I can return." I've been working all my adult life, and I think I'm very eager for success. Nevertheless, the idea of working suddenly feels impossible. Giving birth changed me in ways that were surprising. Steven and I have this strong, symbiotic relationship. Somehow, I can't get over the idea that I may be hurting him by returning.

CLAUDIA: What kind of work do you do?

JOANNA: Wonderful work. I work at a museum in a program I invented. I write plays about art history and give lectures and do all kinds of things to make art come alive. It's the kind of job that's so wonderful that if someone offered me thirty thousand dollars a year to work elsewhere, I'd refuse. The issue isn't the job—the issue is Steven. Funny, before he was born, I never thought I'd be happy staying at home. Once he was there, though, I was amazed to find I could spend hours just staring at him, feeding him. Some of my ambivalence about returning to work comes from my own feelings about my mother. She was a totally committed working mother—the kind of woman who'd die if she had to stay home for more than ten minutes. I have wonderful memories of her being a warm and zany clown, but I want to be different with Steven. She worked six days a week. We saw her Sundays and evenings. I still have some resentments, but even that's not the issue here. What *is* the issue is that my own motherhood is much better than I expected, and I feel sick about going back to work next week. Honestly, I don't know how all of this is going to work out for me.

MARGARET: Joanna, I went through the same thing a couple of weeks ago. It does work itself out—you'll see. While I was pregnant, I was absolutely, unequivocally convinced I'd go back to work right away. The pressures on me to do that were—are—enormous. The hospital where I do my residency is tremendously understaffed, and my not going back would have put a huge work burden on my colleagues. I could just hear people saying to themselves, "Damn women, admit them to the medical profession and they make life harder for everyone!" There was also a very real fear that I'd be hurting my medical career by interrupting training.

Well, what happened was that I was totally unprepared for the reality of motherhood—particularly for the symbiosis you speak of. Unless you grow up in a family where there are lots of children, the first baby you have any real contact with is your own. Me, I naïvely thought it would be easy to go back. I was all primed to return, and then Justin started smiling for the first time—that was when he was a month old—and all of a sudden motherhood seemed so marvelous that all I could think was: "I can't go back and miss all these fantastic subtle things that are happening to him . . . I can't go back because I might damage him."

Well, I did go back, and it was agony. The first day I saw patients. Between visits, I'd run to the bathroom and cry my eyes out. The predominant feeling was one of being physically torn from Justin.

CLAUDIA: Was five weeks too early?

MARGARET: Much too early. But there's so much pressure, and there's no one around to give you advice on what is reasonable. After all, there really hasn't been a generation of American women who were balancing work and family the way we are. When I came home that first night, I swore I'd quit. "I'll take three years off and then I'll resume my residency wherever I can," I told my husband. It was a crazy idea—crazy. You see, I come from a working-class background. Going to school, becoming a physician, expanded my life in ways that are tremendously important to me. If I quit for three years, I wasn't likely later to find a residency that was as good as the one I now hold. It was my husband who finally said, "Go back part time and see how that works out." I did. But it's hard.

ISABEL: I'm also undecided about what to do. I wish I could say, "I'll go back and everything will be all right." Part of why I've been staying at home has to do with the unexpected pleasures of motherhood and the other part with the mixed pleasures of work. I'm on a year's leave that started out as a three-month leave. Now I'm wondering if that one-year leave shouldn't become a three- or four-year leave—which really means giving up my job. Before Miriam was born, I was director of an anti-poverty project in the Bronx; it was something I built through fourteen back-breaking years of knocking myself out for other people. Then Miriam came, and I discovered I was wild about her, and motherhood was far more interesting than it had been advertised to be.

CLAUDIA: What's wrong with the job?

ISABEL: There were problems. My husband, Johnny, was my immediate superior—and people within the program were always trying to play us off against each other. The tension was unbelievable. I worked myself into such a state before Miriam was born that I was developing toxemia and the baby had to be taken by Caesarean. I'm a very driven person, a perfectionist. This program takes 300 percent of my energy. Lately, I've started wondering if I can do all that again. Now that Miriam's here, I'm not sure I can be a first-class project director and a first-class mother. Miriam's more important to me than anything else on earth.

CLAUDIA: Does anyone here feel an obligation to return to work based on— well, feminism? For the past ten years many women have been fighting hard for the right to a career, and now some of you are saying, "Well, my career may not be as important as motherhood."

MARGARET: Oh, I feel that kind of pressure strongly. First, there's such incredible discrimination against women in medicine, even now. A lot of

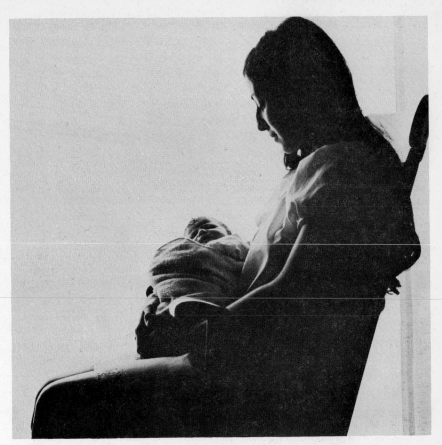

Dilemmas of Motherhood. Motherhood often poses unanticipated problems for career-oriented women. (Photograph by Muckley. Courtesy of Photophile.)

male doctors have a very particular view about what a women's proper place in life is—and they don't see it as competing with them. But even without that, I feel a kind of internal pressure to work. I can't deny that working is a big part of who I am, and, yes, I'd feel I had betrayed part of myself by quitting now.

ISABEL: Listen, I don't just worry about hurting the cause of women if I don't return; I worry about hurting the cause of the *poor*. My program was a very special kind of thing because of the hard work I gave to it. Maybe it's egotism, but I do wonder if things will function without me. The other day one of the staff women called and said, "If you don't come back, I'm quitting. I don't intend to work for some bureaucrat who's going to ruin this thing." Talk about pressure—how do you resist that?

The motherhood thing is going so *well* for me! I've done all the external things that the world says you're supposed to be proud of. I've been "big tough Isabel" all my adult life, and here I am learning these soft female skills, things that aren't easy for me, and I don't want to give them up. Sometimes I wonder if I should have another baby right away, and then I think, "Isabel, you'll never get back to your job." Then I start to think, "Isabel, what's wrong with motherhood as a career for the next five years? You can always try something else later."

CLAUDIA: Can you? I'm wondering if a woman really *can* be the chairman of the board if she interrupts the prime years of her work life.

MARGARET: The way things are set up now, you have to choose. I know that for me, now that Justin is here, certain kinds of career advancements are really difficult. I've had to make peace with that. I'll never be chief resident. I'll probably, for a while, not do interesting research or publish certain kinds of papers that lead to professional advancement. There just isn't time for everything.

ISABEL: Even if there were time, I wonder about energy. I have a limited amount of intense energy to give out. Right now, it's reserved for my daughter.

ALICE: Isabel, your fear is mine exactly. I teach—or I did till Eleanor was born six months ago. When I took a year's leave. I thought I'd use the time to find out what else I wanted to do with my life—beyond teaching. You just have so much energy in a day for being around children. I don't want to come home to Eleanor drained. Well . . . it's all kind of moot, this speculation, because my husband lost his job the other day, and I'm going to have to go back to work. We need the money. Max, my husband, is going to stay home with Eleanor. He's a very loving guy, and I'm glad that it's now possible for a child to have her father raise her, but, still, I'm sad. We'd have both preferred a fifty-fifty deal. This morning we were lying in bed, and we both looked at her and thought about how wonderful she was. Max said, "Wouldn't it be wonderful if society rewarded parenting? Wouldn't it be great if we lived in an ideal world and if parents were given stipends to spend the first few years with their children? Then a baby could have both parents." We feel sad that one of us has to become the predominant parent. I feel particularly sad about going back to teaching.

ELIZABETH: None of you has said anything positive yet about working. For me, enjoyment of my job has been a positive side effect of motherhood. Let me explain. I gave birth to Peter when I was thirty-seven: I'd been married a year, and I terribly wanted the baby. After all, I had waited a long time for the right man. Well, when Peter was born, I took a six-month leave, thinking all along that I wouldn't return to work: I wanted to be home with this marvelous, much-desired child: I also had a lot of feelings about possibly hurting Pete if I went back too early. Well, when I came to the end of my six-month leave, I noted that my life had gotten much too child-oriented. Everything in my day revolved around him. All I talked about was, "Pete did this and Pete did that." It wasn't good for him. It wasn't good for me, the way I constantly concentrated on him. Suddenly, going to a job seemed like the greatest pleasure: being a whole person and not just an extension of a child. Besides, we desperately needed a second income. My husband was married before and has large child-support payments to make. Still, I would have stayed home, taken out loans . . . whatever, if we thought it important for the baby to have me with him all the time.

ALICE: Is your job interesting?

ELIZABETH: Well, it has many interesting aspects, and it is satisfying to me at this time. What it does do is balance my life in a way that full-time motherhood couldn't. I feel proud of myself at work, and my husband does, too. When I get a raise, he just beams—not just because of the extra money, but because I've accomplished something and other people recognize it. Another thing, it's fairly easy for me to go to work because I was lucky enough to find a good school for the baby. He goes from eight-thirty to five-thirty, and there are only five children in the school—it's really not a school but a play group with a qualified teacher. He dances and listens to piano and has contact with people he'd never know if he were just home with me. Believe me, good child care can do a lot to free a woman from the guilt she might feel about returning to work.

JOANNA: I wouldn't feel guilty—I'd feel cheated. I feel a positive desire to be home with Steven! When you work at a paying job, you feel the goodies of accomplishment eighty percent of the time; at home, with my beautiful son, the goodies are one hundred percent.

The truth is that I've changed a lot since Steven's birth. My ambition has slowed down tremendously. It's not that I've abandoned my work; it's just that Steven is first fiddle, work is second fiddle. A lot of feminists try to make me feel guilty about that, and I think that's garbage. It makes perfect sense for my career to take second place right now. There'll be another time, when the baby is older, when work can be the main part of my life. Now, the only way I can think about work is that the income is needed and that I'm keeping in touch with my field for a later period when I'll be more active again. Work's not the essence of my existence. Making Steven a wonderful and secure person *is*. I deeply resent anyone who says this is wrong. Coming from where I came from, staying home with my son is . . . a revolutionary act.

ELIZABETH: Joanna, maybe one of the reasons you find being at home so exciting is because you've had the choice of work or full-time motherhood. My mother never did. Women didn't work. "It wasn't done." She was a fine mother, but she never was in a position to question it. A lot of women of her generation did feel trapped.

MARGARET: I'm wondering if some of the ambivalence women feel has to do with the nature of work. For most people, there's very little in their lives that's unequivocally creative and joyful. A job is rarely that. But then you have this baby and every minute is a thrill.

JOANNA: What you just said, Margaret, doesn't relate to any of us here. Again, for me, it's not a choice of not going back to work because the job is bad, but because mothering is *better*.

ALICE: Wait a second! Some of my anxiety does come from my negative feelings about teaching. I was very dissatisfied. I felt I was more creative than the job required. For a while my husband and I talked about starting a business that would sell children's clothing and serve as a child-care center at the same time. The store would give us a chance to fuse our interests and also split the child rearing more evenly. But when Max lost his job, my ambivalence about teaching disappeared. I had no doubt about returning to work to maintain my family's security. Still, this horrible feeling sank into the pit of my stomach: "I'm not going to be with my baby all day. I don't want to go back to school."

CLAUDIA: Since we all agree that parenting is fabulous, and since no one here has a million-dollar trust fund, can we talk about some of the social changes that would make it easier for women to have both a family and work? Perhaps the ideal would be to have husbands and wives sharing everything equally?

ALICE: In theory, that would be ideal. But society's institutions aren't set up to accommodate working parents who want to share. The Board of Education in New York does allow fathers to take a year's paternity leave, but they are about the only employer I've ever heard of who does that. If you want to share a child and have both parents work part time, lots of luck. Just about the only way you can do that is to be self-employed.

JOANNA: Jim and I did a lot of talking about sharing our baby fifty-fifty. We sat down with paper and pencil and very quickly discovered that two half salaries didn't make for one whole one. On paper what we had were two less-than-half salaries and no benefits. We finally concluded that the way things were set up a family needs at least one full-time salary to survive on.

ISABEL: And that salary tends to be the husband's salary. Last year Johnny and I started thinking about how we could share the baby more. The speculation ended the minute we realized he earns twice what I do. In most families, men tend to earn twice the wife's salary. You can say it's unjust and unfair, but when you've got three mouths to feed and all kinds of new expenses, plus the problems of inflation, you go with the bigger salary. And then you end up with a situation like the one I have. Johnny is working, as he always has, eleven, twelve hours a day. He isn't sharing in the day-to-dayness of the baby in any meaningful way. He's crazy about her, but he can't be as involved as I am. It's lucky that I'm adoring motherhood because otherwise I *would* feel trapped.

ALICE: Claudia, you asked earlier what kinds of social changes we'd like to see to make us feel less anxious about work. One obvious answer is: an adjustment in employment practices so that parents could afford to split child rearing.

CLAUDIA: What about switching roles . . . having the man stay at home?

ALICE: That's what Max and I are doing—though it isn't exactly our first-choice solution. I guess you could say that we're lucky that times have changed enough for that to happen and be a positive experience. For me, it's easy because Max is a really good father. He has two daughters from his first marriage, and he's always been wonderfully responsible and loving with them. Still, knowing that Eleanor is in good hands isn't enough. *I* want to be there, too. I feel I'm going to be missing out on something big by going back to work. I probably won't see the first time she gets up and walks or any of that.

JOANNA: Even if my job paid enough for us to divide the child rearing, I wouldn't want to go back full time. You know, ever since Steven was born, I find myself accepting all these values that I thought I'd rejected years ago. Like: "The man should be the breadwinner." and: "The woman should stay at home." A few months ago Jim suggested the possibility of *his* staying home full time and my going to work. I was horrified! While I thought it might be wonderful for Steven to have his father mothering him, I was jealous.

MARGARET: Jealousy is really natural. *I* feel jealous of everyone who spends any time with Justin . . . my husband, the baby-sitter. When you have a new baby, you go through falling in love, and when you're in love, you get jealous.

CLAUDIA: What you're saying makes me think that it's very difficult for people to change traditional sex roles.

JOANNA: Well, all I know is that I had great ambitions for us not to take on sexist roles, and somehow it's happened. Most of it has to do with my being at home and Jim working. I do a lot of the housework because when he gets home I want him to spend as much time as possible with Steven. I don't know if there's any solution.

CLAUDIA: To change the subject slightly, I'm wondering if some of these anti-work feelings come from the fact that adequate child-care facilities are few and far between. How can anyone pursue a career with peace of mind when it's so terribly hard to find somewhere decent to leave the child?

MARGARET: That was part of our problem. When we were looking for some arrangement for Justin, everything seemed like a nightmare. First, there was something so unreal about setting up a financial arrangement with a stranger to have him or her do the most precious work on earth for you. How can you put *that* on a monetary basis? Then, there's the fact that day care for infants is impossible to find—and, besides, we didn't want day care for a baby as young as Justin. At first we interviewed potential housekeepers, but they were all disasters—people I'd be afraid to leave him with for two minutes. In the end, we were lucky in finding a woman in the neighborhood who had some children of her own and who adored having a baby in the house. Actually, the search for a good solution depressed me as much as going back to work did. That first day on the job I was convinced I was hurting Justin by sending him to a baby-sitter. Oh, the guilt! Then, when I picked him up, I found this smiling baby and I was even more depressed: He was happy without me!

ISABEL: It's too facile to say, "If there were good day-care facilities, then one could go back to work in peace." Sure, good day care is an absolute necessity for those tens of thousands of women who have to work: but the availability or the lack of it doesn't make much difference to those of us who are contemplating staying home because we want to.

ALICE: I disagree. I think some of the answer lies in having day-care centers at places of work—like they have in Scandinavia. Then you could be with your child during lunch and during coffee breaks, and you wouldn't feel so torn.

ELIZABETH: All I know is that Peter and I are both better off now that he's at his little school. His life is wider because he gets more experiences than he'd get with just me. It wasn't easy to find a good place for him, and without it I could forget working. A housekeeper would be too expensive: her salary would eat up mine. This way I go back to work knowing he's in a good situation, and I come home and I'm fresh and ready to give him lots of love.

CLAUDIA: Earlier Joanna suggested that people these days have reversed themselves: In the past the woman who worked was ostracized: now it's the woman who stays home.

JOANNA: What I meant is that all this feminist pressure to work negates how really wonderful motherhood is.

generation creates a new *Zeitgeist* and develops a new tone and style; but each generation of adolescents does so by recombining elements that are provided by the generation of adults.

First, then, a look at the interrelation between adolescents and adults, i.e., the structure of the relationship within which they socialize each other. The adolescent tasks are by their very nature well-designed to exert regressive pulls on parents. Consider two examples.

1. The child at puberty is confronted with a radical restructuring of the internal environment. The infusion of hormones into the system stimulates new drives, moods, and fantasies. The psychological problem for the youngster is the integration of these new realities into a developing concept of the self. The fact of adult genital capability requires a restructuring of his interpersonal world and of his experience and expression of love. The adolescent must learn to integrate sex with love and affection. Until this point the incest taboo has required the child to segregate sexual feelings from ties of love, since the significant loves to this point have been members of the child's own family.

The problem for the parents, on the other hand, is to keep sex and love neatly segregated in the face of the child's palpable new sexuality. And this is no easy trick. Here is the parent, accustomed over the years to a relationship of closeness, affection, tenderness with his child—a relationship uncomplicated by sexual conflicts. Now all of a sudden what had been taken for granted and filled with pleasure is disrupted by the subtle intrusion of sexuality. The tickling, the sitting on daddy's lap becomes overcast with a hint of danger, conflict, the need for controls where none previously needed to be invoked.

2. The adolescent task presses the youngster to withdraw cathexis from the family and to reinvest it in the peer group where he experiments in forming and dissolving relationships and group attachments and begins the work of identity formation—of detecting continuity in the self in the face of discontinuity of the interpersonal setting. A side feature of this process—and absolutely necessary as an accumulation of cathexis and energy for the large work of discovering or creating a self—is a significant measure of narcissism. The youngster becomes self-absorbed.

The parents, meanwhile, are exactly at that stage of development in which the self is defined by its roles and relationships to others. They measure themselves by their interdependencies and mutualities. They are nothing if not workers, parents, marriage partners, citizens, friends. The network of interdependent relationships forms, for the generative adult, the meaning of life and the definition of self. When the child pulls out of the family—at least emotionally and perhaps also geographically—the parents are left with their parenting needs and behaviors dangling. They need to parent and they need the parent role as one of their self-defining elements. But there is no longer a child to receive the parenting, no longer a reciprocal to their parent role.

Berry's World

Reprinted by permission. © 1979 NEA, Inc.

What do parents do in this situation? Ideally they recognize interdependence as a relationship of many forms and say to the child by their behavior: now your needs require a *new* kind of relationship, a new stage of our developing interdependence. You need to have freedom to explore and form yourself outside the bounds of the family. I will give you this freedom, this distance. I will also grant you new recognition as an autonomous being. What you need from me has changed. That you need something remains.

And ideally the child will have the sensitivity and empathy to give the parents room and credit for their new form of parenting.

But things are not always so ideal, and even in the best of circumstances the shift in relationship is likely to be experienced by the parents as a loss. No matter how we phrase it and no matter how likely particular parents are to enjoy a newly based and more adult relationship with their children, the fact is that they have lost the little child and the baby they once enjoyed—their youth, along with the expectations and unjaded hopes they had when that baby was little. The emerging adulthood of one's children must at some level register as the signal of one's own decline.

So parents respond variously when their children withdraw their emotional chips. Some make use of old mechanisms learned in previous encounters in which a threat was posed by the other. They may identify with the child in a paradoxically reversed repetition of their identification in childhood with an overwhelmingly powerful parent. Though the roles are reversed, the threat and the process invoked are the same. They may—as increasing numbers of women have done in the last ten years—return to their own identity task and regroup emotional resources for a new self-investment and self-definition. They may decide to take up painting, or find a new career opportunity, or look to the issue of refurbishing their marriage relationship which, having given and stretched to accommodate children, may by this time have become quite threadbare except in the area of their intense parallel concern with child-rearing.

However they respond in the long run, the parents must experience separation from the child—and mourn the loss. Depending on the particular conditions of separation and the extent to which the child's emerging adulthood represents a shocking discrepancy between the parents' aspiration and accomplishment, it will leave the parents either ready to move on to a new stage in the parent role or dashed and disillusioned with life.

In my experience—and despite all of our popular mythology about the controlling mother who cannot give up her children and tries with all her means to keep them dependent—it is fathers who suffer adolescents' separation most acutely. Often, I think, the child's assertion of autonomy comes as a ruder shock to the father who has not been so intimately involved as the mother has in the child's many smaller departures during childhood. It also often comes—this first and final move toward independence—at a time when the father is having to face the fact that he is not going to realize all of his ambitions in work—that point when many men look at themselves in the mirror and ask, "Is this all there is?" The combination of disappointment in work and loss of control of the child can precipitate a crisis or a period of acting out which in turn can lead to dissolution of the family.

I will come back to the family and discuss ways in which both child and parent can be helped to accept the changing nature of their relationship without rejecting the relationship and their interdependence as such. But here, on the level of culture, let us consider ways in which contemporary critics in our society have conceived adolescence and responded to it, and how their views differ from those of other times and other cultures.

What I want to note first in the views of the Handlins, Midge Decter, and other critics of youth is the fact that they no longer assume the narcissism of adolescence to be part of a developmental phase which has clear limits. Their apparent fear is based on the assumption that the features they find appalling in the young—narcissism, marginalism, unwillingness to postpone gratification—are historical phenomena which mark this generation and will continue as their style throughout adulthood and old age. They attach such characteristics to various causal forces—Dr. Benjamin Spock and child-centered techniques of child-rearing, affluence, the liberalism of parents in post-World War II America. But whatever the cause, it is viewed as a historical stamp which distinguishes this generation of young from all which have gone before.

They do not, in other words, attach the traits they dislike to a stage in normal life development but rather to the generation as such and for all of life.

In earlier periods this is not the way people thought about adolescence. People were highly aware of adolescence as a stage, even if they had no name for it. Those who were young, yet physically mature, sexual but not included in the institutional structures that allowed legitimate sexual expression, were seen as special, as possessing energy and powers which were without channels in the organized life of the adult community. All recorded societies seem to provide some mechanisms for organizing these powers in the service of the group life or at least of neutralizing their potential for destructiveness. Natalie Davis and other historians have catalogued the courts of misrule and other youth groups and have described their functions.

In the past people complained of youth. We are all familiar with the wonderfully contemporary-sounding quotations from Plato and other philosophers down through the ages inveighing against the young. They all share the general message that the generation about to take over is dissolute, without character, and going to hell in a handcart.

What they do not share with some of today's critics is the latter's finality, a time perspective which extends across the life span. All of the early complaints clearly see adolescence or youth as finite and their problems as eventually dissolving in the responsibilities and privileges of adulthood to which youth will eventually succeed. The traditional complaint was one of timing—that youth were not moving briskly enough to the inevitable next stage in their development. Plato, George Bernard Shaw, and Booth Tarkington all saw the youth of their day as self-centered, self-indulgent, and irresponsible. But they say nothing final or historically absolute about such traits. In their conceptual scheme, youth was a stage with a beginning and an end, and the end of the offending traits would come when this youth cohort, like all cohorts before, took its place as adults. No one doubted that youth would end and adulthood would take over.

What distinguishes contemporary complaints about youth and adds to the weight of anxiety they carry, is the sense they have that adulthood may *not* be inevitable, that adolescents may never grow up, that the character of the contemporary cohort of youth may have been marked by historical factors so indelible that youth will never mature but will carry self-absorption and irresponsibility along with them into adulthood and beyond.

Why? Why are we so apprehensive about our young? Why do we doubt that they will grow up just like all previous generations? Is it really, as Midge Decter claims, because our desire to make life beautiful and nurturing for them in childhood was really a cover for lack of commitment—that we made their lives beautiful in order not to have to cross them, to take the role of ultimate authority, and that in essence we abandoned them by this choice?

Or is our fear not perhaps grounded on the fact that our concepts of the goal of growth—adulthood—have become shaky and unclear? In earlier generations people worried less about youth getting stuck at their stage because they could see quite clearly what other generations had come to, they knew that adulthood would overtake the young, and they were satisfied with their vision of what that adulthood would be.

In our time, on the other hand, the image and definition of adulthood has become confused. Does adulthood mean commitment, restraint, mutuality, responsibility, and abandoning the idea of "instant gratification"? But where do we find these characteristics in adult life, and where do we find adults who not only practice such virtues but derive both satisfaction and self-definition from the practice? In the husbands and fathers who leave their families in middle life because they have found their true love and have answered their question, "Is this all there is?" with a resounding "No" and gone off to start a new family? In the women who leave families because they now discover an inner voice or talent which they must realize? In an economic system that urges people to "go now, pay later" and stimulates needs and desires which can only be gratified on an installment plan if at all? In political leaders who excoriate the young for their laziness, lack of ambition, immorality, and searching for the easy way, but all along are themselves accepting bribes and using their high offices to reap illegitimate, easy, and instant rewards? In the adults who frequent encounter groups, vacation at Esalen, and dress like adolescents? . . .

Data on the values, attitudes, and personal integrations of youth have been accumulating now for twenty-five to thirty years. The generalization that emerges most clearly from the studies is that, by and large, the values and identities of youth will strongly reflect parental values and identity. In studies of political and religious attitudes, of delinquency, alienation, radicalism, and of broad patterns of adjustment, the results point to the same conclusion. If our children reject the idea of having children it is because in our parenting of them we have not communicated the joys of parenting. If they do not accept authority unquestioningly it is because we have taught them to think for themselves. If they are self-indulgent and seek instant gratification they have access to adult models who are equally so. If they refuse to grow up it may be that they cannot get a handle on the satisfaction and self-definitions which come from that role.

In a recent article reviewing research in the field, a thoughtful social scientist made the following observations:

> "Child-rearing is no longer a source of personal meaning. In this post-modern era, children may damage rather than enhance their parents' self-esteem by repudiating their central values. Further erosion of parental authority, if it should occur, is likely to be accompanied by an increase in rejection by parents of adolescents; adults may well abandon their parental role earlier in the life cycle. The reduction of legal age status to age eighteen may be a first important step designed to liberate parents from their children."

Who is rejecting whom? And where do we find anything in this statement about the satisfactions of parenthood and adulthood? Parenting is reduced to hardships from which one seeks liberation. In what traditional system were parents promised "personal meaning" from children? The role of parent is in part to transmit meaning to children, to help them discover legitimate sources of personal meaning. No child can make a parent's life meaningful if the parent has not in his own search for meaning discovered the traditional and committing role of parent to be one crucial source of that meaning.

This quotation seems to me to be looking for a rationalization for parents' abandoning the parent role and their children. Are children really rejecting parents' values and authority, or are they rather expressing and giving behavioral form to the parents' lack of commitment and individual self-seeking?

The task for all societies and all parents is to present an image of adulthood which attracts the young and makes the struggle to grow up worth it. Can we develop for our young some such model?

One interesting development over the last ten to fifteen years has been the remarkable turn of the young toward the very old. Beginning with the hippies but continuing on, the youth culture has developed a significant respect for really old people. Old men who, for years, had wandered on our campus with complete anonymity are now approached and engaged in conversation. Young students in graduate school decided that their real interest in socialization and development lay in the upper reaches of age distribution, not in early childhood. Jessamyn West's story, "Sixteen"—about a young woman's growth in response to her grandfather's imminent death—became a favorite.

Gutman theorized that contemporary youth were in many respects psychologically like the very old. *Harold and Maude* became an underground film classic.

What I make of this affinity is another sign of the muddy and ambiguous picture we have of adulthood. The young look to the very old as perhaps the right consultants about adulthood. After all, the old have successfully navigated the period. Perhaps the young are looking for a definition of adulthood with which they can identify.

LILLIAN B. RUBIN

Women of a Certain Age

In this introduction to her book, Women of a Certain Age, *Lillian Rubin speaks eloquently of the dilemmas and conflicts that face the woman in middle age when she has completed her major childraising function and looks ahead to thirty years of life with no crucial life work. What will she do with her days? Rubin describes her own creative and courageous response to the challenge of midlife.*

I am a midlife woman. Like most women of my generation, I gave over much of my adult life to marriage and motherhood. Like so many others, I awoke one day from the childhood dream that I would be forever cared for—that being some man's wife and some child's mother would occupy my mind and my hands for the rest of my life. And I lay on my couch, listened to music, and wept with despair.

I was thirty-eight years old, already divorced and remarried to a man with whom I expected to spend the rest of my life, the mother of a beautiful fourteen-year-old daughter whom I loved dearly. But it wasn't enough. My daughter was busy with her teenage activities, my husband with his career. And I? I awoke each day wondering how to fill the time, wondering how I'd ever gotten into this fix, wondering how I'd ever get out.

But it was only 1962. The women's movement hadn't yet arrived to reassure me that others suffered a similar anguish. Betty Friedan had not yet given my feelings a voice, had not yet given my problem a name. So I suffered silently and, I thought, alone.

Abridged from pp. 1–11 "Of Beginnings and Endings" in *Women of a Certain Age: The Midlife Search for Self* by Lillian B. Rubin. Copyright © by Lillian B. Rubin. By permission of Harper & Row, Publishers, Inc.

I had until then spent my life in and out of the labor force, sometimes doing small jobs, sometimes bigger ones. When restlessness overcame guilt, I went to work. When guilt won out, I quit. In between working for wages, I worked without wages, often putting in longer days and nights in volunteer labors than I would ever have permitted myself to do at paid work. But no complaints. It was better than staying at home wondering how to keep useful and busy. And more importantly, those volunteer jobs—for me, done mostly in the political arena where I have a lifelong interest—kept me connected to the world and taught me skills that I was able to turn into reasonably well-paid work in the period of my divorce.

But here I was, married again and living in another city—four hundred miles from the political community I knew so well, four hundred miles from old friends. Four hundred or four thousand—in such moments in life, they are effectively the same. I felt isolated, lonely, and furious with myself. I had a man I loved and a child I loved. What was the matter with me? Why wasn't I happy? What did I expect of life anyway?

In 1962, I had no answers. But shout at myself as loud as I could, rage at myself as much as I would, none of it helped; nothing abated the restless yearning inside me—a yearning that called for something more, something different, in this life of mine.

I tried to go back to the world of volunteers. But it didn't work. Once having been paid to do the same kind of work, it felt odd, awkward, almost disrespectful to myself to work without pay.

But returning to the paid work force had its own problems. Without a college degree, the only way I could get a job that would interest me was through personal contacts—through people who knew me, people who were willing to put aside bureaucratic regulations because they believed in me. And I had left all of them behind when I married and moved those four hundred miles away.

As I recall that time, I'm met with an inner sense of shock—shock, not because I gave up the life I had built for marriage, but because it never occurred to me not to. I remind myself: It was only 1962, five years before most women even thought such thoughts. And I ask myself: Would I do it differently today? And I ask you: Would you?

I had two choices. One, to pack up and go back to the life I had left. The other, to go to school. Both filled me with dread. Although I had always mourned the fact that I had been too poor to go to college in my youth, at thirty-eight I was scared—scared of competing with talented, well-educated eighteen-year-olds, scared that I'd find I wasn't as bright as I wanted to think I was, as I wanted others to believe. Still, on balance, I suppose the other option looked the worse one. A year later, I went to school—a college freshman at thirty-nine. Eight hard but exciting years later, I left the campus with a doctorate in sociology and postdoctoral training in psychology.

Eight years—years when I was literally buried in my books, years when most family responsibilities took second place to my studies. Even as I write that sentence, I experience again the guilt. And I wonder: Do I really want to let it stand bald and naked that way? Can I really be comfortable telling the world that my family took second place to a term paper? I'm not comfortable, but I'll let it stand because I must if I'm to tell the truth about the price a woman with a family pays when she embarks on such a road.

Eight years of guilt and excitement playing counterpoint to each other—years of finding out who I am, what I can do; years of struggle and years of growth. None of it would have been possible without the support and cooperation of my husband and daughter; none of it possible without their protection, not only from their own needs, but from the criticisms and intrusions of friends and family who warned about the dangers to my marriage, the costs to my child. They were warnings well founded in observation and experience, it's true. When a woman embarks on such a course, her marriage often *is* under threat. But there was something else underlying these expressions of concern from people whose lives touched mine—something related to their own needs and their own resentments because I was no longer able to give them the time and attention they wanted. How often my brother's voice came across the miles of telephone line, anger masking his hurt: "Can I come to visit, or is my forty-year-old sister too busy doing her homework?" How often a friend responded to my inability to make a lunch date with: "Oh come on, surely you don't have to take it all *that* seriously." How often my mother sighed: "Some people are so lucky; their daughters come every Wednesday." And I suffered, even while I understood. On the one hand, she wanted another kind of life for me, a different kind of old age. On the other, her own need, her own emptiness, was intensely felt. And her fantasy still was that I could fill the void in her.

It's true, as Marya Mannes says: "No one believes [a woman's] time to be sacred. A man at his desk in a room wih a closed door is a man at work. A woman at a desk in any room is available." It's true, not only in a room in the family home, but on a college campus as well. Ask any woman who has served on a faculty how often a student will pass a male colleague's office to come into hers with a request. If she asks that student why he or she didn't go to the male professor next door—a man who serves on the same committee, can answer the same question, grant the same request, she's very likely to hear something like: "I didn't want to bother him; he always seems so busy." A man, at work or at home, is the symbolic father, not to be disturbed—too busy, too preoccupied with the large tasks of life. A woman is the symbolic mother—always nurturant, always available—even when she is at work.

It was in 1963 that I started back to school—the only person over twenty-five in any of my undergraduate classes. It was in 1963 that Marya Mannes wrote of the "long burden of guilt" creative women would bear for their desire to do their work. It was in 1963 that she said: "No woman with any heart can compose a paragraph when her child is in trouble or her husband ill; forever they take precedence over the companions of her mind."

Fifteen years have passed since then—fifteen years of political and social turmoil; fifteen years during which, one by one, different segments of the American society have stood and roared their grievances; fifteen years during which women, too, translated their personal injuries into a social movement. At first this new feminism . . . was treated as a bad joke, or passed off as the cry of a few malcontents. Now, . . . it is taken seriously enough to merit an articulate, highly organized, and well-financed opposition.

By the time the 1970s were well under way, however, the great force of radical social protest that had powered the decade before had turned inward— at least for that historical moment. That didn't mean, as some commentators have suggested, that the grievances went away, that people forgot their anger and their pain. It meant that, exhausted from the struggle with powerful institutions that resist change so ferociously, they turned inward for R & R. Only, instead of *rest and recreation,* for the activists of the sixties R & R meant *respite* and *reanalysis*—a reanalysis that sought to understand more firmly how individual consciousness and social institutions interact to maintain the existing structure of social arrangements.

Whatever the initial intent, that turning inward has been capitalized on in the popular commercial culture. The decade of the seventies has become the *Me* decade. Gone, or at least muted, not audible under all the noise, is the old ethos of duty and responsibility to others—exchanged for detailed instructions on how to look out for "number one." Dozens of books now appear regularly, all aimed at reminding millions of readers that their primary duty is to self.

Enter the midlife woman of the late 1970s. In its early years, the women's movement was by, for, and about the young. But these are times in which diffusion—whether in ideas or fashion—works both ways. The styles of the student and the peasant are taken up by the rich; the ideas of the young, embraced by the old. Today's midlife woman had lived by the old rules—rules that promised kudos, congratulations, and fulfillment of self for giving up her own life to meet her responsibilities to others. Now, in the face of a movement that raises serious questions about her life, she wonders: What was it all about? Now, in the face of a culture that exhorts us all to a concern only for self, she asks: Is that really the kind of life I want for me? For my children? Now, in the face of a departing family and a lifetime of empty days, she worries: What am I going to do with the rest of my life?

It's a strange time, midlife, perhaps especially for women—a time of endings, and also a time of beginnings. As with all endings, there's pain, and the sadness of loss. But *this* ending brings with it also relief—relief because a task undertaken is finished, one phase of life done; relief because it presages a beginning.

Beginnings, too, carry with them a complex set of feelings. There's fear of the unknown, and anxiety about the capacity to meet whatever life's new challenges may be. And there's excitement, too—the excitement of a heightened sense of adventure. Life takes on a new charge, an increased energy; there are new possibilities, perhaps to develop potentialities only dreamed of before. Maybe there's even a second chance. . . .

With more of us living longer, healthier lives than ever before, more of us live through a period of middlehood, and more of us must deal with the choices, tasks, and changes that time of life requires. Since we now have fewer children in this eighth decade of our century—2.3 per family compared to 3.3 in the 1900s—women today bear their *last* child younger than before, which means they reach the end of their child*rearing* period earlier as well.

Those two facts alone account for a dramatic change in family life—a change that has important implications for both the marriage relationship and for the way the individuals within it will live their lives. At the turn of the century, the average couple could expect to survive together for just over a year and a half after their last child married. Now, they can expect to live together without children under their roof for just under thirteen years before death takes one of them (most likely the husband) off.

But why talk about marriage when everyone knows that the divorce rate is spiraling crazily? Why worry about who lives together and for how long when everywhere we turn we hear that the nuclear family is dying, that marriage will soon be a relic of an archaic past? The answer: Because some respected population analysts already are predicting that the divorce rate is, at the very least, stabilizing, and possibly heading for a decline. Because right now, well over three-fourths of the population between the ages of twenty and sixty-four are married. Because in almost 85 percent of *all* families, a husband and wife live together. . . . Because even if the rising divorce rate eventually means that one-third of all first marriages are dissolved, two out of three couples will remain married "until death do them part." And finally, because three-fourths of the women and five-sixths of the men who divorce eventually remarry, usually within a three-year period.

And among midlife people—those between thirty-five and fifty-four? Despite the rising divorce rate, 82 percent of the women in that age bracket and 87 percent of the men are married, by far the vast majority of them in stable, long-term first marriages. For the women who live in those marriages, the increasing life span and the decreasing number of years spent in bearing and rearing children have come together to present them with a set of problems and opportunities unknown to earlier generations.

There are today nearly 25 million women in America between the ages of thirty-five and fifty-four—about one-fourth of the total female population of the country, compared to less than 20 percent eighty years ago. If the projections of government demographers are accurate, these figures will increase to almost 40 million and 30 percent respectively by the end of the century. The future aside, today's statistics alone make a powerful argument for attending to the problems of women at midlife. For they are the largest segment of the adult female population.

Twenty-five million women—at least half of them awakening daily to wonder how to fill the time. *Twenty-five million women*—the other half managing to keep busy, often at paid jobs, sometimes not, but, in any case, rarely ever anywhere near to tapping their talents and potential. . . .

LILLIAN E. TROLL,
SHEILA J. MILLER,
AND ROBERT C. ATCHLEY

Families in Later Life

*With greatly increased longevity today, most adults live to see their children
become adults with children of their own. In addition, many adults—particularly women, whose life expectancy is higher than men's—can expect to live
alone for a considerable period in later life. What are the relationships
between older parents and their adult children? How do older persons weather
the loss of a spouse and adapt to life alone? What factors affect the ease or
difficulty of their adaptation? In the following article, a group of researchers
who have studied changes during our life spans consider these and related
questions.*

Adult-Child/Older-Parent Relations over the Life Course

Studies of older-parent/adult-child relations have looked mainly at the
launching stage, when parents are in early middle age, and at aged parents
and their middle-aged children. Furthermore, wide age and developmental
ranges tend to be collapsed into single categories. There is no research on two
categories of parents and children: those where the children are in their thirties
and early forties and those where the children are themselves past middle age.
Findings have been reported on the close links between newly married couples
and their parents. On one hand is the American norm that requires independence of the newly married couple. They are expected to establish a home
separate from both sets of parents *(neolocal)*, raise their children according
to "absolute" criteria for "correct" childrearing and not listen to the "old-
fashioned wisdom" of their grandparents (whom most psychotherapists see
chiefly as malevolent influences on nuclear family integration and childrearing

success), and be economically independent by virtue of the young husband's own efforts and successes. In actual fact, most young couples seem to live reasonably close to both sets of parents, receive help in the form of either services (such as babysitting) or money (more in the middle class), and visit frequently.

At the other end of the age scale is an opposite stereotype. The old parent is believed to want dependence on his adult children, to demand money and services, and to move in with children where possible, though generally to be neglected and unwanted. Again, the facts are just the opposite. Most old parents prefer to live alone, though they live near and see their children frequently and there seems to be as much reciprocity as dependence in services and money, with aged parents continuing to help their children as long as they can.

What happens in the years between? Are the bonds between the nuclear units continued throughout? Or do they loosen gradually and only tighten again as the parents retire? Does the involvement of adult children in rearing their own children loosen ties with their parents? How influential is the adult child's career upon potential changes in ties with parents over the life course? The cross-sectional and longitudinal data we need to answer such questions are practically nonexistent.

The small sample of parents, studied by Lowenthal and associates (1975), who were middle-aged or approaching retirement

> . . . looked back to the time when their children were infants as the period of greatest parental happiness. In so doing, they may in part be indulging in pleasant recollections of their more youthful selves, or reflecting more contemporary experiences of carefree interaction with grandchildren. For the most part, they were nostalgic for a period free of parent-child conflict, a period when, whatever the stresses, the child's dependence on the parents is unquestioned and his expressions of love more frequent and direct . . . for older men the next most satisfying relationships occurred after the children had fully matured.

Some of the consequences of Blenkner's concept of *filial maturity* are important for a life-cycle theory of development. A basic corollary is the reciprocity of the developmental process. For the child to achieve filial maturity, the parent must participate in the process, first in a modeling capacity, and second in a rewarding capacity. There is reason to believe that the inverse is also true. For the parent to continue to develop, the child must participate in the process in both a modeling and a rewarding capacity. In other words, the significance of the parent/child relationship does not end with launching but continues throughout life. Parents and children who continue to develop throughout their lives—to accept their own development as meaningful and satisfying—are helping their children and parents to develop in turn. . . .

Sources of Change

There are several sources of change in adult-child/older-parent relationships. We will discuss retirement, widowhood, and divorce or separation.

Retirement can give older parents freedom to move nearer to their children. But retirement, with its average income decline of 50 percent, can also make traveling to visit adult children more difficult. For the most part, loss of job through retirement is not a source of declining prestige within the family. Those persons who own family businesses, however, can lose a good bit of power and influence upon retirement. For example, farmers who operate two- or three-generation family farms tend to lose their power over economic decision-making when they hand their farms down to their children. Consequently, many older farmers don't completely retire. They give up physical work, but continue to manage the farm.

Widowhood generally increases interaction with children during the bereavement period, but it has little long-run effect except for those widowed persons who move in with adult children or whose adult children move in with them. As we saw earlier, this is not a common pattern.

We do not know how divorce or separation affects adult-child/older-parent relationships. There are a good many ideas that could be studied. Do the children of divorced parents keep in touch with both parents? Is the frequency of contact affected by divorce? Are divorced parents as likely as widowed parents to receive aid from their children? Do older divorced mothers become financially dependent on their children more frequently than widows do? What effect does the timing of the divorce in the adult child's life have on the effect of divorce on parent/child relations? Does divorce affect parent/child relationships for mothers more than for fathers? The list of questions that need study is long.

Summary

Most older Americans have living children, and those who do are in close touch with them. They do not tend to live in the same household unless either parents or children are in such poor health that they cannot take care of themselves or unless financial circumstances make it necessary. That is, all prefer to be as autonomous and independent as they are able, and are happier when they can be so. When help is needed, however, it is available, most often from parent or child, much less frequently from more distant relatives. Parents and their adult children seem to prefer to live near each other, as witnessed by both prevalence and migration data. When they move apart for economic or career reasons, they tend to move closer together again later in life. How much of this enduring relationship is intrinsic strength of bonds, meaningfulness and enjoyment of each other's company, and how much is instrumental duty or obligation motivated by shame or guilt, we cannot say. It is not impossible, however, that all kinds of motives underlie such long-standing and complex relationships. Most ties are strongest between women—mothers and daughters—though ethnic and social class factors may mediate this tendency. Social class may be an important mediating factor in flow of help, with the oldest generation continuing to supply most help—particularly money—in middle and upper classes and the middle generation supplying to both older and younger generations in working and lower classes. Over time, family crises may lead to short-term increase or mobilization of interaction and help. Nevertheless, downward mobility of one member may eventuate in reduced interaction and help in the long run.

Consequences of Widowhood

Higher death rates among men and higher marriage rates among widowers result in five widows to every widower among older people. Thus, we often think of widowhood as something that happens mainly to women. Yet in 1975, almost one fourth of the men over seventy-five were widowed (and not remarried). This proportion has been decreasing recently, however. Since it is reasonable to assume that losing a spouse is a different experience for women and men, we will examine these two situations separately.

Women

In American society, the role of widow is a long-term one, particularly for older women. Actually, young widows are soon considered single again rather than widows. Because young widows are so much in the minority among their age peers, they tend to feel stigmatized. In contrast, older women see widowhood as more normal. Even as early as sixty-five, a third of all women are widows. Thus, the prevalence of widowhood in later life combines with low expectations for remarriage to produce a more definite social position for the older widow.

Even so, the role of older widow is a vague one. Ties with their husband's family may be drastically reduced, yet they are supposed to be interested in keeping his memory alive. They are also not supposed to be interested in men but to associate primarily with other widows or with their children.

Being a widow changes the basis of *self-identity* for those women for whom the role of wife and mother is central, having structured their lives not only in their households but also on the job. In answering the question, "Who am I?" such women would usually have put *wife of* at the top of their list, but many find it harder to do the same with *widow of*. They have also lost the person who supported their self-definition. Husbands who were best friends and confidants may have been very important in making them feel that they were good persons. . . .

[Helena] Lopata (1973) found that widows cope with this identity crisis in different ways. Role-oriented women can turn to other roles, taking a job or increasing their investment in a job they already have. They may also become more involved in civic or social organizations. Those who need confirmation of their personal qualities may become more involved with friends and family, although in a later study Lopata (1977) found that those widows who had not had friends outside the family before their husband died did not tend to acquire any after his death. Widows who base their identity on things rather than on people are often in trouble because they find that their income level is substantially reduced. All of these orientations may, of course, be present in the same person. . . .

Loneliness

The concept of *loneliness* is central to discussions of widowhood, divorce, and old age, although it is not always treated analytically. It is important to distinguish between living alone, feeling lonely, feeling isolated, feeling desolate, and so on. Many people—young and old—who live alone do not feel lonely, isolated, or desolate, and many people who live with a spouse or other relative do feel lonely, isolated, and desolate. Many widows quickly grow accustomed to living alone; more than half of older widows do so and apparently even prefer to do so. They miss their husbands both as persons and as partners in many activities. However, and particularly if they are older, they become involved with friendship groups of other widows and tend to miss their husband's companionship less. In residential areas with a high concentration of older widows, loneliness is reported much less frequently than in areas where such widows are more isolated. In fact, Atchley, Pignatiello, and Shaw found that widows had higher rates of interaction than married older women. And Arling (1976) found that having strong relationships with friends and neighbors was more related to high morale among widows than were ties with family.

The amount and kind of *social disruption* caused by widowhood depends largely on what life activities had been shared with the husband. For example, middle-class women are more likely than working-class women to have seen themselves as part of a husband-wife team, so that their involvement in a wide variety of roles and activities would be impaired by their husband's death.

Widowhood has its most immediate impact on family roles. Contacts with in-laws are usually lost, for example, particularly if children are grown. Contacts with children usually increase for a time, but few move in with their children except as a last resort, preferring "intimacy at a distance." First, they do not wish to become embroiled in conflict over managing the flow of household activity, and after being in charge of their own homes, it is hard for American widows to accept a subordinate position in another woman's house, especially a daughter-in-law's. Second, they do not want to be involved in the dilemmas of rearing children. They feel that they have done their work, raised their children, and deserve a rest.

Patterns of mutual aid between children and parents are often altered, so that older widows usually grow closer to their daughters and more distant from their sons. Because adult sons often feel responsible for their mothers' welfare and because older widows often want to be responsible for themselves, there is great potential for conflict and guilt in the older widow/son relationship. Relationships with the extended family (brothers, sisters, aunts, uncles, cousins, and so on) also change, increasing immediately after death but tapering off within a short time.

The impact of widowhood on friendship depends on the proportion of the widow's friends who are also widows. If she is one of the first in her groups of friends to become widowed, she may find that her friends feel awkward about death and grief—they do not want to face what in all likelihood is their own future. If friendship groups consisted mainly of couples, then the widow may be included for a time, but she will probably feel out of place. The widow may also encounter jealousy on the part of still-married friends.

On the other hand, if the widow is one of the last to become widowed in a group of friends, she may find great comfort among friends who are familiar with her problems. In fact, as a group of women friends grows older, those who are still married may sometimes feel left out because their widowed friends do many things as a group that they do not feel free to join. For these people, widowhood brings the compensation of being among old friends again. In sum, widowhood is easier for older than for younger women.

Churches and voluntary associations organized around interests can provide avenues for increased social contact for widows, since these activities do not usually depend upon having a spouse or being accompanied by a member of the opposite sex. Women's groups are often more comfortable than heterosexual groups because they do not confront widows with being the lone single woman.

Social class is also a factor in adjustment to widowhood. Middle-class women are more likely than working-class women to have balanced their roles of wife and companion and mother. Therefore, the loss of comradeship can often be traumatic for them. On the other hand, middle-class women also tend to have more social options, more nonfamily friends, and more organizational activity, not to mention more personal resources in general. They usually have a more secure income, more education, and more job skills. To balance this in a small way, many working-class women tend to emphasize their mother role more than their wife role, and thus may experience less personal loss. But we must not forget that working-class women have fewer friends, fewer organizational memberships, less money, and fewer personal resources. On the whole, then, working-class widows are much more likely to be isolated and lonely than are middle-class widows.

Among low-income elderly, the widowed were consistently more negative in their self-reports of life satisfaction (Hutchison, 1975). . . .

Class differences are particularly large among blacks. Working-class black women tend to become widowed at even earlier ages than working-class whites. On the other hand, overt hostility between the sexes is more prevalent among blacks, and therefore widows sanctify their husband's memory less. As a result, widowhood brings less emotional distress among working-class blacks than among working-class whites (Lopata, 1973).

There also are considerable *ethnic* and *foreign-birth differences* in the impact of widowhood, though these are complex and vary with the kinds of expectations older women have been socialized for and the congruence between these expectations and the attitudes of younger generations in their family. Foreign-born widows are much more likely to have had the kind of traditional expectations for respect and care which entail greater identity problems when the younger members of their families were brought up to different values. For example, many foreign-born older women were reared in cultural traditions that offer widows a high degree of involvement with extended kin. To the extent that the younger extended kin and in-laws do not share this orientation, there is room for a greater gap between what the older foreign-born widow expects from her family and what she gets. A similar pattern prevails among older widows reared in some areas of Appalachia.

Men

The impact of widowhood on men has received little systematic attention. The literature on this subject is long on speculation and short on systematic research. Nevertheless, it is important to outline both what we do know and what we need to know about being a widower, as a guide for future research.

The role of widower is probably even vaguer than that of widow. Because widowers who have not remarried are not very common in the community until after age seventy-five, their common status does not solidify them into groups. Like widows, they are expected to preserve the memories of their wives and are not expected to show interest in other women. Indications are that many widowers adhere to the former but ignore the latter, as can be inferred from the remarriage rates cited earlier.

Because the male role traditionally emphasizes other roles in addition to that of husband, widowers are probably not as apt as widows to encounter an acute identity crisis when they lose their husband *role*. But men are more likely than women to see their spouse as an important part of *themselves*. In addition, older men are less likely than women to have a confidant other than their spouse and thus can experience painful loneliness.

How older men cope with widowhood's impact on their identity also probably depends, as older women's reactions do, on how the lost relationships fit into the men's *personal goal structures*. Despite current stereotypes about men's overinvolvement with their jobs, there is little evidence that widowhood is any less devastating for men than for women. In fact, it can wreck a man's concept of life in retirement completely. There is little basis for assuming that marriage is less important to older men than it is to older women.

So far, there has been limited study of the impact of widowhood on men's roles outside the household. Glick et al. report that widowers have more difficulty than widows with work during the mourning period. However, they do not differ from widows in isolation from kin or voluntary associations, nor are either widows or widowers more isolated than their married peers. In fact, those who have friends tend to see them more often. When Atchley controlled for social class, he found that widowhood tends to increase contacts with friends among middle-class widowers and decrease them among lower-class widowers. It could be that the large surplus of widows in senior centers and similar social groups for older people (generally used more by working-class than middle-class people) may inhibit the working-class widowers in developing new kinds of community participation. Such widowers tend to be embarrassed and even harassed by the competition among widows for their attention. But beyond this, they are unaccustomed to take the lead in such preponderantly female gatherings. While they may be nominally the leaders there, they are often frustrated and intimidated by the tendency of the women to dominate discussions and other activities.

Petrowsky found that widowers were much less involved in religious activities than were widows, but this is likely to be due to a continuation of sex differences in religious participation established earlier in life. . . .

Very little has been written aboout age, social class, racial, or ethnic variations in the impact of widowhood on older men. Some of the variations noted for widows, however, no doubt apply to men as well. This area is greatly in need of research.

There is currently a controversy over whether widowhood is more difficult for older women or for older men. . . . Berardo is the leading proponent of the idea that older men find widowhood more difficult than do older women. He suggests that men are ill-prepared to fend for themselves—to cook their own meals, keep house, and so on—and therefore end up having to give up their independent households. Berardo also feels that men have more difficulty finding a substitute source of intimacy. He says that courtship opportunities are limited for widowers and that friends and children see them as being too old for "that sort of thing." Berardo feels that widows have the advantage of continuing their role of housewife, a meaningful activity that provides continuing standards for behavior. He sees widows as being much more able to maintain an independent residence and at the same time more able to gain acceptance in the households of their children, should the need arise.

On the other side of this debate, Bell concluded that widowhood was harder on older women than on older men because: (1) being a wife is a more important role for women than being a husband is for men; (2) widows are given less encouragement to remarry; (3) widows face a bleaker financial future with fewer financial skills; (4) widows are more isolated because women are expected not to be socially aggressive; and (5) the lack of available men makes remarriage difficult for all but a few older widows. Recently, however, he has agreed that the problems of survivorship *are* greater for husbands.

This controversy raises several issues in comparing widowers with widows. Between the ages of sixty-five and seventy-four, widowers in general are slightly more likely than widows to live in group quarters such as hotels or rooming houses rather than in independent households; after age seventy-five, there is little sex difference. Widowers who live in their own homes are slightly *more* likely to live alone than are widows. Thus, those men who remain widowers are not significantly less likely than widows to live alone.

Widowers are only slightly less likely than widows to be living with children. When they live in multiperson households, however, widowers are much more likely to be considered the household head.

Berardo made the usual assumptions that jobs are more important to men than to women and that retirement is an identity crisis primarily for men. He saw widowhood as a *cumulative role loss* only for men. Atchley presents a somewhat different analysis. Since he found little evidence that leaving the job at retirement represented an identity crisis for large proportions of either men or women, he concluded that job loss is not a significant source of distress even in widowhood. He suggested that widowhood interacts with retirement to the extent that widowhood wrecks plans for a retirement lifestyle built around being a member of a couple. And this type of interaction between retirement and widowhood is probably as applicable to widows as to widowers.

But what about the housewife role? Berardo feels that the continuity of the housewife role is an advantage for widows. However, what is retained is the role of house*keeper,* not house*wife.* The widow loses the housewife role because widowhood and the empty nest take away her clients. To some women, doing for oneself has less satisfaction than doing for others. There may also be a decrease in the time required for homemaking tasks.

Berardo feels that widowers have more difficulty than widows with finding alternate sources of intimacy because of social norms against courtships and remarriage for older men. But every year nearly 30,000 older widowers remarry, compared to about 15,000 older widows who remarry.

Widowers are much less likely than widows to have had a *confidant*—a very close friend—other than their wives. Therefore, widowers *need* remarriage more than widows do, in order to find a new confidant. As for the social discouragement of remarriage, McKain reports no sex difference in the extent to which children oppose remarriage, even though he does report that children's opposition is a significant obstacle to remarriage.

There can be little doubt that widows are far worse off financially than widowers, especially in the working class. In traditional marriages, the wife is usually ignorant of the family finances and has no training in how to manage money. In addition, the incomes of widows average considerably less than the incomes of widowers. And Atchley's research cited earlier suggests that this poverty is a critical factor for working-class widows.

Atchley found that widowed older people were significantly more often lonely than married older people, and that working-class widowed older people were more often lonely than those in the middle class. He found no significant sex differences, however, in the prevalence of loneliness among the widowed. On the other hand, widowers were much more likely than widows to increase participation in organizations and contact with friends.

Thus, no aspect of widowhood appears demonstrably more difficult for older widowers than for older widows, but widows are clearly worse off than widowers in terms of finances and prospects for remarriage.

BERNICE L. NEUGARTEN
AND KAROL L. WEINSTEIN

The Changing American Grandparent

Styles of grandparenting are distinguished and described in the following article by psychologists Bernice Neugarten and Karol Weinstein. Some of these styles occur more in older grandparents and some are more common among younger grandparents. Suggestions are offered for the study of the grandparent role and the ways in which people are socialized into the role.

Despite the proliferation of investigations regarding the relations between generations and the position of the aged within the family, surprisingly little attention has been paid directly to the role of grandparenthood. . . .

There are a number of anthropologists' reports on grandparenthood in one or another simple society as well as studies involving cross-cultural comparisons based on ethnographic materials. Notable among the latter is a study by Apple which shows that, among the 51 societies for which data are available, those societies in which grandparents are removed from family authority are those in which grandparents have an equalitarian or an indulgent, warm relationship with the grandchildren. In those societies in which economic power and/or prestige rests with the old, relationships between grandparents and grandchildren are formal and authoritarian. . . .

The data reported in this paper were collected primarily for the purpose of generating rather than testing hypotheses regarding various psychological

Neugarten, Bernice L. and Karol K. Weinstein, "The Changing American Grandparent," *Journal of Marriage and the Family,* May 1964, pages 199–204. Copyrighted © 1964 by the National Council on Family Relations. Reprinted by permission.

Photograph by C. Capa. © Magnum Photos, Inc.

and social dimensions of the grandparent role. Three dimensions were investigated: first, the degree of comfort with the role as expressed by the grandparent; second, the significance of the role as seen by the actor; and last, the style with which the role is enacted.

The data came from interviews with both grandmother and grandfather in 70 middle-class families in which the interviewer located first a married couple with children and then one set of grandparents. Of the 70 sets of grandparents, 46 were maternal—that is, the wife's parents—and 24 were paternal. All pairs of grandparents lived in separated households from their children, although most lived within relatively short distances within the metropolitan area of Chicago. . . . As is true in other middle-class, urban groups in the United States, the largest proportion of these families had been upwardly mobile, either from working class into lower-middle or from lower-middle into upper-middle. Of the 70 grandparental couples, 19 were foreign born (Polish, Lithuanian, Russian, and a few German and Italian). The sample was skewed with regard to religious affiliation, with 40 percent Jewish, 48 percent Protestant, and 12 percent Catholic. The age range of the grandfathers was, with a few exceptions, the mid-50's through the late 60's; for the grandmothers it was the early 50's to the mid-60's.

Each member of the couple was interviewed separately and, in most instances, in two sessions. Respondents were asked a variety of open-ended questions regarding their relations to their grandchildren: how often and on what occasions they saw their grandchildren; what the significance of grandparenthood was in their lives and how it had affected them. While grandparenthood has multiple values for each respondent and may influence his relations with various family members, the focus was upon the primary relationship—that between grandparent and grandchild. . . .

Degree of comfort in the role. . . . The majority of grandparents expressed only comfort, satisfaction, and pleasure. Among this group, a sizable number seemed to be idealizing the role of grandparenthood and to have high expectations of the grandchild in the future—that the child would either achieve some special goal or success or offer unique affection at some later date.

At the same time, approximately one-third of the sample (36 percent of the grandmothers and 29 percent of the grandfathers) were experiencing sufficient difficulty in the role that they made open reference to their discomfort, their disappointment, or their lack of positive reward. This discomfort indicated strain in thinking of oneself as a grandparent (the role is in some ways alien to the self-image), conflict with the parents with regard to the rearing of the grandchild, or indifference (and some self-chastisement for the indifference) to caretaking or responsibility in reference to the grandchild.

The significance and meaning of the role. The investigators made judgments based upon the total interview data on each case with regard to the primary significance of grandparenthood for each respondent. . . .

1. For some, grandparenthood seemed to constitute primarily a source of *biological renewal* ("It's through my grandchildren that I feel young again") and/or *biological continuity* with the future ("It's through these children that I see my life going on into the future" or, "It's carrying on the family line"). . . .

2. For some, grandparenthood affords primarily an opportunity to succeed in a new emotional role, with the implication that the individual feels himself to be a better grandparent than he was a parent. Frequently, grandfatherhood offered a certain vindication of the life history by providing *emotional self-fulfillment* in a way that fatherhood had not done. As one man put it, "I can be, and I can do for my grandchildren things I could never do for my own kids. I was too busy with my business to enjoy my kids, but my grandchildren are different. Now I have the time to be with them."

3. For a small proportion, the grandparent role provides a new role of teacher or *resource person*. Here the emphasis is upon the satisfaction that accrues from contributing to the grandchild's welfare—either by financial aid, or by offering the benefit of the grandparent's unique life experience. . . .

4. For a few, grandparenthood is seen as providing an extension of the self in that the grandchild is one who will *accomplish vicariously* for the grandparent that which neither he nor his first-generation offspring could achieve. For these persons, the grandchild offers primarily an opportunity for aggrandizing the ego. . . .

5. . . . Twenty-seven percent of the grandmothers and 29 percent of the grandfathers in this sample reported feeling relatively *remote* from their grandchildren and acknowledged relatively *little effect* of grandparenthood in their own lives—this despite the fact that they lived geographically near at least one set of grandchildren and felt apologetic about expressing what they regarded as unusual sentiments. Some of the grandfathers mentioned the young age of their grandchildren in connection with their current feelings of psychological distance. . . .

Of the grandmothers who felt remote from their grandchildren, the rationalization was different. Most of the women in this group were working or were active in community affairs and said essentially, "It's great to be a grandmother, of course—but I don't have much time. . . ." The other grandmothers in this group indicated strained relations with the adult child; either they felt that their daughters had married too young, or they disapproved of their sons-in-law. . . .

These grandparents imply that the role itself is perceived as being empty of meaningful relationships.

Styles of grandparenting. Somewhat independent of the significance of grandparenthood is the question of style in enacting the role of grandmother or grandfather. Treating the data inductively, five major styles were differentiated:

1. The *Formal* are those who follow what they regard as the proper and prescribed role for grandparents. Although they like to provide special treats and indulgences for the grandchild, and although they may occasionally take on a minor service such as baby-sitting, they maintain clearly demarcated lines between parenting and grandparenting, and they leave parenting strictly to the parent. They maintain a constant interest in the grandchild but are careful not to offer advice on childrearing.

2. The *Fun Seeker* is the grandparent whose relation to the grandchild is characterized by informality and playfulness. He joins the child in specific activities for the specific purpose of having fun, somewhat as if he were the child's playmate. Grandchildren are viewed as a source of leisure activity, as an item of "consumption" rather than "production," or as a source of self-indulgence. The relationship is one in which authority lines—either with the grandchild or with the parent—are irrelevant. The emphasis here is on mutuality of satisfaction rather than on providing treats for the grandchild. Mutuality imposes a latent demand that both parties derive fun from the relationship.

3. The *Surrogate Parent* occurs only, as might have been anticipated, for grandmothers in this group. It comes about by initiation on the part of the younger generation, that is, when the young mother works and the grandmother assumes the actual caretaking responsibility for the child.

4. The *Reservoir of Family Wisdom* represents a distinctly authoritarian patricentered relationship in which the grandparent—in the rare occasions on which it occurs in this sample, it is the grandfather—is the dispenser of special skills or resources. Lines of authority are distinct, and the young parents maintain and emphasize their subordinate positions, sometimes with and sometimes without resentment.

5. The *Distant Figure* is the grandparent who emerges from the shadows on holidays and on special ritual occasions such as Christmas and birthdays. Contact with the grandchild is fleeting and infrequent, a fact which distinguishes this style from the *Formal*. This grandparent is benevolent in stance but essentially distant and remote from the child's life, a somewhat intermittent St. Nicholas.

Of major interest is the frequency with which grandparents of both sexes are either Fun Seekers or Distant Figures vis-à-vis their grandchildren. These two styles have been adopted by half of all the cases in this sample. Of interest, also, is the fact that in both styles the issue of authority is peripheral. Although deference may be given to the grandparent in certain ways, authority relationships are not a central issue.

Both of these styles are, then, to be differentiated from what has been regarded as the traditional grandparent role—one in which patriarchal or matriarchal control is exercised over both younger generations and in which authority constitutes the major axis of the relationship.

These two styles of grandparenting differ not only from traditional concepts; they differ also in some respects from more recently described types. Cavan, for example, has suggested that the modern grandparent role is essentially a maternal one for both men and women and that to succeed as a grandfather, the male must learn to be a slightly masculinized grandmother, a role that differs markedly from the instrumental and outer-world orientation that has presumably characterized most males during a great part of their adult lives. It is being suggested here, however, that the newly emerging types are neuter in gender. Neither the Fun Seeker nor the Distant Figure involves much nurturance, and neither "maternal" nor "paternal" seems an appropriate adjective.

Grandparent style in relation to age. A final question is the extent to which these new styles of grandparenting reflect, directly or indirectly, the increasing youthfulness of grandparents as compared to a few decades ago. (This youthfulness is evidenced not only in terms of the actual chronological age at which grandparenthood occurs but also in terms of evaluations of self as youthful. A large majority of middle-aged and older persons describe themselves as "more youthful than my parents were at my age.")

To follow up this point, the sample was divided into two groups: those who were under and over 65. . . . The Formal style occurs significantly more frequently in the older group; the Fun Seeking and the Distant Figure styles occur significantly more frequently in the younger group. (. . . The same age differences occur in both grandmothers and grandfathers.)

These age differences may reflect secular trends: this is, differences in values and expectations in persons who grow up and who grow old at different times in history. They may also reflect processes of aging and/or the effects of continuing socialization which produce differences in role behavior over time. It might be pointed out, however, that sociologists, when they have treated the topic of grandparenthood at all, have done so within the context of old age, not middle age. Grandparenthood might best be studied as a middle-age phenomenon if the investigator is interested in the assumption of new roles and the significance of new roles in adult socialization. . . .

With the presently quickened pace of the family cycle, in which women experience the emptying of the nest, the marriages of their children, and the appearance of grandchildren at earlier points in their own lives, the expectation that grandmotherhood is a welcome and pleasurable event seems frequently to be accompanied also by doubts that one is "ready" to become a grandmother or by the feelings of being prematurely old. The anticipation and first adjustment to the role of grandmother has not been systematically studied, either by sociologists or psychologists, but there is anecdotal data to suggest that, at both conscious and unconscious levels, the middle-aged woman may relive her own first pregnancy and childbirth and that there are additional social and psychological factors that probably result in a certain transformation in ego-identity. The reactions of males to grandfatherhood has similarly gone uninvestigated although, as has been suggested earlier, the event may require a certain reversal of traditional sex role and a consequent change in self-concept.

CHAPTER TEN

The Child in the Family

Evening star, you bring all things
Which the bright dawn has scattered:
You bring the sheep, you bring the goat,
You bring the child back to its mother.

> Sappho, Frag. 120

The child is father of the man.

> William Wordsworth,
> "My Heart Leaps Up When I Behold"

Children begin by loving their parents; as they grow older they judge them;
sometimes they forgive them.

> Oscar Wilde, *The Picture of Dorian Gray*

Colonial Laws Regarding Children

Colonial law intervened directly in family life and, as revealed in the follow-ing colonial statutes, sometimes took a view of parent-child relations that is shocking to modern sensibilities. A child who was repeatedly insubordinate could, according to a Massachusetts law, be put to death. The punishment was never put into practice in fact, but it must have stood as an awesome reminder of parental rights.

Massachusetts, 1646

If any child[ren] above sixteen years old and of sufficient understanding shall curse or smite their natural father or mother, they shall be put to death, unless it can be sufficiently testified that the parents have been very unchristianly negligent in the education of such children, or so provoked them by extreme and cruel correction that they have been forced thereunto to preserve them-selves from death or maiming. . . .

If a man have a stubborn or rebellious son of sufficient years of under-standing, viz. sixteen, which will not obey the voice of his father or the voice of his mother, and that when they have chastened him will not harken unto them, then shall his father and mother, being his natural parents, lay hold on him and bring him to the magistrates assembled in Court, and testify to them by sufficient evidence that this their son is stubborn and rebellious and will not obey their voice and chastisement, but lives in sundry notorious crimes. Such a son shall be put to death.

Massachusetts, 1654

Forasmuch as it appears by too much experience that divers children and servants do behave themselves too disrespectively, disobediently, and disor-derly towards their parents, masters, and governors, to the disturbance of families and discouragement of such parents and governors: For the ready prevention whereof it is ordered by this Court and the authority thereof that it shall henceforth be in the power of any one magistrate, by warrant directed to the constable of that town where such offender dwells, upon complaint, to call before him any such offender, and upon conviction of such misdemeanors to sentence him or them to endure such corporal punishment by whipping or otherwise as in his judgment the merit of the fact shall deserve, not exceeding ten stripes for one offence, or bind the offender to appear at the next Court of that county. And further, it is also ordered, that the commissioners for the town of Boston, and the three commissioners for towns where no magistrate dwells, shall have the like power, provided the person or persons so sentenced shall have liberty to make their legal appeal to the next County Court, if they desire it in any of these cases.

Laws of the Duke of York, 1676

. . . If any children of servants become rude, stubborn, or unruly, refusing to harken to the voice of their parents or masters, the constable and overseers (where no justice of peace shall happen to dwell within ten miles of the said town or parish), have power upon the complaint of their parents or masters [to] call before them such an offender, and to inflict such corporal punishment as the merit of the fact in their judgment shall deserve, not [exceeding] ten stripes, provided that such children and servants be of sixteen years of age.

U.S. Children Give Families High Marks

Adults are frequently surveyed and interviewed about aspects of their family experience. In a first major study of children's view of the family, Nicholas Zill found that most children are happy with their family life. A few of his preliminary findings are described in the following article from Science News.

Although American children worry about their home and family environment, the vast majority of them view their family as a cohesive, "happy" force, according to preliminary results of a nationwide study of 7 to 11-year-olds. The youngsters' reflections do "not support the position that the American family is in decline," reports Nicholas Zill, project director for the National Survey of Children and senior staff scientist for the Foundation for Child Development, which sponsored the research.

More than 2,200 children and 1,700 of their parents were interviewed in late 1976 by researchers from Temple University's Institute for Survey Research, which conducted the survey for the foundation. The sample is designed to represent the country's 17.7 million children.

"We wanted to give kids a chance to speak for themselves," Zill explains. "In the past, most studies have focused on parents, teachers, doctors . . . with no input from the children. We see this survey as a benchmark—we're trying to see what effects social changes are having on kids, and would like to see [similar] surveys done in the future."

In the youngsters' views, the researchers see an overall positive picture of the family unit, although some children say they are "worried" and "afraid" of aspects of their life both in and out of the home. More than 9 of 10 children pointed to a happy face to convey how they feel about their families. Ninety percent of the youngsters agreed with the statement, "I like being the way I am," and over 75 percent said they were "lucky."

But 8 of 10 also said they worried about their families—that figure rose to nearly 100 per cent in families where the mother described the marriage as "not too happy." "People talk about the increase in separations and divorce in this country—and we do see a detrimental effect on kids in some of these households," Zill says. However, the survey also suggests that having both parents together does not guarantee a child's happiness. In families with both husband and wife present, nearly half of the children wished their fathers would spend more time with them, and more than one-third expressed the same desire about their mothers.

"Apparently it's not the absence of a parent *per se*" that has negative effects on a child, Zill says. The data suggest that a single parent may be better than two in some cases if he or she has adjusted well to that role. But if the single parent felt depressed or nervous about the separation, the child tended to feel bored and lonely. In double-parent families, one of five youngsters in marriages described as "not too happy" by the mother got into fights at school, as opposed to one of ten youngsters from well-adjusted marriages. The most influential factors in a child's well-being hinge on the relationship between husband and wife in two-parent families, or the single parent's own well-being and ability to cope, Zill says.

Parents' education levels have risen steadily during the last decade, Zill says, and this has had a positive influence. Among the children surveyed, the proportion of those reporting they had "interesting things to do most afternoons" (about one-third of the children questioned) rose steadily with parents' educational level.

ANDREW BILLINGSLEY

Raising Black Children

In addition to the usual socialization tasks that all parents face in raising children, black parents have the special task of teaching their children to accept and value being black in a culture of white people who discriminate against them. The challenge, Andrew Billingsley of Howard University says, consists of helping the child to grow up feeling neither self-hatred nor hatred of society, to teach children a moral code in the face of a socio-legal system that "upholds much of this same code, while violating at every turn their basic human rights."

It is often assumed, particularly by liberal intellectuals and sometimes by social scientists and social workers, that what is required of Negro families in our society is essentially the same as what is required of white families. According to this view, it is not the demands made on the family, but the ability of the family to meet these demands which distinguishes Negro family life. If, however, the Negro people are viewed as an ethnic subsociety, it can be appreciated that while there are basic similarities in the requirements of all families in America, there are particular requirements for Negro families, which grow out of three factors: (a) the peculiar historical development, (b) the caste-like qualities in the American stratification system which relegates all Negroes to inferior status, and (c) the social class and economic systems which keep most Negroes in the lower social classes.

For the Negro family, socialization is doubly challenging, for the family must teach its young members not only how to be human, but also how to be black in a white society. The requirements are not the same.

Negro families must teach their children very early in life, sometimes as early as two years of age, the meaning of being black. "Every Negro child I know," says Robert Coles, "has had to take notice in some way of what skin color signifies in our society." A Negro mother in Jackson, Mississippi, put it this way:

> When they asks all the questions, they ask about their color too. They more than not will see a white boy or girl and it makes them stop and think. They gets to wondering, and then first thing you know, they want to know this and that about it, and I never have known what to say, except that the Lord likes everyone because He makes everyone. . . . I tell them that no matter what it's like around us, it may make us feel bad, but it's not the whole picture, because we don't make ourselves. . . . When they ask me why colored people aren't as good as whites, I tell them it's not that they're not as good; it's that they're not as rich. Then I tell them that they should separate being poor and being bad, and not get them mixed up.

She also needs to teach them to separate being *black* and being bad, which is the real problem and much harder to separate.

. . . High-income Negro families who live in white suburbs in the North . . . often must face the same kinds of problems in teaching their children how to grow up black in a white society. Some face it with resignation. "All you can do is make your children understand that some people are just not going to like them," one middle-class suburban Negro mother told the *New York Times*.

> You can tell them that some people are ignorant or something like that, but they still have to get used to it. You can't hide them from reality. We've had the same experience. We had to learn to live with it—they will too. . . .

Other middle-class Negro families take a laissez-faire approach to the problem. An attorney observed:

> We've found it best to more or less leave our children to themselves. Left alone—given enough security—they'll determine where the lines are drawn and how to react to them. We've never really talked to our children about racial problems. . . .

Still other black suburbanites take a more activist role in dealing with the problem. "Of course my son has difficulties," said another father, himself a school teacher,

> and each time we've tried talking with him afterwards. Let's face it, there is an undercurrent of bigotry here, and it's not that far from the surface. We've tried to show our son the difference between his value as a person and the distorted view people may have of him. He was eight when we moved here. We were the first Negroes in any of these buildings. A lot of times he'd come in crying from school or from playing in the courtyard outside. Someone would have told him

something like—"we don't play with niggers" or "coons stink." I'd tell him children often use bad names or say things that aren't true, but he'd have to understand that they needed to do this. It really had nothing to do with him. I think this helped. He's been able to cope with it. I'm not sure, but I think the well-adjusted Negro has to have a clearer picture of himself. The society, too. There aren't any dreams he can rely on.

Hopefully the dreams may be only deferred. It is a constant challenge for Negro parents, at all levels of the ethnic subsociety, to teach their children how to be human and American and black and proud. Even educated middle-class parents who read avidly do not find much help with this problem from psychology books or treatises on child rearing. The books have been written for white parents, to deal with other problems. "The best advice I've had," said one mother, "has been passed along by word of mouth, talking with other Negro parents."

Negro children must be taught not only to distinguish themselves from whites and to accept themselves, but, even more crucial to their survival, they must be taught to deal with white people. There are, of course, a variety of ways both of teaching and doing this; but hatred and fear are often basic mechanisms of survival which go into the socialization of lower-class Negro children. Another Negro mother expressed this problem vividly:

> I guess we all don't like white people too much, deep inside. You could hardly expect us to after what's happened all these years. It's in our bones to be afraid of them, and bones have a way of staying around even when everything else is gone. . . . So if you want your kids to live long, they have to grow up scared of whites; and the way they get scared is through us; and that's why I don't let my kids get fresh about the white man even in their own house. . . . So I make them store it in the bones, way inside, and then no one sees it.

The dilemmas facing the Negro parent in rearing their children in the face of these conflicting demands are deep and intricate. How, indeed, are the ravages of self-hatred to be avoided when a parent may state to a child "It is not you who are bad," but when, for the child's own physical and psychic safety, the obvious corollary, "It is *they* who are bad," cannot be taught? How does a parent impart a moral code to a child when they are surrounded by a socio-legal system which also upholds much of this same code, while violating at every turn their basic human rights?

How Negro parents have resolved these dilemmas is a virtually untouched field of study. While Negro parents have informally shared their experiences with one another, the startling neglect of such important areas of expressive functioning in Negro family life finds us without information which is vital to understanding not only the Negro family, but also a very rich part of the human experience.

MARY ROWE

Choosing Child Care: Many Options

*With more than half of all married women now holding jobs, and with the
number of households headed by single, working women steadily increasing
(see the article by Wattenberg and Reinhardt, p. 372), the issue of child care
for working mothers has assumed new importance. Guidelines and considerations for choosing child care are detailed in the following selection. Mary
Rowe, Special Assistant for Women and Work to the President of the Massachusetts Institute of Technology, gives special attention to the alternatives
couples may choose if they are determined to share child care equally. Particular arrangements will, she says, vary from time to time, depending on
the number and ages of children, cost, time, and distance.*

How to combine various jobs with having children used to be a pretty straightforward issue for most couples. The tendency was to follow one fairly standard
pattern; a few people varied it a little; fewer varied it a lot. This meant that
in most husband-wife families—perhaps 80 per cent of them—there were two
or three or four or more children, with the father as the only breadwinner,
except for pin money brought in by the mother for work done at home. Other
less frequent variations included the mother in part-time or full-time work
outside the home.

In the 1980s in the USA, all indications are that there will be many
different, basic child-care patterns built around changes now manifest in labor
force patterns and fertility. . . .

The full-time labor force participation rate for men has been declining.
It may be down to about 70 per cent by 1990, for a basic 30–35 hour week.

This means that only 70 per cent of all men aged 16–65 will be in paid, full-time work or looking for work, at any given time. Others will be in training, on leave, early-retired, out-of-work, or working as fathers and househusbands.

On the other side of the coin, the labor force participation rate for women has been increasing. It will probably be at least 70 per cent by the 1980s counting part-time and full-time employment. Thus paid work patterns for most women will be increasingly similar to those of most men for most of their lives. This will be especially true for the probable one-tenth of all women who will never marry and the 10 to 20 per cent who we expect will have no biological children. We expect that perhaps another 50 per cent of all women will have only one or two children; they too are likely to lead working lives much more like those of their men than has been true in the past. . . .

Already the modal family has changed enormously. In place of the traditional male-as-sole-breadwinner family (which now accounts for only a third of two-parent families in the U.S.A.), nearly half of all husband-wife families now have both spouses in the paid labor force. In addition to these extraordinary changes in labor force participation we will probably see a further great change in family economics. From the 30 per cent of family incomes brought in by U.S. wives in 1975, we will probably see 40 per cent brought in by the women of the 1980s. And probably at least a fifth of all wives will earn as much as or more than their husbands.

Changes in marriage patterns toward divorce and unusual family forms are expected to continue into the 1980s, although families as such seem here to stay. I estimate that in the 1980s at least half of all children will spend at least two years of their childhood in a 'non-traditional family'. Most of these will be living during such periods with single parents. At any *given* time, probably 75–80 per cent of all children aged 0–16 will be living with two parents, or with parents and step-parents. However, probably more than half will have lived in a family different from the traditional nuclear type for a significant period of their early lives. . . .

By the same token, our values about men and homemaking and child care seem to be changing rapidly in some segments of the population. . . . A large number of American men now appear to have been changing their views very rapidly in the 1970s. A 1976 Gallup poll reports that men who believe in relatively egalitarian marriage are now far more likely to report their marriages as 'very happy'. . . .

In the 1980s more men will become single-parent fathers through death, divorce and adoption. (The proportion of single-parent males has already increased to about a tenth of all single parents.) . . . All these facts will mean that the social and legal rights and expectations of men with regard to child care may be expected to continue to expand during the 1980s. Thus changes in labor force participation, in fertility, marriage, divorce and sex-role attitudes have combined to permit very wide ranges of child-care patterns and customs.

Child-care Arrangements in the Early 1970s

Recent nationwide surveys of child-care arrangements illuminate the very wide variety of child-care patterns now existing. By and large, they vary by age of child, by type of parental employment, by family income, number of children and arrangements available.

To begin with an examination of the traditional norm (that mothers are the chief or only child carers), we find that most mothers *are* basically responsible for the children, although few are completely alone in this endeavor. Only about 3 per cent of all households have a child under 10 and use *no* form of care besides the mother in her own home. And only 7 per cent have a child or children aged 10–13 and report no child care at all. In other words, nearly nine-tenths of all households with children under 14 do use some kind of care, once in a while, other than the mother in her own home.

However, many use very little care other than the mother. About a third of all parents report using care very briefly, for only about an hour per week. Another 30 per cent use care 1–9 hours per week. These brief arrangements usually involve the spouse (52 per cent), an older sibling (30 per cent), relatives in their own or the child's home (33 per cent, 27 per cent). Others include babysitters (26 per cent) and the child alone at home (12 per cent).

Thus, in about 75 per cent of all homes with 0–13-year-olds the mother is the principal and essentially the only caretaker. This is clearly the dominant mode of American child care. This dominant form is mitigated in a major way only by hours children are in school, from age 5 or 6, and by the brief babysitting hours, described above, totaling fewer than 10 hours per week. . . .

Two studies [of households using 10 hours or more of child care per week] indicate that relatives are somewhat more likely to be child carers for children whose mothers are not in paid employment.* But in any case, family is plainly still very important in American child-care arrangments. And families and neighbors combined account for a very high proportion of all child-care hours.

Reading both of these studies and other available data suggests that in about 10–20 per cent of all households where both parents are employed, parents *share* much of the child care. Two-parent homes with a primary househusband are quite rare—under 5 per cent—but homes where men account for substantial child care are now a distinct mode.

*Ed. note: The studies are Unco (1976), *National Childcare Consumer Study* and G. Duncan and C.R. Hill (1975), "Modal Choice in Child Care Arrangements," in Duncan and Morgan, eds., *Five Thousand American Families*.

Day care appears to be somewhat less prevalent than many observers might hope or fear. Recent studies find all *formal* child-care arrangements, taken together, to comprise not more than 8 to 10 per cent of all arrangements, and not more than 20 percent of all major arrangements (those over 10 hours per week). Day care (including nursery school, Headstart, before and after school programs, as well as programs called day care) is a *major* source of child care only for preschool children with mothers in paid employment in the rather rare areas where such care is available.

How to Choose a Child-care Arrangement

How should a young couple choose? . . . Of course parents should choose child arrangements with thoughtful care, finding as many possibilities as they can, and then learning all the details about each possibility. But no one should feel bound to seek the 'one right method', or to feel that any given, careful decision needs to be permanent.

To begin with, most people change arrangements several times. Most parents arrange in-family care, or care by relatives, for infants. For children between one and two, many parents begin to use a different kind of care, often because the major caretaker has gone back into paid employment and needs more hours of care. As the child becomes a preschooler, parents may switch again, often seeking some hours in a formal arrangement, especially if the mother is in paid work. This happens in part because the parents seek a social life and educational setting for their child, especially if it is a first or only child. Counting all kinds of care in addition to the mother in her own home, at any one time 36 per cent of all parents use one kind of child care, 30 per cent two kinds and 34 per cent three or more different kinds of arrangements.

Cost and distance from home are major considerations. About two-thirds of all households pay no cash for child care, but many arrangements are reimbursed in kind; only about a tenth of all arrangements are considered 'free'. And probably half of all substantial arrangements (more than 10 hours) are not cash-paid. Despite the fact that several studies find cost reported by parents to be a 'secondary' consideration, it is clear that actual behavior in choosing child care depends very much on the price of care. With respect to distance from home, about 80 per cent of all child care occurs within 10 minutes of home; fewer than 5 per cent of all parents travel as much as 30 minutes from home for a child-care arrangement. Thus most parents seem to include considerations of time, money and distance with great care.

Another important problem has to do with the reliability of child-care arrangements. Parents in paid employment place a high premium on arrangements which do not break down. . . . In-family care and relatives appear to be the most reliable of care, with 'child takes care of self' and 'babysitters'

Photograph by Glasheen. Courtesy of Photophile.

found to be less reliable. This may be one reason why care at home with relatives is nearly universally reported to be the most satisfactory. However, it is important also to note that there is a clear and separate mode of parents who prefer child-care centers (and their variations) even though sick children often cannot go to them. This is presumably because of the educational and social advantages many parents find in these formal programs.

How important is the availability of different kinds of care? . . . There is some evidence that most parents who prefer and can find a free arrangement, a relative, or who decide that they could themselves split child care, are already doing so, but many who would like to use more formal child-care facilities if they were available have not been able to find them. Unco estimated that perhaps a fourth of all users would change arrangements if they easily could. These data indicate substantial potential demand for more care, for better care and for different options.

Effects on Children and Parents of Child-care Arrangements

There are no easy answers as to which child-care arrangement is 'best' for children. This is partly because it is very difficult to measure any kind of different effects related to specific responsible arrangements. . . . This is true for a variety of methodological (measurement) reasons and because most children are very adaptable. Such evidence as exists suggests that children thrive best when their parents are satisfied with their work lives and child-care arrangements, and when the caretaker is stable and responsive. Obviously, it is enormously important that parents be truly well-informed about a variety of arrangements in order to choose wisely. It is also important that parents continually monitor child-care arrangements in order to prevent abuse and ensure responsiveness to the child's needs. . . .

Which child-care arrangement is best for parents depends on a wide variety of factors. We know that there are many parents who stagger their paid working hours completely in order to care for their children. These parents widely report themselves very dissatisfied with their arrangements, often feeling very lonely indeed, with little waking or sleeping time to share with their spouses. On the other hand, some 'split arrangement' parents, who use an additional child-care arrangement and see each other regularly, are among the happiest parents. Many parents who are essentially in the traditional mode, with the mother as sole caretaker, report themselves much happier about their children's welfare than they would be in any alternative arrangement. Many others would prefer more relief or more time in paid employment. Parents of children with special needs have a particularly serious need of outside support.

The Unco study reported that about half of all parents who would like to change their child-care arrangements would prefer a formal arrangement such as a day-care center. Many others who would like a change but not to day care, have children under two, and would prefer to change to in-home care, preferably with relatives.

Costs and Benefits of Choosing the Egalitarian Mode

The traditional mode and its variations are by now rather well understood. The husband's career comes first in the constellation of both spouses' use of time, and the husband will try to maximize his opportunities, promotions and salary in paid work. . . .

If Roger and Anne choose this model, Roger is likely to allocate his time in whatever way will best advance his career. His time in the home and with children will depend on his work, not on Anne's work or on how many children they have. If Anne, the wife, chooses paid work at all, it will probably be after she stays home for a year or more with the children. She will do nearly all the homemaking. When she does take up paid work, she will, all in all, work 7–10 hours more per week than Roger, counting all paid and unpaid work and commuting. She will also get less sleep than he but will probably have a more leisurely life during some of her hours at home. How she will allocate her time will depend mainly on Roger's day and the children. Her career will be considered secondary, at least until the last child is well on his or her independent way.

But if a couple like Roger and Anne opt for a more egalitarian mode, as a great many U.S. students assert that they wish to do, they will have another kind of cost-benefit reckoning to do, in terms of risks and potential benefits lying ahead. If each of them can find half or three-quarter-time paid work, while the children are small, the family will receive one or one-and-a-half salaries for these years. Suppose each parent works 30 hours a week in a paid job. Suppose further that they use child care 20 to 30 hours per week, including evening babysitting, and that otherwise they split homemaking and child-care responsibilities by dint of some job-staggering. They will each get to know the children and the skills of homemaking; they will have a chance to spend some time alone together, and perhaps even some time at church activities or volunteer work.

These spouses will probably have a much keener sense of each other's lives. The typical 'learned helplessness' of each sex toward the other's role may never develop in Roger and Anne's marriage. As they share responsibilities they may feel much less taken for granted and less lonely than many fathers and mothers. Anne can still be very supportive of Roger's need to relax after the office though she works herself; and Roger can still help out in Anne's areas of domestic responsibility as well as some of his own.

Their family financial security, as well as actual income, will grow more rapidly than if either one were the sole family breadwinner, as lifetime earnings and the ability to find and keep a job depend much more on continuous years in the labor force than on hours per week. Promotions will probably come later for Roger and Anne than for full-time workers. However, each can expect much higher life-time earnings than if he or she drops out for very long for family responsibilities. . . . Though the strains of keeping two jobs going, as well as domestic responsibilities, may restrict their external activities in some ways, we would expect that the quality of life for these two may nevertheless be good; each will have several arenas for friends, status, productivity and self-image. . . .

If either is left alone, through death or divorce, he or she is more likely to survive in both paid work and family life. (Men who equally care for their children have, in practice, more rights with respect to custody and visitation.) One can imagine that, when Roger and Anne retire from child raising and paid work, they will be much more comfortable under circumstances where they both have a wider range of skills and interests. Their mid-life crises may also be less severe, with a wider range of options offered by two sets of skills and two incomes in the family.

Many couples may choose to share family responsibilities this way so completely that neither spouse ever drops out of school or job for family reasons. But other couples may choose to have one or the other spouse a full-time homemaker for a period of time and to alternate who is staying home.

And many couples may need to have both in full-time paid employment, using child care 30–45 hours per week, at least until the youngest child is in school. The important question is the decision, early on, to share homemaking, financial responsibility and child care. Many couples seem to be making the new model work very well.

How to Choose a Child-care Arrangement

Ideally a couple would begin discussing child care as they begin discussing life together. In the opinion of this author, decisions about child-care arrangements are the most fundamental decisions a couple will make in terms of the roles they will occupy in and out of marriage for the rest of their lives. These decisions, especially if the couple has more than one child, are likely to predict how both partners will spend their time for at least 10–15 years.

A couple anticipating a birth will want to take stock of the parents' careers, of their present and anticipated incomes, of all the possible child-care alternatives and of their places of residence and work (in relation to commuting to work and to care arrangements, if any).

They should discuss all possible relatives and friends, and visit and discuss all available alternatives, including trading child-care hours with friends. Many couples may even consider moving or changing schools or jobs to permit easier care arrangements. The major elements of choice will be time of commuting, price of care, reliability of care and special elements of care that a given child may need at a specific time. The price of care should carefully be balanced against the life-time earning expectations of a spouse that would otherwise stay home.

Most comunities have libraries and community health programs with access to Day Care and Child Development Council materials on how to choose child care, how to monitor arrangements, how to evaluate or even become a family day caretaker, how to begin a play group or child-care center, on how to find lists of local child-care facilities, including those with particular ethnic or other characteristics. . . . Reading and talking with local experts is most important in cases where parents and/or children have special needs.

All young parents should keep two major rules in mind: their children are likeliest to thrive if the *parents* are happy about their work and child-care decisions, and if the caretakers are stable, responsive and consistent. Bystanders can nearly always safely be ignored.

BRUNO BETTELHEIM

Communal
Education: The
Case of the Kibbutz

In this article an eminent child psychoanalyst looks at communal child-rearing in the Israeli kibbutz. The kibbutz, a collective agricultural community in which all property is held in common, is run along socialist principles, and child-rearing, too, is a communal responsibility. What were the purposes for which pioneers in Israel designed their child-care system? How well does it meet the purposes and achieve the goals which its founders intended? Bettelheim compares kibbutz child rearing with the experience of American children raised by their parents in nuclear families.

Today, when there exists such widespread dissatisfaction with our educational system, a radically different one might be expected to hold great interest for us—especially one thriving among people like ourselves, of Western background. It is therefore astonishing how little attention has been paid to the fascinating educational venture embarked on . . . by the more radical socialist kibbutzim of Israel: that of the communal rearing of their children. . . .

The success or failure of communal child rearing seems to depend on the size of the group, the adult-child ratio, and, above all, the attitude of those in charge of the children. . . . The children of the kibbutzim are raised in small groups and cared for by a skilled and devoted staff. What happens under such conditions is surely full of implications for our own educational methods.

In this respect the kibbutz is unique. Nowhere else during modern times has a community of highly intelligent and educated Europeans so seriously tried to free the child from a dependence on his natural parents. Within days

Reprinted from *Conmentary*, February 1962, by permission; all rights reserved.

after birth, the child enters the communal nursery. There his own age group takes the place of what we would call his family of origin—for it alone remains stable over the years; the adults who rear the children—nurses, child-care workers, and teachers—are replaced periodically. The nursery group consists of a maximum of sixteen babies—but usually fewer—all housed and cared for together. Older children are organized into smaller age groups and live in cottages within the kibbutz. Having at birth acquired full rights in the children's autonomous society, the child remains a member until his graduation from high school, at which time he is elected to adult membership in the kibbutz if he so desires—and almost all do. It must be added that the child's parents during the years of his education have no individual rights of control or decision over any aspect of his life.

Most published American critiques of kibbutz child rearing . . . declare that the children suffer severely from communal education. Judging on the basis of our own values, these critics find particularly damaging the fact that the children are separated from their parents, do not have their own mothers to minister to them, have to share the attention of their caretakers with several other children, and undergo not infrequent changes in these caretaking persons. These observers are also influenced by reports on the personality development of institutionalized children. We may take John Bowlby as their spokesman when he says that "essential for mental health is that the infant and young child should experience a warm, intimate, and continuous relationship with his mother."

But what exactly constitutes warm, intimate relations and continuity? It is true that the educators in charge of the children in the kibbutz are not always available to *all* the children in their care, and that the care by any one person is intermittent (days off, relief periods, etc.) But during the time the nursery workers are with the children, no other demands whatsoever are made on them—the child has the full attention of the mothering person. The nursery workers receive appreciation for their trained child care; they are relieved of housekeeping duties, enjoy regular periods of freedom from the children, have the stimulation of adult companionship after their day's work is done. Most important, they are not beset by a parent's typical anxieties—the hopes and fears we harbor about children who are ours. . . . Does not a consistent, if only intermittent, mothering nevertheless equip the child with a continuous inner image of mothering? . . .

The most intimate contact between mother and infant is that of breast feeding. Now, while a vast majority of kibbutz mothers breast-feed their babies, the opposite is true of American mothers. Nearly all kibbutz mothers are able to nurse, love to do it, try very hard to stretch out the nursing period for as long as possible. . . .

In contrast, bottle feeding, with much earlier weaning, is the rule of America. Where, we might ask those authors who decry the lack of intimacy between mother and child in the kibbutz, does the child experience the more "functional" intimacy with his mother—there or here? . . .

A first important change occurs when the infant is six months old. He then may be taken from the nursery cottage to his parents' home for about an hour in the early evening. At approximately one year, the child moves from the nursery to the toddlers' house and his group gets reduced in size to about eight. At this age the child may remain with his parents in their quarters for two hours or so every evening, and most of the day on Saturdays.

The child will now live continuously with these seven others—his age peers—until graduation from high school. At about the fourth or fifth birthday, that is at kindergarten age, the group again numbers up to sixteen by the merging of two toddler groups. This enlarged group remains steadily together until they reach high school age and join with others just entering high school.

From the earliest age on, the children learn to interact with little or no adult supervision. If a child is afraid at night, or becomes ill, his companions take care of him: play with him, talk to him, bring him water, and in general reassure him. Having intimately shared his experiences, they know what he is likely to be afraid of; and the anxious child, trusting his comrades, will confide in them.

In a very short while, the child ceases to wake up afraid in the middle of the night, so absolutely secure does he feel with the other children. Group living makes it possible for the kibbutz child to enjoy much more of that inner security which we put so much stress on, but which many middle-class American infants—alone with their anxieties in their own rooms—fail to find.

Yet American observers deplore "the rather unstimulating and frustrating environment of the child under three, and the limited physical and emotional content which he often has with his caretaker." They also deplore that "the child from the earliest age is expected to subordinate his own needs to the needs of the group." But are the children he lives with not a powerful stimulation? Is it frustrating to a child always to have with him a companion, a friend, some other children to watch; or is it a matter of greater contentment to be so often only with adults—or with no company at all? Are elaborate toys and equipment more rewarding than the uninterrupted company of age mates? And are not each child's own needs also those of the group? Why, one may ask, is the *coordination* of needs viewed by the American observer as *subordination?* . . .

The frequency and anxiety with which I am asked about how to get children to share with others suggests that perhaps our children do not learn the lesson early in life of how to coordinate their own needs with those of others for successful relationships.

Kibbutz children are actually much closer to their parents in some ways than most American children—if not to their parents as persons, then as members of the community. It is the kibbutz (that is, their parents' way of life) which is central to all learning, formal and informal, in the children's village. From the toddlers' school on, the children take daily hikes to visit their parents at work. At the machine shops, the barns, the olive groves, the children are stopped by adults, talked to, joked with, praised, perhaps asked to lend a hand, and when met by their parents, hugged. Thus the child is made to feel a welcome and important part of his father's and mother's occupational activities, and those of the whole community—an experience which most American children would envy them greatly. So, too, all big communal events in the kibbutz, such as holiday celebrations, are related to work that parents and children both have a part in (the festival of the first fruits, arbor day, the harvest festival, etc.).

The system of parental abdication in the rearing of the child was fashioned by the founders of the kibbutz movement out of their ideological convictions. Behind it was the idea that those who established the kibbutzim had grown up in a decadent society, injurious to human freedom and dignity. Nor could any society be regenerated, the kibbutzniks believed, except through the regeneration of the individual, who in turn was viewed as being largely the product of the education he received.

The specific objectives of this system of collective education were: (1) to abolish parental authority, particularly the patriarchal authority of the father; (2) to free the female from the impediment of being assigned only a few special roles in society, such as homemaking and child rearing; (3) to perpetuate the value system of the communal society; and (4) to provide the children with the most democratic education possible. It was hoped that freeing the parents of the need to care for and educate their children would bring the parent-child relation to rest mainly on positive emotions. Since, also, the community as a whole would be responsible for his physical well-being, the child would not be beholden to any particular person, and least of all to his parents.

Any system of child rearing can only be judged, of course, by its results, by whether or no those whom it educates behave later in life in accordance with the goals set. . . . Asked to rank in importance the values they wish their educational system to instill in their children, the parents of one kibbutz replied: first and foremost, "work"; after that, in the order of importance, "love and humanity," "responsibility to the kibbutz," "good character," "intellectualism," "socialism," "Zionism," "social participation," "patriotism," and "cooperation." Neither emotional adjustment nor success in competition was mentioned: adjustment was viewed as implicit in achieving the first four of the values given, while personal advancement was contrary to all their values in general (and to the first in particular), since by work they meant cooperative work in the kibbutz. Thus, queried also as to which ambitions they hoped their children would realize, kibbutz members ranked being a good comrade first, and being a good worker second.

From all available evidence, the results of kibbutz education are unequivocal: the stated main goals are achieved. . . . I am convinced that kibbutz education has had a success of a kind that might well lead us to reconsider some of our own assumptions and values throughout the entire field of education.

In the kibbutz classroom, there is no competition for grades; grading does not determine the success or failure of a student—nor is there any grading of teachers, for promotions. The atmosphere is free; to the American observer it often seems chaotic. The children come and go as they please, and there are no specific assignments or homework; I am tempted to say there is only good teaching. Youngsters of all ages are highly motivated to learn, and study without pressure.

On waking in the morning, the children generally read until it is time to get up; they also read at rest times and on many such other occasions. Reading books of their own choosing—generally what we would call serious reading matter—appears to be the children's favorite pastime. As they grow older, they carry increasing kibbutz work assignments in addition to their academic program. By the time they reach senior high school they are doing three hours of daily work in the field or the shops. During the two-month summer vacation, carrying a full daily work load on the kibbutz, high school youngsters also read an average of ten books of history, biography, or science. At graduation, .their educational achievement is far superior to that of the average American high school graduate.

How do these habits and values carry over later on? These children, born of intellectual Jews, when they take their place in the adult kibbutz, devote themselves of their own free will to manual labor in an agricultural settlement often surrounded by hostile Arabs; frequently working ten hours a day to cultivate the desert, they live with a minimum of material possessions, and like the way they live. Both competitive ambition and long-range mobility goals, in our sense, are meaningless in their society.

But what of the primary motive for creating this educational system— that of freeing the child from dependence on his parents? Has this goal been realized too? . . .

The system does indeed work in making the child independent of his parents—only too well for the taste of most Western observers, since they believe that little good can come of such early and radical separation of children and parents. . . .

The relations of these children to their kibbutz parents are to an astonishing degree free of those all too intense ambivalences of love and hate, of
the desired and resented dependencies, which characterized relations between
the founders of the kibbutz and *their* parents—and, I might add, which are
also typical in the relations of white middle-class American children and their
parents. But though the relations of kibbutz-educated children to their parents
and to each other are amazingly uncomplicated, straightforward, and unneurotic, they are at the same time—and here is the rub—comparatively lacking
in intensity. This absence of intensity is viewed with alarm both by investigators and by kibbutz parents themselves. Blood simply is not thicker than
shared emotional experiences; it is the latter that tie people together. The
strong positive feelings of the child who is reared communally are concentrated
on his "family" of upbringing, the children with whom he uninterruptedly
shared all the experiences of infancy, childhood, and adolescence.

I should like to offer here a few speculations which seem sound to me
though I cannot offer any strong evidence to support them. For these kibbutz-
educated children the absence of deep involvement with their parents meant
there was no need to revolt or prove themselves in any way against their
elders—by surpassing them economically or socially or morally—in order to
achieve personal worth. Now, the need for individuation is a correlate of the
fear of anonymity. . . .

In the middle-class American family, the child's deep emotional, economic, and social dependence leads to a personality structure developed in
response to the unique stresses, strains, and rewards that the family imposes.
But the child then feels the need to fight free of dependence on his parents by
developing a unique personality that is different from theirs. This striving
becomes still more urgent where the modern mass society threatens the individual with anonymity.

Kibbutz-educated children feel no such defensive need to develop a unique
personality. Each of them is safe from anonymity because he is well known
to all who count in his human surroundings. . . .

By entrusting the child's total education to workers who are replaced—
though not too often—the kibbutz system prevents him from forming either
positive or negative identifications with the whims, idiosyncrasies, or emotional
constellation of one or two particular adults. Instead it forces him to organize
his life along the consistent patterns and values of the *community,* held in
common by all the adults: the ones who take care of him and the others living
around him. . . .

For the individual kibbutz child, this child-centered system pays off, hand-
somely. Absent are the frustrations of all kinds: dependencies satisfied but
made guilt-ridden; injunctions imposed, together with guilt for transgressing
them; needs projected by adults onto the child, and the anxiously feared and

expected developments. In their place are deep, permanent, extremely meaningful and mutually satisfying attachments of the youngsters to each other. These children who grew up together in the new system readily give for each other—their life's comrades—everything: fortune, even life itself.

That their interest in their parents, by comparison, is hardly equal in intensity should have been anticipated. If we remove ourselves from the lives of our children, they are not necessarily the worse off for it—in some ways perhaps even much better off; but we are then not very important in their lives. Still, this logical consequence is a distinct disappointment to most of the first-generation kibbutz parents. . . .

Yet in other respects these kibbutz parents are richly rewarded. From all descriptions, the children turn into exceptionally courageous, self-reliant, secure, unneurotic, and deeply committed adults who find their self-realization in work and in marriage. . . .

The adults are genuinely fond of children, their own as well as others, and this interest in children develops early. . . . Later, as parents, they are warm and affectionate with their children, but relaxed and unanxious. Yet they have no desire to return to raising them privately at home; they are well satisfied with the way they themselves were communally reared. Not having experienced deep emotional attachment to parents as the core of their own development, and, presently having a full life of their own, they do not feel they are missing anything by being parted from their children. Without doubt or hesitation they place their few-days'-old infants in the autonomous children's society. . . .

I am not suggesting that we adopt the kibbutz educational system. I have a great admiration for the vast expenditure of capital and human resources which the members of the kibbutzim bestow on the education of their children, and for the hardships they are willing to undergo to further their children's schooling, which is given so central an importance in the community. What we might well copy, without further study, is this attitude of seriousness toward the problems of children in their development and education.

CHAPTER ELEVEN

Varieties of Family Patterns

Such duty as the subject owes the prince,
Even such a woman oweth to her husband.

> Shakespeare, *The Taming of the Shrew*

In my coat of many colors that my daddy made for me.

> Black folk ballad

I'll take you home again, Kathleen,
To where your heart has ever been.

> Irish song

ANDREW BILLINGSLEY

Black Families in White America

This article by Andrew Billingsley of Howard University maps some of the variety of family styles among American blacks. Beginning with a description of a middle-class family, the article then distinguishes among different kinds of poor families—the working poor, the non-working poor, the underclass poor. Even among the very poor, families vary widely in such characteristics as authority structure and child-care concerns.

A striking example of the precariousness of Negro middle-class life is the Adams family. They are in many respects a model middle-class American family. Mr. Adams is thirty-four and his wife is thirty-two. They have been married for ten years and have three children, Michael, age six, Dennis, age four, and Denise, age two. An Army veteran with two years of college, Mr. Adams is a professional photographer with a steady income. Mrs. Adams also has two years of college. The family income was $10,600 last year. They have a heavy mortgage on their own home on the edge of a black ghetto.

They have planned their family to suit their economic abilities. They delayed having children for the first four years of their marriage, "in order to get on our feet financially." During those first years she worked as an office secretary while he worked at the Post Office.

In other ways, too, they are a model American couple. He is tall and slender, weighs about 185 pounds; he is good looking, dresses well and tastefully with a slight flair, and is in manner and bearing not exactly aggressive, but, as he would describe himself, "somewhat forward." He is industrious, works hard, likes spectator sports, drives a late model car, and drinks to be sociable. He does not go to church because he is tired on Sunday, likes to work around the house and watch television. Mrs. Adams is also an attractive, well groomed young woman, though perhaps a bit less sophisticated than her husband and not quite as forceful in manner. She pays the bills and takes the children to a Protestant church and Sunday School. She makes most of the decisions about the children. It is, on balance, an equalitarian family.

There are other aspects of their family life which support this middle-class equalitarian mold. He gets out of bed first in the morning, for he is an "earlier riser." He dresses the three children and plays with them until she has breakfast ready. He kisses them all goodbye when he leaves the house. They even have a typical middle-class family problem. She is often not ready for work on time, and he "cannot afford to be late." When they drive to work together in their one car, this causes friction.

But if this is in many respects a model American middle-class, equalitarian family, it is only precariously so. Consider their education. While they are more highly educated than a majority of their fellow Americans, they do not have enough to fortify their middle-class position. Their $10,600 last year put them in a distinctly upper-middle income bracket but it was earned at a high price. As in 90 per cent of Negro middle income families, Mrs. Adams worked to help maintain that family income level. Besides, that income was for last year; this year, in keeping with their middle-class style of life and their concern for the care and well-being of their children, particularly since the aunt who used to live there and care for them got married and moved to another city, Mrs. Adams decided to stop work and become a full-time house-wife. She enjoys the role very much. But this year the family income from Mr. Adams' earnings alone will be $6,400. Now they will still be a middle-class, educated, handsome American couple, but the precariousness of their status and the tenuous hold they have on their economic and social well-being are apparent. Mr. Adams has taken an extra job a few hours a night "so that the washing machine and dryer could be paid for without sacrificing the house payments."

Now Mr. Adams, though still keeping up a well dressed appearance in public, does not bathe quite as often as he used to. Now when he leaves his extra job at night he lingers a bit longer at the tavern than he used to. He even seems to drive his car faster and more recklessly than he did before. . . .

Most Negro families are composed of ordinary people. They do not get their names in the paper as outstanding representatives of the Negro race and they do not show up on the welfare rolls or in the crime statistics. They are headed by men and women who work and support their families, manage to keep their families together and out of trouble most of the time. They are not what might be generally conceived of as "achieving families." They are likely to be overlooked when the white community goes looking for a Negro to sit on an interracial committee, or take a job where Negroes have not been hired

Photograph by MacDonald. Courtesy of Photophile.

before. For they have not gone to college and they are not part of that middle- and upper-class group most likely to come into intimate, daily contact with the white world. At the same time, they are likely to be overlooked by the poverty program and other efforts to uplift the poor and disadvantaged. They often do not qualify to take part in these programs because they are not on welfare. They are, in a word, just folks. They are the great unknowns, typically left out of the literature on Negro family life. Once in a while they appear in fiction, but even then generally as oversimplified stereotypes rather than in all their ordinary, human complexity. And yet, these ordinary Negro families are often the backbone of the Negro community. They are virtually unknown to white people, particularly white people who depend on books and other mass media for their knowledge of life in the most important ethnic subsociety in America today.

. . . A study of 173 families in a Negro ghetto of Hartford, Connecticut, provides considerable support for the above description. The "average" family [was described] as the picture was developed by IBM computers from responses of all study families:

> The family is Negro and Protestant. The mother was born and reared in the rural or semi-rural southern United States. She came to live in Hartford sometime after her eighteenth birthday. The family has two legally married parents and contains 4.7 members. Father is the chief breadwinner, earning $4,800 per year from his employment as a skilled craftsman, steward, or machinist.

Mother, who stays home to take care of the children, perceives them as growing, developing human beings amenable to her control, if only to a limited degree.

The parents want their children to have at least some college education. They hope that their children will become skilled technicians, specialized clerical workers, or go into one of the minor professions—library science, teaching, the arts. The children are involved in at least two organized community activities (Scouts, the "Y," settlement house, etc.). Previous to the summer school project, they had been actively involved in some other type of voluntary educational opportunity program.

Mother has achieved a rather high degree of integration into her neighborhood and is involved in a meaningful (to her) give-and-take relationship with her neighbors. At the present time, she is participating in at least two community activities. She is a registered voter and voted in the last election. She listens to the radio, watches television and reads one of the two Hartford newspapers every day.

The family is geared to obtaining a better life for its children, including more education and more materially rewarding, status-giving employment. Hartford is perceived as a racially prejudiced community and education appears to be considered the primary method for circumventing this prejudice.

Families like these, despite their stability, achievement, and contributions within the Negro community, are often ignored by the wider society because of the general tendency to lump all "lower class" Negro families in the ghetto into a single category and to focus on the most dysfunctional patterns of family life there.

Half of all Negro families may be considered distinctly lower class. They view themselves that way and are viewed by their fellows as such. It should be added, however, that this large group of people is highly differentiated and is by no means a uniform mass. Three distinct groupings within this lower class may be identified, including (1) the working nonpoor, (2) the working poor, and (3) the nonworking poor.

At the very top of the lower class is a group of families headed by men in the semi-skilled, highly paid, unionized, steady industrial jobs. These are members of the *industrial working class.* Families of Negro men holding good steady jobs as truck drivers (in the Teamsters Union), construction workers, and semi-skilled factory workers are in the upper reaches of the lower class. If it were not for the color of their skins and the housing discrimination they face, many of these men would be able to join the ranks of the new majority of labor union members who, it is said, now drive from work to their homes in the suburbs, sit in the backyard drinking martinis, and complain about high taxes. But if this is an elite working class, it is indeed a small one. Less than 7 per cent of Negro working men are truck drivers, constituting about 12 per cent of all truck drivers. But not all of them are members of the Teamsters Union. About 3 per cent are lumbermen, but many of these are in the south where wages are low. Less than 2 per cent are auto mechanics and semi-skilled factory workers. Less than 1 per cent are longshoremen, though they account for a third of the workers in this class, often earning $12,000 to $15,000 a year. When to the secure occupational base of these men and their wives are added the style of life they can afford and a degree of community activity in the church, or lodge, or other specifically Negro institution, their status can be considerably higher than that suggested by the term lower class. The "average" family in the Hartford ghetto is among the working nonpoor. Between half and two-thirds of the families with school-age children in this study meet none of the current official definitions of poverty.

A second category of lower-class Negro families is the working poor. The fact is not generally appreciated in the wider society that the majority of poor Negros live in nuclear families headed by men who work hard every day, and are still unable to earn enough to pull their families out of poverty. Each point of this statement should be emphasized.

1. The majority of poor Negros live in nuclear families, and not in segmented families. Nearly 60 per cent of children in families with less than $2,000 annual income were living with both parents in 1959. If we consider families with earnings between $2,000 and $4,000, the proportion of children living with both parents rises to over 80 per cent. It increases, of course, as income does.

2. The majority of poor Negroes live in nuclear families headed by men and not by women. Among families earning less than $3,000 in 1966, nearly 60 per cent were headed by husbands and fathers. Among those earning between $3,000 and $5,000, the proportion of male-headed families increased to nearly 75 per cent. As income increases the proportion of male-headed families increases.

3. The majority of poor Negroes live in families which are self-supporting and are not supported by public welfare. . . . Thus, nationally about a third of all poor Negroes (3.2 million out of 9.6 million) were supported by welfare. This proportion varies by communities. In Hartford nearly 60 per cent of poor families were self-supporting. These are the working poor. . . .

The working poor families are often headed by unskilled laborers, service workers, and domestics. More Negro men work as janitors or porters in this country than in any other specific occupation. . . . Negro women, who are often heads of families in this group, are even more highly concentrated in low level, unskilled jobs than men. . . . These men and women support families in that dominant segment of the lower class which outnumbers every other class stratum and includes probably a third of all Negro families. It should be noted that these men and women work and support their families on very low wages. . . . Even among female-headed families, the majority of the mothers work and support the family.

So far we have described in socioeconomic terms 80 to 85 per cent of Negro families. We come, finally, to that group on the bottom of the economic ladder who occupy the lowest status in both the general community and the Negro community. These are the *nonworking poor,* that 15 or 20 per cent of Negro families headed by members with less than eighth grade education, who are intermittently if at all employed, and who have very low levels of job skills. These are families often supported by relatives and by public welfare. In many respects, though we describe them as part of the lower class, they may be more appropriately referred to as the *under class,* for like the majority of Negro families a hundred years earlier, they are outside and below the formal class structure. In this sector, the basic conditions of life are most abject. Many of these family heads have not gone beyond sixth grade. . . . Among them are families living in dilapidated housing or, if they are very fortunate, in public housing projects.

Even in the under class, however, there are some variations in life conditions. . . .

To be living poor and black means severe restrictions in the most basic conditions, particularly focused in the areas of family income, education of parents, occupations of family heads, family housing, and health care. And, if the conditions of life in these five crucial areas are not met, the Negro family can not be expected to assume the same structure as other, more achieving and affluent families. And, if they do not have the basic supports for their society in these areas and do not develop the most effective structures of family life, they cannot be expected to meet the functions of family life required of them by their members and their society. And yet, they are expected to do these things. And many are able to perform in a remarkably functional manner. Just as there is variety and range in the basic life conditions and societal supports available to Negro families, there is variety and range in both the structure and function of Negro family life. There is no single uniform style of Negro family life, not even in the most depressed sections of urban ghettos. But if there is not complete uniformity, there also is not random variety. There are patterns, and modalities of life which are eminently tied in to the basic conditions of life, both contemporary and historical.

There are several bases for the patterning of life among low-income Negro families. First, there is geographic patterning. . . . The conditions of life for low-income Negro families are most abject in the rural South, less so in the urban South and less so still in the urban North and West. The ability of Negro families to meet the requirements of society, particularly for achievement, is highly associated with this geographic patterning.

A second basis for patterning is socioeconomic. Even among the lower class, there are at least three major groupings, the *working nonpoor,* the *working poor,* and the *nonworking poor.* Both family stability and family achievement, and thus viability, follow very closely variations in socioeconomic status.

Thirdly, there are patterns in the structure of Negro family life, based on household composition. Thus some families are *basic families* with only the two married adults present. Others are *nuclear families* with two married adults and children. Still others are *attenuated nuclear families* with one adult missing. And each of these three types of primary family groups may be further elaborated into *extended families, sub-families,* or *augmented families* with nonrelatives functioning as intimate members of the household.

Still a fourth type of patterning is related to size. There are small, medium, and large sized families in the lower class. Size may serve as both an obstacle, and a facilitator of achievement depending on the age, sex, relationship, character, and contribution of the various family members.

A fifth type of patterning is associated with authority and decision making in the family. Here there are three distinct groups. There are the vanishing *patriarchies,* where men make most of the decisions in crucial areas of family life. They form a minority among low-income Negro families, but they still exist to some extent. Then there are the resilient *matriarchies* in which the wife and mother exerts an inordinate amount of authority at the expense of or in the absence of the husband and father. This is the second most common authority pattern among low income Negro families, and not the most common as is often assumed. Then, finally, there are the expanding *equalitarians.* These are families in which both husband and wife participate actively and jointly in decision making in the major areas of family life. Their tribes are increasing at the expense of both the patriarchy and the matriarchy. This is the most common pattern of authority among lower-class Negro families today.

A sixth type of patterning has to do with family division of labor. Some families have a more or less strict, traditional division of labor based on sex. The man earns the livelihood, and does little else of the household and family chores. The wife and mother has her work which she performs largely unaided. These are role segmented families. In still other families, however, there is role flexibility and mutual cooperation between husband and wife in meeting the instrumental needs of the family in both the external world and within the family. Still other families have children or other relatives able and willing to participate jointly with husband and wife in these major functions of family life. Among low-income Negro families, the segmented role relationships are probably most common, although, as the above discussion has shown, collaboration is probably more common than is generally thought. Also, when there are older children in the family, they are drafted into service with household tasks, including child rearing tasks, at a much earlier age in these families than among other ethnic subsocieties.

Seventh, and finally, there are patterns of Negro family life reflected in their attitudes and behavior toward the socialization of children. Some low-income Negro families take very good care of their children and inspire and aid them on toward conformity and achievement in the major areas and institutions of life. These are families that are considered to function adequately. They are able to understand, intervene actively in, and manipulate to some extent the plethora of institutions on which they depend and which, often, in themselves, function most inadequately. A second category of families function less adequately. They function better in some areas of life than others; and better at some times than others, and always they function better under some (favorable) conditions than under others. These families may be on and off welfare. Their children may be in and out of trouble. They are engaged in a struggle for respectability, conformity and achievement. Then, at the bottom of life's resources, is a relatively large group of low-income Negro families who have been most deserted by their society. They receive the least supports from the major institutions of society. They are the most victimized by discrimination and poverty and general lack of opportunity. They are, consequently, the most chronically unstable, dependent and deviant. Their children are most likely to get into trouble or to be neglected. These are the problem families and the long term welfare recipients.

But it cannot be stressed too strongly that not all lower-class Negro families are poor. Not all poor families are broken. Not all single-parent families are on welfare. And not all welfare families are chronic problems. A more adequate income structure would remove many of them from the arena of social concern.

These are the major dimensions along which Negro family life is patterned in the other America. They interact with and overlap each other. Families move from one category to another as time and circumstances change. They do this in response to life conditions and in an effort to survive, to conform, and to achieve in a society which expects these ends, but often provides inadequate means to their attainment.

NATHAN GLAZER AND
HERBERT GUTMAN

Black Families:
An Exchange

It is widely recognized that contemporary black families have a high rate of out-of-wedlock births and a high proportion of female-headed households. In 1975, for example, more than 35 per cent of all black families were headed by females, compared to less than 11 percent of white families. However, there is widespread disagreement about the reasons for these patterns in black families. In 1965, Daniel Moynihan, then Assistant Secretary of Labor, attributed what he termed the "instability" of black families to the heritage of slavery, a view that had also been expressed in a book he coauthored with sociologist Nathan Glazer, Beyond the Melting Pot. *Critics of Moynihan and Glazer have pointed out that the differences in family patterns between blacks and whites are not nearly so great if families in similar economic circumstances are compared. In addition, recent research by historian Herbert Gutman has shown that the two-parent, nuclear family prevailed among blacks not only under slavery, but indeed through the 1920s. As the following exchange of letters from* The Nation *magazine shows, Glazer accepts Gutman's historical research, but the two disagree strongly on whether the primary cause of the problems of poor black families today is our welfare policies or continuing discrimination that has resulted in lack of economic opportunities and kept so many blacks in poverty.*

Scholarly Style?

Cambridge, Mass.

I respect Herbert G. Gutman for his monumental scholarship on the black family under slavery and after. . . . But now we move on to the present, and one may still ask: If the poor black family was, as described by Gutman and others, solidly fixed in a supportive network of extended kin—and I do not dispute it—then what could explain what has been happening for the past twenty years? Here Gutman is remarkably silent. He writes, the "familial and kin connections [of black families] have been unconscionably strained in the past four decades," but certainly this strain should have been considerably reduced in the [past fifteen] years, when we have seen major legislation and programs against discrimination instituted, a dramatic reduction in prejudice, a great increase in the number of blacks in good white-collar and professional jobs, a huge increase in blacks going to college. Yet it is just during these past fifteen years that we have seen great increases in black children born out of wedlock and in broken black nuclear families. Whatever the strengths of the black family and kin networks, no one argues that there is no problem when perhaps half the black children being born come into family situations in which there is no assurance of a stable relationship with the father, the assurance that for the rest of the society is symbolized by the commitment of marriage. Gutman and other critics of those of us who have said this is a problem cannot have it both ways; they cannot insist there is no problem because of the strengths of black family and kin networks, and then say there is a terrible problem and that "family and kin connections have been unconscionably strained." Clearly there has been more ingenious adaptation to this strain than bare statistics describing high rates of illegitimacy and family breakup suggest. But the statistics also express a reality, one in which many children are being raised, yes, in a "tangle of pathology." . . .

I agree that, whatever the contribution of the distant past to the situation of the poor black urban family, the contribution of the present is more significant. But those—like Gutman—who insist on this don't tell us *what* the significance of the present for the disastrous condition of the poor black family is. The significance of the present cannot possibly be, as they sometimes suggest, that opportunities for poor urban blacks are now fewer—never have there been more. I believe the evidence strongly suggests that the black family is being damaged now basically by misguided social policies, principally our welfare policies, that create a situation in which stable family life and normal work find massive competition. George Gilder's *Visible Man* describes how devastating this competition is for the Northern poor urban black family. My question was not a rhetorical one: It was an effort to direct attention to a continuing plague, one spread by contemporary social policies, but one to which it is also very difficult to find alternatives. Without continuing the discussion of the poor black family directly, Moynihan certainly has not been derelict in trying to find alternatives to social policies that now seem to be the main continuing cause of a bad situation. And I have given a good deal of my time, too, to pondering what we might do about these policies to strengthen rather than destroy supportive kin networks.

Panglossian Purview*

Nyack, N.Y.

Nathan Glazer's letter invites three brief comments. First, it is welcome news that Glazer now rejects "the legacy of slavery" argument (a historic "deficit" black family structure) so central to his and Daniel P. Moynihan's prescription for black social health in the 1960s. Glazer now writes, "Whatever the contribution of the distant past to the situation of the poor urban black family, the contribution of the present is more significant."

But Glazer's view of the present remains excessively Panglossian. (I leave aside his description of the black middle class except to remind readers of Vernon Jordan's sanguine comment that most middle-class blacks would return to poverty if they missed three paychecks, and of the fact that the aggregate number of blacks in the middle class now is actually shrinking.) Glazer's optimism is misleading. He seeks "present" explanations for the troubles poor blacks and their families experience but insists that such explanations "cannot possibly be . . . that opportunities for poor urban blacks are now fewer—never have there been more." Really? Between 1954 and 1978 the unemployment rate for white youths aged 16 to 19 increased from 12.1 percent to 13.9 percent. Among black youths aged 16 to 19, it increased from 16.5 percent to 36.3 percent. And the unemployment rate among blacks aged 20 to 24 (20.7 percent) doubled in the past decade. The recent suffering among so many poor urban blacks has not been experienced in a setting of expanding opportunity for them. Glazer surely must know these facts. . . .

---

*Ed. note: Dr. Pangloss, in Voltaire's *Candide,* was the tutor who said, "All is for the best in this best of all possible worlds."

HERBERT J. GANS

The Urban Villagers

America is a land of immigrants. Although some observers have called America a "melting pot" in which different nationalities were fused into an "American" people, many European immigrants, particularly in the late 19th and early 20th centuries, moved to ethnic enclaves in America. There they continued their family traditions through several generations. In the following article, sociologist Herbert Gans describes an aspect of the social-ization system of a group of Italian Americans, the urban villagers in Boston's West End. The role of the peer group in this subculture shares certain features of the children's house described by Bettelheim in Chapter Ten.

Generally speaking, the Italian and Sicilian cultures that the immigrants brought with them to America have not been maintained by the second gen-eration. Their over-all culture is that of Americans. A number of Italian patterns, however, have survived, the most visible ones being food habits. In all European ethnic groups, traditional foods and cooking methods are retained long after other aspects of the immigrant culture are given up. This is true also among West Enders. Most of the women still cook only Italian dishes at home, and many of them still make their own "pasta," especially for holiday dishes. . . .

The pattern of heavy eating and light drinking, found in most Latin and Mediterranean cultures, also persists among the West Enders. Thus, rich food rather than alcohol is used to counteract deprivation or to celebrate. Entrées are strongly spiced, and desserts are very sweet. Even so, the food is milder and less spicy than that eaten by their parents. Moreover, West Enders have also given up the immigrant pattern of preparing olive oil and wine at home, and buy the weaker commercially made ones.

The durability of the ethnic tradition with respect to food is probably due to the close connection of food with family and group life. Indeed, food patterns are retained longer than others because they hold the group together with a minimum of strain. Also, there seems to be some association between food and the home. Food preparation serves as an example of the woman's skill as a housewife and mother. When company is present, it enables her to display her skills to relatives and peers.

Another pattern that has persisted into the second generation is language. Most of the West Enders I met could speak Italian—or, more correctly, the special patois of their locality—because they had learned it from their parents, and had to use it to communicate with them. Their children—that is, the third generation—are not being taught the language, however. Also, Italian names are slowly being Anglicized. . . .

There is little, if any, identification either with Italy or with the local areas from which the immigrants came originally. Second-generation people know their parents' birthplace, but it is of little interest to them. . . .

Acculturation thus has almost completely eroded Italian culture patterns among the second generation, and is likely to erase the rest in the third generation. In fact, the process seems to have begun soon after the arrival of the immigrants. One West Ender told me that his Italian-born mother had saved for years for a visit to Italy, but that when she was finally able to go, she came back after a month, saying that she could not live among these people because she was not like any of them. The woman, even though she had never learned to speak English properly, had become Americanized in the West End. . . .

Assimilation, however—the disappearance of the Italian social system—has proceeded much more slowly. Indeed, the social structure of the West End, to be discussed in the next section, is still quite similar to that of the first generation. Social relationships are almost entirely limited to other Italians, because much sociability is based on kinship, and because most friendships are made in childhood, and are thus influenced by residential propinquity. Intermarriage with non-Italians is unusual among the second generation, and is not favored for the third. As long as both parties are Catholic, however, disapproval is mild.

The relationship to the church is also similar to that of the immigrant generations. West Enders are religious, but they minimize their ties to the church. And while the traditional Italian emphasis on the Virgin Mary and the local saint continues, the superstitions based on the anthropomorphizing of nature have faded away.

Judging by the nostalgia of the West Enders for the past, it would appear that the Italian group is no longer as cohesive as it was in the previous generation. They say that in those days, people were friendlier and more cooperative, and that there were fewer individual wants, especially on the part of children. But while they mourn the loss of cohesion, they do not pursue it.

For example, the redevelopment gave West Enders an opportunity to return to a more cohesive community in the nearby North End, which is still entirely Italian. None of the West Enders seemed to be interested, however, largely because of the poorer quality of the housing. The ethnic homogeneity and cohesion of the North End were never mentioned either positively or negatively; for most people it was a place to shop for Italian food, and to visit relatives.

Relationships with members of other ethnic groups are friendly but infrequent. These groups are characterized by traditional stereotypes, to which exceptions are made only in the case of specific individuals. . . . The social distance between ethnic groups was illustrated by one West Ender, who was on friendly terms with her Jewish neighbor. When she spoke of the woman, however, she did not use her name, but called her simply—and entirely without malice— "the Jew."

The Structure of West End Society: An Introduction to the Peer Group Society

While residence, class, and ethnicity may locate the West Ender in ecological and social space, they tell us little about how he lives his daily life. As has already been noted in passing, life for the West Ender is defined in terms of his relationship to the group. . . .

The life of the West Ender takes place within three interrelated sectors: the primary group, the secondary group, and the outgroup. The primary group refers to that combination of family and peer relationships which I shall call the *peer group society*. The secondary group refers to the small array of Italian institutions, voluntary organizations, and other social bodies which function to support the workings of the peer group society. This I shall call the *community*. I use this term because *it,* rather than the West End or Boston, is the West Ender's community. The outgroup, which I shall describe as the *outside world,* covers a variety of non-Italian institutions in the West End, in Boston, and in America that impinge on his life—often unhappily to the West Ender's way of thinking.

Although social and economic systems in the outside world are significant in shaping the life of the West Ender, the most important part of that life is lived within the primary group. National and local economic, social, and political institutions may determine the West Ender's opportunities for income, work, and standard of living, but it is the primary group that refracts these outside events and thus shapes his personality and culture. Because the peer group society dominates his entire life, and structures his relationship with the community and the outside world, I shall sometimes use the term to describe not only the primary relationships, but the West Enders' entire social structure as well.

The primary group is a peer group society because most of the West Enders' relationships are with peers, that is, among people of the same sex, age, and life-cycle status. While this society includes the friendships, cliques, informal clubs, and gangs usually associated with peer groups, it also takes in family life. In fact, during adulthood, the family is its most important component. Adult West Enders spend almost as much time with siblings, in-laws, and cousins—that is, with relatives of the same sex and age—as with their spouses, and more time than with parents, aunts, and uncles. The peer group society thus continues long past adolescence, and, indeed, dominates the life of the West Ender from birth to death. For this reason I have coined the term "peer group society."

In order to best describe the dominance of the peer group principle in the life of the West Ender, it is necessary to examine it over a typical life cycle. The child is born into a nuclear family; at an early age, however, he or she—although girls are slower to do this than boys—transfers increasing amounts of his time and allegiance to the peers he meets in the street and in school. This transfer may even begin long before the child enters school. Thus, one West Ender told me that when he wanted his two-year-old son to attend an activity at a local settlement house, bribery and threats were useless, but that the promise that he could go with two other young children on the block produced immediate assent.

From this time on, then, the West Ender spends the rest of his life in one or another peer group. Before or soon after they start going to school, boys and girls form cliques or gangs. In these cliques, which are sexually segregated, they play together and learn the lore of childhood. The clique influence is so strong, in fact, that both parents and school officials complain that their values have difficulty competing with those being taught in the peer group. The sexually segregated clique maintains its hold on the individual until late adolescence or early adulthood.

Dating, the heterosexual relationship between two individuals that the middle-class child enters into after puberty—or even earlier—is much rarer among West Enders. Boys and girls may come together in peer groups to a settlement house dance or a clubroom. Even so, they dance with each other only infrequently. Indeed, at the teenage dances I observed, the girls danced mostly with each other and the boys stood in the corner—a peer group pattern that may continue even among young adults. A West End girl in her twenties described her dates as groups of men and women going out together, with little social contact between individual men and women during the evening. Individual dating takes place not as part of the group activity, as in the middle class, but only after the group has dispersed. Judging from the descriptions given by young West End men, the relationship then is purely sexual—at least for them.

The hold of the peer group is broken briefly at marriage. During courtship, the man commutes between it and his girl. Female peer groups—always less cohesive than male—break up even more easily then, because the girl who wants to get married must compete with her peers for male friends and must be at their beck and call. At marriage, the couple leaves its peer groups, but after a short time, often following the arrival of the first child, they both re-enter peer group life.

Among action-seeking West Enders, the man may return to his corner, and the woman to her girl friends. But most often—especially in the routine-seeking working class—a new peer group is formed, consisting of family members and a few friends of each spouse. This group meets after working hours for long evenings of sociability. Although the members of the group are of both sexes, the normal tendency is for the men and women to split up, the men in one room and the women in another. In addition, husband and wife also may belong to other peer groups: work colleagues or childhood friends among the men, informal clubs of old friends that meet regularly among the women. In the West End, friendship ties seem to be formed mainly in child-hood and adolescence, and many of them last throughout life.

But the mainstay of the adult peer group society is the *family circle*. As already noted, the circle is made up of collateral kin: in-laws, siblings, and cousins predominantly. Not all family members are eligible for the peer group, but the rules of selection—which are informal and unstated—are based less on closeness of kinship ties than on compatibility. Family members come together if they are roughly of the same age, socio-economic level, and cultural background. How closely or distantly they are related is much less important than the possession of common interests and values. Even among brothers and sisters only those who are compatible are likely to see each other regularly.

This combination of family members and friends seems to continue to function as a peer group for the rest of the life cycle. Thus, each of the marriage partners is pulled out *centrifugally* toward his or her peers, as compared with the middle-class family in which a *centripetal* push brings husband and wife closer together.

The West End, in effect, may be viewed as a large network of these peer groups, which are connected by the fact that some people may belong to more than one group. In addition, a few individuals function as communicators between the groups, and thus keep them informed of events and attitudes important to them all. . . .

The hold of the peer group on the individual is very strong. Some illus-trations of this can be given here. Achievement and social mobility, for ex-ample, are group phenomena. In the current generation, in which the Italian is still effectively limited to blue-collar work, atypical educational and occu-pational mobility by the individual is frowned upon. Children who do well in school are called "sissies," and they cannot excel there and expect to remain in their peer group. Since allegiance to any one group is slight at this stage, however, the good student can drift into other peer groups until he finds one with compatible members. Should such peers be lacking, he may have to choose between isolation or a group that does not share his standards. Often, he chooses the latter. This is well illustrated by children who have intellectual skills but who find that out of fear of peer group pressures they cannot summon the self-control to do well in school.

Life in a peer group society has a variety of far-reaching social and psychological consequences. For example, the centrifugal pressure on man and wife affects the family structure, as does the willingness—or resignation—of the parents in relinquishing their children to their own peer group at an early age. The fact that individuals are accustomed to being with—and are more at ease with—members of their own sex means that their activities are cued primarily to reference groups of that sex. This may help to explain the narcissistic vanity among West End men, that is, their concern with clothes, and displays of muscular strength or virility. It also may help to explain the chaperoning of unmarried women, in fear that they will otherwise indulge in sexual intercourse. Not only does the separation of the sexes substitute for the development of internal controls that discourage the man from taking advantage of the woman, but they replace, as well, those controls that allow the woman to protect herself.

The peer group principle has even more important consequences for personality organization. Indeed, the role of the group in the life of the individual is such that he exists primarily in the group. School officials, for example, pointed out that teenagers were rough and active when they were with their peers, but quiet and remarkably mild and passive when alone. Their mildness is due to the fact that they exist only partially when they are outside the group. In effect, the individual personality functions best and most completely among his or her peers—a fact that has some implications for independence and dependence, conformity and individualism among the West Enders. In some ways the individual who lives in a peer group society is more dependent than the middle-class person. This is true, however, only on a superficial level. . . . Both types are independent, but their independence is expressed in different contexts, and varies in a number of other characteristics.

My emphasis on the role of the peer group should not be taken to mean that it is distinctive to the West End, or even to second-generation Italians. Other studies have suggested that it is a fairly universal phenomenon in working-class groups. Nor does its influence end at this point. Peer groups are found in all classes, but in the middle and upper-middle class, they play a less important role, especially among adults. In the lower-middle class, for example, peer groups are made up of neighbors and friends, and exist alongside the nuclear family, but usually they do not include members of the family circle. Moreover, dependence on the peer group for sociability and mutual aid is much weaker. Also, there is much more interaction among couples and groups of couples. Nevertheless, social gatherings usually do break up into male and female enclaves, and voluntary associations are segregated by sex. In the upper-middle class, social relationships take place primarily among couples, and voluntary associations are less frequently segregated by sex. Even so, social gatherings and activity groups may break up into male and female subgroups. Upper-middle-class women often resent the fact that concentration on the mother role creates handicaps to job or organizational activities in which the sexes work together.

In the lower-middle class, and more so in the upper-middle class, people move in a larger number of peer groups, often formed to pursue specific interests and activities. The West End pattern, in which people spend most of their spare time within the confines of one peer group, is not found here. Consequently, the influence of the peer group on the life of the middle class is much less intense.

LILLIAN B. RUBIN

Worlds of Pain

*Working-class families look at marriage and family life through a screen of
expectations, attitudes, and conventions that differ from middle-class concepts. Sex role distinctions are more openly acknowledged in the working
class: a man is expected to "provide for his family," a wife to maintain the
home and social life. The authority of the husband is more explicitly recognized in the working class. Middle-class women, in contrast, do not speak
of their husbands allowing or not allowing them to make decisions. Despite
these differences, common currents run through family life in both classes.
Both common and disparate themes are subtly analyzed in this selection by
Lillian Rubin, excerpted from her book* Worlds of Pain: Life in the Working
Class Family.

> I guess I can't complain. He's a steady worker; he doesn't drink; he doesn't hit
> me. That's a lot more than my mother had, and she didn't sit around complaining
> and feeling sorry for herself, so I sure haven't got the right.
>
> [*Thirty-three-year-old housewife,*
> *mother of three, married thirteen years.*]

"He's a steady worker; he doesn't drink; he doesn't hit me"—these are the
three attributes working-class women tick off most readily when asked what
they value most in their husbands. Not a surprising response when one recalls
their familiarity with unemployment, alcoholism, and violence, whether in
their own families or in those around them. That this response is class-related
is evident from the fact that not one woman in the professional middle-class
families mentioned any of these qualities when answering the same question.
Although there was no response that was consistently heard from the middle-
class wives, they tended to focus on such issues as intimacy, sharing, and
communication and, while expressed in subtle ways, on the comforts, status,
and prestige that their husbands' occupation affords. Janet Harris, writing

Oklahoma Migrants, 1936. Concepts of a good family life differ among lower- and middle-class families. (From The Depression Years as Photographed by Arthur Rothstein. *Dover Publications.)*

about middle-class women at forty, also comments that she never heard a women list her husband's ability to provide or the fact that he is "good to the children" as valued primary traits. "The security and financial support that a husband provides are taken for granted," she argues; "it is the emotional sustainment which is the barometer of a marriage."

Does this mean, then, that working-class women are unconcerned about the emotional side of the marriage relationship? Emphatically, it does not. It says first that when the material aspects of life are problematic, they become dominant as issues requiring solutions; and second, that even when men are earning a reasonably good living, it is *never* "taken for granted" when financial insecurity and marginality are woven into the fabric of life. These crucial differences in the definition of a good life, a good husband, a good marriage— and the reasons for them—often are obscured in studies of marriage and the family because students of the subject rarely even mention class, let alone analyze class differences.

Still, it is a mixed message that these working-class women send; for while many remind themselves regularly that they have no right to complain, their feelings of discontent with the emotional aspects of the marriage are not so easily denied. Indeed, once the immediate problems and preoccupations of the early years subside, once the young husband is "housebroken," an interesting switch occurs. Before the marriage and in the first years, it is the wife who seems more eager to be married; the husband, more reluctant. Marriage brings her more immediate gains since being unmarried is a highly stigmatized status for a woman, especially in the working-class world. Both husband and wife subscribe to the "I-chased-her-until-she-caught-me" myth about courtship in America; both believe that somehow, using some mysterious feminine wiles, she contrived to ensnare him. It is no surprise, then, that it is he who has more trouble in settling down at the beginning—feeling hemmed in, oppressed by the contours and confines of marriage, by its responsibilities.

With time, he begins to work more steadily, to earn more money. The responsibilities seem to weigh a little lighter. With time, he finds ways to live with some constraints, to circumvent others. For him, marriage becomes a comfortable haven—a place of retreat from the pressures and annoyances of the day, a place where his needs and comforts are attended to by his wife, the only place perhaps where he can exercise his authority. He begins to feel that he's made a good bargain. It's true, it costs plenty. He has to commit to a lifetime of hard work—sometimes at a job he hates, sometimes not. But the benefits are high too; and there's no other way he can get them:

> I like being married now. I don't even feel tied down anymore. I'm out all day and, if I want to have a drink with the boys after work, I just call her up and tell her I'll be home later. When I get home, there's a meal—she's a real good cook— and I can just relax and take it easy. The kids—they're the apples of my eyes— they're taken care of; she brings them up right, keeps them clean, teaches them respect. I can't ask for any more. It's a good life.
>
> [*Thirty-eight-year old plumber, father
> of three, married seventeen years.*]

For his wife, time works the other way. She finds herself facing increasing constraints or, at least, experiencing them as more oppressive. For her, there are few ways to circumvent them—no regular work hours:

> When I was a kid and used to wish I was a boy, I never knew why I thought that. Now I know. It's because a man can go to work for eight hours and come home, and a woman's work is just never done. And it doesn't make any difference if she works or not.

. . . no stopping off for a relaxing moment after work:

> He gets to stop off and have a drink when he feels like it. But me, I have to rush home from work and get things going in the house.

. . . no regular time off in which to develop her own interests and activities:

> I know I shouldn't complain. Bringing home a check and food for the family and keeping a roof over our heads is a lot of responsibility. But it's his *only* responsibility. I work too, and I still have to worry about everything else while he comes home and just relaxes. He has time to do other things he wants to do after work, like getting out there and fooling around fixing his truck, or other projects he likes to do. Me, I don't have time for anything.

. . . no night out she can count on:

> He gets out once a week, at least. I don't always know what he does. He goes to
> a ball game or something like that; or he just goes out with some of the guys. Me,
> if I'm ever dumb enough to take a night off to do something, I pay for it when
> I come home. He can't—or maybe he won't—control the kids, so the house looks
> like a cyclone, and he's so mad at the kids and me, you can't live with him for
> days.

. . . and perhaps more important, no way, short of years of nagging or divorce,
to defy her husband's authority and dicta about what she may or may not do
with her life:

> I begin to worry what's going to happen to me after the kids are grown up. I don't
> want to be like my mother, just sort of hanging around being a professional
> mother and grandmother. So I thought I could go to school—you know, take a
> few courses or something, maybe even be a teacher eventually. But he says I can't
> and no matter how much I beg, he won't let me.

"He won't let me"—a phrase heard often among working-class women.
"He won't let me"—a phrase spoken unselfconsciously, with a sense of resignation, as if that's the way of the world. Indeed, that is the way for most
of these women.

It is not only in the working class that this is true, however. Rather, it is
only there that a *language* exists which speaks of husbands "permitting"
wives. Not once did a professional middle-class man speak about refusing his
wife permission to do something—whether to go to work, to school, or to have
an abortion. Not once was a wife in a professional family heard to say, "He
won't let me." Such talk would conflict with the philosophy of egalitarianism
in the family that finds its fullest articulation among men and women of this
class. But the tension between ideology and reality is high and, as William
Goode writes in *World Revolution and Family Patterns,* ". . . the more
educated men are more likely to concede more rights ideologically than they
in fact grant." The mere fact that the discussion takes place around what men
will "grant" is itself a telling statement. For in relations between equals, one
need not grant rights to another; they are assumed as a matter of course.

To understand the reality of middle-class life around this issue, the shell
of language with which the more highly educated protect themselves must be
pierced. When it is, the behavior with which men effectively deny women
permission stands revealed. Thus, referring to an unplanned pregnancy and
his wife's wish for an abortion, one professional man said:

> It's her choice; she has to raise the kids. I told her I'll go along with whatever she
> decides. [*After a moment's hesitation.*] But, you know, if she goes through with
> it, I'll never agree to have another child. If we destroy this one, we don't deserve
> to have another.

Have you told her that?

[*Defensively.*] Of course! She has to know how I feel.

How did she respond?

She cried and got angry. She said I wasn't giving her much of a choice. But it seems to me she ought to know what the consequences of her actions will be when she makes the decision, and those are the consequences. Anyhow, it's all over now; she's decided to have the baby.

Such are the "choices" that confronted this woman as she struggled to make the decision.

The difference, then, is not that middle-class marriages actually are so much more egalitarian, but that the *ideology* of equality is more strongly *asserted* there. This fact alone is, of course, not without consequences, para-doxical though they may be. On the one hand, it undoubtedly is a central reason why middle-class women are in the vanguard of the struggle for change in the family structure. On the other hand, an ideology so strongly asserted tends to obscure the reality, leaving middle-class women even more mystified than their working-class sisters about how power is distributed in their mar-riages. Thus, the middle-class wife who wants an abortion but decides against it because of her husband's threats, doesn't say, "He won't let me." Instead, she rationalizes:

> It was a hard choice, but it was mine. Paul would have accepted anything I decided, but it just didn't seem right or fair for me to make that kind of decision alone when it affects both of us.

For the working-class woman, the power and authority of her husband are more openly acknowledged—at least around issues such as these. She knows when he won't let her; it's direct and explicit—too much so for her to ration-alize it away.

Such differences in ideology are themselves a concomitant of class and the existential realities which people confront in their daily lives. First, there are important differences in what is expected of wives—in how they relate to their husbands' work, for example—and important consequences that flow from those expectations. Wives in professional middle-class families actually are expected to participate in their husbands' professional lives by cultivating an appropriate social circle, by being entertaining and charming hostesses and companions. Most large corporations, after all, do not hire a middle or top executive without meeting and evaluating the candidate's wife. By definition, the tasks of such a wife are broader than those of the working-class wife. The wife of the executive or professional man must be active in the community, alert to world events, prepared to "shine"—only not *too* brightly—at a mo-ment's notice. Husbands who require wives to perform such services must allow them to move more freely outside the home if they are to carry out their tasks properly.

The working-class man has no need of a wife with such accomplishments since his work life is almost wholly segregated from his family life. His wife has no positive, active role in helping him to get or keep a job, let alone in his advancement. No one outside the family cares how she keeps the house, raises the children, what books she reads, what opinions she holds on the state of the nation, the world, or the neighborhood. Her husband, therefore, is under no pressure to encourage either her freedom of movement or her self-development; and she has no external supports to legitimate whatever longings she may feel. Among the wives of the professional middle class, those longings and the activities they generate are supported by the requirements of the role. A charming hostess must at least be conversant with the world of ideas; an interesting companion must know something about the latest books. But for the working-class woman to develop such interests would require a rare order of giftedness, a willingness to risk separation from the world of family and intimates, and a tenacity of purpose and clarity of direction that few of us can claim.

In other ways, too, the realities of class make themselves felt both inside and outside the home. The professional man almost invariably is more highly educated than his wife—a fact that gives him an edge of superiority in their relationship; not so with his working-class counterpart. The professional man has the prospect of a secure and orderly work life—his feet on a prestigious and high-salaried career ladder; not so with his working-class counterpart. The professional man is a respected member of the community outside his home—his advice sought, his words valued; not so with his working-class counterpart.

Thus, the professional middle-class man is more secure, has more status and prestige than the working-class man—factors which enable him to assume a less *overtly* authoritarian role within the family. There are, after all, other places, other situations where his authority and power are tested and accorded legitimacy. At the same time, the demands of his work role for a satellite wife require that he risk the consequences of the more egalitarian family ideology. In contrast, for the working-class man, there are few such rewards in the world outside the home; the family usually is the only place where he can exercise power, demand obedience to his authority. Since his work role makes no demands for wifely participation, he is under fewer and less immediate external pressures to accept the egalitarian ideology.

Part Four

CRISIS AND RESPONSE

Introduction

The American family, challenged in recent years by ideological and social movements, has been stressed to an unprecedented degree. Divorce has increased significantly (though this may be, as historians have cautioned, only an extension of a long historical trend). Young people are postponing marriage until a later age, and some are choosing not to marry but to form different kinds of "families" which may exclude either sex or children or both. Runaway children and mothers are not uncommon; nor are mothers who are still children themselves. Family violence—child abuse and wife-beating—appear to be increasing, though it is hard to know precisely the extent to which higher statistics represent an increase in actual incidences of violence or an increase in reporting of cases. These and other trends bespeak stress on the institution of the family brought about by rapid changes in our economic and social organization.

In this last part of the book, we consider indicators of stress, some of the ways in which the family and society have responded to stress, and future prospects for the family. In Chapter Twelve, "Signs of Strain," divorce—perhaps the leading manifestation of strains on the institution of the family—is viewed from two different perspectives. Psychologists Judith S. Wallerstein and Joan B. Kelly consider the impact of divorce on the children involved, while sociologist Jessie Bernard considers the effect of our current policies regarding divorce on the future well-being of the couple involved. The stresses imposed on marriage by women's drive for equality are considered from a sympathetic male's point of view in "Confusions of a Middle-Class Husband," by sociology professor S.M. Miller.

Alternatives to the traditional, middle-class nuclear family have been proposed or developed out of necessity in response to changing mores and economic and social conditions. Some of these new forms are considered in Chapter Thirteen.

One increasingly common alternative to the husband/provider, wife/homemaker pattern is the two-career couple. More than half of all married women are in the labor force today. Perhaps most are driven into the job market by economic necessity in a period of double-digit inflation. But many others, including highly-educated middle-class women imbued with the ideology of the feminist movement and attracted by the new opportunities now open to them, want to work in order to fulfill their own career goals. Some of the adjustments that couples must make to accommodate two careers are analyzed by Kathy Weingarten, a psychologist, in "Interdependence."

In contrast to those who "make it together" in two-career marriages are those who must "make it alone" in single-parent households. There are so many of these families today that they have formed an international self-help organization, "Parents Without Partners," with local chapters in communities throughout the United States. Esther Wattenberg, of the University of Minnesota School of Social Work, and Hazel Reinhardt, a demographer, consider the problems of "Female-Headed Families," while author Robert Miner describes in "Man as Mother" what it is like for a man to be responsible for the daily care of a small child.

One possible solution to so many children growing up with only one parent is proposed by Margaret Mead in "Marriage in Two Steps." Reviving an idea that gained currency in the 1920s, the noted anthropologist suggested that there be two kinds of marriage: the individual marriage, which would involve a commitment only to one's partner, and the more permanent parental marriage, which would have as its goal the establishment of a family. The first kind of marriage could, but would not necessarily, be a first, trial step toward the second. The individual marriage would, essentially, give formal status to the arrangements many young people have adopted today, of living together without intending to have children.

The final alternative we consider in this chapter, the commune, is not really a new form; many primitive peoples have some sort of communal living arrangements, and there have been periodic experiments in communal living throughout the history of the United States. But the communes that developed during the late 1960s and early 1970s were a specific revolt against middle-class values and lifestyles. Sociologist Bennett Berger and his colleagues describe one aspect of this counterculture in "Child Rearing in Communes."

A variety of services has developd to support families undergoing change or crisis, and social critics and practitioners in the field of family service have proposed other policies and programs to the government to aid families in performing crucial functions under stress. These are considered in Chapter Fourteen, "Family Services and Public Policy." Psychologist Kenneth Keniston and the Carnegie Council on Children, in "Services Families Need," review the services we currently provide and, finding them lacking, make recomendations for other policies to support the family. The next two articles are concerned with improving marriages, through counseling and marriage enrichment. Marriage counseling has become increasingly widespread today. Formerly a luxury of only the rich, it is now offered through community services in many areas. William J. Lederer and Don D. Jackson, in "Interpersonal Comparison Tests," present a questionnaire that is used with couples seeking marital counseling. Joanne and Lew Koch look at a recent trend, marriage encounter and marriage enrichment, in their article, "The Urgent Drive to Make Good Marriages Better." The last article in this chapter, by journalist Lillemor Melsted, outlines "Swedish Family Policy," which is considered to be among the most advanced in the western world in terms of the financial and practical support it gives the family.

Finally, in the last chapter of the book, we turn to "The Family in the Future." Will the family survive? Will it undergo dramatic changes in form and/or functions? Will we witness another baby boom in the 1980s, as some demographers predict? Will extended families—of kin or non-blood relations—come into prominence as we come to recognize the hazards and hardships of small, isolated nuclear families? Will we eventually see men and women sharing equally the hard work and the satisfactions of building and maintaining families?

The authors of the selections in the final chapter present a variety of answers. Journalist Jane Howard, in "Families," cites the need to be part of a supportive group and sets forth the earmarks of a good "family," whether of blood relatives or not. Judith Bardwick, a psychologist, argues in "Divorce and the Survival of the Family" that families will survive because they fulfill our psychological and emotional needs as well as the need to perpetuate ourselves. In contrast, sociologist Suzanne Keller, asking "Does the Family Have a Future?" thinks that the family may well have outlived its usefulness and, at the least, will undergo radical changes. Educator Mary Jo Bane, however, argues that, despite certain tensions between family and public values, the family is "Here to Stay." And finally, historian Carl Degler admits that the family is "At Odds" with women's drive for individuality and with the values of today's world, but he is optimistic that a resolution of this conflict can be reached.

For all the questioning and experimenting and criticism the family has experienced in contemporary society, the fact is that the family has survived. Battered and bruised though it may be, the family is likely to survive in one form or another in the future. Its functions—humanizing and socializing members and their contacts with the larger society—are too crucial to be left to chance.

CHAPTER TWELVE

Signs of Strain

To have and to hold from this day forward
For better, for worse, for richer, for poorer
In sickness and in health, to love and to cherish
Till death do us part

Book of Common Prayer

Happy families are all alike; every unhappy family is unhappy in its own way.

Leo Tolstoi, *Anna Karenina*

Marriage is like life in this—that it is a field of battle, and not a bed of roses.

Robert Louis Stevenson, *Virginibus Puerisque*

JUDITH S. WALLERSTEIN AND JOAN B. KELLY

Children and Divorce

One out of every two marriages today ends in divorce. What are the effects of divorce upon children? Is divorce less hard on children than a family in which there is constant fighting? Psychologists Judith Wallerstein and Joan Kelly, starting with these questions, studied a group of children whose families were dissolved by divorce. The breakup of the family, they found, had varying effects on children, depending on their age and overall adaptation when the disruption occurred. It is clear that divorce is hard on children, but they survive and manage the effects in time. Their work has been summarized in their book, Surviving the Breakup: How Children and Parents Cope with Divorce.

Divorcing couples and their children constitute a rapidly increasing population whose special needs have been insufficiently recognized, infrequently studied, and poorly served. Thus far, only a fraction of the studies focusing on divorce have examined its impact on children, and interventions specifically addressing the needs of children whose parents are divorcing have been developed slowly. . . .

In their clinical work with children of divorce, practitioners have tended to rely on existing knowledge regarding separation, loss, and mourning. However, although similar in certain aspects to other experiences of loss, divorce departs from these experiences significantly in both its course and outcome. . . .

For the family containing children, divorce is a multifaceted, extended process that alters but does not end the relationships existing among family members. . . . Furthermore, the disruption caused by divorce is often accompanied by primitive angers and impulsive acts on the part of a couple that may not have been part of their behavior or manner of interacting before their breakup. The intrapsychic distress and intrafamilial disequilibrium attendant on a divorce frequently extend over two years or more. . . . In a study that was conducted by the present authors and that will be described in this article, the average length of time required by women to reestablish a sense of stability in their lives after being divorced was 3½ years; 2½ years was the average time required by men.

Thus, for many children, the process of divorce is characterized by initial loss and turmoil, followed by several years of relative instability in which the attention received by them from their parents fluctuates. The decreasing availability of supportive social structures, the weakening of extended-family ties, and the geographic relocation that often follows in the wake of divorce all contribute to the stress that is experienced by the child.

Children are participants affected by at least four related stages or situations in the process of divorce. These are the following: (1) the predivorce family, (2) the disruptive process of divorce itself, including the events leading up to and surrounding the parents' decision to separate, and the transition period immediately following, (3) the changed social, economic, and psychological realities of being reared in a family in which divorce has occurred, and (4) the alterations in the parent-child relationship that take place after the marital breakup. A fifth situation for many children is the remarriage of one or both parents, not infrequently to a partner with children of his or her own. Living through each of these situations and experiences may have short-term or enduring consequences. Each has the potential to interfere with the child's development, just as each represents an opportunity for growth for the child. The duration of stress over time, as well as the rhythm and degree of change, will vary for each child and within each family.

Overall Perspective

Between 1966 and 1976, the rate of divorce in the United States increased by 113 percent. Whereas in 1966 one divorce was granted for every four marriages performed, by 1976 the ratio had changed to one divorce for every two marriages. Indications exist that this spiraling increase in the divorce rate has recently begun to slow down. Nevertheless, nearly one million divorces per year may be expected to be a continuing social phenomenon over the next few years. . . .

Approximately 65 percent of all divorces and annulments taking place in the United States occur in families with children under 18 years of age. Since 1972, each year more than one million children under 18 years of age have been affected by their parents' divorce. It has been estimated that between 32 and 46 percent of the children who have grown up in this country during the 1970s will experience either the separation or actual divorce of their parents.

Not surprisingly, therefore, the proportion of children who live with only one parent has almost doubled since 1960. In 1974, 15.6 percent of all children under 18 were reported to be living with one parent, and of these, nearly one-third were under the age of 6. Significant racial differences exist in this area. Proportionately, more than three times as many black children as white children live with one parent. More than two-thirds of the parents of the six million children who lived with one parent in 1974 were reported to be separated or divorced. The remainder were widowed or abandoned or had never married. Overall, the vast majority of children in single-parent families live with their mothers.

Many families in which divorce has occurred face problems involving diminished financial resources, unemployment, child care arrangements, and social isolation; these difficulties are similar to those encountered by all single-parent families. One major problem that relates to divorce and has been approached uneasily and with mixed success in different legal jurisdictions is how to enforce the collection of child support payments from resistant, unreliable, or absent parents. Delinquency in the regular payment of child support is widespread. In a careful summary of available research, Weitzman reports that "after one year, less than half of the men [studied] are still paying support at all for their children." Moreover, the average amount paid for child support in a sample studied in California in 1972 and 1977 provided significantly less than one-half the cost of raising children during those years.

Levels of income and education are much higher among parents in two-parent families than they are among parents in families with only the mother present. In 1974, 51.5 percent of the children under 18 living in families headed by women were found to be below the poverty level. Even in middle-class families, the decline in the standard of living for divorced mothers and their children is striking and occurs within a brief time span following the marital breakup.

Initial Impact

Divorce becomes real for most children when one parent moves out of the home. However, the full acceptance of this event into the inner world of the child often requires considerable time. In preschool and latency-age children, fantasies of parents' reconciliation can persist even after the remarriage of one or both of the divorced parents has taken place. Prior to adolescence, children rarely perceive their parents' divorce as a welcome relief or a reasonable solution except when they have witnessed frequent physical violence between the parents. . . .

Initially, almost all children and many adolescents experience divorce as painful and as disruptive of their lives, and their suffering is compounded by both realistic and unrealistic fears. These fears are related to the following factors: a heightened sense of vulnerability, sadness at the loss of the protective structure of the family and of the parent who does not retain custody, guilt over fantasized or actual misdeeds that may have contributed to parents' quarrels (although such fantasies are not found in all children), worry over distressed parents, anger at the parent or parents who have disrupted the child's world, shame regarding parents' behavior, a sense of being alone, and concern about being different from peers. For many children and adolescents, the overall initial response to divorce can properly be considered a reactive depression. There is no evidence that these initial reactions are muted or are experienced as less painful because of the high incidence of divorce taking place in the surrounding community.

Despite a wide range of individual differences in the reactions of children to divorce, certain common concerns emerge at the time of parental separation that can be related to developmental considerations and cognitive capacity. Children of preschool and kindergarten age fear disruption of nurturance and possible abandonment by both parents, and their anxieties are enhanced by their cognitive confusion. Youngsters in latency characteristically struggle with painful conflicts regarding loyalty to both parents. Younger latency-age children are often preoccupied with a longing for the father who has left the household, and this longing is often unrelated to the nature of the relationship that existed between father and child before the advent of divorce. In addition to experiencing sorrow and increased worry about themselves and their parents, older latency-age children are often intensely angry at one or both parents. In contrast, the sense of loss experienced by adolescents is heightened by their anxious perception of their parents' sexuality, loneliness, and not infrequent regression.

A child's sex and order of birth in the family can affect the intensity of his or her early response to divorce, particularly since children experience pressure from their parents to provide support or enter into an emotional alliance. Research indicates that the only child feels considerably more threatened than the child who shares the impact of divorce with siblings. Children who are members of interracial or ethnically mixed families may also experience greater strain at the time of their parents' divorce. . . .

Long-Term Outcome

Little is known of the longer-range effects of divorce on children. Early sociological investigations . . . supported the idea that living in the environment of a strife-filled marriage may place children at greater risk than living in a family in which divorce has occurred. However, in a psychological study that was experimental in nature and provided a different perspective, Hetherington found intensified seductive and maladroit behaviors in adolescent girls whose fathers had left the household as a result of divorce, . . . those girls whose parents had divorced when the girls themselves were below the age of 6.

A five-year study conducted by the authors focused on sixty families in northern California in which divorce had occurred. The families studied were predominantly white and middle-class, and they contained a total of 131 children, who ranged in age from 3 to 18 at the time of their parents' separation. At the end of the first eighteen months following their families' breakup, the preschool children appeared to be the most vulnerable and susceptible to developing emotional and psychological problems of those studied. Although most were initially considered psychologically intact, nearly one-half showed deterioration. Children in latency were found to be somewhat more resistant to stress related to their parents' divorce. Nevertheless, eighteen months after their parents' breakup it was found in the case of nearly one-quarter of them that their psychological condition seemed to have become worse or that difficulties they had been experiencing before the divorce had become more firmly entrenched. A surprising amount of vulnerability was found among the adolescents.

Eighteen months after their parents' separation, deterioration among the children studied correlated most highly with continued disorganization in the family, undiminished anger or psychological illness in the parent retaining custody, and insufficient contact with the parent who did not retain custody. In general, boys seemed to be faring significantly worse than girls were at this time. However, this was not true for the adolescents among whom sex differences were not discerned. Fulltime employment among mothers was not per se a significant variable in the outcomes for their children if they were emotionally available to the children when not working. For children who were relatively intact, the resumption of growth and development seems to have been primarily related to the reestablishment of stability and nurturance within the family after the divorce and to the continuity of contact with the parent not retaining custody. Support systems outside the immediate family, whose unavailability was often striking, played a less significant role than expected in the outcomes for the children.

Five years after the beginning of the research, fifty-eight of the original sixty families were again studied. At that time, 34 percent of the youngsters seemed to be doing very well indeed, having regained or recently acquired a sense of well-being and self-confidence. Moreover, these children displayed good adjustment as measured in school, at play, in relationships with peers, and in relationships within the family. Unfortunately, another 37 percent of the youngsters were judged to be suffering from a moderate to severe depression that was manifested in a wide variety of feelings and behaviors, including chronic and pronounced unhappiness; sexual promiscuity; delinquency in the form of drug abuse, petty stealing, alcoholism, and acts of breaking and entering; poor learning; intense anger; apathy; restlessness; and a sense of intense, unremitting neediness. In addition, one of these youngsters suffered from a preoccupation with suicide. The remaining 29 percent of the children had resumed appropriate developmental progress but continued to experience intermittently a sense of deprivation and feeling of sadness and resentment toward one or both parents.

Parents and Children

Divorce brings about significant, complex, and sometimes surprising changes in the relationship between parents and children. This is true of children's relationships with both parents. These changes occur in part as the parent-child relationship breaks free of the context of the marital bond and acquires new meaning within the context of the needs of the separated couple after the divorce. A close tie between a parent and child before the advent of divorce may have reflected the parent's need to maintain distance from a frustrating spouse or a turning to the child for the intimacy that was not available within the marriage itself. Both parents of one-quarter of the children in the authors' study were consistently loving to their children despite the conflicts they were experiencing within their marriage. However, parental needs for closeness with a child may terminate abruptly as the marriage ends, leaving the child feeling bewildered and rejected.

Alternatively, the needs of the parent and child may bring them closer together following a divorce. Some children perceive the distress and loneliness of their divorced parents with maturity and compassion and take increasing responsibility for providing comfort, companionship, and practical help in the household. Others, particularly older latency-age and adolescent youngsters, may be caught up in aligning themselves emotionally with one parent or the other. In such instances, the anger shared by parent and child becomes the basis for malevolent, complex, and organized strategies aimed at hurting or harassing the other parent. Often, the children who participate in these strategies had warm and loving relationships prior to the divorce with the parent who becomes the target of their anger. Nevertheless, these strategic alignments may become consolidated and last for many years.

At the time of separation, many parents are heavily burdened by their own needs and are temporarily unable to perceive or respond to their children's increased needs for parenting and understanding. The authors were startled to discover that 80 percent of the preschool children in their study had not been prepared for the marital breakup taking place in the family. This left them almost entirely alone in coping with the confusing and terrifying departure of one parent.

Hetherington, Cox, and Cox followed forty-eight recently divorced, white, middle-class couples and compared their households, their relationships with their children, and the functioning of their families with those found among a control group of intact families. The households in which divorce had occurred were characterized by greatly increased disorganization and by marked changes in the management of the children, including reduced consistency of discipline, diminished communication and nurturance, and the holding of fewer expectations of mature behavior from the children. Significant attitudinal differences were also found between mothers and fathers in the divorced families, which increased the prevailing inconsistency and confusion. Many of these changes were most pronounced after a period of one year, at the time of follow-up, with some diminution in the more disorganizing stresses noted two years after the time of divorce.

The continuation of contact between the child and the parent who has not retained custody is a crucial issue. Mounting evidence indicates that the maintenance of this relationship between parent and child is of central importance in the psychological adjustment of children within the postdivorce family. Jacobson found that children who spent little time with their fathers during the year after the marital breakup were more likely to develop psychiatric symptomatology than those youngsters who enjoyed more frequent contacts. The findings of the present authors' study point to a significant link between depression in younger children and adolescents and diminished visiting by the children's fathers. Conversely, high self-esteem in all children, especially in older boys, was tied to a good father-child relationship that had been sustained within the structure of visitation.

Contrary to popular expectations, the relationship maintained between father and child through regular visits does not necessarily reflect the predivorce relationship between them. . . . The extent of a father's visiting was greatly influenced by his feelings about the divorce itself, by the age of the children, and by the children's responsiveness; the mother's attitude toward visits made by her ex-spouse was less significant than expected. Overall, fathers are likely to visit younger children more frequently and more regularly than they are to visit older youngsters. . . .

Custody Issues

The most tragic and clinically vulnerable children of divorce are those who become the objects of continued acrimonious legal battles between their divorcing parents. . . . Although no definite statistics are available, the authors estimate that 10 to 15 percent of the divorces of couples with children under 18 are litigated over a variety of child-related issues, primarily custody and visitation rights.

The causes of extended legal contests between divorcing spouses are complex. Legally, these battles can continue indefinitely because a decision regarding custody or visitation is always modifiable by the courts. Psychologically, an individual's rage against an ex-spouse, often expressed in litigation in which the child is the pawn, can apparently remain undiminished by the passage of time or by distance. The fight for a child may serve profound psychological needs in a parent, including the warding off of severe depression and other forms of pathological disorganization.

Although the concept of the "best interests of the child" has become the standard for decisions regarding custody, the explication of this phrase, both in law and in practice, has proved extraordinarily difficult. . . .

The emerging trend concerning issues of divorce is toward formal cooperation between the courts and the mental health professions. Diagnostic and counseling services set up or mandated by the courts have developed in widely separated legal jurisdictions. Furthermore, the network of conciliation courts throughout the United States and Canada has increasingly entered into work with families in which divorce is taking place.

In addition, many social changes have affected custody decisions, and some of these changes may impel the courts to make greater use of the expertise of social workers. Among the changes are the following: (1) an increasing social and legal acceptance of the granting of custody to fathers, (2) a growing interest in awarding joint custody to parents, and increased experimentation with different postdivorce living arrangements, (3) an increased willingness among women to yield custody of their children to their ex-husbands and (4) the emergence of the declared homosexual or lesbian parent who seeks custody. Many of these changes are linked to the changing status of men and women in modern society, to changing roles within the family, and to the women's movement.

In the Schools

Few studies that include observations of children in school have been done concerning the behavioral and affective changes in preschool children at the time of their parents' separation. However, the findings that do exist are consistent. McDermott and the present authors found the great majority of children that they studied to be angry, sad, or forlorn; only in exceptional cases did no change in behavior take place. Angry and distressed responses disappeared in these children within the year following their parents' divorce, except in those youngsters whose overall level of functioning had deteriorated. In regard to these more vulnerable children, nursery school teachers reported a driven need for physical contact, inability to function in a group, and diminished self-esteem.

However, in contrast to these findings regarding preschool children, the present authors found that no straightforward relationship emerged between the intensity of the suffering experienced by children in latency over their parents' divorce and the demeanor of these children at school. About half the children displayed acute behavioral changes visible in a precipitous decline in school performance, newly troubled peer relationships, and moody, irritable behavior. Most children recovered within the first year after their parents' separation, although some developed chronic learning difficulties.

Finally, the response to divorce seemed to be bimodal among adolescents. Some teenagers moved into a coping pattern of highly accelerated social and academic activity at school. Other adolescents began to perceive school as an intolerable burden and as a place where academic and social pressures overtaxed their limited resources. They displayed unaccustomed failing grades, fantasies of dropping out, and intense anger and depression. . . .

Implications

A central and persuasive tenet in psychological and social theory has been the paradigm of the two-parent family, which has been held to provide the average expectable environment for the healthy child. With reference to the new realities represented by families in which divorce has occurred, it is important to rethink many traditional concepts of child development, psychopathology, and intervention theory and develop theoretical formulations appropriate to newly emerging family structures. . . .

The development of social policy concerned with the children of divorce involves issues that are delicate, complex, and perhaps uncomfortable to contemplate. A central issue is the divergence of the wishes and interests of the children from those of their parents in many families in which divorce has occurred. The conventional wisdom of yesteryear was that unhappily married people should remain married "for the good of the children." The conventional wisdom of today holds, with equal vigor, that the marriage in which the adults are unhappy is also unhappy for the children and, furthermore, that the divorce promoting the happiness of the adults will, inevitably, benefit the children as well.

This presumed commonality of perceptions among adults and children and the notion that the experience of the children can be subsumed under the experience of the adults is called sharply into question by the findings of the authors. Five years after the study began, 56 percent of the children surveyed did not consider their postdivorce family to be an improvement over their predivorce household. Despite the unhappiness of their parents, many of these children had been relatively happy and had considered their situation neither better nor worse than that of other families around them. Although most of the parents surveyed felt that their lot had considerably improved despite the stresses they were undergoing, the children and adolescents studied did not as a group experience a comparable improvement in psychological health in the years following parents' separation. These differences in experience cannot be resolved by denying their presence. . . . Unfortunately, neither an unhappy marriage nor a divorce is especially congenial for children. Each imposes its own set of stresses on the children and parents involved.

Within this framework, the time has come to introduce pilot programs rather than broad changes in social and family policy. The social work profession has both the opportunity and the responsibility to develop preventive or early intervention programs directed at particular and immediate times of stress in the divorce process. . . .

Furthermore, in order to fulfill the responsibilities of child-rearing, divorced parents are in need of a network of supportive services that are not now available in the community. These include vocational, financial, and psychological counseling; training and employment opportunities for the newly divorced parents; competent child care; quality afterschool programs; and weekend recreational facilities appropriate to the needs of the parent who is visiting his or her children.

It is fair to say that some major building blocks for the development of informed social policy are lacking. Nevertheless, various conclusions clearly emerge from the work of the authors. The outcome of divorce after several years reflects the success or failure of parents *and* children to master the ensuing disruption, successfully negotiate the necessary transition from pre-divorce to postdivorce life, and create a more gratifying family life to replace the family that failed. Unfortunately, the authors found that a significant number of parents and a greater number of children are failing at different points along the way.

The life cycle of a significant proportion of families in this country is likely to include divorce and remarriage during the next decade. Yet it is a curious phenomenon that family policy in the United States, which has recognized the state's responsibility to offer services in the area of family planning, has left parents to fend for themselves in regard to most of the issues and problems arising after children's actual arrival into the family. Perhaps the time has come to develop a realistic policy that addresses the metamorphoses taking place in the American family and the stressful points of change, for this is essential to ameliorative support and intervention as well as to the overall prevention of problems.

JESSIE BERNARD

Remarriage

Laws regulating divorce date back to the Babylonian Code of Hammurabi about 1750 B.C. *Through the ages, various societies have handled divorce in various ways, some, such as the early Christians, virtually abolishing it, while others, such as some Moslem groups, making it possible for a husband to divorce his wife for the slightest reasons. In the United States today, divorce laws vary by state, but there has been a marked trend in recent years to liberalize these laws. Whereas once the main grounds for divorce were desertion, adultery, or cruelty, many states now grant divorces for incompatibility or by mutual consent. In the following article, sociologist Jessie Bernard looks at the possible effects of divorce laws on the couple involved and on their desire to remarry, and urges the need to strike a balance between too much security and not enough.*

Modern life has knocked the institutional props from under the old type of family; it has attenuated the concept of duty as related to family life. It has left little but the slender support of love and satisfaction to sustain the family as a unit.

In many cases this support is not enough, for modern life does not prepare everyone for the kind of discipline that living in a modern family entails. A marriage that must constantly generate its own support is much more difficult to maintain than one upheld by a sturdy underpinning of institutional props. For all its freedom—indeed, perhaps because of it—the current form of family organization is difficult for the persons involved. Little by little, a body of knowledge about modern family life is being built up, and courses are being introduced into schools and colleges; it is conceivable that in time we may succeed in training people for the kind of marriage and family life required by our present social structure. But as yet we can offer relatively little guidance.

Meanwhile, divorce may be expected to continue. Because as it is now institutionalized divorce is so frequently destructive rather than constructive, a good deal of thought is going into plans and policies for its reinstitutionalization. Lawyers, judges, sociologists, psychologists, marriage counselors, clinicians, and others interested in making law conform with the problems and needs of people have for some time been trying to develop ways and means of rendering divorce therapeutic rather than punitive.

Divorce is more prevalent in many preliterate societies than in our own; yet, although the policy of these societies does not encourage it, it is nevertheless not considered as disorganizing as it is among us, perhaps because in these societies it is usually a transitional rather than a terminal state. The increase in remarriage in our society indicates that divorce is tending to be a transitional state among us as well. But so long as our policy toward divorce remains punitive—so long as we continue to try to make it as difficult, painful, and costly as possible, on the theory that we thereby may lessen it—we shall not be willing to acknowledge the possibility of happiness in a second attempt. But if we come to consider divorce as an attempt to remedy a bad situation, and therefore as a constructive action, we may be able to mitigate some of its most traumatic effects for both the adults and the children involved. In practice, of course, the objections of church, state, and society at large have been unable to alter the basic fact that under the conditions of modern living, people do not have to remain married if they do not wish to do so.

In all our thinking about policy with respect to divorce, the question of motivation must be considered basic. It is argued that the prospect of easy divorce and even possible rewards in the form of remarriage removes much of the incentive to try to succeed in a first marriage. We are reminded in this connection of the Russian experience in the first postrevolutionary decades, during which divorce was made simple and easy; the Russian family in this period became so demoralized that divorce was reinstitutionalized in the thirties on a strict, almost prohibitive basis. Security must be the essential core of marriage.

But security itself poses problems that are by no means easy to solve—some, perhaps, that can never be wholly solved. For security, in industry, government, or family relationships, wears a double face. It has been found to be essential for morale; people seem unable to thrive or function at their best if they feel insecure. They become anxious, fearful, uncertain. But too much security may also have its hazards. People who are too secure may become slothful, complacent, or cocky. They are beyond discipline; they don't have to care. Marriage gives life-long "tenure" to its members; they cannot be "fired" except at great psychological and social cost. As in industry and government, security in marriage may prove therapeutic to some, deteriorating to others.

At the present time we tend to emphasize the positive aspects of security, overlooking its costs to those who must underwrite the security, in industry, government, or family relationships—to the employer who cannot fire an incompetent worker, to the wife who cannot leave a man who beats her. The "secure" spouse who uses the institutional vise to protect himself so that he can degenerate, exploit, or otherwise do as he pleases is taking advantage of the security that marriage offers. Our policy toward marriage and divorce must therefore steer a narrow course between the Scylla and Charybdis of too much and too little security.

S.M. MILLER

Confusions of a Middle-Class Husband

*In this short autobiographical account, S.M. Miller, a professor of economics
and sociology at Boston University, demonstrates to us how the structure of
marriage and our sex role assumptions push people into traditional patterns,
even when their intentions and efforts are grounded in an ideology of equality
between husband and wife, man and woman, mother and father.*

I have never had an intellectual problem with sexism. One reason may well
have been the women who surrounded me as a child—my father's mother,
my mother, and two considerably older sisters—although I know it sometimes
goes quite the other way. My father slept, and my mother dominated—partly
out of force of character and partly, one sister informed me fairly recently,
because of the occupational and other failures of my father. He had tried to
make it in America—and could not. His was the immigrant's rags-to-rags
story. He started as a factory worker, and became a small businessman, only
to be wiped out by the 1921 depression. He worked again as a machine
operator, and then started a dress store, where he did the alterations and my
mother was chief saleswoman. Again his enterprise was rewarded by a depression—this time, that of the 1930s. He went back to working at a machine in
the lowest-paid part of the garment industry, where he stayed until he retired
in his early seventies. From the depression days on, my mother worked as a
saleslady. I was a "latchkey kid" from an early age, warming up the meals
that were left for me by my mother.

My mother was very smart and witty, and so was my older sister. They were obviously intellectually well-endowed, although not well-educated. My mother had a few years of formal schooling; my sister just managed to graduate from high school. (I think I developed my repugnance for credentialism because I recognized that these were two very smart though not well-educated women.)

From this experience, I grew up regarding women as competent and capable of making family and economic decisions. (By contrast, my mother disliked cooking; and it was a shock to me when I began to eat away from home to discover what a bad cook she was.) Women worked and ran things well. On the other hand, there was a notion that people frowned on women's working, so we tried to hide the fact that my mother worked. I think I felt both ashamed that my mother worked and irritated that "society" thought that it was wrong for women to work, especially when their incomes were needed.

Furthermore, sexism was, in principle, alien to the egalitarian and participatory circles in which my closest friends and I were passionately involved. We were out of step with the intellectual climate of the '40s and '50s because of our egalitarian, populist, anti-elitist spirit. We criticized Stalinist democratic centralism and American celebration-style pluralist democracy because of their inadequate attention to equality and participation for all. We could no more subscribe to intellectual rationalizations of a low status for females than we could condone the miseries of oppression and deprivation among other parts of the population.

A third reason I see myself as intellectually escaping sexism has more manifest emotional roots. Looking back, I don't believe that I could have accepted a woman who would center her life completely on me and devote herself to making me happy. (Children were not part of my purview.) At one level, the intellectual: how could one individual be worthy of such dedication by another? At a deeper and, I suspect now, more significant level, I rejected or stayed away from easily giving or male-centered women because I did not consider myself worthy of another person's total devotion or capable of evoking the sentiments that would sustain it beyond the initial impulse. Furthermore, such devotion would demand an emotional response that I possibly could not make. In short, I did not think so well of myself that I could live with (overwhelming) devotion. As a consequence, I was usually involved with young women with strong career goals who were seeking their identity through work, not through family. They were my intellectual equals, if not superiors.

Thus I had a good beginning, it seems to me, for having a marriage that did not embody sexist currents. But I don't see that my current life is very different from that of men who espoused or expounded more sexist values. Years ago a good friend told me that I had the reputation among the wives in our circle of being "an excellent husband"; and he said, "You know, that's

"*Pop, you've got to be more supportive of Mom and more willing to share with her the day-to-day household tasks. Mom, you have to recognize Pop's needs and be less dependent on him for your identity.*"

Drawing by Koren; © 1978 The New Yorker Magazine, Inc.

not a good thing." I now have the feeling that families that openly embrace both bourgeois and sexist values don't live very differently from us. I sense that we are engaged in a "lapsed egalitarianism," still believing in our earlier commitments and concerns about equality, but having drifted from the faith in our daily life.

What Happened?

Probably the most important factor in accounting for the direction we took was our amazing naïveté about the impact of having children—a naïveté, incidentally, that I see today having a similarly devastating effect on many young parents. We just had no idea how much time and emotion children captured, how they simply changed a couple's lives, even when the wife's working made it possible, as it did in our case, to afford a housekeeper.

The early years of child rearing were very difficult. Our first son was superactive and did not sleep through the night. We were both exhausted. My wife insisted that I not leave everything to her; she fought with me to get me to participate in the care of our son and apartment. I took the 2 A.M. and 6 A.M. feedings and changings, for our ideology would not allow me just to help out occasionally: I had to "share," "really participate," in the whole thing. I resented that degree of involvement; it seemed to interfere terribly with the work I desperately wanted to achieve in. Indeed, I have always felt put upon because of that experience of many months.

To make matters worse, I did not know of other work-oriented husbands who were as involved as I with their children. True, I realized that my sons and I had become much attached to each other and that a lovely new element had entered my life; but I resented the time and exhaustion, particularly since I was struggling to find my way in my work. I did not consider myself productive and was in the middle of struggling to clarify my perspective. I looked at the problem largely in terms of the pressure of my job, which required a lot of effort, and, more importantly, in terms of my personality and my inability to work effectively. Although I wrote memoranda with great ease, I wasn't writing professional articles and books.

In retrospect, I think that it was the influence of the McCarthy and Eisenhower years that was more significant in my lack of development. My outlook and interests were not what social science and society were responding to. That changed later, and I was able to savor in the '60s that infrequent exhilaration of having my professional work and citizen concerns merge and of gaining both a social-science and a popular audience and constituency. But I did not know in the 1950s that this would unfold, and I felt resentment.

What I experienced was that, unlike my friends, I was working hard to make things easier for my wife, and I did not see rewards. Yes, she told me she appreciated my effort; but my activities were never enough, my sharing was never full, in the sense that I equally planned and took the initiative in the care of child and house. She was tired, too, and irritated by child care; and, in turn, I was irritated by what seemed to be her absorption in taking care of the children.

And there were always those male friends who did so little, compared with me. I could, and did, tell myself that at some point along the line they would be paying heavy "dues" for their current neglect of their wives' plight, but it was small balm at the time. I wondered if I was not rationalizing my irritation by an intellectualizing metaphor about how one pays prices sooner or later and by a plaintively reassuring injunction never to envy anyone else, for who knew what lurked behind the facade of family equanimity?

Things were further complicated by another factor—less typical of today's young marrieds: my incomplete early socialization as a family member. For example, since as an adolescent and pre-adolescent I had eaten meals by myself, I had developed the habit of reading while eating. (Indeed, I am a compulsive reader, a "print nut"; if there is nothing around to read, I will study the labels on ketchup bottles.) The result was that marriage required a resocialization: I had to learn to talk to someone at mealtimes, and not to turn inward to my own thoughts or to *The New York Times.*

Of course, the reading is only the personal tip of the iceberg of a larger problem of not closing myself to others and becoming inaccessible because of stress or intellectual absorption. I am now, again, in a conscious period of trying to make myself more accessible emotionally to my family, but it is a struggle. For example, when we vacation, I spend the first few days devouring three to four mysteries a day—"decompressing" I call it—hardly talking to anyone. And, of course, when I am at a deadline, or caught in my inability to work out an idea, or just unable to get to work (there are few other conditions for me than these three), I am rather inaccessible, to say the least. I work against this tendency, but don't do notably well. While I do the mundane tasks of the household, psychologically I am often not much there. I think that I am winning the struggle against withdrawal, but what is a giant step to the battler may appear as a wiggle of progress to the beholder.

My wife has accommodated to my dislike of fixing things and "wasting time" on such things—not great matters in themselves, but symptomatic of the process of my disengagement from the burdens of home and family.

From a narrow perspective, I have useful incompetences protecting me from diversions of my energy and focus. I don't like to fix things and don't do them well (or soon). In my youth, in my proletarian near-idealization, I felt Arthur Miller was right when he had Willy Loman say that a man isn't a man unless he can do things with his hands. So I tried adult-education shop courses and the like for a brief time. I went in a klutz and came out a klutz. Now, in a spirit of reactive arrogance or greater self-pride, I boldly assert the counterposition that I believe in the division of labor and prefer to pay for specialized labor. I do little around the house—and that usually long delayed. Since skilled labor is hard to get at any price, things are undone, or my wife does them; but my principle of specialization (for me) remains unimpaired.

Similarly, I have been relieved of the task of paying bills. With my usual speed and my disdain for trivia, I did this job very rapidly and made mistakes. Now my wife spends time doing this task. It is easier, in her view, for her to do it than to keep after me to do a competent job. Failure is its own reward: I have escaped anoher task. Of course, I have been after my wife to have a part-time secretary and bookkeeper and have located several people for her. But she resists, as they do not provide enough help to make it worthwhile. The result is that my personnel efforts reduce my feelings of guilt when she spends evenings writing checks. After all, I did try to get her out of that function. But I am still irritated by her doing the checks—for that act is another indication that she is failing me by not showing our true equality by spending more time on her professional writing and research.

I guess what dismays me and makes me see my marriage and family as unfortunately typically upper-middle-class collegial, pseudo-egalitarian American—especially in light of my own continuing commitment to an egalitarian, participatory ethos—is that I assume no responsibility for major household tasks and family activities. True, my wife has always worked at her profession (she is a physician), even when our sons were only some weeks old. True, I help in many ways and feel responsible for her having time to work at her professional interests. But I do partial, limited things to free her to do her work. I don't do the basic thinking about the planning of meals and housekeeping, or the situation of the children. Sure, I will wash dishes and "spend time" with the children; I will often do the shopping, cook, make beds, "share" the burden of most household tasks; but that is not the same thing as direct and primary responsibility for planning and managing a household and meeting the day-to-day needs of children.

It is not that I object in principle to housekeeping and child rearing. I don't find such work demeaning or unmasculine—just a drain of my time, which could be devoted to other, "more rewarding" things. (Just as I don't like to shop for clothes for myself, even though I like clothes.) My energies are poised to help me work on my professional-political concerns, and I resist "wasting time" on other pursuits, even those basic to managing a day-to-day existence.

The more crucial issue, I now think, is not my specific omissions and commissions, but the atmosphere that I create. My wife does not expect much of me, which frees me for work and lessens the strain I produce when I feel blocked from working. Even our sons have always largely respected my efforts to work, feeling much freer to interrupt their mother at her work. The years have been less happy than they would have been if I had been more involved and attentive and my wife had not lowered her ambitions.

Outstanding academically from an early age, a "poor girl" scholarship winner to a prestige college and medical school, excelling in her beginning professional work, my wife expected, and was expected, to do great things. But with children, she immediately reduced her goals. Of course, medical schools don't pay much attention to faculty members who are part-time or female, and the combination of the two almost guarantees off-hand treatment.

She is now realizing fuller professional development. I have always felt guilty about her not achieving more, so I have nagged her to publish, though I have not provided the circumstances and climate that would make serious work much easier. I have had the benefit of feeling relieved that I was "motivating" her by my emphasis on her doing more, but I have not suffered the demands on my time and emotions that making more useful time available to her would have required. In the long run, I have undoubtedly lost more by limited involvement, because she has been distressed by the obstacles to her professional work. But the long run is hard to consider when today's saved and protected time helps meet a deadline.

CHAPTER THIRTEEN

New Family Forms

Wives are young men's mistresses, companions for middle age, and old men's nurses.

> Francis Bacon, *Of Marriage and Single Life*

No man worth having is true to his wife, or can be true to his wife, or ever was, or ever will be so.

> Sir John Vanbrugh, *The Relapse* (1697)

A second wife
Is hateful to the children of the first;
A viper is not more hateful.

> Euripides, *Alcestis* (438 B.C.)

KATHY WEINGARTEN

Interdependence

Only a generation ago, the two-career couple, in which both husband and wife have jobs outside the home, was quite unusual; today it is the pattern of a majority of marriages. The ability to meet each other's needs for dependence is one set of tools a two-career couple needs to manage their complex life and goals. In the following article, psychologist Kathy Weingarten reports on a study of the way in which couples manage their lives through interdependence and flexibility.

The style of marital interaction to be described here—interdependence—is a coping strategy adopted by two people who choose to share an intimate relationship. For all two-worker families time spent away from the home reduces the time available to maintain the home and family. This results in a need, but also creates the opportunity, for an effective coping style such as interdependence. This paper will discuss the concept of interdependence, drawing on interviews conducted in the fall of 1973 in the Boston metropolitan area, with 54 two-profession couples in three different age groups, some of whom were parents and some of whom were not. . . .

Not atypical is the following vignette. It points up the way in which a single unplanned event—a child's getting sick—draws on the available organizational skill and flexibility of the couple. The scene: Mr. Jones is in his study finishing a speech he will be delivering in New York the next day, while making calls to the usual network of babysitters to arrange for someone to stay with his children for the evening. Dr. Jones is talking with her answering service on the other line to ascertain how high a fever Billy Smith has, while simultaneously heating up a stew for dinner. In an hour, Mr. Jones will drive to the airport, the babysitter will arrive, and Dr. Jones will meet Billy Smith and his parents at a local hospital emergency room.

Meanwhile, at Billy Smith's home, Mr. Smith is calling his wife at her law office to ask her to stop off on her way home and buy a pizza so that they will not have to prepare dinner in case Dr. Jones wants to see Billy that evening.

These situations arise and they put an additional stress on the already stressed two-worker family. In my research, I sought to discover how two-profession families managed to combine their work with family pleasures and responsibilities. Eighteen couples (12 of whom were parents) in each of three different age groups—late 20s, late 30s, and 50s to early 60s agreed to be interviewed jointly for two hours. . . . Their divorce and remarriage rate was 7.4 percent as contrasted with 15 percent for professionals in general. Clinically, to this observer, they seemed to fit well Burgess and Cottrell's 1939 definition of marital adjustment:

> the integration of the couple in a union in which the two personalities are not merely merged, or submerged, but interact to complement each other for mutual satisfaction and the achievement of common objectives.

These couples appeared to be successful at doing something difficult: they appeared to be intensely involved with their career and at the same time not compromising the quality of their relationships, either marital or familial.

How they managed to achieve and sustain this balance was one of the questions posed. . . . With the exception of the answer, 'money,' no two couples responded alike. Despite this diversity, there was a quality to which all their explanations alluded. In fact, one sensed that they all had something in common. The quality was difficult to describe, elusive, yet in the presence of these couples, it was palpable. Words like strength, sharing, mutual respect and regard, help, cooperation, dependence, reliance, activity, energy, taking over, picking up the slack, letting go, give and take, and willpower convey aspects of the quality I noticed. These couples shared a mode of interaction that functioned adaptively in a multitude of situations. Some couples made greater use of it than others. I have labelled that mode of interaction *inter-dependence*. . . .

Interdependence connotes more than merely 'mutual dependence' as Webster's *Third New International Dictionary* defines it. It includes the capacity to be independent in the context of an intimate relationship as well. For couples to create the conditions in their marriage such that feelings of dependence and independence can be recognized and acted upon requires considerable emotional maturity. At times one partner will feel dependent and the other will respond by becoming independent. The partners are able to meet each other's needs by balancing the emotional scale. Interdependent couples are also able to tolerate sustained periods when both partners feel and act dependently or when both feel and act independently. Both situations may generate considerable—though different—strains and stresses on the relationship. When interdependence works, there is sufficient flexibility to accommodate shifting stances frequently. Each person knows there is leeway and feels free to use it. . . . Consider two tense and harassed academics simultaneously coming up for tenure at their respective colleges. It is an anxiety provoking time for both and each feels need of as much care and support as possible: they feel dependent. Both would like dinner made for them; the house cleaned up; the bills paid. The couple realize this period will not continue indefinitely. If they have no children, they are able to make certain compromises, for instance in the timing and preparation of meals, that a couple with children may not be able to make. Whether they sit down and map out a long-term strategy or 'arrive' at one nightly on a continuing basis, the couple works out a way of meeting their career objectives by putting their household and relationship needs 'on hold.' The house does get messy. They are less involved with each other, and yet each wants support from the other. They do not like, but are able to tolerate, both their own neediness and the other's diminished capacity to meet it. They complain to each other and this may become the substance of their contact. They manage, in part, because they retain a firm sense of a different past and they believe that the future will be better.

If they have children, they may decide that whatever emotional reserves they have left from their work must go to meet their children's needs. Part of their vacation money is used to hire a housekeeper to clean the house and prepare the meals, freeing them to be with their children during their leisure hours.

The situation is quite different for a couple who are secure in their careers. Whereas the first couple must accommodate to prolonged and simultaneous dependence, the second may have to adjust to simultaneous independence. The wife's career may involve travel away from home. The husband, a scientist, may be doing experiments that require him to be at the laboratory until the early morning hours. Eager to pursue the exciting developments in their careers, both would like to be away from home for extended periods of time. If they have an interdependent relationship, they will be able to negotiate this. The cost of their independence might be estrangement. Anticipating this, they try to bridge the self-imposed distance. For the wife, this may mean getting up early in order to phone her husband each time she is away from home. They share their excitement with each other, and are able to hear it without feeling left out. They acknowledge how much they miss each other. The husband drives the children to school the days his wife is away, and makes an effort to do something special—if brief—with each one. He knows that his wife will feel better about being away if she is sure the children are happy. If the couple is childless, he may take special care to keep the house neat knowing she'll appreciate his thoughtfulness.

In another situation, a couple find themselves temperamentally at odds with one another. Though the wife usually does the cooking, one evening she returns from work exhausted. She doesn't want to do anything. Nor is she able to be a pleasant companion. She has neither the energy nor the desire to mobilize herself. Her husband pours her a drink and leaves her alone with the newspaper while he improvises a meal, not wanting even to ask her what she had planned for their dinner. He responds to her feeling dependent, in this case a consequence of fatigue, by acting independently; he accepts and meets her need.

. . .[A final] example, a husband does not receive an anticipated government grant, and he has reacted by becoming mildly depressed. He is irritable and glum; he can't energize himself to get things done. His wife accepts his behavior and tries to think of things that will please him. She rubs his back and prepares meals he particularly likes. She does some of his chores—the ones she doesn't really mind—and doesn't nag him about the others. She complains a little to him, but does most of her complaining to a friend to whom she confides her wish that he'd hurry up and snap out of it.

Over the course of a couple's life together it is likely that all [of these] patterns will occur. . . .

To act independently while his wife acts dependently may fit a man's sex-role imagery well in some areas but not in others. That is, it may be comfortable for him to work on an extra project that brings in additional money in order to release his wife from several hours at her job, but he may resist and resent acting independently at other times if it means making out the shopping list or buying the children clothes. . . . Yet both may be necessary to achieve interdependence. One man expressed it this way:

> I'm a lawyer in an old, established law firm. I agree with Women's Liberation and I am committed to sharing work with my wife, the work that's involved in raising our family. But it's hard, let me tell you, it's hard, to explain that an important meeting with a client can't be scheduled on Thursday afternoon because I have to take my son to his piano lessons.

This 40-year-old lawyer felt isolated at his job. None of his colleagues—all men—had the kind of sharing arrangement he had with his wife. This man's stated view of the problem interdependence posed for him was that it left him open to possible contempt or ridicule. His colleagues were liable to notice that he crossed the traditional sex-role boundary and to infer a weakness or submissiveness he did not feel. . . .

Several husbands discussed the discomfort they felt as stemming from their own internalized view of themselves as abandoning 'normal masculine behavior.'

Often at the same time that the husband is coming to terms with acting independently in areas for which he never anticipated taking a primary responsibility, he must face the fact that his wife is acting dependently, that she needs and wants his help. For some men—and women—dependent behavior is difficult to accept in any adult. A man who has married a woman not despite her career but because of it may find it particularly difficult to accept an exhausted, insecure and clinging woman when he feels he has chosen a strong, active, ambitious and achieving woman. The wife's dependent behavior may evoke feelings of shock, anger or disappointment at precisely the moment she most needs his support and encouragement.

The women themselves may share their husbands' chagrin at these 'lapses.' Career women expect a great deal of themselves and often become upset and self-blaming when they do not meet their high standards at all times. . . .

These women's self-chosen lives expose them to pressures, anxieties and tensions that their homemaking sisters experience in smaller, usually less sustained, doses. Career women may be anxious for months while waiting for news of a grant acceptance or job opportunity. The task of accommodating the wife's intermittent dependence brought on by career or any other vicissitudes is a difficult one for both partners.

Men, too, have trouble accepting their dependent feelings and the fact that they may wish to act dependently with their wives. Traditionally, men have looked toward women to meet a multitude of needs—from food to sexual gratification to clean clothes. However, their behavior in their relationships with women has not been defined as dependent but as masculine. Men have had little difficulty accepting these kinds of ministrations from women. It is the perception of the need for support in other areas of their lives, such as their emotional life, that may create internal conflict.

At this time, given that few, if any, adult men have been brought up in non sex-stereotyped environments, dependence may be even more threatening to them than to their wives. Particular women may have rejected a version of femininity that includes dependence as an integral part, but when they act dependently they are contradicting their values only, not society's as well. Men transgress their own and society's views when they act dependently. . . .

The man's dependence and the wife's responsive independence may, at times, be difficult for each. A 35-year-old architect said:

> My husband is not mechanically minded and I am. When we bought our house, I, naturally, handled all the details. It was realistic, but we both chafed. I felt angry at him for weeks and I couldn't figure out why. I was thinking things like 'Look at what this creep is making me do. What's the matter with him?'

Her husband, a professor of English, shared his perspective:

> For the first time I had thoughts like 'she *is* a castrating female,' when I'd hear her argue with the contractor. I felt very inadequate, although I haven't any interest in building and she hasn't read a novel in years!

Unemployment of the husband is one of the situations many couples felt would be exceptionally stressful. The difficulty seemed to stem from the wife's acting independently in an area, principal breadwinner, conventionally stereotyped as masculine. Perhaps the converse of the wife's being the breadwinner is the husband's being the principal parent. This did, in fact, generate difficulty for the few couples interviewed in this situation. The wives expressed sadness over the loss of a role—*mother*, with implications of uniqueness and centrality—they had long expected to fulfill. Rationally, they felt they had an ideal arrangement; emotionally, they felt that things were not as they were supposed to be. The husbands, all of whom enjoyed doing child care, were disturbed by their wives' reactions.

If the obstacles to interdependence are great, the rewards are even greater. Couples who have evolved an interdependent style tended to feel successful in meeting their mutual needs in both the work and family spheres. Although no two styles were exactly alike, age did seem to account for regular differences among couples in the quality of the relationship, including the quality of the interdependence. The older the couple, the more likely that independence would predominate in their relationship.

For the group in their 50s and early 60s, their careers had been well established for years. None faced externally imposed job changes. It was a time to consolidate professional skills, and experience a sense of well-being. In the family sphere, if there had been children, they no longer required the attention they once did. Often for the first time, the career cycle and the family cycle were in harmony. . . .

The younger couples were intimately involved and integrally necessary to the working of each other's lives. This was true whether they had children or not. Yet it seemed that something else besides the exigencies of meshing two lives accounted for the closeness of the younger couples. It was almost as though they needed the closeness in order to cope with the psychological costs of living such complex lives. The husbands and wives needed each other to unwind, to celebrate, to commiserate, to clarify and to sympathize. The different quality of interdependence developed by the younger and older couples reflected family and work life-cycle differences.

Across ages, though, interdependence seemed to provide a critical resiliency. Not all the couples relied on interdependence to the same degree. Some couples were interdependent more of the time and in more situations than other couples. For them, interdependence proved to be the most efficient way of leading their lives. Usually these couples worked out a division of labor based on interest and skill. The jobs that no one wanted were often rotated. The task allocation frequently, but not always, diverged from a traditional, sex-role behavior assignment. . . .

Other couples relied on an interdependent mode occasionally and in some instances. Their primary mode of handling and combining their complex lives took one of two forms: the traditional model or the super-woman model. Couples who organized their lives around the traditional model had a definite, fixed and relatively unchanging division of labor. The couple had been employed full time up until the point that the dual-professional involvement disturbed the desired quality of household and family functioning. At that point the woman reduced or discontinued her employment. She became responsible for the majority of household and child care tasks and her husband became responsible for providing the income. Regardless of the couple's feelings at any one particular time, the pattern of distribution of dependent and independent actions was fixed. If the wife was tired or upset from her day at home, it was still her responsibility to prepare dinner and see to the children's baths. Similarly, the husband went to work every day and took on extra assignments if financially necessary, whether he wanted to or not.

The superwoman model is similar to the traditional model in that the division of labor is fixed, as is the distribution of dependence and independence. In this case, the woman acts independently in all spheres: managing a career, the household, the children, and entertaining with relatively little besides financial input from the husband. He is dependent on his wife for services and her income is necessary to maintain their chosen standard of living.

Couples who are interdependent work hard, not only at the work they do, but also at the process of becoming and staying interdependent. It is not easy. How does interdependence happen?

The prerequisites for interdependence are the same as the prerequisites for success in every aspect of marriage: commitment and trust. Without these, couples are not able to risk as much as they must to achieve interdependence. Once both commitment and trust exist, the next step is for couples genuinely to accept that a full range of behaviors is appropriate for both men and women. . . .

Open communication is the second quality of a relationship necessary to achieve interdependence. Since novel behaviors are often a consequence of developing an interdependent mode of interaction, it makes sense for the husband and wife to discuss frankly how they feel about the new behavior. . . . The painstaking process of verbalizing one's thoughts and feelings is necessary. Nor is this process a one-time or one-year effort; it is perpetually ongoing. It is not always easy, and it is certainly not always fun. Sometimes hurtful things are said. Sometimes one feels raw emotions, divorced from logical thoughts. It is helpful to be able to share in this way too: the rage, the tears, the irrationality, the fears and the ecstasies. In the context of a loving, trusting marital relationship it is appropriate to confide the feelings one may have worked hard over the years to suppress. Letting go may be difficult. It may also be life-enhancing.

Finally, reciprocity . . . is essential for optimal interdependence. To sustain a balance of giving and taking, husbands and wives must individually assume the responsibility of monitoring their own behavior. . . . Usually if couples accept a wide range of behaviors in each other, communicate openly, and wish to share, a balance of one sort or another can be reached.

Interdependence proved to be an effective interactional style for the 54 two-profession couples I interviewed. Some relied on it exclusively, others only at times. It provided an on-going context within which to meet their own interpersonal needs as well as their job and family responsibilities. It seems likely that a study conducted with two-worker families would find a similar style of interaction. All two-worker couples have a pressing need to find an interpersonal strategy that helps them cope with their complex lives. Interdependence works.

ESTHER WATTENBERG AND HAZEL REINHARDT

Female-Headed Families

"Only 6 percent of American families fit the traditional definition of a working husband, a wife who is a full-time homemaker, and two young children," according to Esther Wattenberg, of the School of Social Work at the University of Minnesota, and Hazel Reinhardt, a demographer. One form which has increased dramatically is the female-headed family. The article that follows looks at the reasons for the increase, variety among female-headed families, and some of the economic and life conditions of such families.

The decline of the archetypal family dramatically challenges the concept of what is "normative" in the United States. Only 6 percent of all American families fit the traditional definition of a working husband, a wife who is a full-time homemaker, and two young children. Certainly dynamic trends are reshaping American families, and evidence of new family formations is emerging in the national demographic data that follow:

1. *A shift in the timing of marriage.* The proportion of women between ages 20 and 24 who remain single has almost doubled since 1960, increasing from 28 to 48 percent.
2. *A rise in the rate of women who have never married.* For women aged 25 to 29, in 1970, 11 percent were single; in 1978, 18 percent were single.
3. *A rise in the rate of out-of-wedlock births.* In 1960, 5 percent of all births were out of wedlock; by 1975, the percentage had risen to 14.

Esther Wattenberg and Hazel Reinhardt, "Female-Headed Families: Trends and Implications." *Social Work,* Vol. 24, No. 6, November 1979, pp. 460–465. Excerpted and reprinted by permission.

4. *A dramatic growth in the number of households.* Since 1970, the number of households has increased by 20 percent. In addition, for the first time in the history of the United States, more than half (53 percent) of all households consist of just one or two people. This reflects a propensity for individuals to maintain independent households at all stages of life. Separate households include those now maintained by widowed men and women, by young couples no longer "doubling up" with relatives, and by single-parent families.

5. *A change in the rates of marriage, divorce, and remarriage.* First marriages per 1,000 single women aged 14 to 44 and remarriages per 1,000 widowed and divorced women aged 14 to 54 have decreased since 1972. Divorces per 1,000 married women aged 14 to 44 have increased since 1972.

6. *The steady increase in the number of families with older members.* This category includes households with an aging parent with aging children. Fifteen percent of the females who head families are 65 years old or more. Five percent of female-headed families have at least two members over 65 years of age, in some cases representing two generations.

7. *The growth of two-income families.* In 1970, 51 percent of the families had both spouses working; by 1976, this figure rose to 57 percent.

8. *The increasing number of female-headed families.* Between 1970 and 1978, female-headed families increased by 46 percent. Families headed by teenage mothers are a subgroup in this category.

Female-Headed Families

Perhaps the most dramatic statistic is the unprecedented increase in the number of female-headed households with children. Of all American families, 13 percent are headed by single, separated, divorced, or widowed women. Children living with only one parent rose from 12 percent in 1970 to 17 percent in 1977. One of every six children in the United States is living in a family in which, because of death, divorce, separation, or an out-of-wedlock birth, the father is absent. Moreover, the trend is accelerating. Since 1960, families headed by a mother living alone with her children have increased by 81 percent. It should be noted that male-headed families without a wife present currently represent only 3 percent of all families. Many of these may include families headed by elderly siblings or comprising three generations. Although becoming more common, the single-parent male-headed family with children under 18 currently represents such a small proportion of all families that it cannot be accurately measured.

Female-headed families now represent the single largest subgroup of the population that lives below the poverty level. More than half of these families depend on welfare payments as a source of income. Concern for their economic welfare has prompted a number of studies and analyses, and continued research of the trend is clearly indicated to understand its impact on public expenditures, as well as on the social consequences of this major alteration in the formation of the family. Study should be made, for example, of the effect of a father's absence on a child's development.

One striking characteristic is the transient nature of female-headed families. It is inaccurate to think of women who head families simply as women "between husbands," and recent studies reveal dynamic changes in their lives. They move on and off the welfare rolls, in and out of marriage, in and out of poverty, and in and out of the labor market. Data on female-headed families are more like "snapshots." Major events such as marriage, separation, divorce, widowhood, remarriage, and the birth of children create life-shaping circumstances that determine whether women can control their economic and social fate. The multiplicity of these events in the lives of female heads of families contributes to a constantly shifting array of living arrangements.

Although individual women may appear and disappear in the statistical constellation of female-headed families, the total number is expanding. Why families headed by females between the ages of 15 and 44 are increasing has been examined by Glick and Norton, as well as Cutright. Glick and Norton note that the 1970s is the decade in which the baby-boom generation has come of age, therefore the number of adult females in the population is larger. Furthermore, although the tendency to form female-headed families has been particularly pronounced among younger women and among those who are black, the growth of such households is substantial among all segments of the population. Cutright, however, after examining census data from 1940 to 1970, asserts that the current number of such families may be no greater than in the past. He contends that living arrangements in past decades obscured the dimensions of this particular family formation, for example, the tendency of mothers to live with relatives as subfamilies distorted the count of the actual number of female-headed families. Cutright concludes that the contemporary propensity for both white and nonwhite women aged 15 to 44 who have children to form separate households, along with the increase in population, contributes to the statistical rise in the number of these families. He contends that changes in marital stability over the past three decades for both white and nonwhite families contribute only minimally to the rising statistics. Whether this analysis will hold for the seventies must await the 1980 census data.

Marital Instability

Marital instability, nevertheless, is an important factor in demographic data. It is predicted that almost one of every three marriages among younger couples will end in divorce. Several factors are involved in the increasing number of marital dissolutions: readjustment to peacetime after the disruptive Vietnam War, the women's movement, the increased participation of women in the labor force, a general cultural expectation emphasizing self-fulfillment and consequently a lower tolerance for an unhappy marriage, and a general shift in attitudes toward divorce that is reflected in the more liberal attitudes of the churches and in the legislative introduction of "no-fault" divorce.

Although complex factors in personal and cultural circumstances influence marital behavior, three demographic elements appear to have decisive effect: income, age, and mobility.

Income

Examination of the effect of income on marital stability involves such factors as absolute level of income, earning stability, sources of income, income relative to peers, socio-economic effects of occupational status, length of marriage, race, and region of the country. The issue is further complicated by the observation that a wife's income may affect the stability of a marriage differently than a husband's income. Although positive correlation has been found between a husband's or family's income and the stability of a marriage, the effect of a wife's income may provide her a degree of independence that offsets this.

Income maintenance experiments in Denver and Seattle indicate that short-term changes in socioeconomic conditions affect marital decisions in low-income populations. Overall, income maintenance increases the rate of marital dissolution. For black, white, and Chicano women, the greatest increase occurs at the lowest levels of support. Income maintenance also affects remarriage, but these statistics vary by race and ethnicity. For Chicanos, the rate of remarriage decreases as the level of support increases. For blacks and whites, income maintenance has no discernible impact on the rate of remarriage.

Apparently, given a slight boost in economic resources, poor women no longer feel compelled to remain in unhappy marriages. Given feasible options, they will make rational decisions to improve the quality of their lives.

Sawhill, examining data from a longitudinal study of 5,000 families in Michigan, found that each $1,000 increase in the earnings of wives led to a 1 percent increase in the separation rate. Evidence also exists that two spouses earning high incomes have a much lower rate of marital dissolution than lower income groups. Undeniably, however, a source of income enables women and children to form families on their own if they choose or are required to do so. In Levinger's study of couples who had applied for divorce, the critical variable between those who reconciled and those who did not was the wife's level of income. The lower her income, the more likely it was she and her husband would reconcile.

Wolf and MacDonald, however, examined a range of variables and concluded that it is the wife's evaluation of her husband's role as breadwinner and the stability of his income, rather than the absolute level of income, that influenced marital disruption. Sawhill's examination of the Michigan data extends the point by concluding that the level of a family's income does not assure greater marital stability.

An associated issue concerns the degree to which unemployment rates relate to marital dissolution. Several studies affirm the finding from the Michigan data that men who have experienced substantial job instability are about twice as likely to separate from their wives as those who have not. It is not clear whether unemployment per se with its loss of self-respect and family respect or the loss of income contributes more to separation. Sawhill tentatively concludes, however, that it is *employment* rather than income that is critical to the stability of the family.

Another question is whether Aid to Families with Dependent Children (AFDC) plays a role in the increase of female-headed families by providing resources to women who have separated and their children. Honig found that a 10-percent increase in the level of welfare benefits increased the proportion of female-headed families by 3 or 4 percent. Is it the *amount* or *availability* of welfare that affects separation? Are welfare payments simply higher than a male's earnings? Do AFDC benefits precipitate or facilitate the dissolution of an intolerable marriage? In a sample of 451 welfare mothers in New York City, Bernstein and Meezan reported that the most important reasons the women gave for the dissolution of their marriages concerned their husbands' involvement with drugs, alcohol, and other women and physical abuse. Only 12 percent cited "financial problems" as the primary reason for dissolution.

In summary, the relationship of income to marital stability poses a serious challenge for further investigation. The conceptual framework for these studies involves at least two hypotheses. One, the family can be viewed as an economic unit. The research hypothesis is that the transfer of income within the family affects its stability. Studies then involve how resources are transferred from family members who work in the marketplace to those who do not (most often women and children), the effect of the wife's working, and the effect of resources available outside the family. Two, the family can be viewed as a source of status for its members, the research hypothesis being that family stability is associated with fulfillment of self-esteem. Studies involve the influence of income on role performance. An individual's satisfaction with the role of breadwinner or additional earner (as in the case of women who work outside of the home in a two-income family) is measured and correlated with factors such as education, social class, occupation, and income.

Age

The highest rate of separation, desertion, and divorce is experienced by individuals between the ages of 20 and 29. The correlation between early marriage and marital instability is affirmed by recent findings that teenagers are twice as likely to get divorced as are those who marry in their 20s. Furthermore, the proportion of women divorced in their early 20s has more than doubled in little over a generation. Norton and Glick estimate that 25 to 30 percent of the women currently in the early stage of marriage (in their late 20s) will end this first marriage in divorce. It is estimated that for each year of a person's life in which getting married is delayed, the annual separation rate is reduced by 0.1 percent.

Age is also related to the rate of out-of-wedlock births. The proportion of children born to unmarried women has steadily risen. In 1960, 5 percent of all births were out of wedlock; by 1975, the proportion was 15 percent. Although birth rates are declining for older unmarried women, the out-of-wedlock birth rates for women aged 15 to 19 are rising. Two factors are involved in the alarming number of "children giving birth to children." One is the proportion of young women "at risk" in the population as the tail end of the postwar baby boom comes of age; the second factor involves behavior that arises from social forces not yet understood. It is projected that [in] 1980 the number of unwed mothers will have increased by almost a third from the 1965 level.

Examination of the population receiving AFDC reveals that in 1975 over 50 percent of the women were under the age of 29. The age of heads of families is also related to a family's economic status. During the 1970s a clear shift in the ranks of the poor occurred. The number of elderly poor diminished while families headed by females aged 14 to 24 became the majority of poor families. Young people receive the lowest income, experience the highest rate of unemployment, and obtain the fewest benefits associated with a job, yet these same youngsters must deal with the high costs of raising families. This economic "squeeze" combines with the unseasoned abilities of younger people to cope with the stresses of early marriage and, perhaps, explains the frequency of marital disruptions among the young.

Mobility

Although data are scattered and partial, emerging trends indicate that mobility is also a factor in marital instability. Interstate migration is dominated by individuals aged 20 to 29. Residential stability is measured by the length of time one lives in the same house. Recent census data reveal that the mean income of female-headed households decreased as geographical mobility increases. This is especially apparent for households headed by black females. Grumm examined the relationship of interstate migration to recipients of AFDC and found that interstate migration had a destabilizing influence on families. Although the effect of moving within states, counties, and neighborhoods is not documented clearly, it is possible to speculate on its impact. Leaving a supportive network of relatives and friends, facing economic insecurity in the search for a new and better job, and adjusting to an unfamiliar environment, all contribute to marital stress, dissolution, and subsequent pressure on the resulting female-headed families.

Remarriage

Although data indicate an increase in the rate of divorce, 60 percent of all marriages are expected to last. Moreover, although basic transformations in the institution of marriage are under way, strong evidence exists that society's preference for individuals is still a married state. This does not necessarily mean, however, one marriage to the same partner throughout life. A high rate of remarriage accompanies American society's high rate of divorce.

Essential data on marriage reveal that 67 percent of divorced women subsequently remarry, the highest rate of remarriage occurs during the first year after a divorce, only 40 percent of widowers remarry, only 15 percent of women whose marriages terminate after age 40 remarry, the average woman spends about six years as a divorcee, and black widows over 40 who are on welfare are least likely to remarry. The increasing rate of remarriage has not kept pace with the mushrooming rate of divorce, however, and the number of female-headed families has grown. It is estimated that 33 percent of divorced women will remain on their own. Furthermore, remarriage does not guarantee stability: demographers predict that 44 percent of second marriages will also fail. . . .

A small, discernible trend has been emerging since the last decade, that is, women who choose to remain unmarried mothers. Twenty-five percent of participants receiving AFDC are women who have never married and who have children. Although this trend has not been studied extensively, current research is examining the relationship of women's economic opportunities to their single marital status and to the postponement of marriage by young women seeking advanced education and careers. In addition, studies concern young women born at the beginning of the baby boom coming of age who choose single parenthood because, through fluctuations in the birth rate, they are confronted by a scarcity of traditionally preferred slightly older men. This trend presents challenging questions for research and analysis.

TABLE 1. PRIMARY SOURCE OF INCOME FOR FEMALE-HEADED FAMILIES

Income	Percentage of Female-Headed Families
Alimony and child support	7
Employment	28
Social security payments	12
Other income transfer progams	2
AFDC	51

SOURCE: Compiled by the authors from Beverly Johnson McEaddy, "Women Who Head Families: A Socioeconomic Analysis." *Monthly Labor Review,* 99 (June 1976), p. 3; and U.S. Bureau of the Census, "Money Income in 1976 of Families and Persons in the United States,"*Current Population Reports,* Series P-60, No. 114 (Washington, D.C.: U.S. Government Printing Office, 1978), pp. 125–127.

Analysis

. . . The economic status of female-headed families has attracted considerable attention. It is paradoxical that, at a time when other trends suggest the improving status of women, female heads of households account for the largest proportion of economically disadvantaged persons. (See Table 1.) (From 1970 to 1974, the number of *poor* families headed by women rose 21 percent; at the same time those headed by men declined 17 percent.) This country's economic and social welfare institutions have failed these women. . . .

In 1975, with the passage of Title IV-D of the Social Security Act, the government became formidably involved in the issue of child support. That law requires that three steps must be completed when an individual with dependent children applies for public assistance. The absent or noncustodial parent must be identified and located, a program of support based on the ability of the noncustodial parent to pay must be established, and the arrangements for support must be implemented. . . .

It appears that in almost every circumstance the plight of the single mother worsens after divorce, and at the same time the father enjoys a higher standard of living. A man's remarriage complicates the situation. To whom do support payments belong? To his first or second family? The data are indeed grim. Almost one-half of court-ordered payments are delinquent and in one-half the cases, the absent father has not even been located.

The extent to which the government can and should strengthen enforcement of child support is debated vigorously. One position is that, when the father is poor, coercive support procedures erode the informal network of support that does in fact exist in families with very low income. It is argued that it may be more valuable for a father to retain this relationship than contribute a negligible amount of child support. Others argue that children have a right to their father's economic support regardless of the amount and that both parents—not just the mother—should bear financial and social responsibilities for children. It is clear that research which attempts to measure the costs and benefits of vigorous child-support enforcement needs to be developed. Such research should examine the effect of enforcement on the father's relationship with his children.

Discrimination in women's employment has received extensive scrutiny, including examination of disparities in the wages of men and women, occupational segregation, unemployment, the dual labor market (high wage, stable job market versus low wage, part-time, seasonal job market), and the role of human capital (attributes of education, skills, and experience of individual and worker). These studies generally conclude that even great effort on the part of female heads of families does not help to reduce poverty and dependence. Their situation will not change as long as these women face a labor market that regards them as a source of cheap labor.

To the extent that AFDC supplements the poor wages that women workers earn, the possibility exists that the government is institutionalizing a permanent underclass of cheap labor. . . . Is AFDC the least expensive and most effective way of supporting a low-skilled labor supply? Is the mandatory work requirement under AFDC guidelines simply a harassment for women who cannot manage the rigors of a job *and* parenting? How long can discrimination so clearly based on gender be tolerated in the labor market? For women who rely on AFDC as a sole source of income, in almost half the states payments are below the state's own determination of need. . . .

Unemployment figures also show that female-headed families are economically disfavored. . . . Of the unemployed women heading families, only 18 percent had a family member with a job. Watts and Skidmore conclude, "If a breadwinner is defined as someone with dependents who is the only family member in the labor market, a higher proportion of working women who head families now fill that role than working husbands."

The economic status of women is inferior, whether they are working or not. Women are discriminated against by the economic institutions that control their lives. To reverse the pauperization of female-headed households will require sustained attention to discrimination in the labor market, and will require a redefinition of unemployment in recognition that women's work within the home is essential.

Conclusion

The eighties will be a transitional decade. The traditional family with a mother and father is still predominant. However, the single-parent family is a unit in its own right. It also may be a stage, preceding a reconstituted or "blended" family. It is clear that demographic data point to vivid realities in changing family composition, and individuals vary in their capacity to cope with these changes.

Traditional female socialization does not prepare women never to marry, or for the loss of their role as wife, the demands of raising children alone, or the stress of "single again" identities. When women separate, they show classic symptoms of distress compounded by economic helplessness. Women are slowly adapting to this reality, however. There is a new woman emerging on the social landscape. Encouraged by the egalitarian ideology of the women's movement, having realistic expectations of themselves, and valuing their own independence, single mothers may live with confidence and even zest.

There appears to be an irresistible urge to rush to judgment on national family policy. The impact of single-parent families on child development, however, is complex and ambiguous. Studies have not been able to recommend a single direction for social policy. Beginning research has been good. But the consequences for children in changing family formations require sustained attention.

ROBERT MINER

Man As Mother

Until recently, the "single parent" in a "single-parent household" was almost always a woman—the mother. Some of these mothers were widows; some had never been married; others had been deserted, and many had been awarded custody of their children by the courts in divorce proceedings. As the popular and poignant movie Kramer vs. Kramer *revealed, except in rare circumstances, the courts have traditionally assumed that a child belongs with his or her mother. This pattern is beginning to be challenged, however, and in many states even single men can now legally adopt children. It is thus likely that we will see more single-parent, male-headed families in the years to come. The feelings of a father in assuming a traditionally female role and in caring alone for a small child are movingly described in the following article by Robert Miner, author of* Mother's Day.

Once, when I came to collect my three-year-old from day care, the director pulled me aside to whisper that my daughter was disturbed. It seems she kept crying for her father—inappropriate and unhealthy, thought the director. "Would you worry if she cried for her mother?" I asked. Of course not, she answered. "Well," I said, "I *am* her mother."

It wasn't always so. I had the delicious luxury of being a mere father, detached and amiable, for about two years—just long enough, it turned out, for my two kids' mother to use herself up caring for them single-handed.

Then it was my turn.

Like many men of this era, I had to be forced into mothering by the unilateral withdrawal of a woman. That woman, I know now, was running for her life from the crushing institution of motherhood, but she did me a profound service in the process. She forced me into a fierce and unrelenting experience that changed almost everything about me—a kind of open-heart surgery, performed without anesthesia, by rows of sharp, tiny teeth.

For two years as a father I had been genial and tolerant. Two weeks into motherhood and I found myself shaking a toddler in fury above my head. When I realized I was shaking a beautiful, fragile child the way a dog shakes a snake, I put the kid down and something inside me gave way.

In the months that followed I found myself terminally exhausted. Children are engines of fatigue. Merciless as any natural force bent upon its business, they hacked away at my masculine facade, uncovering rage and guilt, unthinkable intimacies and vulnerabilities, weaknesses, potentials for evil I had never admitted to myself. I became ramshackle and cantakerous, a bitch and a fishwife, watched always by the large solemn eyes of children who soon learned to duck any time I raised my hand.

If I'd had time and energy I might have been appalled with myself—as I'd been appalled at my wife before me and at the wives of our friends. Or I might have tried to remember those awesome moments with children when I first learned how the touch of naked baby skin could breach the barricades built by years of trying to be the man I thought I was supposed to be.

As it was, I was preoccupied, exhausted.

Once I overslept and found the baby's crib smeared with excrement and zinc-oxide paste. I never overslept again. Once I became too engrossed in work upstairs, only to find my toddler several acres and a frantic hour away, wading up to his waist in a stream. Once I walked for two days and two nights with a feverish infant who would only stop crying that way. I remember seriously debating whether if I just knocked her head a little against the fireplace she might stop so I could sleep.

No one told me mothering would be a trial by ordeal.

Yet somewhere out of all the storms and chaos a strange amphibious change took place. I found myself a sister among mothers, women no longer an alien species to me. Something in the semaphore of caring for children signaled deep seismic messages, and I found we spoke the same language, felt the same feelings. We understood the loneliness and despair of trying to survive with children in a society that seemed at best indifferent, often extortionate, and usually dead hostile to our needs.

What I am trying to say is that the effects of a typical woman's experience on a traditional male psyche can be elemental. Lifetimes of being a single parent—and women are single parents, married or not—made me angry, guilty, desperate, and dangerous. My insulated middle-class male persona was not prepared for this fall from innocence, and it shattered. Excruciating, but finally no great loss. Instead, motherhood created a rare opportunity for a man, the chance to feel an intimate working part of the lives of my children. Caring for them deepened my emotional repertoire. Breaking and entering as only children can, they ransacked all my closets of deception and defense, making me more vulnerable to the feelings of others and sensitive to their needs, and mine.

To learn that cost me a marriage and—I lie awake nights wrestling with this—maybe the future happiness of my children. Once again a child has paid the price for a parent to grow up. But maybe this time there is a difference. Out of fear, guilt, and a manipulated sense of pride, women have kept motherhood a secret from each new generation of mothers. Only this mother happened to be a man. And this mother keeps no secrets.

MARGARET MEAD

Marriage in Two Steps

Recognizing that the family has at least two important functions—providing and regulating sexual expression and socializing children—the late anthropologist Margaret Mead suggests that perhaps we need two different forms of marriage. People who want a love relationship but no children would have an individual marriage, the goals of which would be intimacy and the partners' growth. It would be relatively easily dissolved and would not entail legal obligations for economic support of one partner by the other. A second form, parental marriage, would be undertaken only after a successful individual marriage and would imply a lifelong or long-term attachment through children. Mead offers the suggestion as a way to insure the child's right to permanence in family relationships.

Perhaps we can catch a glimpse of what we might make of marriage and parenthood if we think in terms of a new pattern that would both give young couples a better chance to come to know each other, and give children a better chance to grow up in an enduring family. Through what steps might this be accomplished?

It should be said at once that changes as important as those involved in creating a new style of marriage can never be brought about through the actions of a few people, or even all the members of a single group. In a democracy as complex as ours, in which one must always take into account a great diversity of religious, regional, class, and national styles, success will depend on contributions made by all kinds of people. Many ideas will arise out of discussions in the press, from the pulpits of many churches, on television, in the agencies of government, in the theater, and in commuity organizations.

Some will come from those whose work brings them face to face with the failures of the present system and who are aware of the urgent need for new forms. Some will be shaped by the actual experiments in which lively, imaginative young people are engaging. And still others will arise out of the puzzlement and questions of the people who listen to the suggestions made by all those who are trying to become articulate about the issues. Out of all these discussions, carried on over a period of time, there will, I hope, evolve the kind of consensus that will provide the basis for a new marriage tradition. We are still a long way from the point at which we can consider the new tradition in such pragmatic terms as its formal social framework—in law and religious practice. No one, it should be clear, can write a prescription or make a blueprint for a whole society.

What I am doing here is advancing some ideas of my own as one contribution to an ongoing discussion. First I shall outline the goals that I personally hope we may reach.

I should like to see us put more emphasis upon the importance of human relationships and less upon sex as a physical need. That is, I would hope that we could encourage a greater willingness to spend time searching for a congenial partner and to enjoy cultivating a deeply personal relationship. Sex would then take its part within a more complex intimacy and would cease to be sought after for itself alone.

I should like to see children assured of a lifelong relationship to both parents. This, of course, can only be attained when parents themselves have such a relationship. I do not mean that parents must stay married. As long as early marriage remains a practice, it must be assumed that some marriages—perhaps many marriages—will break down in the course of a lifetime of growth, mobility, and change. But I should like to see a style of parenthood develop that would survive the breaking of the links of marriage through divorce. This would depend on a mutual recognition that co-parenthood is a permanent relationhip. Just as brother and sister are irrevocably related because they share the same parents, so also parents are irrevocably related because they share the same child. At present, divorce severs the link between the adult partners and each, in some fashion, attempts—or sometimes gives up the attempt—to keep a separate contact with the children, as if this were now a wholly individual relationship. This need not be.

Granting the freedom of partners to an uncongenial marriage to seek a different, individual commitment within a new marriage, I would hope that we would hold on to the ideal of a lifetime marriage in maturity. No religious group that cherishes marriage as a sacrament should have to give up the image of a marriage that lasts into old age and into the lives of grandchildren and great-grandchildren as one that is blessed by God. No wholly secularized group should have to be deprived of the sense that an enduring, meaningful relationship is made binding by the acceptance, approval, and support of the entire society as witnesses.

At the same time, I believe, we must give greater reality to our belief that marriage is a matter of individual choice, a choice made by each young man and woman freely, without coercion by parents or others. The present mode of seeking for sex among a wide range of partners casually, and then, inconsistently, of accepting marriage as a form of "choice" arising from necessity, is a deep denial of individuality and individual love. In courtship, intensity of feeling grows as two people move toward each other. In our present system, however, intensity of feeling is replaced by the tensions arising from a series of unknown factors: Will pregnancy occur? Is this the best bargain on the sex market? Even with sexual freedom, will marriage result? Today true courtship, when it happens, comes about in spite of, not because of, the existing styles of dating and marrying.

These goals—individual choice, a growing desire for a lifelong relationship with a chosen partner, and the desire for children with whom and through whom lifelong relationships are maintained—provide a kind of framework for thinking about new forms of marriage. I believe that we need two forms of marriage, one of which can (though it need not) develop into the other, each with its own possibilities and special forms of responsibility.

The first type of marriage may be called an *individual marriage* binding together two individuals only. It has been suggested that it might be called a "student" marriage, as undoubtedly it would occur first and most often among students. But looking ahead, it would be a type of marriage that would also be appropriate for much older men and women, so I shall use the term *individual marriage*. Such a marriage would be a licensed union in which two individuals would be committed to each other as individuals for as long as they wished to remain together, but not as future parents. As the first step in marriage, it would not include having children.

In contrast, the second type of marriage, which I think of as *parental marriage,* would be explicitly directed toward the founding of a family. It would not only be a second type but also a second step or stage, following always on an individual marriage and with its own license and ceremony and kinds of responsibility. This would be a marriage that looked to a lifetime relationship with links, sometimes, to many people.

In an individual marriage, the central obligation of the boy and girl or man and woman to each other would be an ethical, not an economic, one. The husband would not be ultimately responsible for the support of his wife; if the marriage broke up, there would be no alimony or support. The husband would not need to feel demeaned if he was not yet ready, or was not able, to support his wife. By the same token, husband or wife could choose freely to support the other within this partnership.

Photograph by Craighead. Courtesy of
Photophile.

Individual marriage would give two very young people a chance to know each other with a kind of intimacy that does not usually enter into a brief love affair, and so it would help them to grow into each other's life—and allow them to part without the burden of misunderstood intentions, bitter recriminations, and self-destructive guilt. In the past, long periods of engagement, entered into with parental consent, fulfilled at least in part the requirement of growing intimacy and shared experience. But current attitudes toward sex make any retreat to this kind of relationship impossible. In other societies, where parents chose their children's marriage partners, the very fact of meeting as strangers at the beginning of a lifelong relationship gave each a high sense of expectancy within which shared understanding might grow. But this is impossible for us as an option because of the emphasis on personal choice and the unwillingness to insist on maintaining a commitment that has failed.

Individual marriage in some respects resembles "companionate marriage" as it was first discussed in the 1920s and written about by Judge Ben Lindsey on the basis of his long experience in court with troubled young people. This was a time when very few people were ready as yet to look ahead to the consequences of deep changes in our attitude toward sex and personal choice. Today, I believe, we are far better able to place young marriage within the context of a whole lifetime.

Individual marriage, as I see it, would be a serious commitment, entered into in public, validated and protected by law and, for some, by religion, in which each partner would have a deep and continuing concern for the happiness and well-being of the other. For those who found happiness it could open the way to a more complexly designed future.

Every parental marriage, whether children were born into it or adopted, would necessarily have as background a good individual marriage. The fact of a previous marriage, individual or parental, would not alter this. Every parental marriage, at no matter what stage in life, would have to be preceded by an individual marriage. In contrast to individual marriage, parental marriage would be hard to contract. Each partner would know the other well, eliminating the shattering surprise of discovery that either one had suffered years of mental or physical illness, had been convicted of a serious crime, was unable to hold a job, had entered the country illegally, already had children or other dependents, or any one of the thousand shocks that lie in wait for the person who enters into a hasty marriage with someone he or she knows little about. When communities were smaller, most people were protected against such shocks by the publication of the banns. Today other forms of protection are necessary. The assurance thus given to parents that their son or daughter would not become hopelessly trapped into sharing parenthood with an unsuitable mate also would serve as a protection for the children not yet born.

As a couple prepared to move from an individual to a parental marriage they also would have to demonstrate their economic ability to support a child. Instead of falling back on parents, going deeply into debt, or having to ask the aid of welfare agencies, they would be prepared for the coming of a child. Indeed, both might be asked to demonstrate some capacity to undertake the care of the family in the event one or the other became ill. Today a girl's education, which potentially makes her self-sustaining, is perhaps the best dowry a man can give his son-in-law so he will not fall prey to the gnawing anxiety of how his family would survive his death. During an individual marriage, designed to lead to parental marriage, a girl, no less than a boy, might learn a skill that would make her self-supporting in time of need.

Even more basic to the survival of a marriage, however, is the quality of the marriage itself—its serenity, its emotional strength, its mutuality. Over long years we have acquired a fund of experience about good marriages through the inquiries made by adoption agencies before a child is given permanently to adoptive parents. Now, if we wished to do so, we could extrapolate from this experience for the benefit of partners in individual marriages but not yet joined in parenthood and for the benefit of infants hoped for but not yet conceived. And in the course of these explorations before parental marriage the ethical and religious issues that sometimes are glossed over earlier could be discussed and, in a good relationship, resolved. Careful medical examinations would bring to light present or potential troubles, and beyond this, would help the couple to face the issue: What if, in spite of our desire for a family, having a child entails a serious risk to the mother, or perhaps the child? What if, in spite of a good prognosis, we, as a couple, cannot have a child? And then, even assuming that all such questions have been favorably resolved, it must not be forgotten that in all human relationships there are imponderables—and the marriage will be tested by them.

As a parental marriage would take much longer to contract and would be based on a larger set of responsibilities, so also its disruption would be carried out much more slowly. A divorce would be arranged in a way that would protect not only the two adults but also the children for whose sake the marriage was undertaken. The family, as against the marriage, would have to be assured a kind of continuity in which neither parent was turned into an angry ghost and no one could become an emotional blackmailer or be the victim of emotional blackmail.

Perhaps some men and women would choose to remain within individual marriage, with its more limited responsibilities; having found that there was an impediment to parental marriage, they might well be drawn into a deeper individual relationship with each other. And perhaps some who found meaningful companionship through parenthood would look later for more individualized companionship in a different kind of person.

By dignifying individual relationships for young people we would simultaneously invest with new dignity a multitude of deeply meaningful relationships of choice throughout life. First and foremost, we would recognize parenthood as a special form of marriage. But we would also give strong support to marriage as a working relationship of husband and wife as colleagues, and as a leisure relationship of a couple who have not yet entered into or who are now moving out of the arduous years of multiple responsibilities.

By strengthening parenthood as a lasting relationship we would keep intact the link between grandparents, parents, and children. Whether they were living together or were long since divorced, they would remain united in their active concern for their family of descendants. The acceptance of the two kinds of marriage would give equal support, however, to the couple who, having forgone a life with children, cherish their individual marriage as the expression of their love and loyalty.

The suggestion for a style of marriage in two steps—individual marriage and marriage for parenthood—has grown out of my belief that clarification is the beginning of constructive change. Just as no one can make a blueprint of the future, so no one can predict the outcome of a new set of principles. We do know something about the unfortunate direction in which contemporary marriage is drifting. But we need not simply continue to drift. With our present knowledge, every child born can be a child wanted and prepared for. And by combining the best of our traditions and our best appraisal of human relations, we may succeed in opening the way for new forms of marriage that will give dignity and grace to all men and women.

BENNETT M. BERGER,
BRUCE M. HACKETT, AND
R. MERVYN MILLAR

Child Rearing in Communes

One of the alternatives to the nuclear family is the commune, a concept that developed, in its contemporary form, out of the hippie movement of the sixties. In the article that follows, a group of sociologists report on their study of child rearing in communes. They note that mother and child tend to be the basic family unit, with men joining and leaving frequently. The authors contrast commune child raising with that found in middle-class nuclear families. While there is much less attentive child raising in the commune, the children do grow up. These hip communes contrast sharply with the much more structured communal patterns of the Israeli kibbutz, described in Chapter Ten.

Family Structure and Sexual Relations

Everything we have said about the children of the communes occurs in the context of hippie relationships and family structures, and it is important to understand these because they contain the seeds of the potential future of the commune movement.

The most important single feature of hip relationships is their fragility. We mean by this not that many of the relationships don't last; quite the contrary. In several of our more stable communes couples have been "to-gether" as long as the commune has existed (two to three years) and sometimes longer. We mean, rather, that there tend to be few if any cultural constraints or structural underpinnings to sustain relationships when and if they become tension-ridden or otherwise unsatisfying. The uncertainty of the future hovers over hip relationships like a probation officer reminding the parties of the necessary tentativeness of their commitments to each other.

Very few nuclear (mother-father-child) units, for example, are legally married; neither the men nor the women have the kinds of jobs that bind them to a community. Like many of their parents (who theorists have suggested have been highly mobile), they move around a great deal, getting into and out of "intimate" relations rather quickly through such techniques as spontaneous "encounter" and other forms of "up-frontness." And above and beyond these, there is a very heavy emphasis on now—a refusal to *count on* the future as a continuation of present arrangements—and a diffuse desire to remain unencumbered, a freedom *from* the social ties that constrain one.

Yet despite the fact of (and the adjustment to) the fragility of relationships, there are romantic images also superimposed. Although the fragility of old-man/old-lady relationships is a fact, communards of all sorts are generally reluctant to believe in a future of serial monogamy. Many communards, particularly the women, hope for an ideal lover or a permanent mate but tend not to have much real expectation that it will happen. Instead, compensatory satisfactions are found in the *image* of the communal family and household, always full of people, where a group of brothers and sisters, friends as kin, spend all or most of their time with each other, working, playing, loving, rapping, "hanging out"—where wedding bells, far from breaking up the old gang, are themselves so rare that they are occasions for regional celebrations of solidarity when they do ring out.

John Olson, *Life* Magazine, © 1969, Time Inc.

Where it exists, it is the fact of communal solidarity which functions as the strongest support for fragile relations among couples. For when the communal scene is a wholesome and attractive one, as it sometimes is, couples whose relationship is very unstable may elect to stay together in order to share those benefits rather than threaten them by breaking up.

In spite of the fragility of relationships in a system which defines the future as uncertain and in an ideology emphasizing spontaneity and freedom, heterosexual couples are the backbone of most communes, urban or rural, creedal or not. They seem more stable and dependable as members than single people do, if only because their search for partners is ended, even if that ending is temporary. The temporary character of the relationships is more pronounced in urban communes, both, we believe, because the very presence of couples in rural communes is itself generally evidence of more stable commitment, and because of the higher probability in urban scenes of meeting another man or woman who is ready and willing to enter into a close relationship at little more than a moment's notice.

When a couple has a child, their mobility is reduced somewhat, of course, even when the child is the product of a previous union of either the female or the male. But only somewhat, because of the importance of what we call the "splitting" phenomenon, particularly as it applies to men. . . . Children (especially very young ones) "belong" to their mothers, and norms *requiring* paternal solicitude for children are largely absent. What this means is that fathers are "free"—at the very least free to split whenever they are so moved. Since they are not "legally" fathers (even if they biologically are) they have no claims on the child, and since there is generally a strong communal norm *against* invoking the legal constraints of straight society (i.e., calling the police), fathers have no obligation to the child that anyone is willing to enforce. Moreover, no norm takes priority over the individual's (particularly the male's) search for himself, or meaning, or transcendence, and if this search requires a father's wandering elsewhere "for a while" there is nothing to prevent it.

One consequence of this family pattern is the frequency of woman-with-child-and-without-old-man in many of the communes we have studied—although this occurs as often as the result of the woman-with-child arriving on the commune scene that way as it does as a result of her partner splitting. A situation like this does not typically last a long time in any commune we have studied, although it was present in almost all of them. Even when the women involved say they prefer celibacy, there is some doubt that they actually do. One afternoon in a tepee, three young women (without men) with infants on the breast agreed that they welcomed a respite from men, what with their bodies devoted almost full time to the nursing of infants. Within a week, two of them had new old men and the third had gone back to her old one. Celibacy or near celibacy occurs only in those creedal communes whose doctrines define sexual activity as impure or as a drain on one's physical and spiritual resources for transcendence.

But although celibacy is rare and although couple relations are fragile, this should not be taken to mean that sex is either promiscuous or disordered. At any given time, monogamous coupling is the norm in all the communes we studied closely; in this respect hippies tend to be more traditional than the "swingers" and wife-swappers one reads about in the middle class. Although there are communes whose creed requires group marriage (in the sense that all the adults are regarded as married to all the others, and expected to have sexual relations with each other), we have not studied any of these at first hand. But even in communes where coupling is the norm, there seems to be evidence of a natural drift toward group—although this may still be ideologically disavowed.

For one thing, when couples break up in rural communes, it is as likely as not that each will remain at the commune; and this occurs frequently in urban communes too. Without a drift toward group marriage, situations like this could and do cause great communal tensions which threaten the survival of the group. On the other hand, a not uncommon feature of communes is a situation in which over a long period of time many of the adults have had sexual relations with each other at one or another point between the lapses of "permanent" coupling. Under these conditions, group marriage can seem like a "natural" emergence rather than unnaturally "forced" by a creed—a natural emergence which, by gradually being made an item of affirmed faith, can conceivably solve some of the problems and ease some of the tensions generated by the fragility of couple relations and the breakups which are a predictable result of them. Broken-up couples may still "love" each other as kin, under these conditions—even if they find themselves incapable of permanently sharing the same tent, cabin or bed, an incapacity more likely to be explained astrologically than any other way. (Astrology is used to explain "problems" with respect to children and intimate relations between couples.)*

But the widespread presence of women-with-children as nuclear units in the communes is not merely the result of the splitting of men nor an expression of the belief of hip parents in the unwisdom of staying together "for the sake

*We think, indeed, that there is a close relationship between the commune movement on the one hand, and the complex of stirrings in the middle class which includes the Encounter movement, swingers, sensitivity training, and the incipient gestures toward group marriage represented by "wife-swapping." Each represents an attempt to cope with similar problems (e.g., alienation, existential discontents with the prospects or the realities of middle-class life) by groups of people differently situated in the life-career cycle: the communards being mainly college dropouts in their twenties, the others being mainly married couples in their thirties or forties with children and already well into their professional careers, with which they may have become disenchanted.

of the child." The readiness of hip women to bear the child even of a "one-night stand" is supported by a social structure which indicates its "logic." Unlike middle-class women, for example, a hippie female's social status does not depend upon her old man's occupation; she doesn't need him for that. The state is a much better provider than most men who are available to her. And an infant to care for provides more meaning and security in her life than most men could. In addition, these women are often very acceptable to communes as new members. They are likely to be seen as potentially less disruptive to ongoing commune life than a single man; they are likely to be seen as more dependable and stable than a single man; and these women provide a fairly stable source of communal income through the welfare payments that many of them receive. From the point of view of the hip mothers, commune living can be seen as a logical choice; it solves some of the problems of loneliness—there are always others around. And if she wants to go out, there are usually other members of the family present to look after her child, and other males to act as surrogate fathers.

How is it for the children and what will it be like in the future? It is really impossible to say simply and with any certainty. Do the kids seem happy? Healthy? Will they too rebel against their parents? There just isn't any really reliable information, which means that one can say just about anything one wishes to suit one's prejudices.

There are lots of coughs and runny noses, especially in the wintertime. But there's that in suburbia too. They do smoke dope, but it doesn't take very much to get a little one stoned, so there's a built-in thermostat there.

Are they neglected? By the standards of the child-centeredness model in the middle class, we suppose yes. On the other hand, there is reason to be skeptical about the wholesomeness of the middle-class pattern, among whose major consequences are the prolongation of adolescence and dependency, and whose typical figures are nineteen-year-old boys and girls (instead of men and women) who don't know how to take care of themselves.

There seem to be very few "adolescents" visible in communes, although there are plenty of young persons. And if communal living succeeds in abolishing adolescence, it may have been worthwhile after all.

CHAPTER FOURTEEN

Family Services and Public Policy

Nobody who has not been in the interior of a family can say what the difficulties of any individual of that family may be.

Jane Austen, *Pride and Prejudice*

The object of government is the welfare of the people.

Theodore Roosevelt, *The New Nationalism*

KENNETH KENISTON AND
THE CARNEGIE COUNCIL ON CHILDREN

Services Families Need

*In this excerpt from his important report of the Carnegie Council on Children,
psychologist Kenneth Keniston critiques existing policies and programs for
children and the family and suggests guidelines for new policies.*

The present array of publicly supported services for families and children has
developed over decades of emphasis on particular problems, such as the need
to fund foster homes for children whose families cannot care for them, or to
immunize children against diphtheria or polio. Some of these services are
funded and operated entirely at the local or state level; others are managed
at the state level with large federal subsidies in the form of revenue sharing
or block grant funds (which basically provide money without dictating forms);
a few, such as Head Start and Title I, are funded by the federal government.
One survey of federal programs in 1972 showed 280 specifically designed to
help families and children, administered by twenty different federal agencies.
All but twenty-five of these programs provided services as their major function.

Contrary to popular belief, many of these federally supported programs
are not directed only toward poor children and their families. Some programs,
such as school lunches, are available to all, but those who can afford to are
required to pay some or all of the cost. Still other services focus on particular
human needs without regard for ability to pay, including education for the
handicapped, childhood lead-paint-poisoning control, centers for runaway
youths, and programs for the prevention of drug and alcohol abuse. . . .

From *All Our Children* by Kenneth Keniston and the Carnegie Council on Children, copyright
© 1977 by Carnegie Corporation of New York. Reprinted by permission of Harcourt Brace
Jovanovich, Inc.

398

In fact, over three-quarters of the federal programs for families and children listed in 1972 were not intended primarily for the poor, and 35.6 percent of these were completely unrestricted, meant to benefit all comers, including middle-class children if they needed them.

Despite the number of direct service programs to help families cope with their needs, the federal investment in these services is a small proportion of the federal budget. In 1976, the entire budget for family services (as opposed to tax exemptions, deductions, and cash transfers) amounted to about $30 billion. . . .

However important these programs are in specific cases, the problems that have accompanied their piecemeal development are well known: as a nation, we have an inadequate, uncoordinated, and incomplete patchwork of family support services. Services provided at public expense are failing to support families in a number of ways:

Services are unavailable to many who need them. Children entering school are eligible to be screened and treated for physical and emotional problems . . . under the government's Early and Periodic Screening, Diagnosis and Treatment program. In the first nine years of the program, however, fewer than one-quarter of those eligible had actually been screened. . . . Furthermore, of the approximately 2.2 million screened children who proved to need treatment, only about 50 percent ever received it.

A federal program supports special educational services for poor children. Some states and school districts have used these funds to pay for health services related to learning such as diagnostic testing, eyeglasses, and hearing aids. But poor children must be in special classes to be eligible for these health services. If a low-income family had five nearsighted children, only two of whom were in special classes, only those two would be eligible for eyeglasses.

Services are fragmented. A young mother on welfare who becomes pregnant can seek prenatal care from her local health department clinic, but when it is time for the birth, she will be transferred (theoretically with her records but most likely without them) to a public hospital, where she will encounter entirely new faces and a new set of documents. The pediatrician who examines the new baby there will never see the child again. Instead, the young mother now has to take her baby to a "well-child" clinic—but not the same place where she got prenatal care. The well-child clinic unfortunately will not take care of a sick child, so when the baby falls ill she must take the infant to a private physician, whose fee will be paid by the welfare department, or to a hospital emergency room. If the child is found to have a handicapping condition, the child will be eligible for crippled children's services, but these will often be provided at still another place, and paid for with public health funds, which require a whole new set of eligibility determinations. This process, all too typical, would discourage almost any parent from getting that baby the medical care it is entitled to.

Services do not encourage families to stay together. For many years, in order to get welfare, poor families had to prove that the father was absent from the house, which encouraged many poor families to separate or lie. Recognizing this, the federal government in 1972 passed an "unemployed fathers" provision which gave states the option of giving AFDC assistance to families with two parents. But, as of mid-1976, almost half the states had not adopted this provision.

Families with temporary problems such as the illness of a parent may need help caring for their children. Child care during the day in another home or a center is the remedy that disrupts the family least; temporary foster care is more disruptive; placing children in institutions is the most traumatic of all. Yet close relatives who take a child in at times of family stress do not qualify for the payments most welfare programs give to unrelated foster parents; so when money to support the child is a major factor, this federal service policy encourages parents to place their children with strangers or in an institution.

Most services are designed only to treat problems, not prevent them. . . . Medicaid programs in twenty-one states deny prenatal care to first-time mothers, even though studies have indicated that, compared with those who do get care, mothers who receive no prenatal care are three times more likely to give birth to infants with low birth weights, a condition associated with almost half of all infant deaths and with birth defects.

Services are underfunded. The 1976 appropriation for federal child welfare expenditures (which is not AFDC but funds to help state and local welfare agencies provide protective services meant to prevent public dependency and neglect) was more than $200 million short of the authorization enacted by Congress. The appropriations for Title I of the Elementary and Secondary Education Act have never matched the authorizations; in fiscal 1977, the appropriations covered the equivalent of an estimated 39 percent of those children judged to be in need in that year.

Services stigmatize. Overall, the second-class nature of services for the poor is the biggest stigma of all. Specific instances add insult to injury: children who need services but receive them because a court judges them to be "persons in need of supervision" or "children in need of services" may later find that the stigma of their court records outweighs the benefits of any services they get. For example, in forty-seven states truants from school may get services by being institutionalized; but their records may later close job opportunities even if they go back to school. . . .

Principles for Change

Given these problems, it is small wonder that publicly provided social services have received a bad name among both taxpayers and recipients. Yet these problems are not inevitable. The way we provide services to families in this country could be very different if we started from different principles.

1. *Universal Access.* As long as we care about the growth and development of this nation's children, services for all who need them must be the first principle. This means services that are open to everyone—whatever race they are, whatever income they have, wherever they live, and whatever languages they speak. The public has an interest in seeing that everyone has services available and that these meet federal standards of fairness and quality, even if they are privately provided. When the public decides that a service is essential and will be publicly financed for all users, as with education, then everyone should have equal access and get equal benefits. We believe that health care should fall into this category. . . .

Whenever services are in short supply, we believe that priority should be given to families where the well-being of the child and the integrity of the family are in greatest jeopardy for lack of services. For example, if daytime child-care places are in short supply, children with special developmental, emotional, and educational needs should have a high priority. If homemaker services are scarce, families that require these services to prevent placing their children outside the home should have first claims. In practice, we believe this will mean that priority will most often be given to families at the lower end of the income scale, to families who cannot afford to seek the service from private providers.

The same principles—the well-being of the child and the integrity of the family—should determine priorities for the creation of new services when these are needed. And the community itself should determine its own local priorities, within broad federal guidelines, since the unmet service needs of Harlem are likely to be quite different from those of rural Nebraska.

2. *Racial and Economic Integration.* Services should foster, as much as possible, the racial, class, and cultural integration of different families. Having black and white, middle-class and poor children in the same progam not only teaches children about diversity but also builds the breadth of political support that is necessary to sustain adequate support for most services. Integration will be fostered most by making service programs universally available, regardless of family income. In addition, this goal will be helped by better consolidation and coordination of services. Community service centers, for example, ought to be organized to serve families with battered children, children who do not speak English, or children who may need special help to prepare for school—all problems that cut across the lines of race and class.

3. *Convenience and Coordination.* In order to use a service, many families need "secondary support services" such as transportation, baby-sitting, someone who will answer their questions on the telephone, interpreters for those who do not speak English, and public information to let them know what is available. Most current service programs use all their funds for their own basic functions, with nothing left over to provide other kinds of help that will enable families to make use of the services. . . . There should be one place where families can go to find out about the available services they may need, to get proper referrals to the correct services, to make appointments, and to get needed transportation or baby sitters. To provide this, a referral-and-appointment center should exist in every town, county, or neighborhood, depending on the size of the area and the population involved.

Where possible, clusters of related services should be located together or close by each other—on the model of the county courthouse—so that families can go to one location for a variety of related services. When new services are added, they should build on existing service systems that are well accepted. Schools, for example, might also be used for providing health and early screening services.

Coordination should also take place at the federal level, and the government should review the standards it has already set for programs, eliminating discrepancies and conflicting regulations for similar services provided by several agencies.

4. *Maximum Choice.* Service systems should strive to provide families with the widest possible range of options so that they can choose which services will help them most and which provider will suit them best. An illness of one parent may require a visiting nurse, a homemaker, or temporary day care, but families should not be forced to put their children into day care because nurses or homemakers are not available. If they do choose day care, various types should be available: family, group, or center care.

5. *Parent Participation.* Obviously, a good program for migrant-worker families would not be identical to a good program for middle-class suburbanites. The ethnic and cultural traditions of families and communities should be taken into account when organizing and delivering family services. In order to ensure that differences in child rearing and other family patterns are reflected accurately and sensitively in social programs, and to check remote bureaucracies, services should require inclusion of families in policy making, monitoring, and helping run the day-to-day program.

6. *Paraprofessionals and Volunteers.* While good professionals—doctors, teachers, social workers, and the like—are important in diagnosing problems and providing services of all kinds, services should also draw on a range of paraprofessionals and volunteer help. . . .

7. *Prevention and Keeping Families Intact.* A rational and unified system of services should put the prime stress on preventive services and those that disrupt family life the least. It should be as easy for families to go to a clinic for diagnosis and treatment of a mild problem as to the emergency room after the problem has become a serious condition. It should be more attractive for overburdened parents to use day-care and counseling services before they reach the point of harming their child than court-mandated services after the fact. . . . The courts that deal with children should be empowered to order services for families in trouble before things have gotten so bad that a child must be placed in some form of nonfamily care.

Accountability: Increasing Parents' Control

These principles we have sketched out are essentially standards of fairness and quality that we would like to see applied to all service programs, not only those that are government run. Just as restaurants have to meet minimum standards of public health and are not allowed to discriminate against racial minorities, so private service programs should not be allowed to fall below uniform levels. Federally determined standards for all services, some of which we will outline below, should be put into effect nationwide through legislation, where appropriate, and through agency regulations and executive orders as well.

Traditionally, people who provide services, at least those publicly funded, have had to account to their bosses, not their clients, for how well they are doing their job. This means that a father has very little say in how his daughter's day-care center is run, even though he may know more about the center's shortcomings and successes than the bureaucrat to whom they are supposedly being reported. We believe that the traditional enforcement of standards by administrative fiat must be balanced by giving authority and responsibility to the level where the service works. This is why there should be parent representation—which also serves the other purposes outlined above—as well as federal supervision. And parents should be involved in assessing more than just how programs are performing the job they set out to do.

At present, many agencies that operate services do some self-monitoring. Schools, hospitals, and counseling centers, for example, may undertake surveys of the number of people who need their service; they may plan whether to have one center or six; they may count how many of the people who need the service are getting it; they may try to survey how much the service is helping its clients. But in essence this is similar to a business auditing its own books, a practice long outlawed because of the obvious conflicts of interest. . . .

We propose that federal regulations take away from service operators such planning and assessment functions as overall coordination with other similar services, needs surveys, coverage surveys, and evaluations, and require communities to set up "consumers' councils" with heavy representation of parents to perform these auditing jobs. The councils should receive enough federal support to purchase technical assistance such as surveys. Their responsibility should extend to an area no greater than an efficient service "basin," that is, an area about the size of a school district. These councils will have to be independent of any organization that itself provides services. . . .

Consumers' councils would first of all assess the need for services in their area of responsibility; second, survey how well programs are reaching people with those needs; and third, evaluate how well programs are actually alleviating the problems they were set up to solve, and whether they meet federal standards. . . .

The most important tool for making programs accountable for quality is accurate data open to those who evaluate the service and to individuals or groups who wish to challenge a provider of services. Within the bounds of respecting privacy, federal standards should open for public scrutiny the internal information necessary to evaluate how effectively each service program plans and how well it is performing.

At the national level as well, data on the conditions and needs of American families and children must be improved. Most of the major national data-collection systems, such as the National Bureau of the Census and Bureau of Labor Statistics, ask questions about problems, which at least begins to define what services are needed. But these data systems make no effort to connect the conditions for which they gather data to the coverage provided by federal programs to find out whether existing programs are even in place and trying to help. . . .

We believe that the responsibility for watching over standards and performance belongs primarily in two places: at the federal level where the federal intent was formulated, and at the level where the program functions—namely, with the programs' clients who serve on the consumers' council. Neither of these alone can do an effective job of monitoring because federal officials often have no idea of local needs and preferences, and consumers' councils may ignore federal standards and thereby neglect some of the local populations.

WILLIAM J. LEDERER AND DON D. JACKSON

Interpersonal Comparison Tests

The authors of the questionnaire reprinted below were members of a group (led by Gregory Bateson, the eminent anthropologist) which set out in the early 1960s to look for the social sources of schizophrenia. From this group came a radical new approach to psychotherapy—the treatment of a whole family group rather than of the individual alone.

About the same time, other therapists were also discovering that even when they helped an individual child, the cure might not hold when the child returned to the family home. More and more, then, mental health workers began to locate pathology in the family system, and the new family therapy was launched. Lederer and Jackson treat marriage as a system in their The Mirages of Marriage, *from which the following selection is excerpted. This evaluation form is used with couples who seek marital counseling. It is a method for detecting differences and potential areas of conflict between partners, and it can serve to focus discussion with or without the help of a counselor.*

In this section we offer three tests which will aid in determining how close or far apart couples are in their repertoire of values. The amount of difference will indicate the likelihood that the two individuals can form a functional system. Later we will explain how to estimate this.

The tests should be taken by one person at a time in complete privacy. To start the first test, place a piece of white bond paper alongside the first test page. Line up the top of the paper with the top of the page. Now answer the questions by placing an X on the bond paper opposite the horizontal line where it would be put if the answers were being marked in the book. Mark only a single answer for each question, choosing the one which is more true than any of the others. Go through Tests A and B in this manner, using a fresh piece of paper for each page. The instructions for taking Test C are given separately. Be sure to identify each page by writing at the top the number of the corresponding page in the book.

Do not make marks in the book. The second person taking the test would then see your answers, and would be influenced by them.

TEST A

1. I was born
    a. on the Eastern seaboard.   _____
    b. in the Southern United States.   _____
    c. in the Midwestern United States. _____
    d. in the Southwestern United States. _____
    e. in the Western United States.   _____
    f. outside the United States.   _____

2. My place of rearing was
    a. a metropolis.   _____
    b. suburbia.   _____
    c. a medium-sized town.   _____
    d. a small town.   _____
    e. a rural area.   _____

3. My religious background is
    a. Catholic.   _____
    b. Jewish.   _____
    c. Protestant.   _____
    d. Moslem.   _____
    e. none.   _____
    f. other.   _____

4. My parents are
    a. first-generation Americans.   _____
    b. second-generation Americans.   _____
    c. third-generation Americans (or earlier). _____
    d. not American citizens.   _____

5. *The highest annual income earned by my father was*
    a. over $30,000.   _____
    b. over $20,000.   _____
    c. over $15,000.   _____
    d. over $10,000.   _____
    e. over $5,000.   _____
    f. $5,000 or less.   _____

6. *The highest educational level reached by my father was*
    a. grade school.   _____
    b. high school.   _____
    c. college.   _____
    d. graduate school.   _____
    e. a doctoral degree.   _____

7. *The highest educational level reached by my mother was*
    a. grade school.   _____
    b. high school.   _____
    c. college.   _____
    d. graduate school.   _____
    e. a doctoral degree.   _____

8. *My position in the family was*
    a. oldest child.   _____
    b. middle child.   _____
    c. youngest child.   _____
    d. only child.   _____
    e. one of several in middle.   _____

9. *The number of children in my family was*
    a. very large (seven or more).   _____
    b. large (five or six).   _____
    c. average (three or four).   _____
    d. small (two).   _____
    e. only one.   _____

10. *My parents were*
    a. very close in age.   _____
    b. less than five years apart.   _____
    c. less than ten years apart.   _____
    d. less than fifteen years apart.   _____
    e. fifteen or more years apart.   _____

11. *My parents' experience with divorce was that*
    a. neither was ever divorced.   _____
    b. one had been previously divorced.   _____
    c. both had been previously divorced.   _____
    d. they were divorced when I was a child (12 or under).   _____
    e. they were divorced when I was in my teens or older.   _____

12. *In my parents' families (including grandparents and parents' siblings)*
    a. there have been no divorces.   _____
    b. there has been one divorce.   _____
    c. there have been two divorces.   _____
    d. there have been three or more divorces.   _____

13. *In my family rearing the person who seemed most in charge was*
    a. my mother.   _____
    b. my father.   _____
    c. neither parent.   _____
    d. I never thought about who was in charge.   _____

14. *In our community my parents were*
    a. considered important people.   _____
    b. included among the people of some standing.   _____
    c. just average socially.   _____
    d. below average socially.   _____
    e. considered outsiders.   _____

TEST B

I. Past Life Experiences

1. *My family situation consisted of*
   a. living with both of my biological parents.   _____
   b. living with just my mother.   _____
   c. living with just my father.   _____
   d. living in foster homes or with stepparents.   _____
   e. living with my real mother and a stepfather.   _____
   f. living with my real father and a stepmother.   _____

2. *My own family experience was*
   a. warm and pleasant.   _____
   b. pleasant but not intimate.   _____
   c. nothing I can particularly remember.   _____
   d. unpleasant.   _____

3. *As clearly as I can remember my earliest days were*
   a. extremely pleasant.   _____
   b. neither pleasant nor unpleasant.   _____
   c. pleasant, though I was nervous.   _____
   d. unpleasant.   _____

4. *The most pleasant aspects of my childhood are associated with experiences*
   a. with both parents.   _____
   b. with the parent of the same sex.   _____
   c. with the parent of the opposite sex.   _____
   d. with my siblings.   _____
   e. unconnected with members of my immediate family.   _____
   f. I do not recall any particularly pleasant experiences. _____

5. *As a child I was fond of*
   a. reading, solitary hobbies, and daydreaming.   _____
   b. sports and outdoor activities.   _____
   c. being around other people socially as much as possible. _____
   d. no particular interests which I can recall.   _____

6. *During my growing-up period*
   a. I had many close friends.   _____
   b. I had one or two close friends.   _____
   c. I had no friends whom I particularly recollect.   _____
   d. I was a very solitary person.   _____

7. *In my family, my dating*
   a. was something I could easily discuss with my parents. _____
   b. was mentioned rarely, or only in a kidding manner.   _____
   c. was something I did not care to discuss.   _____
   d. aroused considerable conflict.   _____

8. *When I was in high school*
   a. my major interest was in getting good grades as well as maintaining an active social life. _____
   b. my major interest was in maintaining an active social and sports life rather than in getting high grades. _____
   c. I did not want to go to school any longer, and wanted to make money. _____
   d. I felt confused and did not know what I wanted to do. _____

II. Present Life Experiences

1. *Financially and socially I feel the next five years*
   a. will be reasonably successful.   _____
   b. will consist of two steps forward and one back.   _____
   c. are impossible to predict at present.   _____
   d. The future scares me.   _____

2. *About my health at the present time, I would say that*
   .a. I have always had perfect health, and I am certain I'll stay that way.   _____
   b. for the last few years, my general condition has been below par, but I believe I'll regain excellent health in the near future.   _____
   c. for some time now I have had a chronic illness (or disability) which is serious, and the probability of improvement is small.   _____
   d. I don't know for sure. I guess I'm as healthy as anybody, but I haven't had a physical for years.   _____

3. *About my psychological adjustment, I would say that*
   a. I feel fairly secure emotionally.   _____
   b. I am happiest not living alone.   _____
   c. I probably do best living alone.   _____
   d. I do not think about my emotions.   _____

4. *Like many people I am*
   a. sometimes uneasy when I am alone.   _____
   b. sometimes uncomfortable when in a crowd.   _____
   c. sometimes concerned about dying.   _____
   d. hardly ever concerned with such matters.   _____

5. *With regard to children*
   a. I have doubts about how good a parent I would be (am).   _____
   b. I very much want (am very glad I have) a child of the same sex as I am.   _____
   c. I am not sure I want children (like having children).   _____
   d. I do not care what sex the child is, but I do want to have one (or perhaps two or three).   _____
   e. I would like to have at least four or five children.   _____
   f. as far as I am concerned, my marriage would be most successful without any children.   _____

6. *With regard to getting married (being married) at this particular time, I feel that*
   a. since most of my friends are already married, I would like to be (am glad I am) too. _____
   b. marriage would be (is) an important stabilizing influence in my life. _____
   c. the person I wish (wished) to marry will not wait if we do not get married now (would not have waited if we had not married when we did). _____
   d. there is (was) no special reason for marrying now (when I did) but I do (did) not wish to disappoint my friends and relatives. _____
   e. it is (was) as good a time as any to marry. _____

III. The Person I am Thinking of Marrying (Am Married to)

1. *My prospective mate (my spouse)*
   a. is extremely attractive physically. _____
   b. is not unusually attractive physically, but is likeable. _____
   c. is someone I do not think of in terms of physical beauty or good looks. _____
   d. embarrasses me because of his (her) looks. _____

2. *My prospective mate (my spouse)*
   a. comes from a family I greatly admire. _____
   b. comes from a family I feel very much a part of. _____
   c. has so little family closeness I feel sorry for him (her). _____
   d. has very irritating parents, but I can overlook them. _____

3. *With regard to the family of my intended mate (my spouse)*
   a. I am worried that she may become too much like her mother (or he like his father). _____
   b. I am concerned that she may become too much like her father (or he like his mother). _____
   c. I do not feel his (her) parents will (do) play any significant role in our marriage. _____
   d. I do not think he (she) is like either of his (her) parents. _____

4. *I feel that my intended mate's (my spouse's) parents*
   a. are better educated than my family. _____
   b. have considerably more money than my family. _____
   c. are not as socially acceptable as my family. _____
   d. I do not think about them in this way. _____

5. *In the relationship with my intended mate (my spouse) I feel that*
   a. he (she) is more in charge than I am.   _____
   b. we are equally in charge.   _____
   c. I am more in charge than he (she) is.   _____
   d. neither of us is in charge.   _____

6. *With regard to companionship, my intended mate (my spouse) and I*
   a. have many interests in common.   _____
   b. have independent interests, but are tolerant and supportive of each other's activities.   _____
   c. expect to develop interests in common.   _____
   d. seem to have relatively little in common when we are not busy with social activities.   _____

7. *With regard to the question of marriage, my intended mate (my spouse) and I*
   a. have discussed our doubts and fears of marriage.   _____
   b. have had some doubts, but have not mentioned them.   _____
   c. may be afraid of hurting each other by bringing up the question of whether we are making (have made) a mistake.   _____
   d. do not have any doubts whatsoever.   _____
   e. used to have doubts but overcame them.   _____

8. *With regard to our contemplated (present) marriage*
   a. I would like to postpone (leave) it, but am afraid of the consequences.   _____
   b. despite my doubts I prefer to go ahead (stay) with it.   _____
   c. I feel I can overcome any doubts since my love is great enough for two.   _____
   d. I would have doubts no matter whom I was marrying (had married) and should therefore not let these doubts stand in the way now.   _____

9. *With regard to religion*
   a. we are of the same faith and there are no conflicts.   _____
   b. neither of us has had serious religious training, and we do not intend to become involved with any church.   _____
   c. we are of different faiths, but have agreed to rear our children in one of them.   _____
   d. we have opposing religious views, but are tolerant of each other's ideas.   _____
   e. we would have no problems about religion if other people would stay out of our business.   _____

IV. Attitudes Preceding Marriage (For Engaged Couples)

1. My plans for marriage include
   a. a wish to travel as soon as possible.   _____
   b. a desire to move from our present area and establish a
      home elsewhere.   _____
   c. a desire to settle down where we are as quickly as possible.   _____
   d. I have no plans beyond wishing to get married.   _____

2. With regard to traveling and establishing a home
   a. my intended mate's plans include nothing that is incom-
      patible with my own wishes.   _____
   b. we have not discussed this topic fully.   _____
   c. I am leaving the decisions to him (her).   .   _____
   d. he (she) is leaving the decisions to me.   _____

3. With regard to sex
   a. my intended spouse has had experience, but I have not.   _____
   b. I am more experienced than he (she).   _____
   c. It is important to me that he (she) has had sexual expe-
      rience before marriage.   _____
   d. we have both had premarital sex experience.   _____
   e. we are limiting our sex activity until after marriage.   _____
   f. we do not agree on our sex life at present.   _____

4. With regard to having children
   a. I would like to have children as soon as possible.   _____
   b. I would leave the decision about when to have children to
      my intended spouse.   _____
   c. I would prefer to wait several years before having children.   _____
   d. I don't feel this is an important consideration.   _____

V. Marriage and the Future

1. With regard to my occupational or avocational interests
   a. I feel I have the courage to pursue both my marriage and
      my interests, even when they conflict.   _____
   b. I feel I could sacrifice almost anything in order to have a
      happy marriage.   _____
   c. I see no reason for conflict between marriage and my other
      interests.   _____
   d. my intended mate (my spouse) has no ambitions or profes-
      sional commitments which will jeopardize or interfere with
      our marriage.   _____

    e. my intended mate's (my spouse's) devotion to his (her) career interest is something I can easily admire and support.   _____

    f. my intended mate's (my spouse's) devotion to his (her) career is something I hope I can get more enthusiastic about as I understand him (her) better.   _____

2. *With regard to the future with my intended mate (my spouse)*
   a. I sometimes think he (she) may become ill.   _____
   b. I fear that he (she) may become ill.   _____
   c. I fear that he (she) will become superior intellectually or more important than I can become.   _____
   d. I never have had any doubts.   _____

3. *With regard to the future of our marriage*
   a. I am worried about becoming poor.   _____
   b. I am worried about the influence of our in-laws upon us.   _____
   c. I am troubled about the question of how many children we should have.   _____
   d. it sometimes occurs to me that my intended mate (my spouse) might have an affair.   _____
   e. I prefer not to worry about things until they happen.   _____

TEST C

Using a separate sheet of paper, write down in order of preference the three activities listed here which you like most and the three which you like least.

Motion pictures
Competitive sports (tennis, bowling, and so on)
Spectator sports
Outdoor activities (fishing, walking, bicycling, and so on)
Special gatherings with friends
Reading
Art appreciation (listening to music, visiting art galleries, and so on)
Politics
Hobbies (woodworking, sewing, stamp collecting, and so on)
Membership in organizations (school or college clubs, union activities, and so on)
Business or professional activities (beyond ordinary office hours)
Creative endeavor (writing, drawing, singing, acting, playing a musical instrument)
Television

Driving in the automobile
Theater
Night clubs
Dancing
Discussion groups
Civic activities
Being with a few friends of my own sex

When you and your partner compare sheets, first note those activities which neither of you checked and decide whether you are both genuinely indifferent to all of these. Perhaps there are some in this group which you might enjoy trying together.

How to Use the Tests

For Tests A and B lay the two partners' answer sheets for a particular page one on top of the other so that the columns of X's are side by side. Be sure that the tops of the two sheets are even. (See diagram.)

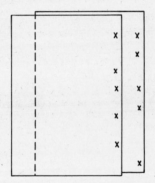

The alternative answers for each question have been arranged in order of increasing differentness (vertically). Therefore, the extent of the vertical distance between the X's for any particular question indicates the degree of difference in cultural and ethnic values between the two people taking the tests.

A scanning of the results of Test C will make the differences in taste between the two people obvious.

In *general,* the greater the gap between the two people in culture and taste, the greater is the likelihood that they will find themselves incompatible and the greater will be their difficulty in forming a highly functional relationship. . . .

This is the rule of thumb, but it is not an absolute law. No generalization about human nature can be absolute, for there is an infinite variety of people, and they relate to each other in an infinite number of different ways. Therefore, the man and woman who have completed the tests should do more than just take note of the differences between them. They should explore them in depth so that they can determine if the "samenesses" can be fully utilized to increase the solidarity of the marriage, and so that they can attempt to turn some of the possibly debilitating differences into advantages, or at least to neutralize them.

One way of achieving these aims is to undertake a *quid pro quo* session, using the information brought out in these tests as the basic material for discussion. Such a session will provide the spouses with a means of beginning, at least, to resolve and adjust differences. But no matter how hard they attempt to be objective, they will have a strong tendency to rationalize. A trusted third party can be helpful in keeping the dialogues on an even keel, and the conclusions objective.

JOANNE KOCH AND
LEW KOCH

The Urgent Drive to Make Good Marriages Better

Part of the personal growth movement has concentrated on marriage and its problems. The marriage-enrichment movement and marriage therapy are described in the following article by Joanne Koch, a writer, and Lew Koch, an investigative reporter. The authors remark on the great popularity of marriage programs and note what seems to be a limitless interest in making good marriages better. What used to be taken for granted as a comfortable and reliable relationship now seems to be under some requirement to become a constantly varied, rich, and "growing" one.

Marriage is better than ever. So say the one million people in this country who are part of the growing marriage-enrichment movement. They know that 40 percent of all marriages will end in divorce, but they are convinced that marriage still offers the best opportunity for satisfying and even exciting relationships.

Marriage enrichment refers to a number of short-term programs—most of them lasting a weekend—for teaching husband and wife how to be more responsive to each other's needs, more accepting, more intimate. Marriage enrichment is not marriage counseling. The couples who attend marriage-enrichment programs are self-referred and self-screened; only those who perceive their relationships as "good" are asked to attend. But within that broad

---

category of good marriages are many "sub-clinical" relationships, as psychologist Herbert A. Otto calls them—marriages fraught with low-level, debilitating problems which are not severe enough to bring couples into therapy—yet.

David Mace and his wife Vera claim to know more about marriage enrichment than anyone in the country. They probably do. The Maces founded the Association of Couples for Marital Enrichment three years ago, on their 40th wedding anniversary, after devoting most of their married lives to helping couples who were in marital trouble. . . . As a founder of Parents Without Partners, Mace often heard divorced people say that if they had known more about how to be married, they would never have had to divorce.

Democratic Grace

The Maces began their enrichment activities in 1973 with 10 couples on a Quaker retreat in the Pocono Mountains of Pennsylvania. They broke the traditional rule of silence between dinner and breakfast and began the spontaneous dialogue and experiments in new behavior that are the hallmark of their Association's workshops. ACME is not Quaker-affiliated. Any religious ceremony during the weekend, even grace before meals, must be agreed upon by the group.

Couples talk about things that concern them. Some husbands and wives can't talk to each other in private, but can talk with the support of the group. The weekend gives them a chance to do that. The Maces may act out some disagreement or conflict from their own marriage. They invite others to share in the same way, but the atmosphere is not threatening. . . . When couples act out their disputes, they learn how to handle them. . . . He believes a key to this discovery process is to have couples find out that all married pairs experience conflict and dissatisfaction.

The weekends have been so successful that the Association has spread. Chapters have been started in all 50 states and in 18 other countries. Working in cooperation with parent-training programs, communication courses, and churches, the Association of Couples for Marital Enrichment offers a democratic, sane and dignified way to make good marriages out of mediocre ones.

Many couple-enrichment programs have religious affiliations. ACME weekends are often conducted under the auspices of a local church. The Marriage Communications Lab, conducted for the past 10 years by Antoinette and Leon Smith, is sponsored by the United Methodist Church. Marriage Encounter began as a Catholic enrichment experience and continues with the support of various religious groups.

But Mace separates these programs from those that have a hierarchical view of marriage: God supreme and His authority extending in a direct line to the husband and then on down to the wife, and finally the children. Brushing aside Marabel Morgan's *Total Woman*—the best-selling work of nonfiction in 1974—as "froth," Mace admits that some men may retain their unquestioned authority and even feel flattered by it, but contends that both the total man and the total woman need warmth, tenderness and love. . . .

But Marabel Morgan is a step ahead of the Maces when it comes to packaging and pragmatism. She knows that millions of Americans already have a hierarchical marriage. Rather than put both spouses through the retraining an egalitarian marriage requires, Morgan offers women her Total Woman course. It is fundamentally sex therapy in the guise of marriage enrichment. It provides sexual permission without insisting on sexual equality. . . . When a woman who has never dared equate eroticism with Christian marriage hears that message, she is released from the bondage of original sin. The word that orgasms are holy is liberating. . . .

"*We parlayed a twenty-seven-year trial marriage into six years of wedded bliss.*"

Drawing by Geo. Price; © 1974 The New Yorker Magazine, Inc.

Pure as Cottage Cheese

Admire and adapt to your husband, she advises, use costumes and alluring nightgowns to surprise him, and remember that "sex is as pure and wholesome as cottage cheese." But never forget that God is the power source, for "Without a power source for heat, for light, for life, your shell is nothing more than a glorified outhouse." . . .

Approximately 20,000 women have paid $15 for the four-week Total Woman course taught in cities and towns across the country. Five dollars goes back to the parent company: Marabel and Charlie Morgan. With course rebates, continuing hardback book sales, and two million copies in the first paperback printing, Total Woman pays considerably better than hairdressing, Marabel's former trade. For women who want a hierarchical marriage or feel they have to remain in one, Total Woman and a similar course and book, *Fascinating Womanhood,* written by Mormon mother Helen Andelin, offer support, encouragement, and a bag full of tricks to keep husbands happy and sexually interested. . . .

Beyond that potent endorsement, straight from God, and the encouragement to crave your husband's body and provide variety in bed, there is little sex education.

The National Sex Forum's totally secular Sexual Attitudes Restructuring program, on the other hand, approaches sex education head on, with explicit films followed by discussion groups that are often segregated by sex. During a Sexual Attitudes Restructuring weekend, many aspects of sexuality are frankly discussed and seen on film: homosexuality, lesbianism, bisexuality, celibacy, masturbation, oral sex, and intercourse. The weekend format was developed to help clergymen, physicians, and social workers discover that they were moralistic as well as ignorant about human sexuality—and then educate them. The crash course in sexuality now admits nonprofessionals, who may attend the weekend or take the same course in four once-a-week sessions (at a cost of about $140 a couple). A more formal program for couples includes homework exercises and reading material, but the popular weekend course simply provides a rush of information and insight in the hope that afterward some integration will take place. Though couples may be asked to share their feelings about sex or some of their sexual fantasies, there is no sexual experimentation during the weekend.

Uncomfortable or Bewildered

About 100,000 people have attended such weekends, according to James Maddock. Maddock, a psychologist who works in the University of Minnesota's Program in Human Sexuality, . . . recommends the Sexual Attitude Restructuring program for spouses who disagree over which one should take the sexual initiative, those who are uncomfortable or bewildered about certain sexual practices, those who can't agree on the frequency of intercourse, and those who are considering or being pushed into a sexually open marriage.

Sex-educator Jessie Potter, who leads some of the S.A.R. weekends, finds that attitudes about sexuality are likely to be expressed during all-male or all-female discussion groups or in a "fishbowl," where men stay in the middle while women sit on the outside and listen. . . . When women and men understand how their sex-role conditioning affects and often limits their sexual relations, they tend to shed their guilt and become open.

"We are looking for a level of intimacy that no other generation has expected out of marriage," says Jessie Potter. But informed sex cannot carry the entire burden for the intimate relations today's couples are seeking. Intimacy requires that each partner understands the other's needs and feelings; it demands empathy.

At Pennsylvania State University, psychologist Bernard G. Guerney Jr. is convinced that empathy is the key element in marriage, a quality that is far more valuable when it comes from one's spouse than when it emanates from a paid professional, no matter how skilled. Empathy, claims Guerney, can be learned by almost anyone. His IDEALS course (Institute for the Development of Emotional Life Skills), which combines behavior modification with techniques from Carl Rogers' client-centered therapy, attempts to teach empathy to married couples at a nominal fee. IDEALS sets forth rules for communication, rules for talking, listening—knowing when to talk and when to listen. Groups of three or four couples work for six months with a trained leader, learning and practicing these rules until they become automatic.

The more concentrated Minnesota Couples Communication Program, developed by Sherod Miller, Elam Nunnally and Daniel Wackman, is a series of four three-hour workshops conducted by couples who are experienced in group work but do not necessarily have degrees in therapy. The four or five couples who come together for an MCCP session are given extensive source materials, published under the title of Alive and Aware. They first hear about the need to become self-aware, to discover just what they think, feel, want and do. . . .

Full Disclosure

After becoming aware of oneself, the next step is to express the self in personal terms, without blaming or depreciating one's mate. . . . Couples learn to make full disclosures, to ask for feedback, and to listen. . . . The 12,000 husbands and wives who have gone through the Minnesota course have learned to recognize the different styles of communicating, and practice matching their intentions with the appropriate style.

Unlike the Total Woman courses, which are run on a semifranchise basis with each group returning some of the money to the central organization, the Minnesota Couples Communication Program and IDEALS charge only for materials. The entire fee goes to the instructors. Research on the Minnesota program, and on other short-term communications-training programs for married couples, suggests that couples do learn to understand their partners, to speak directly, and to feel an increased satisfaction with their marriages.

But such skills do not a marriage make. If a couple is to prevent conflicting wants from turning into major marital rifts, both husband and wife must have the spirit, the will, the intention to love. Marriage Encounter is the only crash course in marital empathy that also tries to rejuvenate that decision to love. Or so it seemed from the numerous couples we interviewed who had attended the encounter. Nearly one million Americans have been through this encounter experience, and we were determined to find out for ourselves if it worked, and why.

We sat in a small conference room of a surburban motel, waiting for the Marriage Encounter to begin. Unlike the other 38 couples who had gathered here, attracted by the promise that they could make their "good marriage better," or inspired by the enthusiasm of couples who had been through the program, we knew exactly what would take place.

We knew most of the 44 hours would be spent writing down our private feelings, exchanging these love letters, and talking alone in our rooms, learning to accept the feelings we had poured onto paper. We knew the weekend would proceed from a period of self-examination and discovery to a concentration on our marriage and then a reaching out to God and the community. We knew there would be some sentimental songs and romantic surprises. We knew the only public sharing of marital problems would come from the three couples who led the group. We knew that despite the presence of the clergy (a priest always goes on Catholic weekends, a rabbi and his wife on Jewish weekends, a minister and his wife on Protestant weekends), religious ritual would be confined to grace before and after meals, a few biblical references, a ceremony in which couples renew their marriage vows. But we weren't sure why these procedures had changed hundreds of thousands of token marriages into love stories.

At first, we stood aloof from the experience, particularly when we were asked to kiss as we went off to write the first reflections in our empty notebooks—women to their rooms, men in the conference room. . . .

But from the nonthreatening, banal exchanges of "your mate's most endearing qualities," we gradually moved to serious self-examination. The chinks in our armor were exposed, not by confrontation before a leader or a group, but simply by the permission to admit weakness in the safety of our private notebooks, the encouragement to exchange our reflections, and discuss them in the privacy of our room. There was no haranguing or public derision meant to knock down our defenses, only the examples of the three couples who expose their own vulnerabilities before the group. They say, in effect, "We stood where you stand now, afraid to risk being open, our masks in place. But we revealed our fears and loneliness and now we accept each other fully. We didn't fall apart; in fact, we are stronger now." . . .

Soured Charm

It was one thing to see charts that showed a drop in satisfaction after marriage, or studies that indicated childbearing often produces feelings of being unloved. It was something else to hear one of the three couples tell how his easy-going charm had soured into sloth and her decisiveness had turned into manipulation. The same qualities that had attracted them to their mates had become sources of distance and conflict. As they spoke, a shared sense of being cheated by what Don D. Jackson and William H. Lederer had called "the mirages of marriage" rippled through the room, giving each couple added confidence and trust when they went off to wrestle with their feelings.

As the day went on, the questions became more probing. All had to admit to areas of spiritual divorce—lessening of gentleness, sarcasm, indifference, loneliness, being taken for granted, or escaping into work or drink or frenetic activity.

All had to drop the masks of good provider, or good mother, or happily married couple. For the first time, each was reaching out in emotional nakedness. The men realized that a quest for intimacy could be masculine, even heroic. They understood that their worship of clock and cash register led only to heart attacks, divorce and desolation. . . .

We sat in the small conference room during that last hour, women and men with eyes brimming, filled with a joyful sense of well-being that one man described as "smiling inside and out." No one wanted to leave.

Is the Marriage Encounter weekend merely an emotional storm, as Robert Ryder, Dean of the University of Connecticut's School of Home Economics and Family Study believes? Or will the experience change the "lifestyle of the entire American community," as one of Marriage Encounter's chief architects, Roman Catholic priest Chuck Gallagher, predicts?

Certainly the 44 hours are filled with emotionalism. The series of 10-minute reflections and 10-minute intimate exchanges builds to an emotional climax and, if couples use the one 90-minute period for that purpose, a physical climax as well. Despite its orgasmic structure and its emphasis on affection and nonverbal communication, Marriage Encounter provides no information about sex. "Sexual relations" is among the 14 subject areas suggested for couples' private dialogues. But with money, health, work, marriage, children, relatives and death also on the list, it is easy to avoid any focus on sexual maladjustment. The three couples who lead the encounter and the priest or religious couple are available for private questions, but they make no pretense at being professional therapists.

Those who object to the lack of concrete information and to the general anti-intellectual drift of the weekend may also be disconcerted by the regimentation: a time for writing, a time for talking together, no discussion of one's marital problems with other couples except during meals or at coffee breaks, and the group is delayed until all have returned to the conference room. After the weekend is over, couples are urged not to reveal the details of their experience. . . . The secrecy surrounding the weekend and the proselytizing by couples who ooze sentimentality make many people wary of the project.

Shared Elation

. . . We found the weekend exhilarating, exciting and educational. We haven't stopped disagreeing; we still suffer disappointments. We occasionally eschew the candor we learned. But when we disagree, or feel misunderstood, we bring out our notebooks, write out how we feel, exchange the books, and begin talking. And we usually find the hostilities being replaced by understanding. When we feel rejected or inadequate, we are now much more likely to share the emotional load. And when one of us is happy, we share the sense of elation more completely than before.

Marriage Encounter has been criticized for too much religious ritual and for too little, but even those who attended weekends run by a different faith did not seem to find the religious aspects oppressive. . . .

We would recommend that a couple considering the experience seek the weekend closest to their religious beliefs. The spiritual atmosphere enhances the experience, giving one a sense of connection to the past. . . .

A vague spirituality and a victory over sexism were not exactly what Father Calvo had in mind when he developed Marriage Encounter in Spain in 1965. . . . [But] if couples do not make church, God, and the community the center of their lives, as Father Calvo had hoped, at least they tend to reorder their priorities, making marriage and family the heart of their existence.

Marriage Encounter advertises itself as being for "couples with a good marriage, who want to make it even better." . . . The concentrated periods of privacy and lack of professional leadership make Marriage Encounter inappropriate for couples on the brink of divorce. When the weekend is successful, it eases a couple into a changed relationship that both desire. In this sense, Marriage Encounter is consistent with the goals of marital therapy.

Unlike encounter weekends of the Esalen variety, after which people go back to their daily lives without any continuing support, Marriage Encounter provides couples with tools that encourage them to continue the enrichment. During the weekend they have practiced full disclosure during the 10 minutes of personal reflection, followed by the exchange of written feelings and a 10 minute dialogue. Few couples continue this "10 and 10" on a daily basis, but many use it frequently. When the weekend is over, each couple is invited to join a nationwide volunteer network. They can participate in community nights, dialogue groups, reunions. They may wish to help with the newsletter, or become couples who greet, phone, write to, clean up after, or entertain couples on subsequent weekends. Eventually they may offer their services as one of the three experienced couples at future encounters. These procedures, added to the initial impact of the experience, have made Marriage Encounter the largest and fastest-growing of the enrichment programs.

Passing Fad

Robert Ryder, who studied 2,000 newly married Americans for the National Institute of Mental Health, follows his dismissal of Marriage Encounter with some suspicions that the enrichment movement may be a passing fad. But he does agree that marriages must be attended to or they will disintegrate. He compares the process by which people drift into marriage with the process by which they drift toward divorce. In both cases they are lulled into believing that nothing of consequence is happening—until it is too late. "People who are married don't take seriously the fact that they are drifting away," Ryder says. "Being married is not an item of security. Either you go on worrying about it, or you'll have something to worry about."

If marriage is defined as an intimate, sharing relationship, most Americans have never had a marriage. For those who wish to move in that direction, marriage enrichment offers the best training for intimacy available today.

LILLEMOR MELSTED

Swedish Family Policy

In this article a Swedish journalist describes programs and practices in child care developing in her country, often considered the most advanced nation with respect to policies designed to support egalitarian family models.

Recently in Sweden, about 6,000 fathers of newborn babies have stayed home each year from their jobs for one month or longer to take care of their infants. This has been made possible through the *parental insurance system.* . . . The system entitles one parent at a time to stay home and care for the baby, while receiving compensation during the first seven months in the form of a *parental benefit,* equivalent to about 90% of ordinary pay. A parent who has not been gainfully employed before the baby's birth receives a certain daily amount, currently Skr 32.* The parental benefit is taxable just like ordinary income and is counted as part of earnings for purposes of qualifying for income-related supplementary pensions. The system also entitles a parent to the same benefit while caring for a sick child under 10 years old. The insurance system is 85 percent financed through employer fees, the rest from central government grants. Parents may divide the leave of absence between them; one of them may use it all, or both may choose to work half-time.

This new system gave fathers a realistic chance to be at home one or more months and take care of their babies. As a rule, those who have taken advantage of this opportunity have chosen to use their leave of absence after the mother has first been at home and breast-fed the baby for a number of months.

Taking "paternity leave" is slowly but surely becoming natural for more and more fathers—although it will still take a long time before everyone uses

*Ed. note: The Swedish Krona is worth approximately 25 cents.

From *Current Sweden,* June 1979, published by Swedish Institute, Stockholm, Sweden.

this opportunity. The proportion doing so is now 10–12 percent. Parents in intellectual professions and families where the mother also has a good income make use of the paternity leave option considerably more frequently than, for example, industrial worker families.

This right to a leave of absence for fathers of newborn babies is only one part of Swedish government family policy. But it can serve here to exemplify developments over the past decade. For it is no longer only a matter of providing subsidies to families with children and ironing out differences in living standards, but also of creating rules which increase equality between men and women. It is a question of providing both sexes with a chance to play two active parts—in the family and on the labor market.

In the opinion of most people in Sweden, a prerequisite to equality between the sexes is that women should be given more space on the labor market and that men receive increased opportunities to share responsibility and influence in the home. This trend has been predicated on a rapid—though still very insufficient—expansion of public child care programs.

Traditional Family Policy

Child allowances and housing allowances are family policy tools which have long been uncontroversial, but whose structure has recently begun to be questioned.

Child allowances were introduced in 1948 and have periodically been increased. Since January 1, 1979, they have amounted to Skr 2,500 annually for each child up to age 16. The purpose of child allowances, which are tax-free, is not to create greater equality between high- and low-income groups, but between families which have children and those which are childless.

There have been recent proposals that a higher allowance be paid for child number three and up belonging to the same sibling group. The background is Sweden's declining birth rate. Fewer and fewer families are having more than two children. Another factor is that it is very hard for families with many children to maintain a reasonable living standard. It is often increasingly necessary for one parent to remain at home. If both parents go out on the labor market, this additional income leads to a "threshold effect" on take-home pay plus benefits, since housing allowances drop, etc.

The different forms of housing allowances paid by both the national and municipal governments are means-tested, and they take account of income, number of children, rent, etc. They were created in order that all families could obtain good housing. About 450,000 families with about 90,000 children today receive housing allowances for rental expenses or for costs incurred to live in their own houses.

Public Child Care

The expansion of *public child care* has become an increasingly important supplement to family policy per se. At the beginning of 1979 there were 134,000 places in *day care centers* (day nurseries), which take care of children aged up to seven during the daytime while their parents are busy with their jobs or studies. In addition there are 77,000 openings in *family day care,* where public authorities pay a "day mother" a salary to take care of several children in her own home. For younger school children, there are 49,000 places in so-called *free-time centers* for after-school recreational activities, as well as 26,000 openings in *family free-time centers*.

The total of 221,000 openings for preschool children should be seen in relationship to the full number of preschool children in Sweden—about 770,000. Roughly 450,000 of these have mothers who work full-time or part-time. Out of all women with children of preschool age, in 1977 about 37 percent worked part-time and 28 percent full-time.

The desire to provide children with good-quality care and to ease the burden on gainfully-employed parents of small children has emerged as an increasingly central political issue. Solutions have been sought along the lines of expanded public child care and increased entitlements to leaves of absence for parents with small children.

Parental Insurance Is Expanded

It was the Social Democrats, while in power, who proposed the parental insurance system which came into effect in 1974.

The system was later expanded by the three-party bourgeois Government. The period of leave became nine months, and special rules were introduced for the final three months. These last months are now covered by "special parental benefits," which may be utilized in a very flexible fashion. A family may choose to take the full leave of absence all at once. But the final three months may also be used bit by bit until the child's eighth birthday. Another model is to use the leave of absence in order to shorten working hours, for example, by half or in order to work six-hour days. In all these cases, the total leave covered by special parental benefits should be equivalent to three months away from full-time work.

This three-month leave should, in principle, be divided equally between the parents. By means of a simple application form, however, one parent—in practice most often the father—can transfer his/her share to the other. Single parents may use the entire leave of absence themselves.

Six-Hour Working Day

Additional opportunities to take time off from work were introduced beginning on January 1, 1979. From that date, all parents were granted a legal right to six-hour working days or a full leave of absence until the baby reaches the age of 18 months. The six-hour day can be retained until the child's eighth birthday. But no compensation is payable for these types of partial leave, which in other words may be taken on top of the nine months' leave paid for by the parental insurance system.

Voluntary Parental Training

The spring 1979 session of Parliament moreover approved a bill saying all parents are to be offered voluntary parental training during paid working hours. Fathers of newborn babies will be invited to the hospital maternity ward for a day to become acquainted with the baby and learn to take care of it. At 10–12 meetings before childbirth and the same number afterwards, parents will meet under expert guidance to discuss the problems and pleasures of parenthood. . . .

CHAPTER FIFTEEN

The Family in the Future

The sum which two married people owe to one another defies calculation. It is an infinite debt, which can only be discharged through all eternity.

Goethe, Elective Affinities

The birthday of my life
Is come, my love is come to me.

Christina Rossetti, "A Birthday"

The family is one of nature's masterpieces.

George Santayana, The Life of Reason

JANE HOWARD

Families

In this excerpt from her book Families, *journalist Jane Howard describes what it takes to make a solid clan or family. The requirements are varied and can be met by a group of people who have no kin ties as well as by a group of relatives.*

"If you're voluntarily childless and alone," said the other Helen, who was from Pennsylvania by way of Puerto Rico, "it gets harder and harder with the passage of time. It's stressful. That's why you need support systems." I had been hearing quite a bit of talk about "support systems." The term is not among my favorites, but I can understand its currency. Whatever "support systems" may be, the need for them is clearly urgent, and not just in this country. Are there not thriving "megafamilies" of as many as three hundred people in Scandinavia? Have the Japanese not for years had an honored, enduring—if perhaps by our standards rather rigid—custom of adopting non-relatives to fill gaps in their families? Should we not applaud and maybe imitate such ingenuity?

And consider our own Unitarians. From Santa Barbara to Boston they have been earnestly dividing their congregations into arbitrary "extended families" whose members all are bound to act like each other's relatives. Kurt Vonnegut, Jr., plays with a similar train of thought in his fictional *Slapstick*. In that book every newborn baby gets assigned a randomly chosen middle name, like Uranium or Daffodil or Raspberry. These middle names are connected with hyphens to numbers between one and twenty, and any two people who have the same middle name are automatically related. This is all to the good, the author thinks, because "human beings need all the relatives they can get—as possible donors or receivers not of love but of common decency." He envisions these extended families as "one of the four greatest inventions by Americans," the others being *Robert's Rules of Order,* the Bill of Rights, and the principles of Alcoholics Anonymous.

This charming notion might even work, if it weren't so arbitrary. Already each of us is born into one family not of our choosing. If we're going to go around devising new ones, we might as well have the luxury of picking their members ourselves. Clever picking might result in new families whose benefits would surpass or at least equal those of the old. The new ones by definition cannot spawn us—as soon as they do that, they stop being new—but there is plenty they can do. I have seen them work wonders. As a member in reasonable standing of six or seven tribes in addition to the one I was born to, I have been trying to figure which earmarks are common to both kinds of families:

1. Good families have a chief, or a heroine, or a founder—someone around whom others cluster, whose achievements as the Yiddish word has it, let them *kvell,* and whose example spurs them on to like feats. Some blood dynasties produce such figures regularly; others languish for as many as five generations between demigods, wondering with each new pregnancy whether this, at last, might be the messianic baby who will redeem us. Look, is there not something gubernatorial about her footstep, or musical about the way he bangs with his spoon on his cup? All clans, of all kinds, need such a figure now and then. Sometimes clans based on water rather than blood harbor several such personages at one time. The Bloomsbury Group in London six decades ago was not much hampered by its lack of temporal history.

2. Good families have a switchboard operator—someone like Lilia Economou or my own mother who cannot help but keep track of what all the others are up to, who plays Houston Mission Control to everyone else's Apollo. This role, like the foregoing one, is assumed rather than assigned. Someone always volunteers for it. That person often also has the instincts of an archivist, and feels driven to keep scrapbooks and photograph albums up to date, so that the clan can see proof of its own continuity.

3. Good families are much to all their members, but everything to none. Good families are fortresses with many windows and doors to the outer world. The blood clans I feel most drawn to were founded by parents who are nearly as devoted to whatever it is they do outside as they are to each other and their children. Their curiosity and passion are contagious. Everybody, where they live, is busy. Paint is spattered on eyeglasses. Mud lurks under fingernails. Person-to-person calls come in the middle of the night from Tokyo and Brussels. Catchers' mitts, ballet slippers, overdue library books and other signs of extrafamilial concerns are everywhere.

4. Good families are hospitable. Knowing that hosts need guests as much as guests need hosts, they are generous with honorary memberships for friends, whom they urge to come early and often and to stay late. Such clans exude a vivid sense of surrounding rings of relatives, neighbors, teachers, students and godparents, any of whom at any time might break or slide into the inner circle. Inside that circle a wholesome, tacit emotional feudalism develops: you

give me protection, I'll give you fealty. Such treaties begin with, but soon go far beyond, the jolly exchange of pie at Thanksgiving for cake on birthdays. It means you can ask me to supervise your children for the fortnight you will be in the hospital, and that however inconvenient this might be for me, I shall manage to. It means I can phone you on what for me is a dreary, wretched Sunday afternoon and for you is the eve of a deadline, knowing you will tell me to come right over, if only to watch you type. It means we need not dissemble. ("To yield to seeming," as Buber wrote, "is man's essential cowardice, to resist it is his essential courage . . . one must at times pay dearly for life lived from the being, but it is never too dear.")

5. Good families deal squarely with direness. Pity the tribe that doesn't have, and cherish, at least one flamboyant eccentric. Pity too the one that supposes it can avoid for long the woes to which all flesh is heir. Lunacy, bankruptcy, suicide and other unthinkable fates sooner or later afflict the noblest of clans with an undertow of gloom. Family life is a set of givens, someone once told me, and it takes courage to see certain givens as blessings rather than as curses. Contradictions and inconsistencies are givens, too. So is the war against what the Oregon patriarch Kenneth Babbs calls malarkey. "There's always malarkey lurking, bubbles in the cesspool, fetid bubbles that pop and smell. But I don't put up with malarkey, between my step-kids and my natural ones or anywhere else in the family."

6. Good families prize their rituals. Nothing welds a family more than these. Rituals are vital especially for clans without histories, because they evoke a past, imply a future, and hint at continuity. No line in the Seder service at Passover reassures more than the last: "Next year in Jerusalem!" A clan becomes more of a clan each time it gathers to observe a fixed ritual (Christmas, birthdays, Thanksgiving, and so on), grieve at a funeral (anyone may come to most funerals; those who do declare their tribalness), and devises a new rite of its own. Equinox breakfasts and all-white dinners can be at least as welding as Memorial Day parades. Several of us in the old *Life* magazine years used to meet for lunch every Pearl Harbor Day, preferably to eat some politically neutral fare like smorgasbord, to "forgive" our only ancestrally Japanese colleague Irene Kubota Neves. For that and other reasons we became, and remain, a sort of family.

"Rituals," a California friend of mine said, "aren't just externals and holidays. They are the performances of our lives. They are a kind of shorthand. They can't be decreed. My mother used to try to decree them. She'd make such a goddamn fuss over what we talked about at dinner, aiming at Topics of Common Interest, topics that celebrated our cohesion as a family. These performances were always hollow, because the phenomenology of the moment got sacrificed for the *idea* of the moment. Real rituals are discovered in retrospect. They emerge around constitutive moments, moments that only happen once, around whose memory meanings cluster. You don't choose those moments. They choose themselves." A lucky clan includes a born mythologizer, like my blood sister, who has the gift of apprehending such a moment when she sees it, and who cannot help but invent new rituals everywhere she goes.

7. Good families are affectionate. This of course is a matter of style. I know clans whose members greet each other with gingerly handshakes or, in what pass for kisses, with hurried brushes of side jawbones, as if the object were to touch not the lips but the ears. I don't see how such people manage. "The tribe that does not hug," as someone who has been part of many *ad hoc* families recently wrote to me, "is no tribe at all. More and more I realize that everybody, regardless of age, needs to be hugged and comforted in a brotherly or sisterly way now and then. Preferably now."

8. Good families have a sense of place, which these days is not achieved easily. As Susanne Langer wrote in 1957, "Most people have no home that is a symbol of their childhood, not even a definite memory of one place to serve that purpose . . . all the old symbols are gone." Once I asked a roomful of supper guests who, if anyone, felt any strong pull to any certain spot on the face of the earth. Everyone was silent, except for a visitor from Bavaria. The rest of us seemed to know all too well what Walker Percy means in *The Moviegoer* when he tells of the "genie-soul of the place which every place has or else is not a place [and which] wherever you go, you must meet and master or else be met and mastered." All that meeting and mastering saps plenty of strength. It also underscores our need for tribal bases of the sort which soaring real estate taxes and splintering families have made all but obsolete.

So what are we to do, those of us whose habit and pleasure and doom is our tendency, as a Georgia lady put it, to "fly off at every other whipstitch?" Think in terms of movable feasts, for a start. Live here, wherever here may be, as if we were going to belong here for the rest of our lives. Learn to hallow whatever ground we happen to stand on or land on. Like medieval knights who took their tapestries along on Crusades, like modern Afghanis with their yurts, we must pack such totems and icons as we can to make short-term quarters feel like home. Pillows, small rugs, watercolors can dispel much of the chilling anonymity of a sublet apartment or motel room. When we can, we should live in rooms with stoves or fireplaces or anyway candlelight. The ancient saying still is true: Extinguished hearth, extinguished family. Round tables help, too, and as a friend of mine once put it, so do "too many comfortable chairs, with surfaces to put feet on, arranged so as to encourage a maximum of eye contact." Such rooms inspire good talk, of which good clans can never have enough.

9. Good families, not just the blood kind, find some way to connect with posterity. "To forge a link in the humble chain of being, encircling heirs to ancestors," as Michael Novak has written, "is to walk within a circle of magic as primitive as humans knew in caves." He is talking of course about babies, feeling them leap in wombs, giving them suck. Parenthood, however, is a state which some miss by chance and others by design, and a vocation to which not all are called. Some of us, like the novelist Richard P. Brickner, "look on as others name their children who in turn name their own lives, devising their own flags from their parents' cloth." What are we who lack children to do? Build houses? Plant trees? Write books or symphonies or laws? Perhaps, but even if we do these things, there still should be children on the sidelines, if not at the center, of our lives. It is a sadly impoverished tribe that does not allow access to, and make much of, some children. Not too much, of course: it has truly been said that never in history have so many educated people devoted so much attention to so few children. Attention, in excess, can turn to fawning, which isn't much better than neglect. Still, if we don't regularly see and talk to and laugh with people who can expect to outlive us by twenty years or so, we had better get busy and find some.

10. Good families also honor their elders. The wider the age range, the stronger the tribe. Jean-Paul Sartre and Margaret Mead, to name two spectacularly confident former children, have both remarked on the central importance of grandparents in their own early lives. Grandparents now are in much more abundant supply than they were a generation or two ago when old age was more rare. If actual grandparents are not at hand, no family should have too hard a time finding substitute ones to whom to give unfeigned homage. The Soviet Union's enchantment with day care centers, I have heard, stems at least in part from the state's eagerness to keep children away from their presumably subversive grandparents. Let that be a lesson to clans based on interest as well as to those based on genes.

JUDITH BARDWICK

Divorce and the Survival of the Family

A psychologist who has done important work on the psychology of women thinks that the nuclear family will survive and gives her reasons in the following article.

If divorce has become so prevalent, for whom would we expect marriage and parenting to be more gratifying than frustrating? Those who are more satisfied than frustrated are people whose histories and family backgrounds have led them to want to marry or have children, who have not been frustrated by finding that family commitments forced them to give up other major interests, and who have not found that in the marriage everyone else's happiness is more important than theirs. Perhaps most crucial of all, satisfied people have realistic expectations of what these relationships require. With a healthy ambivalence, they feel that they gain more from the relationships than they lose. When commitments result in a major loss of autonomy, they will be resented. Most people will be happier if they do not have to give up their own interests when they choose to make a commitment to another person. Such people gain more than they lose in the creation of a marriage and a family because they feel loved and know they belong somewhere. While social values and the forms of marriage are changing, the need for family commitment and loyalty remain.

I think the American family will survive, mostly in the form of the nuclear family, because it is difficult if not impossible to achieve a sense of intimacy, and thus of significant connection and caring, within larger groups. But the

---

stability of the family will require more social changes, so that we may develop specific consensual norms of freedom and obligation in marriage. Several different family patterns will probably evolve as legitimate alternatives.

A number of variations on the stereotypical American family are prevalent enough to be considered normal. Common variations include the extended family in which the couple share household arrangements or child-rearing tasks or both, with other family members. There are many single-parent, especially mother-child, families. There are families that are no longer intact because of death or divorce. There are some rural and urban communal arrangements, which have a long history in this country. And today there are a few experimental arrangements; some are variations of group marriage, others are shared households made up of friends and their children but not necessarily involving sex. One of the more interesting and frequent new family forms involves a divorced woman and her children sharing their home with several unrelated single women. Also common is the sharing of one house by several divorced women and their children. This form has obvious economic and psychological advantages and is likely to become more common, since divorced men tend to remarry younger women.

A further psychological shift will also have to occur away from the one-sided priority of gratifying individualistic needs to an increased awareness of benefits derived from the existence of the relationship. In addition, since many of us have learned that it is psychologically dangerous to be overwhelmingly dependent on any one relationship, there will be pressure upon other relationships, especially with friends and work acquaintances, to provide alternate resources for the security of belonging or the trust of loyalty. We have learned from the social changes of this decade and from recent studies of how adults change that a workable model of marriage and family in the future will have to include expectations of change and of individual flexibility.

Since the family is the institution in which we feel we have more license to act on our own needs, the panoply of anxieties and angers which arise outside are all brought into it. Thus the stresses on the family arise both from the relationship itself and from external strains. In this way the family is a reactive institution, reflecting changes which are taking place in society. The family is the most salient place to experiment with new values or compensate for losses experienced outside.

In this decade we have all become aware of limitations on our lives imposed by rules of marriage and roles assigned because of gender. Especially those younger than 30 are attempting to break out of the cage of traditional restrictions. Yet the drift of change seems reformist and not radical, aimed at modification of an essentially monogamous nuclear family. This is probably partly because of the inertia of large-scale institutions but also because in Western society the nuclear family has met psychodynamically central needs not met in other social institutions. Fundamentally, our needs for belonging are not met elsewhere. Thus, reform of family structure is intrinsically better than total dissolution, because the sense of being a partner in marriage or a child of some specific family provides the grounding of identity that none of our other institutions can. For us, the family is still a unique and irreplaceable source of satisfaction, connecting, and belonging. We do not have other connections that are permanent, indissoluble, and intimate, in which each person belongs as an individual. The passions of the family come from possession and protection and permanence; the family, nuclear or extended, is the group we are a part of, to whom we owe, and from whom we may ask—whether they like us today or not.

Until I, the oldest grandchild, left for college, my whole family lived close to or in New York City. Part of every Sunday was taken up with visiting each other, and of course holidays were family affairs including aunts and uncles, cousins, grandparents, in-laws, and close friends. The dominant figure was one grandmother, an autocratic, illiterate, shrewd woman of absolute conviction and stunning power. Family members lent money to each other, watched over each other's kids, were privy to each other's secrets, were a bastion against the rest of the world—and were also best enemies. One grandfather, after he declared that the man was a crook, did not talk to a cousin for 20 years. With all the costs of emotional turmoil, I miss such intense family involvement. Today, like many middle-class families, my generation is sprawled all over the United States. But I notice that on the few occasions when we get together we *begin* from the premise of family intimacy and belonging. Moreover, I see that even distant members of the family respond to my children, whom they have never seen, from the fact of their family membership. Somehow the connections of blood, which can never be undone, seem more permanent than those of friendship.

While the family is the source of neurosis and the pathologies that come from possession, it is also the source of individuality and the strengths that come from emotional buttressing and the permanent conviction of belonging. The family is the first source of love and the sense of one's importance. It is not only a real organization, but also an idea of place.

The family is where we can most honestly tangle with our emotional present and, especially with children, construct a future. The feminist model of marriage tends toward the stereotype of male family involvement, in which the goals are equal power, equal freedom, and equal self-gratification; there is relative silence about equal commitment, equal dependence, and equal vulnerability. It is in the family, rather than at work, in school, or in friendship, that at psychologically conscious and not aware levels, we are passionate, tenacious, caring, and possessive, as we entangle the anchorages of our total time and total being. Clearly, this is the historically feminine model of family. What we are learning is that this commitment is one that men need too.

Very few families bear much resemblance to the posed portraits of togetherness, replete with fireplace and dog, that arrive at Christmas. And rather few marriages would be described as "happy," in the sense that the percentage of time that the people would describe themselves as joyful is small over the lifetime of a long relationship. But, then, "Are you happy?" is the wrong question. Marriage and thus family are where we live out the most intimate and thus powerful of our human experiences. The family is the unit in which we belong, from which we can expect protection from uncontrollable fate, in which we create infinity through our children, and in which we find a haven. The stuff of which family is made is bloodier and more passionate that the stuff of friendship, and the costs are greater too.

SUZANNE KELLER

Does the Family Have a Future?

In the following article, Suzanne Keller, a sociologist, raises questions about the necessity and value of the family as an institution. The decline in parents' authority over children may make the idea of family life less attractive to men and the family may prove too limiting for women. In any case, she asserts, population control will make families less relevant for us all. This article presents a radical and provocative challenge to ideas we often take for granted.

The malaise of our time reflects not simply a temporary disenchantment with an ancient institution but a profound convulsion of the social order. The family is indeed suffering a seachange.

The family means many things to many people but in its essence it refers to those socially patterned ideals and practices concerned with biological and cultural survival of the species. When we speak of the family we are using a kind of shorthand, a label for a social invention not very different, in essence, from other social interventions, let us say the Corporation or the University, and no more permanent than these. This label designates a particular set of social practices concerned with procreation and child rearing; with the heterosexual partnerships that make this possible and the parent-child relations that make it enduring. As is true of all collective habits, once established, such practices are exceedingly resistant to change, in part because they evoke strong sentiments and in part because no acceptable alternatives are offered. Since most individuals are unable to step outside of their cultures, they are unable to note the arbitrary and variable nature of their conventions. Accordingly, they ascribe to their folkways and creeds an antiquity, an inevitability, and a universality these do not possess.

Suzanne Keller, "Does the Family Have a Future?" *Journal of Comparative Family Studies,* Spring 1979. Excerpted and reprinted with permission.

The idea that the family is universal is highly misleading despite its popularity. All surviving societies have indeed found ways to stabilize the processes of reproduction and child care else they would not have survived to tell their tale. But since they differ greatly in how they arrange these matters . . . the generalization does not help us explain the phenomenon but more nearly explains it away.

In truth there are as many forms of the family as there are forms of society, some so different from ours that we consider them unnatural and incomprehensible. There are, for example, societies in which couples do not share a household and do not have sole responsibility for their offspring; others in which our domestic unit of husband and wife is divided into two separate units, a conjugal one of biological parents and a brother-sister unit for economic sustenance. There are societies in which children virtually rear each other and societies in which the wise father does not know his own child. All of these are clearly very different from our twentieth-century, industrial-urban conception of the family as a legally united couple, sharing bed and board, jointly responsible for bearing and rearing their children, and formally isolated from their next of kin in all but a sentimental sense. This product of a long and complicated evolutionary development from prehistoric times is no simple replica of the ancient productive and reproductive institutions from which it derives its name and some of its characteristic features. The contemporary family really has little in common with its historic Hebrew, Greek, and Roman ancestors.

The family of these great civilizations of the West was a household community of hundreds, and sometimes thousands, of members ("familia" is the Latin term for household). Only some of the members were related by blood and by far the larger part were servants and slaves, artisans, friends, and distant relations. . . .

The fallacy of universality has done students of human behavior a great disservice. By leading us to seek and hence to find a single pattern, it has blinded us to historical precedents for multiple legitimate family arrangements. As a result we have been rather impoverished in our speculations and proposals about alternative future arrangements in the family sphere.

A second common fallacy asserts that the family is *the* basic institution of society, hereby revealing a misunderstanding of how a society works. For as a social institution, the family is by definition a specialized element which provides society with certain needed services and depends on it for others. This means that you cannot tamper with a society without expecting the family to be affected in some way and vice versa. In the contemporary jargon, we are in the presence of a feedback system. Whatever social changes we anticipate, therefore, the family cannot be kept immune from them.

A final fallacy concerns the presumed naturalness of the family, in proof of which a motley and ill assorted grab bag of anecdotal evidence from the animal kingdom is adduced. But careful perusal of ethological accounts suggests that animals vary as greatly as we do, their mating and parental groupings including such novelties as the love death, males who bear children, total and guilt-free "promiscuity," and other "abnormal" features. The range of variation is so wide, in fact, that virtually any human arrangement can be justified by recourse to the habits of some animal species. . . .

Today the family and its social and psychological underpinnings are being fundamentally challenged from at least three sources: (1) from accumulated failures and contradictions in marriage; (2) from pervasive occupational and educational trends including the changing relations between the sexes, the spread of birth control, and the changing nature of work; and (3) from novel developments in biology. Let me briefly examine each.

It is generally agreed that even in its ideal form, the industrial-urban family makes great, some would say excessive, demands on its members. For one thing it rests on the dyadic principle or pair relationship which . . . is inherently tragic and unstable. Whether in chess, tennis, or marriage, two are required to start and continue the game but only one can destroy it. In this instance, moreover, the two are expected to retain their separate identities as male and female and yet be one in flesh and spirit. . . . Nor do children, the symbols of their union, necessarily unify them. . . . And yet their upbringing and sustenance, the moral and emotional climate, as well as the accumulation of economic and educational resources needed for survival, all rest on this small, fragile, essential but very limited unit. . . .

To these potentials for stress and strain must be added the loss of many erstwhile functions to school, state, and society, and with it something of the glamour and challenge of family commitments. Few today expect the family to be employment agency, welfare state, old age insurance, or school for life. . . .

Like most social institutions in the throes of change, moreover, the modern family is also beset by numerous internal contradictions engendered by the conflict between traditional patterns of authority and a new egalitarianism between husbands and wives and parents and children. . . .

One [current] trend, demographic in nature but bound to have profound social implications, concerns the lengthened life expectancy and the shortened reproductive span for women. Earlier ages at marriage, fewer children per couple and closer spacing of children, means: the girl who marries at twenty will have all her children . . . out of the home by her early forties. This leaves some thirty to forty years to do with as personal pleasure or social need dictate. . . . Hence what may in the past have been an individual misfortune has turned into a social emergency of major proportions. . . . Destined to outlive her husband, stripped of major domestic responsibilities in her prime years, what is she to do with this windfall of extra hours and years? Surely we must expect and prepare for a major cultural shift in the education and upbringing of female children. If women cannot afford to make motherhood and domestic concerns the sole foci of their identities, they must be encouraged, early in life, to prepare themselves for some occupation or profession not as an adjunct or as a last resort in case of economic need but as an equally legitimate pursuit. . . .

All in all, it would appear that the social importance of the family relative to other significant social arenas will . . . decline. Even today when the family still exerts a strong emotional and sentimental hold its social weight is not what it once was. All of us ideally are still born in intact families but not all of us need to establish families to survive. Marriage and children continue to be extolled as supreme social and personal goals but they are no longer—especially for men—indispensable for a meaningful existence. As individual self-sufficiency, fed by economic affluence or economic self-restraint, increases, so does one's exemption from unwanted economic as well as kinship responsibilities. Today the important frontiers seem to lie elsewhere, in science, politics, and outer space. This must affect the attractions of family life for both men and women. For men, because they will see less and less reason to assume full economic and social responsibilities for four to five human beings in addition to themselves as it becomes more difficult and less necessary to do so. This, together with the continued decline of patriarchal authority and male dominance—even in the illusory forms in which they have managed to hang on—will remove some of the psychic rewards which prompted many men to marry, while the disappearance of lineage as mainstays of the social and class order, will deprive paternity of its social justification. For women, the household may soon prove too small for the scope of their ambitions and power drives. Until recently these were directed first of all to their children, secondarily to their mates. But with the decline of parental control over children a major erstwhile source of challenge and creativity is removed from the family sphere. This must weaken the mother-wife complex, historically sustained by the necessity and exaltation of motherhood and the taboo on illegitimacy.

Above all, the move towards worldwide population and birth control must affect the salience of parenthood for men and women, as a shift of cultural emphasis and individual priorities deflates maternity as woman's chief social purpose and paternity as the prod to male exertions in the world of work. Very soon, I suspect, the cultural presses of the world will slant their messages against the bearing and rearing of children. Maternity, far from being a duty, not even a right, will then become a rare privilege to be granted to a select and qualified few. . . .

This along with changing attitudes towards sex, abortion, adoption, illegitimacy, the spread of the pill, better knowledge of human behavior, and a growing scepticism that the family is the only proper crucible for child-rearing, creates a powerful recipe for change. World-wide demands for greater and better opportunities for self-development and a growing awareness that these opportunities are inextricably enhanced or curtailed by the family as a prime determinant of life-chances, will play a major role in this change. . . .

The trends that I have sketched would affect marriage, male-female, and parent-child relations even if no other developments were on the horizon. But there are. As yet barely discernible and still far from being applicable to human beings, recent breakthroughs in biology—with their promise of a greatly extended life span, novel modes of reproduction, and dramatic possibilities for genetic intervention—cannot be ignored in a discussion devoted to the future of the family. . . .

We will have to come to terms with changing sexual attitudes and mores ushered in by what has been called the sexual revolution. This liberalization, this rejection of old taboos, half truths, and hypocrisies, also means a crisis of identity as men and women, programmed for more traditional roles, search for the boundaries of their sexual selves in an attempt to establish a territoriality of the soul. . . .

Returning now to our main question—does the family have a future—it should be apparent that I expect some basic and irreversible changes in the decades ahead and the emergence of some novel forms of human togetherness. . . .

Thus if we dare to speculate further about the future of the family we will be on safe ground with the following anticipations: (1) a trend towards greater, legitimate variety in sexual and marital experience; (2) a decrease in the negative emotions—exclusiveness, possessiveness, fear and jealousy—associated with these; (3) greater room for personal choice in the kind, extent, and duration of intimate relationships, which may greatly improve their quality as people will both give and demand more of them; (4) entirely new forms of communal living arrangements in which several couples will share the tasks of child rearing and economic support as well as the pleasures of relaxation; (5) multi-stage marriages geared to the changing life cycle and the presence or absence of dependent children. Of these proposals, some, such as Margaret Mead's, would have the young and the immature of any age test themselves and their capacities to relate to others in an individual form of marriage which would last only so long as it fulfilled both partners. In contrast to this, older, more experienced and more mature couples who were ready to take on the burdens of parenthood would make a deeper and longer lasting commitment. (See pp. 385–391.) Other proposals would reverse this sequence and have couples assume parental commitments when young and, having discharged their debt to society, be then free to explore more personal, individualistic partnerships. . . .

For the immediate future, it appears that most Americans opt for and anticipate their participation in durable, intimate, heterosexual partnerships as anchors and pivots of their adult lives. They expect these to be freer and more flexible than was true in the past, however, and less bound to duty and involuntary personal restrictions. They cannot imagine and do not wish a life without them.

Speculating for the long range future, we cannot ignore the potential implications of the emerging cultural taboo on unrestricted reproduction and the shift in public concern away from the family as the central preoccupation of one's life. Hard as it may seem, perhaps some day we will cease to relate to families just as we no longer relate ourselves to clans, and instead be bound up with some new, as yet unnamed, principle of human association. If and when this happens, we may also see a world of Unisex, Multi-sex, or Nonsex. None of this can happen, however, if we refuse to shed some of our most cherished preconceptions such as that monogamy is superior to other forms of marriage or that women naturally make the best mothers. Much as we may be convinced of these now, time may reveal them as yet another illusion, another example of made-to-order truths.

Ultimately all social change involves moral doubt and moral reassessment. If we refuse to consider change while there still is time, time will pass us by. Only by examining and taking stock of what is can we hope to affect what will be. This is our chance to invent and thus to humanize the future.

MARY JO BANE

Here to Stay

The family operates according to such principles as love, affection, and caring, which often differ from the principles governing the larger society, such as sexual equality and equality of opportunity for all children. This difference leads to a certain tension between family life, with its emphasis on family privacy, and public values. In the following selection, sociologist Mary Jo Bane offers some possible directions that public policy might take to ease the tension, but she does not think it can be entirely eliminated. She is optimistic about the family's ability to manage the residual tension and survive.

The facts—as opposed to the myths—about marriage, child rearing, and family ties in the United States today provide convincing evidence that family commitments are likely to persist in our society. Family ties, it seems clear, are not archaic remnants of a disappearing traditionalism, but persisting manifestations of human needs for stability, continuity, and nonconditional affection. If, indeed, this view of the persisting centrality of family commitments is correct, then the makers of public policy cannot afford to ignore them.

Persistent family commitments generate persistent tensions between important public values. With Americans continuing to live in families and to value the responsibilities and satisfactions of family life, the polity is virtually required to respect family privacy and the family's role in raising children. But other social values—sexual equality, protection of children against abuse and neglect, provision of equal opportunities to children—seem in many situations to require governmental invasion of family privacy. These invasions are not easily justified nor easily implemented in a society with strong family loyalties.

The tensions between family privacy and other values are to some extent resolvable by a public stance that emphasizes the rights of individuals and leaves family roles to be worked out privately. For example, the most workable

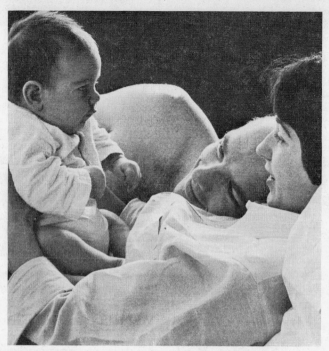

approach to sexual equality is probably to enforce the political and economic rights of women, and to rely on families to work through the power shifts and changing division of labor that political and economic equality imply. The protection of children, a more complicated task because of children's inherent dependency, may be partially dealt with by emphasizing the individual rights of children and designing mechanisms for articulating them. Yet another kind of tension, between family privacy and equal opportunities for children, may also be resolvable within an individualist framework. "Lifetime insurance"— which would make individuals responsible not only for their old age but also for their own childhood care—is a mechanism for equalizing opportunity with minimal intrusion on family privacy. An insurance scheme to provide benefits to single-parent families would also try to reconcile aid to children and non-interference in adult lives by emphasizing the notion of marital disruption as an insurable risk.

Other policy issues can perhaps also be dealt with by focusing on individual rights and inventing mechanisms that provide maximum freedom for individuals to shape their own family patterns. Such approaches are almost certainly more sensible than attempts to force conformity to traditional family patterns. History suggests that laws that, for example, require people to live in conventional families or forbid divorce are neither particularly effective nor particularly necessary. When left to their own devices, and even in the face of some severe discouragements, Americans continue to marry, have children, create homes, and maintain family ties.

There are, of course, some persistent tensions between family society and the polity that cannot be resolved, however much good sense and good will are available. Family life is incompatible with some aspects of equality among citizens. As long as children are raised even partially by families, their opportunities can never be equal; however much resources are equalized, affection, interest, and care remain idiosyncratically centered in families.

Equal treatment is, in a strict sense, also incompatible with family ties. Equal treatment implies an ethic wherein all men and women do unto others as others do unto them; strangers and brothers are treated similarly; and people are judged by what they do rather than what they are. Family loyalty follows quite different principles, treating people on the basis of special relationships, compatibility, and affection. Family members make no pretense of treating each other equally or of treating strangers the same as themselves. Family relationships are nonmeritocratic and based on characteristics over which people have no control. For these reasons some would have us believe that they are incompatible wih modern life and represent an archaic holdover that need not be taken seriously.

Reality cannot, however, be discarded so simply. Family ties and family feelings are integral to the lives of most Americans. The ethic that governs relationships between people who love and care for each other inevitably intrudes into public life, coloring people's perceptions of what they and others ought to do. Policies that ignore this ethic—that imply that public facilities can replace parental care or that the public welfare system is responsible for supporting children—will almost surely be either widely resented or essentially disregarded. Even when family service programs respond to real needs, they are often perceived as undermining the fabric of society. Until such programs are designed to incorporate the very real and very strong values that underlie family life in America, and until they are perceived as doing so, they are doomed to failure.

Delay in designing constructive programs, consistent with family values, for promoting sexual equality and providing adequate resources to ensure some measure of equal opportunity to children serves no one. The historical trend has long been toward greater equality, and it is unlikely to come to a halt now. On the other hand, the strong commitment to family institutions and values, which is such a persistent theme in American society, is no more likely to go away. . . .

CARL N. DEGLER

At Odds

In the following excerpt from his book At Odds, *Pulitzer Prize-winning historian Carl Degler asks the question: Can women realize their individual goals and still maintain the value of the family? Not, he says, until the structure of the family changes. He suggests various ways in which the conflict between individual and family goals might be resolved.*

Children, obviously, are the heart of the problem of reconciling family and career. If both parents have careers—or full-time jobs, for that matter—who takes care of the children? If the answer is that both do—share and share alike—then both careers or jobs may suffer, and the result will be a compromise comparable with that worked out by the couples who alternated in their career moves. If both parents share in child-rearing, then both parents probably will sacrifice full success in the interest of family, too. And that, also, may become a recognized solution for many couples with children.

But long before that point is reached, the question of the husband's willingness to accept such a limitation on his own career or job will have to be faced. At this stage in the analysis, the problem is no longer peculiar to professional or career couples; it applies equally to any couple in which both parents want to work full-time. Michael Young and Peter Willmott, in their book *The Symmetrical Family,* refer to each parent in such a family as having two jobs rather than one. Under the old order in the 19th century, they note, the wife took care of the children and the household while the husband's job was outside the home. Then in the 20th century, as married women entered the paid work force, wives in effect took on a second job, while husbands continued to fill only one. But in a symmetrical family, as Young and Willmott see it, when husband and wife share house and child care as well as having jobs outside, each has two jobs.

When Young and Willmott wrote their book [1975], they were optimistic about the future of the symmetrical family, but so far, in the United States at least, that optimism has a thin basis in fact. The general record of husbands' assuming household tasks, not to mention baby care, is pretty poor. There have been recent efforts, to be sure, to show that men have a kind of "paternal instinct," which encourages many men to want to share the care of children with their wives. James A. Levine, in his recent book *Who Will Raise the Children?,* provides some encouraging examples of male involvement in child-rearing. Yet even Levine has to admit that attempts to institutionalize and thereby encourage such behavior more broadly among fathers have been less than successful. For instance, he notes that though the Board of Education in New York City grants about two thousand maternity leaves each year, in the two years since September 1973, when men first became eligible for child-care leaves, only eight such leaves [had] been taken by fathers. In Seattle only one father has taken a child-rearing leave, and in Berkeley, California, where all municipal employees are eligible for such leaves, at the time Levine wrote not a single father had taken up the opportunity to stay home with his child.

Sociologist Mirra Komarovsky found that, though many American college men in the early 1970s said they believed in egalitarian marriages, they actually expected their wives to stay home to rear the children. They were willing to help, she reported, but certain tasks like diapering, washing, or cleaning they thought should not be expected of them. Jessie Bernard, another sociologist of the family, thought in 1972 that she saw signs of change in men's willingness to assume the care of children. In support of her contention she cited evidence from a popular TV show in 1970. But in subsequent years the evidence has been rather more negative than positive; there just have not been any signs that men are undertaking child care in substantial numbers or that they want to. As Lillian Rubin reported in her study of young white working-class families, men may help around the house, but they invariably see such help as just that, not as responsibilities. "With all the talk about the changing structure of family roles," Rubin wrote, "a close look reveals that when it comes to the division of labor in the family, it's still quite traditional. Over and over, that's the story: He does man's work, she does woman's work." In sum, if there is a strong desire on the part of men to share in child-rearing, it has not been very evident nor widely developed on any class level.

Sociologist William J. Goode has explained that the differences in attitudes and behavior regarding gender equality may be little more than apparent between working- and middle-class men. "Lower-class men concede fewer rights ideologically than their women in fact *obtain* and the more educated men are likely to concede *more* rights ideologically than they in fact grant. One partial resolution of the latter tension," Goode noticed, "is to be found in the frequent assertion from families of professional men that they should not make demands which would interfere with his *work:* He takes precedence as a professional, not as family head or as male; nevertheless, the precedence is his. By contrast, lower-class men demand deference as *men,* as heads of families."

Nor have men in other industrial societies been more interested in personally bringing up children. One sociologist reported that, though it is Swedish government policy to enlist men in work at day-care centers, she did not find in visiting two dozen of such institutions in 1973 more than a single man at any of them, and even so most of the men were either conscientious objectors or older men. Sweden, in short, also has had difficulty in tapping the "paternal instinct."

Another alternative to women as sole child-rearers, and the option most commonly advocated, is some form of institutional arrangement that would permit women to pursue work away from their children. Such institutional child care, usually under government auspices, has been the principal answer of feminists and other advocates of the expansion of career and work opportunities for women. The advocacy has been very recent, however. . . . Prior to 1940 very few friends of women were prepared to defend the employment of a mother of small children, unless necessity compelled her to work. In some respects, Americans have come a long way toward recognizing the hard facts of life for many women—namely, that most married women now work and for reasons considerably more substantial than the need for "pin money." There was a time, and not so remote, either, when no income tax deductions were allowed to working mothers for child care on the ground that such a concession would encourage women to work outside the home! Yet at that time—in the 1950s—millions of mothers of small children were already working. But if that particular refusal to face the facts of women's work has now passed, the overall situation has not altered much. American governments are still reluctant to establish child-care centers, even though it is well recognized that over a third of children under school age are in families in which the mother is employed.

Part of the reason for that reluctance, it is necessary to recognize, is that most working mothers seem to be wary of institutional child care. It is felt, apparently, to be intrinsically inadequate. . . . A detailed study made in 1965 of working mothers with at least one child under 14 reported that . . . almost 88 per cent of the children under the age of six were cared for either in the home of the working mother or in the home of someone else. Less than 6 per cent were placed in a day-care center. Finally, a study in 1971 found only slight change in the pattern of parental behavior in this regard since 1965. At that date about 8 per cent of white working women placed their children in day-care centers; 15 per cent of black working women did. Well over half— 56 per cent—of white working women used care at home by family members or others.

A friend of the day-care-center solution might well argue that this limited recourse by mothers to such care stemmed from a dearth of facilities rather than from a lack of parental interest. But surveys of parental preferences and other signs suggest that cannot be the main reason. Regardless of quality, institutional care never is high on lists of parental preferences. Even more significant as a measure of how parents feel are the results of experiments with low-cost, high-quality institutional care. In all the instances studied, the parental response has been lower than expected. At Gary, Indiana, for example, the highest enrollment of children was 15 per cent of eligible pre-schoolers. In experiments where subsidies were offered, the results were much the same. And even group-care centers located at the work site of the mother, comparable with those widely established in some European countries, have not attracted the interest of working mothers.

Such a history has caused one authority on institutional child care to conclude in 1977 that "evidence accumulates to indicate much less interest on the part of parents in formal day-care centers than the public debate implies." Apparently the majority of mothers prefer to leave their children with relatives or known friends. Other professionals in the field are now becoming much less sanguine about child-care centers as quality institutions, for, to provide care of the level of quality that a mother as an individual routinely provides in her home, day-care centers would have to be much more lavishingly funded than the society or the majority of parents is either able or willing to do. To pay for quality care, sociologist Mary Jo Bane has recently estimated, might well consume half the income of a working mother. From a perspective less friendly to women's aspirations, Selma Fraiberg has written that to provide the kind of care she thinks children deserve "we will need over 2,000,000 devoted and dedicated 'substitute mothers' with professional qual-ifications to serve the needs of 6,500,000 children under the age of six whose mothers are employed." At the moment such persons do not exist in such numbers.

Furthermore, the experience of other industrial countries with institu-tional child care warns us against the easy assumption that the underdevel-opment of institutional care is a peculiarly American deficiency. No country, including the Soviet Union and Sweden, the two societies which have made the heaviest commitment in this respect, has sufficient child-care facilities for all the children of working mothers. And though expense is undoubtedly an important reason in accounting for the disparity, the experience of a number of European countries suggests that it may also stem from the reluctance of women to place their children in such centers. A survey made in England in 1965, for example, showed that two-thirds of working women who were quer-ied left their children with husbands or other relatives. About 2 per cent of children under two years of age, and about 12 per cent of children aged three and four, were in day nurseries there. These are figures somewhat higher than for the United States, but they are not substantially different. Alice Rossi in 1977 noted that "there is a drift in East European countries away from day-care centers for children less than three years old. Not only is such care extremely expensive—the younger the child is, the more costly its care—but there have been rumblings that all is not well in terms of the very young child's welfare in such group-care institutions." Some Czechoslovak researchers suggested that very young children's nervous systems are irritated by the noise and activity of others all day long. The Czechs, she points out, have begun to move "from group care to foster care in private homes and long-leave policies for employed mothers." Even among some Scandinavian countries interest in group care is low. . . .

Gail Lapidus's recent scholarly book on women and work in the Soviet Union warns us that making institutional arrangements for women's family responsibilities can easily work against feminist goals. As she writes, "the conditions of female employment in the USSR are specifically designed to accommodate family responsibilities to a degree that is virtually unprecedented in industrial societies." But pregnancy leaves, arrangements for nursing infants during working hours, and exemption of pregnant women from heavy work or overtime or travel, she also notes, often result in women continuing to shape their work around the family. Under such arrangements, Lapidus continues, "work satisfaction depends less on the content of the work itself than on its convenience in relation to family responsibilities." The higher rate of absenteeism among women than among men Lapidus attributes to women's responsibility for young children when they suddenly become ill. Men's work, on the other hand, is structured around the assumption that men have no responsibility for child or family care; they can even be expected to take work home with them. Not surprisingly, the bulk of the students in evening and correspondence courses in the Soviet Union are men. Nor is it unexpected, Lapidus pointedly observes, "that married women are seriously underrepresented in enterprise activities requiring additional commitments of time and energy, as well as in volunteer movements and in public affairs more generally."

When this recent history of attempted solutions to the question of child care for families with working mothers is projected against the longer history of the family, one possible solution for the future of women and the family suggests itself. It is that we may well be at a point in the history of the family where the high level of child care, to which two centuries of the modern family has accustomed us, can no longer be sustained. For most of human history the care of children has been something performed by women in conjunction with many other tasks. Under the pre-industrial regime, in the main, there were few occasions for women to be physically separated from the child while these other tasks were being performed. Yet, given the variety and sheer physical demands of these other tasks, the mother was never able to concentrate the bulk of her time and attention upon her children. Only during the 19th and 20th centuries has child care been virtually a full-time occupation of mothers. Over the last quarter-century that pattern has been changing rapidly, as married women have sought other uses for their time and set other goals for their lives. Even during the 19th century there was tension between the family's interests and those of women as individuals. Although that tension most commonly manifested itself in relations between husband and wife, today it is most obviously, but certainly not exclusively, apparent between women and children. One measure of it is the enduring debate over child-care centers and working mothers. In fact, the whole field of child psychology rests upon the assumption that the close supervision by a mother is indispensable for a child's successful passage into adulthood. Certainly that has been the burden of the widely influential work of John Bowlby during the 1960s, to mention only the best known. It has been recently and forcefully pressed upon us in Selma Fraiberg's book *Every Child's Birthright: In Defense of Mothering*. Her confidence in her position is almost unlimited. "In this century," she tells us, "we have come into knowledge about children and the constitution of personality that can be fairly placed among the greatest scientific discoveries in history." The field of child study, in short, will provide little help in resolving the dilemma that confronts working mothers. On the contrary, it is likely to make more difficult the achieving of any further recognition of women's interest in activity outside the home.

The recognition and the realization of women's individuality in work will be difficult for an even more profound reason. The central values of the modern family stand in opposition to those that underlie women's emancipation. Where the women's movement has stood for equality, the family historically has denied or repudiated equality. For even in the companionate family of the 19th and 20th centuries, hierarchy has prevailed among father, mother, and children. Few families have treated them equally or assumed them to be equal, even today. Where the women's movement has called for a recognition of individualism, the family has insisted upon subordination of individual interests to those of the group. Even fathers have been expected to share their earnings with the other family members and to shape their lives to such an extent as to provide a living for the whole family. And, finally, where the women's movement has asked for a person to be judged on merit, the family has denied merit as a basis of membership, approval, or love. Indeed, the great appeal of the family has been that it accepts members simply because they are born into the group and not because of what they may achieve or contribute.

To point to these obvious contradictions is but another way of saying that the great values for which the family stands are at odds not only with those of the women's movement, but also with those of today's world. Democracy, individualism, and meritocracy, the values most closely identified with the last two centuries of Western history, are conspicuous by their absence from the family, even with its present modifications. Just because these modern values have been absent from the family, some commentators have called for the end of the family, or at least have predicted its dissolution on the ground that it is anachronistic.

But that conclusion is based upon only half the evidence, so to speak. For if the family, unlike the women's movement, does not reflect modern values, it does embody values that inhere in great social movements like nationalism, ethnicity, racial allegiance, and the great religions of the world. For those movements extol hierarchy and scorn equality and meritocracy. The family, in short, like the great traditional movements, is an anti-individualistic institution. In fact, its denial of individualism is the source of the family's strong attraction for many men and women today. For at least two centuries the best known alternative to the individualism, competitiveness, and egoism that infuse the modern, industrial and urban world has been the family. That has been its strongest appeal as individualism spread from country to country in the wake of commercial and industrial capitalism. As an ideal, at least, the family was truly a "haven in a heartless world," to use the title of Christopher Lasch's recent book. That is also why all the great utopian visions of the 19th and 20th centuries from Marxism, which is the most familiar, to the hippies of yesterday, have taken the family as their model of human order. In the face of an individualistic market economy, the family has seemed the epitome of true humanity and interrelatedness. The very slogan of Communism— "from each according to his abilities, to each according to his needs"—is not only the antithesis of a market economy's conception of human relations, but the central principle of family life. In short, aside from the evidence that Americans still consider the family a central institution in their lives, the very values for which it has stood over the years suggest that it will endure.

Simply because the family is deeply imbedded in American life and is unlikely to fade away, tension between it and the individual interests of women was inevitable. For some two centuries now, Americans have seen that tension rising. Most recently, with the movement into work of married women and particularly with the rise of the women's movement, the tension has reached a new height. Philosophically and practically the family and women's individuality are difficult to reconcile. Many women today find the realization of themselves as persons impossible to achieve within a family situation. Yet most women still consider a family relationship as more important to them than the realization of their own individuality. Obviously, how any individual woman perceives her future is up to her. The family, after all, is at bottom nothing more than a relation between a man and a woman and their offspring.

What they work out for themselves as a mutually satisfying relation today depends in large part upon them. For some people that will mean a continuation of the established relation, with perhaps an opportunity for the woman to work outside the home, though for supportive rather than individualistic ends. For others it may mean abandoning family entirely in pursuit of complete individual fulfillment. The ideal goal, it would seem, would be one in which the values of family and the realization of women's individuality could be reconciled.

Will it be possible for women and men to work out some arrangements—call it family or something else—in which these two goals can be realized? Or must the historic drive for women's individuality stop short of full realization in the name of children, husband, and family? Never before has the tension been so evident or the room for maneuver so narrow. After two hundred years of development, both the future of the family and the fulfillment of women as persons are at odds as never before. Presumably a resolution will come in something less than another two centuries.

Notes About the Authors

Robert C. Atchley teaches at Miami University, Oxford, Ohio, and is a research associate at the Scripps Foundation for the Study of Gerontology. He is coauthor of *Families in Later Life*.

Mary Jo Bane is in the Department of Education at Harvard University, having formerly taught at Tufts University. She was also associated with the Center for Research on Women at Wellesley College.

Judith Bardwick is a Professor of Psychology at the University of Michigan. She is the author of *The Psychology of Women* (1971) and *In Transition* (1979).

Bennett Berger is Professor of Sociology at the University of California, San Diego. He is an associate editor of *Social Problems* and a former editor of *Sociometry*. He is author of *Working Class Suburb, Looking for America,* and *Ideological Work* (in press, 1980); he has written for a wide variety of periodicals from *The American Sociological Review* to *The New York Times Magazine*.

Jessie Bernard, honoris causa, Pennsylvania State University, is author of many influential and important works including *Women and the Public Interest, The Future of Marriage,* and *The Future of Motherhood*.

Bruno Bettelheim is a child psychologist and founder of the Orthogenic School for autistic children in Chicago. He is also a widely published author: *Love Is Not Enough* (1950), *Symbolic Wounds* (1954), and *The Uses of Enchantment* (1976).

Andrew Billingsley is Vice President for Academic Affairs of Howard University. His publications include *Black Families in White America* with Amy Tate Billingsley and *Children of the Storm* with Jeanne Giovannoni.

Robert Coles is a research psychiatrist at Harvard University Health Services. He is also Pulitzer Prize-winning author of *Children of Crisis* (1967–72).

Carl Degler is Margaret Byrne Professor of American history at Stanford University. He is author of *Out of our Past* (1970), the Pulitzer Prize-winning *Neither Black Nor White: Slavery and Race Relations in Brazil and the United States* (1973), and *At Odds* (1980).

John Demos is Professor of History at Brandeis University. He is the author of *A Little Commonwealth: Family Life in Plymouth Colony* and other studies in social history. He is currently completing a book on witchcraft in early America.

Elizabeth Douvan, course coordinator for "American Families in Transition," is Professor of Psychology at the University of Michigan, where she also directs the program on Family and Sex Roles at the Institute for Social Research. She has co-authored a number of books including *The Adolescent Experience* (1966) and *Feminine Personality and Conflict* (1970).

459

Claudia Dreifus has authored three books, all on sex roles and changing ways of life; the most recent is *Seizing Our Bodies: The Politics of Women's Health* (1978). She is the Long Island interviewer for *Newsday;* contributing commentator to "City Edition," a New York PBS program; and a writer for *McCalls, Redbook,* and *Glamour.*

Jean Bethke Elshstain is Associate Professor of Political Science at the University of Massachusetts, Amherst.

Amitai Etzioni is a sociologist and author of works on social organization and social change. He is Professor of Sociology at Columbia University and director of the Institute of War and Peace Studies.

Herbert Gans is Professor of Sociology at Columbia University and senior research associate, Center for Policy Research. He is author of *The Urban Villagers* (1962) and *The Levittowners* (1967).

Nathan Glazer is Professor of Education and Social Structure at Harvard University. Formerly on the editorial staff of *Commentary,* he has been coeditor of *The Public Interest* since 1973. His books include *Beyond the Melting Pot* (coauthored with Daniel Moynihan), *Remembering the Answers,* and *Affirmative Discrimination.*

Ellen Goodman is a journalist who was on the staff of *Newsweek* and the *Detroit Free Press* before joining the *Boston Globe* in 1967 as a columnist and feature writer. Since 1976, she has also been syndicated by the Washington Post Writers Group.

Herbert Gutman is Professor of History in the Graduate Center of the City University of New York, having previously taught at the University of Rochester. He is the author of *Slavery and the Numbers Game* and *The Black Family in Slavery and Freedom, 1750–1925,* and coauthor of *Reckoning with Slavery.*

Bruce Hackett is Associate Professor of Sociology at the University of California, Davis. He is currently studying energy use among the communes in northern California.

Tamara K. Hareven is Professor of History and Director of the History of the Family Program at Clark University. She is also a research associate at the Harvard Center for Population Studies and editor of the *Journal of Family History.* She is the author of numerous articles on the history of the family and aging and of the forthcoming books *Amoskaeg: Work and Life in a Factory City,* and *Family Time and Industrial Time,* on the interaction between the family and industrial work. She is editor of two forthcoming books: *Family Transitions and the Life Course in Historical Perspective* and, with Maris A. Vinovskis, *Family and Population in Nineteenth-Century America.*

Carolyn Heilbrun is Professor of English Literature at Columbia University. She is the author of *Toward a Recognition of Androgyny* (1975) and *Reinventing Womanhood* (1979).

Jane Howard is a journalist and writer whose *A Different Woman* (1975) and *Families* (1978) have become bestsellers.

Morton Hunt is a professional writer interested in contemporary marriage. His books include *The World of the Formerly Married* and *The Affair.*

Don Jackson was before his death a director of the Mental Research Institute and Associate Clinical Professor at Stanford Medical School. He authored *Myths of Madness* and *The Mirages of Marriage* (with Lederer).

Rosabeth Moss Kanter is currently Professor of Sociology at Yale University. She has also taught at Brandeis and at Harvard and has been a fellow and visiting scholar at Harvard Law School. Her books include *Men and Women of the Corporation, Work and Family in the United States,* and *Commitment and Community,* as well as the edited volumes *Life in Organizations, Another Voice: Feminist Perspectives on Social Life and Social Science and Communes: Creating and Managing the Collective Life.* She has prepared impact statements for federal policy and legislation as a member of the Family Impact Seminar in Washington, D.C.

David Kantor is a family therapist and instructor at the Cambridge Family Institute. His book (with William Lehr), *Inside the Family,* reports an intensive study of nineteen families.

Suzanne Keller is Professor of Sociology at Princeton University. She is the author of *Beyond the Ruling Class* (1963) and *The Urban Neighborhood* (1968).

Joan Kelly is Co-Principal Investigator, Children of Divorce Project, Marin Community Mental Health Center, Marin County, California, and has a private practice.

Kenneth Keniston is Andrew Mellon Professor of Human Development at the Massachusetts Institute of Technology. He is author of *The Uncommitted* (1965), *Young Radicals* (1968), *Youth and Dissent* (1971), and *All Our Children* (1977).

Clyde Kluckhohn was at the time of his death Professor of Anthropology at Harvard University. His books include *Culture and Behavior* and *The Navajo.*

Joanne and Lew Koch are journalists who write a syndicated column and published a book called *The Marriage Savers* (1976) about marital counseling.

Christopher Lasch is Professor of History at Rochester University and is author of the bestselling *The Culture of Narcissism* (1979) and *Haven in a Heartless World: The Family Besieged* (1977).

Barbara Laslett is Associate Professor of Sociology at the University of Southern California. She has written extensively on the family, both past and present.

William J. Lederer is a journalist and author (with Eugene Burdick) of *The Ugly American* and (with Don Jackson) of *The Mirages of Marriage.*

William Lehr teaches at the Cambridge Family Institute and has studied "disturbed and normal family milieux" in a participant-observational study of nineteen Boston families.

Jean Lipman-Blumen has taught at the University of California, Santa Cruz, and Harvard University and has been a research associate at the Radcliffe Institute. She has written extensively on the situation of women in our society.

Margaret Mead, America's most distinguished anthropologist, wrote widely about women, children, and the family. Her fieldwork in New Guinea and Samoa gave her rich comparative clues about the possible arrangements for meeting human needs and family life. Among her many important books were: *Coming of Age in Samoa* (1928), *Sex and Temperament in Three Primitive Societies* (1935), *Male and Female* (1949), *Blackberry Winter: My Earlier Years* (1972). She was until her death curator of ethnology at the American Museum of Natural History.

Lillemor Melsted is a political journalist in Sweden and heads the Parliamentary News Bureau of Sweden's Daily Press.

Sheila J. Miller teaches at Miami University, Oxford, Ohio, and is associated with the Scripps Foundation for the Study of Gerontology.

S.M. Miller is Professor of Economics and Sociology at Boston University and author of *Comparative Social Mobility* (1960) and (with F. Riessman) *Social Class and Social Policy* (1968).

Bernice Neugarten is Professor of Human Development at the University of Chicago. She has written *Personality in Middle and Late Life* (1964), edited *Middle Age and Aging* (1968), and conducted a distinguished series of studies of aging.

Niles Newton is a professor in the Medical School, Northwestern University. His research focus has been the birth process and its accompaniments.

Michael Novak is a philosopher, author, and religious educator. He is author of *The Rise of the Unmeltable Ethnics* (1972) and scholar-in-residence at the American Enterprise Institute.

Hazel Reinhardt is Director of Research and Personnel for the Minneapolis Star and Tribune Company in Minneapolis, Minnesota.

Betty Rollin is an author and essayist. Among her works is *First You Cry,* the story of her own confrontation with breast cancer.

Mary Rowe is Special Assistant for Women and Work to the President of the Massachusetts Institute of Technology.

Lillian B. Rubin is a research sociologist at the Institute for the Study of Social Change, University of California, Berkeley, and a psychotherapist in private practice. Her books include *Worlds of Pain* (1975) and *Women of a Certain Age* (1979).

Richard Sennett is Professor of Sociology at New York University. His works in history and sociology center on the family. His books include *Families Against the City* and *The Uses of Disorder*.

Arlene Skolnick is a research psychologist at the Institute for Human Development at the University of California, Berkeley. She is author of a widely used textbook on the family, *The Intimate Environment* (1973) and coeditor (with Jerome Skolnick) of *The Family in Transition*.

Philip Slater is a sociologist and author whose books include the best-selling *Pursuit of Loneliness* (1970), *Earthwalk* (1974), *Footholds* (1976), and *Wealth Addiction*.

Carol Tavris, a freelance writer and social psychologist, was Senior Editor of *Human Nature* and of *Psychology Today,* where she was also Assistant Managing Editor. Her publications include *The Female Experience, The Longest War—Sex Differences in Perspective* (with Carole Offir), and *The Redbook Report on Female Sexuality* (with Susan Sadd).

Lillian E. Troll is a psychologist who studies life-span development. She is a professor at Rutgers University and has written *Development in Early and Middle Adulthood* (1975).

E. Jerry Walker, a Methodist pastor and family therapist, is executive director of the Center for Family Studies at the Dudley House in Duluth, Minnesota.

Judith S. Wallerstein teaches in the School of Social Welfare at the University of California, Berkeley, and is Principal Investigator on the Children of Divorce Project for the Marin Community Mental Health Center, Marin County, California.

Esther Wattenberg is Associate Professor in the School of Social Work at the University of Minnesota.

Kathy Weingarten is a clinical psychologist in private practice and a research associate at the Wellesley Center for Research of Women in Higher Education and the Professions.

Karol Weinstein is a psychologist in private practice in Chicago. She is coauthor (with Lee Rainwater) of *And the Poor Get Children.*

Kenneth Woodward is a senior writer for *Newsweek,* having joined the magazine staff in 1964. He regularly writes the sections on Religion and on Ideas and is author of the 1975 report, "Who's Raising the Kids?" which received the American Psychological Foundation award in 1976. He is also coauthor of a forthcoming book on grandparents and grandchildren.

Suggestions for Further Reading

Chapter 1. Introduction and Definitions

Bernard, Jessie. *The Future of Marriage* (NY: Bantam, 1972). In this book which has become a classic, a famous family sociologist looks at the condition of marriage in our society and speculates about its future. She distinguishes between "his" marriage and "her" marriage and shows that the two are by no means the same.

Blood, Robert O. and D.M. Wolfe. *Husbands and Wives: The Dynamics of Married Living* (London: Collier-Macmillan, 1960). A description of one of the first large-scale studies of married people's definitions and experiences of marriage. Decision-making and power distribution are analyzed and are related to marital satisfaction and experience of marital problems.

Capon, Robert F. *Bed and Board: Plain Talk About Marriage* (NY: Simon and Schuster, 1965). Father Capon looks at marriage in a humanist framework. Humorous, literate and lively, this Episcopal priest's book is a good antidote to many marriage manuals and the writings of social engineers.

Cottle, Thomas. *A Family Album: Portraits of Intimacy and Kinship* (NY: Harper and Row, 1974). A sensitive and engaging description of families from many walks of life. The book explores the joys and tragedies, the comforts and conflicts of family life.

Grunebaum, H. and J. Christ, eds. *Contemporary Marriage* (Boston: Little, Brown, 1976). Essays on the history and contemporary situation of marriage in our culture.

Howard, Jane. *Families* (NY: Simon and Schuster, 1978). A leading woman writer takes a personal odyssey through the many families of kin and non-kin she knows. Wise and witty, the book makes a strong case for our deep need of family connections.

Landis, J.T. and M.G. Landis. *Building a Successful Marriage* (Englewood Cliffs, N.J.: Prentiss-Hall, 1968). A life cycle consideration of family life. Practical, readable guide to problems and issues in marriage with examples and solutions.

Lasswell, Marcia E. and Thomas E. Lasswell. *Love, Marriage, Family: A Developmental Approach* (Glenview, Ill.: Scott, Foresman, 1973). An excellent anthology. Readable integrative essays by experts on all the important topics.

Mead, Margaret. *Male and Female* (NY: New American Library, 1949). A classic statement about the ways in which males and females share or differ in human traits, and the implications these similarities and differences have for relationships between men and women.

Newsweek (May 15, 1978). A major news magazine devoted a large part of an issue to the condition and prospects of the "American Family" in all its many forms. Very readable summary of many views, though occasionally also somewhat superficial.

Rossi, Alice, Jerome Kagan, and Tamara K. Hareven, eds. *The Family* (NY: Norton, 1978). An interdisciplinary collection of essays including Alice Rossi's controversial paper on the biological bases of mothering. Historians, sociologists, and psychologists are represented.

Skolnick, Arlene. *The Intimate Environment* (Boston: Little, Brown, 1973). This introductory textbook on the family is well-integrated and provides excellent definitions and a sound introduction to the study of the family.

Sussman, Marvin. *Sourcebook in Marriage and the Family* (Boston: Houghton Mifflin, 1974). This is a collection of papers by experts in the field. Includes some which are quite technical but many which provide basic information and a developed framework for looking at the family in its various stages and relationships.

Chapter 2. The Family and Social Change

Adams, Bert. *Kinship in an Urban Setting* (Chicago: Markham, 1968). A study of kin contact among city dwellers. The book discusses the central role of the mother in maintaining kinship ties. Fathers are only important in this maintenance process if there are economic ties (e.g., a family business) binding children to the father.

Background Facts on Women Workers in the United States (Women's Bureau, Workplace Standards Administration, U.S. Department of Labor 1970). Statistical analysis of women in the labor force and the relation between work and family status.

Boserup, Esther. *Women's Role in Economic Development* (London: Allen and Unwin, 1970). A comparative analysis of women's labor force participation in various countries by a distinguished Swedish economist.

Carter, Hugh and Paul C. Glick. *Marriage and Divorce: A Social and Economic Study* (Cambridge, Mass.: Harvard Press, 1976). This book presents demographic data on marriage and divorce rates and interpretations of changes which have occurred over the course of the modern era.

Elder, Glen. *Children of the Great Depression* (Chicago: University of Chicago, 1974). Elder has located and studied a large sample of the depression generation and compares their life experience, attitudes, and behavior to other generations of Americans.

Flacks, Richard. *Youth and Social Change* (Chicago: Markham, 1971). Flacks discusses the effects of economic and political change on the family's structure and functioning.

Greven, Philip J., Jr. *Four Generations: Land and Family in Colonial Andover, Massachusetts* (Ithaca, N.Y.: Cornell University Press, 1970). Through a careful analysis of records, Greven reconstructs colonial families and their land ownership and traces the families through four generations. A model of the new social history.

Handel, Gerald, ed. *The Psychosocial Interior of the Family:* A Sourcebook for the Study of Whole Families (New York: Aldine Publishing Company, 1972). An anthology which presents discussion of demographic and social-psychological studies of the family. Contains a number of classic articles.

Lasch, Christopher. *Haven in a Heartless World: The Family Beseiged* (New York: Basic Books, 1977). Modern society both creates and encourages needs for identity and sociability which can only be satisfied in the family, yet at the same time robs the family of the authority and power to meet these needs. Lasch investigates the tragic outcomes of this contradiction.

Laslett, Barbara. "The Family as a Public and Private Institution: An Historical Perspective," *Journal of Marriage and the Family* 35 (August 1973), 480–92. A consideration of the boundaries and conditions of family life and the relationship between the family and the state in the past.

Zaretsky, Eli. *Capitalism, the Family and Personal Life* (New York: Harper & Row, 1976). Originally written as a series of essays, this book analyzes the effects of economic and social structural forces on family life and the individual.

Chapter 3. The Meaning of Family in the Past

Ariès, Philippe. *Centuries of Childhood. A Social History of Family Life* (New York: Knopf, 1962). A classic study, though much better on the family and childrearing in the 18th and 19th centuries than on what preceded it.

Balsdon, J.P.V.D. *Roman Women: Their History and Habits* (London: Bodley Head, 1963). Includes material on marriage and family.

Demos, John. *The Little Commonwealth* (New York: Oxford, 1970). A study of the psychology of the Puritan family in its social and political context.

Duby, Georges. *Medieval Marriage. Two Models from 12th-Century France,* tr. E. Forster (Baltimore: Johns Hopkins University Press, 1978). An interesting short study by one of France's greatest historians.

Flandrin, Jean-Louis. *Families in Former Times. Kinship, Household and Sexuality* (New Rochelle: Cambridge University Press, 1979). Much good detail on French families in the 17th and 18th centuries.

Gordon, Michael, ed., *The American Family in Social-Historical Perspective* (New York: Saint Martin's Press, 1973). Essays on demography, childrearing, family, patterns of migration from the colonial period to the 19th century.

Katz, Jacob. *Tradition and Crisis. Jewish Society at the End the Middle Ages* (New York: Schocken Books, 1971). Chs. 14–15 treat the Jewish family in the 16th to 18th centuries.

Lacey, W.K. *The Family in Classical Greece* (London: Thames and Hudson, 1968). A study of the Greek family from the Homeric period to Plato's day.

Macfarlane, Alan. *The Family Life of Ralph Josselin. A Seventeenth-Century Clergyman* (New York: W.W. Norton, 1977). More readily available than the longer Diary in hardcover, Macfarlane's study gives a beautiful analysis to the relationships among family members in a Puritan rural and urban setting.

Poster, Mark. *Critical Theory of the Family* (New York: Seabury Press, 1978). A historian looks critically at various psychological and social theories of the family (Freud, Marx and others) and offers a model for thinking about the family drawn from European social history.

Rosenberg, Charles E., ed., *The Family in History* (Philadelphia: University of Pennsylvania Press, 1975). A useful collection including essays by Diane Hughes on medieval Italy, Lawrence Stone on England in the 16th and 17th centuries, David Landes on 19th-century France, and Joan Scott and Louise Tilly on 19th-century Europe.

Rossi, Alice, Jerome Kagan and Tamara K. Hareven, eds. *The Family* (New York: W.W. Norton, 1978). An interdisciplinary collection, including historical articles by E.A. Wrigley on England, Natalie Z. Davis on France and Tamara K. Hareven on the United States.

Shorter, Edward. *The Making of the Modern Family* (New York: Basic Books, 1975). Some interesting material on courtship and intimate family life in Europe, though overstates the sexual revolution of the nineteenth century.

Stone, Lawrence. *Family, Sex and Marriage in England, 1500–1800* (New York: Harper and Row Torchbook, 1980). The most useful view of the English family, especially of the artistocratic and wealthy family, in the early modern period.

The Memoirs of Glückel of Hameln, tr. Marvin Lowenthal (New York: Schocken Books, 1977). A delightful picture of family life among the Jews in 17th-century Germany, drawn by a Jewish merchant-women.

Tilly, Louise A. and Joan W. Scott, *Women, Work and Family* (New York: Holt, Rinehart and Winston, 1978). An excellent overview of the family, especially the working class family in Europe from the 18th century on. A good corrective to Shorter.

Tufte, Virginia and Barbara Meyerhoff. *Changing Images of the Family* (New Haven: Yale University Press, 1979). A collection of essays from a variety of perspectives, focusing on *images* of the family in history, the arts, contemporary society, and the law.

Zborowski, Mark and Elizabeth Herzog. *Life is with People. The Culture of the Shtetl* (New York: Schocken Books, 1964), Part IV on the Jewish family in the eastern European village of the late 19th and early 20th centuries.

For further bibliography and recent articles on the family, see the *Journal of Family History,* now in its fifth year, edited by Tamara Hareven.

Chapter 4. Post-Industrial Society and the Family

Bell, Daniel. *The Coming of Post-Industrial Society* (New York: Basic Books, 1973). One of the first analyses of our society to point to the change from a work ethic to consumerism and examine the effects of the change.

Bellah, Robert N. *Beyond Belief: Essays on Religion in a Post-Traditional World* (New York: Harper & Row, 1970). Changes in our social organization have also eroded traditional religious beliefs and commitments. Bellah looks at what happens to spiritual needs when traditional religion no longer serves.

Berger, Peter. *Sacred Canopy* (New York: Doubleday, 1969). Spiritual needs and the search for meaning express themselves in many ways and in different forms. Berger groups these forms under the spiritual canopy.

Cox, Harvey. *The Secular City. Secularization and Urbanization in Theological Perspective* (New York: Macmillan, 1966). A description of changes in our society over the past century and their implications for religion and religious institutions.

Fava, Slyvia, ed. *Urbanism in World Perspective: A Reader* (New York: Thomas Crowell, 1968). An anthology of essays by experts in various fields on the pace of urbanization in various parts of the world and its effects on human life.

Kahn, Herman, *et. al. The Next 200 Years* (New York: William Morrow, 1976). One of our most active futurists and his colleagues project our life conditions 200 years ahead, considering problems which will arise and mechanisms for dealing with them.

Kemeny, John. *Man and the Computer* (New York: Scribners, 1972). The computer extends the power of mind. Discusses how humans will manage this power and work out their relationship to it.

Kuhns, William. *The Post-Industrial Prophets, Interpretations of Technology* (New York: Harper & Row, 1971). Technology has had and will continue to have profound effects on our lives. The effects will, to some extent, be shaped by our interpretation of technology. Kuhns considers some of the leading and conflicting views of technological change which are dominant in our culture.

Muller, Herbert J. *The Children of Frankenstein, A Primer on Modern Technology and Human Values.* (Bloomington: Indiana University Press, 1972). Discusses the ways technology has affected our values and what effects it is likely to have in the future. Asks if humans can control technological advances (e.g., biological engineering) so that they do not destroy our values.

Nisbet, Robert. *Quest for Community* (New York, Oxford University, 1962). Individualism has become so dominant a myth and mode in our society that we are in danger of losing our connections and interdependencies with others. Yet humans need a sense of belonging as well as a sense of self. Nisbet describes our search for community.

Stein, Benjamin. "Whatever Happened to Small-Town America?" *The Public Interest* (Number 44, Summer 1976, pp. 17–26). Stein considers where and how the sense of community, the human values and traditions that marked small town life have diminished with mobility and urbanization.

Toffler, Alvin, ed. *The Futurists* (New York: Random House, 1972). The author of *Future Shock* considers the meaning of forecasting and the preoccupation with the future.

Walker, Charles. *Modern Technology and Civilization* (New York: McGraw-Hill Book Company, 1962). Provides a careful exploration of aspects of modern technological change and the way in which it has affected our world.

Winch, Robert F. *The Modern Family,* 3rd Edition (New York: Holt, Rinehart and Winston, 1971). A comprehensive book about the functioning of the modern American family which includes comparisons to older family forms and recent experiments.

Chapter 5. The Psychological Revolution

Fromm, Erich. *Escape from Freedom* (New York: Rinehart, 1941). A classic analysis of the forces in modern industrial society that lead individuals to want to give up self-direction and follow a leader.

Fromm, Erich. *Man for Himself* (New York: Holt, Rinehart and Winston, 1947). Fromm explores the effects of post-industrial society on human personality. He looks at the dynamics of "the market personality."

Goffman, E. *The Presentation of Self in Everyday Life* (New York: Doubleday, 1959). A sophisticated social analysis of transactions of daily life. Goffman's work is penetrating and startling in its insight.

Hougan, Jim. *Decadence: Radical Nostalgia, Narcissism, and Decline in the Seventies* (New York: Morrow, 1975). A highly pessimistic view of changes in the myths and ideologies by which we live—away from community toward preoccupation with the self.

Howard, Jane. *Please Touch: A Guided Tour of the Human Potential Movement* (New York: McGraw-Hill, 1970). A wry yet thoughtful exploration of the various forms and fads in the human potential movement. It is, above all, respectful of the troubles and needs that lead thousands of Americans to try some treatment to make their lives and relationships better and closer to their ideals.

Marin, Peter. "The New Narcissism," *Harper's* (October 1975). This article introduced what has become a modish interpretation of American society as a society of individual self-absorption and self-indulgence. By reducing the problems of our society to a psychological cause, writers like Marin and Lasch seem to do what Ryan describes (see Bibliography for Chapter Eleven) as "blaming the victim."

Rieff, Philip. *Triumph of the Therapeutic: Uses of Faith after Freud* (New York: Harper & Row, Torchbooks, 1968). A provocative, brilliant analysis of the effects of Freudian ideas on our culture. Argues that the view of life and social organization (e.g., the family) as therapeutic (i.e., releasing the individual to find and express his/her true self) has corroded faith and commitment.

Riesman, David. *The Lonely Crowd* (New Haven, Conn.: Yale University, 1950). With this early book, character interpretation of Americans became a dominant way of looking at social problems. Riesman argued that conformity in American life was the product of a new character type dominated by the need to be liked and socially accepted. The book was nostalgic for the rugged individualism of the nineteenth century. It was a very important influence on our modes of looking at ourselves.

Sennett, Richard. *The Fall of Public Man* (New York: Knopf, 1977). The individual— even the child—used to live in contact with the hurly-burly of city life and in the civic, public arena. In the nineteenth century, people became more and more absorbed in the private sphere of the family. Sennett analyzes the causes and consequences of this change.

Slater, Philip. *The Pursuit of Loneliness* (Boston: Beacon Press, 1970). A best-selling analysis of the ways in which individualism and the artificially stimulated desire for uniqueness have led us as a culture to striking uniformity and, more importantly, to isolation and loneliness. Slater looks ahead and sees some hopeful prospects for constructive change developing.

Wheelis, Allen. *The Quest for Identity* (New York: Norton, 1958). A description of the processes by which humans seek to discover and/or build identities. Considers not only elusive and problematic aspects of the quest but also causes of successful identity formation.

Chapter 6. The Sexual Revolution

Armour, Richard. *A Short History of Sex* (New York: McGraw-Hill, 1970). A sound and humorous treatment of the history of sex, including changes brought by birth control, the Kinsey reports, and the sexual revolution.

Barrell, Gilbert D. *Group Sex* (New York: Peter Wyden, 1970). A study of swingers. Author sees the behavior as an effort to improve marriage heavily influenced by our society's exaggerated, mechanical approach to sex.

Kinsey, Alfred et al. *Sexual Behavior in the Human Female* (Philadelphia: Saunders, 1953). This book, with its companion volume listed below, brought the Victorian era to an abrupt end by exposing the hidden realities of sexual practices. Many critics feel that the books also changed our conceptions of sex, stripping it of romance and mystery and reducing it to "performance" which could be both mechanical and a new area of achievement and anxiety about one's adequacy.

Kinsey, Alfred et al. *Sexual Behavior in the Human Male* (Philadelphia: Saunders, 1948). The first of a series of scientific reports by this famous biologist and his colleagues which became a runaway best-seller despite its authors' intent and dry, scientific style.

Masters, W.H. and V.E. Johnson. *Human Sexual Response* (Boston: Little, Brown, 1966). The first important challenge to the idea that sex is radically different for men and women. The findings reporting that women were capable of multiple orgasm became an important political plank among radical feminists.

Masters, W.H. and V.E. Johnson. *Human Sexual Inadequacy* (Boston: Little, Brown, 1966). A description of the Masters and Johnson technique of sexual therapy for sexual problems.

O'Neill, Nena and George O'Neil. *Open Marriage: A New Life Style for Couples* (New York: New American Library, 1972). This is one of the early and very important pleas for loosening the monogamous bonds of marriage. The authors have withdrawn their plea for sexual freedom of married partners more recently.

Rogers, Carl R. *Becoming Partners: Marriage and its Alternatives* (New York: Delacorte, 1972). An eminent therapist brings his experience to bear on the processes of building satisfying relationships within or outside of conventional marriage.

Smith, J.R. and L.G. Smith, eds. *Beyond Monogamy: Recent Studies of Sexual Alternatives in Marriage* (Baltimore: Johns Hopkins, 1974). A scholarly book which looks at the varied sexual activities and styles of married people.

Tavris, C. and C. Offin. *The Longest War: Sex Differences in Perspective* (New York: Harcourt Brace Jovanovich, 1977). The war between the sexes is analyzed in all its forms through an examination of the evidence supporting the view that women must accept subordination. The authors discuss factors that would lead to a hope for sexual equality.

Chapter 7. The Feminist Revolution

Bernard, Jessie. *Women, Wives, Mothers: Values and Options* (Chicago: Aldine Publishing Company, 1975). Bernard looks at the options available to women, the obstacles they face, and the supports they have in the work of realizing their individual goals.

Bird, Carolyn. *Born Female: The High Cost of Keeping Women Down* (New York: Simon and Schuster, 1960). A sophisticated writer looks at the socialization of girls and young women and describes the ways in which they are discouraged from achieving.

Chodorow, Nancy. *Reproducing Motherhood* (Berkeley: University of California Press, 1978). Each generation of young females is somehow convinced that their appropriate function is a biological one—to reproduce the species. Mothers, by and large, carry out this socialization. Chodorow analyzes how the cycle is continued from mother to daughter.

de Beauvoir, Simone. *The Second Sex* (New York: Bantam, 1961). A classic analysis of the position of women in society and the forces of socialization which have kept women subordinate. Originally published in the forties, it became the manifesto of the new feminism.

Freeman, J. *The Politics of Women's Liberation* (New York: David McKay Company, 1975). A political theorist looks at the position of women and analyzes the women's movement as a political movement for liberation.

Friedan, Betty. *The Feminine Mystique* (New York: Dell, 1964). This very important book called into question the value of restricting highly educated women to the domestic sphere. It was the clarion call to the feminist movement of the 1960s.

Goldberg, Susan. *The Inevitability of Patriarchy* (New York: William Morrow, 1973–74). A book which presents an anti-feminist argument for the necessity of a sexual hierarchy.

Harris, L. "Changing Views on the Role of Women," *The Harris Survey* (December 11, 1975). Public opinion polls during the late sixties and early seventies reveal that popular views of women's appropriate roles in society have changed.

Heilbrun, Carolyn G. *Reinventing Womanhood* (New York: Norton, 1979). Contemporary life does not require extreme division of labor by sex. A distinguished feminist and humanist mounts a plea for recognition of women's capacity to function in all spheres of human activity.

Loring, R. and H. Otto, eds. *New Life Options: The Working Woman's Resource Book* (New York: McGraw-Hill, 1967). An anthology that considers all aspects of women's lives in contemporary society and provides guidelines to women who are playing a role in the labor force at the same time that they are managing traditional family roles.

McGuigan, D., ed. *New Research on Women* (Ann Arbor, Mich.: Center for Continuing Education of Women, 1974). A collection of papers dealing with the new feminist scholarship. Woman and men at work and in family roles are subjected to scientific scrutiny.

Moers, Ellen. *Literary Women* (Garden City, N.Y.: Doubleday, 1976). Part of the new scholarship on women analyzes the portrayal of women in literature. The themes and outcomes of literary works about women depicts the way in which women have been understood and misunderstood in our society. A classic description of women's place in the world of work.

Patai, R., ed. *Women in the Modern World* (New York: The Free Press, 1967). This collection of papers describes the position of women in different industrial cultures throughout the world.

Chapter 8. The Family in Society

Elder, Glen. *Children of the Great Depression* (Chicago: University of Chicago Press, 1974). A study of the depression generation and their attitudes and beliefs in adulthood. An outstanding analysis of the effects of a major historical event on personal and family life.

Hess, Robert D. and Gerald Handel. *Family Worlds* (Chicago: University of Chicago Press, 1959). A theoretical and empirical analysis of family patterns, family interaction, socialization and its outcomes. A very broad and important work.

Kanter, Rosabeth Moss. *Work and Family in the United States* (New York: Russell Sage, 1977). An analysis of patterns of integration between work and family and how they have changed over our history.

Komarovsky, Mirra. *Blue Collar Marriage* (New York: Vintage, 1967). A classic treatise on working class families.

Piven, Frances Fox and Richard Cloward. *Poor People's Movements* (New York: Pantheon, 1977). Describes and analyzes the conditions of life that stimulated political movements among the poor and led, in many cases, to women's assuming the initiative and leadership roles in these movements.

Slater, Philip. *Footholds* (New York: Dutton, 1977). Slater looks at changes in sex roles and family life which have developed in the last decade and discusses where they came from and where they will take us as a society.

Whyte, William H. *The Organization Man* (New York: Simon and Schuster, 1957). An analysis of work-family integration in corporate life.

Zaretsky, Eli. *Capitalism, the Family and Personal Life* (New York: Harper & Row, 1976). A series of essays analyzing the effects of economic and social structure on the family and the individual.

Chapter 9. From Infancy to Old Age: Family Stages

Cain, Lynn. *Widow* (New York: Morrow, 1974). A strikingly honest and poignant autobiographical narrative about widowhood.

Datan, Nancy. "The Narcissism of the Life Cycle: The Dialectics of Fairy Tales," *Human Development* 20, No. 4 (1977). Analysis of family dynamics through fairy tales, discussing the dependency of early infancy and its effect on the parents; the child's transition to sexual maturity; and the child's discovery of adult fallibility and vulnerability. These conflicts, seen in the stories of Hansel and Gretel, Snow White, and The Emperor's New Clothes, are viewed as an inherent component of the process of family development and the succession of generations.

Ginsberg, L. and N. Datan, eds. *Life-Span Developmental Psychology* (New York: Academic Press, 1975). An anthology of articles dealing with various life stages and the problems they present.

Knopf, Olga. *Successful Aging* (New York: Viking Press, 1975). A readable and practical guide which dispels many myths about aging and offers reassuring advice about prospects for a full life in later stages of the life cycle.

Levinson, Daniel, et al. *The Seasons in a Man's Life* (New York: Knopf, 1978). Reports on a major longitudinal study of men as they traverse mid-life.

Liebowitz, Lila. *Females, Males, Families: A Biosocial Approach* (Belmont, Ca.: Duxbury Press, 1978). Critical discussion of "natural" family roles from an evolutionary perspective, including comparative studies of human societies as well as primate families. Dynamic definition of "family" in terms of generational obligations; application of social theory to social policy.

Neugarten, Bernice. *Middle Age and Aging* (Chicago: University of Chicago, 1968). An integrated report of research on mid-life by one of the major research workers in the field. Readable and very interesting.

Rossi, Alice S. "A Biosocial Perspective on Parenting," in A.S. Rossi, J. Kagan, and T.K. Hareven, eds., *The Family* (New York: W.W. Norton, 1978). Creative and critical overview of the biosocial perspective on parent-child relations, drawing on two sources: the biology of parenting, and the bio-evolutionary history of parenting. The author reviews current research on the changing nuclear family and raises questions for future research as well as for policy formation.

Rubin, Lillian. *Women of a Certain Age* (New York: Harper & Row, 1979). In this study of 160 mid-life women, Rubin presents the normal problems of women's mid-life transition.

Sheehy, Gail. *Passages: Predictable Crises of Adult Life* (New York: Dutton, 1976). A more popular presentation of adult life change based on social science research.

Troll, Lillian. "The Family of Later Life: A Decade Review," *Journal of Marriage and the Family* (1971), 263–290. Comprehensive, dynamic overview of the family in later life which stresses the importance of family relationships over the entire life cycle. Broad review of research in the areas of kinship structure, family interaction, intergenerational relations, intragenerational relations, developmental processes. Graphic summary of major studies in the field.

Troll, Lillian, Sheila Miller, and Robert Atchley. *Families in Later Life* (Belmont, Ca: Wadsworth Publishing Company, 1979). Comprehensive review of literature on the family of later life, representing the disciplines of psychology, sociology, and family studies. Includes a critical overview and chapters on older couples, the unmarried person in later life, parents and their adult children, grandparenthood, and siblings. Concludes with a discussion of implications of current research for future researchers as well as social policy.

Chapter 10. The Child in the Family

Ariès, Phillippe. *Centuries of Childhood,* tr. by Robert Baldick (New York: Knopf, 1962). This book stimulated a great deal of interest and lively response. It looks at historical changes in the family and suggests that childhood and adolescence came to be thought of as distinct life stages only in relatively recent times. A fascinating, highly readable book.

Bettelheim, Bruno. *Love is Not Enough* (Glencoe, Ill.: Free Press, 1950). A critical look at American child rearing with particular emphasis on permissiveness. The child, Bettelheim notes, has needs for authority and control as well as for love. The work is based on the author's extensive work with disturbed children.

Bronfenbrenner, Urie. *Two Worlds of Childhood* (New York: Russell Sage, 1970). A comparative analysis of child raising in Russia and the United States.

Coles, Robert. *Children of Crisis,* vols. 1–5 (Boston: Little, Brown, 1964, 1965, 1966, 1967–1977). I. *A Study of Courage and Fear,* II. *Migrants, Sharecroppers, Mountaineers,* III. *The South Goes North,* IV. *Eskimos, Chicanos, Indians,* v. *Privileged Ones.* This remarkable series of books describes childhood, socialization, and family life in the subcultures of America.

Fraiberg, Selma. *The Magic Years* (New York: Scribner, 1959). An early book about childhood from a psychoanalytic viewpoint. Offers advice and guidance to parents.

Kenniston, Kenneth. *All Our Children: The American Family Under Pressure* (New York: Harcourt Brace Jovanovich, 1977). A report by the Carnegie Council on Children on the state of the American family and the policies and programs needed to support families in their crucial task of child rearing.

Spiro, Melford E. *Children of the Kibbutz* (Cambridge: Harvard University, 1958). An early and excellent study of the effects of communal child raising in Israel.

Spock, Benjamin. *Baby and Child Care* (New York: Pocket Books, 1957). The American mother's guide to child rearing since World War II. The book is full of helpful, practical advice but also carries certain ideological bents. Worth looking at as an artifact of our culture as well as a daily guide to child raising.

Chapter 11. Varieties of Family Patterns

Gambino, Richard. *Blood of My Blood: The Dilemma of Italian-Americans* (Garden City, N.Y.: Doubleday Anchor Books, 1975). The tension between the desire to adapt and succeed in America and the equally intense wish to hold on to important ethnic traditions and goals is played out in the Italian-American family.

Gans, Herbert. *The Urban Villagers* (New York: Free Press of Glencoe, 1962). Gans discusses the conflict between tradition and change among Italian-Americans and describes the socialization process that holds succeeding generations in the subculture. At the same time, he sees tradition inevitably eroding.

Gutman, Herbert G. *The Black Family in Slavery and Freedom* (New York: Random House, 1976). Gutman describes changes and stability in the black family since slavery was abolished. Most disruption, he asserts, occurred in the north after the Great Depression and particularly in contemporary urban life.

Jackson, Jacquelyne Johnson. "Sex and Social Class Variations in Black Aged Parent-Adult Child Relationships," *Aging and Human Development* 2, no. 2 (1971), 96–107. Report of a study of the kinship supports of the black elderly.

Krickus, Richard. *Pursuing the American Dream: White Ethnics and the New Populism* (Garden City, N.Y.: Doubleday, Anchor Books, 1976). Among white ethnic groups, the success myth has conflicted with traditions of family solidarity. Out of the conflict have emerged new political themes.

Lewis, Oscar. *La Vida: A Puerto Rican Family in the Culture of Poverty—San Juan and New York* (New York: Random House, 1966). A moving account of conditions of life among bi-cultural people who travel between cultures but always remain in poverty.

Madsen, William. *Mexican-Americans of South Texas* (New York: Holt, Rinehart and Winston, 1964). A careful and detailed case analysis of life conditions and the hardships of poverty and discrimination faced by Mexican-Americans in rural areas in Texas.

Novak, Michael. *The Rise of the Unmeltable Ethnics* (New York: Macmillan, 1972). The melting pot has been more myth than reality. Ethnic Americans have held on to their cultures and traditions with remarkable integrity.

Rainwater, L. *And the Poor Get Children* (Chicago: Quadrangle, 1960). Rainwater considers the forces that operate to prevent family limitation among the poor.

Rubin, Lillian B. *Worlds of Pain* (New York: Basic Books, 1976). A comparative analysis of working-class and middle-class families.

Stack, Carol. *All Our Kin* (New York: Harper & Row, 1974). A case study of support structures among black families living in poverty in the South.

Zborowsky, Mark and Elizabeth Herzog. *Life is with People: The Jewish Little-Town of Eastern Europe* (New York: International Universities, 1952). A vivid, warm description of life in the Jewish ghettoes of eastern Europe.

Chapter 12. Signs of Strain

Bohannan, Paul and Rosemary Erickson. "Stepping In," *Psychology Today,* January 1978. The first report from a study of fathering in step-father families.

George, Victor and Paul Wilding. *Motherless Families.* (London: Routledge and Kegan Paul, 1972). An English study of fathers as single parents. A description of the social, emotional and financial situation of single fathers, with some emphasis on issues of social policy.

Goode, William J. *Women in Divorce.* (New York: Free Press, 1965). (Originally published as *After Divorce,* 1956.) The first and as yet the only large-scale survey of post-divorce adjustment problems.

Levinger, George and Oliver Moles, eds. *Separation and Divorce: Context, Causes, and Consequences* (New York: Basic Books, 1979). A collection of articles, all of good quality, some of them excellent, together representing the best current information and thinking about separation and divorce.

Longfellow, Cynthia. "Divorce in Context: Its Impact on Children," in Levinger and Moles, *Divorce and Separation: Context, Causes and Consequences.*

Visher, Emily B. and John S. Visher. *Step Families: A Guide to Working with Step-parents and Step-children.* (New York: Brunner/Mazel, 1979). A careful review of the problems in second marriages when there are children of earlier marriages. The authors are therapists, organizers and directors of a program for helping step-parents, and step-parents themselves.

Wallerstein, Judith S. and Joan B. Kelly. "The Effects of Parental Divorce: The Adolescent Experience," in E.J. Anthony and C. Koupernik, eds., *The Child in His Family: Children at Psychiatric Risk,* Vol. 3. (New York: John Wiley and Sons, 1974).

———. "The Effects of Parental Divorce: Experiences of the Child in Later Latency," *American Journal of Orthopsychiatry,* January, 1976.

―――. "The Effects of Parental Divorce: Experiences of the Child in Early Latency," *American Journal of Orthopsychiatry,* January, 1976. Wallerstein and Kelly have written several articles based on their experiences in providing short-term help for separating parents and their children. These articles present their findings for latency-age and adolescent children.

―――. *Surviving the Breakup: How Children and Parents Cope with Divorce* (New York: Basic Books, 1980). This volume summarizes many of the authors' findings from several years of research on divorced parents and their children.

Weiss, Robert S. *Going It Alone: The Family Life and Social Situation of the Single Parent* (New York: Basic Books, 1979). A description of single-parent life, together with an analysis of what produces it. The topics considered range from managing a household as a single parent to balancing a personal life with parental responsibility.

Weiss, Robert S. "Growing up a Little Faster," *Journal of Social Issues,* Winter, 1979. A description of the early maturity displayed by some children whose parents have separated or divorced.

Weiss, Robert S. *Marital Separation* (New York: Basic Books, 1975). An empirically based account of the impact of marital separation.

Chapter 13. New Family Forms

Bird, Caroline. *The Two Paycheck Marriage: How Women at Work Are Changing America* (New York: Rawson, Wade, 1979). A popular writer integrates social science information and her own observations to describe how women's movement into the labor force has affected both families and the workplace.

Feinstein, Karen Wolk, ed. *Working Women and Families* (Beverly Hills, Ca.: Sage, 1979). The effects of women's labor force participation on family life; changes in the power distribution in the family.

Hochschild, Arlie. "Communal Living in Old Age," *The Future of the Family,* ed. by Louise Kapp Howe (New York: Simon and Schuster, 1972). A study of the way in which older poor people built cooperative support systems.

Hoffman, Lois Wladis and F. Ivan Nye. *Working Mothers: An Evaluative Review of the Consequences for Wife, Husband, and Child* (San Francisco, Ca.: Jossey-Bass, 1974). An integrated review of research on working mothers.

Kanter, Rosabeth Moss. *Commitments and Community: Communes and Utopias in Social Perspective* (Cambridge, Mass.: Harvard University Press, 1972). A study of communes, both historical and contemporary, and of the factors that lead them to succeed or fail.

Pleck, Joseph H. "The Work-Family Role System," *Social Problems,* 24 (1977), 417–427. A consideration of the many patterns of contact between work and family spheres: conflict, accommodation, etc.

Ross, Heather L. and Isabel V. Sawhill. *Time of Transition: The Growth of Families Headed by Women* (Washington, D.C.: Urban Institute, 1975). Two economists investigate the trend in the last 50 years toward more female-headed households and consider the effects of these trends on the economic conditions of families.

Smith, Ralph E., ed. *The Subtle Revolution: Women at Work* (Washington, D.C.: Urban Institute, 1979). An outstanding book that deals with many different aspects of family-work issues.

Weiss, Robert S. *Going It Alone: The Family Life and Social Situation of the Single Parent* (New York: Basic Books, 1979). A description and analysis of the life and problems of single parents.

Young, Michael and Peter Wilmott. *The Symmetrical Family* (New York: Pantheon, 1974). An effort to describe family structure in contemporary families where both adults work. Both the woman and man will, according to these authors, carry two critical roles.

Chapter 14. Family Services and Public Policy

Bach, George R. and Peter Weyden. *The Intimate Enemy: How to Fight Fair in Love and Marriage* (New York: Avon, 1968). Many marital problems develop from partners' inability to disagree openly, to face and resolve conflict. Hidden tactics and double messages erode the marriage. These authors suggest ways for couples to discover and deal with their conflicts in open and honest confrontation. Many examples and cases are described.

Chilman, Catherine S. *Adolescent Sexuality in a Changing American Society: Social and Psychological Perspectives* (Washington, D.C.: U.S. Government Printing Office. DHEW Publication no. NIH 79–1426, 1978). An analytic overview of all available social and psychological research concerning various aspects of adolescent sexuality in the United States, including trends in sexual attitudes and behaviors, contraceptive use, abortion, illegitimate births, and early marriage. Includes implications for further research as well as suggestions for public programs and policies.

Giele, Janet. "Social Policy and the Family," Ann. Rev. Sociol. 5, *Annual Reviews, Inc.* (1979), 275–302. Presents a condensed overview of major scholarly publications that deal with the theory and development of family policies in the United States. Recommendations are made for further theory development and research. A source of valuable information concerning many of the significant developments in the field.

Gordon, Thomas. *P.E.T. in Action* (New York: Wyden, 1976). Parent Effectiveness Training is described in a reassuring and helpful guide to the problems and pleasures of child raising.

Journal of Marriage and the Family. Special Issue: Family Policy. F. Ivan Nye and Gerald McDonald, Guest Editors, 41 (August 1979), 3. The topics of the various articles include: a variety of definitions of family policy, the role of research in policy-making, economic and employment problems of families, public assistance policies, some policy issues in divorce and separation, etc.

Kahn, Alfred J. and Sheila B. Kammerman. *Not for the Poor Alone: European Social Services* (Philadelphia: Temple University, 1975). Describes ten selected social services programs in five northern European countries designed for the average citizen. Attitudes of the citizenry toward these programs are also discussed. Such services as child care, home helps, visiting health workers are less oriented in Europe (than in the United States) toward crises and poverty.

Kammerman, Sheila B. and Alfred J. Kahn, eds. *Family Policy: Government and Families in Fourteen Countries* (New York: Columbia University Press, 1978). This report on family policies in fourteen countries is a compilation of papers commissioned by the editors in their visits to sixteen countries. Prepared by academics or civil servants in these countries, the papers are uneven in quality and objectivity. The term "family policy" tends to be vague and confused in most countries. Difficulties both in defining and implementing public family policies in most of the nations studied should provide warning to the United States that the issues in this field are complex and fail to yield to simplistic solutions such as establishing a governmental department on families.

Keniston, Kenneth and The Carnegie Council on Children. *All Our Children: The American Family Under Pressure* (New York: Harcourt Brace, Jovanovich, 1977). Two major sections comprise this summarized report of the Carnegie Council on Children. The first section analyzes current conditions of families in the United States. The second section presents concrete proposals for changes in employment policies, the tax structure, income supplements, health care systems, delivery of family services and children's legal status. The authors call for increased economic security and greater parental power in all interactions with other social systems.

Krantzler, Mel. *Creative Divorce: A New Opportunity for Personal Growth* (New York: New American Library, 1973). This work—in many ways the culmination of the personal growth movement—treats divorce as an opportunity for development.

Lederer, William and Don Jackson. *The Mirages of Marriage* (New York: Norton, 1968). This book presents a theory and system for marital change based on the authors' analysis of family systems. Includes many case descriptions and exercises for couples to use to clarify problems and differences and resolve them.

Monroney, Robert M. *The Family and the State: Considerations for Social Policy* (London: Longman, 1976). The central theme of this examination of families and social policy in the United Kingdom is: how much responsibility should government take for assisting families and how much should families assume for themselves. This is a central question for the "welfare state." It is particularly investigated here in respect to the care of the frail elderly and mentally handicapped children. The author recommends policies which provide choices for families in the care of their dependent members and which offer basic public supports for families so that they can better carry out their special functions.

Rice, Robert M. *American Family Policy: Content and Context* (New York: Family Service Association of America, 1977). The author reviews current trends in family formation, historical aspects of various interest groups which have tried to influence social policies toward families, and various current family policy proposals in both Europe and the United States. Critical issues are discussed which are of interest to researchers, policymakers, and practitioners.

Ross, Heather and Isabel V. Sawhill. *Time of Transition: The Growth of Families Headed by Women* (Washington, D.C.: The Urban Institute, 1975). Economists Ross and Sawhill analyze a basic change in American society: the emergence of millions of female-headed families during the past decade. Special attention is given to differences in family structure by race, the possible contribution of welfare to the growth of female-headed families, the consequences for children who grow up in single parent families, and some implications for public policies.

Satir, Virginia. *Conjoint Family Therapy* (Palo Alto: Science and Behavior Books, 1967). One of the early books on family therapy—a system in which problems are located and treated in family dynamics and relationships rather than in the individual.

Shanas, Ethel and Marvin G. Sussman, eds. *Family: Bureaucracy and the Elderly* (Durham, N.C.: Duke University Press, 1977). This book of readings presents a theoretical analysis of the functions of families and bureaucracies in providing services to the elderly. It also includes chapters that describe programs and policies for the elderly in Britain, Israel, the Netherlands, Poland and Yugoslavia.

Social Work. Special Issue on Family Policy 24 (November 1979), 6. Neil Gilbert, ed. Policy-related subjects covered in this special issue include: some pros and cons of family policy, female-headed families, issues in family planning, child care and protection, care and support of the elderly and handicapped, income maintenance, and types of family policy research.

Chapter 15. The Family in the Future

Adams, Margaret. *Single Blessedness* (N.Y.: Basic, 1976). A book that takes a special view of the unmarried status. Sound analysis of available information, and a level-headed assessment of the advantages and drawbacks of the single life.

Bell, Donald. "Up from Patriarchy: The Male Role in Historical Perspective," to appear in Robert Lewis, ed., *Men in Difficult Times* (Englewood Cliffs, N.J.: Prentice-Hall, 1980). This is interesting as representative of the male perspective on role changes.

Bernard, Jessie. *The Future of Marriage* (New York: Bantam, 1973). A very important discussion of marriage which provides both theory and evidence indicating that men and women have very different experiences of marriage.

————. *The Future of Motherhood* (New York: Penguin, 1974). Analysis of the state and prospects of another important family role.

Binstock, Jeanne. "Motherhood: An Occupation Facing Decline." *The Futurist,* 6 (June, 1972). An interesting view of motherhood as just another job threatened by newer trends.

Carter, Hugh and Paul C. Glick. *Marriage and Divorce: A Social and Economic Study* (Cambridge: Harvard University Press, 1970). This book is so knowledge-able and assembles so much good statistical material that anyone wanting to know trends in the family would do well to become familiar with it.

Douvan, Elizabeth. "Family Roles in a Twenty Year Perspective." M.S. Horner, C. Nadelsen, and M. Notman, eds. *Perspectives on an Era* (N.Y.: Plenum, 1980). This paper presents the findings from two national studies of Americans' attitudes and experiences in family roles.

Friedan, Betty. "National Organization for Women Takes a New Turn." *New York Times Magazine,* Nov. 18, 1979, 40, 92 ff. Presents an important point of view and has had considerable impact among young feminists.

Glazer-Malbin, Nona, editor. *Old Family/New Family* (New York: D. Van Nostrand, 1975). This is an anthology of papers, some of them extremely interesting. It is oriented primarily from the woman's point of view but men contribute also.

Howe, Louise Kapp, ed. *The Future of the Family* (New York: Simon & Schuster, 1972). A very readable and comprehensive collection of papers by experts on all aspects of the family.

Libby, Roger W. and Robert N. Whitehurst, eds. *Marriage and Family Alternatives* (Glenview, Ill.: Scott, Foresman & Co., 1977). Another anthology rather more far-out than the others. The subtitle is "Exploring Intimate Relationships" and it is addressed "to those who choose to explore intimacy within and beyond marriage." Whitehurst talks about "present and future potentials in relationships." The inter-play between the radical and conservative point of view is Libby's Epilogue and the response from the Maces is an interesting contretemps.

Levinger, George and Oliver C. Moles, eds. *Divorce and Separation. Context, Causes, and Consequences.* (New York: Basic Books, 1979). See the note for this book in the bibliography for Chapter 12.

Lopata, Helena. *Marriages & Families* (NY: Van Nostrand, 1973). Another anthology. There is a section on Families of the Future. The Rainwater article is especially valuable and so is Margaret Mead's.

Myrdal, Alva and Viola Klein. *Women's Two Roles* (London: Routledge & Kegan, 1956). A classic analysis which argues for women's assuming two roles—in the home and in the labor force. It assumed a level of supportive services which, however, has not developed.

Sawhill, Isabel V., ed. *Women's Changing Roles at Home and on the Job* (Washington, D.C.: Special Report of the National Commission for Manpower Policy Special Report No. 26, September 1978). A fairly high-power anthology of papers given at a conference sponsored by the Labor Department.

Schur, Edwin M., ed., *The Family and the Sexual Revolution* (Bloomington, Ind.: Indiana University Press, 1964). The date of this book gives away its antediluvian perspective. Just a sort of benchmark to show where the future was starting from at a time when marriage rates were declining and divorce rates almost doubling.

Smith, Ralph E. *Women in the Labor Force in 1990*. (Washington, D.C.: The Urban Institute, 1979). This is a fairly technical but well-written statement of how trends are analyzed. It is addressed to those interested in the labor force more than in the family, but it does deal with the implications for child care.

Smith, Ralph E., ed., and Others. *The Subtle Revolution: Women at Work* (Washington, D.C.: The Urban Institute, 1979). This is one of the very best books on the subject. It deals with all of the aspects of the family-work issues. It covers all the relevant research. Chapters 4, 5, and 6 are especially good.

The Family Coordinator, Nov., 1979. This whole issue is devoted to male roles in the family.

A Study Guide
for
American Families
in Transition

by
Helen Weingarten

CONTENTS

NOTES TO THE STUDENT

The intent of this guide is to help both the general reader of family studies and the student enrolled for credit in the thirteenth Course by Newspaper, "American Families in Transition." The Study Guide is not meant to substitute for a critical reading and evaluation of the course material. Rather, its intent is to focus inquiry and stimulate a personal integration of the diverse and sometimes contradictory findings of the family experts whose insights are presented in these materials.

The course materials consist of a series of fifteen newspaper articles written by distinguished scholars in the family field; a Reader or anthology of articles, documents, and book excerpts entitled *American Families* that supplements the newspaper articles; and this Study Guide. Highlighting the themes of the newspaper articles and Reader selections, the Study Guide is organized into four sections that correspond to the four major parts of the course. The major divisions are: (1) Definitions and Historical Background; (2) Forces for Change; (3) Forms and Functions of Family Life; and (4) Crisis and Response. A complete course outline appears on page vii.

Each section of the Study Guide begins with a list of the newspaper articles for the section and the appropriate supplementary Reader selections. This is followed by learning objectives—some of the basic understandings of the issues that the designers of the course hope you will develop. The overview provides a brief summary of the readings and shows their connection, emphasizing similarities and differences among the various approaches to common problems. Key concepts and definitions highlight some of the major ideas presented in the section and explain terms that may be unfamiliar. Two kinds of questions have been provided: factual review questions for each chapter, which will enable you to test your own knowledge of the materials; and essay and discussion questions for each major part, designed to test your ability to integrate facts and use them in a discussion, as well as to serve as a review and stimulus to further thought about the issues.

Although each student will discover for himself or herself how best to use the course materials, we would suggest the following approach:

1. Read the newspaper article every week; clip it and carefully save it for future study and review.
2. Glance over the learning objectives, overview, and key concepts in the corresponding section of the Study Guide. These will call attention to some of the more important points of the newspaper and Reader articles and will help to focus your reading.

3. Read the appropriate selections in the Reader.
4. Reread the key concepts and overview more thoroughly this time.
5. Proceed to the factual review, rereading the articles as necessary to answer the questions.
6. Consider the discussion questions. Suggested guidelines to answers are provided with each question, although there is, of course, no single "correct" answer.
7. Turn back to the learning objectives. Have you met those goals?
8. Check the bibliographies in the Reader for suggestions of further reading on topics of interest.

The concepts raised by the newspaper articles and Reader selections are broad ranging. In developing this course, we did not seek to come up with a single, simple view on such important topics as the functions of family life, the impact of family socialization on individual growth, and the future of the family. Instead, we have tried to illuminate the complexity of the problems that confront family members and families as a whole in contemporary society. In so doing, we hope we have provided some better understanding of the issues of family life and family survival that face us all.

COURSE OUTLINE

Part One: Definitions and Historical Background

1. "Is the Family Obsolete?"
   Elizabeth Douvan

2. "The Family and Social Change"
   Barbara Laslett

3. "The Meaning of Family in the Past"
   Natalie Davis

4. "Post-Industrial Society and the Family"
   Milton Covensky

Part Two: Forces for Change

5. "The Psychological Revolution"
   Philip Slater

6. "The Sexual Revolution"
   Carol Tavris

7. "The Feminist Revolution"
   Catharine Stimpson

Part Three: Functions and Forms of Family Life

8. "Encounters with Modern Society"
   Marvin B. Sussman

9. "From Infancy to Old Age: Family Stages"
   Nancy Datan

10. "The Child in the Family"
    Kenneth Keniston

11. "Varieties of Family Patterns"
    Lillian B. Rubin

Part Four: Crisis and Response

12. "Signs of Strain"
    Robert S. Weiss

13. "New Definitions of Family"
    Joseph H. Pleck

14. "Family Services and Public Policy"
    Catharine Chilman

15. "The Family in the Future"
    Jessie Bernard

PART ONE
DEFINITIONS AND HISTORICAL
BACKGROUND

Articles:

1. "Is the Family Obsolete?"
   Elizabeth Douvan

2. "The Family and Social Change"
   Barbara Laslett

3. "The Meaning of Family in the Past"
   Natalie Davis

4. "Post-Industrial Society and the Family"
   Milton Covensky

Reader Selections:

"Saving the Family"
   Kenneth L. Woodward, et al.
"The Intimate Environment"
   Arlene Skolnick
"Variations in the Human Family"
   Clyde Kluckhohn
"Life in Appalachia"
   Robert Coles
"Family Types"
   David Kantor and William Lehr

"Family Time and Historical Time"
   Tamara K. Hareven
"Stability of the Family in a Transient Society"
   Niles Newton
"The Significance of Family Membership"
   Barbara Laslett

"The Purchase of Brides"
   The Virginia Company in London
"The American Family in Past Time"
   John Demos
"America's Immigrant Women"
   Cecyle S. Neidle
"Genteel Backlash"
   Richard Sennett

"Some Effects of Transience"
   Philip Slater
"The Family and Morality"
   Christopher Lasch
"The Family Out of Favor"
   Michael Novak

1

LEARNING OBJECTIVES

To develop an understanding of

—the functions of the family in society and in the life of the individual

—the impact of demographic changes on family forms

—the historical relationship of family organization and survival

—the results of urbanization and mobility on family life

OVERVIEW

Part One of the course is designed to familiarize the reader with diverse views on the nature of families and how their structure and functions vary in particular social-historical settings. The selections focus on several key questions: What accounts for the durability of the family? What are the individual and societal needs it meets, and how widely can its form vary and still be considered a family? What is the impact of demographic and economic changes on family form and functioning? Did people in the past think about the family, marriage, and childraising in the same way we do today, or have urbanization and secularization in post-industrial society changed the meaning of the family along with its structure and social role?

DEFINITIONS AND HISTORICAL BACKGROUND

How do we make sense of the predictions of family dissolution considering the actual trenchant continuity of family life? Elizabeth Douvan's keynote newspaper article surveys some of the vital issues raised in this debate and introduces readers to basic definitions and concepts in the study of family life and change.

The Reader selections give further scope to the discussion of these issues. "Saving the Family," by Kenneth Woodward and *Newsweek* staff members, presents the statistics and the concerns that have led some observers to argue that the family as an institution is in a state of crisis.

In "The Intimate Environment," Arlene Skolnick describes four basic types or models of family: the nuclear, the extended, the communal, and the cosmopolitan. Each has its own concept of the meaning of "family," and its own view of the role of the individual in the family unit and in society. Clyde Kluckhohn's concerns, on the other hand, are the universals of the family. Regardless of time and place, he says in "Variations in the Human Family," the family has always been an agency for the protection and training of children, and for regulation of sexuality and the reproduction of the species.

The descriptions of the three nuclear families which follow these selections translate abstract concepts into recognizable images. In "Life in Appalachia," Robert Coles portrays a poor, rural, traditional family, in which the father is the unquestioned head of the household. David Kantor and William Lehr, in "Family Types," describe both a highly organized, well-disciplined "closed" family and an informal, egalitarian "open" family.

The family as an idea has motivated our inquiry; as a reality, it has made us what we are.

FACTUAL REVIEW

1. What, according to Douvan, are the two crucial functions of the family in all cultures?

2. What other functions does the modern family serve, according to Douvan?

3. What three major reasons does Woodward give to explain why the family is in trouble?

4. Approximately what percentage of American families conform to the stereotype of breadwinning father, homemaking mother, and dependent children, according to Woodward?

5. How does Skolnick define the traditional family, and how does such a unit differ from other family types?

6. According to Skolnick, what is the significance of a culture defining the individual in contrast to the family as the "irreducible social atom"?

7. What are three types of cultural variation that Kluckhohn identifies?

8. How does Hugh McCaslin (in Robert Coles' article) feel about his sons and their future?

9. What evidence is there in Coles' article that McCaslin is the unquestioned head of the family?

10. As described by Kantor and Lehr, how does a "closed" family differ from an "open" family?

THE FAMILY AND SOCIAL CHANGE

In observing the family in history, we see many changes in the forms of marriage and childrearing as we move from the premodern to the modern era. In her newspaper article, "The Family and Social Change," Barbara Laslett discusses the effects of demographic factors on family life. She argues that the nostalgic ideal of the extended family, with several generations living together, was seldom a reality because few people lived long enough to become grandparents. Looking at such factors as death rates (mortality), life spans (longevity), number of children (fertility), and age of first marriage, she concludes that family relationships are probably more important today than they were in the preindustrial period.

Laslett's Reader selection, "The Significance of Family Relationships," expands on, and statistically documents, this thesis. She describes how industrialization, necessitating the separation of work and home environments, and technological advances, resulting in increased longevity and reliable birth control, have had profound influence on the roles of men, women, and children and on the relations among them. Immigration and migrations through earlier periods of American history meant loss of family contact, interaction, and support for large numbers in our population.

New institutional forms developed to fulfill functions that the traditional family could no longer serve. As Tamara Hareven points out in her Reader selection, "Family Time and Historical Time," the orderly progression of individuals along a life course was one product of industrialization. Childhood and adolescence as distinct stages of life were recognized only when children no longer functioned as economic resources. Like Laslett, Hareven shows how the family, no longer a production unit in post-agrarian society, became the center for nurturance and affection, and the family home emerged as a personal and private sanctuary.

Today societal changes continue to influence family structure and functioning and prompt Niles Newton, in "Stability of the Family in a Transient Society," to ask: "What can we do to stabilize family ties despite modern distraction?" Providing child care allowances and realistic family income tax deductions are just two possible suggestions he offers to bolster the family's role as primary socializer and nurturer of children in a time when a myriad of competing social institutions are available to take over these activities.

FACTUAL REVIEW

1. In comparing the size and structure of today's kinship group with those of past times, what demographic changes does Laslett feel we need to consider?

4

2. How does the percentage of single-parent households today compare to that in the past?

3. According to Laslett, how has the role of parents in the socialization process been affected by urbanization and migration?

4. What does Laslett mean when she calls the family a "backstage arena"?

5. According to Hareven, how do historical forces influence the timing of family events?

6. In Hareven's view, what demographic factors accounted for the appearance of the "empty-nest" stage of development?

7. What does Hareven mean when she talks of the historical importance of a "familistic ideology"?

8. Do individual lives today follow a more orderly or disorderly sequence than in the past? According to Hareven, why is this the case?

9. As we changed from an agrarian to an industrial society, a number of important changes occurred in the family. According to Newton, what are the most significant of these?

10. What social strategies are offered by Newton to stabilize and strengthen modern family ties?

THE MEANING OF FAMILY IN THE PAST

How does family life relate to larger historical forces? In her newspaper article, Natalie Zemon Davis considers the meaning of the family in past eras and its relationship to current family images and ideals. Prior to the nineteenth century, she points out, the family was necessary for survival, and family cooperation took precedence over self-expression and individual aspirations. The patriarchal family, in which both wife and children were subject to the control of the husband/father, predominated. Changes during the nineteenth century, including the separation of work and home, served to strengthen the family and make it a private haven, according to Davis.

The importance of the family unit to the earliest settlers in America is evident in the letters from the Virginia Company to the colonists in Virginia, reprinted in the Reader.

John Demos, in his Reader selection "The American Family in Past Time," traces the continuities and breaks in American family history from colonial times to the present. Like Hareven, he points to the social and economic changes of the industrial revolution as responsible for the recognition of the child as a distinctive individual, not merely a miniature adult. But, according to Demos, the scattering and fragmentation of families predate nineteenth-century changes and have always marked the new world experience. We have always been a nation of wanderers. America was settled by emigres, and the existence of the American frontier continued to provide restless citizens with the opportunity and the incentive to seek their individual fortunes away from family authority and restraint. Thus, Demos argues, the nineteenth-century ideal of the family as a haven and retreat, as a universe or "little commonwealth" unto itself, was an effort to oppose trends that went far deeper and earlier than the pulls of the industrial revolution.

Richard Sennett, in "Genteel Backlash," analyzes the drawbacks which come from this notion of the family as a haven in a hostile universe. While providing some degree of nuclear family stability, the "intensive family ideal" ultimately leads to social helplessness and an inability to understand and address the real causes of social problems, Sennett argues. His description of middle-class backlash against foreign working-class elements provides strong support for his hypothesis.

The idealization of the family and home as a haven from the harsh world depended, as Demos pointed out, partly on the separation of sex roles and the idealization of women. Women, uncontaminated by the working world, presided over hearth and home. That this genteel image was a middle-class concept is made clear not only in Davis's newspaper article, but also in Cecyle Neidle's Reader selection, "America's Immigrant Women." Neidle portrays the harsh realities of domestic life among immigrant women, who, far from being idealized, were often treated little better than slaves. Thus in the nineteenth century, as today, there were wide variations in family patterns in America.

FACTUAL REVIEW

1. According to Davis, what measures were used to ensure the cooperation and obedience of children in the seventeenth and eighteenth centuries?

2. What was the effect on the family of the separation of male work from the home, according to Davis?

3. Why did the Virginia Company ship brides to the colonists in Virginia?

4. Why does Demos call the colonial household a "little commonwealth"?

5. According to Demos, why was the sex-typing of women in colonial times less restrictive than during the nineteenth century?

6. What factors does Demos identify as leading to an intensification of the mother-child relationship?

6

7. What was the relationship of many Slavic women to their husbands, according to Neidle?

8. How does Sennett account for the fear of foreigners that developed among Chicago's middle-class in the late 1880s and 1890s?

9. What is an "intensive family"?

10. According to Sennett, what form of family best nurtures children who can cope with industrialized life?

POST-INDUSTRIAL SOCIETY AND THE FAMILY

What are the consequences of the post-industrial revolution? What happens when the family, as Milton Covensky writes, shifts from being "a long-term production unit" to being "a short-run consumption center"? Covensky argues in his newspaper article that the rise of instant credit, instant foods, instant news, and instant T.V. entertainment promotes a passive personality orientation in search of supplies and satisfactions. If family members are consumers rather than active producers, there is no social need for them to remain together. Urbanization with its rapid transportation, dual careers, and centralized public schools exerts further anti-family pulls.

Christopher Lasch's article in the Reader takes a similar position: urbanization and secularization, which promote reliance on outside societal institutions rather than family loyalties, are seen as a major threat to contemporary families. Both Covensky and Lasch see a need to reinvest the family with a sense of sacredness. Both appear nostalgic for the nineteenth-century view of families as havens from the rigors of industrial society. And both see strong, authoritative families as a solution to social disorganization.

In contrast, Philip Slater, in his Reader article "Some Effects of Transience," sees the mobility fostered by industrialization as providing an incentive for growth in new directions. To Slater, new social conditions demand new forms and provide new opportunities for individual and family development. As transience and the loss of a stable societal role rule out the adaptiveness of personality and/or role specializations which served well in more static societies, we are encouraged to become more flexible and complete individuals. Such changes, however, are not easy to make, and the family forms necessary to support such developments are not likely to be the same as previous models. In particular, transience, by depriving a couple of other enduring relationships, places great emotional demands—and consequently, stresses—on the marital relationship.

Michael Novak, in his Reader selection "The Family Out of Favor," acknowledges the strains inherent in marriage and family life, yet he believes, like Covensky and Lasch, that the family, despite all its problems, is essential to a free society. He shares Lasch's fear of the encroachment of the state; families, Novak argues, best suit human needs. Furthermore, the family provides the individual with a sense of identity and of worth—not just in economic terms, as a provider, but in psychological and emotional terms as well.

It is interesting for the student to speculate on how the roles for men, women, and children, and the family types developed to suit these roles in the post-industrial age, will differ from those patterns and family structures that functioned well in earlier eras. If men and women are not satisfied with defining one sex as workers in the market and the other as caretakers in the home, can we find solutions that will enable people once again to join work and home roles? Novak is representative of a growing group who seek to form an identity that allows for meaningful integration of the diverse roles now available. Thus, while it seems unlikely that the family will disappear, we must recognize that its form will probably change to fit this social-historical time.

FACTUAL REVIEW

1. According to Covensky, what distinguishes a post-industrial from an industrial age?

2. To what does Covensky refer when he talks of people's need for instant gratification?

3. According to Slater, what are some of the positive and negative ways that transience has affected the American personality?

4. According to Slater, what problems are created for specialized personalities in mobile societies?

5. What are some negative effects of permissive styles of childrearing, according to Lasch?

6. What innovation in the education of children did Edward Filene seek to make?

7. Why, in Novak's view, has the family been "out of favor"?

8. What, according to Novak, is the political significance of the family?

KEY CONCEPTS FOR PART ONE

Socialization is the term used to describe the educational, character-shaping process whereby social rules and values, roles and norms are transmitted to individuals in such a way that the person comes to want to do what the social system requires.

Norm is an unwritten group standard for behavior. The violation of a norm usually results in some form of punishment by the social group.

Role is a pattern of attitude and action that is prescribed as appropriate for particular social positions.

Functional Analyses explain why institutions exist or actions occur by reference to their impact on the larger social system. For example, a functional analysis of the nuclear family looks at how this family structure is suited to socialize its members to meet the needs of the society of which it is a part.

Nuclear Family (also called the **Consanguine Family**) describes a family group composed only of a mother, father, and their children.

Extended Family describes a family group that includes other near relatives (often living in the same household) in addition to the nuclear family.

Communal Family describes a family group composed of adults and children who may or may not be related to one another by blood ties.

Cosmopolitan Model is the term used by Skolnick to describe a family model in which individuals relate directly, rather than through their families, to an urbanized, technological society. The individual can fulfill his or her needs in the absence of family association.

Single-Parent Families are families in which one parent is missing, for example, because of desertion, divorce, or death, leaving a single parent to raise the children.

Monogamy refers to the state or custom of being married to only one person at a time. This term used to refer to the practice of being married only once in a lifetime. Today, however, it is not uncommon for one to enter into a number of monogamous unions which last for a limited time. Some have called the practice of marrying, divorcing, etc., "serial polygamy."

Polygamy refers to marriage in which a spouse of either sex may have more than one mate *at the same time.*

Polyandry refers to a form of marriage in which the female may have more than one husband at any given time. **Polygyny** refers to marriage in which husbands may have more than one wife at any given time.

Family of Orientation or **Family of Origin** describes the family of one's origin or birth; it includes one's parents and brothers and sisters.

Family of Procreation refers to the family one forms upon marriage. It describes families formed to procreate or bear children.

Family Types refer to the different patterns of organizing families. These different patterns are influenced by the social setting within which families develop and act. Kantor and Lehr distinguish between **closed family** types, those in which the behavior and energy of all family members are directed within the family system itself, and **open family** types, those in which family members direct their energy and attention to people and institutions outside the family and are receptive to input and stimulation from these outside sources.

Demography is the study of such characteristics of human population as size, growth, age, sex ratios, and vital statistics.

Mortality usually refers to the number of deaths in a given time or place. The mortality rate is the number of deaths per 1,000 persons in the population in a given year. Laslett and Newton point out that the average lifespan (or the age at which one may expect to die) has risen over the past century as a result of decreased mortality. This increased lifespan greatly influenced the form and functioning of the family.

Fertility can refer to an individual's capacity to bear children or to the rate of births within a population. The development and use of birth control technology exerts an enormous influence on the birthrate or fertility of a population.

Classical Family of Western Nostalgia refers to the concept of a self-sufficient farm family, with many relatives and obedient children living under the authority of the family patriarch. Although this type of family was commonly believed to have been typical in the pre-industrial era, recent research has shown that the nuclear family was much more common.

Traditional Societies are usually non-industrial, agrarian social systems where most resource exchanges occur in face to face transactions between the producer and the consumer. In traditional societies the family is both a primary economic institution and a social institution.

Family Time is a term used by Hareven to describe how significant life events can be timed according to family requirements rather than individual schedules. In earlier eras the vital economic role of the family necessitated that individual family members organize their personal lives and time crucial decisions according to family needs. Today, the timing of major events such as leaving home, marrying, and having children is generally influenced by social institutions other than the family and is based more on individual desires and needs.

Ideology is a system of beliefs that influences behavior.

Familistic Ideology, according to Hareven, holds that the timing of decisions such as marriage or leaving home should be based on family needs and concerns rather than on the desires of individuals. The relationships of family members holding these beliefs were based on mutual obligation rather than on personal affection and sentiment. Hareven says that familistic ideology is characteristic of traditional societies.

The Emergence or Discovery of the Child—In agrarian settings, children work alongside their parents and can be considered miniature adults. In an industrialized and diversified economy, however, what a child would do as an adult does not necessarily have any relationship to what his father does. With industrialization, childhood and adolescence thus came to be identified as distinct stages of life. This recognition of childhood significantly affected the role of women.

Industrial Revolution refers to the series of changes from the eighteenth century to the late nineteenth century in Europe and the United States that transformed their economies from primarily rural, farm to urban, factory systems. This transformation had enormous impact on family structure and function, ideology and behavior. The self-sufficient family, which was an economic unit, was gradually replaced by the family in which the father left home daily to earn a wage.

Sentimental Model of the Family (Family as a Refuge) refers to an idealized model of the family that resulted from the separation of the home from the work sphere and public scrutiny. The family came to be viewed as a haven from the harshness of the world of work, leading to the development of impossible ideals that made real family life seem flawed. The sentimental model requires the family to compensate for harsh realities outside the home but does not provide families with the resources or power to do so.

Secularization refers to the tendency to separate daily activities from religious or spiritual influences.

Geographic Mobility refers to the movement of people from one geographic area to another. In America, geographic mobility was encouraged by the existence of an expanding frontier, which many scholars think has shaped the American character. America was settled by persons who immigrated to this land to escape harsh conditions in Europe. We have often been characterized as a nation of wanderers. We have accepted and traditionally had the option of "moving on" when we wanted a change. Demos points out that geographic mobility has had the effect of disrupting families throughout our history. Slater argues that one effect of transience on the American personality has been the promotion of tremendous flexibility; on the other hand, frequently making and breaking relationships can result in shallowness.

Social Mobility refers to the ability of an individual or group to move from one social or class position to another by either gaining (upward mobility) or losing (downward mobility) economic and educational resources. The belief in the existence of upward mobility has been a key element of the American Dream. Sennett describes how intensive family types in Chicago at the turn of the century generally experienced less upward mobility than extended, large families.

Cybernetic or **Information Revolution**—The vast expansion of knowledge and information storage made possible by computers.

Service Sector is that part of the economy concerned with maintenance, communication, and service rather than with production.

Agencies of Mass Socialization are those social institutions and the media that have taken over some of the socialization functions exercised by families in traditional societies. Lasch sees the expansion of institutionalized health, education, and welfare services as poor substitutes for the family. It is, however, important to recognize that the small nuclear family we are familiar with has never had the resources necessary to carry out the diverse functions that other family types could meet. The family Lasch is nostalgic for will only be possible to recreate in today's world if the nuclear family undergoes major change.

ESSAY AND DISCUSSION QUESTIONS

1. What are some features of the family that remain the same across cultures and time?

Suggested Guidelines:

   a. Refer to Douvan's newspaper article and use this as a framework to organize your inquiry.
   b. Considering the family models described by Skolnick, refer to Kluckhohn's Reader selection and discuss important universal features and functions of family life.
   c. Refer to Coles, Kanter and Lehr, and the Woodward case studies and use them to highlight those features that families have in common and family differences.

2. Discuss how the American family has been influenced by economic and demographic changes.

Suggested Guidelines:

   a. Compare the arguments of Laslett (in her newspaper and Reader articles) and those of Newton. How are their concerns similar, and what special points does each make?
   b. Refer to Hareven's Reader selection. Compare the timing of major events by families in different historical eras. In what important areas has major family change occurred? How are these changes related to demographic and economic factors?
   c. Consider Davis's newspaper article. How did the change from an agrarian to an industrial economy affect the family?
   d. Look at Sennett's article. Does he agree with Davis?
   e. Consider Covensky's discussion of the differences between the industrial and post-industrial era.
   f. What do Lasch and Slater say about the effect of the mass market and modern economy on the family?

3. How have the meaning and the functions of the American family changed over time?

Suggested Guidelines:

   a. Consider Davis's description of life on a pre-industrial farm. Was the life of the individual more or less determined by family concerns than it is today?

b. Looking at the Demos and Lasch selections, identify differences between the relationship of the individual and the state in our colonial past and the present. Discuss whether this changing relationship has affected family structure.

c. Compare family life in colonial times and in nineteenth-century Chicago by referring to the selections by Sennett and Demos.

d. Contrast the views of Lasch and Slater on the value and meaning of the nuclear family. How does each view the influence of the nuclear family on the individual?

e. Develop a historical argument that can account for Novak's position that his role as parent and husband is more important that his role as worker.

f. Taking into consideration the Neidle article, discuss the extent to which changes in meaning and function of the family pertained to all elements of society and the extent to which they affected mainly the middle class.

PART TWO
FORCES FOR CHANGE

LEARNING OBJECTIVES

To examine

—family ideology and functioning in the post-World War II era

—developments leading to our culture's preoccupation with individual psychological well-being

—the sexual revolution and its effects on roles and relationships

—the cultural roots and social impact of the feminist movement

OVERVIEW

The psychological revolution, the sexual revolution, and the feminist revolution have deeply affected the structure and functioning of the contemporary family. In this part, these three important social influences on family life and ideology are discussed. Both their historical roots and their current manifestations are traced in order to clarify the impact that each has on social norms, roles, and interpersonal relationships.

THE PSYCHOLOGICAL REVOLUTION

How have individualism and the ideal of personal happiness influenced the modern family? In his newspaper article, Philip Slater argues that neither the permissiveness of the 1950s nor the narcissism of the 1970s is new. Rather, individualism has long been central to the American system of values. After a brief period of collectivism during the depression and war years of the 1930s and 1940s, Americans tried to retreat into the private, secure world of the nuclear family, excluding the concerns of the world outside. Paradoxically, the unintended results of this intense absorption with one's own family, according to Slater, were an increase in divorce, a disillusionment with family life among young people, and the women's movement.

Several of the Reader selections included in this section point to the importance of the industrial revolution and urbanization as primary influences leading to our time's increased focus on the individual rather than on the broader society. With the separation of the home from the work environment, the family no longer concerned itself with its societal responsibilities. Rather, the well-being of family members, considered independently from the social factors determining their adjustment, became the primary focus of family attention. During the late nineteenth century, a kind of family isolation developed among the middle class in response to urban industrialization which continues to influence our ideas of family life. Like Slater, Richard Sennett, in "The Brutality of Modern Families," is concerned with the "intensive family." He describes how this family pattern was supported by an ideology which claimed that nothing meaningful could be experienced outside the family that could not be experienced within. As defensive isolationism was thus transformed into a moral position, the new "ideal" family became exclusionary and cut off from the larger society. This tendency was intensified by the post-World War II move to the suburbs, where people associated only with those similar to themselves and shut out all diversity.

When we begin to think of the family as independent of its social context, we can easily turn our backs on social problems that do not immediately concern us. According to Sennett, our growing reliance on the family for our sense of order and for all our important experiences reflects a fear of the unknown and of the uncontrollable, such as the social disorganization of our inner cities.

Sennett argues that intensive families are unable to tolerate disorder and conflict not only in the larger society, but within the family as well. With their emotions and trust invested so heavily in each other, they regard disharmony within the family as a moral failure. Yet, as Slater points out in his newspaper article, the very isolation and intensity of these families leads to unrealistic expectations, disillusionment, and frequent conflict.

William J. Lederer and Don D. Jackson, in their Reader selection "The Mirages of Marriage," also focus on the emotional demands placed on marriage. They discuss how false myths or unrealistic expectations lead us both to misunderstand the nature of important human relationships and to perpetuate damaging patterns of relating to each other. To Lederer and Jackson many marital difficulties stem from false expectations about love and romance held by those who decide to marry. Unless we begin to understand the social conditions which determine and maintain problematic marriages, they argue, we will continue to create marriages that fail to meet the needs of the marriage partners. While emergence of the intensive nuclear family and the focus on the psychological well-being of the individual can be seen as attempts to solve a particular set of problems related to industrialization, Lederer and Jackson believe that new forms of human relationships are demanded in our post-industrial age.

Philip Slater, in his Reader selection "Women and Children First," and Kenneth Keniston, in "The Weakened Executive," agree with Lederer and Jackson's assessment that the modern family is unable to meet the needs of its members. Focusing on parent-child interactions rather than on the marital couple, each sees the functions of the family and the resources families need to meet these functions as having undergone enormous constriction. Formerly an important educational and economic institution, the family now functions primarily to fulfill the emotional needs of parents and children. Keniston points out, however, that parents still have tremendous responsibility for their children's psychological well-being, though they no longer have the authority or power to meet their children's needs.

In the absence of resources, Slater argues, parents now rely on forms of childrearing which may look permissive but are actually more totalitarian than the directive styles adopted by parents in earlier historical periods. Parents in the past were able to insure obedience because they had real power. Lacking resources to demand compliance, contemporary parents try to influence their children's motives and values. In Slater's view, the isolated mother-child pair fosters the child's adopting the mother's wishes as his or her own goals. Children behave then, or don't, not because of a realistic appraisal of the consequences of failing to live up to the demands of social reality, but because they want to please their parents. As all the authors in this section argue, emotional reasons generally fail to maintain behavior with the same constancy as do other, more objective, rewards. And, as Slater points out, these emotional bonds can create stress for both the child and the mother.

FACTUAL REVIEW

1. According to Slater, what are the differences between the narcissism of the 1970s and that of an earlier period?

2. What were three unexpected results of the preoccupation with family in the post-World War II period, according to Slater?

3. What is the attitude of people in intensive families toward social injustice?

4. How does the intensive family Sennett describes respond to conflict? Why is this the case?

5. List three reasons mentioned by Lederer and Jackson to explain why people actually marry.

6. Lederer and Jackson see Sullivan's definition of love as potentially attainable. What is it?

7. According to Lederer and Jackson, what are the four major elements of a reasonably satisfying, functional marriage?

8. What most disturbed post-World War II parents about their children's behavior, according to Slater's Reader article?

18

9. Slater writes that contemporary American childrearing is no longer focused on the demands of adult social occasions. On what is it now based and why?

10. To Slater, what is the function of "The Story of the Chaotic Day"?

11. Why does Keniston call American parents "the weakened executive"?

12. What factor does Keniston identify as responsible for our contemporary increase in divorce?

THE SEXUAL REVOLUTION

Birth control technology allows human control over an area previously controlled by biology and religion. As it erodes previous authority, it also opens new opportunities. Separation of sex and procreation unhinges the necessary connection between individual sexual expression and the social structure of marriage and the family. Birth control thus reduces societal control over sexual behavior and shifts it to the individual.

In her newspaper article, Carol Tavris cautions us, however, against considering changes in sexual behavior revolutionary. Rather than a sudden upheaval in values, there has been an accelerated evolution in sexual behavior which began, Tavris writes, not in 1960 but in 1900. In her Reader selection, Tavris shows more specifically how our sexual behavior is gradually changing.

Citing the work of the Institute for Sexual Research at Indiana University, Morton Hunt, in the Reader selection "The Affair," also argues that changes in sexual behavior have been primarily incremental. Tavris and Hunt agree, however, that revolutionary changes have occurred in sex-role expectations and attitudes. Over the past decades, marked ideological and normative shifts have occurred regarding behavioral prerogatives of men and women, and expectations for sexual satisfaction.

While Tavris argues that new attitudes toward sex pose new dilemmas, Jean Lipman-Blumen, in the Reader selection "The Dilemmas of Sex," points out that the moral dilemmas that surround today's relationships between men and women are timeless. As technology has created the possibility to meet, communicate, and be sexual with a speed and frequency previously impossible, we are catapulted into intimacy before we are ready. The vulnerability each person experiences in close relationships creates responsibilities—toward oneself and the other. Lipman-Blumen reminds us that why we establish intimate relationships and how we behave towards others are not only personal or feminist, political issues. They are moral and ethical matters as well.

But it is not only our attitudes toward sex that have changed as a result of birth control technology. Our attitudes toward motherhood have changed as well. According to Betty Rollin's Reader selection, "Motherhood, Who Needs It?" the notion that there is a biologically-based maternal wish is propaganda. Being a mother is seen by Rollin to be restrictive for many women, and employment is presented as a workable alternative for female satisfaction.

Like Rollin, Bruno Bettelheim, in "Untying the Family," emphasizes the importance of women being able to decide whether or not to have children. Women's control over pregnancy inevitably affects the marital relationship, according to Bettelheim. Furthermore, once childbirth becomes a matter of individual choice, a heavy burden of responsibility is added to marriage at a time when social and economic reasons for marriage are far less compelling than they were in an earlier era. And the fact that far fewer children are born into today's families means that parenting is seldom a full-time, lifetime job. All these factors, in Bettelheim's view, contribute to a loosening of family bonds.

FACTUAL REVIEW

1. Tavris identifies some of the important findings of the Kinsey studies. What are they?

2. What, if any, differences in the extra-marital experiences of men and women does Hunt report?

3. Tavris identifies a number of changes that have occurred in the premarital sexual experience of women. List three.

4. According to Tavris, in what area have the most revolutionary changes regarding sex occurred?

5. To Rollin, modern technology allows two important activities to be unlinked. What are they?

6. What does Rollin mean by "The Motherhood Myth"?

7. What factors does Bettelheim identify as having weakened traditional family bonds?

8. What moral issue underlies all forms of sexual behavior, according to Lipman-Blumen?

9. In Lipman-Blumen's view, how has technology led to problems of intimacy?

10. What does Lipman-Blumen hold as a basic measure or test of a person's humanity?

20

THE FEMINIST REVOLUTION

Following the period after World War II in which close family relationships, large numbers of children, and domesticity seemed to be unquestioned values, many educated women came to resent their isolation from the civic and occupational "world of affairs." Women from all social classes, moving into the labor force in larger numbers, began to assert new demands for equality of pay and opportunity in the work setting and for equal division of domestic responsibilities at home. As Catharine Stimpson writes in her newspaper article, women's employment and the women's movement changed the rules of family life for many people in our society. Established hierarchical, sex-typed family patterns were disrupted and new family and work patterns began to emerge.

In the early days of the women's movement, many activists attacked the family as an institution perpetuating women's second-class status. Jean Bethke Elshtain's Reader selection analyzes the arguments of the feminists. The result of blaming the family for women's inequality and of making all aspects of personal life a legitimate area of political concern is a "politics of displacement"—a style of politics that confuses a symptom of social breakdown with its cause, according to Elshtain. In her view, the modern family, despite its flaws, remains an important and humanizing source of social support.

Ellen Goodman notes, however, that as non-traditional concepts of family life developed, the women's movement began to talk of having a rich family life as both a goal and a priority. Today pro-family feminists are careful to point out that the family that they support must be different in form from traditional versions. Rigid and narrow expectations that leave men feeling like failures must be broadened so that men are also able to derive self-esteem from their family participation, Goodman writes.

Jessie Bernard's Reader selection, "Changing Family Life Styles: One Role, Two Roles, Shared Roles," also supports changes in traditional family roles. Sex-role expectations that view women's proper place solely as the home and men's proper place solely as the labor market have been replaced by more equalitarian notions, she notes. These notions can be divided into two types: those supporting two roles, worker and mother, for women; and those supporting shared roles, provider and parent, for both men and women. One problem with the two-role ideology, according to Bernard, is that employment and motherhood often come to be viewed as mutually exclusive alternatives. In contrast to Betty Rollin, whose selection appears in the previous section, Bernard supports a shared-role ideology, which holds that full humanity will only be possible for both sexes when both men and women participate in both productive and nurturing activities. Public policy, she urges, should be geared toward supporting shared roles through such measures as adjusting working hours.

Like Bernard, Carolyn Heilbrun believes that if families are to serve the needs of contemporary men, women, and children, parenting must become the work of both sexes. In "On Reinventing Motherhood," Heilbrun also stresses the value of developing alternative support systems for women beyond those which commonly exist. To Heilbrun, the failure of the women's movement to retain momentum is due in part to the fact that support networks for women have been too narrowly based. Women, like men, need networks that encourage the autonomy required to succeed in the labor market. Heilbrun argues that family and friendship systems that function for women in times of crisis have traditionally provided support at the expense of fostering independence. It is the latter quality that must be valued if women are to manage in the world of work; and support networks, beyond the family, must be developed to serve this end.

FACTUAL REVIEW

1. On what issues do feminists disagree? On what issues do they agree, according to Stimpson?

2. What is the attitude of a majority of American women today toward feminism? according to Stimpson?

3. To what is Elshtain referring when she states that our society is experiencing a "legitimation crisis"?

4. What is one important function mentioned by Elshtain that is served by keeping political and personal spheres separate?

5. According to Elshtain, what are three ways in which a politics of displacement renders politics hollow?

6. Why do men today feel like failures, according to Goodman?

7. According to Goodman, how does the feminist definition of family differ from the anti-feminist version?

8. What changes does Goodman cite in the attitude of the feminist movement toward the family?

9. What three things does Heilbrun feel account for the failure of the women's movement to maintain momentum?

10. What are the three different sex-role ideologies identified by Bernard?

11. In what respects is a two-role ideology antinatalist, according to Bernard?

KEY CONCEPTS FOR PART TWO

Individualism is an ideology that holds that the interests and needs of the individual are, or ought to be, ethically paramount over those of the group or the state. Slater calls this belief system, which denies human beings are interdependent, one of our culture's strongest illusions.

Narcissism refers to total absorption with one's self and one's own needs. Some critics argue that individualism is synonymous with egocentrism or selfishness, and that it has led us to become a culture of narcissists who are solely interested in promoting our own gratification and fulfillment without considering the well-being of others. Slater points out that the narcissism of the 1970s stressed sexual and psychological gratification, while that of an earlier period stressed material well-being.

The Me Generation is a term used to describe the narcissistic people of the 1970s.

Permissiveness is a style of childrearing that is relatively flexible and permits a range of behaviors on the part of the child rather than demanding strict obedience to authority and conformity to rigid schedules and rules.

Child-Centeredness refers to a family orientation that focuses on the child and his or her well-being. The physical and psychological well-being of the parents as individuals are sacrificed to give every possible advantage to the child.

The Village Ethic refers to a web of cohesive social relationships involving everyone within the community. Activities are known to all and add up to an organic whole.

Urbanism, in contrast to the village ethic, is a way of life in which separate activities depend on each other but are not organically bound or broadly known. An ethic based on involvement seems harder to maintain; the complexity and diversity of the city overwhelms many of its inhabitants, who may consequently seek refuge from its demands by retreating to suburbia or to urban enclaves of people similar to themselves.

Family Intensity (see **Urbanism**) refers to a kind of family isolationism based on the belief that all that is meaningful can be experienced within the family. The family is looked upon as containing the whole social arena in microcosm. Adherence to this view results in a rise in social isolation and alienation.

Sexual Revolution refers to changing norms and values governing sexual behavior over the past few decades. According to Bettelheim, greater liberalism in attitudes and freedom in sexual expression is due in part to the removal of the fear of the consequences of engaging in sexual relations that modern birth control technology provides. Tavris emphasizes there has been no revolution in sexual behavior.

Premarital Sex refers to sexual relations before marriage.

Extramarital Sex refers to any sexual relations outside of marriage.

Maternal Instinct refers to the belief that the desire to have a child and the activity of mothering a child are inherent in a woman's biological makeup. Rollin refers to the idea of the maternal instinct, and the related notion that women will be fulfilled only as mothers, as **The Motherhood Myth.**

Feminine Mystique is a term coined by Betty Friedan in 1963 to refer to the process by which society convinces women that being a housewife and mother is the only path available for female self-fulfillment.

Antinatalism means being against childbearing. Betty Rollin takes an antinatalist position in her article, "Motherhood: Who Needs It?"

One-Role Ideology is the belief that social roles should be allocated to individuals solely on the basis of a person's sex. According to this ideology, the appropriate role for women is that of homemaker, and for men, that of breadwinner. In contrast, Jessie Bernard describes patterns in which women are both homemakers and workers and men continue to perform the traditional sex-linked male role. Belief in this pattern is called **two-role ideology. Shared-role ideology** holds that tasks should be divided according to one's time and ability rather than according to one's sex. Shared-role relationships are those in which both men and women share the roles of earning income and parenting. Miller describes how difficult it is to implement shared-role relationships even when one supports such a position intellectually.

Dual-Career Families are families in which both husband and wife have careers with intrinsic satisfaction and merit.

Politics of Displacement is a form of politics which mistakes the symptom for the disease. Elshtain sees the radical feminist strategy of translating personal life into a political arena as a displacement. In reducing the personal to political and vice versa, one loses the sense of how particular social structures shape and constrain action. Furthermore, such politics obscure the ways in which individuals can learn to order, direct, and control their actions to realize personal and social goals.

ESSAY AND DISCUSSION QUESTIONS

1. What have been the unintended effects of our attempts to create a comfortable, secure, private nuclear family world in which to retreat and raise our children?

Suggested Guidelines:

   a. Refer to Slater's newspaper article and pay particular attention to how our attempts to solve certain problems have led to the very dangers which we hoped to avoid.
   b. Discuss Sennett's assertion that the modern family is a brutal one.
   c. Refer to the Reader selections of Slater and Lederer and Jackson and identify factors that have led to unrealistic expectations and disillusionment with family life.
   d. Referring to Keniston, discuss whether we can or should attempt to strengthen "the weakened executive." Considering Slater's argument, how might this best be done?

2. Discuss Carol Tavris' assertion that there hasn't been a revolution in sexual behavior.

Suggested Guidelines:

   a. What arguments does Tavris make in her newspaper article?
   b. Refer to the data cited by Hunt and Tavris in their Reader selections.
   c. Compare the arguments of Jean Lipman-Blumen and Betty Rollin on the meaning of intimate relationships.
   d. What does Bettelheim see as a result of changing sexual norms?

3. What are the social forces that have given rise to feminism? Is the feminist solution to social stresses a positive one?

Suggested Guidelines:

   a. Compare the arguments of Stimpson and Heilbrun.
   b. Refer to Elshtain and discuss the limits to the feminist analysis of our society that she identifies.
   c. Refer to the articles by Goodman and Bernard. What solutions do they propose to improve the quality of family life? How do these solutions fit or fail to fit the model of feminism that Elshtain criticizes?

PART THREE
FUNCTIONS AND FORMS OF FAMILY LIFE

Articles:

8. "Encounters with Modern Society"
   Marvin B. Sussman

9. "From Infancy to Old Age: Family Stages"
   Nancy Datan

10. "The Child in the Family"
    Kenneth Keniston

Reader Selections:

"Public Images, Private Realities: The American Family in Popular Culture"
  Arlene Skolnick
"The Institutionalized Family"
  Amitai Etzioni
"Work and Family in the United States"
  Rosabeth Moss Kanter
" 'Til Business Do Us Part?"
  E. Jerry Walker

"Shall I Go Back to Work?"
  Claudia Dreifus
"What Happens to Parents?"
  Elizabeth Douvan
"Women of a Certain Age"
  Lillian B. Rubin
"Families in Later Life"
  L. Troll, S. Miller, and R. Atchley
"The Changing American Grandparent"
  Bernice L. Neugarten and Karol L. Weinstein

"Colonial Laws Regarding Children"
"U.S. Children Give Families High Marks"
  Science News
"Raising Black Children"
  Andrew Billingsley
"Choosing Child Care: Many Options"
  Mary Rowe
"Communal Education: The Case of the Kibbutz"
  Bruno Bettelheim

11. . "Varieties of Family Patterns"
    Lillian B. Rubin

"Black Families in White America"
   Andrew Billingsley
"Black Families: An Exchange"
   Nathan Glazer and Herbert Gut-
   man
"The Urban Villagers"
   Herbert J. Gans
"Worlds of Pain"
   Lillian B. Rubin

LEARNING OBJECTIVES

To understand

—the connection between the family and other social institutions

—how the individual develops within the family and how the form and functioning of the family changes throughout the life course

—the relationship between the child and the family

—the varieties and the range of family types that exist among subcultures
within our society

OVERVIEW

In Part Three, we look at the family from a number of vantage points. First,
we view it in the context of other social institutions. Next we investigate it
from a developmental perspective, focusing on how the family evolves as its
membership and needs change over the lifespan. Third, we look at how children fare in contemporary families. Are we indeed a child-centered society?
What, in fact, does the modern family teach children? Finally, we deal with
the varieties of modern family life. Even if we think of parents and children
living together in one household as a family, families in different parts of our
society vary enormously. Increasing our understanding of this family variation
and its effects are aims of the fourth group of readings in this part of our
course.

28

THE FAMILY IN SOCIETY

We know that families interact with other social institutions. In this section we seek to answer how families have fared in their encounters with government, economic institutions, and the political world.

In his newspaper article Marvin Sussman describes how, in complex societies such as ours, the family acts as the major link between the individual and other social institutions. Although institutions have taken over many functions previously performed by the family, the family serves as an emotional buffer between the individual and the bureaucracies in the larger society. By meeting the individual's needs for a small, supportive group within which to sort out the options provided by other social institutions, the family serves an important integrative function. Furthermore, Sussman points out, the nuclear family remains responsible for the direct care of its dependent members—for children, the aged, and the infirm.

In his Reader selection, Amitai Etzioni expresses somewhat greater concern than Sussman over the trend towards institutionalized educational and welfare services. He views the expansion of public means to care for dependent persons as an unwarranted transfer of social responsibility away from the family. Not all analysts agree with Etzioni; rather than viewing the development of publicly supported services as undermining the family, one can interpret their expansion as supportive of currently overburdened nuclear family resources.

Although, as Sussman emphasizes, the family is held responsible for meeting the needs of its dependent members, Arlene Skolnick points out that the private family lacks social supports for performing this function. Like Demos and Sennett (see Part One), she sees industrial capitalism as having undermined the power of the home at the same time that it has idealized its attractiveness as a place of security and emotional release. Skolnick argues that the popular image of the ideal family as a retreat from the harsh realities of the outside world inevitably led to a sense of failure. Real families could never match the perfection of the ideal. Skolnick sees hope for the future of the family, nonetheless, in our current disillusionment with the self-sufficient family life. She suggests replacing unrealistic and sentimental expectations with an ideology that recognizes that family relationships involve change and conflict and are intimately connected to the society in which they exist. Such realistic views may help us to cope with the strains on the family and motivate us to change the social conditions from which we formerly tried to take refuge.

The Reader selections by E. Jerry Walker and Rosabeth Moss Kanter both focus on work/family conflicts and suggest ways to alleviate them. Walker's approach is psychologically oriented. He looks at the specific difficulties faced by executive families, and he suggests that these be handled through greater sensitivity on the part of corporations to the needs of these families and by more open communication between husband and wife. Kanter, a sociologist, looks at the ways in which the structure and functioning of families in different times have meshed with, or have failed to fit, the needs of the larger economic system. To Kanter, there is an intimate connection between the needs of the labor market and the family forms which become dominant. She suggests that we must actively influence the policies of the organizations which have control over individual and family if we wish to preserve or promote particular family forms.

FACTUAL REVIEW

1. According to Sussman, how does the family serve as a link between the individual and institutionalized bureaucracies?

2. What is the function of the family in regard to its dependent members, according to Sussman?

3. According to Skolnick, what is the function of public images of the family, and how accurately do they represent what actually exists?

4. What are the effects of privacy on the family, according to Skolnick?

5. Skolnick writes that intimate relationships involve two key elements besides love. What are they?

6. Why does Etzioni argue against the extension of institutionalized welfare services to aid children, the elderly, and the infirm?

7. What does Kanter mean when she says families are sources of "particularistic" loyalties?

8. According to Kanter, what are two strategies that organizations may adopt in relationship to families?

9. Kanter identifies a number of areas for future research on work/family relations. Identify three.

10. What are some of the strategies mentioned by Walker to alleviate strains in executive families?

FROM INFANCY TO OLD AGE: FAMILY STAGES

Young people form families and have children. The family has legal, material, and emotional power which it uses to socialize the young and transmit critical values. But children grow up, and, in the natural course of events, middle age parents live to see their children leave home and establish independent lives. In later life parents, not infrequently, come to depend on their own children for support. Thus, as the family moves through stages, from formation, to childrearing, to post-parenting, and, in some cases, to ultimate dependency, new demands and opportunities require individual and family adjustment and change.

Nancy Datan, in her newspaper article, examines nuclear family life and identifies the changing needs of families at critical stages. Family relationships involve a process of continual adjustment on the part of both child and parent. But she points out that, despite developmental shifts, the family is the one social setting that can respond to and affirm its members as individuals through providing relatively unconditional support across the lifespan.

Like Datan, Elizabeth Douvan, in her Reader selection "What Happens to Parents," stresses the continually changing patterns of family relationships. Focusing on the adolescent-parent relationship, she points out that the adolescent becomes increasingly absorbed with his peer group and with himself at a time when parents have defined themselves in substantial measure by their roles as parents. Thus, parents usually experience a sense of loss when the adolescent becomes less dependent on them, and both parents and child need to adjust to a new way of interrelating. Douvan argues that adults today are confused about the meaning of their own lives, yet it is essential that we arrive at a definition of adulthood with which the young can identify if we want them to mature into responsible individuals. Douvan stresses that interdependence between child and parent does not end as children approach adulthood; it merely assumes new forms.

Lillian Troll and her associates, in their Reader selection "Families in Later Life," also stress that most young couples continue to live close enough to their parents to receive help in the form of services and/or money despite our cultural image of mobile, independent, nuclear families. The significance of the parent-child relationship does not end with the child reaching adult status. Rather it continues throughout life and is reciprocal. Even when the parents reach old age and may be widowed, the authors point out, they try to maintain a reciprocal relationship with their children rather than become dependent.

While recognizing the enduring nature of family bonds, Bernice Neugarten and Karol Weinstein find styles of family involvement differ considerably. In their study of American grandparents, they discovered only a small percentage who remain actively involved in the rearing of their grandchildren. To these researchers, "pleasure without responsibility" seems to be the motto describing most extended family relationships in the post-parental stage.

Lillian Rubin's Reader selection may help explain why many grandparents avoid active responsibility for their grandchildren. Although Rubin does not speak directly to this issue, taking a less active grandparenting role can be seen as a possible result of changes brought about by the women's movement. Rubin states that twenty-five million women—the largest segment of the female adult population—are in midlife. Encouraged by recent cultural trends, many have begun to fulfill their needs for self-actualization in activities other than childrearing.

However, as Claudia Dreifus points out, jobs are not always creative and joyful for many women. For middle-class women who have considered themselves sympathetic to feminist concerns, the unexpected pleasures of motherhood, in conjunction with the mixed pleasures of work, create a crisis about how to combine work and parenting that is difficult to resolve. If, as Rollin asserted in "Motherhood: Who Needs It?" (Part Two), there is no maternal instinct, the emotional bonds of the family are nevertheless often stronger than many career-oriented women anticipate.

FACTUAL REVIEW

1. In what sense does Datan believe that "anatomy is destiny"?

2. Why is the family unique among our social institutions, according to Datan?

3. Why do parents experience a sense of loss when their children reach adolescence, according to Douvan?

4. How does Douvan explain the frequent criticisms of today's youth, and how does such criticism differ from age-old complaints about the young?

5. Identify a conflict in roles that creates a crisis for many young women, according to Dreifus.

6. What social changes are suggested in the Dreifus article that may help solve this dilemma?

7. According to Rubin, what evidence is there that the women's movement is now being taken seriously by society at large?

8. Rubin points out that 25 million women face a particular challenge and opportunity for growth. Describe this crisis and account for its occurrence.

9. How would Troll et al. define the concept of "filial maturity"?

10. According to Troll et al., what kind of relationship do most young couples maintain with the families into which they were born?

11. How has the American grandparent changed, according to Neugarten and Weinstein?

12. What are four possible and different meanings that the grandparent role may entail, according to Neugarten and Weinstein?

THE CHILD IN THE FAMILY

In a real sense families are for children, especially in their earliest years when they depend on the family for their very survival. The task of the family is twofold: to instill in children elements of the culture that will prepare them to function in that culture, and to commit children to their society by gradually extending their attachment to the larger world. Socialization, as such, must impart both practical and emotional skills.

Kenneth Keniston, in his newspaper article, discusses basic changes in the structure and functioning of the family that have affected the child and the role of the family in socializing the child. He shows how forces outside the family have an increasing influence on the child. Parents, no longer able to provide directly for all their children's needs, have assumed a new role as general coordinator and harmonizer of these outside influences. But despite these changes, according to Keniston, the basic element of socialization—the special love between parents and children—remains constant.

Although socialization was primarily the parents' responsibility in colonial society, it would be misleading to think that the state took no interest in family matters. As the colonial documents reprinted in the Reader illustrate, the state took a harsh view of disobedience and provided severe punishment—and even death—for rebellion against parental authority.

The authority of the family has unquestionably been weakened in the intervening 300 years, and many experts believe the family itself has been weakened in the process. But a study by Nicholas Zill, reported by *Science News* and reprinted in the Reader, found that the majority of young children continue to view the family as a cohesive and positive force. In the two-parent family, Zill identifies the relationship between husband and wife as the most important factor determining the child's well-being; in the single-parent family, it is the parent's own adjustment and ability to cope.

What will be the effect of increasing numbers of mothers of young children entering the work force? Will day care become another area in which institutions take over socialization functions? Mary Rowe's Reader selection, "Choosing Child Care: Many Options," stresses that use of institutionally based child-care facilities is rare. Eighty-one percent of those using outside sources of child care still seem to prefer relying on relatives or neighbors for family care of some sort, she finds. Rowe identifies changes in labor force patterns and fertility, marriage, and divorce as promoting a considerable shift toward more equal male participation in child care—in values, at least, if not yet in fact. She predicts that the social and legal rights and expectations of fathers with regard to child care will continue to change over the next decade.

Bruno Bettelheim discusses a model of child care, however, that is even more radical than one based on shared parental roles. In the communal child-rearing settings he describes in "Communal Education: The Case of the Kibbutz," children learn to interact with little adult supervision from earliest age on. Group living with a stable set of age peers, rather than consistent care by one's biological parents or parent substitutes, provides kibbutz children with an inner sense of security. Adult caretakers are concerned and present; they are, however, by no means primary.

Bettelheim is careful to point out that we need not follow the kibbutz child-care program. It does produce, he relates, an adult who does not fit our current values. He urges, instead, that we might do well to adopt the attitude of the adult kibbutzim who are extremely serious in their commitment to develop responsible programs of child care and education.

The usual problems of socializing children are complicated for black families by the special dilemma of rearing their children in the face of conflicting demands, according to Andrew Billingsley's Reader selection. Devising child-care strategies and methods that will enable blacks to survive, conform, and achieve in a white society that often discriminates against them presents a particularly difficult socialization challenge.

FACTUAL REVIEW

1. What basic changes have occurred in families that have affected their relationship with children, according to Keniston?

2. In Keniston's view, what essential element in parent-child relationships has remained constant over the years?

3. What penalties were prescribed in colonial statutes for disobedience to parents?

4. According to Zill, as reported in *Science News,* what important effects have social changes had on the attitudes children hold about families?

5. What does Zill identify as the most important factors determining the child's well-being?

6. What are the special problems faced by black parents in socializing their children, according to Billingsley?

7. What three social factors does Billingsley believe account for particular requirements for black families?

8. Rowe says that labor force participation patterns are changing for both men and women. Describe these changes.

9. What percentage of family income are working wives likely to contribute in the 1980s, according to Rowe?

10. What are the major forms of child care used for children under ten, other than that provided by the mother in one's own home, according to Rowe?

11. What factors determine the choice of child-care arrangements, according to Rowe?

12. Bettelheim mentions a number of factors that determine whether communal childrearing will be successful. What are they?

13. What are the major objectives of the kibbutz system of childrearing, and how successfully are they met, according to Bettelheim?

VARIETIES OF FAMILY PATTERNS

Not all families are the same. Most do not even fit the image of the two-parent (one earner, one homemaker), two-child home. The child-centered family is, or was, a middle-class ideal. Some sub-cultures have large families and some have kin networks that provide support and services. Increasing numbers of children are now raised in single-parent homes. The varieties of family patterns in the United States reflect the diverse cultures of its people.

The newspaper article by Lillian Rubin highlights sub-cultural and class variations in American family experience. Although Americans like to think of themselves as a classless society, there are real differences between the working class and the professional middle class. Even if similarities in the outward form of the family exist, childrearing practices, educational philosophy, and the relationship between husband and wife can vary enormously, according to Rubin, depending on the social class to which the family belongs. In her Reader selection, Rubin further explores crucial class differences in one's definition of the good life. According to her research, when material aspects of life are uncertain, they become the dominant family concern. Furthermore, even when working-class men earn a reasonably good living, it is never taken for granted, as it is in middle-class families.

Herbert Gans' Reader selection offers another insight into working-class family functioning. Although peer groups exist within all classes, in middle- and upper-class culture they play a relatively minor role, particularly among adults. The Italian and Sicilian immigrant family, whom Gans calls "the urban villagers," in contrast, maintain primary loyalties throughout their lives to a peer group composed of relatives and friends. Gans discusses the implications of peer group allegiance on both nuclear family relations and on achievement in school and work.

The ideal model of the working-class white family is traditional and heirarchically structured: men work and women take care of the household and children. Men are involved in the world of affairs—women in the life of the home. As Skolnick so convincingly argues earlier in this Part, however, ideology can never fully capture the reality of daily life. Rubin depicts how "ideal" models of family form and function fail to reflect the reality of living for working-class whites. As the Reader selections by Billingsley, Glazer and Gutman highlight, the failure of the American Dream appears even more pronounced for black families in this society.

According to Billingsley, black parents must rear their children in the face of conflicting demands and restrictive opportunities, teaching conformity to a system that exploits them. Although there are many black family patterns, half of all black families are poor; this includes the industrial working class and the working poor. It is not economic oppression alone, however, but institutional racism and educational inequality that also create obstacles to black achievement.

Billingsley emphasizes that most blacks—even the poor—live in nuclear families that are self-supporting and male-headed. Nevertheless there is a high percentage of female-headed households among blacks. In "Black Families: An Exchange," Nathan Glazer and Herbert Gutman debate the reasons for this pattern and the plight of black families.

FACTUAL REVIEW

1. Why does Rubin say that the belief that we can all pull ourselves up by our bootstraps is a myth?

2. According to Rubin, what would most working-class respondents do if they inherited a million dollars? Would middle-class respondents do the same?

3. Does Rubin believe that middle-class marriages are more egalitarian than working-class marriages? Why?

4. What accounts for the different demands that working-class and middle-class parents make upon the schools, according to Rubin?

5. Why does Billingsley believe that middle-class black life is so precarious?

6. What is the most common pattern among black families today in terms of composition and authority, according to Billingsley?

7. To what does Glazer attribute the difficult condition of the poor black family? To what does Gutman attribute it?

8. Gans distinguishes between the process of acculturation and the process of assimilation. What do these terms mean?

9. What is a peer group society, according to Gans?

KEY CONCEPTS FOR PART THREE

Sentimental Model of the Family—See Key Concepts, Part One.

Pluralistic Ignorance refers to widespread ignorance in a social group about what is actually going on in their group. The obscuring of reality results from a gap between private behavior and public norms and images. Much of what goes on within the family is invisible to the public; outwardly, most families try to seem to conform to what they believe are public norms and to images that are presented by the media. Skolnick suggests that false media images, family intensity, and the norm of family privacy are causes of such pluralistic ignorance in the United States.

Expanding Institutionalization is a concept that Etzioni uses to refer to institutions taking over functions previously handled by the family, such as caring for the young, the disabled and sick, and the elderly.

Act as Though Principle, according to Kanter, was a dictate of large work organizations to their members that while they were on the job, they were to act as though they had no other loyalties and no outside life, such as family. It reinforced the separation of work and home spheres.

Nepotism is a favoritism shown to relatives, especially in appointment to desirable work positions.

Flextime or **Flexitime** refers to flexibility in working hours to allow workers time to pursue other interests and fulfill other responsibilities, such as those of parenting.

Family Life Cycle refers to the history and pattern of developmental stages of typical family life.

Developmental Stage refers to a stage within the family life cycle. Throughout the entire life-span, at different periods, individuals are confronted with particular biological and social tasks which demand investment of their time and energy. Mastery of these developmental tasks or opportunities leads to personal growth and permits the individual to confront new challenges and develop further. The time it takes to deal with a particular task such as making the transition from being single to being married, or from childlessness to becoming a parent, is called a developmental stage.

Parental Dethronements is a term used by Datan to describe the series of successive steps by which a child gradually grows less dependent on his or her parents for physical and emotional well-being.

Cathexis is a term (taken from psychoanalysis) used by Douvan to refer to the adolescent's concentration of psychic energy in some particular person, group, idea, or thing. In psychoanalytic usage, narcissism (as described by Slater) refers to that state in which an individual's energy is invested (i.e., "cathected") on the self or some aspect of the self.

Narcissism—See Key Concepts, Part Two

The Empty Nest is the developmental stage of life in which parents whose last child has left home face the challenge of learning to live as a couple again.

The Myth of the Neolocal Family is a phrase used by Troll to debunk the notion that young people upon marriage move to a new location and no longer rely on their parents for emotional and/or financial support. According to Troll's research, the significance of parent-child relationships continues in reciprocal fashion throughout life, although the form and direction of support given changes.

Filial Maturity is a term Troll uses to refer to the capacity of children to aid in their parents' growth and development, just as their parents foster their own maturation and learning. The relationship of parents to children is thus seen as a balanced and reciprocal one, which persists as children grow up and parents grow older.

Styles of Grandparenting refer to the tremendous amount of variety in both the satisfaction derived from the grandparent role and in the ways that different grandparents carry out this function. Neugarten and Weinstein identify five styles: Formal, Fun Seeker, Surrogate Parent, Reservoir of Family Wisdom, and Distant Figure. The Formal grandparents seek to follow proper and prescribed roles. Having frequent contact, they are interested, but leave parenting to the parents—they are not advice givers.

In contrast, the Reservoir of Family Wisdom is authoritarian and a dispenser of advice; he is usually a male patriarch. Surrogate Parents, a female style for the most part, take over child care for working mothers. These three patterns, however, are not the dominant ones today. Fun Seekers, those grandparents whose relationship to their grandchildren is characterized by informality and playfulness, and Distant Figures, those grandparents who have infrequent contact and emerge primarily on holidays in a manner similar to the formal pattern, are the two dominant contemporary forms.

Socialization—See Key Concepts, Part One.

Communal Childrearing is a pattern of rearing children in which the entire community, or specified members of the community rather than just the child's own parents, have the responsibility for much of the socialization of the child.

Kibbutz is a collective agricultural settlement in Israel which practices communal childrearing. Members of the kibbutz are called "kibbutzim."

Class usually refers to how an individual's income, education, and occupation place him or her in a particular social position or status. Rubin says that the notion that America is a classless society is a myth.

Community refers to a group of people (usually, but not necessarily, living in the same geographical area) who share common interests and have an awareness of their relationship to one another.

Ethnic Group is a group of people bound by a common racial, geographic, or cultural heritage.

Acculturation describes a process whereby one group of people, usually an ethnic minority, takes on aspects of the dominant culture without losing a sense of their ethnic identity. Immigrants who choose to speak English in public places and to speak the language of their country of origin at home could be labelled "acculturated."

Assimilation, in contrast to acculturation, involves identity change. When a member of an ethnic minority no longer identifies with his or her ethnic origins but considers him or herself to be "American," writers such as Gans would call that individual "assimilated." Assimilation involves changing one's ethnic loyalties, values, and norms and adopting those of the larger society.

Peer Group Society is one in which an individual's primary source of social support is not the nuclear family but the peer group composed of friends and relatives of the same sex, age, and developmental stage. The "urban villagers" Gans describes is an example.

ESSAY AND DISCUSSION QUESTIONS

1. Should the family remain the major institutional resource for socializing children and handling problems of social deviance?

Suggested Guidelines:

    a. Refer to Sussman. How does the relationship of the family to other social institutions facilitate or hinder its functioning?

    b. Discuss Skolnick's assertion that there is hope for the future in our current disillusion with family life.

    c. Contrast the arguments of Etzioni and Skolnick on the current capabilities of the nuclear family.

    d. What arguments does Keniston make in his Reader selection and in his newspaper article?

    e. Walker and Kantor both focus on the interface between work and family. How does the structure of the work setting influence the family's ability to educate and control its members?

2. What decisions and challenges are presented to individuals at different stages of the family life course?

Suggested Guidelines:

    a. Use Datan's newspaper article to develop a life-span framework.

    b. Refer to Troll et al. and consider their concept of filial maturity.

    c. How are life cycle changes influenced by our current ideological emphasis on individual fulfillment? In this context consider Neugarten and Weinstein's selection on the role of the contemporary American grandparent.

    d. Refer to Rubin and Dreifus. Contrast the difficulties faced by women in the childbearing years with those in the post-parental stage.

    e. Consider Douvan's Reader selection. What are some of the special problems faced by adolescents and their parents?

3. What social factors determine our attitudes toward, and our treatment of, our nation's children?

Suggested Guidelines:

    a. Consider colonial laws referring to the rights of parents and children.

    b. Refer to the article from *Science News* and to Billingsley. What factors account for differences in our treatment of children, and how do social changes affect children?

    c. Consider the child care options described by Rowe and Bettelheim. Can any similarities be found and, if so, what accounts for these?

d. Referring to Keniston's newspaper article, discuss why our experiments with bringing children up in institutions generally have been disastrous.

4. Discuss the meaning and implications of Lillian Rubin's assertion that the class into which we are born generally is the class in which we'll marry and live out the rest of our lives.

Suggested Guidelines:
   a. What arguments does Rubin make in her newspaper and Reader articles? To what does Rubin refer when she speaks of "Worlds of Pain"? Discuss this concept.
   b. Refer to Billingsley. How do black families attempt to cope with their social class position?
   c. What does Gutman say about the factors that tend to keep a large proportion of blacks in poverty?
   d. Discuss how the function of the peer group differs among different cultural groups. What effects would this have on social mobility? Contrast the vision of the working-class world presented by Gans and Rubin.
   e. Refer to the case studies presented in the first section of the Reader by Coles and Kanter and Lehr. Do you see any evidence to support or contradict Rubin's assertion? What does Sennett say about movement from one social class to another in "Genteel Backlash"?

PART FOUR
CRISIS AND RESPONSE

15. "The Family in the Future" "Families"
    Jessie Bernard   Jane Howard

    "Divorce and the Survival of the Family"
        Judith Bardwick
    "Does the Family Have a Future?"
        Suzanne Keller
    "Here to Stay"
        Mary Jo Bane
    "At Odds"
        Carl N. Degler

LEARNING OBJECTIVES

To explore

—the sources and forms of family strain in contemporary society

—the new forms of intimate association which are developing as alternatives to the traditional nuclear family

—how successful services to families have been and what policy changes might improve them

—how the family is expected to change in the decades ahead

OVERVIEW

Rapid social changes over the past decades have imposed strains on the family that are reflected in high rates of family breakdown, in the development of new family forms, and in the proliferation of mental health, welfare, and educational services supported by government. This part of our course considers these responses to changing social conditions and offers opinions on how the family will adapt and evolve in order to survive in the future.

SIGNS OF STRAIN

Divorce has increased dramatically, and there are other signs that the family is under stress. Weiss, in his newspaper article, discusses the factors that may account for the increasing American divorce rate. He concludes that we divorce more frequently, not because we no longer value marriage, but because

44

we give so much importance to the ideal of a happy marriage in our lives. Weiss also considers the traumatic impact of marital separation. Despite the increased frequency of divorce, he cautions, we must remember that the event is always disruptive.

Agreeing with Weiss' assessment of the trauma of divorce, Judith Wallerstein and Joan Kelly in their Reader selection consider the impact of divorce on children. Of the one million divorces which take place annually in the United States, 65 percent involve children under eighteen. Children of divorce initially confront a period of loss and turmoil. Next they usually experience several years of instability in which parental support and attention fluctuates. Even when the post-divorce family stabilizes, Wallerstein and Kelly point out, choices that are good for the parents may not necessarily be good for the children involved.

Of course, what's good for the parents may not be in the children's best interests in non-divorced families as well. Furthermore, what's good for one parent may not be good for the other parent or for the relationship itself. S.M. Miller writes that for most middle-class families, man's absorption in occupational concerns and woman's absorption with children can make decent relationships—much less egalitarian ones—difficult to establish and maintain. He also suggests that to make egalitarian family relationships work, spouses and parents must often give up major commitments outside the family unit.

Since remarriage involves a combining of lives of persons who have pre-existing ties to individuals outside the new unit, remarriage rarely resolves all the tensions of single-parent lives. Step-parent families have problems of their own—many of which stem from the fact that major bonds exist between members of the newly formed family and persons outside it (as with step-children and their non-custodial parent). In her Reader selection, Jessie Bernard considers the strains of divorce and the effects they can have on remarriage, and she suggests that policies toward marriage and divorce should help alleviate these stresses for all involved.

FACTUAL REVIEW

1. What factors does Weiss identify as accounting for the increasing rate of divorce?

2. Weiss talks about "the doctrine of tender years." To what is he referring?

3. According to Weiss, what is the most important factor for children in their post-divorce adjustment?

4. Wallerstein and Kelly identify four related stages in the process of divorce. What are they?

5. According to Wallerstein and Kelly, what percentage of children growing up in the 1970s will experience parental separation or divorce?

6. According to Bernard, how does the support basis of modern families differ from those of other times?

7. What critical factors must marriage policy take into account, according to Bernard?

8. Miller states that he had incomplete early socialization as a family member. What does he mean, and how does this affect his behavior?

9. Although he shared household tasks with his wife throughout their marriage, Miller feels that he failed to do something more important. What did he not do?

10. According to Miller, for what are many young parents unprepared?

NEW FAMILY FORMS

As modern birth control technology has separated sex and reproduction from their necessary connection, new forms of intimate association have developed which do not include child bearing and rearing. Many different groupings and arrangements of people now consider themselves families. What they share and how they differ from traditional family types is the focus of this section.

In his newspaper article, Joseph Pleck makes clear that the nuclear family with the male as sole earner is no longer the dominant family form. Despite the attention given to new sexual arrangements, their impact on the family has not been very significant. However, increased longevity, changing patterns of labor force participation, and high rates of divorce and separation have had a major impact and have led to an enormous increase in both two-earner and single-parent households.

These new family forms require new patterns of membership adjustment and response. In her Reader selection, Kathy Weingarten discusses how a pattern of relating to each other called "interdependence" can help two-career couples cope with the pressures of maintaining career and home responsibilities and of meeting each other's emotional needs. Like Miller in the previous section, Weingarten notes that men are often uncomfortable in assuming major responsibilities for traditionally female jobs, and the degree of interdependence varies widely among couples.

Esther Wattenberg and Hazel Reinhardt look in depth at the growing number of single-parent, female-headed families emerging in our society. They discuss the sources of this trend and look at economic and social welfare policy implications if the trend continues.

46

Although far from a dominant social form, communal families have captured the interest and attention of many citizens and social commentators in recent decades. In their Reader selection, Berger et al. investigate child rearing in communes. Mother-and-child often form the basic family unit in communes, with men frequently joining and leaving. While information isn't totally reliable, the children in the communes seem to be doing all right. The communal families studied are not as child-centered as are typical middle-class families. Berger and his colleagues conclude, however, that the traditional middle-class pattern, with its prolongation of dependency and creation of adolescence, may be less than wholesome. "If communal living succeeds in abolishing adolescence," these authors write, "it may be worth it after all."

Robert Miner also discusses a deviant but growing trend in contemporary America—the emergence of the single-parent, male-headed family. In his Reader selection, Miner movingly details the trials involved and the growth that resulted when he assumed total parental responsibility for his son after the breakup of his marriage.

Although Miner casts his experience in positive terms—he sees his having to parent his son as forcing him to develop into a fuller human being—Margaret Mead is concerned about children growing up with just one parent. In "Marriage in Two Steps," she argues that children's needs can best be met by a lifelong relationship to two mature parents. In order to insure that children can maintain a positive relationship to both parents, marriages that involve the bearing and rearing of children should be considered as a different form from those contracted by adults who are interested in formalizing the bond between them but are not ready to consider having children. Mead believes that if we concern ourselves with investing meaningful relationships throughout life with dignity, there will be less chance that individuals will have children without being prepared to nurture them responsibly as long as they need care.

FACTUAL REVIEW

1. According to Pleck, what two major alternative family types have emerged recently?

2. How do the problems of two-earner families differ from those with a single earner, according to Pleck?

3. What does Weingarten mean by "interdependence"?

4. What factors does Weingarten believe are prerequisite to the development of commitment and trust?

5. What factors account for the rise in female-headed families, according to Wattenberg and Reinhardt?

6. What factors do Wattenberg and Reinhardt believe exert a critical influence on marital stability?

7. What growing social trend is exemplified by Miner's recent experience?

8. Identify and describe the two forms of marriage that Mead would like to see.

9. According to Mead, what must children be assured of as a basic right?

10. What do Berger et al. see as a basic structural flaw in "hip" relationships?

11. What do communal relationships substitute for expectations of permanence, according to Berger et al.?

FAMILY SERVICES AND PUBLIC POLICY

To meet the growing problems of contemporary families, new services, both private and public, have arisen. Increasingly, Americans use mental health services and marriage and family counseling to meet crises and dislocations in family life. Other services, however, such as birth control and abortion, have become political issues in our pluralistic society. Family policy and services are thus designed in a societal context of heated debate.

In her newspaper article, Catherine Chilman explains why family services in the United States are so controversial. She outlines the need for federal programs that will support family well-being. But she also weighs some of the arguments against such measures, including government controls, loss of self-reliance, and financial costs.

Kenneth Keniston, in his Reader selection "Services Families Need," also considers the state of our current family service programs and policies. In his view, family programs are fragmented and underfunded. Furthermore, they stigmatize those they serve, and they are unavailable to many who need them. To Keniston, our family programs undercut family cohesion and vitality rather than prevent family disruption. To combat this trend he suggests that we develop services based on principles of universal entitlement, rather than continuing to fund special remedial programs for persons with special needs.

We can gain a better understanding of the difference between prevention-oriented programs based on principles of universal access and those based on helping families who already manifest special needs by reading Melsted's selection on Swedish Family Policy. The Swedish Parental Insurance System entitles one parent at a time (father, mother, or both in sequence) to stay home to care for a newborn while receiving ninety percent of ordinary pay during the baby's first seven months. Child-care and housing allowances, compensated leave time when a child is sick, public child care in many forms, voluntary parent training courses, and a six-hour working day for parents of young children are just some of the Swedish innovations for creating a pro-family environment through the provision of public services and funds.

Although services designed to improve family functioning have been seen as a matter of private initiative rather than public responsibility in America, supportive family programs are increasingly being designed by a range of mental health, religious, and lay personnel. The Reader selection by William Lederer and psychiatrist Don Jackson presents a questionnaire and exercises they have designed to help couples improve their marriages on their own. In their selection, Joanne Koch and Lew Koch describe the marriage enrichment movement and how participation in a marriage enrichment seminar given under church sponsorship improved the quality of their own marriage, despite their initial skepticism about such programs.

FACTUAL REVIEW

1. According to Chilman, why is the subject of "family policy" so controversial?

2. What are the shortcomings of "family impact" statements, in Chilman's view?

3. What does Keniston believe is wrong with current family service programs?

4. What does Keniston mean when he says programs must be based on principles of universal entitlement?

5. What is the purpose of the Lederer and Jackson "Interpersonal Comparison Test"?

6. What program do Koch and Koch enroll in, and how do they believe it improves their marriage?

7. According to Koch and Koch, what accounts for the success of the bestseller *The Total Woman?*

8. What does traditional Swedish family policy provide, according to Melsted? How does this differ from their family insurance program?

9. In Sweden, what work arrangements support the family?

THE FAMILY IN THE FUTURE

What can we expect for the family in the decades ahead? Will we abandon the family or support it? How will it change?

In her newspaper article, Jessie Bernard discusses how, for all its problems, and with all the experimentation in alternative forms, the family will probably survive and be strengthened by the changes it undergoes.

To Bernard, the accelerated participation of women in the labor force and the rise of feminism will continue to force changes in family structure. She sees a reversal of some of the negative attitudes toward the family that prevailed in the 1970s, and the development of more egalitarian forms of marriage. The question is not whether the family has a future, but what that future family will look like.

In her Reader selection, Suzanne Keller analyzes the forces that are making the family less important as a social institution and less necessary for personal fulfillment. She predicts that there will be a "trend towards greater legitimate variety in sexual and marital experience," and that fewer negative emotions will be associated with these. She also predicts more personal choice in the kind, extent, and duration of intimate relationships and suggests that new forms of communal living and multi-stage marriages will emerge.

Keller is pessimistic about the value of retaining old family models in the years ahead, and she urges us to invent new models and norms that will humanize the future. However, Jane Howard, in "Families," points out that new family associations can learn much from observing and understanding the successes of traditional families and clans. She describes the earmarks of "good families," whether or not the members are related by blood ties. In contrast to Keller, Howard's approach suggests that instead of entirely scrapping old models, we would do well to preserve the good that exists in them and expand on it to build family forms that will be tenable in the future.

In contrast to Howard, Judith Bardwick believes that it is difficult, if not impossible, to achieve a sense of intimacy, significant connection, and caring within large groups—family or otherwise. She is also concerned that feminist models of workable families place undue stress on values such as equal power, equal freedom, and equal self-gratification, with insufficient attention to equal commitment and equal dependence. Feeling that children will get short shrift in alternative family types, Bardwick argues that the nuclear family will and should continue to be the dominant family form. It alone provides the strengths that come from a sense of being loved and belonging.

Carl Degler argues, however, that there is an unavoidable tension between the traditional nuclear family's interests and those of women. Attempts to provide equal career opportunities for women inevitably run up against the dilemma of providing satisfactory child care. The future of the family as we know it and the future of women as fulfilled individuals are inherently at odds, he writes.

However, Mary Jo Bane takes the position in her Reader selection that conflicting values can be reconciled and family forms can be developed that meet the needs of all members if future family policy is designed to take into account these value and interest conflicts. To demonstrate her point, Bane develops hypothetical models for future family policy that incorporate both our commitment to certain traditional family values (such as privacy and choice) and our public commitment to provide equal treatment and opportunities for all.

FACTUAL REVIEW

1. What two movements does Bernard see as accounting for the restructuring of family relationships?

2. What kind of egalitarianism will we be likely to see in future marriages, according to Bernard?

3. According to Bernard, what changes has the feminist movement undergone in recent years?

4. What attributes does Jane Howard believe are essential to all good families?

5. How does Howard define the term "ritual"?

6. What values does Bardwick believe feminist models of the family neglect?

7. Why does Bardwick believe the nuclear family will survive?

8. Keller identifies three fallacies which have impoverished our speculations about future family alternatives. What are they?

9. What are the three main sources of challenge that future families must face, according to Keller?

10. What tensions does Bane see between family privacy and public values?

11. What kind of social policy innovations does Bane believe that we need?

12. According to Degler, how do higher-class marriages differ from working-class marriages, as far as egalitarianism is concerned?

13. What paradox does Degler see as inherent to modern family relationships?

KEY CONCEPTS FOR PART FOUR

Doctrine of Tender Years is the concept that a child too young to care for himself or herself is best off if reared by the mother. This idea gained prominence during the mid-nineteenth century, and since that time has had a strong influence on custody decisions. Prior to that time, it was widely believed that the male parent was the best equipped to rear children in cases of marital separation.

Interdependence is a term used by Weingarten to describe a successful coping style that is adopted by couples where both husband and wife are pursuing a career. Interdependence is characterized by concern for mutual well-being. It allows for times of dependence but fosters personal growth and maturity. In order for two individuals to be "independent in an intimate relationship" (i.e., interdependent) Weingarten feels there must be commitment and trust, open communication, and reciprocity.

Superwoman Model is a model of female performance which requires that the woman perform two roles—homemaker and career women—smoothly, without requiring that the male function in anything other than the traditional male role of breadwinner. Weingarten points out that this is one pattern followed in two-career families.

Individual and **Parental Marriage** refer to two hypothetical marriage forms suggested by Mead as possible alternatives to the single form of marriage that is legally recognized today. Individual Marriages would be contracted by young people who want to make a commitment to each other without accepting family responsibilities. Parental Marriages would involve responsibility for children, the concern being to insure children a lifelong relationship with both parents. Parental Marriage would be more difficult to contract.

Female-Headed Families are those in which the primary wage earner is a woman. It is estimated by Wattenberg and Reinhardt that 13 percent of all families in the U.S. are headed by females.

Egalitarian Marriages are based on principles of equality of rights, responsibilities, and roles of the marital partners. These differ from hierarchical or traditional relationships, which are based on notions of male authority and division of roles according to sex.

Marriage Enrichment, originally developed by marriage counselors David and Vera Mace, refers to a number of short-term, personal growth programs designed to teach couples how to be more responsive to each other's needs.

Often offered under the auspices of a religious institution, marriage enrichment seminars are designed to provide couples with opportunities to explore their feelings, to develop new ways of relating, and to generally improve the quality of their relationship.

Rituals, as described by Howard, refer to the observance of certain set forms by the family group. In her view, family rituals are meaningful performances which express the key themes or connectedness of family life.

Clans traditionally are a group of families or households which claim common ancestry. Based on knowledge learned from studying successful clans, Howard suggests that non-related adults can also form long-lasting associations that serve similar functions of social support.

ESSAY AND DISCUSSION QUESTIONS

1. What factors account for the recent increase in the American divorce rate, and what are its consequences?

Suggested Guidelines:

   a. Refer to Weiss's newspaper article for an overview of this issue.
   b. Consider the impact of divorce on children, referring to the Reader selection by Wallerstein and Kelly.
   c. What strains are inherent in contemporary intact families, according to Miller? What would Weingarten add?
   d. How would innovations in forms of marriage and marriage policy suggested by Bernard improve the situation of divorcing families?
   e. What does Margaret Mead say about the impact of divorce on children? How does she propose to reduce the problem?

2. Why has there been increased interest in alternate family forms?

Suggested Guidelines:

   a. Refer to Pleck's newspaper article. Discuss how current economic and social factor are influencing family forms.
   b. Discuss the implications of female-headed families as detailed by Wattenberg and Reinhardt.
   c. Consider Mead's argument about the needs of children. How would she be likely to view the communal child-rearing arrangements described by Berger et al.? What values do commune dwellers attribute to their "family" form?

3. Some experts argue that government services are needed to strengthen the family. Others argue that the expansion of public services will instead destroy the family. Develop and detail your position on this important debate.

Suggested Guidelines:

   a. Refer to Chilman's newspaper article. What are the arguments she presents for and against government services?
   b. Refer to Keniston and Melsted. Consider the differences between American and Swedish family policy.
   c. Refer back to the articles by Lasch and Etzioni in Parts One and Three. What arguments do they make about the role of the government in family matters?
   d. Consider the selections by Lederer and Jackson and Koch and Koch. What do you think of the value of service programs and courses to improve marital relations? Should such programs be public services? Why?

4. Has the nuclear family outlived its usefulness? Discuss.

Suggested Guidelines:

   a. Bernard's newspaper article describes how two movements are responsible for pressures to change the family. Identify these and consider how they will affect families in the future.
   b. Bardwick would argue that the nuclear family is an essential form. Keller sees it as obsolete. Consider these two contradictory views.
   c. Refer to Degler and consider the implications of his argument that the needs of the nuclear family and the needs of women are inherently at odds.
   d. Howard and Bane both believe there are lessons for the future to be gained from studying the strengths of contemporary families. Discuss their views.

NOTES

NOTES

NOTES

NOTES